A HISTORY OF
MONEY IN
SINGAPORE

First published in 2021 by

Talisman Publishing Pte Ltd
52 Genting Lane #06-05
Ruby Land Complex 1
Singapore 349560
talisman@apdsing.com

www.talismanpublishing.com

Copyright © Monetary Authority of Singapore 2021

Project Co-ordinator
Timothy Auger

Publisher
Ian Pringle

Designer
Stephy Chee

Studio Manager
Janice Ng

Studio Team
Wong Sze Wey
Paul Haines
Jamie Pringle
Annie Teo

Colour separation by
Colourscan Print Co. Pte Ltd

Printed in Singapore by
Colourscan Print Co. Pte Ltd

ISBN 978-981-18-2129-5

Overleaf: An East Indiaman in a gale, c. 1759, by Charles Brooking.

A HISTORY OF
MONEY IN
SINGAPORE

Clement Liew
Peter Wilson

Consultant Editor
Timothy Auger

TALISMAN

CONTENTS

FOREWORD

❦ Tharman Shanmugaratnam ❦
Senior Minister, and Chairman, Monetary Authority of Singapore

This book is a pioneering effort to tell the fascinating story of money in Singapore, from its early days as a trading port to modern times as an independent nation and global city state.

The history of money has always been more than an economic chronicle. It reflects the vagaries of international and regional power, the changing geography of trade and migration, and the evolution of domestic institutions of governance, society and culture. While other studies have explored each of these topics in great depth, this book weaves them together in a holistic narrative of money in Singapore.

The first half of the story covers the time from the precolonial era, when the island was known as Singapura with an active maritime community residing within it, to its days as a British free port, with policies imposed by both the East India Company and the British Colonial Office. It traces Singapore's passage through two World Wars, with the Great Depression in between, and the path Singapore took to attaining self-government. The second half of the book covers independent Singapore, with monetary sovereignty and the financial responsibility that came with charting a future of its own. It includes the 50 years of evolution of the Monetary Authority of Singapore (MAS).

This book should be of interest to several audiences. The numismatists, many of whom are deeply knowledgeable about the specific events behind the notes and coins issued, might appreciate the broader history that is told. Economists and history enthusiasts may both benefit from the insights that come from the many-dimensional account – political, commercial and cultural – of the money that came to be used in Singapore. Finally, the general reader, including citizens or residents of Singapore or those abroad with an interest in the history of the place and the broader Asian region, will surely find the book enlightening and engaging.

The history of money in Singapore, which long predates the country having a currency and central bank of its own, is varied and colourful. One can only hope that the future will be less eventful.

PREFACE

∾ Ravi Menon ∾

Managing Director, Monetary Authority of Singapore

The Monetary Authority of Singapore (MAS) commissioned this volume to commemorate the 50th anniversary of its founding.

MAS is Singapore's central bank. Where money is concerned, MAS's role is to issue the currency, the Singapore dollar, and to undertake monetary policy to maintain its purchasing power. Uniquely among central banks, MAS's monetary policy is centred on managing the exchange rate of the Singapore dollar.

While a central bank is focused on the value of its money, policies about currency – their production and issuance – predate modern central banking by several centuries. The contents of this book attempt to bridge the narrative between the two.

Dr Clement Liew and Associate Prof. Peter Wilson have brought their expertise and deep knowledge to bear on the range of topics covered in this book. Dr Liew is Director of Heritage Services at private research firm Signum Fidei. He adopts a historian's approach to his writing, delving into competing narratives, as well as the rich socioeconomic and political interactions that form the backdrop to the monetary arrangements in the centuries prior to Singapore's birth as an independent nation. Prof. Wilson is Adjunct Professor at the Singapore Management University and has had a long association with MAS. He writes as an economist, applying economic frameworks to analyse monetary developments in Singapore against the backdrop of the international monetary system and the rise of modern central banking.

I would also like to acknowledge Mr Timothy Auger, the project coordinator and consultant editor, who was instrumental in guiding this project through to completion, and the Economic Policy Group at MAS which provided valuable support for this project.

This volume highlights three recurrent principles throughout Singapore's monetary history: openness to trade and capital; ensuring the credibility of the currency; and preserving the purchasing power of money.

These principles are part of MAS's core monetary DNA. They will continue to guide the Monetary Authority of Singapore in the decades ahead, even as it enhances and innovates its operational and institutional arrangements.

ACKNOWLEDGEMENTS

✍ Edward S. Robinson ✍
Deputy Managing Director (Economic Policy) and
Chief Economist, Monetary Authority of Singapore

A small team from the Monetary Authority of Singapore's Economic Policy Group (EPG) conceptualised the publication of this book for MAS's 50th Anniversary celebration as early as 2019. However, developing a book of this scope and ambition would only have been possible with the efforts of many others. I would like to acknowledge and thank the following:

The authors, Clement Liew and Peter Wilson for taking up this monumental project and doggedly staying the course for two years through sometimes challenging circumstances, including the onset of COVID-19. It was a tremendous, seminal effort, as well as a most enriching collaboration.

Timothy Auger, Project Coordinator and Consultant Editor, for careful editing, reviewing, and essential coordination work to keep the project on track and to ensure that this tome could come to fruition. He enriched the book by bringing to bear his personal interest in Singapore and the region's history. His deep experience and expertise provided invaluable guidance for the entire team.

Mr Ian Pringle and the team at Talisman Publishing Pte Ltd, for the marvellous design, proof-reading, and printing work that has brought to life a historical volume that prior to this only existed in our imagination.

Professor John Miksic (National University of Singapore) and Professor Catherine Schenk (Oxford University), eminent scholars in their fields, who provided tremendously useful feedback and insights into specific areas of the book which materially strengthened the earlier drafts.

Mr Janadas Devan, Chief of Government Communications, who shared with us the benefits of his knowledge on events surrounding specific aspects of Singapore's monetary history.

Choy Keen Meng, presently Adjunct Professor at the Singapore Management University, who assisted with birthing the concept for the project, and worked with the authors and Timothy Auger in the early stages to start the book on a strong footing.

Ms Priscilla Ng and Mr Clemence Kng, for assistance in the preparatory stages of the book which included exhaustive efforts in drawing together the folios of internal records that were an invaluable source of reference material for the later chapters.

Ms Tan Yin Ying, for helming the Economic Policy Group's contributions. She provided expert editorial and technical oversight over all chapters from MAS' perspective. Ms Tan also liaised closely with Mr Timothy Auger and the authors, garnering the necessary resources from all across Singapore and beyond – approvals, illustrations, copyright and more – to drive the book to its fruition.

Institutions who have assisted the writers in their research and individuals who have made it possible for them to focus on this project. Dr Clement Liew wishes to acknowledge the assistance of the MAS Gallery team: Eric Lee, Elvan Ong and Karen Tan; help with overseas research provided by Patrick Neo, Cheng Sifan; the staff of the UK Public Record Office, National Archives at Kew Gardens, London; and the staff of the British Library. He is grateful also for assistance rendered by Tim Yap Fuan, NUS Central Library; and advice from Professor Ng Chin Keong. Assoc. Prof Peter Wilson would like to thank Clemence Kng for his time-consuming work in assembling and summarising the vast stock of internal MAS documents which have played such a crucial role in the research for this book. Both authors are also greatly appreciative of the support and patience their wives have given them in completing this massive undertaking.

Institutions and individuals who helped with the sourcing of photographs for the book, including HSBC Archives, Standard Chartered Singapore, the Singapore Mint, and De La Rue plc. A full list of picture acknowledgements will appear later in the book.

Colleagues from the Economic Policy Group: Celine Sia, Andrew Colquhoun, Cyrene Chew, Ng Yi Ping, Vincent Low, Toh Ling Yan and Moses Soh, for their helpful comments on draft chapters and sections of the book, and Soh Wai Mei for the rigorous data checks.

Colleagues from the Corporate Services Department (CSD) and the Currency Department (CD), including Mr Elvan Ong, Mr Eric Lee, Mr Chung Wei Ken, Ms Elena Tan, and others. CSD's heavy logistical and administrative support was indispensable, particular in the midst of a pandemic. CD's sharing of expertise in the currency-related sections of the book and providing access to MAS's Heritage Collection was invaluable. The book would be incomplete and much poorer without your inputs. Carolyn Neo and Kenneth Leong (MAS, London Office) and Kwa Chin Lum (SM's Office, PMO) rendered EPG quick and very useful assistance and advice when needed.

The team would like to acknowledge the Chairman and MD of MAS for their fullest support for this project.

Thanks are due to many others from MAS. All your contributions, great and small, have made this book a fitting tribute to 50 years of MAS working together and serving Singapore in the role entrusted to us.

INTRODUCTION

⁓ Clement Liew ⁓
⁓ Peter Wilson ⁓

The history of money in Singapore began several centuries before the arrival of the British. This island nation has a monetary heritage that dates back to ancient times, one that is closely intertwined with the flows of global and regional trade. These same forces have shaped the development of Singapore from then till the present day. But money mattered not just in the realm of commercial transactions; it was, and is, crucial for the survival and progress of every individual, family, community, society and nation.

This book traces the history of the types of money used in Singapore from pre-colonial times to the present. It is published to mark the 50th anniversary of the founding of the Monetary Authority of Singapore (MAS) in January 1971. The Authority's brief was to consolidate central-banking policy functions previously carried out by government departments, although until 2002 the issue of currency remained in the hands of the Board of Commissioners of Currency, Singapore (BCCS).

There has been voluminous research on Singapore's history by specialist scholars. We do not claim to supplant their work. Rather, our aim is to complement these accounts with a wider view, covering economic, political, social and cultural aspects, and to present the story of Singapore's money in a digestible form for the general reader. We hope the book will be a useful source of information for numismatists, but our perspective is broader than this. Our examination of money goes beyond the physical aspects of currency, to include its role as a medium of exchange, an accounting unit and a store of value in a social context.

Our approach is a dual one: the chronological insights of an historian are combined here with the analytical approach of an economist, drawing extensively on the internal archives of the MAS as well as other documents and contemporary sources. We hope this book will be enjoyed by anyone interested in the rich history of Southeast Asia and its relationship with global powers – Europeans in the colonial era, the United States after World War II and, of course, regional giants such as India and China.

Tracing the history of money in Singapore has revealed several broad themes.

The first is that the story of money in Singapore is inextricably linked to the island's rich heritage within the commercial history of the Southeast Asian region and along the trade routes and networks of East-West trade. Trade has always been the lifeline of Singapore, and this would not have been possible without the currencies that fuelled international commerce. To be sure, the earliest exchange of goods would certainly have been undertaken with some form of barter trade. The advent of global trade – be it the passage of goods along the ancient overland Silk Road, or along the maritime China trade route – meant that larger commercial transactions conducted at greater distances made barter trade inconvenient. Merchants therefore transited to using as their means of payment different types of coinage made of precious metals which possessed intrinsic value. These coins became known as 'specie'.

This book documents the shift in Singapore and the broader region from using commodities as money to commodity-based specie; to paper money; and thence to 'fiat' currency. It analyses policies and practices driven by colonial concerns, and later by the prerogatives of a small but proudly independent nation. The strong trading and financial links between Singapore and Malaysia show why regional ties were so important. Singapore's political separation from Malaysia in August 1965 was traumatic for both parties, as was the failure to retain a common currency in 1967. Yet both sides realised that it was in their best interests to allow each other's currency, as well as the Brunei dollar, to be 'customary tender' in order to avoid serious disruptions to their bilateral trade and banking, and to provide a transitional period before formal exchange rate policy links between Singapore and Malaysia were severed in 1973.

The second theme is that the history of money in Singapore has been greatly influenced by developments in the global economy. This arose because as a small island polity, Singapore did not have its own currency for most of its history. The rise and fall of ancient kingdoms in the region affected Singapore, while developments in the money supply of Song Dynasty China reverberated through the East Indies and the Malay Archipelago. The European powers' search for a direct trade route to China, and the desire to secure that route, propelled the colonial enterprises that took hold in the region and led to the establishment of a free port on the island of Singapore. This free port laid the foundations for the openness of the Singapore economy to trade and capital flows, and has been a major factor underlying Singapore's money and monetary policy. The Spanish silver dollar provided a 'reserve currency' that was accepted by traders all over the world; the Mexican silver dollar, together with the Japanese yen and American trade dollar, would later play this role as well. The 'dollar' therefore became the basis for the currency of the Straits Settlements, of which Singapore was a part, rather than Britain's non-decimalised currency system.

Economic shocks originating outside Singapore have been a recurrent bane of economic policy. The Long Depression of the late 19th century, two World Wars and the Great Depression, affected global commerce and finance. These led to significant challenges to Singapore on the monetary front. They shaped key developments in Singapore's early monetary history, including the issuance of the Straits Settlements' own currency, the shift from the silver to the gold standard, the tokenisation of the currency, and the creation of a pan-Malayan common currency area and currency board. The latter lasted even after the component territories had gained independence from the British, but came to an end in 1967 when the currency 'split' occurred between the Federation of Malaysia, Singapore, and Brunei.

Months after Singapore celebrated the issue of its first currency in 1967, the British government decided to devalue the pound sterling to which the Singapore dollar was fixed. In the 1970s, soon after MAS was founded, there was the breakup of the Bretton Woods system of fixed exchange rates followed by the floating of the pound sterling and then of the US dollar. Singapore had no choice but to follow suit and the longstanding 'anchor' on which Singapore's money and monetary policy had been based was abruptly removed.

Post-independence Singapore has suffered five recessions: 1985–6, 1997–8, 2001–2, 2008–9 and, the most recent and most serious, the COVID-19 pandemic in 2020. In all these cases a primary cause of the downturn was a fall in export earnings, although the COVID-19 episode also owed much to the damaging effects of the virus on domestic consumption and production.

Despite these constraints, Singapore has followed its own development path. This is our third theme. In 1965, when Singapore left the Federation of Malaysia and any hope of automatic trading access to the Malaysian hinterland ended, the decision was made to remove protection and open the economy up to international trade in manufactured goods and promote inward foreign direct investment. Given Singapore's lack of natural resources and the political and economic uncertainties in the region at this time, there was also a need to build up a diversified 'war chest' of external reserve assets. This thinking also lay behind the decision in 1981 to set up the Government of Singapore Investment Corporation (GIC) to invest some of Singapore's reserves for the longer term. The need for these reserves has been clearly highlighted by the COVID-19 pandemic.

Another example is the decision to set up an offshore currency market – the Asian Dollar Market – in Singapore in 1968, despite the fact that Singapore had little relevant local expertise or financial infrastructure to support such an ambitious venture. Yet this turned out to be an important first step in transforming Singapore into a regional financial centre and, subsequently, a global financial centre.

Notwithstanding the constraints, another of our themes is that Singapore has always striven to put in place its own monetary practices, even when official policy dictated otherwise. During the colonial era, the residents of the Straits Settlements rejected 'revenue and rupee' reforms imposed by the East India Company ruling from India, as these measures undermined their trade. They also lobbied hard to secure an adequate supply of currency for the Eastern Trade and for domestic circulation, and these efforts would take on fresh impetus once the Legislative Council was established, permitting a measure of local participation in policymaking. This would lead to the introduction of the Straits Settlements currency board that would issue the Straits Settlements dollar in 1899. However, the ultimate decision-making power still lay in Britain, and the value of the local dollar eventually became pegged to the value of the British pound sterling at a fixed rate. As part of the Sterling Area and the British Empire, Singapore could not use monetary policy to shape its economic trajectory. This remained the case even after World War II, when British currency controls made it more difficult for Singapore and the other colonies to optimise their recovery and economic development plans.

Hence, the introduction of Singapore's own currency in 1967 was a significant milestone in the country's money journey, an expression of self-determination, national identity and historical achievement. After separating from Malaysia and after the currency split in 1967, Singapore retained the currency board system when the norm at that time was for newly independent countries to set up their own central bank. The overriding necessity for Singapore after 1967 was to preserve the purchasing power and stability of the Singapore dollar and to continue to attract foreign capital to the Republic. Even when Singapore did set up its own institution to carry out central banking functions in 1971 – MAS – it chose to leave the issue of currency with the BCCS until 2002, when the BCCS finally merged with MAS. In 1981, Singapore introduced its unique exchange rate-centred monetary policy, in spite of the fact that it was not widely understood at the time by either the financial community or the general public. Over time, the structure for communicating monetary policy was put in place.

Our final theme is the changing form of money in Singapore. Money's role – as a means of exchange, a unit of account, and a store of value – has not changed fundamentally over the years. But the appearance of money has evolved significantly from antiquity to modern times. Early coins were minted out of precious metals such as gold, silver and copper, and over time were increasingly struck in baser metals such as tin, iron, and alloys. Notes, on the other hand, were first issued by banks and later the government. The way they are printed, their quality, and security features have become a critical part of modern currency issuance. By the turn of the new millennium the concept of money had evolved as bank accounts, credit cards and GIRO reduced inconvenience and time spent in withdrawing cash and carrying out basic banking services. Currency itself had become a small percentage of the total amount of money in the economy. This was a fundamental change in the way the public interacted with money, which was no longer just cash in wallets and purses. The development of personal computers, the Internet and mobile phones has accelerated this move to a cashless society. We are now increasingly in a world of digital money, and the powerful effects this trend will unleash on the structure and nature of money and banking are still unfolding.

Overview of the chapters

Chapter 1 describes the historical heritage of the array of currencies found in circulation in Singapore in the early 19th century when the British arrived. It traces how commodity monies became the basis of global trade from the beginnings of East–West trade. Currencies flowed to and across Southeast Asia through the trading networks of antiquity, brought on ships riding on seasonal 'trade winds'. Mariners from the East, and, later, colonialists from the West, carried their nation's coinage and currencies of trade to the region. Chinese cash circulated pervasively and became the circulation currencies of many local kingdoms, communities and port polities in the early part of the second millennium (1001–2000 AD), and it was joined by Portuguese coinage and Dutch copper doits in the latter half of the period. They were already ubiquitous throughout the Malay Peninsula and would have likely circulated in and around Singapore in the centuries before the arrival of Raffles. The maritime commerce that took place across the region for several centuries up till this time used the Spanish silver dollar. All these currencies became circulation currencies in the early days of colonial Singapore.

Chapter 2 examines developments during the time when Singapore was under the oversight of the East India Company, which served on behalf of the British Crown as the administrator of India and its 'eastern' territories. Drawn by the free port status of the island, traders from Europe, the Malay Archipelago, and the Far East transformed Singapore into a global entrepôt for the China Trade. The money and bullion needed to conduct this trade was shipped through Singapore and its Straits Settlements partners. The establishment and extension of European settlements across Asia by the first half of this century also paved the way for European banks and agency houses to establish their branches across the territories along the maritime trade route. This network facilitated the evolution of paper-based financial instruments, which aided commercial transactions between Europe, India, and China. These financial instruments included bills of exchange, promissory notes and even government treasury bills. During some periods, especially when specie was in short supply, these paper instruments became used as 'money' as well.

Chapter 3 covers the second half of the 19th century, when oversight of the Straits Settlements was transferred to the Colonial Office following the demise of the East India Company, through to World War I. During this period, the Straits Settlements came to have its own legislature. However, the laws and policies governing money in circulation was still ultimately determined by the Crown. Although the Straits Settlements had subsidiary coinage minted for their express use, the trade currency of the day remained the silver dollar, which by this period was predominantly the Mexican dollar and the Japanese yen. These were made legal tender in the Straits, while the American trade dollar was accepted to some degree as well. However, the overwhelming concern during this period was the persistent instability of the price of silver, which weighed on the value of both circulation and trade currencies. There was no immediate, clear-cut solution to the problem. By the late 1890s, it was decided that the Straits Settlements should issue its own paper currency, backed by a reserve fund under a currency board, and that this 'dollar' should be pegged to a gold rather than silver price. In the process of transiting to the gold standard, the existing silver coinage began to be tokenised. By 1917, the first subsidiary currency notes were also printed amidst the shortage of strategic commodities such as metals during World War I.

Chapter 4 continues the story of money in the Straits Settlements after World War I through the Great Depression and the dark days of the Japanese Occupation. The most salient monetary changes in this period include the complete tokenisation of the

Straits Settlements currency by the end of the 1930s, and the creation of the Malayan dollar to replace the Straits Settlements dollar. The interwar years also saw the British Empire struggling economically; empire-wide protectionist measures were promulgated, threatening Singapore's free port status. The Great Depression broke out in 1929, providing fresh impetus for 'Empire First' policies. Free trade in Singapore came to an end. When war finally arrived, the Japanese introduced their own paper currency that had no backing whatsoever. The free printing of this 'banana money', coupled with the general shortage of everything during World War II, created the setting for hyperinflation and rendered the Japanese military scrip near-worthless.

Chapter 5 recounts the challenges faced by the residents of Singapore after the Liberation, when they were confronted immediately with a shortage of both non-Japanese money and goods. Although the British eventually put enough Malayan dollars in circulation and while supply networks were gradually restored, the stark reality of the day was that the governments of Singapore and the Malay States had been impoverished by the war even as the need to spend on infrastructure development became urgent. Britain, already indebted by debts incurred during World War I, found its financial position even weaker after World War II. Currency controls were put in place to prevent US dollars and gold needed to service war debt draining from the British Treasury. This led to the creation of a Sterling Area consisting of Britain's existing and former dominions and territories, tying their currencies to the pound sterling. Malaya and Singapore became more determined to transit to self-government with the power to make policies that suited their needs rather than the Empire's. This chapter provides the context to the constitutional developments in the Malay States and Singapore that culminated in the creation of a pan-Malayan polity including Sarawak and Sabah (British North Borneo). In the first instance, these territories, as well as Brunei, came together in a currency union based on the Malaya and British Borneo dollar. The creation of the Federation of Malaysia in 1963 saw Singapore joining with Malaya, Sarawak and Sabah politically, creating the opportunity for ever-closer currency and monetary cooperation. However, both political and monetary union would eventually fail.

Chapter 6 begins with the events following the departure of Singapore from the Federation of Malaysia in August 1965. Prolonged and intense negotiations between Singapore and Malaysia to maintain a common currency failed. A 'split' of the Malaya and British Borneo dollar occurred, culminating in Singapore, Malaysia and Brunei's decision to issue their own currencies. Singapore decided to retain the currency board system. The Board of Commissioners of Currency, Singapore (BCCS) issued Singapore's first currency notes – the Orchid series – in June 1967 and its first coins in November. There were immediate logistical problems to be solved to ensure sufficient supply of the new currency from Britain, and a smooth withdrawal of the old Malaya and British North

Borneo dollar. Crucially, for businesses and individuals, the transition was helped by the Currency Interchangeability Agreement between the three countries, whereby all three countries accepted each other's currency as 'customary tender' at par. We then examine other key events in the later part of the decade which proved to be challenging for newly independent Singapore: the implications of the devaluation of the pound sterling, to which the new Singapore dollar was fixed; the desire by Singapore to diversify its external reserves out of sterling; and Britain's decision to withdraw its military personnel from Singapore by the end of 1971.

Chapter 7 starts with the founding of MAS in January 1971, to consolidate central banking functions which had previously been carried out by government departments, although currency issue was left with the BCCS. There followed a number of events in the global economy which had a significant impact on Singapore: the collapse of the Bretton Woods system of fixed exchange rates; the floating of the pound sterling; the termination of the Currency Interchangeability Agreement between Singapore and Malaysia; and the floating of the Singapore dollar following flotation of the major currencies in 1973. Without an exchange rate anchor, MAS began to develop a framework for 'managing' the Singapore dollar more actively. In the midst of challenge there was opportunity: the collapse of the Sterling Area paved the way for Singapore to liberalise capital controls further, spurring the development of the nascent Asian Dollar Market in Singapore established in 1968. But more 'stormy seas' were to be encountered as the Great Inflation in advanced countries and the global oil shocks of 1973 and 1979 spilled over into higher inflation and unemployment in Singapore. We round off the chapter with some important currency developments in Singapore in the 1970s: Singapore's second series of currency notes – the Bird series; the production of numismatic currency, for both local and international collectors; the growing problem of counterfeit currency; and the arrival of the first ATM on the island.

Chapter 8 covers the two decades 1980–1999, during which Singapore was becoming a newly industrialising economy but suffered two recessions. In the early 1980s there were fundamental changes in the way money was managed in Singapore: the introduction of a unique exchange rate-centred monetary policy, and the establishment of the Government of Singapore Investment Corporation (GIC) to manage a portion of Singapore's external reserves. In October 1984, the BCCS introduced Singapore's third currency notes – the Ship series – and Singapore's second series of circulation coins. The new monetary policy framework was soon tested in 1985 by Singapore's first recession since independence and a speculative attack on the currency. Shortly after, Singapore would be confronted by external political pressures to reduce its balance of payments surplus and allow its exchange rate to appreciate to a greater degree; the pressures culminated in the 'graduation' of Singapore, together with Hong Kong, Taiwan and South Korea, from the US preferential tariff arrangement. We turn next to the 'golden age' of the 1990s with rapid economic growth and low inflation in Singapore, and the removal of almost all the restrictions imposed earlier to reduce the use of the Singapore dollar outside the country. But it was not all plain sailing, as a strong Singapore dollar raised domestic costs and concerns that the economy was becoming less competitive in labour-intensive exports compared to other regional players. In 1992, London-based merchant bank Barings went bust following losses made in its Singapore office by General Manager Nick Leeson. Singapore was not spared the financial and trade 'contagion' from the Asian Financial Crisis of 1997–8. The chapter concludes with the Portrait series of currency notes.

Chapter 9 begins ominously with the new millennium Y2K bug and the bursting of the IT bubble. Shortly thereafter, the BCCS merged with MAS, bringing to an end the currency board arrangements that had defined the issuance of physical notes and coins used in Singapore for more than a century. However, vestiges of the currency board and currency union with the broader region remained in the form of the full reserve backing for notes and coins issued and the Currency Interchangeability Agreement with Brunei. The agreement has been sustained for more than 50 years. Singapore's third series of circulation coins was issued during this period. However, the millennium also brought with it three recessions: in 2001–2 the bursting of the IT bubble, in 2008–9 the Global Financial Crisis, and in 2020 the consequences of the COVID-19 related pandemic. The last two would draw comparisons with the Great Depression of the 1930s. Singapore also became caught up once again in the 'global imbalances' debate – what should be done if some countries have large balance of payments surpluses, other countries have the counterpart deficits, and these are deemed to be excessive? As the new millennium progresses, the focus switches to the rise of digital money. Will private 'cryptocurrencies' pose a threat to traditional central-bank-created fiat money? Should the central bank itself issue digital money? This chapter ends on a series of questions to which there can be no definitive answers at the time of writing.

The history of money in Singapore has evolved alongside the foundation narratives of what has become an island nation-state. The long and winding path which Singapore took to have its own, credible, currency is also a crucial expression of the aspiration to self-determination and independence as a sovereign nation. We believe that in chronicling the past, we have helped to explain the present; in this way we hope that this book will illuminate possible paths in our future journey as a nation. Throughout Singapore's monetary journey there are milestones: they mark critical moments in the island's history that have underlined the importance of proper management of money and financial resources such as our reserves.

The story of money in Singapore is not over; it continues.

CURRENCY AND TRADING NETWORKS IN EARLY SOUTHEAST ASIA

Before 1819

The exchange of goods between persons has taken place throughout the span of human civilisation. Tokens (such as shells) or precious items (such as gold and silver) were used in day-to-day trades within communities and across borders. These eventually became known as 'money'. In ancient Southeast Asia, cross-border trade was by and large a maritime affair, with goods carried on ships borne on trade winds, sailing along extensive networks of seaports that bridged broad expanses of land and water. This cross-border trade was possible because most nations used in exchange the same precious commodities for trade: gold, silver and copper. While the exact nature of ancient Temasek and Singapura's society is not fully clear, it is likely that the currencies used around Southeast Asia and along the East-West maritime trade routes were circulating on the island as well. The advent of European colonialism in Southeast Asia from the 16th century, with the coming of the Portuguese, Spanish, Dutch, and later the British, brought new currencies into the region. After the British planted the Union Jack on the shores of Singapore and a vibrant settlement and entrepôt port arose, these myriad currencies came to circulate on the island.

Economists define 'money' as that which fulfils three functions: medium of exchange, unit of account, and store of value. Ever since individuals or communities started exchanging objects in their possession for other things they desired, the demand for 'money' and the concept of 'trade' have existed. Barter trade is one form of exchange, but the transacting parties need to have what is called a 'double coincidence of wants'. That is, each party has to desire what the other has. However, if both parties to a transaction are willing to use another object to complete an exchange, this eliminates the need for the double coincidence. This other object then becomes the medium of transaction. A common unit of account then exists: both buyer and seller are clear about the price of exchange for a certain good or service. The medium used in a transaction can also serve as a store of value – it can be re-used some time after an exchange without significant loss to its value.

At the core of the pre-modern monetary system was the use of precious commodities, principally metals such as gold, silver and copper, for the production of money. Coins minted from them – also known as 'specie' – would be readily accepted in exchange by traders and consumers outside the territories that produced them. The coins could be melted and recast into the forms of money used by these other communities. Their precious-metal content imparted intrinsic value to them, regardless of the national imprint on the coinage. The weight and purity (fineness) of the precious metals used in the coins could be easily determined, allowing specie to serve as a unit of account. Its durability compared to perishable items also meant that these coins, by and large, could serve as a store of value. In other words, specie was widely accepted as 'money'.

In February 1819, Sir Thomas Stamford Bingley Raffles signed a momentous treaty that paved the way for the establishment of a British outpost on the island of Singapore. On this island, which lay at the crossroads of the East-West maritime trade, a free port was created where trade was not taxed. It attracted a great multitude of people from many nations in the years that followed. Sojourners and settlers alike brought their own money and went about their business unhindered by the lack of a common currency. They simply conducted their business at the bazaar and commercial activities at the port using the different types of money that were already circulating and widely accepted throughout the region.

Our story thus begins with the flow of goods and money across borders, and specifically in the Malay Archipelago, from antiquity to the period before Raffles's arrival on the island.

Chapter opening picture: Detail from The Watering Place at Anjer Point in the Island of Java, by William Daniell, 1794.

Regional trade networks from antiquity to the 1500s

The archetypal early global trading network was the ancient Silk Road. Goods and different types of money flowed along it from Asia to Europe, bringing Han China (206 BC–220 AD) into contact with the Roman Empire (27 BC–476 AD). It was a continuous, linear route, and 'East-West trade' was conducted through intermediaries, with goods transported in a series of shorter legs, passed from one middleman to another.

However, more important for our story were the beginnings of a maritime route established during the reign of the Han Emperor Wu (141–87 BC). This 'Maritime Silk Road' brought the East Indies and India into the East-West trade network. Roman traders would sail to Karachi and Gujarat to purchase Chinese silks,[1] while Chinese traders would make their way to Southeast Asia and the Indian Ocean, bringing gold for the purchase of produce of these regions, and selling items such as silk and porcelain in return.[2] Roman or Arab middlemen using the Maritime Silk Road did not have to travel all the way to China to acquire Chinese products,[3] and the converse was also true. Instead, the commercial ports and settlements of coastal India and Southeast Asia functioned as entrepôts for a wide variety of goods from China, the Middle East, and Europe. As a case in point, Arab, Persian and African traders are recorded as having sailed to Ceylon in the 6th century to sell their incense, perfume, carpets and textiles, while they returned with the Chinese silk and spices available there.[4]

Trade brought great prosperity to many of the ports in the global maritime trading networks, fuelled by the gold, silver and copper (often bronze) specie used for the purposes of exchange. There was a flow of both goods and money. In the first century AD, large amounts of Roman gold and silver coinage passed into the Indo-Pacific region. It has been estimated that 100 million gold coins flowed to India, China and Arabia annually, with India alone receiving 55 million of them.[5] Unsurprisingly, Roman-era coinage has been discovered in archaeological excavations in India, Thailand, Vietnam, China and Japan.[6]

As the East-West trade developed in the centuries that followed, Southeast Asia became more central to several maritime trade networks. Historian Kenneth R. Hall has identified five networks intersecting Southeast Asia dating back to the 10th century AD. Collectively termed the 'Eastern Indian Ocean regional trade networks', these were: the Bay of Bengal Network (Indian Ocean), the Malacca Straits Network (from Sumatra to Siam), the Java Sea Network (East Indies), the South China Sea Network (from China to Southeast Asia) and the Sulu Sea Network (Borneo, the Spice Islands and the Philippines).[7] The most extensive of these were the ones that intersected like links in a chain to form the 'China trade' leg of the Maritime Silk Road, stretching across the Indian Ocean to the coast of China. As Southeast Asia served as a conduit for the

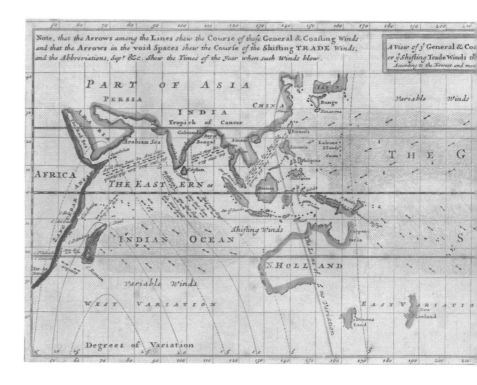

merchandise being traded through the various maritime networks, a wide range of the currencies circulating in the port polities and territories involved in these trades entered the region.

Maritime trade networks were driven, literally, by monsoon winds. Today we associate monsoons with bad weather and storms, and no doubt they were feared even in antiquity. But it was the monsoon winds that propelled sailing ships across the seas, and thus kept global maritime trade flowing – hence the term 'trade winds'.[8] They follow a distinctive half-yearly pattern.[9] For Southeast Asia's maritime trade networks, the winds that crossed the Indian Ocean and the South China sea would have been the most relevant: the Southwest Monsoon (blowing to the northeast) would propel ships from the Indian Ocean to the East Indies from May to October each year, while the Northeast Monsoon (blowing southwest) would propel them from China towards the East Indies from November to April.[10] The regularity and reliability of these winds helped mariners plan stopovers where they could replenish supplies, take shelter and wait for the new monsoon season to start for the second leg of their journey.

The East Indies lay at a point where the Southwest and Northeast monsoons intersected. It was therefore natural for sailing ships to stopover or turn around there. Traders would sell what they were carrying on board their ships and acquire goods brought there by merchants from the other side of the ocean.

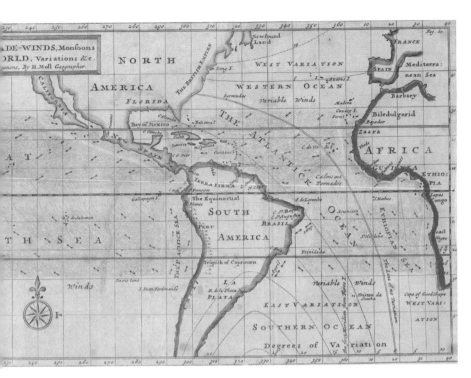

'A view of ye general & coasting trade-winds through the world, variations &c. According to ye newest and most exact observations', by H. Moll, geographer. c. 1715.

The East Indies was not the sole beneficiary of the trade winds. In an era when sailing ships were small, they generally could not survive voyages across the open ocean. Coasting – sailing close to the coastline even for long distances – would have been the modus operandi. Mariners coasting from China to Southeast Asia, for instance, would travel from port to port along the Indo-China coastline and along the east coast of the Malay Peninsula before reaching the Straits of Malacca. From the Indian Ocean, traders similarly coasted until they reached the East Indies. There were two maritime entrances to the China Sea for coasting ships: the Straits of Malacca, and the Sunda Straits. This geography enabled the ports of the Malay Archipelago – not only the East Indies but also the Malay Peninsula and the Philippines – to serve potentially as entrepôt trading hubs, or emporiums, of the Indian Ocean and China trade.[11]

Trade and currencies of the Southeast Asian kingdoms

The Malay Archipelago was, in the first instance, an entrepôt for the East-West trade. From China, the Southeast Asian communities procured goods such as silk, porcelain, copper, iron, salt, and sugar.[12] These were mostly resold to the Europeans and Arabs. At the same time, the archipelago was itself an area of production, offering raw resources and other products sought by Europeans, Arabs, Indians and Chinese. Up to the 18th century, the main items exported from the Malay

Archipelago included local commodities such as spices, aromatics, drugs, ivory, tin, incense, and sandalwood, as well as hundreds of other Southeast Asian products.

The origins of the Malay Archipelago's trade links with China date back to the time of the Tang Dynasty (618–907). By the 7th century, the East Indies was already a 'trading, shipping and transshipment centre' for the maritime trade between China and the territories bordering the Indian Ocean.[13] The main political powerhouse in the region at this point was the Srivijayan Empire (650–1377), which exercised control over Sumatra, the Malay Peninsula, west Borneo, and most of Java.

With Srivijaya's ascendency, for the first time a single polity controlled maritime access to the Malay Archipelago and specifically the East Indies. During this time, the East Indies became a major entrepôt for the China trade.[14] (see map, pp. 64–5.) The port city of Palembang became the empire's political capital and its chief entrepôt, to which the other regional trading centres became feeder ports.[15] Palembang's absolute dominance lasted until the 10th century, after which waves of Chinese junks started trading directly with the main areas of production in the Indies, bypassing the main entrepôt.[16]

Chinese money flowed with the goods being traded. There was an influx of Chinese coinage throughout the archipelago. It peaked between the 11th and 13th centuries, when the trade between the East Indies and Chinese and Arab merchants surged to new heights.[17] Readily available and abundant, the Chinese coins became the most convenient currency for all transactions in the region, including local commerce and the China trade. The output from Chinese copper mines soared: enough copper was mined to mint hundreds of millions of coins in the early 11th century, rising to billions annually by the 1070s. For instance, in 1078 over nine billion copper coins were minted.[18] The East Indies began to

A Javanese trading jong (junk) at Bantam, as shown in di Varthema (1610).

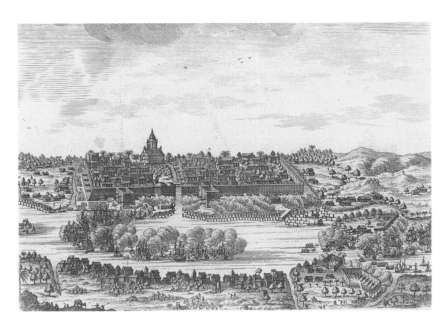

The city of Palembang with its three forts (1659).

import Chinese copper cash directly on a large scale. It was in this context that Srivijaya started using Chinese cash as its currency.

The outflow of copper from China was sufficient to alarm Chinese officials. In 1074, one official was reported complaining about 'foreign ships' carrying away so many copper coins that 'the currency was drained off like waters of the sea into the *wei-lu* [rear gate]'.[19] These 'foreign ships' were probably Arab, Persian or Southeast Asian vessels that had been active in the China trade for several centuries. Chinese private traders also carried copper cash out of China for trading purposes and directly exported the coins overseas as well.[20]

The outflow of copper coins only slowed around 1127, during the Southern Song period (1125–1279), when the Chinese government lost control of their northern territories where the copper mines were situated. This led to the promulgation of a number of imperial edicts in the 12th and 13th centuries prohibiting the export of copper, but they did not prevent the smuggling of copper to the East Indies.[21] The following dynasty, the Mongol Yuan (1271–1368), ceased coin production entirely.[22]

Bronze and copper cash from the Northern Song Dynasty (960-1127), China.

However, by that time there were such large volumes of Chinese copper cash in the East Indies that when the Majapahit Empire (1293–1517) succeeded Srivijaya, it adopted the Chinese Song coinage as the standard currency throughout its kingdom as well. The civil administration even used the Chinese coin to pay the wages of public officials, and levied fines and collected taxes in this currency.[23]

The period of the Majapahit Empire overlapped with the Ming Dynasty in China (1368–1644), which minted coins in only 40 out of the 276 years of its history. From the mid-13th century to the 16th, the main forms of money circulating in China included privately minted coins, 'paper money, coins minted under earlier dynasties, counterfeit coins, and [some] recent official coins'.[24] Nevertheless, the copper cash that was already in the East Indies proved to be very durable. When Ming emissaries visited Java alongside Admiral Cheng Ho in the 15th century, they found copper coins from various dynasties all circulating as current coins.[25] This motley array of copper cash would remain in circulation throughout the next few Chinese dynasties and East Indies regimes and beyond.

During the Majapahit period, monetary developments in China disrupted trade and the supply of copper currency to the East Indies. It has been estimated that over the 14th and 15th centuries the net flow of currency reversed, and Java lost up to two million copper coins to China.[26] The empire's solution was to produce local coinage.[27] Yet, instead of creating a truly indigenous currency, the regime centred at Java simply replicated the design of the old Song cash in tin. The availability of tin in the Malay Archipelago made it a viable substitute for copper, although with the tin coins variations in design emerged. For instance, some Chinese-style tin coins were struck bearing Islamic inscriptions.[28] In the mid-15th century, the Javanese also started using tin bars weighing about one kilogram in commercial transactions.[29] The Majapahit Empire's Chinese tin cash minted in Java were called *picis* – the coins were eventually also produced using lead alloys.[30]

The Javanese-made coins remained in circulation for many years. When the Dutch reached the East Indies around a century-and-a-half later, they found *picis*

The return to Amsterdam of the Second Expedition to the East indies on 19 July 1599, by Andries van Eertvelt.

made of lead at Banten (modern-day Bantam). In fact, after the Dutch established their base at Batavia (today's Jakarta), traders of the Dutch East India Company (Vereenigde Oostindische Compagnie, or VOC) sold 411 tons of lead to a Chinese contractor who was producing *picis* for the place.[32]

It was during the last century of the Majapahit Empire that the Malaccan Sultanate (1400–1511) emerged in the Malay Peninsula. Malacca quickly became an emporium for the East-West trade and an export hub for East Indies produce. It drew large numbers of Arab, Gujarati and Chinese merchants.[33] The Sultanate minted its own coinage, using the main metallic commodity it had in abundance tin.[34] Struck using a base metal, these coins had less intrinsic value, and were probably used only in territories under Malacca's direct control for domestic trade and in administration, and not for its entrepôt commerce.[35] These Malaccan tin coins had Arabic inscriptions, and did not follow the design of Chinese cash.[36]

Indeed, a number of native states on both sides of the Straits of Malacca minted coins of their own, either for political reasons or simply for local usage. While most of them cast their common-use coins in tin, gold specie was also minted. During the reign of Sultan Muzaffar Shah (1445–1459), for instance, the Malaccan Sultanate minted its own tin coins to replace those of the Pasai Sultanate (1267–1521).[37] At around the same time, gold coins (*kupang*) were minted and used in Kelantan and Patani. Kelantan also produced its own tin coinage called *pitis* in the mould of Chinese cash.[38]

Following the Portuguese conquest of Malacca in 1511, the Sultanate was dislodged and from 1528 made Johor Lama its new capital further south. There, Sultan Alauddin Riayat Shah II (1528–1564) minted a set of gold coinage (*mas* and *kupang*) which were used as far afield as Sumatra and Patani, and so became a form of regional trade currency. At the same time, Johor also minted tin coins (*katun*) and circulated these with the gold coins. In 1708, the Terengganu Sultanate (1700–1821) issued its own currency of three coins in the image of the Johor trade coinage. A tin *pitis* was added in the early 1800s.[39] Over at Kedah, from the 17th century to the 18th, the kingdom minted its own gold, silver and tin cash for local use. The design of the tin money was distinctive – it was shaped like a cockerel standing over rings.[40]

Trade and currencies of Temasek and Singapura

Singapore's pre-colonial story is part of a rich tapestry of regional political, economic, and monetary developments. The history of the island once known as Temasek includes colourful and at times contrasting narratives: there is more than one way of constructing a plausible account. Historian Peter Borschberg points out that 'reconstructing the history of Singapore of the pre-1819 period is like working on a gigantic puzzle with literally thousands of little pieces of information that need to be pieced together and made sense of. But unlike a puzzle from a box, it is not known what the final product will – or even should – look like.'[41] There are no contemporary, first-hand, and detailed descriptions of the people and social structures of Temasek or Singapura. Historians are dependent on a diverse range of evidence, from fleeting mentions of the island in documented sources to the interpretation of more recent archaeological finds.

According to one of the earliest readings of the *Sejarah Melayu* (Malay Annals),[42] ancient Singapura – literally the 'Lion City' – was in existence during the 12th and 13th centuries, having been founded by Sang Nila Utama in 1160. In these accounts, he was a prince of a vassal state to the Srivijayan Empire (650–1377). The line of *Rajas* – kings or chiefs – established by Sang Nila Utama ended when the last king of Singapura fled to Malacca in 1252.[43] However, Portuguese and Chinese sources have established the beginning and end of the kingdom at Singapura as 1299 and 1391[44] respectively, consistent with later readings of the Annals that describe Sang Nila Utama as a prince of the Majapahit empire (1293–1517). Parameswara, a Sumatran prince from the same empire, was identified as Singapura's last *Raja*, having established himself after murdering his predecessor King Sangesínga in 1389.[45] He was driven out by either Majapahit or Siamese forces five years later. After fleeing, he went north into the Malay Peninsula, founded Malacca and established the Sultanate there.

Was ancient Singapura a village, town, port, entrepôt or city? The nature of the economic activities conducted there no doubt determined the volume and type of currencies used on the island. One of the most important references to a 'great' Singapura of the old days was provided by João de Barros in his *Da Asia* (1553). Based on 'what the Malay people said', he reported that mariners from the East and West had come to a great emporium on the island. His sources also went on to state that during the time of Sangesínga (1375–1389), the city flourished.[46]

Other accounts of Temasek/Singapura paint a more diverse picture. Wang Dayuan, a trader from China, ventured west and in 1349 recorded his observations in a book, *Daoyi zhilüe* (a short account on the islands of the barbarians). Wang noted the presence of pirates at Temasek who would allow empty Chinese junks to pass unmolested – however, when the ships returned fully loaded, the pirates would attack the Chinese mariners *en masse* as they neared the Carimons, a group of islands southwest of Singapore.[47]

In his 16th-century account, Portuguese observer Tomé Pires reported that there was an active maritime population known as the Celates[48], or Orang Laut (the 'sea peoples' in the local vernacular) who were present from Malacca down the coast of the Malay Peninsula as far as Bintang in Java.[49] They were also in Singapura. What was the nature of their activity on the island? The Orang Laut would have had intimate knowledge of the seaways of the region. According to de Barros, Parameswara was able to cement his position at Singapura because he was aided by his followers from Java as well as the Orang Laut. When hostile forces attacked the island to punish Parameswara for killing Sangesínga, the Orang Laut facilitated his departure from the island. They followed him up north and they founded a settlement which eventually grew to become the Malaccan Sultanate.[50] Pires also noted that the Orang Laut had served the Malaccan king as rowers. Pires recorded that the Orang Laut were 'corsairs' – privateers or pirates – who did not accept monetary payments for their services to the king, only expecting food.[51] He further documented accounts that Paramjcura (Parameswara) 'had no trade' at all; his people 'fished, planted and plundered'.[52] Conversely, if the oral tradition recorded by de Barros about a great emporium in Singapura is accurate, there may have been a time when as an economically active polity and trade emporium existed on the island before it was abandoned by Parameswara and deteriorated into a pirates' den.

According to another narrative more widely adopted in recent years, Temasek in the 14th century was a great entrepôt and emporium following the decline of Srivijaya. The island, like other ports such as Lambri in Aceh and Pengkalan Bujang in Kedah, became a regional entrepôt. While Temasek served the South China Sea region as a key collection centre for the products of the Malay Archipelago, the other two ports catered more to trade in the Indian Ocean.[53] Archaeological evidence lends support to the hypothesis that Temasek was a market and transshipment centre for bulk commodities from China, and also a source of demand for high-quality items, testifying to the settlement's prosperity.[54] Items unearthed during excavations of the northern bank of the Singapore River have led archaeologists to believe that Temasek produced some of its own metal implements and engaged in glass recycling.[55] Other finds have included Chinese porcelain, stoneware and earthenware, hinting that a vibrant trade in foodstuffs between China and the region took place, with basic commodities such as rice, wine and salt imported from China despite the fact that they were also produced within Southeast Asia itself.[56]

Other archaeological finds may help us arbitrate between the different narratives. Ancient coins were discovered within the boundaries of old Singapura as early as 1819. While clearing the grounds of the 'plain' (the present-day Esplanade), Lieutenant Henry Ralfe of the Bengal Artillery found several old Chinese coins at the old earthen wall known as the Old Lines. This wall was the largest and most visible built object left on the island by an ancient regime.[57] It stretched almost a mile long, from the beach front right up to the base of the Singapore Hill (later known as Fort Canning Hill).[58] Only one of the coins was in good condition – the rest crumbled when touched. The Chinese characters inscribed on it indicate that it was struck during the reign of the Emperor Huizong (1100–1126) in the last years of the Northern Song period.[59] The good coin was probably made of bronze, and those that crumbled made of iron,[60] as these two metals were used for minting Chinese cash during this period.

The next significant discovery of old coinage on the island involved John Crawfurd in 1822. Prior to his appointment to the administration of Singapore, Crawfurd (see p. 44) explored the territory. He walked around the top of the Singapore Hill, where he surveyed what was left of ancient Singapura. Among the remnants, Crawfurd found several 10th- and 11th- century Song-dynasty brass coins. He believed that the presence of these coins was evidence that the Malays were established on the island from the 12th century. He pointed out that Chinese coins were already in circulation in the Indies before the region's conversion to Islam, and before the beginning of direct trade between Europe and the Malay Archipelago.[61]

In 1829, a decade after the British founded a trading post in Singapore, the island's resident military doctor, William Montgomerie, found some Chinese coins while laying the foundations of a building. Montgomerie identified them as Song coins produced during the reigns of the emperors Huizong (1100–1126) and Lizong (1224–1264). In the doctor's view, their presence suggested that the Chinese had come as traders to the island from 'very early' times.[62] This contrasts with Crawfurd's opinion that the coins he found on the hill merely confirmed what was general knowledge at that time: that is, the peoples of the Malay Archipelago were using Chinese coinage from the time of the Srivijayan Empire.

Vintages of Song Dynasty coins found at Singapore shortly after the arrival of Raffles in 1819.

Top row: Song Yuan Tong Bao, Emperor Taizu period (960-976).

Middle row: Zhi Ping Yuan Bao, Emperor Yingzong period (1063-1067).

Bottom row: Yuan Feng Tong Bao, Emperor Shenzong period (1067-1085).

One reason for this difference in interpretation may be the location of the coin finds. While we do not know exactly where Dr Montgomerie's coins were found, the circumstances suggest that it was probably on the 'plain', where the old town or bazaar of Singapura had been situated.[63] This interpretation is supported by Lieutenant Ralfe's finds of 'China-ware and shells' on the plain – items that could have been traded or used in trade.[64]

The finds around the plain and on the hill may suggest a settlement pattern in Singapura that could be commonly found across the East Indies. Large, diasporic Chinese communities would not typically settle or live close to the indigenous communities. Instead, they would reside within their own kampongs under their own chieftain at the periphery of the indigenous town. Meanwhile the local ruling elites would occupy a central site. However, the two communities might freely interact in the marketplace.[65] This would probably have been the situation in Singapura.[66]

What conclusions can be drawn from the various finds of Chinese coins? The coins were minted in the period from the 10th century to the 13th. Clearly, both traditions as to the origins of Singapura – whether based on the Malay Annals or on the Portuguese and Chinese records – are compatible with the age of the coins found. The fact that some of the finds pre-date the Singapura of both accounts attests to the extent that Chinese coins had circulated across various dynastic periods. For instance, during the Song, Yuan and Ming dynasties, coins from earlier periods and regimes were still in circulation.

The questions remain – how did the coins come to be in Singapura and who was using them? If Pires's records are to be believed, the Orang Laut community living at Singapura neither used money as a means of exchange, nor conducted trade. In the reconstruction of Temasek's past as a great regional emporium, however, Singapore's ascent was contingent on its engagement in Chinese maritime commerce. The coins found were therefore interpreted as evidence that there was a significant Chinese settlement on the island whose population 'were more likely to adopt Chinese coins as a medium of exchange to facilitate transactions with traders from China'.[67] Supporting this contention, scholars have cited Wang Dayuan's *Daoyi zhilüe*, noting that there were Chinese inhabitants at Longyamen (translated as Dragon Teeth Strait), a geographical feature linked with Temasek. Associated with this was the broader proposition that the general population of Temasek could have used Chinese cash as a form of domestic currency.[68] The island's 'golden age' would have come to an end at the beginning of the 15th century, when it ceded its regional emporium role to Malacca.

But the story of money in ancient Singapura is still incomplete. In 1837, a group of convicts were clearing the marshes along the banks of the Rochor

Representation of
the tin coins found in
Singapore in 1837.

River about five-and-a-half miles from town. In the process, they discovered a glazed earthen vessel filled with 1,000 ancient coins made of tin. It was sunk two feet into the mud, some 15–16 yards (about 14 metres) from the river's edge. On the obverse of each coin was the symbol of a lion rampant, and on the reverse a dagger or a sword. None of the international traders in Singapore at that time could identify the coins or determine their provenance. They believed that the contents of this vessel could well be linked to the 'former history of the island', that is, the time when the island was called Temasek, and later Singapura.[69]

What is certain is that these coins were produced for a non-Islamic polity. The lion rampant strongly suggests Hindu influence, while the kris (a traditional Javanese dagger) points to the polity's connection to Javanese culture. The tin coins were probably cast during the time of the Majapahit Empire (1293–1517), partially coinciding with the period when Singapura was a major polity, according to Portuguese historical accounts. It has been established that some time from the late 14th and early 15th centuries, the Majapahit resorted to minting Chinese cash from tin when supplies of the copper coins from China dwindled. This would also be consistent with the period when most of the polities in the Malay Archipelago started creating their own tin-based coins. With Singapura so tightly enmeshed in developments in the region, if there had been an active political entity remaining on the island after Parameswara's departure, it would probably have used tin cash coins as well. The Malaccan tin coins minted during the reign of Sultan Muzaffar Shah (1445–1459) were almost identical in diameter to the coins found at the Rochor River. The lion rampant design on the newly discovered coins might suggest that they were linked to the 'Lion City' heritage of Singapura.

The earthen vessel in which the coins were found provides the last clue to the time origins of the currency. The people of the Majapahit period are known to have kept their coins in earthen containers. Many of those found in Indonesia had slits for inserting coins. They came in various forms, the most popular of which were boar-shaped. It is possible that the earthen vessel recovered in 1837 originated at the time of Singapura.[70] Given its sheer weight, filled as it was with coins, it was unlikely to have floated down from the coast.

Many questions still remain. If the tin 'lion' coins were produced during the Singapura era, why were they not found with the Chinese coins among the ruins of the ancient kingdom? Were the coins struck just before Parameswara's expulsion from Singapura, and could this be the reason why no more were produced and circulated? Did Singapura have a back-story that is yet to be uncovered? There is much we still need to learn about Singapore's early history.[71]

Trade networks and seaports of the European colonial powers

Historically, there were two main categories of maritime city entrepôt in Southeast Asia. First, there were the seaports that also functioned as capitals of kingdoms, such as Palembang in the Srivijayan Empire (650–1377) and Malacca in the Malaccan Sultanate (1400–1511).[72] Most of these arose in the 15th century or earlier.

The second group arose from the 16th century onwards, as colonial port cities. The overland Silk Road had been closed by the Ottomans in 1453. At the same time, Venice formed a treaty with the Mameluke sultans of Egypt to purchase pepper and other Southeast Asian spices. As this disrupted the free flow of spices

Pioneering Portuguese navigator Bartolomeu Dias.

to the West, the European powers were impelled to develop a direct maritime trading route to China by establishing their own bases.[73] In 1488, Portuguese explorer Bartolomeu Dias became the first to round the Cape of Good Hope. A few decades later, the Portuguese, led by Vasco da Gama, discovered the Europe-to-India sea route. This allowed the Europeans to sail directly to China. For the first time, a true Maritime Silk Road linked East and West, a single linear route comparable to the overland Silk Road. Many of the port cities in this second group originated as concessions from indigenous powers, such as Macao and Madras; or were built over the site of ancient cities that had been conquered and annexed, like Goa and Malacca. They formed a string of seaports serving the maritime networks of European empires.

Before 1800, the main ports of this network linking India with China included Surat and Goa in western India; Ceylon (today's Sri Lanka) in the Indian Ocean; Malacca, Bantam, Batavia, Palembang, and Manila in Southeast Asia;

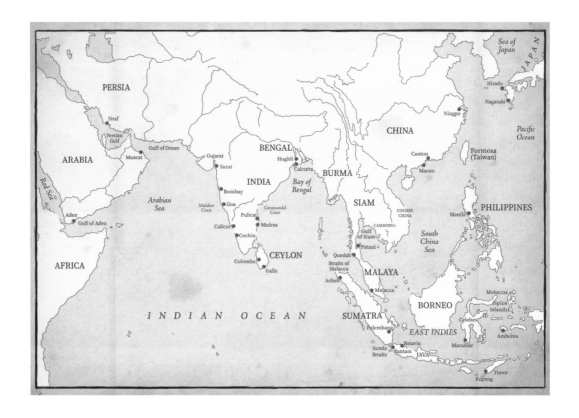

Major seaports
and settlements
on the Indo-Pacific
maritime trade
route up till 1800.

Canton, Macao and Nagasaki in East Asia. Through them flowed commodities, currencies, bullion, early bills of exchange and promissory notes, all contributing to the development of East–West maritime trade. When the Portuguese first took control of Malacca, it became their main commercial station in the Straits of Malacca. The Dutch turned Batavia into the biggest port city in the Indies, even though it had already gained control of Malacca from the Portuguese.[74]

The colonial powers and their currencies
Portugal and Spain

The Portuguese arrived in the Malay Archipelago in the early part of the 16th century. They defeated the Malacca Sultanate, and occupied Malacca from 1511 to 1641. There, as well as at a number of other newly conquered territories such as Goa and Colombo, the Portuguese established mints to make coinage for their eastern maritime empire. Initially, the Malacca mint struck gold (*catholico*), silver (*malaquese*) and several tin (*bastardo*, *soldo* and *dinheiro*) pieces,[75] while the other mints produced gold, silver and copper coinage.[76] The accounting currencies used at Malacca, *tangas* and *patacoes*, were similar to those used at the other Portuguese stations

Barter trade and non-metallic money

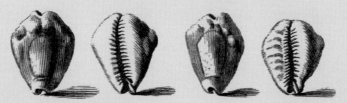

A drawing of cowrie shells, as shown in Gualtieri (1742).

Although specie was the main medium of transaction for many European nations for centuries, in several communities all over the world barter trade, or the use of non-precious commodities as money, was the norm. As European galleons following in Vasco da Gama's wake plied the maritime trade routes, around the Cape of Good Hope, along the coasts of the Indian Ocean and through to the China Sea, they came across these alternative systems of exchange.

John Saris was the chief merchant on the first English voyage to Japan. While he was *en route* to Bantam, a storm blew up, compelling the ship to take shelter and restock provisions at Madagascar. They found that the local peoples did not use money, but they managed to use a tin spoon and a small piece of brass to barter for a fat ox and a sheep.[77]

On a voyage to Surat in India, William Finch, an English merchant under the East India Company, observed that the indigenous peoples of Sierra Leone used the *gola*, a fruit the size of a walnut, as money. The higher the payment required, the more fruits would be given. The fruit would then be shared out and chewed, before being discarded.[78]

Cowries were widely used as money within the Indian Ocean area even before European merchant ships arrived.[79] In Bengal from the 14th to the 16th century, the shells were used side-by-side with the Sultanate's silver currency.[80] In the 16th century, the Portuguese started mass imports of cowries from Maldives to Bengal to enhance the supply of money. When the British colonial administrators gained control of the territory, they simply continued using cowries as a subsidiary currency within the broader rupee currency system, partly because they were short of copper.[81] The ready availability of the shells, therefore, provided some level of stability to the Bengal currency regime. The use of cowries as money lasted until the 19th century.[82]

in India.[83] Through these forms of specie, Portuguese Malacca introduced to the Malay Archipelago currencies that were different from those already in use in the region.

While the Portuguese were discovering the direct maritime route to the Indian Ocean, the Spanish sailed westwards, seeking an alternative route to China. They arrived at the Americas. The Spanish had their own currency, a *real de a ocho* or 'piece of eight', struck in silver. The conquered civilisations of the Americas proved to be a ready source of the bullion which the Spanish used to mint new reals and so underwrite their trade with China. The Portuguese were familiar with the real, and they themselves had introduced it to China; however it became

MALACKA.

The town of Malacca, c. 1665, by Johannes Vingboons.

Tin *dinheiro*,1521-7 (above) and *bastardo*, 1545-8 (below) minted at Malacca by the Portuguese.

widely used in the latter only after the Spanish reached the Philippines in 1565. Deploying galleons sailing out of Manila, the Spanish started exporting their reals in shiploads. In 1597 alone, Manila transported about twelve million reals to China.[84] The acceptance of the real grew internationally, and it also became known as the 'Spanish silver dollar'.

The success of the Spanish silver dollar in China made it the trade dollar of choice for merchants conducting the maritime China trade. The weight and fineness of the coin's silver content imparted to it a high value, and the Spanish colonial mints in the Americas produced a steady supply of the specie. The real was very effective as a store of value, suffering little debasement over the centuries.[85] In the 16th century, its growing popularity coincided with an increase in demand for silver not only in China but also in Europe. In order to acquire products from the Far East, the Europeans were trading intensively with Arab merchants, who preferred payment in silver rather than gold.[86]

Unlike Spain, Portugal did not have silver mines in its colonies from which it could obtain the bullion it needed to underwrite its trade with China and India. As the supply of silver coins in the region fell short of what was required, they resorted to drawing on silver from Portugal, which put a serious strain on their home nation. Although the mint at Goa struck 'Malacca' silver coins to support the Portuguese colonies in the East Indies, these coins were quickly taken up by Chinese traders and none were left. In 1569, it became policy that all Spanish silver dollars earned in Portugal's Indian territories were to be melted into bullion, and no silver coinage would be minted.[87] Silver collected from the Japan trade at Macao was also used to finance Portugal's purchase of gold and silk from China.[88]

However, the drain of resources from Portugal would eventually prove unsustainable. The Portuguese empire was running short of specie for its own use; there was no question of it minting more coins to displace existing currencies in the East Indies. Consequently, the currency of Portuguese Malacca made little impact on the region. Indeed, the Chinese coins and their local variations had remained the main subsidiary currency in the Indies. Because of the shortage of precious metals, the mint at Malacca was eventually reduced to producing only tin coinage, and by the early 1600s it was closed. Financially crippled, the Portuguese empire would shortly lose most of its colonies to the Dutch.[89]

Spanish dollars minted in Peru, 1790 (above) and Mexico, 1748 (below).

The Portuguese in Malacca created a dual currency system: the colonial power would mint a form of 'local' money for domestic trade and administrative use in the colonies, while the Spanish silver dollar would be used in maritime trade, especially with China. This was a forerunner of the currency system used by the other colonial powers in the region, including Britain after it set up a trading outpost on the island of Singapore in 1819 (see p. 34).

How was Singapore situated in this context? The early-20th-century British colonial administrator Warren D. Barnes suggested that, since records show that there was a *shahbandar* (harbourmaster) at Singapore in the 17th century, there must have been an active port on the island.[90] It was also noted that the *shahbandar* also held the title of 'Sri Raja Negara', or 'Raja Negara Selat, Ketua Orang Laut' or

---

Trading foreign currency

It was common for the early sailing ships to carry chests containing the specie needed for trading in the East. Sometimes the coins were sold – great profits could be made in places where certain coins were in short supply. John Saris was residing in Bantam between 1603 and 1605. He provided an account of how Chinese coins – mainly made from brass and tin alloys – had been imported from China because Bantam did not coin its own money. The imported cash was traded as a commodity that could be purchased with Spanish silver dollars, and vice versa. The supply of Chinese cash fluctuated with the junk season, and it would depreciate in value against the silver dollar with the arrival of new cash supplies, and appreciate during the off-season.[91] Bullion was regularly traded as well. Ships *en route* from the China seas to the Indian Ocean were often laden with Japanese silver, as well as bars of copper, aluminium, gold and tin from Malacca.[92] Because of their weight and bulk, bullion and chests of specie were often used as ships' ballast.[93]

'Orang Laut Batin' – that is, he was the 'leader of the Orang Laut sea nomads in and around the Straits'. Certainly, in this light, Singapore was not 'a backwater at this point in time'.[94] Others have concurred, contending that Singapore was a settlement of some size in the 16th and 17th centuries, 'larger than a village but smaller than a city'.[95]

The Dutch

The Dutch East India Company (Vereenigde Oostindische Compagnie, or VOC) first established a foothold in the East Indies in 1605 at Amboina (Ambon), when it captured the Portuguese fort on the island. Although the VOC's power centre became Batavia (today's Jakarta), on the island of Java, it went on to conquer most of the other ports in the Portuguese maritime empire. In essence, the Dutch took over the Portuguese commercial networks, but unlike the Portuguese they had supplies of bullion.[96]

One-guilder coin minted in the Netherlands, 1763.

In the years immediately after 1605, the VOC financed its spice trade and its colonial ventures in the East Indies with bullion and specie brought directly from Holland. However, this placed such an enormous strain on Dutch finances that the VOC instituted a new policy in 1619, requiring that profits made in the East Indies from its trades with India and East Asia be used to pay for goods sent to Holland.[97] Although the Dutch quickly came to dominate the global trade in spices,[98] the profits earned by the VOC were insufficient to fund its China trade. The Company therefore continued to ship bullion from Holland even as it sourced for silver in Japan, exporting Chinese silk to the Japanese in exchange. In the decade from 1630 to 1640, of the 3.2 million florins' worth of gold and silver bullion arriving at Batavia from Holland and Japan, nearly three-quarters came from the latter.[99]

The Dutch currency eventually became known as the guilder (or gulden), and with the arrival of the VOC, guilders became familiar in the region. However, guilders were only struck in Holland. When the VOC established a mint in Batavia, it struck other specie meant for trade and the administration of its territories in the East Indies. There was the silver Batavian crown, which was subdivided into 48 stivers.[100] The crown also came in denominations of half- and quarter-crowns, equivalent to 24 and 12 stivers respectively. Gold Java ducats and silver Java rupees were struck subsequently. The mint also counter-stamped special marks on specie imported from abroad. For example, gold ducats originally minted in Holland were counter-stamped with B for Batavia, Indian and Persian silver rupees were stamped with words denoting 'Java' or 'Dutch rider', and gold *cupang* from Japan were stamped with a lion to filter out counterfeits.

However, the bullion supply situation deteriorated from the 1640s to the 1680s, when the VOC faced stiff market competition from Zheng Cheng Gong

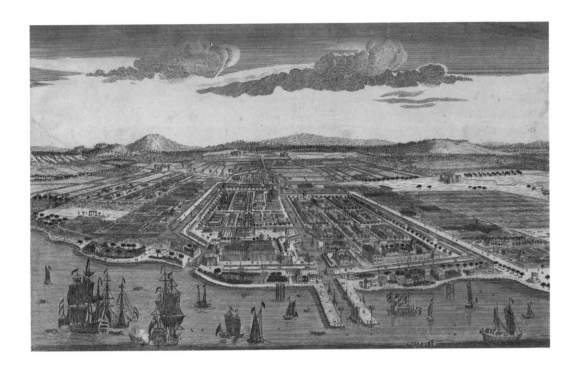

The town of Batavia (today's Jakarta) in 1780.

(Coxinga), a Ming loyalist and rebel against the Qing Dynasty (1644–1912). This forced the VOC to double the amount of bullion shipped directly from Holland.[101] Then, in 1685, the supply of silver from Japan ceased when the shogunate banned the export of precious metals.

Consequently, during the second half of the 17th century, the VOC sought to alleviate the bullion shortage by instituting a monopoly on trade in the East Indies. Chinese junks that had previously bypassed Dutch ports to trade directly in the Malay Archipelago could no longer do so, and had to deal with the VOC. An example was made of Macassar, which was bombarded and occupied in 1660 for having traded directly with the Company's rivals. Bantam – previously the premier entrepôt in the East Indies for the pepper trade – was subjected to a blockade and its trade diverted to Batavia. After this, every port in Sumatra dealing in pepper was required to send all consignments of the spice to the VOC.[102] The Dutch eventually achieved complete control of the Indies and of trade through its ports. However, it could not enforce its monopolistic policies beyond the archipelago.

Despite these measures, the drain of bullion from Holland continued. When war with France broke out in 1688, a large number of Dutch *fluyts* (cargo-carrying sailing ships) had to be redeployed back to Europe. This handicapped the VOC's seaborne trade in the East Indies. Towards the end of the century, the Company made the ultimate decision to cease direct trade with China and depend solely on the Chinese junks bringing supplies to Batavia annually.[103]

European 'factories' (trading posts) at Canton (Guangzhou), China, c. 1805. Qing China restricted all European trading activities to Canton from 1757. This was known as the Canton System.

Faced with a persistent shortage of specie and bullion and an increasingly weak financial position, the Dutch began issuing paper money. In 1782, government bonds were sold with an interest rate of six per cent and used as money.[104] The VOC and private traders also issued bills of exchange in the East Indies for commercial transactions. The bills were denominated in Dutch guilders and made out to be drawn in Holland, but could only be redeemed there at a steep discount and an inferior rate of exchange (see **Paper money**, opposite). This incentivised bearers of the bills to keep recirculating them within the region rather than redeeming them in Holland, providing the Dutch a perfect financial instrument for trade without the need to export bullion or specie directly to Asia for payments.[105] In 1770, of the 4,281,742 rupees imported from Holland to Java for the Eastern trade, bills of exchange on Holland made up 33 per cent of the entire sum, with the rest comprising bullion and specie.[106] Captain Bligh of *Mutiny on the Bounty* fame noted in 1789 that these were already used extensively at Batavia.[107] After the VOC ceased to trade directly with China, it conducted its opium trade out of the East Indies. To pay for the opium, the Dutch at Batavia began offering 'paper' bills or bonds at a 15–18 per cent discount, redeemable only at the 'Batavia Castle' (the fort).[108] Thus the Dutch avoided having to keep a large supply of specie to pay for purchases all across the Indies, and the VOC could manage the circulation of commodity coinage within the region. Using various forms of paper money consequently reduced the flow of silver out of

Paper money: discounts and negotiations in October 1789

'Paper money is the currency of Batavia, and is so understood in all bargains. At this time, paper was at 28 per cent discount: there is likewise a difference in the value of the ducatoon, which at Batavia is 80 stivers, and is in Holland only 36 stivers: this occasions a loss of 21¼ on remittance of money. It therefore follows, that if any person at Batavia remits money by bills of exchange to Europe, they loss [sic] by the discount and exchange 49¼ per cent.

'Those who have accounts to pay, can give unexceptionable bills on Europe, will find a considerable saving by negotiating their bills with private people who are glad to give them a premium of 20 per cent at least.'

Source: William Bligh, *A Voyage to the South Sea, undertaken by command of his majesty, for the purpose of conveying the bread-fruit tree to the West Indies, in His Majesty's ship the Bounty*, pp. 257–9.

Holland. This helped mitigate the adverse balance of payments position caused by the loss of Japanese silver to fund the Eastern trade.

Separately, since the 18th century, a bank of circulation had already been established at Batavia, issuing paper money in the form of bank bills. It was linked to a lending operation, of a kind associated with the Lombards of northern Italy, that loaned money on pledges. A fee of five rixdollars was charged for opening an account, and the bank issued a stamped bank bill for money deposited (it was said that this bank had 2–3 million rixdollars in capital). [109, 110] The bank bills could then be passed on in exchange.

After the VOC had established its regional hegemony, it sought to standardise the currency used in the East Indies. Its mint at Batavia had produced multiple coins and counter-stamped several foreign coins, and the currency situation was chaotic. Starting in 1724, it began importing Dutch copper coins (*duiten*, or doits) directly from Holland. These were circulated within the Java hinterland from 1730. In the years that followed, the doit was legal-tender and massive volumes of the coin were brought to Java.[111] This currency regime continued beyond the dissolution of the VOC (1798–9), when the Dutch government took direct control of the East Indies.[112] However, these efforts at standardisation within the region failed. Within Java alone, many kinds of currency circulated at disparate rates of exchange: gold and silver coins, including Spanish silver dollars, Indian rupees, and other older coins,[113] not to mention a range of subsidiary coinage.

Over the years from 1789 to 1815, Europe lived through the French Revolution and the Napoleonic Wars. The wars resulted in the subordination of

Bank note issued in the Dutch East Indies, 1815.

Holland to France, and the creation of the Batavian Republic (1795–1806). In 1811, the Dutch left the East Indies to concentrate its efforts on the war in Europe, and the British occupied Java to prevent the Dutch colonies in the Indies from falling into the hands of the French.

Thomas Stamford Raffles was made the administrator of Java and one of his first acts was to reorganise the island's chaotic currency system. He made the Dutch stiver the unit of account against which current coins in circulation were valued. Using the Spanish dollar as the standard silver coin, Raffles introduced a new silver Java rupee in 1813, of the same degree of fineness as the old Java rupee (11.5 grams). Thus, one Java rupee was worth 30 stivers or 120 doits.[114]

As the Napoleonic Wars came to an end, the Dutch returned to the East Indies in 1816. They found the currency situation as chaotic as it had been when they had left five years earlier. To remedy the situation, in 1817 they instituted a new currency policy. First, the copper doit was made the main subsidiary currency for residents of the East Indies. Second, the new government decreed that its silver coins in Asia were to carry a premium of 20 per cent over their value in Europe to account for shipping costs and higher demand in Asia.[115] This imposition of a premium by decree led to an increase in the value of Dutch coinage in the Indies. Consequently, there was great demand for copper doits in the rest of Asia, as the doits were subsets of the Dutch silver coins. The result was a scarcity of the doit in circulation. At the same time, one Dutch guilder was also made equal in value to one Java rupee.[116]

To address the dearth of doits, from 1817 the mint at Surabaya started producing copper coins in three denominations: the half-doit, doit, and double doit. Additionally, in the following decade, hundreds of millions of doits were imported from Holland. However, amongst the imported coins were a large

Above: Dutch copper doit, 1790.

Below: Javanese rupee, 1803.

Weights and exchange rates

The use of weight as a basis for determining the value of precious metals has been fundamental in their use as money in various forms. In Sumatra, gold dust, rolled up in parcels, was used widely as a form of currency, even more so than coins. The amount of dust had to be weighed when transactions were conducted, so most people on the island had to carry a small scale with them.[117]

The ability to weigh and measure precious metal content was particularly important in a context where more than one type of currency was used for trade in any given place. In China and the East Indies, one could find Chinese, Dutch, Spanish, British, and Japanese currencies, and a host of subsidiary coinages.[118] A mutually agreed rate of exchange between the various currencies would be necessary for any transaction to proceed. One monetary practice in place at Canton was to weigh the coins used in trades. Hence, it could be determined that the current worth of a Spanish silver dollar at Canton in the 1760s was seven *mes* and four *kanderins* (a Chinese currency used only in accounting).[119]

number of counterfeits, as the unscrupulous sought to capitalise on the artificial premium enjoyed by the coin in Asia.[120] From the 1830s the influx of doits and their counterfeits throughout the region would eventually prove destabilising for traders in the archipelago (see p. 47).

To relieve the acute shortage of money further, the Dutch government in Java printed new paper money in the form of 'Treasury notes'.[121] Although these widely circulated notes solved the initial problem, their continuous issuance soon led to a drop in their value. In 1826, the Dutch authorities began to withdraw the notes, and planned the creation of the Java Bank to issue promissory notes instead.[122]

Given the dominance of the Dutch in the region, by the beginning of the 19th century guilders become the main currency for trade *within* the Malay Archipelago, and copper doits a major subsidiary coinage.[123] However, the Dutch continued to use the Spanish silver dollar when trading goods coming from outside the region, such as Chinese goods coming into the East Indies on junks.

What of Singapore at the time when the Dutch were expanding their control over the region? While it may have had a settlement and port at various times in the 16th and 17th centuries, by the early 18th century, the island seemed to have been lightly populated. In 1703, the Sultan of Johor offered the island of Singapore to British 'country trader' Alexander Hamilton.[124] Hamilton's description of what the island had to offer was fairly detailed, suggesting he had walked around it. While he acknowledged that Singapore could be 'a place for a company to settle a colony on, lying in the centre of trade, and being accommodated with good rivers and safe harbours, so conveniently situated', he made no mention of any habitations there, nor did he mention the presence of a *shahbandar* at that time.[125]

Eastern Side of Pulo
Penang, or Prince of
Wales Island, with Fort
Cornwallis, 1810.

The British

Unlike the Dutch, who had gained control of most of the East Indies, the British
had only a couple of fort settlements in the region before the 19th century:
Bencoolen (on the west coast of Sumatra) and Prince of Wales Island (later
known as Penang), established in 1685 and 1786 respectively. As an outpost of
the British East India Company's administration in India, Bencoolen adopted the
currency system used in the latter for official purposes. However, that meant a
great deal of diversity. There were rupees, sattellers silver, sooco or sukus, reals,
and shillings. The sicca rupee (issued by Bengal) was the main unit of account.[126]
Within the Indies, Bencoolen paid for spices partly in Dutch guilders and partly
in kind.[127] By the early 1800s, when Bencoolen's export of pepper to London had
reached a thousand tons annually, it imported Indian rupees to pay for purchases
of the spice, and when there was a shortfall of Indian money the difference was
made up by bullion.[128]

In response to the general shortage of coinage, Stamford Raffles, as
Lieutenant-Governor of Java, had Bencoolen issue rupee coinage of gold, silver
and bronze (copper doits), struck at Surabaya. The British government had
used 305,210 pounds of copper to mint over 500,000 pieces of copper doits
for circulation within Java. The assistant mint-master at Surabaya revealed that
owing to a shortage of metals, the initial batches of doits struck had used metals
from 'obsolete cannon'.[129]

On Prince of Wales Island (later Penang), the Spanish silver dollar was the
main accounting, circulation and exchange currency until 1826. In 1787/8,
Penang introduced a subsidiary coinage called the 'pice' which had been minted

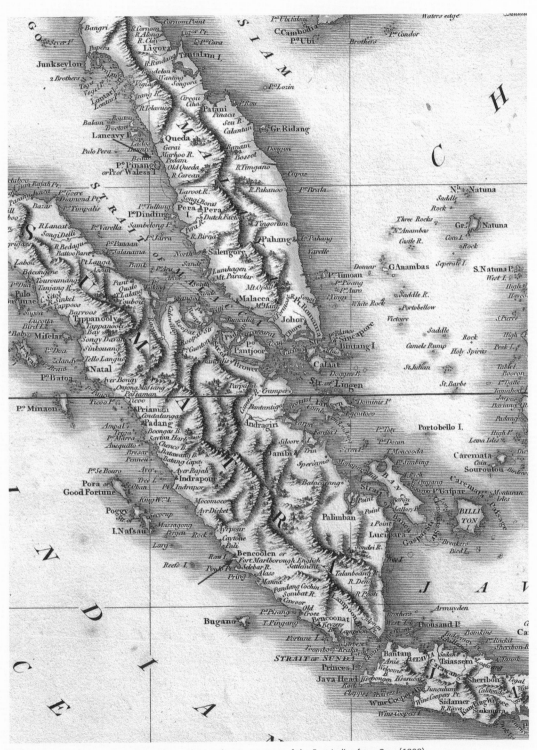

Penang and Bencoolen, as shown on a map of the East Indies from Cary (1808).

Penang coins: half
pice (left) and one
pice, 1787.

in Calcutta. Critically, the pice was equivalent to a hundredth part of a Spanish
dollar.[130] Having subsidiary coinage as fractional parts of the silver dollar would
come to be prized by merchants not just in Penang but in the Straits Settlements
as a whole, because of ease of conversion to the dominant trade currencies of the
19th century (see p. 68). When a shortage of copper pices arose, Penang struck tin
pices that were still denominated as fractions of the silver dollar.[131]

Alternative, non-official coinages were also created as a response to the
shortages. British merchants along the Straits of Malacca circulated their own
coinages around the turn of the 19th century,[132] although these were not legal-
tender. By then, the Indian mints were refusing to produce any copper coins
except for the fractional denominations of the rupee. A number of British
merchants took it upon themselves to commission a private mint (the Soho Mint
in Birmingham) to produce their own tokens. These private coins functioned
as subsidiary currency in British trade in the Indies, albeit unofficially.[133] The
merchant tokens were clearly meant for use in the Indies-Indian-Arabic spheres
of trade, and it has been suggested that the Arabic dates and scripts on these
coins were for the benefit of pilgrims from the East Indies heading to Mecca.[134]
Although the merchant tokens bear the date 1804, some scholars have suggested
that they were produced later, mainly around 1830–32.[135] However, the acute
shortage of specie and other forms of money in the early part of the 19th century
makes it likely that the tokens were minted closer to the 1804 date. Collectively,
these would come to be known as Straits Settlements Merchant Tokens.[136]

In retrospect

The Malay Archipelago has long played a critical role in global maritime
trade. It was the maritime gateway to the East Indies where the trade winds
met and trade networks intersected. The entrepôts and feeder ports of the area
were not just conduits or transshipment hubs for goods from the West and
China; they were also the means by which resources and produce from the
region were put into the trade networks and thence to markets all over the
world.[137] What is clear from the archaeology finds and documentary accounts
of Temasek or Singapura is that an active maritime polity existed on the island

Num. Chron. Ser.III. Vol. XV. Pl.VI.

Tokens commissioned by British merchants in the Straits Settlements
and Malay Archipelago, as shown in Ellis (1895).

for a century or more. The fortunes of the communities living on the island would have risen with the flourishing trade and growing prosperity of the wider Malay Archipelago.

With maritime trade came the money needed for it to function. The preferences of the trading nations would determine the nature of the currencies accepted in international exchange. This was true of Roman specie and Chinese copper cash in antiquity, and Dutch silver guilders, paper money, and Spanish silver dollars after the European powers began sailing directly to Asia. The flows of bullion and specie would bring great prosperity to the nations that saw overall inflows, and financial stresses to those experiencing outflows. In some instances, the drain of financial resources was enough to fell empires.

At the same time, reliance on an external form of money, and critically the bullion to produce specie, was often a point of vulnerability. As we have seen in this chapter, the evolution of money and innovations in the forms it took were often driven by the need for a stable and sustainable supply of both bullion and currency. When China was able to supply the copper cash needs of its partners for their trade with it and for their domestic use, there was little disruption to economic activity in the region. When the stream of coinage from China ceased, every local kingdom had to find alternatives. In pre-modern Southeast Asia, the nations on both sides of the Straits of Malacca simply minted replacement coinage using tin. The Dutch attempts to secure bullion and mint their own coins would also prove inadequate given the strong demand for money; they resorted to issuing paper money to mitigate the situation. In this context, the Spanish silver dollar minted from an abundant supply of silver from the Americas served as a global public good: it was readily available, stable in value, and widely accepted in transactions. Over the course of the 19th century, it would increasingly serve as a unit of account.

A common theme in the story of money in the region is the inadequate supply of currency for local use at the marketplace, whether it was Chinese copper cash, tin and lead cash, or copper doits. Because it took time to produce coins or to import them from abroad, supply rarely adjusted alongside demand, and the value of subsidiary currency could fluctuate quite sharply. Minting such coins locally, and shifting away from precious metal content, either by debasement or by producing coins in a base metal that was in ready supply locally, was one solution. In the centuries to come, shortages would recur, and governing authorities would shift towards using ever baser materials for the production of subsidiary currency.

When Stamford Raffles arrived in Bencoolen, there was already an abundance of metallic currencies already in circulation throughout the region. In the East Indies, various forms of money were employed as international trade dollars, as accounting currency, as trade currencies used only within the region, and as money for purchases at local bazaars. The rest of the Malay Archipelago shared this multicurrency situation,[138] as Raffles would have been aware when people started to gather in Singapore from 1819. There was no one dominant polity in the region which could mandate greater uniformity in currency use, nor was such uniformity deemed necessary. Although the monetary 'non-system' was an eclectic hodgepodge that had arisen as a result of trade, politics, and expediency, the local people and merchants engaged in the maritime trade networks of the region were well-adapted to such a situation.

COMPANY, EMPORIUM AND EMPIRE
(1819–1857)

Modern Singapore began as an outpost of the British East India Company (EIC). Even when Singapore became part of the larger polity of the Straits Settlements from 1826, it still did not have its own currency, and a basket of regional currencies continued to circulate on the island. The most abundant of these was the Dutch copper doit, which had become the main subsidiary currency in the Malay Archipelago. It was only in the late 1840s that the EIC minted a copper coinage for the Straits Settlements' own use. Meanwhile, the Spanish silver dollar remained the main trade currency of the day. In the 1840s, the Anglo-Indian banks established branches across the Straits Settlements, issuing bills of exchange, banknotes and promissory notes, which became paper-based financial instruments that would help fuel East-West trade from the mid-19th century. At this stage, Singapore had no control over currency arrangements, and was confronted with ill-suited policies imposed on it by the EIC authorities. This was a fundamental issue that would characterise Singapore's monetary journey until it gained independence from British rule more than a century later.

W hen Thomas Stamford Raffles reached Singapore at the end of January 1819, the island was formally a dependency of the Johor Sultanate, which was then in a 'chronic state of dissolution'.[1] This disarray was due to a succession dispute between the Sultan and his older brother, Tengku Long, whom the Sultan had bypassed in ascending the throne. In light of this dispute, Raffles instead negotiated a deal with the Temenggong,[2] who was resident on the island. The outcome of this engagement was the recognition of Tengku Long as the 'rightful' Sultan of Johor. As a result of the deal, Raffles secured the right to establish a 'factory' – a 'trading establishment at a foreign port or mart'[3] – on the island of Singapore under the East India Company (EIC). For several years, the Sultan and Temenggong remained the *de jure* authority of the island.[4] Singapore only became a full British colony in 1824 when Britain signed the Anglo-Dutch Treaty with Holland. This recognised Singapore as being within the British sphere of influence in the region, and paved the way for the cession of the island in that same year. The EIC, which had a Royal Charter to represent the British Crown in the East (see **The East India Company and its royal charters**, p. 36), was therefore responsible for the administration of Singapore. As the EIC's main centre of government was in British India, Singapore was viewed effectively as part of India, and did not have the status of a British Crown colony. Singapore was combined with Penang and Malacca to form the Straits Settlements in 1826, and Penang became the seat of government of this new polity.

Chapter opening picture: Detail from Singapore waterfront from the sea, c. 1848, from an oil painting by an unknown artist.

Map of India, 1837, showing the extent of East India Company administration. As shown in the *Imperial Gazetteer of India* (1908).

Under EIC rule, Singapore had to adhere to the regulations and policies promulgated for the Indian subcontinent, including those related to currency and taxation. Although the rupee was established as the legal-tender currency for transactions throughout British India, this policy did not necessarily result in uniformity in monetary matters. Other currencies were in circulation. Each of the Presidencies (administrative units of British India)[5] – Bengal, Bombay and Madras – had its own version of the rupee until the 1830s. Penang and Bencoolen had their own coins, minted for local use.

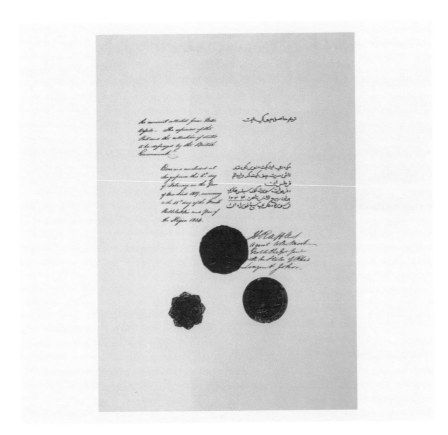

Page from the Record of the 1819 Treaty of Friendship and Alliance, signed on 6 February 1819 by Sir Stamford Raffles and Singapore's Malay rulers, Sultan Hussein of Johor and Temenggong Abdul Rahman.

In India itself, the rupee was used in administration (e.g. for accounting purposes, or for paying taxes, fines, and purchases of land), for trade within the territories on the subcontinent, and for day-to-day use. Within the Malay Archipelago, the situation was quite different. The preferences of buyers and sellers, and the ready availability of various types of money, would determine the medium of transaction. The Malay Archipelago was a colossal entrepôt. Merchants in the Archipelago would need to have Dutch doits and guilders to trade in the East Indies, and Chinese cash to pay for goods offloaded from Chinese junks. For global trade, the use of a standard silver dollar remained the norm – for the first half of the 19th century, this was generally the silver dollar issued by Spain.

Governing from Calcutta in Bengal, the EIC introduced general policies appropriate to its territories within the Indian subcontinent. However, these policies did not always dovetail with conditions in the Straits Settlements, especially with regard to trade, money and revenue. Under the EIC regime, Singapore's free-port status and its currency practices came under constant pressure. This led to resistance from the local merchant community which lobbied for the transfer of the Straits Settlements from British India to the Colonial Office in London.

The East India Company and its royal charters

The East India Company (EIC) was established on the last day of 1600 following a petition by a group of London merchants to Queen Elizabeth I. The Queen granted the company a Royal Charter, entitling it to trade

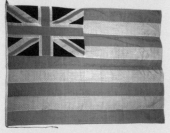

in the East. It was therefore an incorporated trading company from the start, and grew enormously without effective competition from non-chartered English traders.

As British interest grew in the East, the EIC developed capabilities for the protection of the trading networks that stretched from Africa via India on to China. After a succession of military victories within the subcontinent during the mid-18th century, the Company became the *de facto* governing body of British India. From having only 3,000 troops in 1750, the EIC expanded its army to 26,000 in 1763, and 67,000 by 1778. At its height in 1803, the EIC had

The ensign of the East India Company.

260,000 men under arms. The EIC had also its own naval fleet which included warships, but was composed mostly of armed trading vessels known as East Indiamen.

In 1793, the EIC received a new Royal Charter renewing its trade monopoly in India for another 20 years. This time, the Charter specifically established the Company as an agent of the Crown. That is, it was acting officially on behalf of the British government in political matters and not in its own right. The Charter Act of 1793 gave the EIC authority to grant licences to persons to trade in India. These covenanted licensees were known as 'country traders', and the arrangement opened the doors for shipments of opium to China.

With the Charter Act of 1813, the Company's trade monopoly in India came to an end, with the exception of the China tea and opium trades. This was a first step towards opening up the Eastern trade to merchants not associated with the Company. The EIC's monopoly on the trade of tea and opium with China ended when the Parliament in London passed the Government of India Act of 1833, which abolished the commercial role of the Company. From that year onwards, it was a purely administrative organisation.

In the early 19th century, the territories of Bencoolen, Penang, and Singapore were all considered part of the 'eastern settlements' of British India under the EIC. When the British exchanged Bencoolen for Malacca in 1824 under the Anglo-Dutch Treaty, Malacca also came under administration from India. From 1826, Penang, Singapore and Malacca were administered collectively as the 'Straits Settlements'. The EIC's control of India came to an end in 1858, when the British Crown took direct control of its territories on the subcontinent. Responsibility for the Straits Settlements was transferred to the Colonial Office in London in 1867.

East India House, in Leadenhall Street, London, home of the East India Company.

India and the Straits Settlements up to the 1830s: administrative and political structure

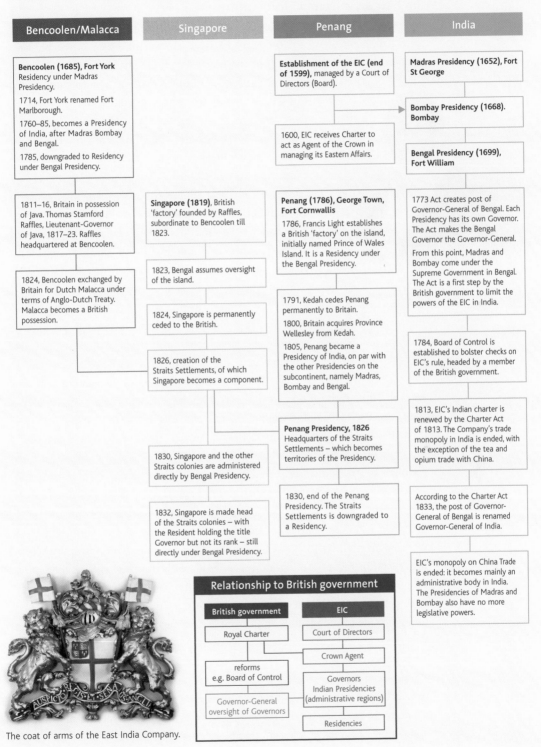

Bencoolen/Malacca	Singapore	Penang	India

Bencoolen (1685), Fort York
Residency under Madras Presidency.

1714, Fort York renamed Fort Marlborough.

1760–85, becomes a Presidency of India, after Madras Bombay and Bengal.

1785, downgraded to Residency under Bengal Presidency.

Establishment of the EIC (end of 1599), managed by a Court of Directors (Board).

1600, EIC receives Charter to act as Agent of the Crown in managing its Eastern Affairs.

Madras Presidency (1652), Fort St George

Bombay Presidency (1668). Bombay

Bengal Presidency (1699), Fort William

1811–16, Britain in possession of Java. Thomas Stamford Raffles, Lieutenant-Governor of Java, 1817–23. Raffles headquartered at Bencoolen.

1824, Bencoolen exchanged by Britain for Dutch Malacca under terms of Anglo-Dutch Treaty. Malacca becomes a British possession.

Singapore (1819), British 'factory' founded by Raffles, subordinate to Bencoolen till 1823.

1823, Bengal assumes oversight of the island.

1824, Singapore is permanently ceded to the British.

1826, creation of the Straits Settlements, of which Singapore becomes a component.

Penang (1786), George Town, Fort Cornwallis

1786, Francis Light establishes a British 'factory' on the island, initially named Prince of Wales Island. It is a Residency under the Bengal Presidency.

1791, Kedah cedes Penang permanently to Britain.

1800, Britain acquires Province Wellesley from Kedah.

1805, Penang became a Presidency of India, on par with the other Presidencies on the subcontinent, namely Madras, Bombay and Bengal.

Penang Presidency, 1826
Headquarters of the Straits Settlements – which becomes territories of the Presidency.

1830, end of the Penang Presidency. The Straits Settlements is downgraded to a Residency.

1773 Act creates post of Governor-General of Bengal. Each Presidency has its own Governor. The Act makes the Bengal Governor the Governor-General.

From this point, Madras and Bombay come under the Supreme Government in Bengal. The Act is a first step by the British government to limit the powers of the EIC in India.

1784, Board of Control is established to bolster checks on EIC's rule, headed by a member of the British government.

1813, EIC's Indian charter is renewed by the Charter Act of 1813. The Company's trade monopoly in India is ended, with the exception of the tea and opium trade with China.

According to the Charter Act 1833, the post of Governor-General of Bengal is renamed Governor-General of India.

EIC's monopoly on China Trade is ended: it becomes mainly an administrative body in India. The Presidencies of Madras and Bombay also have no more legislative powers.

1830, Singapore and the other Straits colonies are administered directly by Bengal Presidency.

1832, Singapore is made head of the Straits colonies – with the Resident holding the title Governor but not its rank – still directly under Bengal Presidency.

Relationship to British government

British government		EIC	
Royal Charter		Court of Directors	
		Crown Agent	
reforms e.g. Board of Control		Governors Indian Presidencies (administrative regions)	
Governor-General oversight of Governors		Residencies	

The coat of arms of the East India Company.

Free trade, currency and empire

Singapore's location on the East-West trade route meant that it could help secure British interests along the Straits of Malacca. As we have seen in the previous chapter, its position at the tip of the Malay Peninsula placed it at the maritime entrance to the East Indies, where traders congregated to exchange goods and purchase commodities. However, these strategic attributes were not the only reasons why Singapore developed into the 'Emporium of the East'.[6] Raffles's master stroke was to establish a free port where commerce was not taxed. This gave passing traders an incentive to call at Singapore rather than other ports in the region.[7] Colonial port cities established earlier, such as Portuguese Malacca[8] and Dutch Batavia, had operated under regimes that imposed taxes on the value and volume of trade. The Dutch, in particular, had enforced monopolistic policies, forcing passing junks and European ships to stop at Dutch ports, and so were able to control the flow of trade and imports, and maximise taxation revenue from exports and imports (see p. 23).

Sir Thomas Stamford Raffles, in an engraving, 1824.

Raffles's action ran contrary to the mercantilist spirit that had always motivated the EIC and its Dutch counterpart, the Vereenigde Oostindische Compagnie (VOC).[9] As we have seen, the EIC was itself caught up in mercantilist practices from the mid-18th century to the early 19th, namely enforcing a monopoly of the China tea trade, and restricting the sale of tea in Britain to Company traders.

Raffles had his own ideas for a British 'factory' (trading post) at Singapore.[10] He envisaged a free port where merchants were left alone to conduct their commercial affairs, unencumbered by restrictions and taxation.[11] This *laissez-faire* system (the term originated in 18th-century France) is the ideological antithesis of mercantilism, and it was rapidly gaining adherents in Britain at the time.

It helped that in the early years of the free port, the EIC authorities in India were in no position to impose a unified currency policy on Singapore. From the outset, merchants calling at Singapore were able to use, without hindrance, the various currencies preferred by their counterparts in the China and Malay Archipelago trades. Intersecting at Singapore were other regional networks that brought trade to the island.[12] Ships from both China and the Malay Archipelago sailed to ports along the Straits and picked up what they needed to carry home.[13] The forms of specie used in these trades were not only the Spanish silver dollar but also the dominant currencies of the region including Dutch guilders and doits, as well as Chinese cash. Most of these currencies were accepted in the Straits ports where there were always traders willing to receive specie of their home nations, which they could take back with them.

Two Malay prahu, in an engraving by Thomas and William Daniell, 1810.

Imports of gold dust to Singapore, May–December 1830, as reported in the *Singapore Chronicle*, 20 January 1831.

The prospect of untaxed trade and the ability to pay and receive widely accepted currencies made the Singapore port very attractive to mariners and merchants plying the China and Malay Archipelago trade networks, and they brought with them a wide variety of goods and money.

Activity in the 'Emporia in Imperio'[14] – the emporium within the empire – took off. Singapore quickly became a significant entrepôt for the China trade. A year after its establishment, it was also able to capture much of the Archipelago trade being shipped through the Straits of Malacca (see **Singapore supersedes other regional ports**, p. 40). By mid-1820, it was estimated that the total value of trade passing through Singapore had reached nearly two million Spanish silver dollars.[15] From April 1820 to April 1821, imports and exports involving 'Chinese junks and native vessels' alone were estimated at around 885,000 and 914,000 dollars respectively, for a total of nearly 1.8 million dollars.[16] In 1823, the value of all exports through the Singapore port was estimated to have reached around 5.6 million dollars.[17] A year later, the value of exports and imports flowing through Singapore had risen to 6.6 and 6.9 million dollars respectively.[18]

Trade needed financing. Initially, the EIC used bullion from the Britain to underwrite its trades in the East. This could not be sustained indefinitely. Britain's preference was that the purchase of Chinese goods should be financed by profits earned from the China trade – the Dutch had used their profits from the spice trade in a similar way (see p. 20). The EIC had realised early on that there was profit potential in opium-dealing. It was noted in Singapore's Master Attendant's ledger for April 1820–

GOLD DUST.

This precious metal forms one of the most valuable of our Imports. The quantity annually brought into the Settlement by native traders is of such an extent that we are induced to give it particular notice.

The principal portion comes from Pahang on the east coast of the Peninsula, and is mostly brought here in the Sampan Pucats which trade between this and Pahang. Indeed it forms the most valuable article of Export from that port. The Pahang-gold, we believe, is considered superior to all other brought into the Settlement.

The following is a statement of the quantities which have arrived since May last, from the different ports, from whence Gold Dust usually comes; we have no doubt that more has been brought privately by natives when was not reported, at the office of the Registrar of Imports & Exports:

From Ports on the E. coast of the Peninsula.

Pahang	bunkals	4,235
Calantan	"	300
On Borneo.		
Sambas	"	1,508
Pontiana	"	645
Succadeo	"	20
Banjar	"	27
Soongai Raya	"	417
Cota Ringin	"	5
Passar	"	55
On Sumatra.		
Jambie	"	104
Campar	"	160
On Celebes.		
Kyle	"	560
From Neighbouring Islands.		
Palo Tambelan	bukls.	12	
Rhio	"	9	
Lingin	"	10	31
	Total bunkals	8,104
	or Catties 405, bukls. 3	

The greater part of this immense quantity is sent to Calcutta, where it forms a good remittance for Opium and other Articles imported from Bengal.

April 1821, that non-European ships alone had imported and exported close to half a million Spanish dollars' worth of opium through the port at Singapore. This made opium the single most valuable item in the Archipelago trade.[19] By 1827, Singapore's import and export of opium alone were valued at 1.2 million and 868,955 dollars respectively, making the commodity the highest-earning item at the time.[20] When the EIC's tea monopoly ended, the need to find an alternative source of funds to finance the China trade became all the more pressing.[21] The sale of opium could supply the EIC with the necessary silver, avoiding the need to tap Britain for financial resources.

Private sources of financing also emerged. In addition to the EIC traders, free-trading merchants from Europe not affiliated to the Company were also participating in the China trade. They made the British ports in India and the Straits, including Singapore, their centres of operation. Many were owners of trading firms and agency houses that imported manufactured goods from the West into the region and shipped local goods out, taking a commission in the process, and amassing significant sums of capital. With their branches in Britain, India and the East, they could provide local merchants with access to trade capital, warehousing facilities and conveyance opportunities, as well as business networks.

Singapore supersedes other regional ports

Although Singapore stimulated the intra-regional trade of Southeast Asia, its gains were at the expense of other regional ports, which saw a significant drop in commercial activities.

In the early 1820s, until the establishment of Penang and Singapore, Malay and Bugis proas used to exchange their produce at Junkceylon (today's Phuket). Queda (Kedah) was 'formerly a place of considerable trade; but since the establishments at Pulo Pinang [Penang] and Singapore, the Malay proas have carried the greater part of their trade thither, for the European and country ships bound to China'. At Pahang, 'trade is scarcely deserving of attention since the establishment of the settlement at Singapore'.[22]

Malacca was particularly affected. Singapore's second Resident,[23] John Crawfurd, who was appointed in June 1823, noted that Malacca had historically owed its prosperity to its status as the only port in the Straits offering a degree of security for life and property.[24] EIC ships from India bound for China used to call there for supplies, and to purchase goods. However, the Dutch had eroded the attractiveness of Malacca as a port by employing a 'rigid system of exclusive trade',[25] and its trade had been dwindling. The development of Penang dealt it a further blow; Singapore 'completed its fall'. In the words of a London newspaper report of 1820, 'The Dutch Settlement at Malacca declines as Singapore advances.'[26] According to another report in the same year, there were quite a number of Chinese junks in the Singapore harbour while not one had visited Malacca.[27] The decline of Malacca was also evident from the amount it was collecting in import and export duties. In 1819, these amounted to 50,000 Spanish silver dollars.[28] Two years later, duties had more than halved to 23,000 dollars, and they fell further to just 7,000 dollars in 1823. By this time, Malacca had become a feeder port to the Singapore entrepôt, exporting mainly Malayan produce to the island instead of conducting its own international trade. For instance, through the 1820s Malacca became the main source of Singapore's imported food.

Gambier and pepper plantations in the northern and western parts of the island, as seen in this portion of the map by the Survey Department, Singapore (1885). Gambier and pepper plantations were found all over the island in the 1840s-50s. They were the twin pillars of the Chinese cash crop plantations in early Singapore, providing pioneering immigrants employment which helped pay for their passage to this part of the world as indentured labour.

They made Singapore not only an emporium for traded goods but also a centre of finance for the China trade.

The establishment of Singapore, Penang and Malacca as critical nodes in the network of British maritime ports in the East gave the EIC the means to transfer securely the monetary resources required for trade,[29] and profits earned from it.

The EIC headquarters in Calcutta used these secure port networks to move bullion to China in order to fund the Company's China trade. From the early 1820s, it was also sending consignments of Spanish dollars to the Singapore treasury,[30] which became a critical link in this financial network.

The mercantile community profited from the port and its associated financial networks. By virtue of the silver dollars flowing in, the Singapore treasury became a source of trade dollars for merchants and the agency houses operating on the island. In early 1823, for instance, following a tender submission by Messrs Harrington & Guthrie, William Farquhar, Singapore's first Resident, supplied them with thousands of Spanish dollars.[31] Discounts in favour of the government were applied in this tender to cover the cost of transport, the amount the administration had paid for the specie, and some profit for the government.[32] The security offered by the British port network also enabled free-trader merchants to engage in the import and export of specie and bullion themselves.[33]

Portrait of William Farquhar by M. Gauci, after John Graham-Gilbert. Lithograph. 1830.

Singapore thus had much to offer. Its geographical location provided the ideal place for ships to stop over, its free-port status drew merchants, and the British provided the capital and financial networks that facilitated trade. As a result of these advantages, the island of Singapore became central to the China and Archipelago trades.

Money in Singapore

Broadly speaking, the different types of currency used in the Straits served three purposes. The first was local administration, such as the payment of taxes and transactions involving the authorities. Second, there was day-to-day use by the average resident, including for shopping at the local bazaar. Third, there was regional and international trade with merchants of the many different nationalities with which Singapore traded. Currencies generally accepted for the first two purposes are known as 'circulation currencies', while those used for the third purpose are 'trade currencies'.

However, there are other ways of categorising specie. 'Subsidiary currency' was specie of smaller denominations – for example, a fractional denomination of a rupee, guilder, or silver dollar. Different types of subsidiary currency would have been used to varying extents in administration, at the local bazaar, and in international trade, depending on the value of the transaction concerned. 'Accounting currency' was used by parties such as agency houses, banks, or the government. Transactions themselves were not necessarily carried out in the accounting currency, though they would have been recorded after conversion into it.

As an outpost of British India, it was expected that Singapore would use the rupee as the currency of administration. In practice, however, the EIC did not impose a specific currency policy on the island when the British 'factory' was first established. From 1819, Singapore was for a time under the supervision of Fort Marlborough at Bencoolen, where Raffles was the Lieutenant-Governor. The first Resident of Singapore, William Farquhar, sent the settlement's accounts to Raffles every quarter.[34] They were kept in Spanish silver dollars.[35] Farquhar also instituted a system of licensing, or 'revenue farms', to fund the administration of the settlements (see **Revenue farms**, p. 44). The taxes collected were also in Spanish dollars.[36] It was therefore Raffles and Farquhar who made the Spanish silver dollar, rather than the Indian rupee, the currency of administration. This practice may have gone unchallenged during the first years of the settlement simply because up to 1823, Singapore was under the oversight of Bencoolen, where Raffles wielded authority.

What was the situation on the ground? Several months after the British 'factory' was established, Farquhar decided that the following would be accepted as circulation currencies in Singapore: the Spanish silver dollar, Dutch guilder, Java rupee, and all British India rupees, except for the sicca rupee issued by Calcutta. As for subsidiary currency, local merchants by and large used Dutch copper doits till the mid-1840s. Not only were the doits in abundance across the Malay Archipelago, but the Straits Settlements also imported the coins directly from England.[37] Meanwhile, the Spanish silver dollar was the most valued trade currency. Up to 1823, when Raffles left Singapore for the last time, India had only sent Spanish dollars to the Singapore treasury.[38] The treasury in Singapore kept the revenue and reserves of the island's administration.[39] This was consistent with the way the EIC saw Singapore up to the early 1820s – it was to be considered a commercial settlement, and therefore the EIC were willing to supply it with silver dollars for trade.[40] However, going into the mid-1820s, guilders became the island's main trade currency with the region as the much-valued Spanish dollar became scarce.

Revenue farms

As a free port, Singapore did not enjoy the revenue from customs duties that the commerce at its port might otherwise have provided; and there were no agricultural enterprises on the island that could have been taxed for income.[41] Although Raffles's provisional treaty with the Temenggong specified that the Malay chiefs were entitled to part of the revenue derived from any customs duties collected from native vessels,[42] no such collection was undertaken. Raffles had instructed the first Resident, William Farquhar, that there was no need to impose any duties on trade at the time.[43] Farquhar kept faith with Raffles's instruction. However, a need remained for the administration to generate income for the maintenance of the settlement, policing, public works, and port facilities, as well as to honour the treaty obligations.

By November 1819, Farquhar was left with no option but to write to the governing authorities in India. He proposed implementing consumption taxes on selected items by licensing their sales through 'revenue farmers'. The EIC authorities replied that Farquhar should not incur excessive municipal expenses. If a significant number of people were to settle on the island, then Farquhar should not lose sight of the fact that commerce was the 'chief object of the eastern settlements' and he could introduce moderate custom duties to derive revenue for his outpost.[44] This instantly placed Farquhar in a dilemma, as following Calcutta's advice would have ended free trade at Singapore.

Farquhar then wrote to Raffles. But before he had received a reply, in March 1820 he had already instigated a revenue-farm system for opium, requiring persons wanting to retail prepared opium to seek permission first. Other revenue farms were introduced.[45] The revenue they raised removed any need to impose customs duties and provided a critical source of funds for Raffles's town planning and rebuilding efforts in 1822-3.

Government revenues from licensing farms, 1830-41 (Spanish dollars) [46]

Farmed Items	Years										
	1830	1831	1832	1833	1834	1835	1836	1838	1839	1840	1841
Opium	3,279	3,390	3,440	4,000	5,060	4,800	4,570	4,860	4,050	5,440	6,250
Spirits (Arrack)	1,735	1,620	1,765	1,610	2,130	2,135	1,920	2,220	2,420	3,185	3,750
Pork	820	550	660	670	550	690	740				
Seerih	575	490	570	490	560	500	525	510	582	637	715
Toddy	80	76	65	90	99	70	112	114	133	266	184
Market Chinese	397	340	355	359	360	382	402	390	375	440	750
Market K. Glam		86	98	111	120	94	107	65	80	88	90
Pawn Brokerage	162	120	160	140	100	180	180	260	268	300	295
Total Revenue	7,042	6,672	7,123	7,470	8,970	9,031	6,636	8,119	7,908	10,356	12,034

This diverse range of coins presented challenges to the island's administrators. The actual values of the various currencies, when used locally, had to be determined by complex conversion rates to the Spanish silver dollar. These rates were subject to fluctuations and discounts.[47]

To facilitate domestic trade and administration, John Crawfurd, Singapore's second Resident, advocated minting a local circulation currency. This was the first serious effort to create a money for Singapore. Crawfurd's proposal was in line with earlier practice in British colonies such as Bencoolen and Penang, which had their own forms of coinage (see p. 26). It was not his intention to replace the Spanish silver dollar, which he declared 'legitimate', or legal-tender, for international trade. Instead, he wanted to establish a single currency for use at the bazaar and for government transactions locally.

In July 1823, Crawfurd proposed to the Bengal government that 'small bronze' (mostly copper) and 'silver coinage', denominated in fractional parts of the Spanish dollar, be minted for Singapore's use. By mid-1824, the Calcutta Mint had created the dies, and some copper and silver specimens were even struck. However, nothing more was done, as it was at this juncture that the government in India began to consider making all its eastern possessions use the rupee.

John Crawfurd in a photo taken in the 1850s.

In 1826, Penang, Malacca and Singapore were combined into a single administrative entity, the Straits Settlements.[48] Penang, already an Indian Presidency, was given a new Royal Charter and became the capital of the Settlements.[49] This arrangement lasted until 1830. As the Straits Settlements was a Presidency within the EIC governmental system, it was *required* to use the rupee in all official matters. The Penang Presidency promulgated regulations accordingly and imposed the rupee on the component territories of the Settlements.

In 1827, the Penang government attempted to impose the use of Calcutta's sicca rupee as the main currency of the Straits Settlements generally. This was met with great resistance by the merchants of Singapore. The residents of the Straits had come to the region to trade and work, and it was convenient for them to hold the currencies of their home town or money that was widely accepted in trade. Local merchants had to acquire the currencies that their trade counterparts desired, which as far as the Malay Archipelago and China trade networks were concerned, was *not* the rupee. Forcing the residents of the Straits to adopt the rupee would have been an inconvenient and costly affair.

Replica of the 1824 coin for Singapore, reproduced in 1919 during Singapore's first centenary.

The merchants petitioned against the move and brought the issue before the British Parliament in 1827, where they succeeded in forestalling the sole use of the rupee.[50] As a result, during the Presidency, several currencies continued to be used for accounting and international trade: the British pound, Spanish silver dollar, and sicca rupee. The currencies in circulation included an astonishing variety of rupees: the Surat rupee, the Furruckabada rupee issued by Uttar Pradesh-North India, and the rupees issued by Madras, Bombay, and Ceylon. Critically, however, the widely used Dutch guilder was permitted to remain as a circulation currency.[51] Penang itself had given up its free-port status from as early as 1801, and it only readopted free trade when it became the seat of government of the

One rupee coin issued by the Bombay Presidency and a gold two-mohur coin issued by the East India Company.

Straits Settlements in 1826.[52] Consequently, it felt free to propose revenue policies, such as payment of port dues, which would have been challenging for Singapore's free-port status.[53]

The Penang Presidency ended in 1830. The number of circulation currencies in Singapore continued to grow. In the 1830s, one could find Spanish silver dollars and gold doubloons, a variety of Indian rupees, Dutch guilders and copper doits, the Java rupee, copper coins from territories such as China, Cochin-China and Madras, Sycee silver from China, Javanese and Siamese tecals, gold mohurs from India, and even cowrie shells[54] (see p. 17). And there were still more! The myriad currencies in use at that time seems astonishing today, and they reflected the diverse origins of the traders, sojourners and settlers in the early years of the settlement. As one can imagine, the simple act of shopping at the local bazaar would have been a very complicated affair, necessitating multiple exchange calculations between a host of currencies. The need for a standardised currency to serve as a common unit of account and medium of transaction was clearly present.

Adding to complexity on the monetary front was the presence of paper money. Although different types of paper money issued by the Dutch were already circulating widely throughout the East Indies, there is very little information about them being used in Singapore.[55] Their usefulness would have been confined to the East Indies trade, as with the guilders and doits. In any case, the local government in Singapore could not issue bills of exchange or any form of treasury or paper notes on its own. Although banks could issue 'banknotes', which were bills of exchange or promissory notes stating the sums that the bank had undertaken to guarantee, there was no bank on the island until the 1840s.

Whatever the situation was with the Dutch paper money, other forms of paper money soon emerged on the island. As a sub-unit of the British India treasury, the Singapore treasury could accept payments for bills of exchange issued by the treasuries of any of the Indian Presidencies. In this way, bills of exchange issued by the India government drawn on Calcutta were sold through the

Singapore treasury. These bills provided the local mercantile community a paper payment facility which could be used for commercial transactions or for remitting funds.[56] A variety of other paper instruments were available on the island for merchants to use, including private bills of exchange meant to be encashed at other places[57] and promissory notes issued by the Indian government in the 1820s. Redeeming the bills or promissory notes for specie normally incurred a discount, or a loss,[58] but that was a regular feature of the contemporary monetary system that would have been factored into business considerations. What mattered most in this instance was the security and convenience provided by these paper-based financial instruments.

Given this mind-boggling variety of currencies, after Singapore assumed the leadership of the Straits Settlements in 1832, it applied for authorisation from Bengal to set rates of exchange. This it obtained a year later, when the Supreme Government in Bengal sanctioned use of the 'Twelve Tables' – a table of rates of exchange for all the Indian rupees and the Spanish dollars, in all the British settlements in the Straits of Malacca.[59]

Twelve Tables, in the *Singapore Chronicle*, 24 January 1833.

Currency woes and barter trade

Singapore used the Dutch copper doit as subsidiary currency until the 1830s. The doit had also become the subsidiary coinage of the Malay States which traded directly with Singapore. However, the Dutch authorities had never planned for the expansion of the doit as a regional currency. There was therefore a strong underlying demand for doits in the wider Malay Archipelago in excess of what the Dutch were supplying for use by the East Indies.[60] To keep its own trade going, the Straits Settlements had to import doits from Britain.[61]

In the 1810s and 1820s, the Dutch East Indies monetary system experienced upheaval. The Dutch had over-issued paper money throughout the Indies during the Napoleonic Wars to make up for a shortage of silver guilder coins. In 1827, a new Commissioner General arrived in the East Indies to deal with the problem. He carried the Dutch King's orders to cease the circulation of the bills, redeeming them in doits and in other paper securities such as bonds, instead of silver. However, the Dutch treasury and government offices stopped accepting doits in payments. These actions rendered the doit unviable and created grave difficulties for all the traders in the Malayan Archipelago. The underlying value of the doit collapsed, but since there was no other

Singapore Free Press and Mercantile Advertiser, 8 August 1844.

Seizure of Copper Doits.

A great seizure of counterfeit coin has been made at Birmingham by the police, in the workshops of Mr Taberrer, and Messrs Calley and Co., where was found a very large quantity of counterfeit coin, made to resemble doits, and supposed to be intended for exportation to the Dutch settlements. "It appears," says the *Birmingham Journal* "that several *highly respectable* merchants in the town have been in the habit of exporting these coins, not aware of the consequence; and that from one house alone *two tons weight* were sent out a few weeks ago. That this seizure will put a stop to the traffic there can be little doubt, as the penalty for every piece of coin so made is 10*l.*; and if inflicted in the present instance, it would require little short of two millions sterling to pay the fines incurred.

readily available subsidiary currency in the Archipelago, demand for the coins remained. In terms of copper content the coinage became increasingly debased, and counterfeiting was uncontrolled.[62]

The problems with the doit aside, a different kind of currency woe emerged at around the same time. In 1827, a general scarcity of specie emerged in China as well as the East Indies. This affected the opium trade in China and drove the East Indies to depend more on promissory notes.[63] By 1828, the shortage of trade currencies was also afflicting Singapore, and many trades were conducted on a barter basis.[64] The following years brought little relief. In the 1830s, the general lack of silver specie and subsidiary copper coins led to the return of barter trade within the Straits (see table, opposite). In 1834, there was so little subsidiary currency circulating in Singapore for domestic use that the sale of theatre tickets became problematic because people could not find enough low-denomination coins to pay for small items.[65]

In order for barter trade to occur, there had to be a 'double coincidence of wants'. Goods exchanged in barter were therefore less liquid than money, which did not rely on the double coincidence. Of course, a merchant could take a risk, hoping that demand for a particular good would increase in the future, and accept in barter items he did not necessarily want at that point in time. In this way, a system of credit based on barter between merchants and local shopkeepers was also possible and did operate in Singapore. However, repayments in kind could be unsatisfactory. Debtors might delay delivering the goods, and the items might be inferior in quality to what was promised under the terms of credit. Consequently, while barter trade and in-kind payments were necessary stop-gap measures during a specie shortage, they involved significant frictions to trade and often imposed losses on creditors, threatening their financial viability. What was needed was a liquid medium of transaction that relieved the frictions to trade, and a clear, common unit of account such that creditors and debtors would not quibble over whether the quality of goods offered constituted adequate repayment. In other words, more 'money' was needed in order for Singapore's commerce to thrive.

The specie shortage continued to worsen, and in April 1835 the European merchants of Singapore held a public meeting at which they decided to introduce and enforce their own policies on trade and money.[66] They had already identified the key reason for the dearth of coins in Singapore, and no doubt this was mirrored across the Malayan Archipelago: Chinese merchants at Singapore only sold for cash, and paid only in kind. They were therefore constantly withdrawing specie from circulation in Singapore. The Europeans declared that goods would henceforth not be accepted as payment; trade could only be conducted on a cash basis.[67]

How credit really worked – a Singapore resident's perspective

'A Chinese shop-keeper comes to a godown, purchases 1,000 pieces Long Cloths at a stated price, and, in barter, agrees per his promissory note to pay – in lieu of cash, which from causes I will attempt to explain, is of reputed scarcity in Singapore – in such staple as Tin, Pepper, Coffee, Sago, and etc. at market rate, in 3 or 4 months, but it seldom happens (even with the most creditable Chinamen in the Bazaar), that he fulfils, to the strict letter, his engagement. Instead of 3 or 4 months, he pays you in 5 or 6, or even 6 or 7 months, and instead of giving the articles agreed for, the piece-good house is often obliged to accept of inferior or different descriptions of produce, in order to 'get out' with a bad or doubtful customer. Why give credit to such fellows, you will say, if one is obliged to wait so long for payment after the note is due, and besides be obliged to accept of other articles than those agreed for? In reply I should say, that the Chinese shop-keepers, who are our chief, or in fact our only purchasers; are nearly all alike notorious bad paymasters; and custom has sanctioned this dilatory system.'

Source: *Singapore Chronicle*, 21 February 1835.

Snapshot of barter transactions in international trade in 1831

Dates	Nature of barter trades conducted in Singapore
20 January 1831	Siamese sugar sold in barter for cassia (cinnamon)
10 March 1831	Iron for produce
17 March 1831	Siamese junks arrived with sugar, salt, rice and coconut oil – sold to the Chinese in barter for cotton piece goods and cotton yarn
28 April 1831	Chinese junks on return trip to China would accept barter for their goods, pepper, tin and more
14 July 1831	British piece-goods for Siamese sugar, plates for coffee
21 July 1831	British piece-goods for Siamese sugar, stick lac (sealing wax) for Java coffee
28 July 1831	Piece-goods for sugar, tin, coffee
4 August 1831	Chinese merchants exchanging coffee for British and Indian piece-goods, and pepper from the West Coast of Malaya
15 September 1831	Cotton twists for middling (flour) and tortoise shells
22 September 1831	Piece goods for produce
29 September 1831	Opium for pepper
13 October 1831	Madras piece-goods for tin, bees' wax for opium
20 October 1831	Rice for Bengal piece-goods
3 November 1831	British piece-goods offered in barter for produce, tortoise shells – taken by British merchants in barter for payment of debts
10 November 1831	Japanese copper from Batavia for opium, Indian piece-goods for Siamese sugar
17 November 1831	Cassia (cinnamon) for tin and Siamese sugar
1 December 1831	Siamese sugar for opium

Source: Commercial Remarks in the *Singapore Chronicle* for 1831. The dates are the newspaper's publication dates.

Monetary solutions:
local banks and credit, paper money and coinage

Recurrent specie shortages had demonstrated that an exchange and credit system based on barter was inferior to one based on money. However, the European merchants' attempt in 1835 to address the shortage of specie in Singapore was a temporary measure at best. If the outflow of specie was a structural issue affecting the broader Malay Archipelago, then a more enduring solution would be to boost the local supply of money in circulation so that merchants could have the liquidity, the means of exchange, and the credit needed for their commercial transactions.

The logical move was to expand the local availability of paper money and develop means of trade financing without actually using specie. The first institutions to fill the monetary gap were the agency houses in Singapore. The oldest such house in Singapore was set up by Alexander Johnson in 1819, and by 1821, there were eight British houses.[68]

As the agency houses developed their trade networks, they established branches that extended from Britain to India, along the Straits of Malacca and thence to China. These branches did not just support their shipping and trading activities; they also became conduits for money transfer and financing. The agency houses employed 'compradores', Chinese agents closely familiar with the local market and the creditworthiness of local customers and suppliers – a system that was operated by international banks even into the 20th century. The agency houses were therefore also well-placed to issue promissory notes, bills of exchange, and letters of credit

IMPORTS.
COMPARATIVE STATEMENT OF THE TRADE WITH THE UNDERMENTIONED PLACES, BETWEEN THE YEARS 1836-37 AND 1837-38.

Names of Places.	1836-37. Sp. Drs.	1837-38. Sp. Drs.	Increase. Sp. Dlr	Decrease. Sp. Dlrs.
From Great Britain.	1,720,426	1,652,457	"	67,969
" Foreign Europe.	58,036	9,516	"	43,520
" United States	100,298	50,980	"	49,318
" Rio de Janeiro	2,725	"	"	2,725
" Mauritius	12,917	28,720	15,837	"
" Calcutta	1,401,907	1,669,794	267,887	"
" Madras & Ports in C. Coast.	272,556	379,400	106,844	"
" Bombay	235,351	301,607	66,256	"
" Arabia	2,220	25,361	23,141	"
" Manila	94,048	213,305	119,257	"
" Ceylon	8,120	17,949	9,829	"
" China	790,735	659,272	"	131,463
" Java	892,961	1,037,157	144,196	"
" Rhio	148,394	124,282	"	24,112
" Siam	225,969	381,516	155,547	"
" Cochin China.	94,918	70,908	"	24,010
" Sumatra	220,981	321,890	100,909	"
" E. S. Peninsula.	423,200	368,777	"	54,423
" W. S. Peninsula.	32,140	44,051	11,911	"
" Borneo.	266,689	289,056	22,367	"
" Neighbouring Islands &c.	159,845	117,573	"	42,272
" Bally	91,382	83,097	"	8,285
" Celebes & other Eas. Islands.	273,242	310,181	36,942	"
Total Sp. Drs.	**7,528,990**	**8,156,852** **7,528,990** **627,802**	**1,080,959** **453,097** **627,802**	**458,097**

Value of imports expressed in Spanish dollars (*Sp. Dlrs*), according to the *Singapore Free Press and Mercantile Advertiser*, 21 June 1838.

that could facilitate larger-value transactions.[69] In this way, they performed crucial financial functions in the initial decades of the Singapore colony when no bank had yet been established on the island. These houses also became local agents of foreign banks. In 1836, A.L. Johnston & Co. advertised that they were agents selling bills at 60 days sight drawn by Bank of Scotland.[70] Following close behind was G. Kinnear, Maclaine Fraser & Co., who presented themselves as agents of Bank of Australasia, which had a Royal Charter to issue bills and notes for circulation.[71]

Banknotes were an important form of paper money. A bearer of the note could bring it to the issuing bank to redeem for specie. Several proposals to establish local bank branches began from 1833, but these failed to come to fruition. In late 1840, however, the branch of the Union Bank of Calcutta was established near the Singapore River. It offered a full range of banking facilities: mercantile credit, post bills issued on Calcutta at three days' sight in exchange for its own notes held by parties desiring to remit funds to Calcutta; and bullion remittances to Calcutta, Bombay and Madras. It also made loans collateralised with pledged assets or deposits.[72] Crucially, the bank issued banknotes. By 1843, it had put into circulation 400,000 dollars' worth of notes throughout Singapore;[73] each note could be redeemed for its equivalent value in silver dollars. Unfortunately, the bank's headquarters in Calcutta ran into trouble, and the Singapore branch folded in the same year.

The next bank to operate on the island was the Oriental Bank Corporation, which incorporated a branch locally in May 1846. It offered a range of services similar to the Union Bank, but it stood out in that it was transparent about the state of its assets and liabilities.[74] This imparted a greater degree of confidence in the bank's management, and thus in the banknotes it issued. The Oriental Bank's first promissory notes in Singapore came in denominations of five and 100 dollars. They had imprints in four 'native languages – Chinese, Malay, Bengalee and Tamil'.[75] In fact, at this point, the bank had a charter only permitting it to issue banknotes in India; however, it went ahead to issue them in Singapore. In 1851, the bank formally received a Royal Charter permitting it to function as a full British bank in the region with the capacity to issue banknotes. By then, it had already put 70,000 dollars' worth of notes into circulation in the Straits.[76]

The Royal Charter under which the bank operated was governed by the British Bank Charter Act of 1844.[77] The act required all chartered banks issuing notes to keep in reserve bullion or specie equivalent to a third of the value of all notes issued.[78] The accounts of banks issuing banknotes had to be published on a regular basis.[79] After the Oriental, other banks were also granted Royal Charters allowing them to issue

A 10 dollar banknote issued by the Oriental Bank, 1885.

banknotes in the Straits Settlements. These included the North Western Bank of India (1855), the Chartered Mercantile Bank of India, London and China (1855),[80] the Chartered Bank of India, Australia and China (1861), and the Hongkong and Shanghai Banking Corporation (1881). The Hongkong Bank was the last entrant into the local banknote market, and it had to use the bank's paid-up capital to guarantee the notes.

Having a bank in Singapore did not just benefit the mercantile community. The first banks on the island also accepted deposits from the local government and paid out interest. Following the Bengal government's practice of depositing its funds with the Bengal Bank and the Oriental Bank in 1848,[81] the Singapore Municipal Committee from 1849 deposited the Municipal Fund with the local branch of the Oriental Bank.[82] British authorities used bank networks to transfer funds as well. By the mid-19th century, the commercial banks in the British territories had become partners in the colonial enterprise.

The local banknotes and other paper securities provided the Straits Settlements with the monetary resources to carry on its commercial activities. However, the need remained for a more stable subsidiary currency than the copper doit. From the perspective of the Dutch government in the region, although the doits were intended to be a subsidiary currency for the Indies, they soon became the main circulation currency as a silver specie shortage emerged from the 1820s, while the value of paper money depreciated.[83] Concurrently, the Bank of Java ramped up circulation of a paper currency called the *kopergeld*, or 'copper money', valued at 100 notes to one guilder. It was perhaps hoped that these paper notes could become a stable subsidiary currency for the East Indies in place of the doit. The first tranche was issued in 1828, the second in 1838, and then another in 1842-5. Whatever their impact on the East Indies was, the notes were not widely taken up by Malayan merchants, who still preferred the copper doit for their Indies trade.

Even in the 1840s, the Dutch East Indies government found itself unable to improve the doit situation. The counterfeited or debased doits had fallen sharply in value against the Spanish silver dollar, and their continued use threatened to destabilise not only Singapore's economy[84] but commerce in Europe as well. In 1837, the EIC authorities in India made a second attempt to impose the general use of the rupee in the Straits Settlements. While this could have resolved Singapore's subsidiary currency conundrum,[85] the merchants of Singapore were adamant that they would not accept India's currency. Instead, they proposed the creation of a currency specifically for the Straits' use.

In 1844, a law was passed that allowed the creation of a local British coinage for the Straits Settlements.[86] The EIC began to make plans to mint the coins for the Straits,[87] but no further concrete steps were taken. Despite the problems caused by the doit, the Singapore Chamber of Commerce feared that an outright ban on the coin in 1844 would leave the public with insufficient copper coins for everyday use. Moreover, as the entire trade of the Malay Archipelago depended on Dutch copper doits supplied through Singapore, the Chamber was also concerned that suppressing the Dutch coins at this point would create severe problems for merchants involved in regional trade. It pointed out that the situation was not simply caused by the counterfeiting of the Dutch doits alone but also by the fact that the British government did not supply the Straits Settlements with its own coins.[88] It seems that for the merchants at that point in time, producing the new coin was a far greater priority than banning the unviable doit. The new Straits coins only became a reality when the Governor of the Straits Settlements raised the matter to the Bengal Government in early 1845, reiterating the threat to the economy of the Straits represented by the debased doits. In any case, by the middle of that year, the Dutch government had decided that the old doits should be completely withdrawn.[89] Hence, the peoples of the Malayan Archipelago were presented a *fait accompli*. A new subsidiary coinage *had* to be created.

A copper doit 1793.

The EIC could not create a new currency series without access to a reliable source of copper for the purpose. The British had annexed the territories of Arakan, Tenasserim, Assam and Manipur during the First Anglo-Burmese War in 1824; these lands contained copper mines. Hence, the decision was made to use copper from Burma (Myanmar) to mint the first coins of the Straits Settlements.[90]

The first EIC Straits Settlements copper coins were finally issued in 1847. These became known as the 'EIC coins' as 'EIC' was the main inscription on the face.[91] The first consignment to be delivered comprised the following denominations: one cent (10,000 dollars'-worth), ½ cent (20,000 dollars'-worth) and ¼ cent (20,000 dollars'-worth). In 1848, the legal-tender status of the copper doits in the Straits Settlements was revoked.[92] From 1 January 1848, the EIC coins became the only copper coins that could be received in the treasuries of the Straits Settlements. Meanwhile, the Spanish silver dollar continued to be the currency of international trade.[93]

While the introduction of a stable copper currency was considered a great boon generally, several Chinese merchants expressed trepidation over the loss of the doit's legal-tender status.[94] They undoubtedly possessed a great number of doits and their businesses had been conducted in this coin. They feared the new copper coin might hamper their trading activities, especially since they were not certain if an adequate supply of EIC coins would be made available. Consequently, they came together and drafted a petition to the Governor. The Chinese Brotherhood (*huey*, or 'secret society') also added their voice. Many of their associates were coolies in the plantations in the island's interior; what little they earned was paid in doit. They believed that the Chinese mercantile leadership had failed them in not preventing the impending calamity. So, after a discussion in their *huey* meeting, their representative, Tan Kam Long, drafted an open letter to the government demanding an assurance 'that the prohibition of copper tokens [the doit] cannot be legally enforced'.[95]

Meanwhile, the Dutch authorities ceased producing doits in the East Indies in 1845; thereafter new ones were imported into the region. However, there were still an estimated 4.7 billion Indies-minted doits in circulation throughout the Indies.[96] These doits were ultimately not withdrawn, but remained in circulation throughout the 19th century, despite having become severely debased in value.[97]

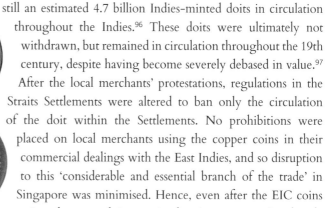

Half-cent coin (above) and one-cent coin (below), approved in 1845 by the East India Company and issued in 1847. The coins feature a portrait of Queen Victoria.

After the local merchants' protestations, regulations in the Straits Settlements were altered to ban only the circulation of the doit within the Settlements. No prohibitions were placed on local merchants using the copper coins in their commercial dealings with the East Indies, and so disruption to this 'considerable and essential branch of the trade' in Singapore was minimised. Hence, even after the EIC coins were issued, copper doits remained an important regional trade currency for Straits merchants.[98] Yet, local merchants continued to complain about difficulties and losses suffered in the change of currency from January 1848.

Banning the doit as a circulation currency within the Straits Settlements had a much greater impact on the lower-income, non-merchant classes. As the doit had been the only subsidiary coin used throughout Malaya, it was the main coinage used day to day, and was the currency in which most coolies and plantation workers were paid.

The introduction of the EIC coin in place of the doit led to unintended inflationary consequences that eroded the purchasing power of these groups. For every silver dollar the labourers were paid previously, they would have received, on average, 600–700 doits after exchange rate conversion. They would then spend these copper coins. However, the smallest denomination of the EIC coin was a quarter-cent, and there was a fixed rate of 400 quarter-cents to a dollar. Hence, earning a dollar's worth of wages meant that workers would only receive 400 coins when they changed a dollar for copper coins to spend. Although, on the surface, this meant that the new EIC coinage was of greater value than the old doit coinage, it also meant that the lowest amount that could be spent at the local bazaar had now gone up from a sixth or seventh of a cent to at least a quarter of a cent. Consequently, the cost of living rose with the new coinage, and this hurt the lower-income groups.[99] Although the merchants holding large amounts of doits could continue using the coins for their East Indies trade, coolies and plantation workers had to exchange them for the new EIC cents as the doit was no longer to be circulated in the Straits. The currency reforms, while necessary given the widespread debasement and counterfeiting of the doit, were making the poor poorer.

Chinese remittances

A letter-writer at work, from Seah (1847).

From the 1830s, Chinese gambier and pepper coolies toiling in the jungles of Singapore made an annual trek to town to send letters and remittances to their families in China. They relied on the help of fellow countrymen from the same province returning to China on the departing junks following the change of the monsoon winds. These 'carriers' or agents were called 'seu pe ke' (in Teochew). The remitter gave an agent a 10 per cent commission for his trouble; the agent could carry specie or invest the sum in goods which he had to sell after arrival back in China, and then forward the exact sum that the remitter had entrusted to him.

All classes of immigrants sent remittances – the merchants in hundreds of dollars, the coolies in units of ten. In some years, about 70,000 Spanish dollars could be sent annually, while in bad years, the amount might fall to 30,000–40,000. As most of the Chinese coolies were unable to write, they paid itinerant public letter-writers who set up stalls in the streets to pen their messages. The letter-writer was paid 3–6 cents per letter. When the time came for the junks to leave, there were as many as 40–50 letter-writers operating along the streets.[100]

Emporium vs empire

From the birth of the Singapore settlement, there had existed a tension between the interests of the 'Emporium of the East' and the prerogatives and needs of the overarching authorities of the British Empire, filtered through the Crown's agents, the East India Company. The Indian authorities' policies were essentially orientated to further the EIC's commercial activities, and to enforce adherence to the monopolies it enjoyed. Even after all its monopolies had been stripped away, the EIC continued to be the governing authority for all the British India territories, including the Straits Settlements. As the Company became less involved in commerce and more occupied with the responsibilities – especially the financial burdens – of government, it would prioritise raising revenues from a range of taxes, even if these had an impact on trade.

From this perspective, free-trading Singapore was at odds with the policy priorities of EIC-governed India. While Singapore defended its free-port status and the right to use currencies it found most useful for trade, the EIC authorities would time and again attempt to impose taxes on trade or introduce the currency systems of India to the Straits Settlements. The island first experienced this under the Penang Presidency.

In the second half of the 1830s, the Supreme Government in Bengal attempted to impose 'revenue and rupee' regulations. It directed the Governor of the Straits Settlements in January 1836 to 'prepare a draft Act and schedule for levying duty on Sea Exports and Exports of the Straits Settlements'. The duties raised were supposed to fund expenses incurred as a result of dealing with piracy in the Straits,[101] but this meant the salaries of the court staff and judges involved in prosecuting pirates rather than spending on naval forces to combat piracy.[102] Some in Singapore believed that the so-called 'anti-piracy' measures were simply a pretext for the imposition of customs duties.[103] After all, Singapore already generated enough revenues from its licence farms to pay for these additional measures.[104] The Singapore mercantile community held a public meeting in February 1836, and decided to send a petition against the move to the EIC's Board, as the proposed customs taxes would have ended Singapore's free-trade status.[105] The merchants' resistance to the threats to free trade was immortalised in a rallying cry that appeared in almost every issue of the *Singapore Chronicle* from May 1836 to the end of that year: '*This being a Free Port, there are no duties on imports and exports, and no port charges on vessels.*' The Board replied in October 1836 that it had already instructed the government in India not to impose levies on the trade of Singapore.[106] The 1836 affair showed that the merchants on the ground could influence tax policies as well as currency matters.

The Supreme Government was not oblivious to the situation in the Straits. In fact, during a tour of the Straits of Malacca in 1829, the Governor General had stopped over at Singapore, where he had asked the mercantile community what he could do to help 'improve commerce in this place'. The merchants duly submitted a list of concerns, and chief among these was that the absence of a local currency had inconvenienced trade.[107]

Nothing more was done on the currency front until 1835, when the authorities in India unified the multitude of rupees in circulation.[108] Up till then, the silver rupees of the various Indian Presidencies had differed in value, reflecting their varying weight, fineness and size.[109] However, the reforms were focused on improving the Indian currency system rather than addressing the concerns of the

Above: A standardised EIC one-rupee coin (the Company rupee) issued in 1835.

Below: A quarter-anna, a subdivision of the Company rupee, also issued in 1835.

Straits Settlements. The Singapore press had noted that Calcutta had already sent Ceylon the new 'Company rupees' to replace the sicca rupee;[110] it was an omen of things to come for the Straits. Then, in 1837, with the battle against customs duties barely over, Calcutta attempted to impose the use of the newly standardised rupee in the Straits Settlements, threatening the already fragile currency situation in Singapore at that time. The Singapore merchants, having formed a Chamber of Commerce in 1837, rejected this currency reform for the same reasons they had given in 1827. Once more, they proposed minting a local copper currency for the Straits Settlements.[111] The rupee plan was not implemented and nothing more was done at this point.

Spanish silver dollar, 1770.

Between 1837 and 1854, the government in India made further attempts to force the Straits Settlements to adopt the rupee as its main circulation currency, and even replace the use of the Spanish silver dollar for trade. Things came to a head in September 1854, when the authorities introduced a Currency Act making the rupee legal-tender in the Straits Settlements.[112] Earlier in the year, in January, Calcutta had pre-emptively held back supplies of the EIC copper coins that it regularly sent to the Straits,[113] while in February it sent a consignment of rupees to the Singapore treasury.[114] Consequently, when the Currency Act was introduced in the latter half of the year making the half pie – a fractional denomination of the rupee – legal-tender alongside the Straits copper coins, local merchants were presented with a *fait accompli*.[115] This caused great dismay and consternation.[116] The EIC's response was to send the Straits Settlements a 'last' consignment of Straits coins in early 1855, and to declare that *only* rupees and coins of the rupee's subdivisions – annas and pies

– would be delivered thereafter. The treasuries of Calcutta and Madras then sent 50,000 rupees worth of annas over. Even after a year, however, only 2,490 rupees worth of annas had been issued across the Settlements: locals were unwilling to use them, and there were not enough copper cent coins to change for annas.[117] Despite the low rate of take-up for the annas, the Indian government persisted and continued to withhold Straits coinage.[118] This coercive move was a precursor to India's plan to implement the Stamp Act in the Straits Settlements, which required that stamps be denominated in Indian currency.[119] The measures were met with widespread protest throughout 1856. In 1857, the EIC was forced to rescind the currency reform.[120]

In retrospect

Broadly speaking, British officials in Singapore in this period had decided for themselves what was workable and necessary when considering their response to policies emanating from India. In 1819, the EIC had neither dictated to the settlement the local currency to be used, nor provided any guidance on how the settlement could earn the revenue needed for its running. This allowed the early administrators to maintain Singapore's free-trade regime and to permit the use of a vast array of currencies relevant to needs of merchants and residents in the Malay Archipelago.

However, this situation would be disrupted time and again when the EIC attempted to impose policies drafted in India on the settlements along the Straits of Malacca without considering local circumstances and needs. The Straits Settlements was ultimately subordinated to a higher authority in India, and the policies and legislation thereof would always put the needs of the subcontinental 'centre' before those of the Straits 'periphery'. The Straits Settlements was an ocean away from India, while Singapore in particular had a very different approach to commerce from the East India Company. Consequently, the Straits would suffer from the EIC's practice of implementing a one-size-fits-all policy tailored for India's needs. For the rest of the EIC period, the administrators and resident communities would find themselves struggling to maintain those freedoms; and the India 'centre' would, time and again, attempt to strip away those freedoms in the name of its policy priorities.

The challenges that Singapore faced on the monetary front were not due simply to the imperatives of the Empire. They also arose from the fact that the specie that Singapore used in domestic and international trade was not its own, and it could not mint more coins to meet its needs. In the face of a recurring specie shortage, local monetary solutions had to be found. The private sector innovated, introducing various forms of paper money, including banknotes, while the EIC was eventually compelled to create a local subsidiary copper coin for the Straits

Settlements. Going into the latter half of the 19th century, Singapore's need to have a reliable supply of money for trade and local purposes would only increase, as the island faced increasing volatility in the value of the silver dollar, banking crises, and a perennial shortage of subsidiary currency.

EIC rule would come to an end in 1858, and the Straits Settlements would eventually come to be governed directly by Britain. While the Company would no longer be able to coerce the Settlements to adopt policies detrimental to its commerce, the residents of the Straits would soon realise that regardless of the colonial governance structure, the broader needs of the British Empire would still be a major factor when it came to designing policies – currency or otherwise – for the Straits Settlements.

A view of Singapore from Mount Wallich, by Percy Carpenter, 1856.

FROM COMMODITY MONEY TO TOKENISATION

(1858–1919)

Singapore's monetary journey from the second half of the 19th century to the end of World War I was marked by significant change in the nature of global commerce; in the political economy of the British Empire as a whole and within Malaya; and in the international monetary system. The advent of steamships led to the decoupling of maritime commerce from trade-wind cycles. Together with the Second Industrial Revolution, these propelled a surge in world trade during the last decades of the 1800s. It was in this period that banknotes and other securities began taking the place of specie as circulation currencies. However, a spate of bank failures in the last decades of the century led the British to conclude that its colonies should have their own currencies to use as money rather than rely on a basket of foreign specie. This led to the creation of the first government-issued currency notes, the Straits Settlements dollar, while the increasing tokenisation of commodity monies followed shortly after. The Straits dollar also became legal-tender in the Malay States. This was the genesis of the shared currency used by Singapore and the Malay States throughout the 20th century.

The latter half of the 19th century ushered in fundamental changes to the global technological, geopolitical and monetary landscapes. The interplay of these forces swept Britain and its overseas possessions along with its currents.

On the technology front, sailing ships gave way to steamships. Steam power, as well as other technological innovations, played an important role in driving rapid increases in the international flow of goods, people, capital and information. Commerce across the world accelerated since maritime trade no longer had to follow prevailing seasonal monsoon winds. The opening of the Suez Canal in 1869 connected the Mediterranean Sea to the Red Sea and Indian Ocean, sparing mariners from Europe the need to circumnavigate the African continent and sail round the dangerous Cape of Good Hope. This shortened the time needed to complete a cycle of maritime commerce, and reduced the logistical commitments and costs associated with conducting trade across the oceans.

The Anglo-Chinese wars (1839 and 1856), also known as the Opium Wars, led to the opening of a number of Chinese port cities to European maritime commerce.[1] Opportunities for Western trade opened up well beyond the boundaries of the long-established Canton trade system, transforming the nature and scope of the China trade fundamentally. Western banks and agency houses established a presence in these treaty ports, forging commercial and financial networks linking Europe, the Indian subcontinent, Southeast Asia, and China.[2] The western mercantile houses also brought new technologies such as telegraphic communication that led to new ways of conducting business and transferring money. The dynamism imparted by these innovations to global commerce, finance, travel and communications was vividly captured in Jules Vernes's *Around the World in 80 Days*, written in 1872.

Chapter opening picture: Battery Road, 1936. View from Commercial Square (Raffles Place) towards Collyer Quay, at the corner of the Hongkong and Shanghai Bank.

SS *Benvenue*, an iron steamship, 1883. Steamships carried sail as an additional power source.

The opening of the Suez Canal, 16 November 1869, as shown in *The Illustrated London News*, later hand-coloured.

The last quarter of the 19th century is considered the zenith of the British Empire, marked by British intervention and expansion into various eastern and other territories deemed strategic.[3] In the case of maritime Southeast Asia from the 1860s, the British did not just use negotiation and treaties to gain territory; they resorted to direct conquest and annexation. This was the beginning of what historians have called the British Forward Movement in the region.[4]

In the 1870s, the forward policy took the form of interventions in several Malay States. The Residential System was introduced in four States: Selangor, Perak, Negeri Sembilan and Pahang. These became Protected Malay States,[5] and were unified into one administrative area, the Federated Malay States (FMS), in 1896.[6] Thereafter, Britain extended its reach: by the 1900s, the remaining states other than Johor had come under British influence as the Unfederated Malay States, and Johor joined this grouping in 1914. Up till this point, each of the Malay States still had its own Sultan and system of government. Coming under the umbrella of British colonial rule altered the states' political economy. Now, for the first time, pan-Malayan economic policies could be introduced, and the adoption of a common currency became feasible for use across the Straits Settlements, the 'Federated' states, and the 'Unfederated' states.

On the monetary front, the latter half of the 19th century saw the ubiquitous Spanish silver dollar make way for the Mexican dollar and other silver specie, while the use of paper-based financial instruments such as banknotes and bills of exchange became widespread in global commerce and were used to an extent in local circulation. Nevertheless, these were not without problems. A shortage of the Mexican dollar emerged in the 1870s, while the shift away from a bimetallic

Map of the 'East India Islands', published c. 1903.

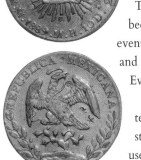

Mexican silver dollar, 1889: 8 *reales*.

monetary system (see p. 78) caused the value of silver with respect to gold to fall for several years. The Straits Settlements would be beset by uncertainty over the supply of trade currency and instability in its value. Meanwhile, the stability of currency notes issued by banks was also undermined by a series of recessions and bank runs over the course of the Long Depression of 1873–96. The dependence on commercial banks to issue and guarantee banknotes had become a risk to global commerce and local money supply. These problems eventually led to the creation of a British trade dollar for the Straits Settlements and its own government-issued currency notes towards the end of the century. Eventually, the Straits Settlement would shift to the gold standard.

The early 20th century saw the emergence of British Malaya as a single territory intimately linked to the Straits Settlements and the British-protected states in Borneo. These three territories had deep economic ties and already used currencies in common. The issuance of the Straits Settlement dollar in the first decade of the 20th century meant that a readily available common unit of account and medium of exchange was now available; by the 1910s, the Malay States, Sarawak, British North Borneo and Brunei had made the Straits Settlements dollar the sole legal-tender in their territories. This led to the *de facto* 'Straits dollarisation' of the region.[7]

With the end of East India Company (EIC) oversight of the Straits Settlements in 1858, the policy centre that shaped developments at Singapore was anchored in London. However, this period was also marked by increasing local input and participation in policies, including on financial and monetary matters. As a Crown colony, the Straits Settlements set up a local legislature, established a currency board with its own reserves, and issued its own currency. These were major achievements of the people of British Malaya and the Straits Settlements in their long journey towards self-representation within the colonial regime.

Becoming a Crown colony

The East India Company's role as an agent of the British Crown overseeing the administration of India came to an end following the Indian Mutiny that had begun in 1857 and revealed the serious deficiencies of Company rule in the subcontinent. In 1858, the Crown assumed direct control of India, making it a Crown colony.[8] Merchants and officials in Singapore had awaited this day for years, hoping for an end to attempts to establish regulatory uniformity between India and the Straits. They had resisted the EIC government's efforts to impose Indian regulations on the Straits Settlements, including those on taxation, currency, and even law and order. These Indian regulations and ordinances, if implemented, would impinge on development of the Singapore free port. The business community in Singapore had long fought for the separation of the Straits Settlements from India; they accused the EIC of failing to understand the conditions in and needs of the British settlements situated along the Straits of Malacca.[9]

However, the removal of the EIC changed little for the Straits Settlements. Although the British government had taken over administration of India, the Straits were still ruled from the subcontinent, and not directly from London. The change did not mean that the needs of the Straits Settlements were finally getting due attention.

The British government was especially concerned that its colonies were dependent on Britain for financial resources, including the supply of specie. A severe shortage of British copper coinage in the Straits Settlements, in particular, had begun in 1855, when the EIC were trying to force the Settlements to use the rupee, and withheld the sending of Straits copper coins[10] (see p. 57). This shortage persisted beyond the abolition of EIC rule in 1858. From 1857 to 1859, the situation deteriorated to the point where all the 'current' silver and copper coinage used at the bazaar had been shipped to Singapore through Britain.

The Straits Settlements was sending Britain projections of its specie needs based on estimates of currency usage in the three territories; however, a copper-coin shortage was inevitable because the residents of the Malay States were also using Straits coinage as their own subsidiary currency. With the constant 'leakage' of subsidiary currency to the Malay Peninsula, there was just not enough to go around.[11] The Straits residents felt that the solution was to establish a local mint

The British presence in the Malay Archipelago

British settlements in the Straits of Malacca
1786 Station established at Penang, ceded to Britain in 1791.
1819 Station established at Singapore. Formally ceded to Britain in 1824 after the Anglo-Dutch Treaty.
1824 Malacca transferred to British rule.
1826 The three stations merged to form the Straits Settlements.

British Borneo
1848 Labuan ceded to Britain.
1888 Brunei becomes British protected State.
1888 North Borneo becomes a British protectorate.
1888 Sarawak becomes a British protectorate.

British Malaya
1874 Intervention started: Selangor, Perak, Negeri Sembilan and Pahang (Federated Malay States from 1896).
1909 British gain influence over Kedah, Perlis, Terengganu and Kelantan (Unfederated Malay States).
1914 Johor became a British protectorate and a member of the Unfederated Malay States.

One-cent, half-cent and quarter-cent coins, 1862: the first post-EIC India Straits Settlements coin issue.

at Singapore or at Bengal to produce Straits copper coinage.[12] This proposal was rejected,[13] but the authorities in India committed the mints at Calcutta and Madras to sending the Straits between 92,000 and 102,000 silver dollars' worth of existing EIC Straits copper coins. These would arrive in early 1859.[14] By the beginning of that year, coins were enjoying a premium of 3–5 per cent on the dollar: that is, an individual would not get the full hundred cents per dollar changed, but would get three to five cents less. Although the premium had halved from the rate in the preceding two years, it was still significant, and imposed a heavy burden on lower-income groups.[15] So great was the need for the coinage amongst the local traders, that every coin was taken up soon after its release. Despite this, the scarcity of Straits copper coinage persisted.[16]

The Crown authorities in India continued to send copper coins over, including a new consignment of 140 boxes of coinage in January 1861.[17] The first post-EIC India Straits Settlements copper coinage was finally struck and circulated in 1862. The arrival of these new coins relieved the currency shortage for a number of years at least.

These episodes made clear the factors that dictated monetary developments in Singapore at that time. First, the specie 'shortage' was not simply due to supply problems, but due to preferences. The residents of the Singapore free port were accustomed to dealing in silver dollars, and in the decade following the issuance of the EIC coin, they had come to appreciate the convenience afforded by decimalised subsidiary coinage. Although technically the Straits could have used alternative coins available in the region, such as Dutch silver guilders and copper annas, the degree of acceptance of, and confidence in, a currency were still important determinants of what would be used in circulation locally. While the preference for decimalised currencies remained, and for as long as the specie supplied did not come in the form demanded, a 'shortage' would persist. Second, even after the abolition of EIC rule, Singapore was administratively still an extension of British India. The Straits Settlements still had no power to formulate its own policies and regulations.

Preferences and authority could be at odds at times, leading to the situation in which the Spanish dollar remained the preferred trade and silver circulation currency in the Straits Settlements, even as the Settlements' authorities kept accounts in 'company rupees'[18] and India made further attempts to impose new taxes on its eastern colonies.[19]

While ordinances enacted in India also applied to the Straits, exemptions could be given. This was the case with the Income Tax Act which India passed in 1860, introducing income tax to the subcontinental territories for the first time.[20] The tax had been mooted to raise revenue in order to cover the losses suffered during the 1857 Indian Mutiny. The residents of Singapore reacted instantly to the news of India's plan and sent a petition for exclusion even *before* they were informed if they were subject to the new tax. The Straits Settlements were subsequently informed that they were not included.[21]

But exemptions were not always forthcoming, as was the case in the Stamp Act of 1863. Indian taxpayers who were subject to income tax and customs duties had been paying for the Empire's troops and fortifications within its territories, which included the Straits Settlements.[22] The Straits had not been charged for military expenses. Then in 1863, India introduced the Stamp Act, whereby taxes would be collected whenever the government affixed revenue stamps on official or legal documents. This time round, the colonial authorities rammed through the implementation of the stamp tax in the Straits. It was envisaged that the additional

A wood engraving showing a group of Malay youths diving into the water to retrieve coins at the New Harbour (renamed Keppel Harbour in 1900). First published in *The Illustrated London News*, 1872. Hand-coloured later. It was customary for travellers to toss a coin into the sea before setting off on their journey, in the belief that it would bring luck and safety.

revenue derived would enable the Straits Settlements to cover 'all of their own expenses', including defence.

The residents of Penang and Malacca came together with their Singapore brethren in a show of unity to oppose yet another India tax.[23] However, their resistance proved futile as now it was the Crown they faced, and not the old EIC. Their misgivings with regard to this new tax were proven well-founded even before its first day of implementation. The stock of stamps sent in October 1862 ahead of the 1 January 1863 implementation date were all denominated in rupees, and no rates of exchange were attached. The Straits Settlements had previously complained about the EIC's attempt to implement a stamp tax in the 1850s (see p. 57); the new stamps would likewise inconvenience a society that had got used to transacting in dollars and cents.[24] The stamps were made mandatory for all bills of exchange, bills of lading, shipping orders, invoices and even promissory notes. It touched, and added frictions and costs to, almost every level of commercial life. This eroded Singapore's free port status.

The only way for the Straits Settlements to have policies geared towards its own needs and conditions was to achieve a measure of self-determination. Consequently, although the residents of the Settlements initially viewed the stamp tax as a hindrance, they soon came to embrace it as the tax revenues it raised boosted the Settlements' ability to be financially independent. An improved financial standing would aid their bid to separate politically from India and become a Crown colony ruled directly from London. As a Crown colony, the Straits Settlements would have its own governor and legislative council (comprising appointed and elected members), institutions that would provide some measure of self-determination, formulate policies and pass local regulations. Of course, the Crown and British Parliament would retain final authority on all matters.

An earlier request that the Straits Settlements be transferred to the direct control of London under the Colonial Office had failed on financial grounds. In May 1861, after the near escape from the Income Tax Act and amid rumours of an impending stamp tax,[25] a number of Singapore merchants formed a committee to raise in London the question of the transfer. The committee was informed unreservedly that '...the Straits did not pay their own expenses, the Transfer was inadmissible'. The British government's position was that its colonies needed to share the burden of maintaining the Empire's military infrastructure. Hence, Singapore's bid for the Straits Settlements to become a Crown colony hinged on the Settlements' ability to cover the costs of administration and development, including outlays associated with the maintenance of convict and military establishments.[26] While the Straits Settlements' revenues from revenue farms (see p. 44) and municipal collections were more than sufficient to cover local expenses,[27] they were unable

The Queen's profile

The British monarch's profile had featured on the British coins used in the Straits even before the Crown assumed direct control of India in 1858. The copper coinage minted for the use of the Straits Settlements, dated 1845 and circulated from 1847, had the name of the EIC on one side, with the profile of the Queen and the words 'Queen Victoria' on the other (see p. 54). The 1862 coins bore similar features, but the reverse face was inscribed 'India. Straits. 1862'.[28] These reflected the new reality of the Crown's rule in India in place of the EIC, as well as the relationship the Straits Settlements had with India at this time. Struck at the Calcutta Mint, this coinage was the last series circulated before the Straits Settlements became a Crown colony. It was only a decade later when the Straits Settlements was a new Crown colony with its own legislature, that the subsidiary currency issued was inscribed with the full name of the colony for the first time – 'Straits Settlements'.[29]

to cover the cost of the garrison and convict establishments, which had hitherto been borne by the colonial treasury.[30]

Following the implementation of the stamp tax however, the financial situation had fundamentally changed as revenue collection increased significantly from 1862-3.[31] Consequently, a second committee was formed to pursue the transfer anew.[32, 33]

At the end of 1863, the Colonial Office appointed Sir Hercules Robinson, the Governor of Hong Kong, to review and recommend how the transfer of the Straits Settlements could occur. However, before his report was completed, the War Office intervened and accelerated the transfer process. By 1866, Singapore was considered by the War Office as an alternative base for the Hong Kong garrison, where the mortality rate of troops and their families had been high.[34] When Robinson submitted his report, it was quickly reviewed and the recommendation for the Straits to come under direct Crown rule was accepted.

Crucially, Robinson recommended also that the Straits Settlements' public accounts be kept on dollars and cents (decimal) standards, and that dollars and the subdivisions thereof were to be the only legal-tender currency in the Straits Settlements. The required silver and copper specie would be procured from England after the transfer. The report stated that 'Local ordinances should be passed, accommodating the postal rates and stamp revenue to the currency of the colony.'[35] This last point was the most important for the residents of the Straits, as it meant that the Straits could have some say with regard to their own currency policies and practices.

On 1 April 1867, the Straits Settlements became a Crown colony.[36] On this day, the Straits Settlements' first colonial governor, Sir Harry Ord, passed Act No. IV of 1867 – 'An Act for declaring Dollars and proportionate parts of Dollars in Silver and Copper to be legal-tender.'[37] Along with the Straits Settlements' attainment of Crown colony status, the primacy of decimalised currency in Singapore was permanently secured.

Even as the Straits Settlements was struggling with the persistent shortage of subsidiary currency, a dearth of silver specie emerged in 1864. From that year, less silver came from Europe as the continent went into a recession that culminated in a financial crisis.[38] Agency houses in China were also remitting reduced amounts to Singapore. At the same time, the French government in Saigon was selling in Singapore bills of exchange on France. However, the money paid did not come back to the island but was sent to Cochin China instead. This effectively also drained silver specie from Singapore in the longer term.

Silver dollar struck in Hong Kong, 1867.

Beyond the specific shortage however, more fundamental changes in trade currencies were taking place. By the late 1850s, the Mexican silver dollar was increasingly replacing the Spanish dollar as the main dollar of the China trade (see **From the Spanish to the Mexican dollar,** below). Its growing dominance could be seen in Hong Kong: that colony had its own ten-cent bronze coins

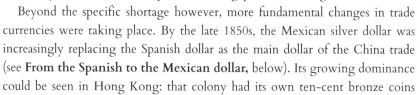

From the Spanish to the Mexican dollar

The Spanish silver dollar was first minted in 1497, and was denominated in *reales*, the unit of currency used in the kingdom then. The coin was worth eight *reales*, and so also came to be known as a 'piece of eight' or peso. Subsequently, English merchants gave the name 'Spanish dollar' to the coin.

The bountiful silver mines of Spanish America provided the bulk of the ore from which Spanish silver dollars were eventually minted in abundance. From as early as 1535, Spain had established a colonial mint in Mexico to produce its silver dollars, and eventually set up ten other mints in the territory. Over the years, Spain established more mints in the other colonies, but the principal Spanish mints were those in Mexico City, in Lima, Peru, and in Potosí, Bolivia. It was estimated that by 1821, more than two billion silver dollars had been struck in the silver mints of Mexico alone.[39]

As Spain's eminence in global affairs and trade rose, so the Spanish silver dollar became widely accepted and ubiquitous, prized for the fineness (purity) and weight of its silver content, and its uniformity. This specie thus became the money that fuelled international commerce; a foreign currency used by nations all over the world in trade with one another, but especially in the China trade. With the conclusion of the Mexican War of Independence, Mexico gained control of the colonial mints, and began producing its own silver dollars. However, this did not end the dominance of the Spanish dollar as the trade currency of the day. It remained the preferred currency for several more decades before being displaced by the Mexican and other dollars in the latter half of the century.

The Hong Kong Mint, 1866-8.

minted in England,[40] and the coin's value was exactly a tenth part of the Mexican dollar. This was the genesis of the Hong Kong dollar system.[41] This 'convenient' copper coinage was also highly coveted in Singapore; the only fear was that the local chettiars or moneylenders might not exchange them for their true metal value.[42]

Concerned with the rising cost of acquiring Mexican silver dollars and shipping them to Hong Kong, Sir John Bowring, the colony's fourth governor (1854–59), proposed establishing a local mint. The Hong Kong Mint opened in 1866 and struck Hong Kong silver dollar coins. This specie quickly became one of the silver dollars current in the Straits, although it was never popular enough to displace the Mexican dollar. At the same time, the mint took over production of the Straits copper coins. It also released subsidiary silver coins, popularly called 'small silver coins'. These appear to have made their way to Singapore as well.[43] Together with the India-Straits copper coins, the small silver coins could have mitigated the scarcity of copper coins. This is probably why there were fewer complaints about subsidiary currency shortages in the Straits in the 1860s.

The arrangement with the Hong Kong Mint lasted till 1868, when it closed.[44] Britain then took over minting of the Straits Settlements coins from 1871.[45] In that year, the Straits Settlements also created its own series of silver subsidiary coinage in denominations of 5, 10 and 20 cents. Befitting the territories' status as a Crown colony, it was also the first time the inscription 'Straits Settlements' was used,[46] with no qualifiers regarding 'India' or the 'EIC'. More pertinently, the decision to have a silver subsidiary currency was made by the local legislature, the Straits Settlements Legislative Council, which had debated the merits of having the coins in the Straits.[47] The local councillors also worked with the Colonial Treasury[48] and Royal Mint on the matter.[49] These initial steps in

Subsidiary coins minted in Britain for the Straits Settlements from 1871 onwards.

making decisions on currency for the Straits Settlements laid the foundations for the Singapore authorities' considerations as to the introduction of a local dollar within the next two decades.

While the introduction of alternative subsidiary coinage was meant to alleviate the copper coin shortages, the reality was that production, delivery and dissemination required time. Even after the coins arrived, their uneven distribution to different places and across different times of the year resulted in premia being applied on the exchange of copper coins already in circulation, with severe repercussions for the Straits residents, especially those on lower incomes. In mid–1872, Malacca reported that it faced such a severe copper currency shortage that Indian moneychangers in the colony were applying a four per cent premium on coins exchanged from dollars. Up till this time, the government had yet to send Malacca additional supplies of copper coins or the new small silver coins, and the only sign of hope was a news report in the Penang papers that a consignment of the new silver coins was already on its way from Liverpool. A broadly similar premium was being applied in Singapore and Penang,[50] and this was an improvement over the beginning of 1872, when Penang's rate was five per cent. The reasons for the 'squeeze' at the beginning of that year were partly seasonal: the Chinese tended to hoard copper coins before the Chinese New Year in order to have more cash during the festive season.[51] Structurally however, a great amount of Straits copper coinage had 'leaked' to the Malay States for circulation there.

Banks, money and sustainability

None of the banks in Singapore in the 19th century were 'local banks' in the true sense of the word. Nearly all of them had to be incorporated in Britain, or they would have been established by a Royal Charter to allow them to conduct their affairs, including the issuance of banknotes and promissory notes. These pioneering banks were branches of European banks which nominally had business and operations stretching from India to China, but there were also those that functioned as local agents of the London-Indian banks.[52]

By the early 1850s, the Oriental Bank Corporation had become the most established bank in Singapore, as the bank branches that came before it had already folded or withdrawn from operating on the island. Consequently, the Oriental Bank served as the bank of the local government. When the small silver coins (5, 10 and 20 cent silver pieces) finally arrived in 1873, the government appointed the Oriental as the local bank at which people could exchange these coins for dollars.[53]

More chartered banks were established locally from 1855, when the North Western Bank of India and the Chartered Mercantile Bank of India, London

Banknotes issued by the Mercantile Bank (5 dollars, left) and a specimen note from the North Western Bank of India (100 dollars, right).

LIABILITIES AND ASSETS OF THE ORIENTAL BANK.
LONDON, 1ST APRIL, 1846.

Deposits and other Liabilities......	£ 766,090	4	5	Cash and Government Securities....	£ 348,883	8	9
Bills Outstanding................					657,746	11	7
Cash, Credits & Loans on Security ..					406,711	2	1
Reserved Fund..............	106,950	1	1	Dead Stock........	7,446	13	1
Nett Stock....	605,126	9	7	Balances due by other Banks....	57,378	18	9
	£1,478,166	15	1		£1,478,166	15	1

(Signed) EDW. LANGLEY,
Actg. Acct.

(Signed) G. W. ANDERSON,
Chairman.

By Order of the Board,
WM. ANDERSON,
Interim Manager

Oriental Bank, Singapore, 9th June, 1846.

Liabilities and assets of the Oriental Bank, *Singapore Free Press*, 25 June 1846.

---

and China established branches in Singapore.[54] These three banks were the main financial institutions which issued banknotes as circulation currencies while offering traditional banking services such as discounting, deposit-taking, and exchange.[55] As the early 'exchange banks' of Singapore and the Straits Settlements as a whole,[56] they cashed bills of exchange or redeemed paper money for specie[57] across their network of branches in different continents, charging a fee or premium for their services.

Following the establishment of the Straits Settlements Legislative Council, the local government formulated regulations identifying three London-based banks with local branches as the official exchange banks of Singapore. These were the Oriental Bank, the Mercantile Bank, and the Chartered Bank, the North Western Bank having withdrawn its operations.[58] The three were the main 'Eastern Banks' engaged in the China trade,[59] and they were already extensively issuing banknotes in the Straits. Like the agency houses of the day, these banks had established branches across the length of the China trade route; they could easily settle payments and complete the 'exchange' within the margins of their books without having to physically conduct exchanges between different forms of the monies.

Straits Times and Singapore Journal of Commerce, 26 December 1854.

NORTH WESTERN BANK OF INDIA.
Registered under Act XLIII, of 1850.
HEAD OFFICE, 4, COUNCIL HOUSE STREET, CALCUTTA.
JOHN O. B. TANDY, *Manager.*
W. H. RIPLEY, *Deputy Manager.*
AGENCIES.
LONDON, 24, Gresham House, ROBERT McKIM, Agent.
MUSSOOREE, North West Provinces, WILLIAM FREETH, Agent.
BOMBAY, 1 Forbes Street, JOSEPH RICH, Agent.
SINGAPORE, 19, Malacca Street, DAVID DUFF, Agent.
BUSINESS OF THE SINGAPORE AGENCY.
DISCOUNTS.
The Agency discounts Mercantile and Private Bills and Notes, payable in Singapore which bear two approved names unconnected in General Partnership, or bearing only one name if accompanied by the Deposit of adequate collateral Security.
DEPOSITS.
The Agency receives Deposits and allows Interest on the same, until further notice, as follows, viz :
3 ℔ Cent ℔ Annum on Deposits and repayable at 3 Months notice.
4 do. do. do. and repayable at 6 Months notice.
5 do. do. do. and repayable at 12 Months notice.
N. B. Notice of withdrawal will be dispensed with, *only* when the money is required to pay for the Agency drafts on the Head Office or the branches.
The Agency opens Current Deposit Accounts with Individuals and Firms, and allows Interest on their minimum monthly balance if not less than $444.44, at the rate of two ℔ Cent ℔ Annum. The accounts are balanced half yearly, on the 30th June and 31st December.
EXCHANGE.
The Agency grants Drafts at the Exchange of the day on the Head Office, the other Agencies, and on the Union Bank of London, and Purchases or collects Bills payable in Europe, Calcutta Mussooree and Bombay.
DAVID DUFF,
Agent.
North Western Bank of India,
Singapore. 20th Dec. 1854.

A 5-dollar banknote (left) and a 50-dollar post bill (a type of promissory note) issued in Singapore by the Chartered Bank of India, Australia and China.

They were able to sell, issue and accept bills of exchange which could be encashed in places where they had branches. These bills functioned like paper money, and for their bearers, they reduced the need to always hold specie or bullion to complete commercial transactions.[60]

The Eastern Banks also printed and issued banknotes which could be used in trade in the absence of specie. The notes were printed with a face value and could be used as money for trade insofar as they were accepted by the parties receiving them in transactions. Unlike gold, silver and copper specie, paper banknotes were a purely 'token' form of money with no intrinsic value. Their worth came from the fact that they represented a claim on something of value. Hence, banknotes had to be backed by specie or bullion held by their issuing institutions, and they had to be 'convertible'. That is, a bearer of a banknote would expect to be able to approach the issuing bank and redeem it for specie or bullion of equivalent value. The stability, value, and usefulness of banknotes rested on this guarantee of convertibility, which was, in turn, underpinned by Britain's Bank Charter Act

Announcement of an 'Act to regulate the Issue of Bank Notes', 19 July 1844.

of 1844[61] (see p. 51). Specifically, the Act required issuing banks to keep a reserve ratio of bullion or species to the notes issued.[62] There was also a requirement that the accounts of banks circulating notes be made known to the public on a regular basis.[63] In an era when paper money coexisted with specie money, the absence of backing to guarantee convertibility would have diminished confidence in the notes, eroding their usefulness as an alternative money to specie.

Paper money was a convenient solution when the supply of specie was unstable. However, recessions and financial panics, or crises, could and did happen; banks, and their ability to back the notes, would be affected. During severe downturns that spilled over into financial crises, the British government took the extreme step of suspending the reserve requirement to the dollars in circulation, so as to ease pressures on the banks. It did so in 1847, 1857 and

1866. Despite this, three banks with branches in Singapore went bankrupt and folded during the 1866 Panic: the Asiatic Banking Corporation (1862–1866), the Commercial Bank Corporation of India and the East (1864–1866) and The Bank of Hindustan, China and Japan (1862–1866).

Another crisis occurred in 1873, which led to Britain suspending the requirements of the Charter Act once more. The 1873 Panic marked the beginning of what, with hindsight, has come to be known as the 'Long Depression' (1873–1896). This was characterised by two decades of trade depressions, economic recessions, and banking crises. The adverse financial and economic situation meant that by the 1870s, banks were drawing on their Reserve Funds more frequently to cover normal operations; the otherwise idle reserves were simply too attractive not to dip into. In April 1876, despite the economy being in the midst of a slowdown,[64] all three of Singapore's note-issuing banks declared significant dividends for which they had to seek funding to pay out.[65] The Oriental Bank drew from its Reserve Fund to pay the declared dividends as well as to cover losses in 1877. Although it attempted to restore the 'borrowed' sum a year later,[66] due to the continued trade depression the bank's Reserve Fund was wiped out by the end of 1878.[67] As for the Mercantile Bank, it came close to bankruptcy in the later part of the decade as the loans it made went sour.[68] In 1878, the bank held significant silver deposits and a large amount of paper rupees. With the price of silver falling persistently and when the Indian government unexpectedly increased the supply of paper bills,[69] the bank lost £45,000 on its silver deposits and £44,745 on its paper rupees.

Snapshot of banknotes in circulation by issuing bank (dollars)*
(in accordance with the terms of the Royal Charter of Incorporation)

Reporting period	Oriental Bank	Chartered Bank	Mercantile Bank
August 1869	220,400	193,850 Specie in reserve 100,000	190,518
January 1870	208,000	209,800 Specie in reserve 100,000	214,583
December 1871	309,285	355,025 Specie in reserve 150,000	337,680
March 1872	276,375	411,195 Specie in reserve 150,000	312,475
July 1874	273,000	622,475	466,880
August 1875	221,935	676,571	N.A.

*Although data on the reserves held by the Oriental Bank and the Mercantile Bank for these years was not always published, it was often noted that the banks held bullion in reserve as required under the terms of each bank's Royal Charter.

Sources: *Singapore Free Press*, 25 June 1846, 1 March 1849, 15 February 1850, 2 February 1860, 9 August, 25 October 1866, 13 December 1884; *Straits Times Overland Journal*, 16 March, 18 June, 10 September, 8 October 1869, 17 January, 15 June 1872, 22 August 1874, 27 May 1879, 28 June 1880; *Straits Times*, 30 September 1856, 12 February 1870, 13 April 1872, 4 September 1875, 11 March 1876, 17 August 1878, 17 July 1880; *Straits Observer* (Singapore), 5 July 1875; *Daily Times*, 23 May 1879, 2 February 1880; *The Government Gazette*, 9 May 1879.

The shift from bimetallism to gold

Part of the difficulties the banks faced in the 1870s was due to falling silver prices.[70] The year 1872 marked a severe blow to bimetallism, the regime whereby governments sanctioned the unlimited monetary use of both silver and gold at a fixed exchange rate. In that year, the German Empire, which had been 'bimetallic', de-monetised silver and shifted to a gold standard. It began selling its silver in France, which remained on the bimetallic régime and was committed to maintaining the fixed rate of exchange between gold and silver despite Germany's actions. Eventually, France placed limits on the minting of silver dollars in 1873. Without this move, Gresham's Law (named after the 16th-century economist Sir Thomas Gresham) – the principle that 'bad money drives out good' – would have been operative: Germany would have exchanged its silver (the 'bad money') for gold (the 'good money') at a fixed rate in France, and the Germans would have 'swallowed up' France's gold and driven it out of circulation there. Bimetallism would have collapsed in France, and the republic would have been forced onto a silver standard. The US introduced the Coinage Act in 1873 which ended the right of holders of silver to have the bullion struck into dollar coins accepted as legal-tender. This act shifted the US onto the gold standard as well.

The various nations' actions caused the silver price of gold to rise; that is, silver depreciated relative to gold. This led to bankruptcies in Europe, and in May 1873, the Vienna Stock Exchange crashed, precipitating the Panic of 1873. The banks in Singapore, with their holdings of silver specie and bullion in reserve, were also affected.

Beyond the financial crisis, scholars have argued that France's move to restrict the coining of silver signalled to markets that the country could not credibly commit to bimetallism in the long run. This cemented the decision for other nations to adopt the gold standard,[71] which, in turn, would guarantee the continued decline in demand for silver relative to gold, cause the price of silver to weaken further, and make it even less attractive as a store of value and medium of transaction. Between 1873 and 1893, the price of silver relative to gold fell a total of 40 per cent.[72] The shift to a world where currencies would be set on a gold standard would pick up momentum following the events of 1873.

The Chartered Bank was the most prudent of the three. While the Oriental Bank dipped into its Reserve Fund in 1878 to cover the 1877 dividends and losses, the Chartered Bank channelled its profits for that year into its Reserve Fund to bolster its contingency buffers.[73] In that year, it was able to utilise £25,000 from its Reserve Fund to cover exchange contingencies. The bank took care not to invest this fund in special securities and retained £1,781,313 cash in hand. As a result, though the Chartered Bank also suffered during the downturns in the 1870s, it weathered the period better than the other Eastern Banks.[74]

The stresses of the 1870s made clear that requiring financial institutions to keep in reserve funds to back issued notes was no guarantee of stability. Banks could potentially use their reserves for other purposes, and if they became insolvent, there was no recourse for the holders of the banknotes they issued.

Despite this, entering the 1880s, there was still a quiet confidence in the local banking system and in the paper monies issued. In 1880, the banks of Singapore

The Mercantile Bank began to issue notes in Singapore in 1861, but the printer's records show that the 500-dollar denomination was not printed until 1864.

500-dollar specimen note. This denomination was first issued by the Mercantile Bank in Penang and Singapore in 1861.

100-dollar note issued by the Hongkong and Shanghai Bank in Singapore. The term 'manager' suggests it was issued no earlier than 1881 (when the bank was authorised to run a full branch). Between 1877 and 1881 the notes bore the word 'agent'.

10 dollars, the earliest known note issued by the Hongkong and Shanghai Bank in Singapore, c. 1866.

10-dollar note issued in 1882 by the Mercantile Bank, the only bank ever to issue notes in Malacca.

50-dollar note produced by the Mercantile Bank in Singapore.

had in circulation a total of 2.5 million dollars' worth of notes.[75] It was generally believed that chartered banks could not and would not issue notes in excess of their paid-up capital.[76] Yet, rumours persisted that the three Eastern Banks were considering a merger to ride out the bad times.[77] Not put off by the challenges, more institutions entered the scene: in 1877, the Hongkong and Shanghai Banking Corporation established its Singapore branch, offering deposits and granting bank drafts for London, Europe, India, Australia, America, China and Japan. It did not offer exchange services when it first started.[78] By 1884, the Hong Kong bank had a paid-up capital of 7.5 million dollars and a Reserve Fund that stood at 4.4 million dollars. The local branch began offering discount services for local bills and exchange services.[79] Crucially, the bank began issuing banknotes after the Legislative Council passed the Hongkong and Shanghai Bank Ordinance in 1881.[80]

Singapore Free Press, 3 March 1896.

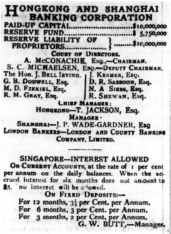

By the late 19th century, several million dollars' worth of banknotes were circulating in the Straits Settlements.[81] These notes had clearly gained ground as an accepted form of money and were very useful for conducting international trade. Yet, a number of questions remained around their function and their stability. First, with the notes typically being issued in larger denominations of five dollars and above, could paper money truly serve as circulation currency and be put to daily use in the Straits? Second, in light of the problems the note-issuing banks were facing, were they the most appropriate institutions for printing and issuing notes on behalf the government? Or should the government issue paper money itself?

One-dollar note issued by the Hongkong and Shanghai Bank in 1872 in contravention of the terms of its charter.

On the first question, it is only when the money that is used in higher-value commercial transactions is also accepted at the bazaar, and by the government, that it becomes circulation currency. If banks were able to issue one-dollar notes, this would make paper money ubiquitous in the economic life of the residents of the Straits (see **Banknotes as circulation currencies**, opposite) The Hongkong and Shanghai Bank came close to this ideal in the 1870s. Established in Hong Kong in 1865, the bank had mistakenly issued one-dollar banknotes in Hong Kong in 1872, flouting the terms of its charter which stated that the bank could not print notes worth less than one pound sterling in value. The bank offered to withdraw the notes in 1873. However, the Secretary of State allowed the notes already printed to remain in circulation, but only within Hong Kong. When the bank sought to establish a branch in Singapore in 1876, the Colonial Office acceded on the condition that the bank withdrew these one-dollar banknotes if the government should eventually issue the one-dollar government notes. The bank agreed, and it opened its Singapore branch in the following year.[82] Hence, in 1877, Singapore had a bank with 226,000 dollars' worth of one-dollar banknotes in circulation, although these were still by and large confined to Hong Kong.[83]

However, the most compelling reason for the main banks of Singapore to continue issuing banknotes for commercial transactions, and indeed to increase their reach into circulation currency, was that there were significant profits to be made in the process. When the British government mooted producing a British dollar for the empire's Eastern trade in the 1880s, this potentially threatened the banks' profits from note issuance. Consequently, they lobbied for the right to produce their own one-dollar banknotes in order to make the notes more ubiquitous in everyday economic life.[84] Note issuance was worthwhile business for the banks as long as it lasted;

Banknotes as circulation currencies

Banknotes were typically issued in the larger denominations – five dollars and above. A survey of a broad range of goods and services indicates that it was possible for five-dollar or even ten-dollar notes to be used for transactions occurring at a lower-than-daily frequency, or for purchasing consumer goods that would have been considered luxury items for that time, such as a whole chicken, or shoes from Robinsons. The average monthly wage of a white-collar employee was 50-75 dollars in 1891,[85] and spending 5-10 dollars in a single purchase would have constituted a very significant expenditure – even more so for blue-collar workers. Clearly, a one-dollar note would be more useful, although subsidiary currency would still be needed to make change.

Prices of goods and services, 1880-1896

Year		Price
	Fees and charges for services	
1880	House rental at Bally Lane	4.50 dollars per month
1881	House rental at Amoy Street	8 dollars per month
	House rental at Cross Street	10 dollars per month
1883	School fees (girls' school)	1 dollar per month
		4 dollars (including music lessons)
		10 dollars (for boarding students)
1893	Boys' boarding school quarters	36 dollars per month
	Admission fees, musical performance	0.75 dollars
	Entrance fees for Golf Club	2 dollars per entry, 1 for monthly subscription
1894	Season tickets (three shows) for opera at the Town Hall Theatre	7.50 dollars
1894	Hotel room, budget	1.25 dollars
	Prices of consumer items	
1884	Rice paddy, 1 picul (60 kg)	1.30-1.60 dollars
	Large chicken	3.40 dollars
	Large duck	3.60 dollars
	10 eggs	0.13-0.14 dollars
	1 lb mutton	0.22-0.25 dollars
	1 catty beef	0.10-0.125 dollars
	Potatoes, 1 picul (60kg)	4 dollars
1890	Shoes from Robinsons	2.50 dollars
1891	Sherry, 1 case	10 dollars
1896	Envelopes, 1,000 pieces	0.75 dollars

Sources: *Singapore Daily Times*, 4 May 1880; *Singapore Daily Times*, 25 Mar 1881; *Singapore Daily Times*, 25 March 1881; *Straits Times Weekly Issue*, 20 June 1883; *Straits Times*, 19 May 1884; *Straits Times Weekly Issue*, 20 August 1884; *Daily Advertiser*, 7 October 1890; *Singapore Free Press* (Weekly), 1 September 1891; *Singapore Free Press*, 7 July 1893; *Singapore Free Press*, 16 December 1893; *Singapore Free Press*, 20 May 1893; *Straits Times*, 6 September 1894; *Singapore Free Press* (weekly), 24 March 1896; *Mid-Day Herald and Daily Advertiser*, 15 November 1897.

Nevertheless, a case can be made that banknotes were being used to some degree as circulation currency in the 19th century. There were two runs on the Mercantile Bank, in 1872 and 1892, and in both instances, reports indicate that the crowds rushing to cash their notes for specie were Chinese shopkeepers.[86] It is reasonable to think that the shopkeepers had accepted the notes as payment for goods sold. In 1897, the Assistant Postmaster-General reported that people were remitting monies home by physically posting banknotes abroad. He complained that the practice was 'inexcusable' considering that the Post Office provided money-order services.[87] It may be the case that these individuals already had banknotes on hand and did not want to incur extra charges by purchasing money orders.

they knew full well that the dollar note, as well as any larger-denomination notes, would have to be withdrawn if the government ever introduced its own paper currency. With more than three million dollars' worth of banknotes in circulation in mid-1882, growing to more than four million by January 1884, the major banks of the Straits had much to lose if they could no longer issue banknotes.[88] Meanwhile, the Malay States were using the notes issued by the banks of the Straits Settlements. For the local banks, the States were a growing market for their notes. Consequently, the note-issuing banks resolutely opposed the introduction of a Straits Settlements government paper currency.[89]

On the second question, the concern was whether commercial banks had sufficient scale and stability to bear the risks and responsibility of issuing paper money for the Straits Settlements. On this, there was no consensus. A segment of the populace believed a government-issued note would be safer and offered better protection for lower-income groups; others argued that the banks were safer because they had reserves. In any case, they said, the colonies ought to support their own banks.[90] This should make a bank-issued note as safe as a government note.

In the event, when the first note-issuing bank with a branch in Singapore failed, the weight of the argument shifted decisively in favour of a government-issued British dollar for the purposes of Eastern trade.

In 1884, the Oriental Bank was bankrupted. As we have seen earlier, the bank had faced severe challenges in the early 1870s that persisted for several years. By the end of 1878, the Reserve Fund backing the bank's notes in circulation had nearly been exhausted.[91] On 3 May 1884, the run on the Oriental Bank at Calcutta started. On 4 May, the bank stopped all payments. By 5 May, the Oriental's deposits had fallen by £1.5 million from the sum on its last published balance sheet.[92] In Ceylon and Mauritius, where the bank was entrenched and dominant, the government had to intervene to guarantee the Oriental's banknotes.[93] On the same day, the bank closed its doors in preparation for liquidation.[94] The oldest of the Eastern exchange banks[95] had fallen.

The contagion spread quickly. In Hong Kong, Chinese businesses refused to accept the Oriental's banknotes. In the morning of the crash, these notes were almost 'unnegotiable', but later, they were let go at 15-20 per cent discount. The rush on the bank was so intense and the withdrawal of deposits so large that the Hong Kong branch had to suspend payments. Then a run on the Chartered Bank in Hong Kong started.[96] The most asked question of the day was, 'Who will collapse next?'[97] Singapore was also affected. When news of the Oriental's difficulties in India and Ceylon arrived, holders of the Oriental's notes from as far as Johor started making a beeline towards Singapore. Large crowds gathered outside the Oriental and the other banks, hoping to redeem their banknotes. The panic was halted by coordinated action: before the Oriental opened its doors for payments on the morning of the bank run, the managers of the other banks had already met and agreed to accept and cash the Oriental's notes. By noon, calm had returned.[98] Although the Oriental was quickly reconstituted as the New Oriental Bank Corporation,[99] it faced severe challenges and rapidly depleted its reserves in the years that followed.[100] It collapsed once more in 1892 and was liquidated the year after.

With hindsight, it is clear that the run on the Oriental had triggered a run on all the banks because the confidence in the entire system of note issuance had been shaken. The Oriental had the smallest issuance and distribution of banknotes in the Straits;[101] this was perhaps why the coordinated action by the other banks was effective in halting the run. What would happen if a larger bank were to fail?

Following closely behind the Oriental's failure was the collapse of Singapore's second oldest surviving bank, the Mercantile Bank. A run on the Mercantile on 12-13 June 1892 forced it into liquidation. A previous run on the bank in 1872 had ended without grave consequences. When it was made known then that a major debtor of the bank had failed, a large gathering of the Mercantile's depositors (which included a significant number of sojourners and migrants to the region), even those from outside Singapore, rushed to the bank to redeem their banknotes. The Mercantile Bank was helped by the Chartered Bank, which accepted and cashed its notes. In 1892, however, the bank suffered another run. Following a vicious rumour, a great number of Chinese *towkays* (the Hokkien term for business owners) descended on the bank before opening hours to redeem their banknotes for specie. As before, other banks assisted by accepting and cashing the Mercantile's notes.[102] At the other end of the Malay Peninsula, the rush at the Penang branch of the Mercantile Bank was far more chaotic amidst rumours that the bank would soon stop payments. A great panic ensued, leading many to offload their banknotes with a 25 per cent discount. When the dust settled, 200,000 dollars had been withdrawn. The bank was re-capitalised and reborn as the Mercantile Bank of India (Limited), but it had lost its Royal Charter and could no longer issue banknotes.[103]

After withdrawing a bank note from circulation, the Hongkong and Shanghai Bank would keep a half-note on file for record purposes.

Into 1893, therefore, the Chartered Bank was the only one of the original three exchange banks still standing. It and the Hongkong and Shanghai Bank were the only two remaining banks with the right to issue banknotes in the Straits Settlements. From the mid-1890s, both banks ramped up the number of notes in circulation across the Straits to make up for the shortfall left by the failed banks. In January 1884, the combined banknote issued had amounted to just over 4.3 million dollars,[104] but by September 1896, these two banks alone had issued 6.9 million dollars in banknotes.[105]

Towards the end of the decade, the Colonial Office would decide to produce a British silver trade dollar and a Straits Settlements dollar paper money, thereby eliminating the need for privately issued banknotes for commercial transactions and as local circulation currency (see p. 81). However, as it would take time to put the newly issued government specie and paper money in circulation, banknotes were still needed in the transition period to augment the money supply. Consequently, on the eve of the release of the Straits paper currency, the Chartered Bank was allowed to increase its circulation of banknotes by an additional one million dollars.[106]

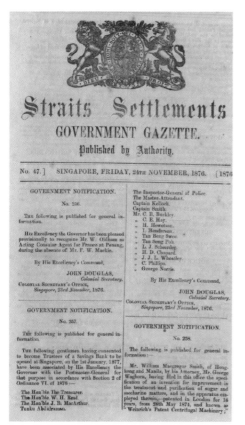

Trustees appointed in 1876 to oversee the new Post Office Savings Bank, as announced in Government Notification No. 257 in the Straits Settlements Government Gazette.

Banking and saving with the government

The government first conceived the idea of having a savings bank attached to the General Post Office in 1874.[107] It was thought that the institution would 'encourage frugality amongst people with small income', and it would eventually have a loan office that would earn enough profit to pay for the establishment and provide good interest to depositors.[108] A Legislative Council Subcommittee was appointed two years later to review the matter, and in September 1876, the Council passed the Savings Bank Ordinance to incorporate the bank and establish a trusteeship to oversee it.[109] The Post Office Savings Bank finally opened for business on 16 January 1877,[110] with a capital of 14,000 dollars. It paid depositors interest of 5 per cent per annum while charging 7 per cent for loans.[111] Limits were also set to ensure that the bank remained a savings institution for lower-income individuals: each depositor could only put a maximum of 250 dollars a year in the account, and the account could never exceed 750 dollars.[112]

The Savings Bank did not have shareholders. As it did not issue banknotes, it was not required to hold a Reserve Fund. The bank's deposits were invested to earn income, and policies pertaining to interest rates and investment of deposits initially also came under the Postmaster-General.[113] However, as this officer was himself a member of the civil service, the Colonial Office in London was the ultimate authority governing the Post Office and its subdivisions, including the Savings Bank.

Within a year of the bank's opening, the Colonial Office intervened and instructed that the bank be reorganised under a new ordinance. The Secretary of State in the Colonial Office considered the trustee model unsound, and it was not in line with the norms of the Post Office Savings Bank in England. He wanted the deposits of the Saving Bank, which had hitherto been invested locally, to be remitted to Britain where they should be invested in government securities. The world had been undergoing a severe economic downturn in the 1870s, and Britain's public finances in the later part of the 19th century were very strained.[114] It is perhaps not surprising that the 'home government' expected support from its colonies. In addition, the Secretary of State was of the view that the British colonial administration should oversee the bank directly.[115] Hence, the Trustees body was to be abolished.[116] A new ordinance had to be passed to implement these changes, but this required the previous ordinance to be repealed. The Post Office Savings Bank would cease to be, and a new entity, the Government Savings Bank, would take its place.

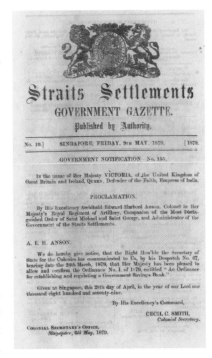

Ordinance for establishing and regulating a Government Savings Bank, 6 May 1879.

The General Post Office, built in 1873. It subsequently shifted to the Fullerton Building site in 1928.

The new Savings Bank Ordinance became law in 1879. The original Post Office Savings Bank was 'closed on the coming into operation of this Ordinance', and the Government Savings Bank took its place on 10 May 1880.[117] The management of the bank was transferred from the Postmaster-General to the Colonial Treasurer.[118] There was an initial panicked reaction to the closure of the Post Office Savings Bank, which led to a withdrawal of deposits.[119] However, the situation quickly calmed because there was strong underlying demand for the bank's services, while the bank's management responded to stem the flight.

NOTICE.

Depositors in the Savings Bank are reminded to send in their passbooks between January 6 and 20, 1908, for audit, in compliance with the Rules and Regulations under the Savings Bank Ordinance. Passbooks may be forwarded free by post to the Superintendent of the Bank.

W. G. BELL,
Postmaster-General,
Straits Settlements.

Government Savings Bank,
Singapore, January 6, 1908.
28

The Government Savings Bank: notice to depositors, *Straits Times*, 18 January 1908.

Aside from a cut in the interest paid on deposits to 4 per cent, little else changed in the new Government Savings Bank. It was still only open twice a week between the hours of 11 am and 2 pm, and depositors had to bring along their deposit books when using banking services. The Government Savings Bank was still located in the General Post Office building, where the original Post Office Savings Bank had opened its first branch.

The Government Savings Bank evolved to become a full 'branch' of the General Post Office despite being under different management following the 1879 reorganisation. Within the Post Office establishment, the Money Order and Postal Order department was a significant revenue generator, and it handled even more cash than the Savings Bank (see table opposite). By the turn of the century, the Savings Bank was popularly considered a part of the Money Order Department,[120] although it was a separate entity directly under the control of the Colonial Treasurer. In 1907 a new Government Savings Bank Ordinance was passed, repealing the 1879 ordinance.[121] It essentially placed the Government Savings Bank under the care of the Postmaster-General, making official what had already been practised. The linkage between the two institutions was strengthened in 1909 by the appointment of a single person to oversee the two 'departments' of two different government services. W.H. Threlfall was appointed Superintendent of Singapore's Money Order Branch as well as the Manager of the Government Savings Bank at the Post Office.[122] In 1923 an ordinance would be passed to change the name of the Government Savings Bank back to 'Post Office Savings Bank'.

Combined, the resources of the two Post Office departments were formidable. The network of government post offices in the British Empire allowed the Straits Settlements' post offices to arrange for and serve as conduits for the transfer of money across borders, a function that hitherto could only be performed by the exchange banks with their branches across the world. The savings banks of the Post Office could also undertake cross-border interbank transfers, and indeed its money-transfer facility was extended in 1907 to include the Bahamas, British Guiana, Canada, the Federated Malay States, Jamaica, Malta, Southern Rhodesia, throughout the Straits Settlements and Trinidad.[123] Where the chartered banks' money-transfer services were previously largely accessible only by merchants and other banks, now any individual or owner of a small or medium-sized business could perform money transfers and access basic banking services by walking into the General Post Office or a local post-office branch.[124]

Straits Settlements postal service money and postal orders: value and volume

| Period | Value of money orders (Straits dollars) | Postal orders | | Notes |
		Number of transactions	Value of transactions (Straits dollars)	
1906	—	50,440 Singapore 82,750 Straits Settlements	1,066,848 Singapore 1,776,600 Straits Settlements	The Straits Settlements Post Office had handled FMS's money-order transactions with India, China and Ceylon until this year. For postal orders, Straits Settlements Post also bought these from London and distributed some to the FMS. However, from 1906, the FMS bought POs directly from London.
1908	2,173,145	—	—	Money order rates: For British North Borneo: 1% commission or minimum 5 cents. For Australia, New Zealand, Hong Kong, Siam and Kelantan: 1½% commission or minimum 10 cents.
1910	2,471,629	—	—	Money-order business with Britain, India, Johor, Australia, Kelantan, Siam and British North Borneo increased.
1918	5,321,844	—	—	97,214 dollars in revenue from telegrams.
1919	5,795,930	—	—	21,772.66 dollars in revenue from telegrams.

Sources: *Singapore Free Press*, 24 July 1909, 19 October 1920; *Straits Times*, 15 July 1911, 14 July 1913; *Eastern Daily Mail*, 29 May 1906; *Malaya Tribune*, 23 October 1920.

Although the government's savings bank did not operate like commercial banks in providing exchange services and loans, it was not fully shielded from the impact of exchange-rate fluctuations. In 1920, the stability of the Post Office and the bank was tested when the price of silver rose amidst weak supply. This had caused the value of the Indian rupee to appreciate vis-à-vis the Straits dollar, and the rate for money transfers rose: whereas the two currencies had been at parity before, at one point it became possible to get only 80 rupees per 100 Straits dollars with bank drafts and 90 rupees with money orders.[125] These fluctuations hurt the 'man in the street'. The depreciation of the Straits dollar against the rupee meant that Indian coolies remitting money home from the Straits had to send more dollars to ensure their families had enough rupees.[126] The stronger rupee and an ongoing trade depression also led to a sudden rush to withdraw deposits from the bank in early 1921, placing it under extreme pressure. The Acting Colonial Treasurer had to ask the Legislative Council to sanction a 50,000-dollar loan to the bank to tide things over; almost a month after this request, a further sum of 100,000 dollars was approved.[127]

The importance of the Government Savings Bank to the colony went beyond allowing lower-income individuals the opportunity to save and earn interest. The Empire-wide branches of the British postal service, and thus the savings bank, served as a complementary commercial-financial network that facilitated the international flow of money alongside the banks. The fact that the savings bank could come into existence and operate for the benefit of the average resident in the Straits demonstrated that the Straits Settlements' attainment of Crown colony status played a crucial part in allowing it to shape its own financial policies. However, the intervention by the Colonial Office would have served as a reminder that the policies enacted by the Straits government could not be entirely independent of the priorities of the imperial establishment.

Number of depositors, value of total deposits, and value of average deposit account in the Straits Settlements Government Savings Bank

Year ended December 31–	Depositors	Deposits (dollars)	Average deposit account (dollars)
1881	289	21,359	73.90
1882	356	26,200	73.59
1883	453	34,710	76.62
1884	559	51,009	91.25
1885	631	58,493	92.69
1886	645	56,674	87.86
1887	745	64,008	85.91
1888	844	67,891	80.44
1889	1,275	71,506	56.08
1890	1,036	72,036	69.53
1891	1,260	86,772	68.86
1892	1,378	103,648	75.21
1893	1,568	116,241	74.13
1894	1,647	130,976	79.52
1895	1,688	141,059	83.56
1896	1,867	185,587	99.40
1897	2,021	206,406	102.13
1898	2,244	233,302	103.96
1899	2,404	244,853	101.85
1900	2,504	246,742	98.53
1901	2,745	276,555	100.74
1902	2,951	305,517	103.53
1903	3,078	331,482	107.69
1904	3,109	320,283	103.01
1905	3,310	317,065	95.79
1906	3,571	330,569	92.57
1907	3,696	339,854	91.95
1908	4,017	367,039	91.37
1909[a]	4,267	380,981	89.29

[a] From special report of U.S. consul, June 16, 1910.
The value of the Straits Settlements dollar fluctuated until 1906, but for the purposes of this table the present value, $0.56775833, was used in reducing to United States dollars.
'Compiled from Statistical Abstract for the Several British Colonies, Possessions and Protectorates'

Source: National Monetary Commission (1910), 'Notes on the Postal Savings-Bank Systems of the Leading Countries', Document No. 658.

Government-issued dollars for the Straits Settlements

Meanwhile, there was a pressing need to alleviate the uncertainty caused by an inadequate supply of silver dollars for trade and the volatility in silver prices. For most of the century, almost every nation involved in the China trade had used common 'foreign' silver dollars – Spanish, Mexican, and even American and Japanese silver dollars. Many of the territories from around the China Sea and the Malay Archipelago, including the Straits Settlements, the Malay States, and British Borneo, had used these currencies as circulation currencies within their own borders. However, the specie was often issued by nations over whose currency policies their users had no control.

For the British in the mid-19th century, there were two options: for Britain to create its own silver coinage to guarantee an adequate supply of trade dollars, or to have affected colonies switch to a gold standard. In 1863, the Governor of the Straits Settlements actually articulated his support for a trade dollar for the territories.[128] However, this was just before the Straits Settlements' transfer, and there was no local legislative body to pursue this endeavour. The trade dollar produced by the Hong Kong Mint in 1866 was intended as a solution, but it was unfortunately not popular with the merchants of the China trade, and it never gained traction. This is perhaps unsurprising: while a dollar was meant to be of equal value across the different varieties of specie issued by different nations, the weight and purity of silver inherent in each series of dollars differed, making some coins preferred to others (see 'Legal-tender' table, p. 90).

The Hong Kong Mint closed in 1868, and the Mexican dollar remained the trade currency of the day. However, when a scarcity of Mexican dollars emerged in 1872 and affected business and commerce,[129] calls arose for the British to issue their own dollars for the China trade.[130] With few alternatives, the Japanese yen and American trade dollars also came to be accepted as current in the Straits during this time.[131]

In April 1878, the Japanese government applied to the Straits and Hong Kong governments to make the yen legal-tender in the two colonies. This sparked a debate about whether the British should issue their own trade dollars or continue to rely on currencies issued by other nations. No action was taken, and the supply of Mexican silver dollars remained scarce. In 1877 the Hong Kong banks petitioned for the minting of a British trade dollar. This call was reiterated in 1886 by the Auditor General,[132] who recommended having a British trade dollar.[133] The Singapore Chamber of Commerce complained about the inconvenience of depending on foreign coins, and wrote to its Hong Kong counterpart on the matter. The Hong Kong chamber responded with an offer to join the Singapore chamber in submitting a proposal for a British trade dollar to the British government once more.

An 1884 American trade dollar (left) and an 1874 Japanese one-yen coin (right). The weight and fineness of the silver in both coins are inscribed on their faces.

In 1887, the Japanese government made an offer to mint a silver dollar for Hong Kong and the Straits Settlements for a 1 per cent seigniorage fee.[134] This was not taken up, but in an effort to establish some measure of exchange stability in the Straits, the Home Government issued a Queen's Council order in October 1890 listing a basket of specie which was to be considered legal-tender in the Settlements. These coinages were classified into two divisions. The Mexican dollar was declared the 'Standard Coin', while the American trade dollar, Japanese yen and Hong Kong dollar were recognised as 'Other Coins' (dollars and subsidiaries) also considered legal-tender in the Straits Settlements.[135] By 1893, the situation had become so desperate that Hong Kong was itself considering making the yen legal-tender, a proposition it had flatly rejected 15 years previously. There was a growing concern that the failure to act now might lead to higher costs in future if

Legal-tender: 'Standard Coin' and other coins, as notified in the Straits Settlements Government Gazette, 5 December 1890.

PART ONE.
Standard Coin.

Coin.		Metal.		Millesimal Fineness.	Standard Weight.		Minimum Weight.	
					Grains.	Grammes.	Grains.	Grammes.
Mexican Dollar...	...	Silver	...	902·7	417·74	27·070	413·563	26·799

PART TWO.
Other Coins.

1. Ratio to Standard Coin.	2 Coin.		3. Metal.	4 Millesimal Fineness.	5. Standard Weight.		6. Minimum Weight.		7. Limit of Tender.
					Grains.	Grammes.	Grains.	Grammes.	
1	American Trade Dollar...	...	Silver	900	420·00	27·215	415·800	26·943	None
1	Japanese Dollar or Yen...	...	,,	900	416·00	26·957	411·840	26·688	,,
1	Hong Kong Dollar 1st Issue	...	,,	900	419·052	27·150	414·862	26·879	,,
1	Do. do. 2nd Issue	...	,,	900	416·00	26·957	411·840	26·688	,,
·50	Do. Half Dollar 1st Issue	...	,,	900	209·50	13·575	207·405	13·440	,,
·50	Do. Do. 2nd Issue...		,,	900	208·00	13·478	205·920	13·344	,,
·50	Straits Settlements Half Dollar	...	,,	800	209·52	13·576	199·044	12·898	2 Dollars
·20	Do. Twenty Cent Piece		,,	800	83·81	5·430	79·620	5·159	,,
·10	Do. Ten Cent Piece	...	,,	800	41·90	2·715	39·805	2·580	,,
·05	Do. Five Cent Piece	...	,,	800	20·95	1·357	19·903	1·290	,,
·01	Do. One Cent Piece	...	Copper or mixed metal.	—	144·00	9·331	—	—	1 Dollar
·005	Do. Half Cent Piece	...	,,	—	72·00	4·665	—	—	,,
·0025	Do. Quarter Cent Piece		,,	—	36·00	2·333	—	—	,,

Mexico were to apply export charges on its dollars or if Japan raised minting fees. Even worse – the Mexicans and Japanese could cease minting silver dollars in the near future, and there would be no more silver dollars for the Eastern Trade.[136] Things had come to a head. It was time to take a stance on the creation of the British trade dollar.

The Colonial Office appointed a six-member Currency Commission to review the currency situation in the Straits Settlements and Hong Kong. They presented two options. The first involved the continuation of free silver, or specie minted by others. However, this meant adopting the Indian rupee, or continuing to use the Mexican dollar, which was the cause of the problems in the first place. The second option was to create a British trade dollar, which would follow the prevailing price of silver.[137] The Commission decided on the latter. The Bill for the new coinage was brought before the Straits Settlement Legislative Council in 1894, and by October that year, the British government informed the Straits and Hong Kong governments by telegraph that the Indian mints would strike their silver trade dollars, and they would receive these by 1895.[138] On 27 October, Secretary of State for the Colonies Lord Ripon wrote to the Governor of the Straits Settlements a letter that was then laid before the Legislative Council:[139]

Sir, I had the honour to inform you by telegraph on the 13th instant that the proposal to coin a British Dollar at the Indian Mints has been sanctioned and the new coin will be issued for circulation in the Straits Settlements and in Hongkong. The issue will take place under a joint agreement into which the Chartered Bank of India, Australia and China and the Hongkong and Shanghai Banking Corporation have undertaken to enter, and under which they guarantee to the Indian Government a payment of one per cent on a minimum coinage of five million dollars annually, to be supplied to the Banks on production by them of bullion; the agreement to be for one year in any case and to be terminable thereafter at six months' notice. No expense in connection with the coinage will be thrown upon the Colonial Governments of the Straits Settlements and Hongkong, except the preliminary cost of making the dies, which can be divided equally between them. It has been decided, on recommendation of the Banks, that the Dollar shall be of the same weight and fineness as the Japanese Yen, and Hongkong Mint Dollar....

British trade dollar, 1895.

Not long after the British decision on producing a trade dollar, Japan went onto the gold standard, and the silver yen was demonetised at the end of 1897.[140] This left the Japanese with a great stockpile of silver coins which they attempted to offload to British banks, who could present the silver at the India mints for coining into British trade dollars. Fearing that the Japanese might flood the market with discontinued silver yen coins and impede the progress of the trade dollar, the British government rescinded the yen's legal-tender status. The Legislative Council passed an ordinance to stop the importation of the yen; the penalty for violation was a fine or imprisonment.[141]

Parallel to the discussion about the British trade dollar was the prospect of the government issuing a paper currency for the Straits. In 1893, the Governor of the Straits Settlements raised the issue when he informed the Secretary of State for the Colonies that the remaining two banks – the Chartered Bank and the Hongkong and Shanghai Banking Corporation – could not produce enough banknotes for the Straits Settlements, although they had around seven million dollars' worth of banknotes in circulation in the mid-1890s.[142] Moreover, they were unable to cover adequately each other's banknotes, given that they were only required to hold in reserve a third of the value of their own notes in circulation. In light of the recent bank failures, it seemed clear that government-issued notes would be more secure than notes issued by the banks.

The government proceeded to introduce a British trade dollar to augment the supply of current silver dollars for the Straits Settlements to use in the Eastern Trade. By the time the specie finally came to Singapore, the Colonial Office was deliberating giving the Straits Settlements its own paper dollar notes, but for a different purpose: the paper money was to improve the supply of stable local currency.[143]

Another issue linked to the introduction of government-issued paper money for the Straits Settlements was the position of the Malay States vis-à-vis this new currency. Prior to the 1890s, the Malay States had already been using

Remitting paper money

Around the 1900s, both government notes and banknotes were afflicted by 'mutilation'. The Chinese, in particular, would send banknotes or government notes through the post. The most secure way to do this was to send half the note first; only after the first portion was received would the second be dispatched. The note portions would then be reassembled and redeemed. There were so many instances where one half was lost in mail, or of the notes being cut and joined wrongly, that the government found it necessary in 1900 to publish rules and regulations for redeeming such notes.

Source: *Singapore Free Press* (Weekly) 19 April, 21 June 1900; *Singapore Free Press* 17 April 1900.

GOVERNMENT CURRENCY NOTES

The substance of the rules published for the encashment of defective and mutilated notes is (1) The parts of the note must be neatly and securely fastened together. (2) The number and series must, as a general rule, be decipherable. (3) Mis-matched halves, or halves alone, will be paid for when the second half comes into the Treasury.

Conditions for cashing in spoiled currency notes, *Singapore Free Press*, 16 June 1900.

currencies circulated within the Straits Settlements, which including the copper and silver subsidiary coin series, and banknotes issued by the Straits Settlements banks. Indeed, strong demand for money in the States was part of the reason for the specie shortage in the Straits. While the matter of the new paper currency was still in discussion with the Secretary of State, the Governor of the Straits Settlements began negotiations with the government of the newly formed Federated Malay States (FMS) to join in the issuance of the Straits Settlements' paper currency. This involved nominating commissioners, circulating notes, and guaranteeing the notes. Given this approach to the States, the early model of the note which the Governor attached in his exchanges of correspondence with the Secretary of State and the Malay rulers of the FMS included features associated with the Malay States: the tiger image which would subsequently be printed on the stamps of the FMS, and in the corners of the note's design

four krises (traditional Malay daggers) representing the four federated states.[144] But unbeknown to the Governor, the Secretary of State would ultimately forbid the inclusion of the FMS in the new currency scheme, deeming it *ultra vires*.[145] The FMS was an administrative amalgamation of four Malay states under British protection and not a Crown colony like the Straits Settlements. The States were still sovereign Malay polities with their own rulers who could not be made legally responsible for the notes issued.

Above: Two postage stamps, issued by the Federated Malay States (left) and by Pahang (right), one of the FMS.

Below: A proof of a Straits Settlements currency note (1895), featuring a tiger and four krises.

In any case, change was on its way. The Currency Note Ordinance, 1897, Ordinance VIII of 1897,[146] was a major reform for the Straits Settlements. It provided for the creation of a Board of Commissioners of Currency, Straits Settlements, with three commissioners, all based in Singapore.[147] The three would have the authority to issue notes in exchange for current silver coins. Each Straits dollar would be equivalent in value to a silver dollar. The coins collected would then form the seed capital for the Note Guarantee Fund, of which two-thirds was to be held in cash (specie) and the remaining third invested in Indian or British securities. The income earned from investments could be used for the costs of operating the currency system and to create a Depreciation Fund, which would be drawn on to cover any 'depreciation' in the value of invested capital. The currency commissioners were therefore tasked to oversee the issuance of Straits currency notes, and the management of the reserves that backed this paper money.[148]

Straits Settlements
currency notes,
5 dollars and
10 dollars, dated
1 September 1898.
They started
circulating on
1 May 1899.

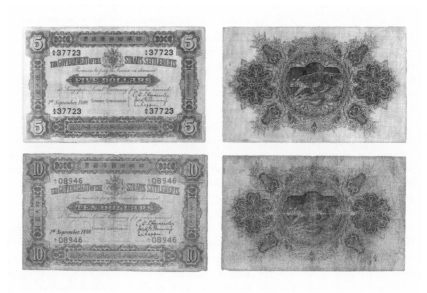

Conceptually, currency notes adequately backed by a reserve fund comprising specie and securities would have imparted necessary confidence in the government's paper money and made it useful as 'money'. However, some members in the Legislative Council wanted to go further: if the notes were to be genuinely 'exchangeable' for specie, then holders of the notes had to be able to redeem them at locations within the Straits Settlements other than Singapore.[149] The council members were assured that the government would consider establishing a branch of the Currency Commissioners' office at Penang at a later date. However, plans for the Penang branch were scuppered barely a year later as it would have been too costly to operate.[150] Consequently, the notes could only be redeemed at Singapore.

The first Straits Settlements currency notes arrived from Britain in denominations of 5, 10, 50 and 100 dollars, and started circulating on 1 May 1899. By the end of the year, this had increased to 3.9 million Straits dollars, against a specie reserve of 2.7 million dollars. At the beginning of 1900, 4.2 million dollars' worth of currency notes had been issued, and 2.5 million dollars more were on their way to the Straits. However, government notes could not fully replace banknotes as yet: at this juncture, there were still about 8.4 million dollars' worth of banknotes in circulation.[151]

The advent of government notes brought about changes to the monetary system of the Straits on two major fronts. First, it led to the eventual withdrawal of privately issued banknotes as circulation currency. Second, it led to the Malay States' formally adopting the Straits Settlements dollar as their currency.

When the British trade dollar was first introduced in 1895, the banks in the Straits had in circulation several million dollars' worth of banknotes. The Hongkong and Shanghai Bank's issuance limit alone was 10 million dollars.[152] Up till the passing of the 1897 Currency Note Ordinance, the two remaining note-issuing banks in

the Straits had 7.3 million dollars of banknotes in circulation, and the Chartered Bank was seeking to increase its limit by another million.[153] This was the zenith of banknote issuance in the Straits. In 1899, the Hongkong and Shanghai Bank was taken to task for circulating banknotes with a value exceeding the bank's paid-up capital, and it was required to cancel the excess banknotes. It began this process in early 1900 but was unable to complete it because there were insufficient government notes to replace the withdrawn banknotes. The government accordingly advised the Secretary of State not to renew the ordinance allowing the bank to issue banknotes.[154] Over time, both the Hongkong and Shanghai Bank and the Chartered Bank continued to reduce their outstanding stock of notes,[155] and their right to issuance eventually ended in December 1904 and August 1908, respectively.[156]

The introduction of the Straits Settlements dollar notes also brought to the fore the fact that the British Protected Malay States of Selangor, Perak, Negeri Sembilan and Pahang, and Johor did not possess their own currency and had always depended on foreign currencies, including the subsidiary coins and banknotes of the Straits Settlements.[157] With the formation of the Federated Malay States (FMS) in 1896, the British in Malaya were confronted with the challenges and opportunities presented by unified administration of the states, including on the currency front. When the first Straits Settlements currency notes were issued in May 1899, the FMS formally declared the notes to be legal-tender in

6. During the year the Reserve Vault was opened to give out coin to two Banks in exchange for Notes, the total amount of encashment being $175,000.

The ordinary daily encashment of Notes at the office of the Commissioners has been done from a small advance, the Notes received during any day being exchanged with the Banks for more coin.

7. Currency Notes were issued as follows during the year:—

				$
(1). Chartered Bank of India, Australia and China, Singapore	...			600,000
(2). Do. do.		Penang		100,000
(3). Hongkong and Shanghai Banking Coporation, Singapore	...			185,000
(4). Sarawak Governmen t	...	...	...	80,000
(5). Treasurer, Straits Settlements	...	...	...	20,000
(6). Assistant Treasurer, Penang	...	...	...	100,000
				1,085,000

As the Federated Malay States draw their supplies through the local Banks, the above figures do not show separately the amount absorbed by these States.

Institutions distributing currency notes in Singapore and the region, from Report on the Working of the Currency Note Issue, 1904.

9. The average monthly circulation of the local Banks for the last seven years has been as follows :—

				$
1899	...	...	...	8,082,209
1900	...	...	...	6,713,133
1901	...	...	...	5,473,755
1902	...	...	...	4,966,518
1903	...	...	...	4,176,913
1904	...	...	...	2,918,136
1905	...	...	...	1,866,215

The decrease is mainly due to the Hongkong and Shanghai Banking Corporation gradually withdrawing its local issue.

Decline in bank note circulation, 1899–1905, from Report on the Working of the Currency Note Issue, 1905.

A Straits Settlements
five-dollar note dating
to 1901, a year after
the size of the note
was reduced.

the States, and began formulating the rules and regulations relating to their use there.[158] This was a unilateral decision. The Straits Settlements was not a party to the legislation – indeed, the Straits government passed a new currency-note ordinance in 1899 expressly specifying that the Protected Malay States were not part of the arrangement.[159] The Straits dollar was therefore not a jointly created common currency for both the Settlements and the FMS, but it was a currency used in common.

By the turn of the century, there was still no sign of the one-dollar note. A dollar was the lowest denomination used in international trade, equivalent to the value of the ubiquitous silver dollar coins. Yet, it was also of a value small enough that it could be used to an extent in everyday transactions and at the marketplace. The Straits government was convinced that the five-dollar note should be the lowest denomination issued.[160] The most significant development here was the reduction in size of the first five-dollar note. This occurred in 1900 and was done to lower the cost of producing currency and to make the notes more convenient to carry around.[161] The government refrained from issuing a one-dollar note at this point.

A stable local currency

While the introduction of the British trade dollar alleviated the monetary constraints on trade and the issuance of the Straits Settlement dollar provided a steady supply of local currency for the Straits economies, there remained the issue of the volatility in the value of silver. The obvious solution was to shift to the gold standard. The Currency Commission of 1893 had clearly deliberated the issue when deciding on whether to issue a British trade dollar. When Lord Ripon wrote to the Governor of the Straits Settlements in 1895,[162] he had noted that the members of the Commission were all in favour of retaining the silver standard.

There were numerous push and pull factors that led to the eventual shift to the gold standard in 1903. By the turn of the century, the bulk of the commerce transacted through the Straits had been with countries and territories already on the gold standard.[163] In 1900, for instance, import and export transactions with countries on the silver standard were valued at around 212 million dollars, while trade with gold-standard countries had reached 330 million dollars. With an increasing number of countries going onto the gold standard, trade denominated in silver dollars had become less profitable, and revenues earned in silver dollars were always subject to conversion losses when exchanged to gold-standard currencies. On the ground, the impact of the depreciation was palpable. In 1888, one dollar (whether silver dollar or its banknote equivalent) was worth three shillings, where the latter was linked to gold. By 1903, the same dollar was only worth 1½ shillings. India had shifted to the gold standard late in the century, and similarly, while 100 dollars could fetch 225-232 rupees in the

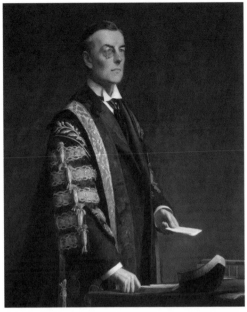

1880s, it could only be changed for 118-120 rupees by 1903. Indian workers paid in dollars backed by silver in the Straits were consequently getting far less in terms of their home-country currencies.[164]

The Governor of the Straits Settlements determined that it was necessary to examine whether the colony should shift to the gold standard. At his behest, the Secretary of State for the Colonies, Joseph Chamberlain, appointed another Straits Settlements Currency Commission in 1902 to look into the application of a gold standard not just in the Straits, but in the Federated Malay States as well, and to determine how to go about it.[165] The commissioners began their inquiry in London, on 13 November 1902, and continued receiving feedback until February 1903.[166] Meanwhile, the Straits Settlements Legislative Council had already started reviewing past commissions' reports and examining the currency models in other parts of the Empire, such as Ceylon and India.[167] The Commission finished their work within the first quarter of 1903,[168] and recommended the creation of a local dollar with a fixed value relative to the British gold sovereign for the Straits Settlements and the FMS.[169]

Hitherto, the Straits had always operated on a silver dollar basis, and transiting to the gold standard therefore required, as an intermediate step, fixing the value of a local silver dollar relative to gold. The monetary historian Lee Sheng-Yi has analysed the plan, breaking it down into four stages.[170] First, create a new local silver-dollar coin whose volume the government could 'control and manage'. Second, separate the exchange value of this coin from the bullion underlying it. This can be done through legislation prohibiting export of the new dollar coin

The Right Honourable Joseph Chamberlain, Secretary of State for the Colonies 1895–1903, in a portrait by Harrington Mann, c. 1900.

and the import of other dollars, and demonetising other silver dollars by melting them down into bullion. Over time, should the price of silver continue to fall relative to gold, the coin will become more of a 'token': that is, its value when used in transactions will not be determined by the worth of the bullion embedded in it, but by the number stamped on its face. As a token, the new dollar coin will simply be akin to a metallic form of paper money. Third, fix the exchange rate between the Straits dollar and the British gold sovereign. Although this exchange rate technically specified the rate at which the local currency could be exchanged for the gold sovereign rather than gold *per se*, the common understanding at the time was that with so many countries on the gold standard, it was easy to express one territory's exchange rate against another, without going through the intermediary of a measure of gold. Fourth, accumulate a stock of gold reserves to back the local currency.

The Legislative Council accepted the report and spent most of July 1903 reading and passing the Currency Note Ordinance 1899 Amendment Bill,[171] as well as finalising the design of the new coin which 'carries the head of the King in his golden crown, and his title *Edward VII King and Emperor*'.[172] It was during the discussion on the design of the new silver coin that the Governor suggested that the new Straits dollar should be one-sixteenth smaller in diameter than the British trade dollar to distinguish the new from the old.[173]

The creation of government currency notes earlier had already provided two contingency instruments: the Note Guarantee Fund (1899) and the Depreciation Fund (1902).[174] The funds had amassed a sizeable stash of old Mexican and British trade dollars which the Commissioners had collected in exchange for their paper notes, and this provided the government a perfect source of bullion with which to mint the new local silver dollar coin. The process of melting down the trade dollars and minting them into new Straits dollar coins would also demonetise these alternative silver coins, enabling the Straits to take the next two steps in the transition. After the first batch of new coins had been minted, they were returned to the reserve fund, and the next batch was then sent out for melting and minting. Over time, most of the old silver trade dollars in the funds were replaced with the new Straits dollar coins. With the government-issued currency alone remaining in circulation in the Settlements, it was relatively easy to fix a rate of exchange between the Straits dollar and the gold sovereign without causing great disruption.[175]

The reminting of the first batch of old coins was undertaken in July 1903 by the Bombay Mint for a 1½ per cent seigniorage fee.[176] The minting of the first batch of new coins was completed by early October, and these were sent back to the Straits by steamship. They were quickly put into circulation through the banks and the treasury.[177]

Straits Settlements dollar coin, 1903.

The rollout of the new silver coin encountered a number of teething problems in those early days. The Mexican silver dollars and the British trade dollars were still in circulation in early 1904, and they hindered the take-up rate of the new Straits silver dollar coin.[178] Accordingly, the government proclaimed on 23 August 1904 that from 1 September, that these two forms of silver specie would cease to be legal-tender in the Straits Settlements, as part of the larger legislation to demonetise all 'foreign' coins. Following this, the prohibition placed on the export of Straits dollars was withdrawn on 5 September so as to allow the new coin to flow freely. The second step towards the gold standard had been implemented.[179]

A major milestone was reached on 17 March 1905 with amendments made to the Currency Note Ordinance of 1899, to allow the Currency Commissioners to issue notes in exchange for gold at a rate to be determined by the Governor and approved by the Secretary of State. The gold received would form part of the Note Guarantee Fund, and could be invested or used to buy silver to be re-minted. The profits from minting would be placed into a Gold Reserve Fund instead of the Note Guarantee Fund.[180] The Straits Settlements was now just one stage of legislation away from the gold standard. All that was left was for the Governor to fix a rate of exchange between Straits dollars and gold. This day came on 29 January 1906 with the passing of the Currency Ordinance 1899, Amendment Ordinance 1906, which fixed the rate at which the Currency Commissioners could exchange Straits dollar notes for gold at 60 dollars for seven gold sovereigns, making each dollar equivalent to two shillings and four pence.[181] With this, the Straits Settlements was officially placed on the gold standard.[182]

Looking back, the role of government-issued Straits Settlements dollar notes cannot be overstated in the currency reforms of the early 20th century. The notes were not printed simply to replace banknotes;[183] they also provided a crucial liquidity buffer when the old silver specie was withdrawn for re-minting into new Straits dollar coins. Indeed, the Note Guarantee Fund had been a source of old silver specie used in the re-minting. It is unclear whether the colonial authorities had in mind the optimal monetary arrangements for the Straits Settlements when they embarked on government note issuance, or whether policies simply evolved organically in response to the pressing needs of the day. The fact of the matter is that the government notes were critical in the birth of the Straits silver dollar,[184] which in turn, was indispensable in putting the Straits Settlements on the gold standard.

Although the years between 1903 and 1906 could come across as a haphazard lurching from one currency standard to another,[185] in reality a paradigm shift had occurred without great fanfare. The Straits Settlements, including Singapore, had moved from relying on foreign currencies for trade and circulation locally, to having its own trade dollar and its own government-issued money. In particular, the journey towards the gold standard, which required stricter monetary controls that led to the demonetisation of other currencies in the Straits, carved out the space for local currency to become the sole legal-tender in the Settlements.

The monetary reforms in the Straits ran parallel with the political evolution of the region. As the British colonial sphere in the Malay Archipelago expanded, it created an enlarged British economic sphere in which the component territories had access to each other's markets and financial institutions, leading to closer economic and financial links between the Malay States and Singapore. Having a common currency serve as a unit of account, means of exchange, and store of value simply made sense. The Straits Settlements dollar thus became a public good that the neighbouring British-held territories wanted to use; the consolidation of the British colonial presence over the region created an enlarged policy sphere that made such an arrangement possible.

Sarawak first expressed interest in formally adopting the gold-backed Straits dollar as soon as the Report of the 1903 Straits Settlements Currency Commission was released.[186] The restriction placed on exporting the new dollars from Singapore in 1903 and the demonetisation of all other currencies in 1904 posed a serious problem for Sarawak as it became a challenge to acquire the dollars needed for trade with the Straits Settlements. Consequently, Sarawak made the decision to make the Straits dollar its standard currency. On 30 November 1904, it declared that its treasury would only accept the Straits dollar.[187] Initially, Sarawak had to use gold to purchase currency notes from the Straits, but it eventually negotiated for silver to be accepted.[188] Singapore allowed Sarawak a narrow window of time[189] in which to dispose of its stock of old silver coinage through Singapore, for which it would obtain Straits dollars in return. By September 1904, the Sarawak treasury had replaced most of its old dollars and received half a million Straits dollars from Singapore. In 1903, Selangor adopted the new Straits dollar. Its State Council passed legislation prohibiting the importation of Mexican and British trade dollars, Japanese yen and all copper and bronze coins issued by British North Borneo, Sarawak and Brunei.[190] Brunei and British North Borneo (Sabah) adopted the Straits dollar as legal-tender in 1906. The Sultan of Brunei subsequently prohibited the importation of the Mexican and British trade dollars, and decreed that Straits dollars in Brunei could not be exported to places outside the territories of Singapore, Sarawak, British North Borneo and Labuan.[191] Likewise, the Governor of British North Borneo also made it illegal to export Straits Settlements coins from his territory.[192]

A local currency created for the Straits Settlements had become the only legal-tender in the Straits and several other states in peninsular Malaya and the British

An illegal exchange

'The Colony is making a poor speculation in allowing its dollars (silver) to be swapped for North Borneo copper tokens. The *modus operandi* is something like this: A native merchant goes to a North Borneo treasury, and draws, on personal security or otherwise, a sum of copper of, say, from $5,000 to $50,000. This is ostensibly to purchase produce for the Singapore market. He is a known man and gets long credit from the North Borneo Treasury, long credit acting as a handsome discount. These coins are not spent on produce, but are conveyed direct to Singapore, where the importer, by using the moneychangers to work the coins off, giving these men a fair commission, secures for himself a handsome return, in silver, on the investment. The process is repeated ad infinitum, and the importation of "duits" is a thriving industry.'

Source: *Singapore Free Press* (Weekly), 28 September 1897

territories in Borneo. This created what amounted to a Straits dollar area in the first half of the 20th century.

Fixing the stability of the dollar dealt with only some of the currency issues confronting the government. The situation with subsidiary coinages in the Straits was more chaotic and acute than with the silver dollar. The Straits had suffered decades of severe copper coinage shortages since the mid-19th century, which the government attempted to alleviate by creating subsidiary silver coins. In the 1880s, British North Borneo and Sarawak had become British protected states, and they introduced significant volumes of copper coins into the Straits.[193] These coins were known as 'duits', recalling the problems with the Dutch doits in the earlier part of the 19th century. The situation swung in the opposite direction. During the shortages in the 1870s, a dollar could only be changed into 97 copper cents; with the surfeit in the 1880s, 102 cents could be obtained per dollar.

Although the government had fixed a value to each coin, the reality in the local bazaar was very different.[194] Pawnbrokers refused to take copper coins except at a discount. In 1891, when Penang underwent a downturn, shopkeepers and opium revenue farmers found themselves in a quandary: they held an estimated 60,000 dollars' worth of copper coins which the banks would only accept with a 2 per cent discount.[195] When the run on the Mercantile Bank occurred in 1892, and many banknote holders were looking to offload their notes in a hurry at up to 25 per cent discount, the opium revenue farmers gladly exchanged their copper coins for the banknotes.[196] Each side probably thought it was making the financially more prudent move.

A copper infestation, Singapore Free Press and Mercantile Advertiser (Weekly), 28 September 1897.

machinery for prevention more effective than a *Government Gazette* Notification.

On the question of the amount of foreign copper coin here, we give the following figures of varieties of coins found in $3.50 of coppers taken entirely at random:

Straits cents *(duit Queen)*	146
East India cents (date 1845)	12
(date 1862)	19
British North Borneo *(duit Sandakan)* ...	111
Sarawak unperforated *(duit Raja Brooke* or *Kepala gundal)* ...	49
Sarawak perforated *(duit lobang)*	3
Brunei *(duit Brunei)*	4
Hongkong cents *(duit Hongkong)*	5
English half-penny	1
	350

The native names for these coins are given in brackets. The dates of these India coins are given to show the persistence of coins of considerable age. Cents half a century old still abound. This will interest those who consider that with a strict prohibition of importation, alien coins would in time cease to be in circulation in the Colony.

10. The following is a list of remittances made for investment during the year from the Coin Reserve Fund.

The total was $1,007,974.01, i.e.,

(a) To the Crown Agents for investment in Gold Securities :—

	$ c.	Rate.	£ s. d.
June 27th, 1905 ...	503,937 01	1/11/¼	50,000 0 0
July 4th, 1905 ...	503,937 00	1/11/⅛	50,000 0 0
	1,007,874 01		100,000 0 0

13. The amounts due to the Depreciation Fund in respect of investments made in Gold and Silver Securities each year since the commencement of the Note Issue are:—

	Amount Invested. $ c.	At One per cent. $ c.
1899. In Gold Securities ...	636,000 00	
„ Silver „ ...	628,365 05	
Total ... 1,264,365 05		12,643 65
1900. In Gold Securities ...	545,337 01	
„ Silver „ ...	147,958 58	
Progressive Total ... 1,057,660 64		19,576 61
1901. In Gold Securities ...	550,000 00	
„ Silver „ ...	98,890 01	
Progressive Total ... 2,606,550 65		26,065 31
1902. In Gold Securities ...	2,236,596 35	
„ Silver „ ...	829,014 15	
Progressive Total ... 5,672,161 15		56,721 61
1903. In Gold Securities ...	600,000 00	
„ Silver „ ...	Nil	
Progressive Total ... 6,272,161 15		62,721 61
1904. In Gold Securities ...	Nil	
„ Silver „ ...	Nil	
Progressive Total ... 6,272,161 15		62,721 61
1905. In Gold Securities ...	1,007,874 01	
„ Silver „ ...	Nil	
Progressive Total ... 7,280,035 16		72,800 35
		$13,250 95

17. The balances after paying all the expenses of management and the one per cent. of the Coin taken out for investment to the Depreciation Fund were as follows :—

On the actual Working of the Year.	$ c.	Carrying forward Balance.	$ c.
1899 debit for year ...	60,317 07	Total debit to end of 1899 ...	60,317 07
1900 credit „ ...	3,872 22	„ „ 1900 ...	56,444 85
1901 „ „ ...	28,561 92	„ „ 1901 ...	27,882 93
1902 debit „ ...	32,817 18	„ „ 1902 ...	60,700 11
1903 credit „ ...	84,856 89	Credit „ 1903 ...	20,490 11
1904 „ „ ...	91,911 74	„ „ 1904 ...	112,401 85
1905 „ „ ...	101,079 86	„ „ 1905 ...	213,481 71

An additional sum of $3,666.67 was included in the working account during the first three years and eight months for rent of Vault but this was stopped at the end of 1902 under instructions from the Secretary of State. The Depreciation Fund was begun in 1902.

18. At the annual audit held in March, it was ascertained that the difference between the Coin taken out for investment and the market value of securities amounted to $347,580.83 after taking into account the sums already paid out of revenue and the Depreciation Fund. Owing to a proposal to bring in legislation for the payment of the whole of the net proceeds from the investments into the Depreciation Fund instead of one per cent. of the Coin taken out for investment as at present and for removing from the revenue of the Colony the liability of making good this difference year by year, no order for payment of the difference out of revenue was forthwith made by the Governor as required by the Ordinance. The Bill to effect these objects met with

Left: Reserve funds in gold and silver, from the Report on the Working of the Currency Note Issue, 1905.

Right: Investments of the Depreciation Fund, gains and losses, from the Report on the Working of the Currency Note Issue, 1905.

Following a ban on 'foreign coins' in 1891-2,[197] a greater number of Straits copper coins was returned to Singapore.[198] However, the foreign coins continued to circulate locally. A survey of the Singapore bazaar in 1892 found that 45 per cent of the coins in circulation were not Straits Settlements coins but copper cents from India, Sarawak and British North Borneo.[199] Critically, there was a glut of these coins.[200] It was known that a Chinese merchant had put 20,000 dollars' worth of copper coins into circulation in 1892.[201] The foreign copper coins that 'infested' the Straits Settlements were brought not by sojourners, settlers, visitors or merchants, but by individuals looking to make a profit by exchanging them for Straits currency.[202] As long as there was money to be made, this trade in currencies would continue. The Straits government's solution was to demonetise all coins except the ones produced and controlled by the Straits government, and this was done in 1903. By then, however, market forces were already leading people to shift away from the use of copper coins as money as the value of copper cash fell so much that people in the Straits started melting them to make wash-hand basins instead.[203]

One of the aims of the currency reforms of the early 20th century was to ensure that the Straits Settlements had a steady supply of local currency whose value was stable and not depreciating alongside the falling price of silver. The shift to the gold standard certainly resolved the issues associated with the latter. Moreover, the currency board held several funds – the Note Guarantee Fund, the Depreciation Fund, and the Gold Reserve Fund – which, on paper, enhanced the stability of the new Straits dollar, could instil confidence, and provide a safety net for the holders of the currency notes and the government as well. As a safeguard built into the original Currency Ordinance, the government could choose to make good the difference between the value of notes issued and the value of reserve funds, by drawing from the local revenue to top up the losses incurred by the Note Guarantee Fund's investments. All these factors suggested that the gold-backed Straits dollar notes would be a very stable form of currency well-suited for local circulation.

However, inherent in this system were two critical assumptions: first, that the funds would be secure; and second, that gold prices would not suffer the extent of fluctuation and depreciation that had afflicted silver.[204] Events proved otherwise.

In the first instance, the value of the Note Guarantee Fund's investments started to fall. In early 1900, the securities held by the commissioners depreciated by nearly 25,000 Straits dollars amidst geopolitical upheavals: this was the year of the Boer War in South Africa, the Boxer Rebellion in China and a period of unsettling disturbances in India.[205] Each of these episodes involved Britain and was taking place in areas where Britain had investments. Then the unimaginable happened: the gold price of silver began to rise (i.e. gold depreciated against silver), while investments in India recorded losses.[206] The value of the currency board's investments at the end of December 1904 was 6.3 million Straits dollars, having fallen by 873,441 dollars. The investment portion of the Depreciation Fund also suffered losses in the same year.[207] In 1905 alone, the government had to 'advance' more than a million dollars from the treasury to cover losses sustained by the currency board's securities investments. Of course, the government could not continually tap into the revenues of the Straits Settlements to make good the fall in the value of the currency reserves. It therefore amended the ordinances governing note issuance several more times[208] to give itself the flexibility of deciding whether to 'top-up' the funds. This relieved the government of responsibility for the colony's currency burden.

The Straits Settlements one-dollar note, first issued in 1906.

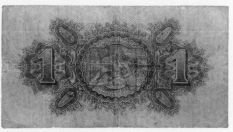

The local government had already created a Gold Reserve Fund in 1905, separate from the Note Guarantee Fund, to hold gold reserves as part of the Straits' shift to the gold standard.[209] The question soon arose as to whether it would be prudent to keep a gold reserve in Singapore itself rather than having all the colony's gold kept in London. Arguably, until Straits dollars could be exchanged freely for gold, the Straits Settlements could not be said to be fully on the gold standard. From this perspective, the Straits was still 'not quite there yet'.[210] More financial resources were needed to facilitate the accumulation of gold reserves.

To attain this, the government decided to produce more money using fewer resources. This led to the introduction of the previously-withheld one-dollar Straits Settlements note on 13 November 1906. It was also decided that a smaller Straits dollar silver coin should be minted. In October 1907, the treasury shipped 12.3 million 'large' Straits silver coins (36.5 mm) to be reminted into 'smaller' dollars (34.2 mm). It received 16.3 million new dollars in return. The plan was to reduce gradually the weight and fineness of the silver in the coins in such a way that they became pure 'tokens', and to replace the old dollars with their gold equivalents over time. The tokenisation process was therefore in line with the steps necessary to fully shift to the gold standard. The losses arising from demonetising the large dollars would be covered by the Gold Standard Reserve Fund established in 1907, which had been built up from profits on the issuance of the new smaller dollars in that same year. The same was done with the Straits Settlements subsidiary silver coinage minted since 1871 – the small silver coins were to be withdrawn and sold at their bullion value. When the new 34.2 mm silver dollar had been put into circulation, the government would also withdraw all current subsidiary silver coins and replace them with coins of the same size and weight but composed of silver of only 600 millesimal fineness, down from 800. The profits made from this operation would be credited into the Gold Standard Reserve Fund. It was a scheme that required a length of time to complete (see **Tokenising the silver Straits dollar and the gold standard**, opposite).[211]

In this way, the Straits government embarked on turning the Straits silver dollar into an increasingly tokenised coinage, albeit one that still held significant silver content. It was reported that Chinese shopkeepers in the Straits initially refused to accept these coins. They doubted that the smaller dollar was worth its face value, and they could not understand the concept of a token coinage.[212]

Meanwhile, a 'gold' storm started brewing in the latter half of 1906, when the price of gold weakened. Falling prices triggered a surge in demand for gold in India. Local banks responded by redeeming government currency notes, and the gold they obtained from the currency board was shipped to India.[213]

Tokenising the silver Straits dollar **and the gold standard**

The road taken to tokenising the coins of the Straits Settlements was closely tied to the initiatives to set the Straits dollar on the gold standard. Crucially, the printing of the one-dollar note in late 1906 enabled the introduction of the smaller one-dollar coin in March 1907 to occur without disruption.[214] This was because the government could seamlessly call in old Straits silver coins for re-coining into the smaller, new ones without disrupting the supply of money in the Straits.[215]

At the same time, tokenisation was part of the British government's strategy to stabilise the currencies used in its colonies at a time when the global price of silver was volatile. Winston Churchill, the Under-Secretary for the Colonies at this time, declared that the stability of the Straits currency would be threatened unless the fineness of silver in the dollar coins was reduced; the only other way was to abandon the Straits dollar's fixed exchange rate with the British currency. The first option was chosen. The British government did not see this as a debasement of the Straits dollar, because Straits Settlements currency – whether printed on paper or minted on baser alloys – was redeemed on the basis of the face value of the note or coin.[216]

When the first Straits Settlements silver dollar was struck in 1903, it weighed 416 grams and had a millesimal fineness of 900. When the dollar coin's size was reduced in 1907, the silver content was also lowered – the weight of the dollar coin had been reduced to 312 grams, while that of the half-dollar was now 156 grams. The millesimal fineness of both coins remained unchanged. In 1909, the silver content of the subsidiary silver 20-cent coin was adjusted down to 600 millesimal fineness. During World War I, the weight of the dollar coin was further reduced to 260 grams and its half-dollar to 130 grams. The millesimal fineness of the silver in these coins was lowered to 500. Crucially, bronze and nickel coins were struck in place of some of the copper denominations.

The millesimal fineness of the Straits silver dollar coin was raised to 600 and 750 in 1925 and 1938 respectively when the economies of the Straits Settlements and the Malay States were booming. However, by this time currency notes had become the main circulation medium. Silver specie, including those coins with higher precious metal content, was mostly kept in reserve. As war broke out in Europe and Asia in the late 1930s and the 1940s, and the global demand for gold, silver and copper as strategic commodities surged, the path to fully token money was fully established.

The 1903 and 1907 Straits Settlements one-dollar silver coins.

Prior to this, the currency commissioners had managed to accumulate £954,730 of gold in August 1906. By December, only £127,169 remained in the vault. The redemption of the currency notes went hand-in-hand with the fall in the value of the Note Guarantee Fund, and the net result was that the money supply in the Straits contracted with concomitant appreciation pressures on the local dollar. The value of a dollar rose from 2s 4d to a one-time high of 2s 4½d in January 1907, before weakening to 2s 3⅝d in late 1907. It only returned to the value of 2s 4d in August 1908.[217] The decline in the price of gold continued. From September 1907 to January 1909, the value of gold assets held by the Straits currency board declined by 65 per cent.[218]

In the latter part of 1908, the Netherlands Indies demonetised their stock of almost two million Straits dollars issued prior to the shift to the gold standard. The Indies then required a significant supply of the new dollars. The Northern Malay States were about to become part of British Malaya at around this time, which meant that they would join the Straits dollar area as well. Faced with the prospect of having to increase significantly the issuance of Straits Settlement notes, the currency board had to find more gold resources to back the money printed. Instead, another run on the board's gold reserves started, amidst a financial crisis in the East in 1908.[219] Just the year before, the Board of Commissioners of Currency had acquired more gold reserves to fund the development of the Tanjong Pagar Dock. In September 1907, the gold in the vault had increased to £511,897.[220] However, in April 1908, the Singapore treasury vault had only 5,418 dollars' worth (£632 2s) of gold left.[221] The Singapore gold reserve had been nearly wiped out.[222]

By this time, it had become increasingly clear that paper money was fast becoming the predominant circulation currency in the Straits, while gold and silver specie were increasingly kept in reserve and locked up in vaults. The currency board managed to replenish its gold holdings after the 1907/8 episode, and gold eventually came to dominate the reserve funds' composition, befitting the fact that the Straits dollar was on the gold standard. However, most of the gold assets were held in London.[223] The currency board's investments in securities continued to lose money, making the cash component of the reserve funds even more critical to the smooth functioning of the currency system. The transition of the old monetary regime based on specie to one fuelled by currency notes was well under way.

World War I and emergency notes

In the 1910s, the growing importance of paper currency, by comparison with commodity coinages, reached the point where currency notes were simply accepted as 'currency' – money in and of themselves – rather than being valued because they represented a claim on specie. There was therefore no longer a need for the 'paper' or 'note' descriptors. While these had highlighted the token nature of the paper money, people had got used to keeping notes and transacting with them, rather than redeeming them for specie.

World War I (July 1914 to November 1918), also known as the Great War, was fought mostly in Europe. Hostilities ended in 1918, but the war was formally concluded when the Treaty of Versailles was signed on 28 June 1919 during the Paris Peace Conference. Britain itself went off the gold standard in 1914 in order to print more notes during the war; it returned to the standard in 1925, only to leave it again during the Great Depression.[224]

When war started in mid-1914, strategic commodities became scarce almost immediately. They included both specie and coins minted from baser metals, and the metals used to produce the coins. With no alternative, demand for circulation paper currencies rose.[225] At the end of January 1915, there were 48.5 million Straits dollars' worth of currency notes in circulation. By mid-1917, this had climbed to 85.1 million dollars.[226]

However, there was still no alternative for subsidiary coins. The scarcity of subsidiary currency persisted for more than a year before the government decided that it should release its own paper subsidiary notes. These were not sanctioned by the Colonial Office. So, in October 1917, the Singapore treasury turned to the Government Printing Office in Singapore and the Survey Department of the Federated Malay States based in Kuala Lumpur to print these contingency subsidiary notes on normal paper.[227] These 'emergency' notes were crudely made and not expected to survive serious handling.[228] The authorities seem to have thought that giving them a revenue stamp, or 'chop', might endow them with a semblance of legitimacy. In the event, a crowd descended on the Treasury at Empress Place to claim their 10-cent notes.[229] The notes were of such poor quality that local Chinese leader Dr Lim Boon Keng declared them a disgrace.[230]

Dr Lim Boon Keng, c1910s.

This policy was hardly appropriate to the real needs of the 'Straits Settlements dollar area'. A shortage of local subsidiary notes persisted, especially within the Malay States. The private sector began to fill in the gap. There were many reports of Chinese towkays, particularly in Perak, printing their own subsidiary note series in 5-, 10-, and 20-cent denominations.[231] The Chinese Chamber of Commerce in Ipoh was said to have issued a 10-cent note. In Kampar, Perak, a number of shops issued their own note series, and the proprietor of one, a Mr Lam Loo King, issued subsidiary notes bearing his image and even serial numbers.[232] The government told these enterprising individuals and organisations to withdraw their notes.[233]

The scarcity of subsidiary monies during the war years was reminiscent of the copper-coin shortages that plagued the Straits Settlements throughout the 19th century. Even after the war ended, this shortage persisted. A local resident cheekily labelled the state of affairs 'a small-change famine'.[234] With metals still short in supply, the British home government eventually printed subsidiary notes for the Straits Settlements and Malay States. These were of higher quality and better accepted by the local population.[235]

There was a need to find a more enduring solution to the 'small change' problem that had frequently plagued the Straits Settlements even during the time of the East India Company. The Straits Settlements dollar notes were already 'tokens' with no inherent value; their worth lay in their claim to the specie backing them. The silver content of the Straits Settlements dollar coin

Top and centre: The 1917 10-cent and 25-cent notes were printed by the Survey Department of the Federated Malay States. The revenue stamp was stamped on the back of the 1917 10-cent note.

Below: The 1919 10-cent note was printed by Thomas de la Rue & Co. in Britain.

struck in 1903 had been reduced over time, and its purity was also lowered. Subsidiary paper notes had demonstrated their usefulness during the Great War; tokenising the small-denomination coins and producing them using baser metals was the logical remaining step towards ensuring a more resilient supply of coins for the Straits.

In retrospect

The period from the mid-19th century to the early 20th was a time of transformation. It corresponded with the Second Industrial Revolution. The technological advances of the day and the emergence of a group of industrial economies reshaped the contours of global commerce. These forces supported the expansion of the British Empire, but it was also in the last quarter of the 19th century that the Empire reached its zenith.

During this period, commercial banks and agency houses emerged as partners in the British Empire's commercial enterprise. Their branches across the empire provided financial instruments that helped fuel international commerce – bills of exchange, promissory notes, telegraphic transfers, exchange services and facilities, and more. Banknotes from these institutions began circulating within the United Kingdom's eastern colonies, which had no paper currencies of their own. However, by the late 19th century, it had become clear that these commercial institutions could not sustainably guarantee a supply of currency notes that was stable in value. By the time the Long Depression ended, many of the more established banks had folded, and with them, confidence in bank-issued notes. Against this background, the British government explored providing its colonies two types of money: first, a silver trade dollar for its eastern trade, in which the Straits Settlements had a share; second, a local currency for the Straits Settlements, one that was partly based on a paper dollar.

With the Straits Settlements notes and currency, the Crown colony was on a parallel journey to progressively tokenise its circulation currency. Tokenisation was a key step in the process of shifting the Straits dollar onto the gold standard. The government managed to peg the value of the local dollar to the pound sterling at a fixed rate of 2s 4d; it was the pound sterling itself that had a fixed price to gold. The Straits currency board began the process of building up its gold reserves. It was thought that shifting away from the silver standard to gold would provide the Straits currency much-needed stability. In reality, the prices of both metals, and thus the value of the currencies backed by them, proved to be volatile.

Nevertheless, with the new Straits dollar notes and coins, an increasingly tokenised currency system began to be established in the Straits. By the first two decades of the 1900s, the notes had come to be used as 'money' in and of itself, with little or no reference to the silver or gold that had been so critical to the commercial life of the Straits just a few decades earlier. This monetary journey would culminate in the issuance of a new currency – the Malayan dollar – as we shall see in the next chapter.

CURRENCY AND FINANCES IN CRISES AND WAR

(1920–1945)

The British Empire emerged from World War I greatly weakened and encumbered by debt. Britain turned more protectionist, especially when the Great Depression hit, and the needs of individual colonies became subordinated to the needs of the Empire. Britain's colonies had to impose tariffs vis-à-vis non-Empire goods, which threatened Singapore's free trade. This period saw the continued tokenisation of coins, and this trend culminated in the issuance of the Malayan dollar to replace the Straits dollar. Financial considerations, notably the fiscal buffers that the Straits Settlements' currency reserves provided during the recessions of the 1920s and '30s, were a deciding factor in the shift. Under this new currency arrangement, the Malay States would become full partners in the currency board that issued money used in the Malay States and the Straits Settlements, and enjoy a share of the revenues derived in the process. When the Japanese Occupation started, the Imperial Army circulated 'banana notes' that were not backed by any assets. This currency would become worthless even before the war ended, as persistent shortages of essentials drove accelerating inflation, exacerbated by overprinting of the notes.

The years 1870–1914 saw the rise of industrial and economic centres other than the United Kingdom; these nations began to pose a serious challenge to Britain's political and economic heft in the world. This was the period of the Second Industrial Revolution. Territorially and militarily, Britain's empire reached its peak towards the turn of the 20th century. The Great War that broke out in 1914 signalled the beginning of the end of British hegemony. Emerging from the hostilities, the British Empire faced economic and political challenges. The country was laden with war debt,[1] Its share of commerce in the Americas and in East Asia was eroded by both the US and Japan.[2] The British also faced growing dissent in the colonies, with calls for self-rule or full independence.[3] Domestically, unemployment surged as production in the wartime industries of coal, iron, steel, and shipbuilding eased.

The British Empire's diminished capacity was evident in its inability to maintain a naval force commensurate with its global aspirations. The defence plan for its far-flung colonies and dominions involved maintaining only a single fleet, the Home Fleet, which was to be based at home and dispatched to flashpoints only when needed. The Singapore Naval Base was constructed as an operational platform, dock and shelter for the Royal Navy's use in the event that it was sent to the Far East.

Recovery efforts after the end of World War I were geared towards restoring pre-war prosperity and order,[4] and for a while it seemed as though some sense of economic normalcy was returning, as Britain went back onto the gold standard in 1925. However, in 1929 the Great Depression struck, and the 1930s offered little respite for Britain and its colonies[5] as the crisis devastated their economies. Prices, production, and trade plunged. The fiscal revenues of the Malay States and Straits Settlements fell sharply. In a bid to restore competitiveness, Britain abandoned the gold standard once more during the Depression. The Straits Settlements dollar's value was tied to the pound and depreciated alongside it. Under pressure to stimulate and promote commercial activities, Britain and its major colonies leaned towards protectionist policies, promoting an imperial preference system and a campaign within the 'Commonwealth of Nations', as the Empire became known from 1926. The rallying call resounded to 'Buy British' and 'Buy Empire'. This involved Britain and its territories raising tariffs on goods produced outside the Empire, making goods produced within it relatively cheaper, and therefore, more competitive. Britain was no longer supporting free trade. The political economy of the Straits Settlements was affected, as well as that of the Malay States that traded through the Straits ports. A conundrum arose: should the needs of the Empire, or the economic mainstay of the Archipelago – namely, free trade – come first?

Meanwhile, from 1931, signs of another global war were surfacing once more. In Europe, the National Socialist German Workers' (Nazi) Party had grown in

Chapter opening picture: Raffles Place in the 1920s. Facing the camera is the Chartered Bank building.

The Commonwealth of Nations, or the British Empire, prepares to celebrate the coronation of King George VI in May 1937.

popularity and was on the cusp of seizing power.[6] In the Far East, Japan invaded Manchuria. These threats led the allied western powers to divert resources needed for economic recovery towards preparations for war.[7] Against this backdrop, it was a logical step to free up the much-needed financial resources hitherto bound up in backing the currency and embedded in specie and money containing alloys of precious metals. This meant reducing the backing of the Straits Settlements dollar, lowering the silver content of Straits coinage, and circulating more paper currency notes. While these trends had already been visible in the earlier part of the 1900s, they now accelerated. The Straits Settlements' currency became increasingly tokenised, a process that culminated in the issuance of a fully tokenised currency for the Straits and the Malay States: the Malayan dollar. Whereas there had been a silver Straits dollar coin to anchor that currency's underlying value, there was no such specie-based tether for the new currency, although it was pegged to the pound sterling.

When the Malay Peninsula and Singapore fell to the Japanese in the early 1940s, the residents of these territories were forced onto a fully fiat currency that had no backing and represented no claim on anything of value. The Japanese 'banana notes' included subsidiary paper notes. There was no coinage with any metal content, precious or otherwise. Banana money was thus a truly token money – its intrinsic worth was only that of the paper it was printed on. The Japanese Occupation would bring about severe hardship and disruption, and its impact on the domestic financial system would have severe repercussions in the years to come.

A changing global economy and the Singapore entrepôt

Singapore's entrepôt economy, fuelled by the free trade policy established by Raffles, was foundational to the island's success in the 19th century. In the first half of that century, Singapore's role in facilitating the China trade made it the most significant entrepôt in the Malay Archipelago. However, the contours of global trade began to change in the second half of the century, and the nature of trade through the Singapore port evolved too. With the onset of the Second Industrial Revolution in the 1870s, processed commodities and manufactured goods carried by steamship became the mainstays of global trade. These items were produced by emerging industrial states such as the United States, Japan and Germany, and the goods traded included iron, steel, tools, paper, petroleum, chemicals, rubber, tin, bicycles, automobiles, engines, telecommunication equipment, and more.[8] These displaced the old trade flows of silk, tea, spices, porcelain and opium, carried on

The Straits Settlements coat of arms, on the wall of the Tanjong Pagar railway station, opened in 1932.

ships propelled by seasonal monsoon winds. Heading into the 20th century, global maritime commerce had become more multifaceted in terms of the composition of goods traded, and more internationalised with regard to the number of economies actively engaged in trading. Against this backdrop and contemporary technological advances, global trade expanded by 300 per cent from the late 19th century to the early part of the 20th.[9]

Trade through the Straits ports increased by an even larger 800 per cent.[10] In the later 1800s, the trends highlighted at the beginning of the previous chapter came together powerfully to bear on the evolution of the Straits Settlements. Although steamers had been calling at Singapore since the 1840s, they were mostly mail and passenger ships: they carried limited cargo as they had to haul their own coal fuel as well. Steamships only became a viable form of cargo conveyance when more dry docks and coal depots were set up in maritime ports from the 1860s. Singapore became a critical port of call on the steamship network with the establishment of the Tanjong Pagar Dock Company,[11] which built wharves with coal supply facilities.[12] The next critical milestone was the opening of the Suez Canal in 1869, which only steamships could use. The canal further reduced the time it took for a ship to travel between Europe and Asia. Politically, the British 'Forward Movement' (see p. 63) from the 1870s onwards led to intervention in the Malay States, paving the way for their

One of the few surviving tin dredges: the Tanjung Tualang Dredge No. 5 in Batu Gajah, Kinta District, Perak, Malaysia. Built in 1938, it weights 4500 tons.

economic development. In due course they would trade with the world through the Straits Settlements ports.[13]

A key outcome of direct British involvement in Selangor, Negeri Sembilan, Perak and Pahang from 1873[14] was that capital and labour from the Straits Settlements flowed into these territories.[15] This turned the hitherto small-scale extraction of tin in these States into extensive, large-scale mining operations. The use of tin-plating in the production of tin cans to contain food had been an important innovation in the 19th century, and demand for tin sheets had risen exponentially as canning methods developed. To capitalise on the demand for tin, the Straits Trading Company was established in 1887 in Singapore to mine, smelt and export tin from the Malay States.[16] The company imported tin from the Malay Peninsula and sent it to smelting factories established on Pulau Brani. The finished tin sheets were then exported. Most of the commodities originating in the Malay States were exported through Singapore and, to a lesser extent, Penang. Right through World War I, the Straits Settlements ports were responsible for handling 80 per cent of all imports into, and 67 per cent of exports from, these four Malay States, which became administratively united as the Federated Malay States (FMS) in 1896.[17] In the early part of the 20th century, to meet the demands of the booming automobile industry that required rubber tyres, Malayan rubber joined tin as one of the chief commodities produced in the FMS and exported through the Straits Settlements. Tin and rubber became the

Dredging tin – buckets in action.

The chimneys on Pulau Brani were part of the Straits Trading Company's tin smelter.

Singapore, Keppel Harbour.

twin pillars of the Malayan economy,[18] generating significant spill-overs that benefitted Singapore.

Singapore remained a significant emporium and entrepôt well into the 20th century. The value of imports and exports of the Straits Settlements rose more than tenfold from 42.5 million dollars and 34.0 million dollars respectively in 1870 to 425.8 million dollars and 397.3 million dollars by 1915.[19] However, trade was no longer as focused on China – it had become more internationalised. Singapore was shifting its focus towards exporting to meet the needs of the western industrial nations, while importing these supplies from the region. Between 1870 and 1915, the value of imports and exports from India and China (South and East Asia) fell by 32 per cent and 43 per cent, respectively. By 1915,

Rubber-tapping, an image on the tiled wall of the Tanjong Pagar railway station.

only 12 per cent of the Straits Settlements' exports were going to East Asia, down from close to 20 per cent in 1870.

Meanwhile, the Straits' exports to the western nations increased thirteen-fold over the same period. The growth of Malaya's imports into the Straits was even greater, with the 1915 level more than 30 times that in 1870. The import of tin[20] and rubber[21] from Malaya into Singapore smelters and processing plants would have contributed to most of this increase. The western nations had, together, accounted for a third of the value of the Straits Settlements' imports and exports in 1870. By 1915, their share of the Straits' imports had fallen to below 15 per cent, but their share of exports had risen to above 50 per cent. At 97 million dollars, the US was the Straits' largest export market, while Britain followed close behind. Combined, the value of the Straits Settlements' exports to these two nations in 1915 was 81 per cent of its exports with the West, and one-third of its total exports.

Straits Settlements foreign trade, 1870 and 1915

Distribution of Straits Settlements foreign merchandise trade

Zones	Imports		Exports	
	1870	1915	1870	1915
Southeast Asia	44.4%	67.9%	42.9%	35.8%
South and East Asia	23.0%	19.1%	17.8%	10.6%
Western nations	32.5%	14.8%	37.4%	53.4%

Distribution of Straits Settlements Trade with Southeast, South, and East Asia
Percentage of total trade and value (thousands, Straits dollars)

Zones	Imports		Exports	
	1870	1915	1870	1915
Southeast Asia of which:	44.4% 18,907	67.9% 289,429	42.9% 14,587	35.8% 142,508
Malaya	10.0% 4,244	30.0% 127,978	4.3% 1,462	14.2% 56,399
Netherlands East Indies	16.6% 7,065	16.3% 69,566	18.2% 6,164	14.9% 59,203
Siam	8.8% 3,735	11.9% 50,646	8.9% 3,011	3.7% 14,662
Burma, Indo China, British Borneo, rest of East Indies	9.1% 3,863	12.7% 41,239	8.6% 3,950	3.1% 12,244
South Asia	11.4% 4,835	5.3% 22,399	5.8% 1,959	5.8% 23,229
East Asia	11.6% 4,945	13.9% 51,077	12.0% 4,711	4.8% 19,178
Total	67.4% 28,687	87.0% 362,878	60.7% 21,257	46.5% 184,915

Distribution of Straits Settlements trade with Europe and America
Percentage and value of total trade (thousands, Straits dollars)

Zones	Imports		Exports	
	1870	1915	1870	1915
Britain	27.7% 11,778	8.6% 36,510	24.6% 8,340	19.2% 76,535
Europe	3.9% 1,667	2.8% 12,115	1.2% 407	8.5% 33,748
America	0.04% 19	1.6% 3,719	10.9% 6,959	24.4% 97,044
Others	0.9% 384	1.7% 7,328	0.7% 238	2.7% 5,264
Total	32.5% 13,848	14.8% 59,672	37.4% 15,944	53.4% 212,591

Source: Chiang Hai Ding, *A History of Straits Settlements Foreign Trade, 1870–1915* (Singapore: National Museum, 1978), pp. 85-90. Figures may not add up precisely due to rounding.

The Mercantile Bank of India building in Raffles Place – it was replaced in the 1920s.

This diversification of Singapore's entrepôt economy could perhaps explain the abandonment of the British trade dollar that had been created for the Eastern trade (see p. 91). By the early 20th century, the Straits Settlements was doing more trade with the Malay States than with East Asia. Consequently, it made sense to create a dollar that would be used generally within the Malay States as a local regional currency, and that could also serve as a common unit of account. This was more feasible than creating a replacement trade dollar; in any case, such a dollar would never have reached the circulation levels of the Spanish, Mexican and American dollars or even the Japanese yen.[22]

'Empire first' or free trade?

The Straits Settlements dollar – both specie and notes – was a stable currency that the Straits and other Malayan governments were able to maintain for several decades, and even through the Great War. Yet, by the 1930s, Britain decided that it had to reconfigure the popular Straits dollar into a new Malayan dollar.

Why did this occur? The answer lay in the very strength of the Straits Settlements dollar itself. Although the British government had over time turned the dollar into an increasingly token form of money, the currency remained widely accepted. This was clearly not due to any intrinsic value in the notes and coins. Instead, the acceptance of the Straits dollar as 'money' rested on its substantial reserve backing, which imparted stability to its value and earned it the confidence of the public. The currency reserves, which were mostly invested, also provided the Board of Commissioners of Currency, Straits Settlements,

Shipping Conferences: cartels against free trade

A factor behind the changes in shipping routes and thus trade patterns was the anti-competitive behaviour of shipping companies. In the second half of the 19th century, shipping firms serving similar markets or plying similar routes would band together to form associations known as Shipping Conferences, the objective being to reduce price competition between members and to protect markets from outsiders. They colluded, fixing freight rates and sometimes even routes and destinations. The Conferences were effectively cartels that could cut rates and so force out competition, and then raise prices. There was no Conference among operators of vessels sailing to the Straits Settlements until 1897. The previous year, shipping rates to London had plummeted in the midst of a trade downturn. This led shipowners to organise the Straits Homeward Conference.[23] The effects were felt instantly. The Conference inhibited the entrepôt trade of the Straits, causing a loss of trade for the colony – so much so that the Singapore Chamber of Commerce appointed a commission to investigate the situation.[24] Although this led the Straits Settlements Legislative Council to pass the Freight and Steamship Ordinance in 1910 to stamp out the oligopolistic practices of the Conference, the law did not receive the King's assent, and the shipping cartels wielded too great an influence on the British government for reforms to be made. By 1930, leading members of Singapore's European community were asking 'if we cannot rid ourselves of this octopus which is strangling this Colony'.[25]

The heart of the problem was that freight companies that were part of the Conference had offered shippers and merchants rebates. They had established a fund equivalent to five per cent of the value of freight heading 'homeward' (usually Europe) in ships plying Conference routes. This fund was disbursed as a 'secret rebate' to six or seven large firms responsible for 60 per cent of Singapore's trade if they chose to send their cargo via established Conference shipping lines. The rebates were not offered to parties deviating from the preferred routes. As a consequence, steamers from America plying the Pacific route at the turn of the century seldom sailed beyond Hong Kong. Steamers coming out of New York were forced to use the Suez Canal to reach the Straits, and this led to higher overall shipping costs.[26] Government action in the Straits failed to curtail the activities of these organisations. Instead of enforcing the law, Sir John Anderson, the then Governor of the Straits Settlements, made a secret pact with certain parties – specifically the Homeward Java and Homeward Straits Conferences and the New York Steamer Company – to exclude certain Straits produce from the Conference rebate system and to abolish the secret rebates for the routes into the Straits.[27] In return, he repealed the 1910 Bill.

with positive returns. These translated into additional income for the Straits government – useful during downturns. The British Empire in general, and British Malaya in particular, viewed the strength of the Straits government's finances with some degree of envy. Hence, when the government of the FMS experienced great financial difficulties through the late 1920s, the question arose: should the better-off members of the British Commonwealth such as the Straits Settlements render assistance to the others? Put more explicitly, should the colony or the Empire come first? And for that matter, should members of the Empire support each other?

In the context of British Malaya, 'Empire first' sentiment manifested itself as a mix of protectionist and nationalist fervour as early as 1925. Then, the Secretary of State for the Colonies expressed the view that the colonies needed to give preference to British or Empire produce.[28] Similar sentiments in Britain itself led to the creation of the Empire Marketing Board (1926–1933), stressing 'the value of imperial unity'.[29]

Empire Marketing Board promoting goods from the colonies.

Meanwhile, other financial pressures were coming to bear on Malaya. The tin and rubber industries had become the twin pillars of the Malay States economies, and accounted for a large part of their government revenues. However, these commodities would prove to be the States' 'Achilles heel' – commodity prices could slump as well as boom. For instance, when the FMS government revenues fell across the board between 1912 and 1913, it was noted that deteriorating rubber prices had had the greatest impact.[30] In 1928, the price of rubber fell to an all-time low following the end of the Stevenson Rubber Restriction Scheme[31] which had been put in place in 1922 to manage the level of rubber production in Malaya and so control prices. The failure and abandonment of the scheme precipitated a further decline in rubber prices.[32] Concurrently, revenues earned on rubber duties fell from 1927 to 1929, while the expenses of the FMS government rose continuously.[33] Falling duties were the result of sharp contractions in the States' trade, which declined in 1928 by 25 per cent from its 1927 level and 32 per cent from two years before.

Wall Street crashed on 29 October 1929, sparking the onset of the Great Depression. A worldwide economic downturn led to a general collapse of trade. Between 1929 and 1932, the total value of Malayan trade (which included Singapore) had more than halved from 1.8 billion Straits dollars to 0.7 billion dollars.[34] The FMS was particularly hard-hit by the Depression because of its dependence on rubber and tin. As an internationalised entrepôt, Singapore similarly could not escape a downturn. During 1929, the business environment on the island deteriorated severely. In June of that year, when large-scale Chinese firms started to fail, almost 4,000 houses fell empty, not rented out. Rents declined by 25 per cent.[35] This weighed heavily on the Singapore mercantile community. In 1930, it was reported that 5,000 Chinese men in Singapore were jobless and fast becoming destitute. Deflation spread from overseas to Malaya. Reflecting these trends, the stock of Straits Settlements currency notes in circulation fell from 115 million dollars in 1928[36] to 67 million dollars by the end of July 1933.[37]

Straits Settlements currency notes and coins bearing the portrait of King George V (reigned 1910–1936)

1 dollar (1935)

5 dollars (1935)

10 dollars (1935)

50 dollars (1925)

100 dollars (1927)

5 cents

10 cents

20 cents

Impact of the Great Depression: value of Malayan trade[38] (millions of Straits dollars)

Year	Imports	Exports	Total
1925	1,008	1,290	2,298
1929	899	931	1,830
1930	724	674	1,398
1931	402	405	807
1932	380	366	746

The Depression had a major impact on the finances of the FMS government as customs duties on tin and rubber accounted for a significant portion of government revenue. In contrast, the Straits territories were free ports that did not collect customs duties, and they were therefore less affected as far as this source of government revenue was concerned. In addition, the multiple reserve funds held by the Straits government played no small part in augmenting government finances during a time when the Depression was weighing on revenue collection. For instance, in 1930 the Straits government's revenues of 32.4 million Straits dollars was insufficient to meet its expenditures of 39.2 million dollars. However, the 6.8 million dollar deficit was fully covered by the government's reserves, which stood at 83.2 million dollars at the beginning of the year. The healthy reserves balance was, in part, due to a 19 million dollar transfer from the Currency Guarantee Fund to the Treasury.[39] As a result, even after funding the deficit for 1930, the Straits coffers still held reserves amounting to a significant 76.4 million dollars at the beginning of 1931.[40]

It had been accepted that during World War I, policies regarding security and defence, commerce and monetary regulations, among other matters, would be co-ordinated at the pan-Malayan level, which included the Straits Settlements, the Malay States and the British territories in Borneo. A question was whether this should also be the approach with regard to the economic difficulties affecting these territories, such as the Great Depression. Britain had already achieved hegemony across Malaya and by this time, the Governor of the Straits Settlements, Cecil Clementi, held concurrently the position of High Commissioner of the Federated Malay States, British North Borneo (Sabah), Brunei and Sarawak.[41] Clementi envisaged that British Malaya should weather the storm of the Depression as a collective: that part of the Empire which had the means should help the part that was in need.

It was in this context that in 1932 Clementi called for a pan-Malayan customs union, to ensure common regulations and tariff rates across the various territories.[42] As the ports at the Straits Settlements did not levy duties on trade, this proposal created great resistance amongst the Straits residents.[43] There were clearly two divergent economic philosophies at work in different parts of British

The 1932 Ottawa Conference[44]

After World War I, trade between the United States and the British Empire boomed, but in the 1920s, the Empire as a whole had a sizeable trade deficit with the US. Not only were many of its goods unable to compete with American products, but the onset of the Great Depression in 1929 left Britain and its colonies and dominions in dire straits economically. They gathered for a month-long meeting from July-August 1932 at Ottawa, Canada, to formulate an action plan. Participants included leaders and representatives of Canada, Australia, India, the Irish Free State (Ireland), Newfoundland (part of Canada from 1949), New Zealand, Southern Rhodesia (today's Zimbabwe), South Africa and the United Kingdom. Known as the British Empire Economic Conference or the Imperial Economic Conference, the grouping acknowledged the failure of the gold standard which Britain had abandoned a year earlier when it had insufficient gold reserves to support the pound.

The conference members agreed in principle to implement an 'Imperial Preference' policy that promoted trade among members of the Empire at preferential terms while maintaining tariffs against others. That is, members enjoyed lower tax rates as compared to non-members. The Ottawa arrangements, which were to last five years, were formalised in eleven bilateral agreements. In this scheme, Britain allowed continued free trade in most goods produced by its colonies and dominions while it imposed new tariffs on certain imports from non-members. On the other hand, Britain's dominions and colonies could apply tariffs against British produce only in instances when inferior products had to be blocked. Otherwise, they were committed to buy within the grouping first. Essentially, the Ottawa agreements provided members with 'sheltered markets' during the Great Depression.

Whilst the conference marked the beginnings of a protectionist regime within the British Empire, co-operation within the grouping provided some relief for its members as part of the sterling group. They constituted a sterling bloc. This helped stabilise currency fluctuations, as members of the bloc placed most of their exchange reserves in London, making it easier for members to obtain loans from London's financial markets.

Malaya: free trade and protectionism.[45] Making common policies for these very disparate parts of Malaya would prove challenging.

The governments of the Straits Settlements and the FMS did not immediately opt for protectionist measures in 1929. The FMS government had depleted its reserves even before the onset of the Depression. It had fewer options than the Straits as to how it would cover its operational deficit going into the 1930s. Initially, it undertook a series of austerity drives, cutting spending and conducting massive retrenchment exercises.[46] The situation improved somewhat only when exports began rising once again from 1933. In that year, exports increased to 400 million Straits dollars while imports declined to 358 million dollars, giving the FMS economy its first positive balance of trade since the start of the Depression.[47] With trade improving again, from the fiscal perspective the ability to impose more tariffs and boost trade within the Empire was very attractive.[48]

Meanwhile, Britain adopted another course of action: it abandoned the gold standard in 1931 and officially ended its free trade policy the year after.[49] Going off the gold standard allowed the pound sterling to fluctuate according to market forces. It depreciated. Most British colonies, including the Straits Settlements, had currencies pegged to the pound and hence to the price of gold. Abandoning the gold standard and having depreciating currencies made exports from the Empire cheaper to the rest of the world, while making imports from outside the Empire dearer. This would stimulate intra-Empire trade and encourage exports to the rest of the world, while checking imports and the resultant outflow of silver.

A further step was taken to ensure that foreign goods would be more expensive: increasing tariffs on non-British goods and services. These policies were set in motion in July 1932 when Britain convened an Imperial Economic Conference in Ottawa, Canada, bringing together 'the Dominions, Britain's largest Empire partners' to formalise and coordinate the 'Empire First' initiative. Britain had hoped that its dominions would 'clear away most barriers to trade within the Empire so as to increase Imperial unity without further damaging international trade'. However, the Conference partners were unwilling to offer outright preferences for British imports. They were prepared to raise external tariff rates, but not reduce or remove tariffs for within-Empire goods.[50] Nevertheless, trade within the Empire rose markedly in the 1930s.[51]

Though British Malaya did not sent a representative to Ottawa, the FMS declared in November 1932 that it would adhere to the spirit of the conference and 'buy Empire' as well as adjusting its tariff regime in line.[52] By the end of 1932, Sarawak had also begun implementing preferential tariffs on Empire goods. Examples of tariffs prevailing in Sarawak at this time included a 30 per cent tariff on cars and a 10 per cent tariff on cement and electrical products imported from outside the Empire, compared to the 20 per cent and 5 per cent imposed, respectively, for such items imported from within the Commonwealth.[53] In 1933, the FMS government, which had already put in place a plethora of taxes during the Depression, also imposed preferential taxes: a five dollars per 100 lb duty was imposed on milk imported into the Straits Settlements, while the Empire received a preferential two-dollar rate for milk imported from within the Commonwealth.[54]

Although Singapore had already committed itself to giving preference to some costlier British produce months before the Ottawa Conference,[55] it did not ultimately adopt the tariff arrangements, given the Straits Settlements' free-port status. Singapore was concerned that such tariffs would inevitably mean taxes 'on the necessities of life for the labouring classes'. These concerns soon proved valid: while there was no significant difference in the cost of living as between the FMS and the Straits Settlements in 1932–3, after the Malay States adjusted customs duties in line with the recommendations of the Ottawa Conference, the cost of living there increased significantly.[56] The Malay States had imposed taxes on necessities earlier in order to rectify their fiscal shortfall, and implementing the new tariffs raised prices of everyday items imported from outside the Empire even further. Compared to the Straits, the Malay States felt that they alone were left 'to carry the burden of Empire'.[57]

Faced with such differences in philosophy and approach to taxation between the Straits Settlements and the Malay States, the High Commissioner (Governor) Cecil Clementi pressed further to standardise policies and practices in both the territories under his authority. Despite the earlier opposition to his call for a pan-Malayan customs union, he nevertheless set up a Customs Duties Committee composed of unofficial members to look into the matter anew. This committee did not support his plan. The governor then appointed an official committee to consider whether Singapore and Penang could be excluded from the customs union if it were implemented. This committee also was not supportive of the idea. In its report, submitted in February 1932, it was made clear that its objection to the proposal was less about a customs union in itself, but more about the general imposition of taxes on all trade. While the advantage of free trade within the customs union was not disputed, the committee was concerned that tariffs would hurt trade with territories outside the union. The committee observed that the foreign trade of Malaya, except for a small part carried on junk and rail, was concentrated through Straits Settlements ports: Singapore, Penang and Malacca.[58] By early 1933, Clementi's customs union proposal was effectively dead.

Promoting both the tin and the pineapple industries, an Empire Marketing Board poster.

Malayan trade through Straits Settlements ports, 1923–4
(millions of Straits dollars and percentage of Malaya's total trade)

Ports	1923		1924	
	Imports	Exports	Imports	Exports
Straits Settlements ports	555.7	611.1	625.0	662.4
FMS ports	20.3	54.6	26.6	54.3
Non-FMS ports	1.6	4.1	1.7	3.8
Total	577.6	669.7	653.3	720.5
Straits Settlements ports' share of Malaya's trade	96%	93.5%	93%	92%

Source: *Straits Times*, 31 December 1925.

Collyer Quay in the 1930s. Left to right: the Union Building (later renamed the Maritime Building), the Hongkong Bank building (the second on the site); the former Chartered Bank building in Battery Road, occupied later by the Bank of Taiwan and then the Bank of China; and the Fullerton Building, which housed the GPO and other government offices from 1928.

As it turned out, there would be no near-term return to tranquil periods during which free trade could thrive. Even after the dark clouds of the Great Depression had passed, another global war was looming on the horizon. Geopolitical and strategic considerations meant that free trade, particularly with potential enemies, would not be brooked. Consequently, the Straits Settlements faced enormous pressure to conform to the Empire's trade directives in the 1930s, and this only intensified following the Japanese invasion of mainland China in 1937.[59] Emergency regulations, which also imposed restrictions on trade, soon followed the outbreak of war in the European theatre. The Straits Settlements had no choice but to set aside the defence of its free trade regime. Nevertheless, the needs of the divergent development models of Singapore and of Malaya would become an issue again decades later.

The repeated failures to introduce a customs union exposed critical fault lines in British-ruled Malaya. Although there were essentially two contrasting economic philosophies, reflecting the different development paths of the Straits and the FMS,[60] one path was more aligned with the realities confronting the Empire since the 1920s. Economic and financial crises before, during and after the Great Depression brought these fundamental matters to a head: the Empire would always come first, over the needs of individual colonies.

Therefore, while the Straits Settlements managed to avert inclusion in a customs union, it would lose the battle in another pan-Malayan initiative: a common currency. The Malay States were already using the Straits Settlements currency as legal-tender. However, they had no part in the currency board. Consequently, while the Straits government bore the liabilities associated with currency issuance, it also reaped the profits from it; these were not available to the

Malay States. Given the growing tendency of the British authorities at all levels to put 'Empire first', the Straits could no longer defer sharing the profits earned on its currency reserves with the largest user of its money, the FMS, especially since the latter needed additional financial support.

Malayan economy, dollar, and preparation for war

The growing importance of the FMS's trade with the Straits Settlements made it only logical to establish a monetary system that formally encompassed the two territories. Although the States had unilaterally passed legislation making the Straits Settlements dollar legal-tender at the turn of the century, they were ultimately users, not co-owners, of the currency. This *status quo* was maintained for several decades until the Great Depression provided new impetus for monetary reform.

One of the most compelling reasons was the divergent financial standing of the FMS and the Straits Settlements. By the 1920s, a number of reserve funds in both the FMS and the Straits Settlements had helped supplement government revenues. These included the Opium Revenue Replacement Reserve Fund, set up in order to 'wean' the governments of these territories from their reliance on revenue from opium. However, the most important and lucrative fund, which the Malay States did not have, was the Currency Guarantee Fund which underpinned the issue of the Straits Settlements dollar.

The variance in how the FMS and Straits Settlements started and managed their respective opium replacement funds explains in part the differences in the fiscal challenges confronting the two territories. The Federated Malay States set up its fund with an initial seed funding of 10 million dollars in 1925, and committed to contributing around 15 per cent of its annual revenues from opium into the fund. The fund was then deposited in London. From 1926 to 1929, the FMS added around two million dollars a year. By the end of 1929, the 18.4 million dollars added to the fund had risen in value to 20.6 million dollars.[61] However, just before 1929, FMS government expenditures increased unexpectedly by 12 million dollars. Consequently, pressure mounted for the government to discontinue its annual contributions into the fund.[62]

The FMS did not immediately respond to this pressure, even though the Great Depression broke out a few months later. Initially, the government requested a cut in its contribution rate from 15 per cent to 7½ per cent. Despite this, and notwithstanding the imposition of a slew of additional taxes, the FMS government still did not have enough revenues to fund expenditures, and the budget deficit grew.[63] From this point, the FMS drew on its reserves in the opium replacement fund to bail out its troubled assets, and ceased to make further contributions.[64]

Opium and revenue: dependence and dependency

It has been said that the British Empire in the 19th century was built on the opium trade. Opium sparked the wars that led China to open up to western commerce on a large scale from the 1840s. The trade in opium contributed to mass addiction to this drug not only in China, but in the ports through which opium passed, including the Straits Settlements. A large number of opium addicts in the Straits Settlements were coolies who toiled at the harbour and in gambier and pepper plantations. They consumed the drug to alleviate physical pain and to distract their minds from daily hardship. In the late 19th century, rickshaw coolies in the town resorted to opium – they typically wore no shoes while working and were constantly injured. Many of the coolies also believed that opium could cure tuberculosis, malaria and venereal disease. Consequently, men addicted to opium could be found in almost every lodging house in Chinatown. The 1908 Opium Commission found that only two per cent of the rickshaw coolies were opium smokers when they arrived in Singapore; after coming to the island, up to 40 per cent, or 8,000 of them, became addicts. A similar percentage of the Chinese coolies in the Malayan coal mines were also addicted.[65]

A barefooted rickshaw puller takes a break.

By 1923, there were 423 government-run shops where opium could be purchased over the counter. A conservative estimate put the average number of Chinese customers per shop at 377.[66] This meant that the government-operated opium shops alone catered for almost 160,000 opium smokers. With so many 'patron-addicts', it is no wonder that the sale of opium for consumption was generating a significant proportion of local government revenues by the turn of the century. In 1900, opium-derived revenues stood at 1.5 million dollars out of total revenues of 2.4 million dollars. The proportion of opium revenues increased to two-thirds by 1906, generating 4.2 million dollars out of 6.3 million dollars in total revenues.[67] Municipal works had to be curtailed when opium revenues fell in 1909.[68] By 1914, opium revenue still accounted for 57 per cent of the local government's total revenues. At this time, the average daily wage for a labourer was 60 cents, of which 32 cents would be spent on the drug.[69]

There was a need to end this dependency on opium revenues. In 1907, the government-appointed Straits Settlements Opium Committee recommended abolishing the revenue-farm system for opium in Singapore, as well as introducing other restrictions on its sale. Following the Hague Opium Convention of 1912 and the Geneva Opium Agreement of 1925, the British Empire agreed to end taxation on opium consumption as a revenue stream. The local government would no longer have an incentive to undertake what had amounted to blatant promotion of the habit. By 1926, the legislature and ruling councils of the Federated Malay States, Straits Settlements and the state of Johor had established Opium Revenue Replacement Reserve Funds in their respective territories.[70] Although the Funds were meant to help British Malaya avert financial fallout in the absence of opium revenues, they became a critical source of reserves during the Great Depression, and for the Federated Malay States in particular. By January 1933, the Chief Secretary of the Federal Council was warning that the government would have to carry out a 'raid on the Opium Revenue Replacement Fund' in order to continue with expenditures planned for the year.[71]

The Straits Settlements' Opium Revenue Replacement Reserve Fund had a very different trajectory. To begin with, the Straits' seed funding was three times that of the FMS, and the Straits government committed to contributing a more sustainable 10 per cent of annual opium revenues to the fund each year. This reduced the risk that the contribution rate might need to be cut during downturns. Moreover, the seed amount for the Straits' fund was drawn entirely from accumulated surpluses in its reserves,[72] whereas the FMS had to draw part of the sum from its current revenues. The divergent approaches to the opium fund arose from the very different financial and economic structures of the two territories. The Straits colonies had built up deep reserves for contingencies as they had little or no natural resources and could not derive revenue from the lucrative maritime commerce passing through their ports. The FMS, on the other hand, had a vast hinterland with extensive agricultural potential and mineral resources that gave it natural sources of wealth. In this context, the FMS preferred to place duties on its imports and exports to raise revenues rather than to build up reserves and rely on investment income. Given its stronger financial standing, the Straits government was able to continue making contributions into the Opium Revenue Replacement Reserve Fund throughout the Great Depression. The fund grew from 43 million Straits dollars in 1928 to 62 million dollars in 1935.[73]

As a consequence of its financial approach, the Straits government had not just the opium replacement fund but other reserve funds that helped it to remain solvent despite falling revenues and budget deficits during the Depression years. Aside from the sums in the Currency Guarantee Fund, the Straits government had, on the eve of the Depression, reserves amounting to 64 million dollars. Of this, 53 million dollars (not including the opium fund) was held in liquid assets that could be drawn at short notice. It was initially projected that the value of this portion of the reserves would rise to 75.5 million Straits dollars by the end of 1929, but the realised sum came up to 91.5 million dollars.[74] Consequently, when the Straits government projected a sizeable 21.9 million dollar deficit for 1932, it had more than enough resources to cover the shortfall.[75] The reserve buffers would remain ample throughout the decade.[76] The Straits Settlements was able to wean itself off its dependence on opium revenue.[77, 78]

As for the Currency Guarantee Fund, the Straits government controlled it through its Board of Commissioners of Currency. However, the Malay States felt they were entitled to a share of the profits earned by the currency board. After all, the size of the assets held by the board was tightly linked to the stock of notes and coins issued; this in turn determined, in part, the value of profits earned on assets invested as well as on seigniorage. From this perspective, the profits of the currency board were partly due to the Malay States, which by the 1920s had become the largest users of the Straits currency. The importance of the

Malay States to the currency board became apparent: whenever the FMS suffered downturns, the circulation of the Straits dollar declined accordingly. In January 1926, for instance, the currency board had 163 million dollars' worth of currency notes in circulation. By February 1927, when Malaya's imports and exports started contracting, the stock of Straits dollar notes in circulation fell to around 131 million dollars.[79]

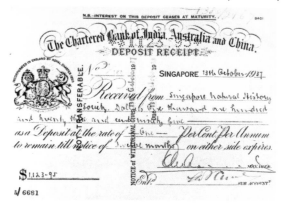

A deposit receipt issued by the Chartered Bank in October 1937.

Adding to the pressure for monetary reform in the 1930s was an emerging pan-Malaya policy promoted by the British, reflected in the Malayanisation movement of the day. Though the general idea was constantly articulated in the period before World War II, there were no clear tenets or ideological concepts as to what Malayanisation exactly entailed. It was clear that its geographical scope would include both the Straits Settlements and the Malay States. Contemporary public debate on the matter included ideas such as Malayan citizenship for all including non-Malays,[80] pro-Malay policies,[81] having Malay as the *lingua franca*,[82] assimilating non-Malays into the Malay culture,[83] and more. The Straits Settlements Legislative Council believed that the aim of Malayanisation was to create a strong Malayan[84] polity by knitting 'our permanent population of all races ultimately into a united Malayan community inspired by Malayan consciousness and patriotism and by undivided loyalty to this country and the British Crown'.[85] Many in the Straits were not in favour of it, and some members saw it as Governor Cecil Clementi's attempt to reintroduce the customs union.[86] The state of Johor noted that 'Some Malayanisation is merely co-operation, some merely co-ordination, while the rest is either unification or tending to unification' and it rejected 'any policy which produces or tends to produce uniformity or centralised control throughout Malaya'. Despite these objections from the Straits Settlements and Johor, from the perspective of the British and the Malay States the time seemed financially and politically right to gather the Straits Settlements, and thus its resources, into a broader pan-Malayan entity and so strengthen the collective as a whole.

And so it came to pass that while a currency in common, the Straits Settlements dollar, had worked well, the question arose in the 1930s whether a common currency would better serve the needs of the collective. Financially, for the Malay States to receive an equitable share of the earnings of the Straits dollar, they would have to be partners in the currency board issuing the monies. Politically, the creation of a common currency and common currency guarantee fund would reflect the centralising tendencies at the heart of Malayanisation.[87] It was in this context that former civil servant and international finance expert Sir Basil

The Legislative Council in session, 1940.

Blackett received an appointment to form a Currency Commission in 1933, to look into the situation in the Federated and Unfederated Malay States, the Straits Settlements and Brunei as a whole.[88] Blackett was directed specifically to look into how the Malay States could participate in the 'profits and liabilities' of the Straits Settlements' currency board.[89] Having come to the region and examined the situation, he concluded that if the *status quo* did not change there would be no economic progress for the communities across the various territories.[90] Blackett returned to London towards the end of 1933 and by mid-1934 he had completed his review. He recommended a currency union that would include the Straits Settlements, Brunei and the Malay States. The combined territories would constitute a single Malayan polity with joint ownership of the currency.[91] This proposal was celebrated by residents of the Malay States who considered it an end to decades of 'injustice'; they would now have a rightful share of the profits earned from the issuance of a currency they had been using since 1899. The Straits residents, on the other hand, believed that the Malay States had 'cast envious eyes' on the profits of the Currency Guarantee Fund.[92]

Blackett's report was endorsed. Putting it into effect proved to be a somewhat convoluted affair: the Currency Bill was sent to the Straits Settlements Legislative Council in February 1937, leading to the Currency Ordinance, 1937 (Chapter 219) that authorised the creation of the Malayan dollar.[93] This ordinance was repealed in 1938 and redrafted into the Currency Ordinance, 1938.[94] Having crossed the legislative hurdles, the Board of Commissioners of Currency, Malaya, was formally established in October 1938

½ cent   1 cent

5 cent   10 cent   20 cent

Malayan dollar coins: the 1 cent, 5 cent, 10 cent, and 20 cent coins were minted in 1939 and issued in 1940; the ½ cent coin was minted a year later. The obverse of the coins bore the portrait of King George VI, who ascended to the throne in 1936.

with the financial secretary of the colonial government in Malaya, H. Weisberg, as its first chairman. Thereafter, the Straits Settlements' financial and currency policies were effectively subsumed within, and subordinated to, the policies of the Malay States.[95]

Under the terms of the new currency board, the Straits Settlements held an equal share with the Federated Malay States at 37 per cent each of the assets, liabilities, and thus profits. The other Malay States, and Brunei, were given a total share of 26 per cent. The Currency Guarantee Fund of the Straits Settlements currency board was absorbed into a similar fund backing the new Malayan dollar. As compensation to the Straits government for all the past input into the Currency Guarantee Fund, 33.4 million dollars was transferred from the fund to the Straits government's coffers.[96]

The Malayan dollar notes and coins were equal in value to those of the Straits Settlements dollar and were intended to be one-for-one replacements. The new notes issued would be unlimited legal-tender: that is, they could be used to discharge obligations of any amount.[97] The Board of Commissioners of Currency, Malaya made plans to issue the new currency in 1939. However, the notes and coins, which were dated 1939 and had been expected to be delivered that year, did not arrive till 1940. This was because the British rearmament programme had led to industrial backlogs, and most of the workers at the Royal Mint had been diverted to arms production.[98]

One aspect of this new currency that by and large escaped notice was that the new dollar was not simply the old Straits Settlements dollar issued under a new name and currency board. In the original Straits currency, the one-dollar Straits Settlements silver coin had been created deliberately to serve as a link with the foreign silver trade dollars used at that time, which had historically served as the international benchmark for exchange. As the British began tokenising the Straits Settlements one-dollar coin (see p. 105), its link to the silver dollar became less important than its declared value (2s 4d) against the pound sterling. By the time the Malayan dollar was conceived, the residents of Malaya and the Straits had long grown accustomed to using government-issued paper notes and token coins, and there was no longer a need to mint a specie coin. The Malayan dollar was thus from its inception the first fully tokenised currency for the Straits and the Malay States.

A set of scales used for weighing coins.

The first Malayan coins (in denominations of one, five, ten, and twenty cents) were minted in alloys of copper and of silver. They were ultimately made available on 18 March 1940. Following the trend established under the previous currency board, the millesimal fineness of the copper or silver content in these coins was reduced compared to their Straits Settlements dollar antecedents. At the Singapore treasury at Empress Place, 750,000 dollars' worth of these new coins were distributed, and the old Straits Settlements coins, with their image of King George V,[99] began to be withdrawn from circulation.[100] The new Malayan notes, in denominations of one dollar (green), five dollars (blue) and ten dollars (plum) were projected to arrive in December 1940.[101] However, it was only in late March 1941, that the first Malayan dollar note to be circulated to the public arrived. It was the ten-dollar note; the government had held back release of the one- and five-dollar notes. The official reason was that there was an insufficient number of the new notes.[102] Instead, as there were still plenty of one- and five-dollar Straits notes in stock, these were issued to replace existing soiled notes.[103]

In the run-up to World War II, another key aspect of the monetary history of Singapore and the Malay States was the monetary resources they brought to bear on the overall war effort. Between July 1937 and February 1939, it was estimated that overseas Chinese worldwide had raised at least 100 million Chinese dollars for the China Relief Fund sent to Chungking, the wartime capital of the Republic of China. More than half this amount came from Asia; Malaya, together with the East Indies, led this contribution.[104] By January 1941, the overseas Chinese had raised over 300 million Chinese dollars for the fund.[105] In March 1941, Tan Kah Kee, as chairman of

Malaya Tribune, 28 August 1937

AN APPEAL TO ALL CHINESE

CHINA RELIEF FUND

To All Chinese is this Appeal made.
It is the cause of humanity that now calls for support and to this noble cause we hope that all Chinese will rally.
Relief is sorely and urgently needed.
Every little contribution will be appreciated and all will be gratefully acknowledged.
All contributions should be sent to:—
CHINA RELIEF FUND COMMITTEE OF SINGAPORE,
43, Bukit Pasoh Road, Singapore.

Money changing colours

It has been suggested that the failure to issue the 1940 one- and five-dollar notes was due to the fact that war between Britain and Germany had already commenced. According to one source, 'Of the 27,000,000 one-dollar and 5,600,000 five-dollar notes planned for circulation some 500,000 one-dollar and 100,000 five-dollar notes were lost when the cargo ship the SS *Eumanes* was sunk by the Germans.'[106] Another account states that 'in November of 1940, the cargo ship SS *Automedon* encountered the German raider *Atlantis* and came under fire, the first shells hitting the bridge of the SS *Automedon* killing its captain and all of its officers'. On board apparently were 700,000 one-dollar notes and 500,000 five-dollar notes. It is difficult to say conclusively whether any of the Malayan dollar notes were on board the SS *Automedon*; the ship was scuttled by the Germans when they decided it was too badly damaged to tow.

When news of this incident reached the British, they almost immediately halted the release of the 1940 green one-dollar and blue five-dollar notes, issuing only the ten-dollar note in mid-1941. It is not clear whether the timing was coincidental or whether they were genuinely concerned that the one- and five-dollar notes had been compromised. In any event, new paper dollar notes with different colours were produced in 1941. The one- and five-dollar notes swapped colours – the former was now blue while the latter was green – and the ten-dollar note became red rather than plum. The colours for these denominations would endure into the future when Singapore began issuing its own currency.

1 dollar

5 dollars

Green one-dollar and blue five-dollar notes printed in 1940
– their issuance was halted.

10 dollars

The plum ten-dollar note printed in 1940 – the only note
of the three denominations to be issued in 1941.

the Southeast Asia Federation of the China Relief Fund Committees (International), announced to the delegates of the Overseas Chinese Conference held at Great World in Singapore that the combined overseas Chinese had, to date, remitted 1.5 billion dollars in Chinese currency to China.[107]

It was remarkable that these funds could continue to flow from Malaya to China. By late 1937, Japan's invasion of coastal China had disrupted most commerce and remittances, and it was virtually impossible for petty remittances to be sent to small villages in the provinces. Some remittance shops and agencies in China had to cease operations. It was at this juncture that the Oversea-Chinese Banking Corporation (OCBC) came to the rescue by providing remittance services to China from Malaya and the Dutch East Indies. OCBC was formed in 1932 when Chinese Commercial Bank Ltd merged with Ho Hong Bank Ltd and Oversea-Chinese Bank Ltd. For a reasonable charge, the bank ensured that deliveries were made with a reply, and it guaranteed a refund if the money was not delivered. It even offered to act as agent for the remittance shops if they encountered difficulties and needed help.[108]

Tan Ean Kiam, rubber magnate. He was a managing director of the Oversea Chinese Bank, one of three that merged to form OCBC in 1932.

In September 1939, after the beginning of the war with Germany, British authorities put in place foreign exchange controls throughout Malaya. Anyone wishing to send more than 100 dollars abroad in the form of currency notes or bank orders had to seek advice at a bank or the post office and state their reasons for sending the funds. Travellers needing more than 500 dollars in foreign currency needed permission from the Financial Secretary. However, the British made special provisions for remittances for the China Relief Fund, although they limited the total amount that could be sent per month to 500,000 Straits dollars.[109] Subsequently, the monthly limit was raised to 750,000 dollars so that the Federated Malay States' China Relief Fund could speed up sending the three million–dollar surplus it was still holding.

Headquarters of the Ho Hong Bank, Kling Street – one of the predecessors of OCBC.

The Straits Settlements and the Federated Malay States would help to fund not only China's war with Japan but also British war efforts in general. After all, Malaya had an 'arsenal' in the form of foreign exchange, a vital modern weapon.[110] Exports of rubber and tin had enriched the private sector. In 1940, Malaya had a trade surplus with the United States in excess of 550 million Malayan dollars, arising from 592 million dollars' worth of exports against only 38 million dollars in imports.[111] Malaya's exports to the US had risen from only 322 million dollars the year before, due mainly to the increased imports of the tin and rubber that the US was accumulating in reserve. Potentially, the British authorities could purchase foreign exchange

Pre-war Chinese remittances[112]

From 1881 to 1913, the number of Chinese migrant workers sailing to Singapore from Hong Kong rose from 37,000 to nearly 103,000. Chinese immigrants in Singapore remitted money to their families in China by junks that were leaving on their return voyage, through various means: entrusting the money to a comrade who made enough money to revisit his native land, delivering the money through a passenger known to the remitter, or paying an agent who made it his business to take care of such remittances. The agent was paid according to the way in which the money was remitted. If it was in cash, he received a ten per cent commission. However, he could also invest the money in the form of goods, on the condition that he paid over in China the exact sum of money that was entrusted to him by the remitter. Chinese hotels also offered a variety of services for their customers such as handling customs procedures, transfer of luggage, purchase of steamer tickets, locating lost relatives or friends and even remittance services.

Remittance was also a significant part of the business for Singapore's famed medicinal shop Eu Yan Sang. It was conducted along dialect lines. After the coolies gave Eu Yan Sang their money, they were issued receipts, which were then couriered to their home villages in China. These receipts could then be exchanged for cash at any of the firm's outlets abroad. Eu Yan Sang's services were very reliable, and their receipts eventually came to be used like banknotes – in certain Chinese provinces in the 1920s they were in fact preferred to banknotes.

A remittance receipt issued by Eu Yan Sang.

from the exporters in return for local currency. In this way, they would be able to accumulate the US dollars needed to purchase ammunition and other strategic materials. Britain also took the step of requisitioning all US securities held by British citizens, reimbursing them in sterling.[113] In January 1941, wartime finance regulations in Malaya made it compulsory for anyone holding gold in bullion or coins to sell them to authorised dealers.[114] Britain would use the gold to purchase foreign exchange for its wartime purchases.

Ironically, while Malaya had abundant financial resources to help support China and Britain in the various theatres of war, the territory as a whole was running short of small change. This had been a recurring issue in the history of the Straits Settlements and the Malay States, and had cropped up during World War I. When the new Malayan copper and silver alloy coinages began circulating in March 1940, they quickly became scarce. The situation deteriorated as the months passed. Things came to a head in July. It was reported that the residents of Ipoh and the surrounding villages were so short of the new Malayan dollar coins that it was difficult to buy goods from small traders. The Chinese Protectorate had to issue circulars warning shopkeepers and dealers not to hoard silver alloy coins.[115] Bus conductors could not give change, forcing riders to pay for a more expensive ticket than they needed. The Malacca treasury was so short of coins that it wired the Singapore treasury for 20,000 Malayan dollars' worth of small change. To keep businesses going, many innovative solutions sprang up. The Land Office, as well as coffee shops in Johor, began accepting postage stamps in lieu of small coins.[116] Instead of small change, market stall owners in the State issued credit notes that could be used to offset purchases on another day.[117] At the Great World amusement park in Singapore, ten-cent cash coupons were used in place of coins. Patrons with leftover or balance coupons could exchange these for cash on the way out.[118]

The scarcity was so severe that it started a panic in July 1940, when several hundred people gathered one morning at the Singapore treasury to change notes for small silver coins; some had come to change as much as 50 dollars' worth of notes. The treasury gates had to be closed. The crowd eventually left after receiving in exchange a mix of coins and subsidiary notes printed during the era of the Straits Settlements dollar. The shortage had arisen because people were hoarding coins thought to contain precious metals, especially silver. In response, the government had to use loudspeakers and leaflets to explain that there was no shortage of silver and there was no need to hoard the coins. In the midst of this chaos, the government issued another currency regulation that prohibited the melting of silver coins and hoarding. Infringement could result in six months' jail and a 500-dollar fine. Metals found on culprits would be confiscated. The police were given the power of enforcement.[119]

A call rang out for the government to issue subsidiary notes as they had done during World War I.[120] With no real solution to the shortage in sight, in late 1940 the government issued the first of a series of notes denominated in Malayan cents. The ten-cent note debuted in September 1940[121] and most of the other denominations followed shortly after. An exception was the one-cent note, only issued a year later when the paucity of copper alloy coins became so acute that the Malayan government had no option but to follow the Hong Kong government's actions and print a note for such a small denomination.[122]

Even this was not enough to relieve the situation, and out of desperation in August 1941 the government began recirculating the old half-cent Straits Settlements coins.[123] It was reported in the same month that the Singapore treasury was working with bus companies to issue 20,000 one-cent coins every day to bus conductors. However, these quickly disappeared from circulation, and few, if any, were returned.[124] In addition, 'strange coins' had begun appearing on buses, including small Japanese coins, Australian halfpennies, and Thai coins. Passengers were attempting to use these to pay their fares, and it appears that they were accepted, a telling testimony to the severity of the coin shortage.

Malayan dollar subsidiary notes, 1940-41

Notes printed in 1940 by the Survey Department of the Federated Malay States

10 cents

25 cents

Subsidiary note denominations subsequently printed by Thomas De La Rue & Co. in Britain in 1941

1 cent

5 cents

10 cents

20 cents

50 cents

Enemy at the gate

The Imperial Japanese Army landed at Kota Bharu (Kelantan) on 8 December 1941. Despite attempts at a counter-offensive, by 31 January 1942 it had reached the Causeway, the gateway to Singapore – the supposedly impregnable 'Gibraltar of the East'.[125] From 8 December 1941 until the island's surrender on 15 February 1942, Singapore suffered numerous air raids. Besides the bombs, one of the first signs of impending disaster was the flood of British and Malayan individuals, families and institutions into Singapore. Government departments of the Federated Malay States set up temporary offices at the premises of the Colonial Secretariat in Singapore,[126] and the state

Before the invasion, air raid wardens douse an incendiary bomb in Raffles Place as a demonstration to raise awareness.

treasuries of Selangor and Negeri Sembilan operated from Empress Place, where the Singapore treasury was located.[127] Following close behind these official institutions were the branches of Malayan banks seeking the relative safety of Singapore, notwithstanding the air raids.

And so, in the last days before Singapore fell to the Japanese, most of the monetary resources of the Malayan government treasuries and banks were carried to the island. Much of it was then transferred to London for the duration of the war. The joint headquarters of the postal savings banks of the Straits Settlements and the Federated Malay States transferred its assets, deposits and records to the General Post Office (GPO) building in Singapore for safekeeping after its own

Smoke rises following an air raid.

Women and children prepare to go aboard ship, 1 February 1942.

building was damaged by bombing. For the Straits Settlements Post Office Savings Bank, this reversed an earlier shift to Kuala Lumpur following the merger of the postal systems of the Straits and the States in 1926. This momentous move to Singapore took place on Christmas Day, 1941. The savings banks had already emptied their vaults and invested most of the assets and deposits through the London financial markets, 'beyond enemy reach'.[128] Nevertheless, the headquarters retained sufficient financial resources within Singapore that many customers from Malaya congregated at the GPO to withdraw their deposits before being evacuated. They created a 'run' on the Post Office Savings Bank on days when it rained bombs. As a contingency, in case the Singapore GPO building suffered damage like the savings banks' Kuala Lumpur headquarters, there were plans for a 'shadow' at an alternative site, to ensure that customers could be served till the end.[129]

The Oversea-Chinese Banking Corporation had closed down its branches in the Malay Peninsula by mid-December 1941, and directed all enquiries to its head office in Singapore.[130] The Chartered Bank's branches at Penang, Alor Star, Sitiawan and Taiping were also shut and their services were handed over to the bank's Singapore office. At the same time, the Mercantile Bank of India also relocated the operations of their Kota Bharu (Kelantan) agency to Singapore.[131] The Hongkong and Shanghai Bank's Sungei Patani sub-agency was also closed in December 1941 and its operations transferred to the Singapore branch. According to one account, a European rubber-plantation manager in a southern Malay State kept his labourers working while Japanese forces were making their way down the peninsula. In late December 1941, he sought to pay his labourers for work done. As all the banks had already moved to Singapore, he made a trip to the island amidst the evacuees, withdrew his money, and headed back across the Causeway against the flow of humanity, back to his plantation.[132]

Amongst the British banks operating in Singapore and Malaya, the Hongkong and Shanghai Bank was quick to decide what course of action to take with the enemy nearly at the gate. The Bangkok branches of the Chartered Bank and Hongkong and Shanghai Bank had been commandeered by Japanese forces almost immediately after the first air raids hit Singapore.[133] The prospect that more branches and more financial resources could be captured by the Japanese, as well as the possibility of reprisals,[134] was not lost on the Hongkong Bank. Not long after the air raids started, it was the one of the first to shift its head office from Singapore to London,[135] and it even sent out a general call for the people of the Malay Peninsula to transfer all their valuables out of Malaya if they could.[136] This would prove prescient. In any case, the operations of the British banks in Malaya and Singapore had already been compromised, as most of their British staff had been called up for local defence duties when the invasion started.[137]

When war broke out on the Malay Peninsula in December 1941 and supplies became uncertain, many retailers instantly raised prices. The Singapore Municipality issued a warning on 12 December 1941 to all 'eating houses, meat shops, bakeries … all people selling "human food and drink"' that their licences to operate would be cancelled if they were found selling products at prices above those prevailing as at 6 December 1941. The Food Control Department then put up a public notice to inform one and all of the Food Control Ordinance that ensured that every district in Singapore had an Area Office to guarantee food supply. They issued rice cards and fixed retail prices in their respective zones.[138] Nevertheless, numerous shopkeepers and stallholders continued charging high prices, despite the threat of official action. Having no other options, long queues formed to buy food at exorbitant prices, so that families would not go hungry.[139]

This growing desperation sat oddly with the surreal atmosphere that pervaded some parts of the island as late as January 1942. While the bombs were falling, theatres continued their shows, Robinson's department store stayed open, Raffles Hotel continued hosting dinner and dance events even up till the island was cut off, and Cold Storage was still selling frozen food, promoting 'chilled mutton, cutlets, legs, loin, chops, shoulders'.[140] Cold Storage apologised to its customers for not being able to bake French loaves in the latter part of January 1942, but offered white loaves instead.[141] It was at this time that 400 cabaret girls, members of the Singapore Cabaret Girls' Association, fearing a loss of livelihood, sent a petition to Governor Shenton Thomas appealing against any

Just three days before the fall of Singapore, *Daily Express*, 12 February 1942.

Churchill announces bad news, *Daily Telegraph*, 16 February 1942.

emergency action that might close the New World entertainment grounds, including its cabaret.[142]

Inflated prices and profiteering at this time was due to more money chasing fewer goods. The supply situation was getting tighter by the day. The solution was to ration items which had become scarce. Petrol rationing had already started on 1 March 1941 when the war in Europe and China had caused shortages of strategic items including fuel. Since petrol had to be imported, it was hoped that curbing non-essential consumption would limit unnecessary expenditure of foreign exchange that could be better used to finance the British war effort.[143] The situation became so dire that, with effect from 1 January 1942, the already meagre petrol ration was halved.[144]

As for food, the government initially demurred on rationing, preferring simply to call on people to consume less. In mid-January 1942, it called on the people to consider having 'two meatless days a week'.[145] However, the situation worsened rapidly as the Japanese army advanced down the peninsula. By the time the Japanese started dropping incendiary bombs on Singapore on 22 January 1942,[146] food kitchens had been set up. For some time, Chinese temples had been keeping stocks of food to feed the homeless, and now they provided for those affected by the bombs. The government had taken over a school to serve cooked rice for five cents a plate. In some areas, the authorities took over eating houses to operate communal kitchens – one of these opened in the New World's boxing arena at Jalan Besar.[147] Towards the end of January 1942, the government requisitioned 12 vehicles, mostly lorries, and converted them into mobile canteens.[148] It was around this time that the authorities issued the ominous call for the people 'to start growing their own vegetables'.[149] By the last day of January 1942, when the Japanese had already reached the Causeway, the Food Controller of Malaya issued an order that from 8 February 1942 ration cards would be necessary for the purchase of frozen meat and butter: these would be available only from 13 food supply offices, including Cold Storage and John Little.[150]

After a week of bombardment along Singapore's shores, on 8 February 1942 the Japanese troops crossed over to the island. By 12 February, the invading forces had reached Bukit Timah Road, near the Chinese High School. At this point,

General Officer Commanding (Malaya) Arthur Percival informed Governor Shenton Thomas that the situation was critical. Accordingly, the governor ordered the destruction of key communications installations but stopped short of calling for a surrender to save more lives in a battle already lost. He told Percival that he needed to make arrangements for the contents of Singapore's treasury vault, to prevent them from falling into Japanese hands.[151] By 13 February, it was reported that people in the rural areas of Singapore had already stopped accepting Straits and Malayan dollars.[152] The Malayan currency board's warnings of penalties for this behaviour would have no bite. On 14 February, after the last ship had departed the harbour, all evacuation efforts ceased.[153] General Percival surrendered Singapore to the Japanese on 15 February 1942, and the conquering Japanese renamed the island 'Syonan-to'.

Lieutenant-General. Arthur Percival.

Occupation currencies

The Japanese Imperial Army arrived with a plan for government which they implemented systematically, an approach no doubt honed by the Japanese experience as colonial masters and administrators earlier in the century.[154] A central part of the plan was to restore socioeconomic order to the conquered regions so as to allow their continued development under Japanese hegemony. A key step was the speedy distribution of Occupation military scrips to prevent disruption to the circulation of currency, and so pre-empt a complete breakdown of economic activity in the new Nippon colonies.

To this end, Japanese army units started circulating money that they printed in every territory that had been subjugated. There was evidence of this in late December 1941 when bills circulated by the Japanese, which the British labelled as 'fake notes', found their way behind British lines during the battle for Malaya. Money, even 'fake' money, flowed faster than the army in the Malaya campaign.[155] Then, the Japanese Military Administration (JMA) allowed the existing stock of Straits Settlements and Malayan dollars to remain in use. Because issuance of the Malayan dollar notes had been slow before the war broke out, the Straits dollar was still in circulation.[156] Accordingly, at the start of the Occupation, the Japanese Commander of the Dai-Nippon Army issued a decree declaring that the currency in Malaya would be the military dollar issued by the Nippon Government, and that Straits currency and Malayan dollar notes were permitted to be circulated at parity with the military notes. At this point, it was estimated that almost 200 million dollars' worth of the pre-Occupation Straits currency was in circulation.[157] This was now 'absorbed' into the new monetary system.

Japanese decree on the military scrip as the only legal-tender in Syonan-to, although Straits currency notes would be accepted at par 'for the time being'. *Syonan Shimbun,* 23 February 1942.

DECREE

1. The sole currency in Malaya shall be the Military Dollar Notes issued by the Government of Nippon. The Straits Currency Notes, however, shall be for the time being allowed their circulation with the equal parity to the military notes.

2. Any person who uses or receives any currency other than those prescribed above, who defames, falsifies or alters the Military Dollar Notes and the Straits Currency Notes, or who disturbs their circulation shall be liable to the extreme penalty of the military law.

For the interest of one and all in Malaya, I proclaim the above mentioned. Never disobey.

Given this date the 25th day of the 1st month of the 2602nd year.

COMMANDER OF THE DAI-NIPPON ARMY.

Banana notes

Banana notes without serial numbers printed using portable printers

5 cents

10 cents

50 cents

1 dollar

5 dollars

10 dollars

100 dollars

1000 dollars

Banana notes with serial numbers printed in Japan

1 dollar

5 dollars

10 dollars

The Japanese also allowed a large quantity of Straits Settlements silver and copper coins to remain in circulation. However, there is no mention of these coins in contemporary sources. Most of these metallic coins were probably melted down during the Occupation years as they were more valuable as raw materials. Copper coins, in particular, would probably have been turned into copper wires and copper wares as these fetched a fortune in the days of scarcity and restrictions.[158]

The strategy of allowing the currency of the previous regime to remain in circulation was a shrewd one. It ensured that a ready and adequate supply of money was still available when the Japanese began administering newly occupied territories. The invaders showed a degree of past experience in territorial conquest, occupation and administration, and they understood what the necessary conditions were for the continued governance and restoration of economic activity. In contrast, the British liberation forces' immediate repudiation of the Japanese currency notes in 1945 was to create utter chaos (see p. 164).

From the start of the Occupation, it was declared that each military dollar would have a par value similar to the Straits Settlements and Malayan dollars. The military notes would also come to be used in the other British territories that the Japanese conquered, including peninsular Malaya, North Borneo, Sarawak and Brunei. They were popularly known as 'banana money' because of the banana-tree motif on the ten-dollar notes. The first Japanese military scrips circulated were the one-, five- and ten-dollar notes. Subsidiary currency notes were also issued in September 1942 in denominations of one, five, ten and fifty cents. In early 1943, the Japanese authorities established the Malai (Malayan) Bankers' Council (MBC) and gave it oversight of matters pertaining to the currency of Malaya. As economic conditions worsened in the occupied territories, the MBC would issue the 100-dollar note in 1944, and a 1,000-dollar note in 1945.

The full extent of Japan's machinations on the monetary front would only come to light during the War Crimes Trials in October 1946. It was revealed during the proceedings that the Japanese had made plans as early as January 1940, almost two years before the bombing of Pearl Harbor on 7 December 1941, to flood allied territories that they intended to occupy with their military currencies. Another trial document revealed that on 16 January 1941 a request was made within the Japanese government to produce 'original plates of military currency to be used in certain unspecified areas', which turned out to be the Philippines, Dutch East Indies, Malaya, Borneo and Siam.[159] Two months later, the Japanese War Ministry also asked the Financial Bureau to print Dutch and British currency notes worth up to 39 million yen (equivalent to eight million dollars in 1941), and these were to be made ready by the following month.

The revelation of Japan's pre-war monetary preparations shed light on the provenance of the 'fake notes' that the British found circulating in the northern part of the peninsula during the Battle of Malaya. These notes were numbered because they were printed in Japan well before hostilities started. They were therefore ready to be put into circulation even before the battle had been concluded. The notes without serial numbers were those printed on the go, using mobile printing machines attached to Imperial Army units. Invasion troops were given currency notes printed by these mobile presses as they advanced. Japanese officials interrogated after Liberation revealed they could not and did not keep track of the banana notes printed by the mobile presses. They had only reported the total weight of paper used. This information enabled British officials to estimate that, in all, the Japanese had printed 7–8 billion dollars in banana money for Malaya during the Occupation years.[160]

Resetting the financial system

Following the initial shock-and-awe tactics adopted for the restoration of order on the streets[161] and Operation *Sook Ching* (literally 'purge through cleansing') from 18 February to 4 March 1942 that had sent thousands of Chinese to their deaths, the Japanese administrators began focusing on the economic affairs of the island. By gaining control over the supply of currency, the JMA had the means of ensuring that the general population could acquire basic necessities. At the same time, given that shortages would be likely in times of conflict, the Japanese authorities also took measures to stem price increases – shortages of necessities and spiralling inflation might have spurred widespread social disorder, and challenges to their authority.

At least in the first few years, the military authorities tried to control expansion in the supply of banana money. The JMA in Singapore did not print any military scrip in denominations larger than ten dollars till late 1944, when the first 100-dollar banana notes were printed.[162] However, there was still a great number of Straits and Malayan currency notes in circulation in 1942.[163] Although the availability of these notes had helped prevent a total breakdown in economic activity during the initial phase of the Occupation, the general shortages of the day meant that there was still too much money chasing too few goods. Hence, while the Japanese allowed the currency of the old regime to remain legal-tender, through various means they began withdrawing a substantial number of these notes.

The Japanese targeted the Chettiars, the traditional financiers of the Indian community. Initially, the Chettiars were made to surrender their Straits dollars in exchange for banana notes, but many of them chose not to do so. Those who buried their money kept them safe, but many simply hoarded their cash. Several suffered the misfortune of betrayal and the false accusation of having been pro-British, and the *kempeitai*, the Japanese secret police, confiscated all their stashes of Straits currency. After liberation, these Chettiars fought for restitution, and even petitioned the Colonial Secretary for fair treatment. Besides the lost money, most of them lost all their investments during the war.[164]

At the same time, the Japanese authorities forced the Chinese community's leadership to 'donate' 50 million Straits dollars as atonement for its part in the pre-war anti-Japanese movement in Malaya. The Singapore Chinese had to raise 10 million dollars while the Chinese in the Malay States had to fork out the remaining 40 million. When the Chinese community leaders missed their April 1942 deadline for presentation of their 'gift', the Japanese set up an Overseas Chinese Association (OCA) in June 1942 in every Malay State and in Singapore to 'better organise' the Chinese leadership in their fundraising efforts. The Singapore OCA decided that members of the community had to contribute a percentage of their assets to raise the requisite funds. To comply, many had to sell belongings; having just witnessed *Sook Ching*, they were too afraid not to. By late June 1942, the combined OCAs had only raised 28 million dollars. The Japanese then directed the OCA leadership to 'borrow' the remaining sum from the Yokohama Specie Bank. On 25 June 1942, Lim Boon Keng and 57 Chinese leaders in Malaya presented General Yamashita a cheque for 50 million dollars at the steps of the Municipal Building.[165] This compulsory donation was a punitive measure meant to send a message to the local Chinese leadership; the community and its leaders were no doubt financially weakened by the affair.[166] However, the official spin then was that in removing this sum from circulation, the 'donation' was a part of the broader effort to check inflation.[167] Of course, only 28 million dollars had truly been removed from general circulation – the balance was already sitting in a Japanese-operated bank.

Receipt for 'donation', issued by the Japanese authorities to the Overseas Chinese Association, 19 May 1942.

Other more 'creative' ways of withdrawing money from circulation soon followed. In September 1942, the military government introduced in Singapore a lottery known as the Syonan Syoken.[168] In reality, it was another form of forced donation. In the first lottery, the million tickets put up for sale at a price of a dollar had a twist. Quotas were assigned to each ethnic community: 600,000 tickets had to be taken up by the Chinese, a total of 300,000 by the Indian, Malay and Arab communities, and 100,000 by the Eurasians. The daily newspaper *Syonan Shimbun* would trumpet that the lottery had successfully withdrawn 700,000 dollars from circulation, since 300,000 dollars disbursed in lottery prize monies had to be netted off from the one million dollars taken in ticket sales.[169] In 1943, another government lottery, the Konan Saiken, was launched. It would take place every month until the Japanese surrender.[170] The Japanese claimed that the lotteries were necessary to absorb 'excess purchasing power'. The inflation, they declared, was the fault of Chinese merchants, who had excess currency on hand after cashing in their stocks before the fall of Singapore; and the fault, too, of the British, who had pumped money into the local economy while ramping up spending on defence works prior to Singapore's surrender. Similar lotteries were launched also in the

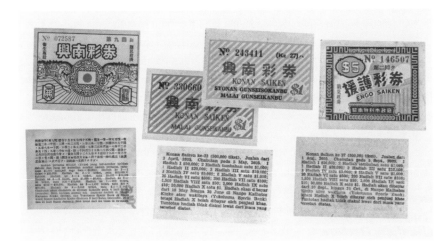

Lottery tickets issued in 1944 (left) and in 1945 (middle and right).

Malay States, the East Indies and in Borneo.[171] While the money collected from the lotteries was banana notes, unlike the OCA's 'donation' which was made in Straits dollars, the net impact of removing excess Japanese military notes from circulation was still considered necessary by the JMA. After all, the banana notes were not considered worthless until later in the war; there was already a shortage of goods, and leaving the military notes in the economy would have exacerbated inflationary pressures.

Not long after introducing its 'monetary measures' to deal with inflation, the JMA progressively restarted the local banking system. Two Japanese-operated banks with local branches, the Yokohama Specie Bank and the Bank of Taiwan,[172] were chosen to kickstart the banking sector. The Syonan-to Chinese Banks Joint Board of Control was duly formed and it restarted five Chinese banks in May 1942: Oversea-Chinese Banking Corporation Ltd, Sze Hai Tong Banking and Insurance Co. Ltd, Ban Hing Lee Bank, Lee Wah Bank Ltd and the United Chinese Bank Ltd. These Chinese banks were given a loan of ten million Straits dollars by the Japanese-operated banks to restart operations.[173] Together they had two immediate functions. They were to absorb the notes that had been 'over-issued' by the British before the surrender in order to check inflationary trends, as well as to put liquidity into the hands of those who needed to access pre-war savings to repair homes and restart businesses.[174] Bank customers who held deposits from before the war were allowed to draw on part of their savings, in banana notes. However, the banks were initially permitted to refund only 15 per cent of their customers' pre-war deposits. By

Top: *Syonan Times*, 9 September 1942.

Bottom: *Syonan Shimbun*, 12 December 1944.

The Syonan Times

WEDNESDAY, SEPT. 9, 2602.

Anti-Inflation Measures Beneficial To Public

A STATE of inflation is said to exist where there is plenty of money but no means of converting it into goods simply because of a lack of such goods. The surest remedy is to withdraw such surplus money from circulation by taxation, borrowing, or other means by the government of the country.

In Malaya we have already had two excellent mediums whereby inflation has been prevented, the first the voluntary gift of $50,000,000 by the Chinese to our Government, and the second, the Syonan Syoken Lottery. The first withdrew from circulation $50,000,000; the second will withdraw $1,000,000 or more correctly $700,000, since $300,000 will be distributed in prizes in the lottery.

The Chinese are far and away the richest community in Malaya and the $50,000,000 donated by the Chinese means that the Chinese community's ability to spend or purchase has been reduced by $50,000,000. The Syonan Syoken Lottery will withdraw another $700,000 from the general public. The Chinese are included, but the Chinese who participate in this second means of averting inflation need not necessarily be the same group who donated the $50,000,000.

BENEFITS THE POOR

Anyway, it means that a total of $50,700,000 has been withdrawn from circulation and that all classes of people have had their purchasing power reduced by that amount, thus averting inflation. Now if that amount had not been withdrawn it would have meant that $50,700,000 would have been floating about looking for a means of conversion through its purchasing power into goods—in the present wartime circumstances of shortages of transport facilities it stands to reason that there is a very limited amount of goods available for purchase—the prices for such goods would have sky-rocketed to the stratosphere of price levels, bringing in its train every dodge and subterfuge known to price profiteers and as a result terrible suffering and distress amongst the poor.

It will be seen therefore that the withdrawal of this $50,700,000 has reduced the people's purchasing power by that amount, lessening price fluctuations and thereby greatly benefitting the poor people who are able to purchase their necessities of life at a price within the reach of their limited means. Our Government has therefore followed the wisest course in the circumstances—a course which, whilst it denies the opportunity of big profit making to the rich, provides a large measure of relief to the poor. That is, it brings the greatest amount of good to the greatest number of people.

Those With Money Urged To Buy Less, Eat Less, Save Excess Funds

BEST WAY TO HELP REDUCE LIVING COSTS

By Syonan Shimbun Staff Reporter

TOUCHING on current food problems, at the informal round-table conference held at the Konan Club last week between leading members of local communities and the Syonan Shimbun (English edition), which was attended by Mr. H. Ikegami, managing editor of the Syonan Shimbun, Lieut. Shindo (Hodo-bu) Mr. Asami (Press Censor), Dr. C. J. Paglar, Tuan Onan bin Haji Siraj, Dr. P. T. Nathan, Mr. G. H. Kiat and Mr. T. Hope, it was suggested that people should strive to consume a minimum of everything, so that there would be sufficiency for all.

November 1942, this was raised to 40 per cent. In the meantime, the island's three Indian banks had also reopened. It was only after the banking system had been 'restored' in September 1942 that the Post Office Savings Bank was permitted to resume operations; of course, this would be underpinned by a loan from the Japanese-operated banks. Customers were permitted to withdraw an initial 100 dollars in Japanese military scrip, and thereafter up to 50 dollars semi-annually.[175]

It is noteworthy that the Japanese restarted the Malayan banking system by pumping liquidity into local banks. After all, the original sum – including stashes of Straits and Malayan dollars – deposited into many of these banks had already been taken out of Singapore and the Malay States. In short, depositors were allowed to withdraw monies they did not deposit, even though the banks from which they withdrew their money were no longer the same institutions with which they had placed their funds before 1942. They were similar only in name.

Malaya's Monetary System Works Very Smoothly And Efficiently, Leading Syonan Bankers Declare

FAR-SIGHTED POLICY OF ADMINISTRATION FOSTERS BRISK AND LIVELY TRADE

THE present monetary system in operation throughout Malaya continues to work very smoothly, thanks to the far-sighted policy adopted by the Military Administration.

Leading local bankers 'praise' the military administration's monetary measures. *Syonan Shimbun*, 30 October 1942.

The banks operating during the Occupation had no reserves, the local money circulating had no backing, the Savings Bank was not part of the Post Office system, and the banks were all standalone institutions no longer linked to their parent institutions in London or elsewhere. They were also delinked from the international exchange system, connected instead to an alternative created within the Japanese Empire. The Japanese had no option but to take this route if they wanted to re-establish some form of banking system locally, albeit one operating on banana money. Hence, while it was not entirely propagandist for the Japanese to declare that they had successfully 'restored' the banking system,[176] it would perhaps have been more accurate to say that they had created a new one.

However, it has to be said that the local banks that resumed operations were essentially providing facilities for deposit withdrawals; they were not geared towards providing credit. The Japanese establishment was fully aware that, unlike the Japanese-operated banks, the other institutions were hardly in a position to finance economic activity. Hence, they created the Shomin Kinko (People's Treasury, or People's Bank) to offer loans to owners of cottage industries (small enterprises), fishermen, farmers, petty traders and any small-timers who needed funds to repair or recover their businesses. The first Shomin Kinko was opened in Penang in June 1942 to help revive 'kampong industries'.[177] According to official Japanese information, by October 1942 the Penang Shomin Kinko had already lent 150,000 dollars to 3,000 families. The hope was that with this alternative source of funds, the people would not have to resort to moneylenders. By September 1942, Singapore had its own Shomin Kinko. The Japanese authorities announced in November that year that the People's Bank in Singapore had already given loans totalling 25,000 dollars to 140 families to help start or restart businesses or trades. In the following year, the number of families receiving these 'soft loans' rose to 490. They had received 84,000 dollars in credit, half of which went to government and mercantile employees to settle debts and rebuild homes, while the rest went to small traders and farmers.[178]

The JMA's final step in revamping the domestic financial system and restarting the local economy was to establish an exchange system for its conquered territories. This new system would be based on the international rate of exchange between military and local dollars in the occupied territories and the Japanese yen. Japan had already taken the yen off the gold standard in 1931 and informally linked it to the pound sterling from 1932.[179] In 1939, it pegged the yen to the US dollar,[180] but, in January 1942, the Japanese unpegged the yen from any foreign currency. In any event, they would have found it increasingly difficult to secure US dollars and to use them in trade. As Japan moved beyond China into Indochina and the rest of Southeast Asia from 1939 onwards, the United States had imposed embargoes on it and ratcheted them up over time. These effectively cut off Japan's access to strategic commodities such as oil, steel and ammunition, and compromised its industries. To secure supplies and provide markets for its goods, Japan became all the more determined in its plans to conquer Asia. The 'Greater East Asia Co-Prosperity Sphere' was a cornerstone of the plan, whereby Japan and the territories it had conquered would form a single, self-sufficient trading bloc. A critical step towards achieving 'co-prosperity' was making the military scrip and local currency in each territory on par with the others. Strategically, this provided Japan the means to purchase commodities and other natural resources from the conquered territories without expending 'real' foreign currency assets (such as the US dollar or pound sterling): it could simply pay in military scrip or in yen. Interchangeable currencies with fixed exchange rates would also facilitate regional trade and restart the supply networks that once connected the region. It was believed that this would go some way towards relieving shortages of goods and thus curb rampant inflation.[181] Japan claimed that this was its way of making East Asia 'commercially independent' from the rest of the world, and would enable the peoples of the region to throw off the 'shackles' of Western colonisers.[182]

Enforcement of the Japanese authorities' exchange-rate proposals required controls on money and capital flows. A preliminary set of regulations governing the exchange of currencies was introduced on 1 July 1942 under the 'Rules for the Control of Travellers' Expenses within the Occupied Territories'.[183] It dictated the amounts that individuals could carry as they travelled between occupied territories, and how local banks in each state should deal with the military notes it received. A formal system of exchange between Malaya and Sumatra was introduced on 1 November 1942. Within this system, a one-for-one exchange rate was established between the Straits Settlements dollar and the Netherlands Indies

Postage stamp celebrating the 'Greater East Asia Co-Prosperity Sphere'.

guilder (also known as the gulden). Critically, the system forbade discrimination between the local currencies and their military scrip equivalents. This effectively put banana dollars and military guilders on par with each other and with the underlying currencies. As the banks within the restored local banking systems were not exchange banks, the Japanese authorities created 'exchange houses' across Malaya and Sumatra to control the rate of exchange between the currencies.[184] Dollars, guilders, and their military equivalents could be exchanged one for the other only for trade, remittances to family, and travel. Changing amounts in excess of 100 dollars or guilders required approval of the exchange houses, which in turn required the submission of an application form.[185] In September 1943, the Japanese also fixed the rate between the Japanese currencies and the Thai baht.[186]

Controls were also applied to remittances. While the fact that one could remit money during the Occupation years might be surprising, it is easy to forget how extensive the Japanese Empire had become by 1942: it exercised hegemony over an area stretching from the eastern seaboard of China through Southeast Asia, at its southernmost extent almost reaching India, notwithstanding a significant stretch of Pacific Ocean. Over this vast area, it was possible to manage postal services, foreign exchange, customs and trade, as well as remittances.

In a sense, the Japanese Empire provided a framework for the resumption of certain cross-border economic activities. Not long after the East Indies had been completely subdued, remittances between Java and Japan became possible.[187] By October 1942, remittances were allowed from Malaya to Hong Kong. The first wave saw 1,000 applications to transmit around 500,000 dollars abroad. However, each family was permitted to send 50 dollars per month, which meant that the first thousand applicants could only send a total of 50,000 dollars in the first month.[188] By December 1942, residents of Malaya could make remittances to Shanghai. These funds could only be sent through the Overseas Chinese Commercial and Industrial Bank which was established in that same month for the purpose.[189] By late 1943, the limit on remittances to China was raised to 100 dollars per transfer.[190] By mid-1944, the situation with regard to international payments was getting close to pre-war 'normality': the Post Office started offering money orders to Japan and the East Indies, although permits were required if more than 30 dollars a month was being sent.[191] Just as the British colonial authorities had linked up their empire through the postal system and the fund transfers through it, so the Japanese Imperial Army was doing the same.

NOTICE

TOMI KANREI No. 2 (Syowa 17, September 29)

REGULATIONS FOR THE EXCHANGE OF MALAYA & SUMATRA CURRENCIES

To provide for the exchange of Malayan currencies (Military Dollar and Malayan Dollar) into Sumatra currencies (Military guilder and Dutch guilder) and vice versa, the following Regulations have been laid down:—
1. As from November 1. 2602, the following money changing offices will be established for the purpose of changing Malayan currencies into Sumatra currencies and vice versa: Head Office, Syonan; Branch Offices, Penang, Malacca, Medan, Pakan Baroe Palembang.
2. Any person desiring to exchange currencies of an amount exceeding One hundred Dollars or Guilders, should present his application to any of the above-mentioned offices on an application form as per specification.
3. No commission will be charged or collected for the exchange of currencies.
4. Persons in Malaya in possession of Guilders and persons in Sumatra in possession of Dollars should immediately exchange their currencies into Dollars and Guilders respectively at the above mentioned offices.
5. Travellers proceeding to Sumatra from Malaya and vice versa should before departure apply to a bank for Letters of Credit and/or Demand Drafts or alternatively should apply to any of the above mentioned offices for their requirements in Guilders or Dollars respectively.
6. All persons are strictly forbidden to buy or sell or to deal in these currencies either for the purpose of speculation or profiteering by way of fluctuations or differences in the rate of exchange.
7. These Regulations will be enforced as from the date of promulgation.

Regulations for exchanging between Malayan and Sumatra currencies. *Syonan Shimbun,* 10 October 1942.

Shortages, privation and hyperinflation

Rampant inflation on the ground reflected grave shortages of essential items due to war. The Japanese military administration was in a bind. The war it was waging had completely disrupted all economic processes in the occupied territories. As a result, international and domestic trade, agricultural production, transport, travel, and industry had ground to a halt, causing widespread shortages. While the JMA put in place measures to withdraw excess money from circulation, it also applied outright price, quantity and cost controls to curb inflation. However, the shortages were so severe that these measures would ultimately fail.

DECREE

1. The prices of goods in each district of Malaya shall be kept at the prices that precede the outbreak of the GREAT ORIENTAL WAR. Any article cannot be dealt in with a higher price than the above-prescribed.
2. Every market or shop shall put up a price list of goods to show prices with a most easy way to see.
3. Any person who violates the above two provisions or trades in cunning business, who hides or hoards goods hesitating to sell. shall be liable to the extreme penalty of military law.
   For the interest of everyone and all in Malaya, I proclaim the above regulations.
   (Given this 1st day of the 2nd month in the 2602nd Imperial year.)
COMMANDER OF THE DAI-NIPPON IMPERIAL ARMY.

The Japanese military administration decrees that prices should be kept at pre-war levels. *Syonan Shimbun*, 23 February 1942.

At the beginning of the Occupation, the JMA imposed price controls on all food items. This was done to 'prohibit the upward trend of the price of commodities compared to before the war'. A table of prices of regulated food items was published in the press during the height of the *Sook Ching*, at a time when few people would have tried to circumvent controls.[192] Quantity restrictions followed shortly afterwards. This meant limiting demand through rationing and controlling the supply chain. The first essential item to come under restriction was rice. On 10 March 1942, the Japanese military authority issued Military Administration Department Notice No. 17. Approved rice wholesalers were appointed and retailers could get their supplies only from them. Rice retailers had to be licensed as well. Those wanting to buy rice had to register with the retailers nearest their homes. Under the initial arrangement, retailers could sell each person bearing a red ration card no more than five *kati* per head per week, up to a maximum of 20 *kati* per head per month.[193]

Relaxation of the regulations did not mean the end of shortages. If anything, they worsened. Food supplies became very low and tapioca leaves, roots and rice became the staple diet of the average Singapore resident. Despite the official announcement in 1942, the actual disbursement of weekly rations in that year consisted of only 2½ *kati* of rice per person (10 *kati* per month). By the middle of the year, salt, sugar, oil and flour had joined rice on the ration list.[194] Although condensed milk was not rationed, it became a controlled item that could be sold only to families with infants under one year old, as well as to the sick and elderly. If the milk was being purchased for a baby, families were required to show the child's birth certificate; they had to be registered by the retailer, who had to keep records of the number of tins purchased. The maximum per family per month was 10 tins or 14 ounces.[195]

It was probably hard to find a single retailer who sold all the rationed or controlled essentials. Many people would have had to purchase supplies from several retailers 'near where they resided'. In any case, there was no guarantee that a single shop would hold enough stock for all the people in the queue each

Queuing for essential food supplies such as rice.

day. Controls meant at times that no one could buy more than a week's rations at a time. This meant that people had to join several food queues several times each week, if not every day. As the Occupation went on, shortages became more and more acute, and these daily food queues became ever longer and more frustrating.

Ration cards for buying rice and cooking oil.

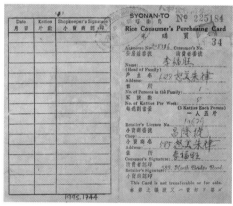

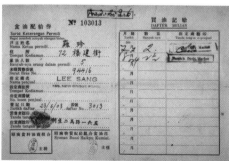

In May 1942, the authorities added cost controls to the price control regime. Stall rentals were lowered by 20–30 per cent compared to pre-war rates within the municipal area. This failed to dampen inflation. The black marketeers paid no rental anyway and continued to dictate prices regardless of any price schedules. Nevertheless, the military administration tried to enforce price controls in the markets, taking to task any stallholder who flouted the regulations.[196] As time passed and queues worsened, a police presence in markets became increasingly necessary for enforcement of the rules and the maintenance of public order.[197]

By late 1943, it was clear that the JMA's battle to keep prices and inflation down was failing.[198] Co-prosperity had not materialised; instead there was widespread privation. Even though many people had started little gardens to grow food following a 'Grow More Food' campaign announced in 1942,[199] these were supplementary foods and did little to alleviate general shortages and rising prices. Supplies dwindled

THE SYONAN TIMES, WEDNESDAY, FEBRUARY 25, 2602, SYOWA 17   **Page 3**

NOTIFICATION

MARKET PRICES

Syonan, Feb. 25th, 2602.

ACCORDING to a notification of the Administration Office of Syonan Island the following order prohibits the upward trend of the price of commodities from what they were before the Great Oriental War. This order takes effect from Feb. 23, 2602.

Hereunder are indicated the maximum prices of various commodities to be observed in Syonan Island.

Anyone who purchases or sells any commodity above the prices hereunder indicated will be severely punished.

BY ORDER.

MEAT

Beef steak	Katti	45
„ stew or curry	„	40
Fillet steak	lb.	90
Mutton, Australian	„	48
Java Goat Flesh	„	58
Malacca	„	—
Pork, lean	Kati	60
„ lean and fat (1st quality)	„	44

POULTRY

Capons (locally reared)	Kati	75
Ducks	„	30
Fowls	„	50
Hens (locally reared)	„	55
Pigeons, domestic, fledged	pair	—
Pigeons, domestic, unfledged	pair	—
Pigeons, wild	Each	—

EGGS

Duck, fresh	10	31
Fowl, fresh	10	42
Duck, preserved Uncooked	10	27

FISH, FRESH

Bawal Puteh (Pomfret)	Kati	1.50
Bunga Ayer (mixed small fish)	„	15
Chenoharu (hard tails)	„	—
Kuran (threadfins)	„	65
Merah (snapper)	„	60
Parang (dorab)	„	30
Pari (ray)	„	12
Prawns, large, salt water	„	70
Tenggiri, (Spanish mackerel)	„	50
Terubok, (herring)	„	—

FISH, DRIED & SALTED

Aruan, (ikan Siam)	Kati	26
Kuran	„	33
Parang	„	—
Prawns, (1st quality)	„	47
„ (2nd quality)	„	36
Sepat, Saigon large	„	22
Sotong, (cuttlefish) Saigon	„	96
„ „ Nipponese	„	—
Tenggiri	„	—
Terubok, (fishroe)	„	—

VEGETABLES

Beans, French	Kati	22
„ long	„	08
„ sprouts (taugeh)	„	03
Beetroots, Chinese	„	—
„ Javanese	„	12
Brinjals, (trong)	„	07
Cabbage, Batavia	„	12
„ China	„	—
Carrots, Batavia	„	15
„ China	„	—
Cucumber	„	06
Mustard (saw)	„	09
Potatoes, Australia	„	10
Pumpkin (labu merah)	„	04
Spinach (bayam)	„	04
Tomatoes, Chinese	„	—
„ Java	„	15
Yam (Keladi)	„	07

FRUITS.

Bananas (pisang hijau)	10	12
„ („ keling)	10	12
„ („ mas)	10	12
Cocoanut	each	04
Limes, large (about 30 to kati)	Kati	05
Limes, small (about 60 to kati)	„	08
Oranges, sunkist	each	10
„ Siam	Kati	24
Pineapples	Each	06

CURRY STUFFS.

Chillies, fresh	Kati	20
Cloves (Chingkeh)	„	45
Coriander (ketumba)	„	14
Garlic (bawang puteh)	„	14
Mace (bunga pala)	„	—
Nutmeg (buah pala)	„	—
Onions, Bombay	„	08
„ Siam (small)	„	09
Pepper, black	„	10
„ white	„	10
Tamarind (assam Java)	„	07
Turmeric fresh (kunyet)	„	05

SUNDRIES.

Blachan (No. 1)	Kati	14
Bread	lb.	10
Butter, Australian (in tin) Iceberg	„	55
Butter, Australian (fresh, Cold Storage)	„	64
Cocoanut Oil	Kati	08
Coffee Beans	„	—
Coffee, Ground (in tin) John Little Co.	lb.	75
Dhall (Cawnpore, yellow)	Kati	08
Flour wheaten Frog Brand	„	09
„ Australian	„	—
Ghee, No. 1 Madras	„	—
Cooking Oil	„	32
„ No. 3 Calcutta, MOS	„	—
Gingelly Oil	„	20
Ginger, fresh	„	11
Gula Malacca, large	10 pieces	08
„ „ small	„	05
Ice	10 lbs.	05
Lard	Kati	25
Milk, fresh	pau	—
Rice No. 1 Rangoon	gantang	—
„ „ 1 Siam	„	—
„ „ 2	„	61½
„ „ 3	„	—
„ glutinous (pulut)	„	—
Salt	Kati	02
Sauce, Chinese (medium)	quart	20
Sugar, white, 1st quality, No. 26	Kati	06
Tea, Ceylon Gold Leaf	lb.	1.50
„ (leaf medium quality)	„	70
Tea, Ceylon (dust)	„	70
Vinegar, Chinese	quart	20
„ European Morton's	„	65

The 'Administration Office of Syonan Island' announces price caps for key commodities, 25 February 1942. The *Syonan Times* was also variously known as the *Syonan Shimbun, Syonan Sinbun,* or *Shonan Times.*

'Grow More Food'

The drive to grow more food and achieve self-sufficiency was a critical wartime strategy for Malaya under the British and for the Japanese. During the course of 1941, even before the Japanese Imperial Army had set foot on the Peninsula, various authorities, including the Sultan of Perak and Singapore's Municipal Commissioner, had exhorted people to grow more food for themselves. Making the colony self-sufficient would aid 'Britain's ultimate victory'.[200] 'The Grow More Food campaign is really a war effort and I can picture the day when Government will feel greatly relieved to know that the people of Singapore are self-supporting in the matter of vegetables,' said the Commissioner.[201]

In April 1942, the JMA declared its aim for Malaya to attain food self-sufficiency. After the initial conquest, a different kind of war was being waged: against food shortages and inflation. The military government blamed the British for the food shortages in Malaya, arguing that the latter's focus on devoting land and resources to economic development (that is, the tin and rubber industries) had resulted in Malaya becoming reliant on imports for all manner of essential foodstuffs: rice from Thailand and Burma, salt from Aden, Java and Thailand, flour from Australia and oil from China.[202] In August of that year, the authorities announced their new food policy. All available land, including idle farms and 'enemy-property rubber plantations', would be turned over to food cultivation. The initial seeds were sown for what amounted to collective farming. A 'Back to the Land Scheme' was started in Singapore, and by September some 500 families had been 'settled' on farms set up in Yio Chu Kang, Geylang Serai, Bukit Timah and Pasir Panjang. The farms would be expanded and 500 additional families were expected to be 'settled' in the following year. The Japanese envisaged that within a few years, Singapore would be entirely self-sufficient for its table vegetable needs, 40,000 tons a year.[203]

Reality fell woefully short of forecasts. Inflation remained rampant. From the last quarter of 1943, the *de facto* collectivisation efforts were stepped up. The military administration sent thousands of people from Singapore to Bahau in Negeri Sembilan and Endau in Johor to establish food-growing settlements. The first supplies of fruits and vegetables came to Singapore from Negeri Sembilan in late 1943, and were sent to the Orchard Road Market for distribution. The new produce was sold at cost price and ended up being some 50 per cent cheaper than that grown locally.[204] As for the Kandang Kerbau Market, which had remained open throughout the Japanese Occupation, there was little food on sale until December 1943, when it started selling produce from Bahau.[205] From February 1944, other markets on the island started receiving shipments from Bahau.[206] In August 1944, Kandang Kerbau Market was also made a distribution centre for newly hatched chickens for the district. These could only be purchased with ration cards that were meant to help the population with their own food consumption, and resale was forbidden.[207] The People's Park Market was chosen as one of the hatchling distribution centres for the Kreta Ayer area in August and November 1944.[208]

'Grow More Food' also operated at the individual level. 'Experts' were sent to schools to instruct students how to grow vegetables. They cultivated empty plots near their homes every day after school, growing mostly tapioca, sweet potatoes and yam.[209] In early 1944, propaganda films encouraged the people to grow more staple food, particularly sweet potatoes and tapioca.[210]

further in 1943; the rice ration was formally cut to 14 *kati* per month in August, and then to 12 *kati* in September. By November, men were down to 12 *kati* a month; women and children received 9 and 6 *kati*, respectively. Sugar and salt saw similar reductions.[211] As food shortages across the island became increasingly acute, the administration intensified its 'Grow More Food' efforts to improve food supplies both centrally and at the individual level.

Over time, the fundamental supply issue reasserted itself in the form of higher prices. As the shortages involved essential items, demand was inelastic and there were limits as to how far down it could go to relieve inflationary pressures. Neither price nor quantity controls could resist the forces of inflation, especially in the later Occupation years when enforcement became more difficult. Increasingly, people turned to the black market where prices were not

SPECIAL NEWS
'SAVINGS INCREASE THUS PRICE DECREASE'
For depositors of
FIRST FIXED DEPOSIT with BONUS.
Who Will be the Luckiest Person To Win...$10,000.00?
WITNESS YOUR LUCK ON THE DAY OF DRAWING
to be held at the Kyoei Gekijo at 11 a.m.
on Monday, 15th May, 2604.

controlled, and the supply of goods in the controlled markets dried up. A sure sign that inflation was out of control was the rise of barter trade. To be sure, the practice had begun in 1942, when the Japanese started using rice to pay for work. Later, although the purchase of controlled rations still required banana notes, as prices continued rising the military scrip became less valuable than the commodities it could buy. Under these circumstances, barter became a key part of many daily activities.

As inflation worsened, people were offered bonuses for saving. *Syonan Shimbun,* 10 May 1944.

By 1944, high inflation in the early years of the Occupation had turned close to hyperinflation. Japanese attempts to control money, prices, and supplies of essentials had failed. Prices had already risen to such a degree that the authorities decided to print higher-denomination banana notes. The decision was not made by the military leadership but by a civilian body. The Japanese central bank of the region, the Nampo Kaihatsu Kinko (Southern Region Development Bank), granted the Malai Banking Association (as the MBC was also known) on 1 April 1943 the authority to issue new notes in place of the old military ones.[212] More than a year later, at the end of October 1944, the MBC issued a new ten-dollar banana note. They had the same design as the old notes but differed in colour and paper quality.[213] The first 100-dollar notes soon followed on 1 January 1945, and the 1,000-dollar note some time after that.[214] These new notes were printed at the Government Printing Office, off Upper Serangoon Road. Documents found after Liberation showed that in three months the Printing Office had printed close to 3.9 million dollars'-worth of 100-dollar notes and had delivered them to the Syonan government. And the Japanese authorities had wanted more.[215] By January 1945, when Allied air raids over the island started, enforcement of price controls had almost disappeared along with the availability of essentials. Just as had happened when the Japanese bombing started three years earlier, local merchants started hoarding goods and prices skyrocketed once more.

Faced with hyperinflation, the authorities resorted to more desperate measures. From late 1944 onwards, they ramped up attempts to remove excess currency in circulation through the local banks. In February, the MBC and the Savings Bank introduced schemes to encourage depositors and new customers to put more money in the banks. The association offered 'Fixed Deposits with Bonus' that gave depositors an additional 2½ per cent interest as well as cash bonuses.[216] This was followed by a Savings Encouragement Drive that promoted saving as a way of lowering the cost of living.[217]

In February 1945, a member of the Overseas Chinese Association's Savings Encouragement Committee was put on the radio to expound: 'A thrifty man with savings is more to be trusted because he makes a good head of his family and is a good citizen and an asset to his country. Remember, what we spend, we lose, what we save, we have. Let us therefore take fullest advantage of the various facilities offered on such generous terms and by doing so, we shall be contributing our little quota in co-operating with the Authorities.'[218] Days later came another message: 'The importance of savings during peace time is recognised as a thrift measure but savings during wartime is a paramount necessity. Financial experts have proved time and again that national savings keep down inflation and help to stabilise prices, thus keeping down the cost of living. Therefore, all citizens should realise their responsibility and make it their duty to save whatever they can…. Going to cinemas, theatres and places of amusement often, smoking more cigarettes than is good for one's health, taking strong drinks, these are all not necessary and can be easily lessened. It has been computed that $2 saved a week by abstaining from amusements will yield $104 in 52 weeks or $1,040 in ten years.'[219]

In July 1945, the Savings Bank offered a further Savings Encouragement Bonus Prize of 50,000 dollars and additional bonuses ranging from 50 dollars to 10,000 dollars for people starting new fixed-deposit accounts.[220] Following this, two new lotteries were announced in Singapore in 1945, the Engo Saiken and Yeh Poh lotteries. The former was in aid of air-raid victims,[221] and the latter for the running of the newspapers.[222] The Koa Saiken lottery was introduced to Negeri Sembilan and Selangor in the same year.[223] It is uncertain to what extent these lotteries truly aided anyone, but certainly they were attempts to withdraw money from circulation and so to curb inflation. At this they failed.

The common narrative about inflation during the Japanese Occupation of Singapore is that the overprinting of banana notes not backed by any reserve rendered the notes valueless, so much so that it took a wheelbarrow-load of banana notes to buy a loaf of bread. This is an incomplete story, as rising inflation was also due to persistent supply shortages. The issuance of higher-denomination notes in 1944 and 1945 would only have reinforced an already vicious inflationary cycle. It was impossible to tame the inflation monster without an improvement in the supply situation. Otherwise, holding down price increases at one point would only have caused them to burst out at another.

In retrospect

The consequences of World War I were like powder kegs that ultimately ignited a second world war. In its aftermath, many of the main actors in Europe were diminished, militarily or financially. Great Britain, in particular, although emerging victorious, was encumbered by a war debt that would not be fully redeemed until the early 21st century. Efforts in the 1920s to restore the pre-war monetary and economic *status quo* proved futile; the ensuing Great Depression simply put an end to the era where many countries pegged their currencies to the value of gold and it put an end to the free-trade regime that the British Empire had espoused for almost a century.

In Malaya and Singapore, fault lines emerged, arising from the tension between giving preference to members of the British Commonwealth in commercial dealings and adhering to free trade. These stymied initial attempts to co-ordinate economic planning that would have enabled the pan-Malayan collective to weather the crisis of the day. With the prospect of another devastating global war on the horizon, and with the needs of the broader Empire becoming more pressing than the preferences of a single colony, the component territories of Malay underwent monetary union and created a common currency, the Malayan dollar. This put an end to the Straits Settlements dollar's dominance as a regional currency that had lasted since the 1900s. A common currency was suited to the needs of the Federated Malay States, which were in financial difficulties in the early 1930s, as they could then share in the profits from issuing a currency of which they had become the major user.

The Straits dollar had become increasingly tokenised over the decades, and the Malayan dollar was the region's first fully tokenised currency. When the invading Japanese army arrived, they introduced their own token money; it was fully fiat, and its value was not backed by reserves. At the beginning, the military notes – banana money – prevented outright collapse of socioeconomic activity within the so-called Greater East Asia Co-Prosperity Sphere, but there was never an adequate way of addressing the persistent shortages of food and all other essential goods. Inflation became hyperinflation; enforced 'donations', increasing saving, and growing more food within Malaya did little to alleviate the situation. The Japanese exacerbated the situation by printing even more notes in larger denominations when inflation spiralled out of control in 1944–5.

Unbeknown to the population then, Liberation was just around the corner. When it finally came in late 1945, money would, perhaps surprisingly, become a matter of life and death. But in this instance, it was the shortage of money that would become the critical issue.

CHAPTER 05

FROM LIBERATION AND RECOVERY TO SELF-RULE

(1945–1964)

Liberation did not end the misery and privation of war. Shortages persisted in Singapore and the Malay States till the mid-1950s. Most people lost their savings as the 'banana notes' were not recognised by the returning British authorities. Although, the British quickly reintroduced the Malayan dollar to restore the money supply, there was never enough in the initial period, and the dearth of subsidiary currency remained acute for many years. The need for rehabilitation spending and to build the social infrastructure for a booming population further diminished the already-weak financial standing of the Singapore and Malayan governments. The ongoing Malayan Emergency also threatened economic development and drained much-needed resources. The Singapore government sought to shore up its fiscal buffers and build up reserves anew. The idea was mooted for a common currency for what remained of British Southeast Asia: Singapore, Malaya and the Borneo territories. As the territories moved towards self-government and even independence, it was believed that the enlarged franchise would lend stability and strength to the local currency. Singapore would undergo political union with Malaya, Sabah and Sarawak to form the Federation of Malaysia in 1965. However, neither political nor monetary union would last the decade.

The people of Singapore lived through more than three-and-a-half years of hardship under Japanese rule. The first sign that the British would return came in late 1944, when the United States, having secured a foothold in the Philippines,[1] launched bombing raids directly over Japan and most of Southeast Asia. By January 1945, the Allied air raids over Singapore had begun. As early as 1943-4, the Allies had foreseen that they would retake the occupied territories, and they began thinking about the post-war future.[2] In mid-1943, the Colonial Office in London established the Malayan Planning Unit to plan for post-war government and policies. It made plans for the creation of a new pan-Malayan political entity to be known as the Malayan Union,[3] and also formulated currency policies for the territories that had formed British Malaya.[4]

Parallel to the Allies' political plans was a series of financial initiatives that would culminate in the Bretton Woods Agreement to rebuild the international monetary system. It was clear to the Allies that almost every nation in the world would be confronted with the need to rebuild after the war, and would require financing. Countries that had borrowed great sums to fund their war efforts also needed to repay their debts. Britain, for example, had borrowed heavily from the United States under the Lend-Lease scheme, under which it had received oil, weapons, ammunition, ships, planes and more. The resultant debt was crippling, and would have to be repaid in US dollars. There was therefore a pressing need to coordinate international financing and monetary arrangements to ensure that recovery was possible and repayment sustainable. To this end, experts in monetary and financial matters from the Allied nations held several meetings even prior to 1944, in an attempt to reach a common basis for the post-war international monetary order. They reached an agreement on 21 April 1944, and released a 'Joint Statement by Experts on the Establishment of an International Monetary Fund' on the same day. This paved the way for further negotiations. On 1 July 1944, representatives of 44 Allied nations met in a hotel at Bretton Woods, New Hampshire. After weeks of discussion, the delegates signed the 'Final Act of the United Nations Monetary and Financial Conference' to establish the International Bank for Reconstruction and Development (IBRD) and the International Development Association, which together constituted the World Bank.

The seeds of the International Monetary Fund (IMF), a transnational organisation meant to supervise the international monetary arrangements that would be put in place after the war, were also planted during the Bretton Woods conference.[5] The IMF was formally constituted in December 1945, when 29 countries ratified the Articles of Agreement. The newly dominant US had a greater say than the British in the matter: the US dollar would be a central currency in a new global system of pegged exchange rates, and the dollar itself would be pegged to a fixed price of gold. This system of exchange rates came to be known as the Bretton Woods system.

Chapter opening picture: The people of Singapore celebrate the return of Allied forces, September 1945.

All members of the system agreed to fix their exchange rates to a level against the US dollar, although small deviations – up to ±1 per cent – were permitted. However, the peg could be changed in the event of severe balance of payments difficulties, and the adjustment process would be overseen by the IMF. The Bretton Woods Agreement would define the international monetary arrangements for Britain and its colonies for years to come, although the colonies' monetary policies and practices would once again be subordinated to the needs of the British Empire as well.

The period after the war ended saw the emergence of a bipolar world order, characterised by tension and even outright conflict between the Western and Communist blocs. In Malaya, open hostilities broke out during the Malayan Emergency (1948–1960). This had a severe impact on the fiscal position of the Malay States throughout the 1950s.

When the British liberation forces returned to the region, they established a British Military Administration (BMA) that governed Singapore/Malaya from September 1945 to April 1946, when civilian government could be restored and made functional. When the handover took place, the plans formulated by the Malayan Planning Unit were implemented and a new polity, the Malayan Union, was created. It comprised what were formerly the Federated Malay States, the Unfederated Malay States (including Johor) and two of the territories that had made up the Straits Settlements, namely Penang and Malacca. With this change, the Straits Settlements was no more. Singapore became a British Crown colony in its own right. In 1948, the Malayan Union was reconstituted to form the Federation of Malaya.[6] The Federation would go on to achieve independence as a sovereign nation in 1957, an event that eventually helped to bring the Emergency to an end, although more sporadic violence would continue for some time yet. Singapore itself would achieve limited self-government in 1955,[7] and full internal self-government in 1959. In 1965, the Federation of Malaya, Singapore, and the former British territories of Sabah and Sarawak would merge to form the Federation of Malaysia. Singapore would, for the first time since 1819, be independent of British rule.

Liberation and the restoration of the Malayan dollar

Liberation came swiftly in September 1945, soon after the US dropped two atomic bombs on Japan. Two weeks after Emperor Hirohito's surrender announcement, the British returned to Malaya, retaking first the island of Penang in late August 1945. On 30 August, nine Royal Australian Air Force planes landed in Singapore, bringing supplies and an advance party to prepare for the formal Japanese surrender and freeing of Allied prisoners of war. The British fleet reached Singapore on 4 September, and a day later Allied troops landed to reoccupy the island. The formal surrender ceremony took place on 12 September at the Municipal Building, the present-day City Hall (now part of National Gallery Singapore).

Malaya, including Singapore, was placed under the BMA as an interim measure pending the restoration of an effective civilian government.

Before the first British troops landed, Japanese forces in Singapore and on the Peninsula faced increasing lawlessness on the streets. There were attacks on Japanese police and military, and on people suspected of having been collaborators. Elements in the population were seizing arms and food supplies by force. Anticipating the Japanese surrender, some resorted to looting and others to mischief.[8] Even after British troops had landed, looting continued for several days.[9] Meanwhile, in the few days immediately after the British had returned, the Japanese 'banana money' continued circulating across Malaya.[10] On 7 September 1945, the BMA made its first proclamation as regards the currency that would have legal-tender status in the liberated territories: it included currency notes inscribed with the words 'Government of the Straits Settlements' (that is, those issued by the Board of Commissioners of Currency, Straits Settlements), except for 'denominations of $1,000, $10,000 and for those less than $1', as well as notes issued by the 'Board of Commissioners of Currency, Malaya', except for denominations of less than one dollar. Coins issued by these authorities were also legal-tender up to a limited amount.[11] Individuals holding 1,000-dollar and 10,000-dollar notes had to turn them in with a written statement as to their origins. If the means of acquiring the notes was found to be lawful, the holder would receive the full value in notes of smaller denominations.

There were several problems with this proclamation. In the first instance, not many people still had pre-war currency. During the Occupation, the Japanese military authorities had taken various measures to absorb pre-war currency while disbursing only military scrip in return, and the financial system had come to be based mainly on banana notes. The only currency many people had in their hands and as savings in the bank was banana money. The few who still had pre-war money hoarded it or used it for speculation.[12] The Japanese military scrip was conspicuously missing from the list of legal-tender currencies in the BMA's 7 September proclamation. This led to uncertainty. By Saturday, 8 September, with still no official statement about the banana notes,[13] panic spread across the island and prices of every item denominated in banana notes skyrocketed, creating an inflationary crisis that appears to have surpassed the hyperinflation experienced during the last phase of the Occupation. As a case in point, a *kati* (about 600 grams) of pork that cost 30 cents before the war, and which cost 400 Japanese dollars in the black market during the Occupation, was priced at 1,500 Japanese dollars on 8 September 1945.[14] Shopkeepers reportedly demanded 100 dollars for an egg. The situation had spiralled to such an extent that by Sunday, 9 September 1945, retailers no longer accepted banana notes. Banana money had become worthless. The people of Malaya started throwing them away. The currency was dumped in the streets. Many discarded notes were seen along South Bridge Road and Cross Street.[15] As a result, from 10 September 1945, a crisis ensued: half a million people in Singapore suddenly had little or no currency to use as money. This 'currency upheaval'[16] exacerbated an already volatile situation. There was anger among the local

SINGAPORE'S CURRENCY UPHEAVAL

Japanese Dollar Thrown Into The Waste-Paper Basket

BUT MALAYAN DOLLARS NOT YET IN CIRCULATION

There were half a million people in Singapore yesterday asking, "What do we use for money?"

The great majority of the population of this city suddenly found themselves unable to buy food for immediate needs, and many thousands were literally without a cent of real money in their pockets.

A HUNGRY DAY

Yesterday at midday an employee of the Straits Times went out to get a meal. Riding a bicycle, he went all the way from North Bridge Road to Tanjong Pagar, visiting stalls and streets of Chinatown well-known for their restaurants. Nowhere in his search was he able to buy any food, although he had British Malayan money in his pocket, and he came back as hungry as when he left.

Many hundreds of Government and Municipal employees who came in from outlying suburbs yesterday to get themselves registered with their departments went without their tiffin, it being impossible to find a food stall or coffee-shop or restaurant doing business anywhere in the vicinity of their offices.

people, not only because the Japanese notes no longer had legal-tender status, but because there was no alternative currency available.[17] Those who held only banana notes were left destitute.

The British had in fact begun circulating an alternative currency, the Malayan dollar, shortly after their return to Singapore. The troops coming ashore were already receiving their pay in Malayan dollars from 8 September.[18] But where did these notes come from? There was a significant store of currency in India. These notes, dated 1 July 1941, had been printed before the war but had never been circulated.[19] Within a few days of the British return, eight tons of currency had been delivered to Singapore. However, transporting and circulating a truly adequate supply of Malayan dollars to fully replace the banana notes required time. Only retailers or merchants stood a chance of being able to exchange their goods for the new currency, and even then, businesses had few goods which they could trade or sell initially. Not every worker could find work or quickly return to their old jobs. There were therefore very few avenues through which the currency could circulate throughout the economy and the broader population.

This put the British in a conundrum. Restoring the monetary system in Malaya with a stable currency backed by reserves was the ideal, but it would be a protracted process. On the other hand, allowing the banana notes to remain in circulation would have been unacceptable; not only was it important to remove all vestiges of the Occupation, but also the banana

Left: Straits Times, 10 September 1945

Right: Straits Times, 11 September 1945.

Straits Times, 11 September 1945.

SINGAPORE INFLATION

COLUMN ONE shows normal prices of essential foodstuffs in Singapore in the former British Malayan currency before the war.

COLUMN TWO shows the prices in Japanese paper money of those commodities in the black market in Singapore, before the fall of Japan.

COLUMN THREE shows the astronomical effect of the announcement that the Japanese money was worthless. The prices quoted here were those demanded on Saturday, when there was a general scare about the Japanese currency but some market stall-holders and shopkeepers were still accepting it, not yet having fully understood the official announcement.

Yesterday the Japanese money was absolutely worthless everywhere in the city.

		Pre-War (British $)	Black Market (Jap. $)	(Jap. $)
Pork (per kati)	..	30 cts.	$400	$1,500
Fish	..	20 cts.	$320	$ 800
Beef	..	20 cts.	$150	$1,000
Sugar	..	4 cts.	$ 60	$ 225
Kankong	..	1 ct.	$ 6	$ 50
Eggs (Hen)	..	3 cts.	$ 15	$ 100
Mutton	..	30 cts.	$125	$1,500
Coffee Powder	..	10 cts.	$ 45	$ 150
Coconut Oil (1 bottle)	..	12 cts.	$120	$ 200
Bean Curd	..	1 ct.	$ 4	$ 30
Prawns	..	60 cts.	$250	$ 840
Bean Sprouts	..	2 cts.	$ 25	$ 150
Green Peas	..	6 cts.	$ 90	$ 500
Chillies (fresh)	..	14 cts.	$100	$ 200
Dry Chillies	..	10 cts.	$200	$ 400
Onions	..	7 cts.	$225	$ 500
Sauce—Chinese	..	10 cts	$ 40	$ 150
Salt Fish (bilis)	..	10 cts.	$ 45	$ 150
Coconut	..	2 cts.	$ 12	$ 150

Malayan dollar notes printed 1941, circulated 1945

1 dollar

5 dollars

10 dollars

notes were not backed by any reserves. While the military scrip was technically the liability of the Japanese government, there was little expectation that holders of these notes could lay claim to anything from the Japanese at this time.[20] From the British point of view, the residents of Malaya should have anticipated that the banana notes would be useless when the former returned. Hence, when on 8 September the press reported that British officials had declared that 'the Japanese Dollar is worth no more than the paper upon which it is printed',[21] the BMA made no effort to qualify that statement. It was only on 14 September 1945 that the BMA's Chief Financial Advisor declared that the people should not be surprised by the non-recognition of the Japanese notes. After all, this policy had been announced in Allied pamphlets airdropped over Malaya before the war had ended.[22]

Raffles Girls' School in a sorry state at the end of the Occupation.

Circulating the new Malayan dollar through wages paid to the military services was only one part of the larger BMA strategy. The British also began paying civilians employed by the administration and military services in new notes, and the first week's wages were paid in advance.[23] The military administration also advanced Malayan dollars to businesses which supplied them when they restarted operations. These businesses disbursed the new money in their payrolls. For instance, this was done in the first week after Liberation, when Fraser & Neave and Malayan Breweries reopened with more than 1,000 people employed. By 10 September, these firms had paid, and therefore circulated, wages amounting to more than 12,000 Malayan dollars. Still, it took time for the majority of the population to receive the new currency.

The military authorities also placed Malayan dollars in bank branches in order that the public could have access to them.[24] However, using financial institutions in the immediate post-war years to circulate currency was not a straightforward exercise. As the Japanese had 'Nipponised' the financial system and replaced all local currency with banana notes, all deposits had come to be denominated in military scrip. While this did not affect the western banks, which were closed throughout the Occupation, the Chinese and Indian banks, which had reopened during those years, had paid out and received deposits in banana notes. The money held by these banks was duly declared worthless. The deposits made with the Post Office Savings Bank during the Occupation were also not recognised by the government, although withdrawals were. This meant that if someone had 100 Straits Settlements dollars in a savings account before the war, any additional deposits of banana notes were simply disregarded. However, withdrawals of banana notes from the account made during the Occupation period were recognised as legitimate and were offset against the pre-war Straits dollar balance. Naturally, this became a significant source of grievance for local depositors. Their position was simple: the government should simply recognise both legs of the transactions or ignore both. If deposits made in banana notes were not considered legitimate, how could the bank take into account withdrawals in banana notes made during the war years?

Reinstating the Malayan currency was the means by which British planners hoped to restore stability to the domestic monetary system. However, the re-establishment of the pre-war dollar system did not in itself deal with the financial disruption caused by the Occupation. The losses suffered by the residents of Singapore and Malaya were in both pre-war Straits dollars and Occupation banana money. The Singapore Chinese community's reparation claims pertaining to lost property and money seized by the Japanese was estimated at 68 million Straits dollars. Meanwhile, the wages and gains from trade which the community had earned over three-and-a-half years of Occupation, amounting to 271 million banana dollars, simply vanished when the British annulled the notes.[25] As for the Chinese in the rest of Malaya, their losses were estimated at 200 million Straits dollars. For their part, the Malay States claimed an even larger two billion Straits dollars.[26] The Singapore Chinese Massacre Appeal Committee also added a claim for 50 million Straits dollars, the amount the Overseas Chinese Association had 'donated' to the Japanese[27] (see p. 148). Hardly any of these claims were repaid, if any at all. Instead, the residents found themselves losing twice over: first under the Japanese military authorities, and again under the BMA.

The wartime plan for post-war Malaya and Singapore also included arrangements for them both to remain in a monetary union, as had been the case before the war.[28] This entailed restoring the Board of Commissioners of Currency, Malaya, with its headquarters again in Singapore. This arrangement was incorporated into the Malayan Union Ordinance that took effect on 1 April 1946, on the same day the BMA handed authority back to a civilian government. The reconstituted currency board would have two commissioners: the financial secretaries of the Malayan Union and of Singapore.[29]

There were several fundamental differences between the pre- and post-war monetary arrangements. Under the pre-war regime, the Malayan dollar was simply pegged to the pound sterling at 2s 4d, even as the pound spent a number of years off or on the gold standard during the first few decades of the 20th century.[30] Under the Bretton Woods system, the Malayan dollar was still pegged to the pound, but the pound now had a fixed parity against the US dollar. Only the US dollar could be exchanged for gold at a constant rate. The link between the local currency and gold was now more indirect than before, although not fully eliminated. At the same time, given Britain's strained post-war finances, it could not afford to use precious metals to mint circulation coinages. While the pre-war Malayan dollar coins were minted from silver alloy, the new coins minted

War reparations in currencies and non-currencies

The British authorities in Malaya would spend years attempting to settle claims and recover losses (on behalf of the people) from the post-war Japanese government, albeit with little success. Unfortunately, the route taken in 1946 was first to assign an exchange value between the Japanese scrip and the Malayan currency. This was in order to establish some basis of calculation for the claims the Allies made with the incumbent Japanese government. It was determined that every Japanese dollar was worth 25 per cent of the pre-war Straits currency. In all, the British attempted to claim 500 million Straits dollars as reparations for 3½ years of Occupation.[31] This staggering amount only represented what all the people had lost in assets and property during those years, and did not include any compensation for the lives lost. Of course, with every aggrieved nation making claims, no one would ever recover a single cent from the Japanese.

In the end, the onset of the Cold War played a part in determining the final outcome of the Malayan claims. At this point, Britain and America needed Japan as an ally in the Cold War, and consequently the claims against Japan were never pursued to their conclusion. By 1947, the only reparations Malaya had received from Japan were a number of demilitarised warships moored at Seletar, including Japanese destroyers and escort ships. With great shortages still afflicting Malaya, the British Malayan government was also content to receive reparations in kind. After all, purchasing goods from Japan, which was in a US-dollar area,[32] would require scarce US dollars that Britain needed to fund its war debt. Consequently, the Malayan government was only too ready to accept machine tools and other goods from Japan, items which they could not buy given the currency controls in place (see p. 178). In the end, the British government in London simply decided to make a token claim of 10 million Malayan dollars on behalf of Malaya, Sarawak and North Borneo; the sum could be paid in kind. The first part 'payment' of this sum, comprising 1.14 million dollars' worth of Japanese produce, arrived in Singapore in February 1950.[33]

for Malaya in 1947 and sent in 1948 were made of pure copper (one cent) or cupronickel (5, 10 or 20 cents). The new post-war cupronickel coins contained no silver, but were still called 'silver coins' because of their appearance, despite having no precious metal content.

What was to become of pre-war coins and subsidiary notes? When the BMA first took charge on the island, it was clear that there was a pressing shortage of currency in general. The administration therefore preserved the legal-tender status of coins with silver content if they had been issued by previous currency boards (for example, the Straits Settlements coins). However, this policy failed to alleviate the shortage of subsidiary currency. Although on paper there were still millions of Malayan dollars' worth of old silver and silver alloy coins in circulation, in reality such coins had become scarce.[34] It was believed that since 1941, people had been hoarding coins with silver content. Many had been melted down and turned into ornaments. Consequently, from September 1945, measures were taken to release more subsidiary coins into the economy.[35] Subsidiary notes that had been printed during World War I,[36] as well as in 1941 during a recurrence of coin shortage,[37] were subsequently also allowed to remain in circulation.

Malayan coins made of cupronickel, bearing the portrait of King George VI

5 cents (1950)　　　　　　　10 cents (1950)　　　　　　　20 cents (1950)

Although the British had introduced the new cupronickel and copper coins in 1948, the public clearly had their own ideas as to what they wanted to hold as money. In 1947, there were more than 314 million copper one-cent coins in Singapore, ready to be injected into the Malaya and Singapore economies. So great was the stash that the Board of Commissioners of Currency, Malaya said there was 'enough weight in the copper coins stored in the Singapore treasury vaults to sink a battleship'.[38] Yet, in late 1948, the board stopped issuing one-cent coins.[39] Post-war inflation had rendered them irrelevant. They had almost 'no purchasing power', and no one wanted to use them.

From 1948, with more cupronickel coins in circulation, the government started withdrawing most of the old paper subsidiary notes still in circulation.[40] By August 1948, all 5-cent, 10-cent, 20-cent and 50-cent paper notes issued before the war were demonetised, despite being fairly popular during the Lunar New Year festive season.[41] Nevertheless, it was reckoned that 50 million pieces of pre-World War II paper currency still remained in circulation in 1950. Then the unthinkable happened. The cupronickel coins introduced to replace the old silver coins and paper notes also became scarce in 1950 when a sudden shortage of the metals in Britain halted further coin supplies from the Royal Mint. Faced with a shortage of 10-cent coins, the Singapore treasury began reissuing the 1941-vintage 10-cent notes in 1950 (see p. 138). By November the following year, more than two million had been placed into circulation.[42] It was not until the end of 1952, when the supply of cupronickel coins had stabilised, that all coins and subsidiary notes issued prior to 1947 could finally be demonetised.[43]

Battling prolonged inflation and shortages

Meanwhile, other challenges remained. The shortage of currency was one thing; the general dearth of almost everything else was another. All basic necessities, including food, healthcare, employment, housing, transport, and more, were sorely lacking. Chaos and disruptions continued at every level as the British struggled to impose law and order. Almost everyone faced great uncertainty and

Postscript: banana notes and Straits Settlements dollars

Though declared worthless and discarded by many in the days after Malaya was liberated, the story of banana money did not end there. Even up to a year later, there were still some relatively remote places on the Malay Peninsula where people continued to use the Japanese military scrip – they had yet to receive any currency issued by the British authorities.[44] Similarly, over in the East Indies, British forces reached the archipelago months before their Dutch allies made their way back, and in the interim the military authorities allowed the locals to continue using their Japanese *pisang* ('banana' in the vernacular) notes. In fact, the Japanese military scrip issued in the East Indies was assigned an exchange value against guilders issued by the Dutch authorities in Java.[45] For instance, in October 1946 100 dollars in Indies banana notes could be exchanged for three such guilders.[46] The banana notes were not completely outlawed there until mid-1948.[47]

Meanwhile, stashes of banana notes emerged in the months after Liberation. In October 1945, 300 tons of banana notes with a total face value of 500 million Japanese dollars were found dumped in Kuala Lumpur. In 1946, the Malayan Union government discovered 3,000–4,000 cases of banana notes stored at the godowns of the Bungsar Paper Mill in Kuala Lumpur. The Japanese had not had time to circulate them. Initially, the BMA had wanted to sell them for pulping or as souvenirs, and a tender was called. Then the government changed its mind and the tender was cancelled. It was decided that all the notes should be burnt instead.[48]

Besides the banana notes, the Straits Settlements dollar had remained legal-tender throughout the Occupation years. While few civilians held much of the pre-war currency, it turned out that the Japanese had plenty. During the surrender in September 1945, the British military found in the personal possession of Japanese civilians and soldiers a total of three million dollars in Straits currency. These were instantly confiscated.[49] The BMA also recovered millions of Straits dollars that the Japanese had kept in bank vaults across Malaya.[50] For instance, in October 1945 it discovered a large consignment of jewellery and Straits currency in the Perak Treasury. There were in total 95 boxes and several sacks containing 1.25 million dollars in Straits notes and 200,000 dollars' worth of coins.[51] It seems likely that a fair number of these notes would have been part of the 50 million dollars that the Japanese had coerced the Chinese community of Singapore and the Malay States into 'contributing' during the Occupation.

Another curious incident involving Straits Settlements dollars occurred in late September 1945. When HMS *Rotherham* arrived at the port of Singapore, its commander, Captain Hilary Biggs, was informed that the Japanese Naval Headquarters at the Sembawang dockyard wanted to formally surrender one million Straits dollars to a naval officer. Biggs sailed the HMS *Rotherham* into the dockyard where he found the Japanese Naval Headquarters staff awaiting his arrival.[52] When he stepped ashore, they officially surrendered the cash. Captain Biggs assigned his cashier to receive the money. This sum, however, remained with the dockyard's cashier until 1947, and was subsequently forgotten by the Admiralty.[53] The tale of what happened to the cache is a story in itself; what is interesting here is that such a large sum was kept at the Japanese Naval Headquarters.

The discovery of the Straits notes in the possession of Japanese men and women at the time of surrender lends credence to the view that the Japanese were hoarding, and perhaps even using among themselves, Straits dollar notes and coins, because they recognised that the currency was a valuable financial resource. If true, then this would have been Gresham's Law by *diktat*: the Japanese were deliberately driving the 'good money' out of the local financial system into their own hands even as they forced the general population to use banana notes that had no intrinsic value and represented no claim on anything as such.

Japanese 'banana' note used to pay taxi fare

PASSENGERS have on occasion bolted from taxis without paying the fare; some have underpaid. But for the first time a cabby has been cheated with an old war-time Japanese "banana" note.

The taxi driver, aged 50, took three men from Waterloo Street to Bukit Merah Central recently. At the end of the journey, they handed him an unfamiliar-looking green note.

To the cabby's question, they said the note was a new one issued by the Singapore Currency Board.

He realised later that the note dated back to the Japanese occupation period.

Police are investigating.

Straits Times,
10 October 1985

some form of privation. The general sense of panic and despair that people felt when their currency holdings and deposits were declared worthless is understandable.[54] Given the lack of employment opportunities, how were people

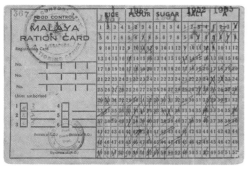

Rationing card for rice, flour, sugar and salt, 1952–3.

expected to earn any of the new currency? Certainly, while Liberation brought an end to the bloodshed, it did not bring an end to the hardship.

Given the extreme situation, the BMA found it necessary to introduce food-control measures just as the Japanese had. In the initial phase from 10 September 1945, when the shortage of money and goods in the market was at its worst, essentials such as salt, sugar and rice were given out for free, until there was enough Malayan currency in circulation. Price controls were then imposed, and the people were permitted to buy necessities at fixed prices and with ration cards.[55] As a result of these measures, food prices fell.[56] The military administration announced that it would put an end to the distribution of free food items by the end of the month, presumably because it assessed that enough new Malayan dollars had been placed into circulation. However, the Singapore Chinese Chamber of Commerce appealed to the British to continue distributing free rations into October.[57] The authorities did not agree as regards Singapore, although it did continue distributing necessities in several Malay States beyond September.[58]

By mid-October 1945, Singapore and Malaya were once again facing runaway price increases. Although the supply situation for foodstuffs and other staples had gradually improved, prices had not weakened commensurately: these goods had been secured because higher prices were being offered in Singapore, and as the items often passed through the hands of multiple middlemen who marked up prices further, the final price to the consumer remained high.[59] Eventually, the balance between money and goods in the economy tilted: Malayan dollars were being injected into the economy faster than supply conditions were improving. Money in circulation was growing more quickly than the supply of goods available for purchase. At this point, it was clear that prices might never return to pre-war levels. The British had little choice but to heavily subsidise rationed essentials or risk a complete breakdown of socioeconomic order in Singapore and the Peninsula. The BMA sought to benchmark the price at which the general public could buy rationed staples to pre-war wage levels. Accordingly, from 1 November 1945, it fixed the price of rice at 8 cents per *kati* even though the rice had cost 20 cents.[60]

The BMA made efforts to increase the supply of food and to relieve transport bottlenecks. On the supply front, the authorities tried to source for rice from alternative sources such as Brazil and Egypt. The conflict in Southeast Asia had affected traditional rice-supplying areas, namely Siam, Indochina and Burma.[61] Damage to these territories' rice-growing areas during World War II had severely limited their ability to restore production to pre-war levels.[62] Transport bottlenecks were also leading to higher food prices. There were not enough transport ships, while the fuel required for land, air and sea transport was in short supply, given the rebuilding efforts taking place all over the world. When food prices began rising again in October 1945, the BMA acquired more lorries to resolve the supply bottleneck. While this might have ensured that more food arrived more quickly where it was needed, the lorries required scarce fuel to operate; the capital and running costs of the lorries would have added to the underlying cost of the food and resulted in higher prices were it not for the subsidies in place.[63] As for sea transport, enterprising private traders came up with innovative ways of shipping food to Singapore from the region.

In these difficult times, profiteers saw opportunities in the black market. It was well-known that sailors and merchantmen conducted trades on the side that circumvented food regulations and price controls. Ships would arrive carrying staple supplies, but even as the cargo was being unloaded at the dock on one side, a portion was being offloaded separately on the other side for the black market. 'Goods came down, and money up.' People thus found ways around the rationing restrictions, and black marketeers were willing to take risks in return for profits of

The last junk fleet sails once more

Moored off the waterfront in wartime Singapore were hundreds of Chinese sailing junks that had become obsolete in the era of motorised shipping. During the Occupation years, they had been given a new lease of life. The destruction of the Japanese merchant fleet by the Allied naval forces pushed the Japanese to turn to these antiquated ships for the transport of necessities to Malaya. After all, they did not require many resources to run – just good winds and fair weather.

When the war ended, the junks were marshalled once again. In September 1945, Malaya had 2,204 junks and sampans carrying its regional trade. According to a press report, 'They brought in the first boat-loads of fresh vegetables, fresh spices of the Indies and fresh fish of which Malaya had seen but little for three years.' Throughout the last months of the year, when food was scarce and prices soaring, the junk fleet helped to keep non-rationed supplies flowing, preventing already astronomical prices from rising even further. By February 1946, it was

A Chinese junk sailing at sea, 1946.

estimated that the junk trade had imported into Singapore more than 20 million Malayan dollars' worth of produce. An average of 70 ships sailed into and out of Singapore daily. The Malaya food run was perhaps the last large-scale journey of the Chinese junks that had once been ubiquitous along the shores of Singapore.[64]

up to 500 per cent.[65] These profit margins were, in a sense, a true measure of inflationary pressures in the post-war economy. The seemingly affordable official prices of items available through the rationing system were by no means the genuine prices experienced on the ground.

In November 1945, the BMA set up a special committee to examine the inflation situation in Malaya.[66] However, real progress was not made until responsibility for government in the Malayan Union and Singapore had been handed over to civilian authorities. In May 1946, the governments of the Malayan Union and Singapore appointed a new committee to look into wages and the cost of living in Malaya. Heading it was C.J. Pyke, the economic adviser to the Union government.[67] By the end of June, the Wages and Cost of Living Committee, which became known as the Pyke Committee, had published its findings and recommendations for the two territories. It concluded that some financial assistance was in order in light of the hardship faced by the people. The committee recommended that all government employees be given a special relief, or temporary allowance, of 10 Malayan dollars a month, or 10 per cent of their basic pay as at 1941, up to a maximum of 35 dollars. The prices for essentials would be controlled. Retailers would be required to display prices, and inspectors would be appointed to enforce the measures. The government would set up more venues for the sale of fresh food and necessities and to provide meals. Specifically, the committee recommended the creation of public canteens styled after Britain's post-war 'Public Restaurants', to sell low-cost meals. These would be operated by the government's Welfare Department.[68]

On the whole, although the government's aid measures were welcomed, not all its initiatives had the desired impact. The special monetary relief offered by the authorities did little to assuage the concerns of government employees. Prices of food had risen by 600 per cent from pre-war levels, yet the relief amounts were capped at 10 per cent of pre-war pay.[69] The workers expressed their dissatisfaction and requested more help, but the government's position was that increasing wages at this point would drive inflation up further and impede recovery efforts. However, the government's food-control regulations, which fixed prices and regulated exports out of Singapore, saw a greater measure of success. The permission of the Food Controller was necessary if anyone was to export food to places other than Malaya. The Singapore government assigned Food Control Inspectors to oversee prices and ensure compliance by retailers.[70] In 1946, there were 300 of these officers operating across the island. In the following year, there were still 103 officers on the job. It was only by the beginning of 1949 that the number of Food Control Inspectors had dwindled to 26, and their job scope had become confined largely to ensuring that the prices of rice, sugar and flour were set at reasonable rates.[71]

THE MORNING TRIBUNE, Monday, September 22, 1947

SINGAPORE FOOD PRICES: OFFICIAL

Morning Tribune,
22 September 1947.

The official wholesale and retail prices of all food commodities are stated below and the public are warned not to pay anything more. It is regarded as an offence against the Food Control Proclamation to do so and the maximum fine of $1,000 may be imposed on anyone violating this rule.

	WHOLESALE	RETAIL
RICE other than those in respect of which an import permit has been issued by the Government or by the Government of the Colony or by the Government of Malayan Union	$ 24.40 per picul	0.25 per katty
SUGAR	31.30 per picul	0.32 per katty
WHEAT FLOUR Imported on Govt. account	$ 24.30 per picul	0.25 per katty
BREAD		0.25 per lb. loaf
TINNED BUTTER		
12 oz tin		1.00 per tin
16 oz tin		1.30 per tin
24 oz. tin		1.95 per tin
2 lb. tin		2.40 per tin
MEAT (Mutton-Australian) locally slaughtered (any cut)		0.75 per lb.
OILS (Coconut)		0.35 per katty
RED PALM OIL	31.08 per picul	0.35 per katty
POWDERED MILK		
"Klim" 16 ozs.	101.00	1.90
"Dari Gold" 16 ozs.	40.40	1.90
"Klim" 2 1/2 lbs.	119.00	4.50
"Klim" 5 lbs	90.70	8.50
Beverage & Infant Foods	WHOLESALE	RETAIL
Ovaltine 1 lb.	20.00 per doz.	1.90 per tin
Ovaltine 1/2 lb.	11.50 per doz.	1.10 per tin

MINERAL WATERS	Consumption on premises	Consumption off premises
Soda Water	0.25 cts.	0.15 cts.
Ordinary Sweet Aerated water	0.30 cts.	0.20 cts.
Fruit Crushes & special products	0.40 cts.	0.25 cts.
BEER Locally brewed, Small (reputed pint) bottle	0.85 cts.	0.65 cts.
Large (reputed quart.) Bottle	1.65 cts.	1.20 cts.

INTOXICATING LIQUOR Maximum Prices

Johnnie Walker—"Black Label" Hepburn & Ross, "Red Hackle," Scotch Whiskies	12.45 per reputed quart bottle
Hedges & Buttlers "Vat 250" Scotch Whisky	11.95 "
Gin	10.25 "
"Queen Elizabeth" Scotch Liqueur Whisky	12.45 "
"Grand McNish" Scotch Whisky	11.95 "
Other Scotch Whiskies	10.95 "

TOBACCO	Per lb.	Per 1/4 lb.	Per 2 oz.	Per 1 oz.
Player's No Name	12.40	3.10	1.55	—
Three Castles Mild	12.40	3.10	1.55	—
Craven Mixture	11.60	2.90	1.45	—
Capstan Navy Cut Medium	11.20	2.80	1.40	—
Richmond Smoking Mixture	10.40	2.60	1.30	—
Three Nuns	12.40	3.10	1.55	—
Old English Curve Cut Player's Navy Cut	11.20	2.80	—	—
Medium	11.20	2.90	1.40	—
Gallaher's Rich Dark Honey-dew	11.20	2.80	1.40	—
Flakes Medium	11.20	2.80	1.40	—
Bulwark Cut Plug	10.40	2.60	1.30	0.65
St. Bruno Flake	10.40	2.60	1.30	0.65
Sir Walter Raleigh	10.40	2.60	1.30	—
Craven Curly Cut	11.60	2.90	1.45	—
Blackcat	11.60	2.90	1.45	—
W/C Barrey's	11.60	2.90	1.45	—
Punchbowle	11.60	2.90	1.45	—

CIGARETTES

BRANDS:	1000 stks.	50 stks.	20 stks.	10 stks.
Caspero Specials	60.00	3.00		
State Express "555", Player's No. 3, Pall Mall de Luxe, Black and White Magnums, Churchman's No. 1, Turkish No 5.				
Craven "A", Wills "Gold Flake", Player's Medium, Du Mauier, Ardath Filter, Martin's Non-throat, Pall Mall Medium, Consulate, Black and White Standard, Garrick, Gerard Cavalcade, and Craven Plain	35.00	1.75	.75	.35
Capstan, Senior Service, Grey's, Virginia House, Gallahers de Luxe, White Horse, Abdullah Imperial, Preference, Astorias	30.00	1.50	.60	.30
Double Ace, Pirate, Rough Rider, Torch Light, Woodbines, Flask, Releigh, Flag, Three Birds, and Gun Boat	25.00	1.25	.50	.25
MEALS IN ESTABLISHMENT	20.00	1.00	.40	.20

Maximum price of one meal in an establishment — $2.50
COFFEE (One cup approximately 1/4 pint)
Unsweetened without milk — 0.05
Sweetened with milk — 0.10
Sweetened without milk — 0.10

In June 1946, the government started its first People's Restaurant. It was at Tiong Bahru and provided meals to the public for 35 cents each.[72] Additional outlets were opened in Telok Ayer and Outram Road by the end of the year. Six central kitchens, known as the People's Kitchens, provided 8,900 meals every day to the People's Restaurants.[73] However, the main clientele of the People's Restaurants turned out to be labourers who could still afford a 35-cent meal because they were earning wages. In December 1946, the Welfare Department would open its first 'Family Restaurant' to cater to members of poor families who did not earn wages – each meal cost only eight cents. The Welfare Department kept prices affordable by purchasing surplus army food at low prices. The first Family Restaurant opened within the Maxwell Road market that month, supplying 2,500 meals a day.[74]

By January 1947, the Welfare Department's restaurants were providing 10-cent breakfasts,[75] and the People's Kitchens sold bulk meals directly to the public. At the same time, the government created Child Feeding Centres for the very young across the island, the first of which was set up next to the Family Restaurant.[76] At this point, the island experienced a general decline in food prices. Accordingly, the People's Restaurant's 35-cent meal was reduced to 30 cents, while the People's Kitchen reduced the price of its bulk meals from 30 cents to 28 cents.[77] The Singapore government's efforts to provide workers and their families with low-cost meals had effectively checked the black market in foodstuffs. Of course, there were still supply problems. As a case in point, soon after the BMA handed control over to the Malayan Union and Singapore, rice rations were reduced. On 17 August 1946, Singapore's rice rations were lowered again to just 2.6 ounces per adult per week, while the Union's rations fell to 1.6 ounces. This led to an outcry, with some exclaiming that their rations were 'Not enough even for a fowl!'[78] The Malayan Union increased the price of rationed rice and reduced flour rations in January 1947.[79]

Price and rationing controls became important tools in the efforts to mitigate the effects of inflation and general shortages. However, the BMA could not possibly keep prices unrealistically low for an extended period, nor could it promise a constantly adequate supply of essentials. In the open market, prices remained higher than the average wage-earner could afford. Consequently, even when price controls were in place, the prices of essentials would be adjusted periodically to better reflect market prices. Similarly, the amount disbursed as rations would also be adjusted from time to time in response to the general supply situation on the island. In the absence of supply buffers, prices became very volatile, adjusting sharply with fluctuations in local supply. For instance, the reduction of rice rations in 1946, and the concurrent rise in open market prices, were partly due to the

Mobile rationing unit
at Nee Soon.

fact that a vessel from Brazil carrying 9,000 tons of rice to Singapore had unexpectedly offloaded half its cargo at Ceylon, where there was a food crisis.[80] On the other hand, in July 1949, when sugar supplies from Taiwan reached Singapore, the price of sugar fell.[81]

Ultimately, runaway inflation could only be tamed if there were lasting improvements to the supply situation. Although Malaya was still Singapore's largest supplier of fruits and vegetables going into 1948, fresh food had to

be imported from Australia and China – countries that were not part of the US dollar bloc – in order for food prices to stabilise and moderate.[82] In early 1948,

Farming in Singapore in the 1950s.

the price of 'free' rice (that is, rice that could be bought legally on the open market rather than that sold under ration restrictions), as well as fruits and vegetables, fell by 50 per cent.[83] However, with the outbreak of the Malayan Emergency, food supplies were once again disrupted. Up till that point, around 400,000 Chinese squatters in Malaya had been the primary suppliers of vegetables to Singapore.[84] They produced more than 14 million Malayan dollars' worth of produce annually that was shipped to Singapore.[85] However, the authorities became concerned that these farmers were supporting communist insurgents in Malaya, and therefore took steps to relocate them away from rural areas. This affected work on the farms, and no new vegetables were planted. In this context, food imports from Australia had become even more important. At the same time, the people of Singapore began growing their own vegetables again – the 'Grow More Food' movement had returned (see p. 156). By 1949, the island had 15,300 acres of land under vegetable cultivation.[86] Most of this fresh food could be sold on the open market.

As a result of the efforts to reduce transport bottlenecks and diversify food sources, the supply situation began to improve significantly, stemming the rapid increases in food inflation seen in the immediate post-war years. In 1949, it was observed that the price of free rice, at 38 cents per *kati*, had fallen to levels almost on par with the price of rationed rice, which was 30 cents per *kati*. Some people found it no longer necessary to use their ration cards.[87]

Currency and import controls

The BMA's efforts were directed at securing the territories and restoring law and order. Consequently, the task of restoring the post-war economy mainly fell to the civilian governments of Singapore and the Malayan Union. Measures to restore trade and commerce only started after basic needs of the population had been met, such as circulating new Malayan dollars and distributing food.

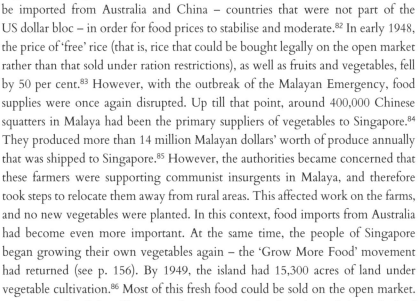

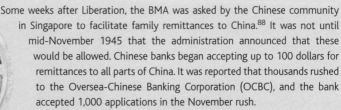

Restoring remittances

Some weeks after Liberation, the BMA was asked by the Chinese community in Singapore to facilitate family remittances to China.[88] It was not until mid-November 1945 that the administration announced that these would be allowed. Chinese banks began accepting up to 100 dollars for remittances to all parts of China. It was reported that thousands rushed to the Oversea-Chinese Banking Corporation (OCBC), and the bank accepted 1,000 applications in the November rush.

However, the authorities then made it clear that approval from London was required before remittance services could properly resume, and the money already collected by OCBC was not sent out.[89] Approval finally came in the following January for the funds collected by OCBC to be forwarded, but no new remittances could be collected until the government had ensured that exchange control regulations were being followed.[90] It took two months for official clearance to be given, and then the maximum each family could send per month was fixed at 45 dollars.[91]

The OCBC logo still graces the façade of a former branch in South Bridge Road.

However, these efforts would take place within the broader financial context confronting Britain and the Empire, just as had been the case before World War II. Britain had a crippling war debt amounting to more than 200 per cent of its GDP, and this had to be paid in US dollars. At the same time, the US had become a global industrial powerhouse, and was exporting many of the items needed for rebuilding. In the Bretton Woods world, the US dollar had become an important reserve currency used in international transactions. With the pound sterling made fully convertible for 'current account' purposes after the war,[92] many nations holding sterling balances in Britain started to exchange pounds for US dollars to buy goods from America or to service debt owed to others. This outflow significantly reduced Britain's own US dollar reserves, which it needed to repay its large war debts. To conserve its foreign exchange resources, Britain continued its wartime currency controls domestically and in its colonies and maintained restrictions on the movement and transfer of sterling.[93] It created a sterling-based economic area comprising itself, its colonies and its dominions. Within this 'Sterling Area', the various territories could trade and acquire strategic resources using sterling or currencies pegged to it, rather than US dollars. It was with this consideration in mind that the BMA had declared in September 1945 that the 'new' Malayan dollar it was introducing would be backed by sterling.[94] With one stroke, Singapore and Malaya were inducted into the Sterling Area.[95]

In Singapore, the BMA required that permission be sought for the import and export of any currency, whether local or foreign; offenders risked imprisonment if they broke these rules.[96] The limits applied to both travellers who needed some foreign currency and people seeking to remit monies to families overseas.

This necessitated tightening the definition of 'foreign currency'. It was ultimately determined that Sterling Area currencies should not be considered 'foreign', while those that were (or had been) legal-tender outside Malaya would be 'foreign'.[97] The new ordinance that was passed placed further restrictions on the purchase, loan and sale of foreign currencies and gold, including securities. Restrictions on imports were tightened to conserve foreign exchange.[98] Those who were still holding foreign currencies were required to sell them to banks. It also became harder to send money from sterling to non-sterling areas.[99]

Import controls were becoming the instrument of choice to prevent the 'leakage' of US dollars from the Sterling Area. In early 1946, when a merchant used US dollars to buy American goods in Singapore, he was arrested and charged.[100] In 1947, as Britain's economic crisis at home worsened, the Singapore government imposed an absolute ban on the import of US goods.[101] Singapore and Malaya were subjected to an austerity plan to control imports of luxury goods.[102] To prevent merchants from flouting the existing ban, the Singapore and Malayan Union governments issued the Prohibition of Imports Order specifically to halt the importation of luxury goods from the broader

BANNED GOODS

These goods are banned by the new "import austerity" measure:
Chemicals: Acetic Acid, Boric Acid and Superloid (Ammonium Alginate).
Constructional Materials: Galvanised Iron Sheets and Zinc and Steel (constructional)
Hardware: Boat Spikes (galvanised), Bolts and nuts, hinges, iron hoop and nails, panel pins. Tinman's rivets, saws, galvanised staples, copper and shoe tacks.
Machinery and Motors: Accounting machines, adding machines, calculating machines, cash registers, dictaphone equipment, outboard motors, refrigerators, tractors and welding equipment (electric).
Miscellaneous: Asphalt, cork and cork manufactures, crown cork, electrodes, hog casings, lamps including kerosene and Miners' carbide, pencils, slate, plywood, resin (synthetic), Manila rope, rubber colours, scythe handles, sharpening stones, port and sherry.
Glass bottles, milk bottles, cinema equipment and film, jewellers' files and saws, powered milk, paints, photographic equipment, newsprint—in reels and in sheets.

'Banned goods',
Malaya Tribune,
13 July 1949.

Guilders and the junk trade

The Chinese merchants running the junks that carried food from the East Indies islands could circumvent currency controls because they used old Dutch guilders. These had become the sole legal-tender in Java following the return of the Dutch to the East Indies after Japan's surrender. A means of exchange between guilders and Malayan dollars was possible,[103] and in early 1946, the exchange rate in Singapore was 0.60 Malayan dollars to a guilder.[104]

Immediately after the war, when many Chinese fled the Indies because of hostilities between Indonesian nationalists and the returning Dutch, they deemed the guilders worthless and dumped most of their holdings of the currency. When the Dutch authorities were regaining control over territories in the East Indies archipelago in 1947, they lifted an earlier ban on ships navigating the waters around Java and Sumatra. All junk traders plying the area were required to pay export duties in guilders. Overnight, the value of Dutch guilders in Singapore soared,[105] and the currency became highly sought after in the Singapore black market.[106] By 1948, rubber importers were buying up guilders to pay for rubber shipments from Borneo.[107] After the Netherlands recognised Indonesian independence in 1949, guilders held by local Chinese merchants soon became 'junk'.

Rubber processing, still an important industry in 1952.

US dollar area and reiterated the official position that locals had to import from within the Sterling Area.[108] Some European firms in Singapore reportedly resorted to barter trade to obtain the items they wanted from US-dollar economies such as the Philippines.[109] Controls were eased slightly in 1949 when both governments jointly published an Import Guide specifying whether the importation of particular US goods was permitted.[110] However, the British authorities in London took things one step further by imposing additional controls to stabilise the Sterling Area currencies. Without consulting the local governments or legislatures, London unilaterally excluded from the list a large number of luxury consumer items such as textiles, photographic films and refrigerators. Purchase permits were only granted for machinery, generators, motors, pumps, construction steel, linseed oil, lubricating oil, and scientific instruments.[111]

Simply put, the immediate post-war economic recovery strategy for Singapore-Malaya was to spend sterling and earn US dollars. While commercial imports were only permitted from early November 1945,[112] efforts to revive industries that earned foreign exchange only began in earnest from early 1946, when the rehabilitation of tin mining and rubber industries commenced.[113] As tin and rubber were strategic commodities necessary for rebuilding, global demand for them was very strong in the post-war years. These two industries not only generated employment and supported economic recovery, but also earned significant foreign exchange.[114] By late 1947, Singapore's economy was beginning to show signs of recovery, and in the following year its production of processed rubber reached an all-time high. In 1949, the export industries as a whole received an unexpected boost: Britain devalued the pound against the US dollar by 30 per cent. The Malayan dollar only strengthened marginally against the pound; it therefore weakened significantly against the US dollar, and the territory's exports, including tin and rubber, became cheaper for non-sterling countries. The tin and rubber industries went on to post record exports, earning significant amounts of US dollars in the process. The Korean War boosted demand for the two commodities even further, bringing a mini-economic boom to Singapore in 1951.[115] Aik Hoe & Company Ltd, the largest rubber firm in Singapore in the post-war period, became one of the largest in the world,[116] large enough to survive an 850,000 Malayan dollar fine for flouting currency control laws in a trade deal worth US$3.7 million.[117]

The US dollars generated by the colonial economies would help to offset the cost of dollar imports, but any surplus could not be retained locally to finance rebuilding and rehabilitation efforts. All Britain's colonies – including Singapore and the Malayan Union – were required to contribute surplus dollars to the 'empire pool'. The sums could be substantial: in the first half of 1950, Malaya's exports of tin and rubber, mainly to the United States, netted the Union 362 million Malayan dollars, or US$121 million. Since Malaya only paid out US$20 million for imports from US dollar areas, it had earned an additional US$101 million for the Empire. When the US approved an extension of the Lend-Lease Agreement and offered Britain a further US$3.8 billion via the Anglo-American Loan Agreement in mid-1946, the civilian governments of Singapore and the Union hoped that exchange controls would be lifted and that they would be able to retain more of the surplus US dollars for their own needs, such as the acquisition of rehabilitation goods.[118] However, Britain did not accede to their request, and the loan turned out not to be enough, as evidenced by the forced devaluation of the pound just a few years later.

The 1949 devaluation

In September 1949, Britain shocked the world by devaluing the pound sterling by 30 per cent. In 1948, the country found its gold and US dollar reserves dwindling, and by the first half of 1949, they were nearly exhausted. The Chancellor of the Exchequer, Sir Stafford Cripps, informed the British Parliament that the crisis had been 'in great part due to a reduction in the income of the whole Sterling Area from sales to North America'. US dollars were required for trading with the United States, but as the Empire as a whole was earning fewer dollars than it was using, Britain and other Sterling Area territories had to sell their gold and silver reserves to acquire the US dollars needed for imports. In addition, Britain also needed US dollars to repay its war loans. With hindsight, it is clear that Britain had pegged the pound sterling to the US dollar at an excessively strong exchange rate. The pound had become overvalued given the state of Britain's economy and international debt obligations. By 1949, the drain on the reserves was unsustainable. Devaluation was the only option.[119]

The import and exchange controls meant that post-war rebuilding in Singapore and the Malayan Union was more expensive than it should have been.[120] Given the preferential trade arrangements within the Sterling Area, Singapore and the Malayan Union had to contend with inflated import costs – local businesses could only pick suppliers on the basis that they accepted sterling currencies, and not because they were more trustworthy or their goods were cheaper or of better quality.[121] The shortage of US dollars impeded the reconstruction of the Singapore Harbour at Keppel because the British refused to allow the local government to procure steel outside the Sterling Area.[122] In the end, Britain's US dollar shortage proved to be a serious constraint on its colonies. Nevertheless, having the advantage of possessing two strategic commodities that had driven their economies since the early part of the 20th century, Singapore and the Malayan Union emerged from the post-war economic slump faster than many other British territories.[123]

The Malaya and British Borneo dollar

The Malayan currency board reconstituted in April 1946 was a new entity, and not simply the prewar currency board – which involved a partnership between the Malay States and the Straits Settlements – restored. In the 1946 board, there was no representation from the defunct Straits Settlements. Instead, Singapore stood alone in the arrangement vis-à-vis the Malay States. Correspondingly, Singapore's share of the resources of the board was reduced. However, even the 1946 arrangement did not remain the status quo. The composition of the currency board evolved alongside the growing tide of independence movements. After World War II, Britain's colonies began pursuing constitutional change and the right to self-determination. India gained independence in 1947, Burma and Ceylon (today's Myanmar and Sri Lanka) in 1948. In the 1950s, British Southeast Asia comprised just the Federation of Malaya, Singapore, Brunei, North Borneo and Sarawak.

As early as January 1947, British North Borneo (Sabah) joined currency talks in Singapore to decide if it wanted to join the Malayan currency board.[124] Sarawak and Brunei also discussed the prospect of membership. The Malaya, British Borneo Currency Agreement was signed in 1950 between 'the governments of the Federation of Malaya, the colonies of Singapore, Sarawak and North Borneo and the government of the state of Brunei'. This agreement was basically a geographical extension of the 1938 currency agreement that had created the Malayan dollar to include Brunei, North Borneo and Sarawak. With new members participating in the currency board, the agreement devised a new formula for distributing its profits: the Federation of Malaya would receive 65 per cent, Singapore 29 per cent, Sarawak 3.5 per cent, North Borneo 2 per cent, and Brunei 0.75 per cent.[125] The same proportions would apply when determining each territory's share of the board's assets and liabilities. The board was composed of the financial secretaries of Singapore and the Federation, an officer appointed jointly by Sarawak, North Borneo and Brunei, and two others appointed by all territories.[126] The financial secretary of the government of Singapore would chair the board. The new currency would be the Malaya and British Borneo dollar.

The newly constituted currency board was formally established on 1 January 1952 as the Board of Commissioners of Currency, Malaya and British Borneo.[127] However, to convey a sense of continuity and stability, much was kept the same. The new dollar would have the same value as the old dollar. Singapore remained the site of the board's headquarters.[128] To maintain a high level of confidence in the new currency, the British authorities backed it by more than 100 per cent of assets, just as the Malayan dollar had enjoyed 110 per cent backing in sterling-denominated assets.[129] As it would take time to design and produce the new Malaya and British Borneo dollar notes and coins, it was decided that the old ones issued by the currency boards of the Straits Settlements and for Malaya would remain legal-tender until the new currency was released in 1954.[130] Brunei had been using the Straits Settlements and Malayan dollars as legal-tender before the agreement, even though it had no part in the currency board. While Sarawak and North Borneo did have their own currencies, the Malayan dollar was also used as a circulation currency. With the new agreement in place, the Malayan dollar would be made legal-tender in the two territories until the new common currency was issued.[131] It was decided that rather than requiring people to queue and exchange old notes for new, the Malaya and British Borneo dollars would be circulated as replacements for damaged Malayan dollar notes returned by the banks to the board.[132] It was envisaged that this would reduce disruptions as much as possible and give the public time to get used to a new currency.[133]

In January 1952, the Board of Commissioners of Currency, Malaya and British Borneo took over the responsibility of issuing a single currency for its member territories.[134] A month later, it met to discuss plans and designs for the new notes and coins.[135] In January 1953, the first concrete step towards changing the currency was taken when the Board of Commissioners of Currency declared that all coins minted and circulated in 1948 and before would no longer be legal-tender. Although, from 1950 on, the former currency board had printed ten-cent notes in response to a severe shortage of subsidiary currency, it would no longer do so.[136]

The new Malaya and British Borneo dollar notes were printed in the United Kingdom. Following the death of King George VI, Queen Elizabeth II ascended to the throne in 1952, and her portrait would be featured on the new notes. Consequently, the notes became known as the 'Queen's notes', and they would gradually displace the old Malayan dollar 'George's notes'. Given the nature of the rollout, George's notes remained in circulation even as the Queen's notes were gradually being issued.

Currency issued by the Board of Commissioners of Currency, Malaya and British Borneo, bearing the portrait of Queen Elizabeth II

1 dollar

5 dollars

10 dollars

50 dollars

100 dollars

1000 dollars

1 cent

5 cents

10 cents

20 cents

50 cents

The Malaya and British Borneo dollar was the last British currency to be issued in what remained of British Southeast Asia. The Queen's notes, however, were not simply physical manifestations of the last vestiges of Empire. Given the nature of the currency board and the Malaya and British Borneo dollar's peg to the pound sterling, the currency preserved a strong, direct link to Britain through the board's reserve and currency policies. For instance, the Currency Agreement of 1950 stipulated that the Currency Fund backing the new notes and coins had to be invested in British or British Empire securities other than those of the seven participating governments.[137] Such an asset composition was logical as long as the Malaya and British Borneo dollar was pegged to the pound sterling and not to any other currency such as the US dollar, but it did mean that the member territories would hold fewer US dollars – an increasingly important reserve currency – than they might desire in their reserves. Even though the United Kingdom eased up on the policy in 1954, it continued to exert pressure on its colonies not to diversify out of sterling. The 1950 Agreement was the main factor determining the currency allocation of Singapore and the Federation's reserves all the way through to the 1960s.

Cost of recovery and development

When the British military handed over administration to the civilian governments of the Malayan Union and Singapore in April 1946, the two governments assumed responsibility for their respective jurisdictions, making territory-wide policies in the areas of excise and customs, education and healthcare, while being in charge of enforcing law and order, facilitating trade and commerce, and overseeing transport and communications infrastructure. With the handover, the two governments had sight of the true status of their finances: against the pressing need to underwrite the rebuilding and rehabilitation of critical infrastructure, the situation was dire. Right from the outset, the cost of operating government and building for recovery was daunting as the economies were not functioning fully, and revenues and incomes were very low. Consequently, the reserves built up in the pre-war years risked being depleted.

The Malayan Union had inherited the Federated Malay States' reserves of £24 million that had been deposited in London – this would have been equivalent to around 206 million Malayan dollars at the exchange rate of £7 per 60 dollars. They had 20 million dollars in accrued interest earned during the war from their share in the Malayan Dollar Currency Guarantee Fund. The Union's projected expenditure for 1946 was 225 million dollars. However, revenues would only come to 75 million dollars. Covering the 150 million dollars would have considerably eroded the reserves.[138] As the year progressed, the Union government's estimate of its deficit fell to the still considerable sum of around 121 million dollars. To fund this, it drew on a significant portion of its reserves, leaving just 13 million dollars by the end of 1946. The government borrowed a further 32 million dollars to cover contingencies.[139]

The Singapore government was likewise in a bind in 1946. To be sure, the revenue sources from before the war were still yielding funds, including the excise taxes and Singapore's share of the income earned on the Opium Revenue Replacement Fund. On paper, the situation appeared manageable; the deficit was expected to be around 10 million Malayan dollars, and Singapore's share of the profit of the Currency Surplus Fund after the war would be sufficient to meet this. At the end of the year, the reported shortfall in the government's finances was small, at only 300,000 dollars.[140]

However, even before the year was out, the governor of Singapore warned that there was a need to raise taxes.[141] The initial expenditure plans for 1946 covered only nine months, as the government had only taken over in April. He made it clear that recurrent expenditures for the full calendar year would certainly be higher. He emphasised that the windfall profit from the currency fund would not be repeated in 1947. Though it was not known at the time, Singapore would fail to secure the 10-million-dollar profit from the Currency Surplus Fund to cover its shortfall due to 'accounting difficulties'.[142] More crucially, as the government went about the business of administration, it realised it would incur significant outlays as a result of the food subsidies under the rationing scheme. These had not been planned for when the initial budget figures were announced, as the government had no way of knowing the severity of the situation when it first came into power. Taking all these circumstances into account, it was later revealed that

Finances of the City Council of Singapore

While the colonial government was responsible for the island as a whole, the Municipal Commission was the main body responsible for the maintenance and development of the Singapore township. In 1951, the town centre was given the status 'City of Singapore', and responsibility for it came under the Municipal Commission, now renamed the 'City Council'.[143] The Municipal Building was renamed 'City Hall'. The Council now had to undertake the tremendous task of rehabilitating a war-damaged township, especially water, gas and electrical infrastructure and services. It required more funds than its revenue streams could provide.

The main sources of municipal revenues were electricity and gas tariffs and assessment rates (property taxes). In 1950, collections from electricity and gas provided the City Council 24 million Malayan dollars for its 1951 budget, and rates brought in another 20 million dollars.[144] Although revenues increased throughout the next few years, expenditure needs rose more, and the council had to borrow money to meet its budget commitments.[145] While the council had its own reserves, in the face of repeated deficits and increased borrowing, the drains on these intensified. By 1957, the council had only around 20 million dollars left in its reserves, less than a fifth of its annual budget.[146]

the true state of the 'working deficit' in 1946 was around 12 million dollars. Even this estimate excluded expenditures on rehabilitation, which was debited from the loan account; from as early as June 1946, the Singapore government had borrowed 25 million dollars through bonds to fund such spending. As the Acting Financial Secretary observed in August 1947, 'The budget deficit as shown in the printed estimates for 1946 gives a very false impression.'[147]

In one aspect, however, Singapore differed slightly from the Malayan Union. Given the severity of its deficit, the Union not only borrowed money but raided the principal in its reserve funds, though it did not take the entire sum. Singapore's deficit was smaller, and given the substantial sums it had in reserve, the government could choose to tap on income and profits earned on the reserve funds. While it did draw on its current account deposits, it did not eat into the book value of the underlying investments excessively. Remaining shortfalls were covered by borrowing. Reflecting on these financing decisions, the Acting Financial Secretary for the Singapore government commented that 'Some part of our reserves are preserved at the cost of paying interest on that overdraft.'[148]

Constitutional developments in the 1950s would see the emergence of a local government with a degree of political mandate and policymaking authority. On 2 April 1955, following elections for the Legislative Assembly, the Labour Front formed a government with David Marshall as the Chief Minister. Although the British colonial authorities retained control over internal security and foreign affairs and were still the final authority in legislative matters, the new local government had its own ministers who oversaw their respective ministries. They took charge of policy areas that had previously been the purview of the colonial government, such as education and healthcare. Singapore had achieved limited local self-government, and was beginning its journey towards full internal self-government, which it would attain in 1959. The responsibility for rehabilitating Singapore as a whole therefore shifted from the colonial government to the local government under Marshall, and later Lim Yew Hock. Within the decade, from 1950 to 1959, the government's expenditure increased almost threefold from 97 million dollars to 275 million. However, revenues did not keep pace, and deficits became the order of the day when the governments were planning their budgets. This forced the governments to adopt measures such as cutting back infrastructure projects or raising tax rates.

Entrance to the Singapore Constitution Exposition, 1959.

The spending needs were urgent and palpable: beyond rehabilitation works, there was a need to enhance the infrastructure of both Singapore Town and the island as a whole. The population was increasing rapidly. The composition of the communities, which before the war were typically made up of sojourning migrants coming to Singapore for employment, had shifted. Now the population was more settled; more people were deciding to put down roots on the island and call it home. At the same time, there was an urgent need to educate youths who had missed out on schooling during the Occupation and who were now making up a large body of over-aged students attending school. This was exacerbated by a post-war baby boom. Consequently, the government had to build more homes and an increasing number of schools. It had to improve living conditions: this would require investment in sanitation, water, electricity, health, and transport infrastructure.

Base ordinance depot workers donate money to the Singapore Anti-Tuberculosis Association (SATA), 1956.

Singapore revenue, expenditure and budget balance, 1949–60[149]
(millions of Malayan dollars and Malaya and British Borneo dollars)

Year	Budget estimates tabled for approval			Revised estimates		
	Revenue	Expenditure	Budget balance	Revenue	Expenditure	Budget balance
1949	103.8	97.2	6.6	–	–	15.4 (actual)
1950	100.3	106.7	-6.4	110.5	104.4	11.7
1951	113.3	126.7	-13.4	152	143.5	8.5
1952	155.3	192.1	-36.8	193.8	157.2	36.0
1953	189.7	204.6	-14.9	209.6	236	-26.4
1954	204.7	236.8	-32.1[a]	below 227	240.0	over 13
1955	208	230	-22	201	199	2
1956	208	231	-22.7	216	231	15.3
1957	217.8	254.7	-36.8	235.7	241[b]	2.0
1958	242	277	-35.0	248	251	-3
1959	243.6	268.5	-24.9	258	257	1 (actual)
1960	269.2	275.3	-6.1	–	–	37

[a] Adjusted to -9.6 million dollars after excluding select items such as revotes.
[b] The adjusted expenditure sum was 232 million dollars.
[c] The actual budget outturn was a surplus of 21 million dollars.

Source: *Straits Times*, 20 October 1948, 20 October 1949, 14 October 1950, 17 October 1951, 7 November 1951, 15 October 1952, 21 October 1953, 13 October 1954, 8 November 1955, 5 November 1956, 5 December 1957, 4 December 1958, 26 November 1959, 30 November 1960.

Just how pressing were these post-war needs? Take education. In 1947, there were more than 160,000 children of primary school age and 80,000 of secondary school age. By 1949, the island's primary schools could still only accommodate 110,000, and the secondary schools 8,000. Unless the situation changed, over the longer term the domiciled population of the island – Singapore's future citizens and labour force – would largely be uneducated or educated only up to primary level. In 1949, the government conceived the 'Ten-Year Education Plan' to build new schools and expand existing ones.[150] It spent 22.2 million dollars on education in 1949, nearly ten times the amount spent in 1948. Having spent so much so early on the plan, the government had to introduce a 'Supplementary Five-Year Education Plan' in 1950 to raise additional funding. By 1956, the annual amount spent on education had increased to 58 million Malaya and British Borneo dollars. Reflecting on the state of affairs in 1960, Dr Goh Keng Swee, by then Minister for Finance in a Singapore with full internal self-government, declared that 'to give every child a place in school and higher education for all those who deserve it', the government might have to foot an annual bill close to 180 million dollars.[151]

A child at school, 1957. Increasing expenditure on education was an urgent priority.

As for housing, most of the population did not own the properties in which they lived. The majority of the population were pre-war migrants who were only now choosing to put down roots in Singapore. In 1954, some 500,000 people, equivalent to half the island's population, were slum-dwellers.[152] Many were living in squatter colonies. Singapore in the 1950s was described as 'a city of striking contrasts' as the colony's housing was at the same time of 'the highest and lowest standards'.[153]

The roots of Singapore's post-war housing crisis could be traced back to the pre-war policy of not building public housing. The colonial authorities at that time did not consider it their responsibility to provide basic needs such as housing for migrants, and this was left largely to the private sector. The Municipal Council did have budget allocations for housing, and the council's infrastructure department, the Singapore Improvement Trust (SIT), constructed living quarters. However, the original objective of the SIT was to provide accommodation for labourers and municipal staff employed by local authorities *within* the municipality. The SIT was not tasked to extend its reach to the rest of Singapore (the Rural Board had responsibility for those areas). Nor did it aim to provide mass housing, even though some housing developments were reserved for the resettlement of residents displaced as a result of its urban redevelopment activities in the core town areas. In the immediate post-war period, when the SIT resumed operations, it prioritised its urban improvement works. In reality, these were mostly rehabilitation works, and not the construction of new homes for the increasingly settled population.

The only way to eliminate slums and the dismal conditions of squatter colonies was to create modern urban centres outside and away from the overcrowded Singapore Town. The government's main building project in the mid-1950s was Queenstown, the island's first satellite township[154] – 70,000 people would be resettled in this 'New Town'. In 1953 it was projected that constructing Queenstown would cost 80 million Malaya and British Borneo dollars. The SIT had already been taking loans in increasing amounts,[155] and once the estimates for Queenstown were revealed, it was clear that housing and resettlement efforts would put a serious strain on government finances for years to come.

There were no proper utilities in the rural areas, where few people had access to basic amenities such as clean water. Neither the City Council nor the Rural Board had the finances to remedy the situation. Providing clean water outside the municipal limits was a serious challenge. For instance, in the 1950s, none of the houses in Geylang Serai had piped water, and everyone had to take turns collecting water at standpipes. At the Alsagoff Estate and Geylang Serai, around 40,000 residents shared a total of five standpipes. Government officials at this time noted that the Geylang district resembled the slums of Chinatown. Conditions were so bad that when a fire broke out in the area in 1954, there were no standpipes nearby to supply water to the fire engines.[156] By 1955, there were still fewer than ten standpipes for the entire Geylang district. The provision of clean water and adequate sanitation remained wholly inadequate until the government made progress in relocating slum-dwellers to newly built public housing estates with the necessary amenities.

Left: A slum in Bukit Ho Swee, 1947.

Right: Conditions in 1949: living, sleeping, cooking and ablutions in one room and on the pavement.

David Marshall's Labour Front government found that it could not tackle problems such as the lack of waterpoints in Geylang immediately, no matter how desperate the shortage had been. The People's Action Party (PAP) came into power in 1959 and the following year established the Housing and Development Board (HDB) to handle public housing matters. The new government committed a staggering 210 million Malaya and British Borneo dollars to the construction of 52,000 housing units.[157] However, much more needed to be done. Going into the 1960s, there were still a quarter-of-a-million slum-dwellers within Chinatown alone who needed resettlement.[158] The number of squatters in Geylang Serai would continue to rise through the decade, reaching 100,000 by 1971.[159]

Singapore Improvement Trust flats under construction in the late 1940s.

Travelling bank [160]

In June 1951, the Post Office Savings Bank created 'banks on wheels', and sent these to the rural districts to offer deposits and withdrawals services to villagers who had no access to banking facilities. These were vans converted internally to resemble banking counters. The deployment of the mobile banks was a prelude to Savings Week, officially launched on 2 July 1951 and touted as Singapore's biggest postwar savings campaign to date. The mobile banks visited all the rural districts of the island which had no post office branches. Staff would follow the vans, encouraging people to save with the bank. It pioneered the use of savings stamps and savings cards, thousands of which were printed for schoolchildren to encourage them to save small amounts. These would eventually become very popular with children who bought ten-cent postage stamps to paste onto the stamp cards. When they had filled their cards with 20 stamps, the children would hand their cards to the school, and these would

Pupils at the Bukit Panjang Government School open accounts with the mobile Post Office Savings Bank.

then be sent to the nearest bank branch where the value of the stamps pasted on the card would be credited to the children's accounts. Most adults simply opened an account with just a dollar at the mobile bank. Each account had a limit — individuals could deposit up to 4,000 dollars in a calendar year, up to a maximum of 10,000 dollars for the account as a whole.

Economic development; restoring income and reserves

In light of the Singapore government's national development needs, strengthening Singapore's finances was a critical priority. A pre-war attempt to introduce an income tax in 1940 had failed,[161] but as the post-war fiscal situation deteriorated, the government pushed through the Income Tax Ordinance on 4 December 1947 without much consultation with community leaders. The governor gave his assent a week later. Concurrently, the Malayan government rushed through its own Income Tax Bill and gazetted it on 15 December 1947.[162] Although both governments announced that the first year of assessment for the payment of income tax would begin on 1 January 1948,[163] Singapore's actual tax assessment did not begin until November that year. All in, about 40,000 individual tax returns and 1,000 corporate returns were received in Singapore, yielding income tax receipts of 33.2 million Malayan dollars.

This was a useful start to putting Singapore on a firmer fiscal footing, but it would not be enough. Public expenditure accelerated in the 1950s. Although the government turned to borrowing to cover the deficits, it could not do so without limit as interest had to be paid on the bonds it issued. The reserves of the currency board were finite, and the amounts available to the authorities to draw on proved inadequate. For instance, by the end of 1949, the Currency Fund had a surplus of 6.2 million dollars, of which Singapore's share was only a quarter.[164] This was equivalent to slightly over one per cent of the government's revenues for the year, a veritable drop in the pond. Likewise, profit and income earned from the Opium Revenue Replacement Reserve Fund was negligible when compared to government expenditure. Critically, going forward, there would be a limit to how

A sign guides passers-by to a branch of the Post Office Savings Bank, as part of a campaign to encourage saving.

The cost of the Emergency

Communist activity during the Malayan Emergency: A train is ambushed by communist guerrillas, and a bus is set on fire.

Dealing with the Emergency put the financial resources of Malaya under tremendous strain. While rubber prices boomed, this was no issue; but when they slumped, national deficits could be sizeable. Towards the end of 1953, Malaya was thrown into financial crisis. Rubber prices fell as the Korean War ended. The deficit in 1953 was 222.5 million Malaya and British Borneo dollars, and the projected expenditure on Emergency-related matters *alone* for the next year was 200 million dollars.[165]

Brunei was first to respond to the Federation's plight, offering a 40 million-dollar loan. Singapore followed with an outright donation of 5 million dollars, which eventually expanded into a 10-year interest-free 30 million-dollar loan. The United Kingdom contributed 51 million dollars to fund the Malayan government's fight against terrorism.[166] Over the next two years, the Federation's expenditure on account of the Emergency remained high, ranging between 134 million and 168 million dollars.

The situation was clearly not sustainable, and financial considerations, among others, drove the Federation to accelerate its push for independence, as this would deprive the Malayan Communist Party of the political justification for the uprising. Chin Peng, the Party's leader, had already declared that his forces would cease hostilities if Malaya gained independence and controlled its own internal defences and security policy.[167]

much the reserves could be tapped before doubts would be raised over the backing of Singapore and Malaya's currency. As the Federation of Malaya achieved independence and Singapore gained full internal self-government within the decade, ensuring the continued stability of the Malaya and British Borneo dollar would become a matter of credibility for both the new nations.

It was clear to the governments of the Federation and Singapore that they needed to find more stable sources of revenue. The Korean War (1950–1953) had had a positive effect on the finances of both governments while it lasted. The Western Allies (United Nations) forces used the docks of Singapore to service and repair their naval ships. Their troops came ashore, and generated consumption-related revenues. In addition, strategic commodities such as tin and rubber saw a surge in prices during times of conflict. Tax revenues and duties on the sale of rubber abroad picked up as demand and prices rose sharply during the war. For instance, when US demand for rubber surged towards the end of 1954 and Soviet demand suddenly picked up in 1955, the price of rubber soared, turning the Federation's projected budget deficit of 148 million dollars for the year into a 26 million-dollar surplus.[168] However, receipts slumped when the conflict ended and rubber prices fell.

In retrospect, while rubber and tin remained critical to the Malayan economy in the 1950s, the extreme swings in rubber prices, in particular, resulted in a degree of instability in the Malayan government's revenues. But at least the Federation had natural resources that could generate regular income streams, even if these were volatile. By contrast, Singapore had no natural resources that it could monetise year after year. A projected deficit had turned into a surplus in 1952 when the government suspended some development projects. Meanwhile the Singapore government experienced a windfall in 1958 when it transferred Christmas Island to Australia for 20 million Malaya and British Borneo dollars, and so alleviated the extent of the deficit. However, it clearly could not keep postponing needed infrastructure projects, nor could it continuously sell land to top up revenues.[169] These realities were not lost to the World Bank's International Bank Mission that visited Singapore and the Federation in 1954. In its 1955 report, the mission recommended that both territories raise personal income and company taxes.[170]

Still more than full backing

The Korean War-induced boom in Malaya and Singapore was reflected in an increased supply of currency in circulation. Nevertheless, the currency board had more than enough assets to accommodate this: at the end of December 1953, it had 765 million Malaya and British Borneo dollars' worth of notes and coins in circulation and 810 million held in reserves, equivalent to a backing of 106 per cent.[171] This was still well above the 100 per cent backing requirement, and the stability of the local currency was not in doubt. However, other questions were raised: did the currency require such a high level of backing? Would the excess funds in the board's reserves be better deployed for badly needed infrastructure development? The British government in London was aware that its colonies were confronting this issue, and that many of them needed to maximise fiscal resources as they advanced towards self-government or independence.

In early December 1954, Britain declared that its 'Crown Colonies and Protectorates' were no longer required 'to keep a full 100 per cent sterling cover for their notes and coins'. For the Malaya and British Borneo currency board, with holdings in excess of 100 per cent, this was an opportunity for the governments to spend more out of their reserves.[172] However Singapore and the Federation decided not to risk reducing the asset backing of the dollar at this stage,[173] given its importance in underpinning confidence in the currency.

It was in this context that the government in Singapore sought to adjust its tax framework so as to better balance its budget and build up its reserves. However, its hands were tied to an extent because the Tax Department established to collect income taxes operated on a pan-Malayan basis. Both the Federation and Singapore governments would collect income taxes from those of each other's citizens who were residing in their territories. Singapore would transfer to the Federation taxes collected from the Malaya's citizens and businesses in Singapore, and vice versa. The Singapore government's net income tax collection in 1956 was 70.4 million dollars, after deducting the 11.7 million that was transferred to the Federation.[174]

The strain of falling revenues and increasing deficits soon came to a head. In 1956-7, Singapore was expecting continued large deficits in excess of 20 million dollars. The Federation's fiscal situation was more dire: the budget deficit of 90 million dollars in 1956 was projected to rise to an estimated 111 million dollars in the following year. Without remedial measures, it was anticipated that Malaya would have to cover two years of revenue shortfall by drawing more than 200 million dollars from its reserves, leaving it with only 170 million dollars by the end of 1957.[175] Consequently, both the Federation and Singapore governments began independently exploring changes to their income tax legislation. To be sure, the governments realised that the people of both territories, especially those who earned income from both sides of the Causeway, would be inconvenienced by having separate tax laws and regulations. There were also concerns that taxation policies would be used by either government as economic tools to implement protectionist policies.[176] However, both governments ultimately placed more weight on fiscal flexibility, including the ability to shore up their own finances. By mid-1957, it had become clear that Singapore and the Federation were headed for 'tax separation'. Preparation for splitting the joint tax department began.[177] The formal separation was announced in December 1958, and enacted in January 1959.

Singapore exercised its newfound independence in tax policy. It announced that from 1959, the maximum personal income tax rate would be increased to 50 per cent, and the company tax rate raised from 30 per cent to 40 per cent. It also put up the duties on cigarettes and tobacco.[178] The increase on these two items made sense: previous years' budget estimates suggested that they would account for a quarter of revenues.[179] The Federation likewise increased the company tax rate to 40 per cent and raised petroleum duties, but it did not lift personal income tax rates in line with Singapore. Economic and financial circles in Singapore were surprised that the government had raised income tax rates as much as it did.[180] One banker when interviewed reckoned that as company tax

Office mechanization in the pre-digital age.

rates remained the same across the two territories, the higher rates 'would not unduly affect trade and commerce'; however, given the lower personal income tax rates in Malaya, investors 'could be expected to choose the Federation' over Singapore.

A cheque-writing machine, designed to combat fraud.

The Singapore government also sought to reduce expenditure. As early as 1953, the post-war government had dabbled with an 'austerity budget',[181] but this meant delayed rehabilitation works and infrastructure development. Government staffing and wages were another prime area for trimming; the government saw a perfect opportunity to reduce long-term staff costs by having locals replace British expatriates in the civil service.[182] While compensation for repatriation would be a heavy cost up-front, it would greatly reduce the government wage bill over the longer run.[183]

The PAP came to power in mid-1959, and, demonstrating the new cabinet's seriousness about trimming unnecessary expenditure, a Cabinet Budget Committee was established, comprising Prime Minister Lee Kuan Yew, Deputy Prime Minister Toh Chin Chye and Minister for Finance Goh Keng Swee. The committee drew up an action plan to reduce public-sector wage costs. The first step was to cut ministers' and parliamentary secretaries' allowances by 600 dollars and 400 dollars respectively.[184] Then, the government slashed the variable allowances of 6,000 civil servants; at the same time, those whose basic pay had been around 600–700 dollars a month had their wages cut by at least 200 dollars a month. Allowances enjoyed by City Council employees were capped at a maximum of 350 dollars, while those for government servants were kept to 400 dollars. As part of the cost-reduction exercise, the government also froze all civil-service vacancies.[185]

A more indirect but enduring means of stabilising government finances was to grow the tax base. In the context of post-war Singapore, this meant encouraging industrial development to provide mass employment and spur economic growth. As more people earned incomes and companies made profits, government revenue would increase. But how would Singapore industrialise, if it lacked indigenous technology and did not have a significant industrial base of its own? The government concluded that Singapore needed an 'injection' of fresh foreign capital.

Britain had led the way in promoting investment in Malaya in 1957, when it exempted British companies from paying taxes in London from profits earned on British territories overseas.[186] Later that year, Sarawak introduced its own bill to grant income tax relief for companies investing in the state, and North Borneo shortly followed suit.[187] In May 1958, the Federation of Malaya also started discussing a bill to grant foreign companies two years of tax relief and the

Minister for Commerce and Industry JM Jumabhoy (centre) visits the Shoemakers' Cooperative Industrial Society, 1957.

Pioneer Industries (Relief from Income Tax) Bill was tabled in its legislature a month later.[188]

It was not until October 1958 that Singapore's Minister for Commerce and Industry, J.M. Jumabhoy, raised in the legislature proposals for support of the island's own 'Pioneer Industries'.[189] As Jumabhoy noted, the Bill, which offered five years of tax relief for new investors, was 'more liberal than those now being offered by the Federation Government'.[190] Some members of the legislature demurred, hoping to work with the Federation instead of competing with it for investments and economic growth. But the government as a whole seemed to think that attempts at co-operation might flounder, given the earlier failure of Singapore's efforts to gain trade concessions.[191] The Relief from Income Tax Ordinance was eventually passed in January 1959.[192]

Industrialising a nation would take time. Income tax relief was certainly no panacea for the public finances. As the PAP government was confronted with a prospective deficit in 1960, calls soon rang out for Singapore and the Federation to work together for their mutual benefit. Some even called for a merger of the two territories.[193] In September 1960, in an effort to entice industrial players to take up Singapore's 'pioneer status' offer, Minister for Finance Dr Goh Keng Swee added six more industries and four more products to those eligible for tax relief.[194] A month later, four companies, bringing with them an investment capital of 76.5 million dollars, were granted pioneer certificates, creating 630 much-needed new jobs.[195] Singapore was on its way to industrialising. It was

Minister for Finance Dr Goh Keng Swee signs pioneer certificates at the Fullerton Building, 1962; Looking on are EDB chairman Hon Sui Sen, next to Dr Goh, and Dr Albert Winsemius, representing the United Nations.

Ships at the Singapore wharves before the container age.

diversifying its export sector, and government finances were becoming less reliant on the tin and rubber industries.

As colonies within the Sterling Area, Singapore and the Federation of Malaya had complied with Britain's directive to impose exchange controls and so conserve scarce US dollars. In reality, the shortage of dollars was not confined to British Southeast Asia: every other nation in the region needed foreign exchange for its own development needs in the 1950s and was using exchange controls for that reason. The restrictions could affect any potential outflows of foreign exchange. However, since the import and export of goods were linked very directly with the loss and gain of precious foreign currency, exchange controls often created barriers to trade and could appear protectionist in nature. At times, they would invite retaliation.

In 1953, for instance, it was discovered that Thai traders were attempting to pay their Singapore counterparts with ticals instead of sterling. The central bank (the Bank of Siam) had been temporarily unable to supply them with sterling as a result of Thailand's reduced trade earnings.[196] To secure Singapore and Malaya's foreign currency earnings, in mid-1953 the two governments imposed new exchange rules on businesses conducting trade with Thailand. The rules were fiercely resisted by local business communities worried that the restrictions would cripple trade even further. Indeed, even before the measures had been announced, Malaya's trade with Thailand had fallen from 43 million Malaya and British Borneo dollars in March 1953 to 32 million dollars in April. The chairman of the Singapore Chinese Chamber of Commerce argued that anything that interfered in the entrepôt trade was 'bad for the Colony's future'. For Singapore to be effective as an entrepôt, it 'must be untrammelled by regulations of this kind'.

Trade with the region continues at Boat Quay in the 1950s.

Singapore's trade with Indonesia in the early 1950s was also affected by such issues. After World War II, Singapore was operating as an entrepôt and processing hub for Indonesian produce. Following an agreement with the United Kingdom in 1948, Singapore and Indonesia shared all foreign exchange earned from the re-export of goods imported into Singapore from Indonesia. Under the sharing formula, Singapore would take 80 per cent of the foreign currency earned from the value added from processing Indonesia's natural resources into manufactured goods for export. In 1951, Indonesia demanded that the formula be revised to ensure a fairer division of currency earnings. Furthermore, Indonesia claimed that Singapore had mistakenly included certain categories of goods that were not imported from Indonesia, and had also failed to reflect the barter trade between Singapore and areas in Indonesia which had no banks. Consequently, the agreement was revised: Singapore was to get 70 per cent of the foreign exchange earned in trade and only 30 per cent of the value of barter trade. This adjustment earned Indonesia an additional US$2 million annually.[197]

Subsequently, in early 1955, when Indonesia found itself very short of motor vehicles and spare parts, it set aside 20 million rupiahs' worth of foreign currency for the purchase of spare parts.[198] However, the Indonesian government soon realised just how big a strain this placed on its stock of foreign currency. Singapore was identified as a source of relatively affordable second-hand cars that Indonesian buyers were importing, free of taxation, and foreign currency was therefore flowing from Indonesia to Singapore. The Indonesian government slapped import taxes of up to 200 per cent on this business as it considered cars luxury items – the country needed to conserve its foreign exchange for importing essentials.[199]

By 1954, the British government was no longer controlling the colonies so tightly in respect of foreign exchange, and had started relaxing exchange rules on imports for certain territories. However, the Federation government maintained tight exchange controls for Malaya.[200] In that same year, the Singapore government's Imports and Exports Committee recommended continuing controls for another year.[201]

For Singapore, a greater threat to trade was looming as Malaya advanced on the road to becoming an independent nation, upon which it would become 'foreign' to Singapore, which was still a British colony, and tariffs would be imposed on Singapore's exports to Malaya. It appeared for a brief moment that the two territories could co-operate and find a solution to this problem: in 1956, the Chief Minister of the Federation, Tunku Abdul Rahman, suggested that they should work together to their mutual benefit. He went as far as to suggest that Singapore should join the Federation. While the Labour Front government in Singapore feared that the island might lose out from such a union, they feared losing even more if Singapore were to be considered a territory foreign to an independent Federation, deprived of easy access to the Malayan market.[202] Throughout 1957, Singapore pushed hard in negotiations for trade concessions from the Federation, hoping for a partial or complete relaxation of duties on manufactured goods exports, such as soap, biscuits and canned foods.[203] Singapore failed to secure trade concessions with Malaya at this time, and discussion on further cooperation faltered.

Education minister Ong Pang Boon (third from right) and EDB chairman Hon Sui Sen (extreme right) attend the opening of a factory near Havelock Road, 1964.

Moneychangers of Change Alley

Beside banks, one could always turn to moneychangers for exchange needs. In 'old Singapore' people headed to Change Alley for the best rates. The earliest record of the Alley as a place of business dates back to the 1890s, when it was just a thoroughfare between Collyer Quay and Raffles Place. By the 1920s, it had become known for the petty traders who set up a table or simply a groundsheet to sell or barter goods. They included moneychangers, many of whom were Indians.

The Alley was conveniently close to Johnston's Pier. In 1933, the old pier was replaced by Clifford Pier. These piers were the main landing places for people arriving and departing by sea. Small craft would often carry them out to larger vessels moored in the harbour. The moneychangers of Change Alley were well placed to serve the needs of travellers. Most were relocated by the government in the 1990s, many of them into the adjacent building, The Arcade, where they remain today.[204]

Moneylenders of Market Street

A Chettiar moneylender.

Indian moneylenders have an important place in Singapore's financial history. They were the financiers of ordinary folks who had no access to banks. They played that role right up to the late 1950s, when the government passed legislation to regulate their business practices. At that time, there were still about 2,200 Sikh, 200 South Indian and 300 Chettiar moneylenders in Singapore. The Chettiars were the most well-known. In the old days, many could be found along Market Street. Several would operate in a single shophouse, each with his own wooden platform and a seat, inside which he kept records and cashboxes. While they were particularly important to the Indian petty traders known as 'Maricars' or 'Kakas' (Tamil or Malabar Muslims), they also lent to the Chinese and others. In most cases, promissory notes would be used as a commitment to repayment. After World War II, the Indian moneylenders would typically charge an interest rate of 48 per cent for unsecured loans and 36 per cent for secured loans. From September 1959, the government required each moneylender to register with the state and fix interest rates at 18 per cent and 12 per cent for secured and unsecured loans respectively. Moneylenders were also required to have lawyers endorse the loan documents for borrowers who did not speak English. By the end of that year, few of them had registered themselves as a business. Those who did were mainly Chettiars.

Things changed on 1 August 1959, when both governments lifted all restrictions on direct imports from US dollar areas. This was a step closer to freeing up trade and securing economic stability.[205] With a wider variety of goods flowing in, the cost of national development, as well as the cost of living for the general public, eventually went down. Singapore's business community welcomed the move as it was expected to boost the island's entrepôt trade.

The notion that Singapore needed freer trade to secure economic progress was still espoused unreservedly on the island, as it had been since Raffles established a free port on the island (see p. 38). Reflecting on the rapidly growing population and the desperate need for development resources, Sir Ewen Fergusson, a nominated member of the Singapore Legislative Assembly, made a trenchant observation on the challenges confronting the island in 1959: 'The great danger and fear is that the demands will outstrip our natural resources and that we will not be able to preserve even the present standard…. To be able to sustain that same standard of living for a greater number of people each year will be a success, not a failure, but it is a desperate problem as the teeming thousands of the teenage population press their needs on the economy…. But, there are restrictions on what can be done. The complete lack of basic wealth in the shape of fuel, minerals, fertile soil and all the natural accompaniments which could serve a growing and developing country force our endeavours into specialised fields…. Singapore trades or it languishes.'[206] Such thinking continues to shape the island's political economy to this day.

Central Bank conundrum

As the Federation of Malaya advanced towards independent nationhood, the question arose: what kind of monetary authority would be appropriate to its needs? There was a debate as to whether it should have a central bank, create its own currency board, or continue with the existing monetary arrangements.

Chief Minister of Singapore David Marshall (right) departing for London to discuss full internal self-government for Singapore, 1956.

Having attained limited self-government, the people of Singapore were equally vocal in articulating their ideas for the future. When Chief Minister David Marshall was in London with his delegation in 1956 to discuss full internal self-government for Singapore, he expressed support for the creation of a joint central bank for Singapore and the Federation, which shared a common currency. He had previously observed in September 1955 that this was one way to make Singapore a financial centre – the 'London of the East' in his words.[207] Local financiers also expressed support for a central bank.[208]

According to Marshall's conception of a pan-Malayan central bank for the Federation and Singapore, the existing currency partnership with Sarawak, North Borneo and Brunei would be terminated, although these territories would be welcome to join in the central bank if they should so wish. However, the North Borneo government did not support joining a central bank with Malaya. It was prepared to end existing currency ties and print its own notes and coins, should that be necessary.[209]

In June 1956, the governments of the Federation and Singapore released a report prepared by G.M. Watson, deputy chief cashier of the Bank of England, and Sir Sydney Caine, economic advisor to the Singapore government. It 'strongly recommended' the establishment of a joint central bank to 'regulate the currency issue, maintain monetary stability, and influence the money market and credit situation in accordance with government policy'.[210] The report noted that if separate central banks were created for Singapore and the Federation, the currency union would break up, and this could lead to a loss of confidence in the Malaya and British Borneo dollar in the interim. It recommended retaining the present currency area and use of the Malaya and British Borneo dollar. As the populations of both territories were already familiar with the currency, such a course would minimise disruption.

The report proposed creating a joint central bank with an initial seed capital of 25 million Malaya and British Borneo dollars. The Federation and Singapore would put up the funds in the ratio of 3:2 respectively, based on the size of their budgets, trade and banking sectors, and the distribution of physical currency. When the central bank was created and the existing currency board wound up, the surplus assets of the board would then be transferred to the central bank and parked under a General Reserve Fund. Under a joint central bank, it would be vital for the Federation and Singapore to harmonise their financial policies.

Working at the Chung Khiaw Bank, 1960.

Alongside the report, the two governments issued a joint public statement to the effect that they had discussed, and agreed on the desirability of, establishing a central bank together based on an agreement between both sides. However, it was stipulated that no final decision on the 'form and organisation of such a banking system' would be made until the constitutional status of both territories became clearer. Despite the report's recommendations and its favourable reception, by 1958 the initial ardour had cooled. The Federation had meanwhile gained independence as a sovereign nation. There was fervent support for 'Malayanisation', and calls within the Federation to rename the Malaya and British Borneo dollar the 'ringgit'. Bankers and traders in Singapore balked at this, arguing that confidence in the currency lay with the word 'dollar', which had a long history dating back to the Spanish silver dollars of the 19th century and beyond.[211] In addition, the vision of co-operation as articulated by Tunku Abdul Rahman in 1956 had faded, and there was a new sense of competition, as evidenced by Singapore's failure to secure trade concessions in 1957. At the same time, a burgeoning desire for greater flexibility on the fiscal front had led both governments to implement divergent tax policies. And looming in the background was a growing awareness that while the economies of Singapore and the Federation were closely intertwined, they were also extremely different, by virtue of different natural resource endowments and comparative advantages.

A piggy bank – or rather a lion bank – for savers.

Malaya continued with plans for its own central bank. In May 1958, Dato Abdul Razak bin Hussein, the then deputy prime minister of the Federation, announced that the Malayan government would establish a central bank by early the following year. He emphasised that Malaya would remain within the existing currency area. However, the new central bank would eventually issue a new currency to 'reflect [Malaya's] status as an independent sovereign state'.[212] Out of consideration for its partners in the currency area, who would have the opportunity to remain inside a currency union with the Federation, the notes of a new currency would be 'neutral' – bearing neither the Queen's image nor that of the Yang di-Pertuan Agong. Although the prospect of a joint central bank was no longer on the table at this juncture, the Singapore government's economic and financial advisors took the view that it should not proceed with its own central bank. They felt that Singapore's small size meant that such an institution could not perform the functions of a central bank, such as being banker to the government, on a cost-effective basis.

Malaya forged ahead with its preparations, and the Federal Council passed a law paving the way for the creation of a new federal central bank. Bank Negara Tanah Melayu started operations on 26 January 1959.[213] Malaya remained within the Malaya and British Borneo dollar area, and at this early stage there was no discussion of a plan for the Federation to issue a new currency. The currency board operated as normal. However, in acknowledgement of the Federation's independent status, after Bank Negara Tanah Melayu was inaugurated, the design of the Malaya and British Borneo notes sent from Britain did not feature the British monarch. These notes were also circulated in Singapore from 1959 until it began issuing its own currency.

Symbols

When the Board of Currency Commissioners, Malaya and British Borneo issued new notes in 1959, these did not bear the image of Queen Elizabeth II. The design featured patterns based on traditional shapes found in Malayan silver engravings as well as elements of life and places in Malaya. In 1961, the currency board released a ten-dollar note that featured images including a farmer ploughing a rice field. This was followed by a new one-cent coin in 1962 embossed with two krises on one side and the numeral '1' and the word 'cent' in the centre with the inscription 'Malaya and British Borneo 1962' around the edge on the other side. Coins minted in 1961, when Singapore, Sarawak and Sabah were still British colonies, still bore the image of Queen Elizabeth II. (see p. 185) It took some time for these coins to be withdrawn; in 1964 they were still circulating in what had become the Federation of Malaysia.[214]

1 dollar

10 dollars

The Malaya and British Borneo notes issued after Malaya's independence,
featuring local symbols in place of the Queen's portrait.

Old Chinese traditions

There was a time when many Chinese people in Singapore did not trust western financial institutions such as banks or agency houses to help them make payments or remit funds to China. They kept their silver and copper in secure boxes at home or even in mattresses or pillows. One of Singapore's most famous Chinese community leaders, supposedly on the island before Raffles arrived, was Tan Che Sang. He is said to have slept on a tiger skin laid over chests filled with his silver. In the 1930s, many Chinese *amahs*, or domestic helpers, kept their hard-earned cash in their pillow or wrapped in a handkerchief or cloth tied to their waist. These were generally known as money belts. For most *amahs*, the cash in their belts was their entire worldly wealth. Chinese hawkers also liked to keep their money close to them, especially if they were unlicensed. It was not until the 1950s that 'blue-collar' workers started to see the advantage of putting what little wealth they had in banks. However, while some started bank accounts, others simply rented deposit boxes to keep their valuables and cash safe.[215]

Towards Malaysia

In February 1960, the Board of Commissioners of Currency, Malaya and British Borneo convened a meeting with 27 delegates from the six countries and territories in Kuala Lumpur. The delegates agreed to amend the 1952 Currency Agreement, removing the need for the board to defer to Britain in all matters relating to decisions and changes made to the existing currency system.[216] The Federation of Malaya was fully independent by this time, while Singapore and Brunei had attained internal self-government in 1959. Sarawak and North Borneo were also progressing along the path to self-government. The members of the currency board had 'come of age'. Reflecting the changing political status of the members, the 1960 agreement also provided for the first time for every member – the Federation, Singapore, Brunei, Sarawak and North Borneo – to have its own representatives on the board.[217]

Malayan/Malaysian premier Tunku Abdul Rahman.

For Singapore, the agreement meant an erosion in its relative position on the currency board. To be sure, Singapore and the Federation would still hold three votes per representative, while the others would have only one vote. However, whereas Singapore previously held one out of five seats on the board, it now had only one out of seven: the Federation would have two seats, reflecting its 'senior' status as the only independent nation on the board, while Brunei, Sarawak and North Borneo would have one seat each. There would be one independent member. Previously the Singapore representative had been the chairman of the board; under the new agreement, this position would now be taken up by one of the two representatives from the Federation. The board's headquarters would move from Singapore to Kuala Lumpur.[218]

Given the close cooperation between the board's member territories, as well as their long-standing political and economic links, it was reasonable to think that a closer union between them all would one day occur. Indeed, the legislation for Bank Negara Tanah Melayu provided for Singapore and other territories to come within its jurisdiction. Not all the territories' leaders were convinced that the political calculus for such a union made sense. Despite this, on 27 May 1961, at a meeting with foreign correspondents, Malaya's Prime Minister Tunku Abdul Rahman broached plans for a union of the Federation, Singapore, North Borneo, Brunei, and Sarawak. The prospect of being part of this new political entity – a 'Mighty Malaysia' – was welcomed by the Singapore government under Lee Kuan Yew. For several years now, it had grappled with the tensions arising from having to both cooperate and compete with the Federation. All the while, it had felt keenly the vulnerability imparted by the smallness of the Singapore market and the island's lack of natural resources. The failure to secure trade concessions

The Singapore office of Bank Negara Malaysia at Empress Place, 1964. This building formerly housed the currency boards of Malaya.

from Malaya no doubt amplified these concerns. Brunei subsequently pulled out of the Malaysia discussions. The remaining territories faced significant political hurdles in getting their populations to agree to what Singapore would later call 'Merger', but these were eventually overcome. On 16 September 1963, Singapore officially joined with Malaya, Sarawak and North Borneo to form the Federation of Malaysia. For the first time in a century-and-a-half, the island was fully free from colonial rule, albeit still not fully independent.

The Malaya and British Borneo dollar remained the currency of Malaysia, but a new institution had taken up residence in the Empress Place building that had formerly housed the headquarters of many generations of currency boards: the Singapore branch of the Malaysian central bank, now known as Bank Negara Malaysia.[219] The dual existence of both the Board of Currency Commissioners and Bank Negara Malaysia would not continue for long: there was a provision in the agreement to allow any government to lodge a 'Notice of Replacement' and withdraw from the currency board at 18 months' notice.[220] When the Federation of Malaya gained independence in 1957, it was already thinking of issuing its own currency eventually, though this had been delayed for a time by the formation of Malaysia. Now that the work of political union had been completed, and all the component territories were fully independent of British rule, the desire to issue a new, local currency grew stronger. Moving into the 1960s, the Singapore and Federal governments would intensify their efforts to make a currency union with a new currency issued by Bank Negara Malaysia a reality.

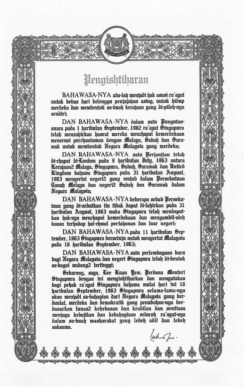

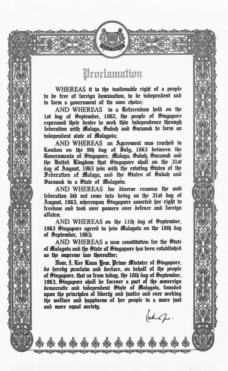

The proclamation of Singapore's merger with Malaysia, signed by
Prime Minister Lee Kuan Yew: in Malay, English, Tamil and Chinese.

In retrospect

Following World War II, Singapore was enmeshed in a new international monetary system under Bretton Woods, with the local currency, the Malayan dollar, pegged to the pound sterling, which was fixed to the US dollar and thence to the price of gold. In the post-war world, Singapore's journey towards a full fiat currency was near-complete.

The events of the 1950s shaped the Singapore government's thinking about fiscal deficits and reserves. Having seen the British government and the Singapore Labour Front government grapple with the challenges of financing deficits in potentially unsustainable ways – issuing debt, selling land, or dipping into the reserves, the PAP government made it clear that it would pay for necessary government spending *and* reduce the deficit. It would control debt issuance, raise taxes where needed, seek to cut unnecessary and ineffective expenditure, and work doubly hard to grow the tax base by industrialising the economy and lifting employment. And it would seek to rebuild its reserves where possible. Fiscal prudence would be the hallmark of the Singapore government in the decades to come.

Even as Singapore became a part of Malaysia, there was a growing sense among the public and within the leadership that the island would only ever be a junior partner in any co-operative endeavour with Malaya. The fact that it had attained independence from Britain only by entering political union with Malaya underscored that fear. Singapore was 'too small' – too small to survive politically and economically apart from Malaya; too small to confront geopolitical and economic shocks by itself; too small to have its own central bank, and by extension its own currency.

Singapore would surprise the world – and perhaps itself – in each of these areas, as the next chapter will show.

NEW NATION, NEW CURRENCY
(1965–1969)

In 1965, Singapore left the Federation of Malaysia, amid economic uncertainty.
Nevertheless, both countries continued working towards a common currency.
This involved tense negotiations, and concerns over the ownership of the reserves
ultimately led to the breakdown. A currency split was inevitable, and there was
a need for separate monetary authorities. Singapore retained a currency board
system, as a safeguard against profligate government spending, consistent with the
PAP's emphasis on prudence and hard work. Crucially, the government believed
that a currency board would maintain confidence in the new currency and enhance
Singapore's ability to access international capital markets as part of the PAP's
development strategy. The BCCS was established in 1967 as the currency-
issuing authority. The Singapore dollar was pegged to sterling, and a currency
interchangeability arrangement was established with Malaysia and Brunei. When
Singapore's new currency appeared – the Orchid series of notes – there were
challenges associated with redeeming the old currency. This was partly a consequence
of the devaluation of sterling in 1967, following which Singapore and Malaysia
decided not to devalue. Some holders of the old Malaya and British Borneo dollars,
still pegged to pre-devaluation sterling values, were hit. Internationally, the US
dollar had substantially supplanted the pound sterling as the world's main reserve
currency, and Singapore's partial diversification of its reserves out of sterling was a
harbinger of the way it would manage its reserves in the future.

Afew weeks before the second anniversary of the formation of the Federation of Malaysia, at 10 a.m. on 9 August 1965, Radio Singapore made an announcement that would forever change the lives of millions of Singaporeans: Singapore had left the Federation and become an independent state. The news was confirmed by Singapore's Prime Minister Lee Kuan Yew at a televised press conference at 4.30 p.m. the same day. Singaporeans were shocked. After all, the ruling People's Action Party (PAP) had repeatedly denied any suggestion that they would seek independence from Malaysia. Two months before the break, Lee himself had declared that separation was out of the question. When it did happen, there was disquiet among some members of the cabinet, many of whom still had deep roots in Malaysia and had been kept in the dark about the negotiations. Finance minister Goh Keng Swee, who had played a prominent role in negotiating the separation agreement, was probably among the few cabinet members, perhaps the only one, who thought that the political merger with Malaysia in 1963 had been a mistake for both sides.[1]

Lee Kuan Yew holds a press conference to announce the separation of Singapore from Malaysia in 1965.

Whatever misgivings the general public or the politicians might have had, a unified front was maintained. There were no protests on the streets, and some businesses in Singapore were happy that they would no longer have to pay Malaysian taxes! Despite some initial reluctance, all members of the Singapore cabinet signed the separation agreement, remained unanimous in publicly supporting the decision, and did not break ranks. Malay remained Singapore's national language and an ethnic Malay, Yusof bin Ishak, became Singapore's first president. The PAP continued to leave open the option of future reunification, and even Malaysian Prime Minister Tunku Abdul Rahman, who had initiated the split, thought that Singapore might one day return to the Federation. The British Commonwealth also accepted the split with good grace, although the Australians were concerned about a revival of the Indonesian 'Konfrontasi' and British newspapers thought it was a disaster for Britain's foreign policy in Southeast Asia.

The split left its mark on Singapore's economic and political future. We now know how successful Singapore has become, but at the time, the prospects for an independent Singapore were much more uncertain. Before the separation, both Singapore and Malaysia had been committed to expanding their manufacturing sectors with joint tariff protection against the outside world. Given Singapore's very small domestic market, it was thought imperative that its exports could be freely traded to the Malaysian hinterland. But now, there was no longer any guarantee of free access to the Malaysian market. Singapore would have to become useful to the world by removing its own tariff barriers and attracting

Chapter opening picture: National Day Parade, 1966. President Yusof bin Ishak (third from the right on the vehicle) reviews the parade, accompanied by Dr Goh Keng Swee (second from the right).

PRIME MINISTER,
SINGAPORE.

PROCLAMATION OF SINGAPORE

WHEREAS it is the inalienable right of a people to be free and independent;

AND WHEREAS Malaysia was established on the 16th day of September, 1963, by a federation of the existing states of the Federation of Malaya and the States of Sabah, Sarawak and Singapore into one independent and sovereign nation;

AND WHEREAS by an Agreement made on the seventh day of August in the year one thousand nine hundred and sixty-five between the Government of Malaysia of the one part and the Government of Singapore of the other part it was agreed that Singapore should cease to be a state of Malaysia and should thereupon become an independent and sovereign state and nation separate from and independent of Malaysia;

AND WHEREAS it was also agreed by the parties to the said Agreement that, upon the separation of Singapore from Malaysia, the Government of Malaysia shall relinquish its sovereignty and jurisdiction in respect of Singapore so that the said sovereignty and jurisdiction shall on such relinquishment vest in the Government of Singapore;

AND WHEREAS by a Proclamation dated the ninth day of August in the year one thousand nine hundred and sixty-

PRIME MINISTER,
SINGAPORE.

- 2 -

five The Prime Minister of Malaysia Tunku Abdul Rahman Putra Al-Haj Ibni Almarhum Sultan Abdul Hamid Halim Shah did proclaim and declare that Singapore shall on the ninth day of August in the year one thousand nine hundred and sixty-five cease to be a state of Malaysia and shall become an independent and sovereign state and nation separate from and independent of Malaysia and recognised as such by the Government of Malaysia.

Now I LEE KUAN YEW Prime Minister of Singapore, DO HEREBY PROCLAIM AND DECLARE on behalf of the people and the Government of Singapore that as from today the ninth day of August in the year one thousand nine hundred and sixty-five Singapore shall be forever a sovereign democratic and independent nation, founded upon the principles of liberty and justice and ever seeking the welfare and happiness of her people in a more just and equal society.

Dated the 9th day of August, 1965.

foreign investment; this was an unusual path for developing countries, many of which pursued protectionist strategies at that time.

Despite the political separation, Singapore and Malaysia were closely interlinked economically and financially. Generally speaking, people in both countries favoured continuing a common currency and banking system because of the convenience they provided for business and the cross-border remittance of funds. A common currency and banking system could act as a bridge between the two countries, keeping them together in a way that politicians had failed to do in 1965. However, Malaysia and Singapore would embark on increasingly divergent paths for economic development. It was against a rapidly evolving backdrop that negotiations for a common currency between Malaysia and Singapore took place and failed, although subsequently the two countries, together with Brunei, came to an agreement to keep their currencies interchangeable.

As was the case before World War II, political and economic dynamics would ultimately determine Singapore's monetary and currency arrangements. The years following 9 August 1965 would see an interplay of forces unleashed at Independence – namely Singapore's urgent push for survival following the loss of its trading hinterland and the political tensions with its nearest neighbours – with its long-standing relationship with Britain, formerly its colonial master, as well as

The Proclamation of Singapore, issued on 9 August 1965, declaring that the island had become an 'independent and sovereign state and nation' following its separation from Malaysia.

with still-deep financial and economic links with Malaysia. These would shape the policies that Singapore would adopt as a newly sovereign nation with much to prove to the rest of the world.

The currency split from Malaysia

As seen in the previous chapter, Singapore had, as part of the British Empire, shared a common currency with Malaya, Sarawak, North Borneo and Brunei issued by the Board of Currency Commissioners, Malaya and British Borneo. After becoming independent in 1957, the Federation of Malaya established its own central bank, Bank Negara Tanah Melayu, with plans to issue its own Malayan currency. In 1960, the joint currency board was reconstituted to take into account not only Malaya's independence but also Singapore's attainment of internal self-government in 1959.

In view of the long-standing, close relationship between Malaya and Singapore, informal discussions began concerning future currency arrangements. In 1960, Malayan officials wrote to Singapore, suggesting that the Federation might be willing to extend the circulation of the Malayan dollar to it under the Central Bank of Malaya Ordinance of 1960.

It was clear that a common currency was an absolute necessity for the smooth running of trade and banking operations between the two territories. For Singapore officials, however, there were concerns as to whether the institutional set-up of the currency-issuing authority meant that it risked financing government budget deficits, which could lead to high inflation.[2] In this respect a central bank faced much greater risk than a currency board. If Singapore were to join in this endeavour, a number of conditions would have to be met, including its concurrence with any changes in the reserve backing of currency issuance, any change in the parity of the currency against the pound sterling, and any change in the automatic convertibility of the currency into sterling. In addition, any profits from note issuance (i.e. the value of the currency notes less the cost of producing them) should be divided equitably between the two governments. Singapore held the view that if it were to withdraw from an agreement subsequently, there would have to be guaranteed conversion into sterling assets at the pre-existing rate for all Malayan dollar holdings in Singapore.

The Malayan side accepted Singapore's position as the 'only way possible', but were concerned that the sovereignty of the Malayan government would be limited if the concurrence of the Singapore government had to be sought at each decision point. They would, however, refer the matter to the Malayan cabinet, and if there was agreement, talks could commence.[3] Differences in the two countries' positions were evident even at this early stage. For instance, Malaya's proposals were an indication that it envisaged a single federal authority that would issue currency and carry out monetary policy, based in Kuala Lumpur but with a branch in Singapore.[4] Although Bank Negara Tanah Melayu would consult with the Singapore government on matters affecting the common currency, it did not believe it practicable to be accountable to two governments.

Internal proposals for Bank Negara Tanah Melayu's currency issuance indicate that the Malayan government was fairly flexible pre-merger,[5] and was willing to give Singapore veto rights over two critical issues it had raised: currency-backing and the exchange rate. Many of the issues discussed in 1960 would surface again when Malaysia and Singapore entered into formal joint-currency talks six years later.

In 1963, Malaya joined with Singapore, Sarawak and North Borneo (eventually Sabah) to form the Federation of Malaysia. The currency board was reconstituted to incorporate the new territorial designations of its members, and plans for a Malayan Federation currency were shelved. But the currency board agreement included a clause that allowed any of the national authorities to give an 18-month notice to leave the arrangement and issue its own currency. Despite this proviso, the intention was to allow the renamed Malayan central bank, Bank Negara Malaysia (henceforth referred to as BNM), eventually to take over responsibility for issuing the currency for the Federation as a whole. The statutes of Bank Negara Tanah Melayu, when it was formed in 1959, had already allowed for the extension of its jurisdiction to other territories, including Singapore, Sarawak, and North Borneo. These entities were expected to join Malaya in a political union, as they eventually did. There was thus every expectation that BNM would eventually replace the currency board as the sole currency issuer for an enlarged Federation of Malaysia. The federal authorities took steps to that effect the following year.

On 12 December 1964, the authorities in Kuala Lumpur lodged a 'Notice of Replacement' with the currency board, to the effect that they would issue their own currency through BNM on 12 June 1966, in line with the 18-month notice period required. Singapore, as a member of the Malaysian Federation, would have been in full agreement with these plans. However, before the notice period had elapsed, on 9 August 1965, Singapore separated from the Federation. Consequently, Singapore now reverted to its pre-Malaysia status and the currency board arrangements as per the Malaya and British North Borneo Currency Agreement of 1960. Three days later, Brunei informed Malaysia that it would issue its own currency, and so the multi-party common-currency plan collapsed into a bilateral discussion between Malaysia and Singapore. A decision on the Malaysian side was urgent, since their commitment to issue a new currency left little time for complex arrangements. Printers in London wanted to get their orders for the new currency by mid-August 1966, well ahead of Malaysia's revised deadline for issuance on 12 June 1967.

Lim Kim San, Minister for Finance (second from left), tours the factory site of Malaysia Associated Industries at Jurong, 1966.

Within a week of Separation, Malaysia's finance minister Tan Siew Sin proposed to his Singapore counterpart Lim Kim San that import controls between the two countries that had been implemented post–Separation be abolished. On this issue at least, Singapore would be accorded a 'special position' that Malaysia had not offered 'to any other trading partner, either inside or outside the Commonwealth'.[6] Lim and Tan met at the Commonwealth Finance Ministers' Conference in October 1965, as well as on the sidelines of the annual meetings of the International Monetary Fund (IMF) and the World Bank, where they agreed they should do everything possible to maintain close economic links. They also decided to approach the IMF for technical advice, and a mission led by the director of the IMF's Central Banking Service, J. V. Mladek, visited Malaysia and Singapore from 25 November to 9 December 1965 and released its report on 1 March 1966.

This desire to maintain close links extended to having a common currency. On 8 November 1965, Lim Kim Sam wrote to Tan Siew Sin suggesting that to maintain public and international confidence in the economic future of the two countries, the currency should continue to be controlled by a currency board, with suitable modifications to take into account the changed circumstances. An alternative arrangement might be for Singapore and Malaysia to share a central bank under joint control which would then issue the currency for the two countries.[7]

Malaysia rejected the option of continuing a common currency board. A currency board was comparatively inflexible, as it reduced the government's macroeconomic policy options, and was deemed unsuitable as a monetary authority for a newly independent country. Malaysia proposed that since BNM had built up a store of central banking expertise since its foundation in 1959, it should continue to operate in Singapore and issue currency for both countries, while keeping its Singapore operations legally separate from those in Malaysia. On matters of policy, Singapore's finance minister would be consulted, and the country would be represented on the board of directors. The external reserves would not be divided but would be kept in separate accounts and the bank's assets in Singapore would belong to the Singapore government.[8]

Singapore, however, was concerned that in the event of a termination of the arrangement there could be some doubt about the ownership of the reserves. Politically, it would be difficult to persuade Singaporeans to accept a foreign institution as their central bank. On the other hand, Malaysia's proposal provided an interim solution in anticipation of possible future political reunion, and time for Singapore to build up expertise in central banking. Thus 'to avoid closing the door to economic cooperation', the government felt that agreement in principle could be given, subject to safeguards regarding the country's sovereignty and control over its external reserves.[9] This view was duly conveyed to Malaysia. On 17 December 1965, Singapore reiterated its desire to continue with a currency board system, and emphasised that under any alternative arrangement it would need binding assurances that in the event of termination, it would have immediate access to its external reserves.[10] These reserves comprised the government's accumulated budget surpluses that had been invested abroad, as well as Singapore's share of the stock of gold and foreign-currency assets held by the Board of Commissioners of Currency, Malaya and British Borneo.

The Malaysian government understood clearly that Singapore would have a 'presentational problem' with regard to a common currency: how would it look if the currency to be circulated in Singapore were the Malaysian dollar, or if BNM were to operate locally? It also noted Singapore's concerns regarding the reserves, and agreed to revise the original proposal so that the reserves attributable to each country would be separately controlled and managed. In the event of termination of the agreement by either party, Malaysia agreed that the whole of the assets and liabilities in Singapore according to the books of BNM would be at the discretion of the Singapore government. This could be achieved by maintaining separate accounts with the depositories of BNM's reserves abroad, such as the Bank of England.

At this stage, the public was reassured by the fact that the talks were ongoing and advice was being sought from international agencies, such as the IMF. There was optimism about a successful outcome. Also, unnamed 'experts' quoted in the *Straits Times* in Singapore felt that it was in the interests of all territories to share a common currency so that 'each will have a fair say in policy matters'. Assurance was found in the expectation that regardless of the outcome, any new currency for Singapore – whether issued by BNM or issued by Singapore itself – would still be tied to sterling and fully backed by foreign reserves.[11]

On 9 May 1966, negotiations reached a milestone: Singapore's Minister Lim Kim San wrote to the governor of BNM stating that the revised proposals were acceptable in principle and could form the basis for detailed negotiations.[12]

Formal negotiations between the two governments began on 10 June 1966 and were adjourned on 5 July. The Singapore delegation was led by the permanent secretary at the finance ministry, Sim Kee Boon, while the Malaysian delegation was headed by Abu Bakar Samad, acting secretary to the treasury. The team from BNM was led by Governor Ismail bin Mohamad Ali, who chaired the meetings. The IMF sent two representatives, U Tun Thin and U San Lin, to provide technical advice.[13] By all accounts, the 11 meetings were intense but interpersonal relationships were relaxed. At this stage little information about the talks was given to the public.

On 6 July 1966, a detailed Working Draft Agreement was produced for the consideration of both governments.[14] This provided for a common currency with a similar design except that the Malaysian issue would be designated the 'M' series and the Singapore issue the 'S' series. Both would be legal-tender in either country.[15]

This draft agreement contained several amendments that sought to meet Singapore's concerns. The Singapore branch of BNM would form a separate accounting and operational unit with its own external reserves and balance sheet, and would be under the immediate control of the Singaporean deputy governor of the bank. Although not in the draft agreement, it was also agreed that Singapore would have control over its own currency issuance, with instructions to be given to the printers that no order would be valid unless countersigned by the Singapore deputy governor. Both finance ministers would have to be consulted before any alteration could be made to the exchange rate of the common currency, its convertibility into foreign currency, or the external reserve backing of the currency. Moreover, any change in the parity of the currency without the consent of both governments would constitute a termination of the agreement and both

Malaysia's Prime Minister Tunku Abdul Rahman (second from right) and Minister of Finance Datuk Tan Siew Sin (right) at Paya Lebar Airport, 1963.

finance ministers would have a veto over monetary and banking policy in their respective territories.[16]

On the face of it, the agreement seemed to satisfy many of Singapore's key demands. Although there were still some worries behind the scenes, the Singapore government decided that the best course of action was to prolong the negotiations and work towards modifying the agreement over time.[17] Crucially, there were concerns that there would be some doubt about the ownership of Singapore's reserves if the agreement were to be terminated, and that Malaysia would be able to amend the Central Bank of Malaysia Ordinance to allow the parity and convertibility of the Malaysian dollar to be varied. Furthermore, it was not clear if the appointment of the governor of BNM would require Singapore's concurrence.

Then, on 11 July, the Singapore government received a letter from BNM Governor Ismail stating that while the value of the land in Robinson Road on which the proposed Singapore branch of BNM would be sited would be credited to the account of the branch, the legal title would remain in the name of the bank. From the Malaysian point of view, the Singapore branch was not a legal entity and, therefore, could not own assets. The governor would therefore like to have an explanation as to how the land was to be transferred to BNM.

This was a 'bombshell' for Singapore. According to the interpretation embedded in the letter, the government would, in effect, be handing over legal ownership of all the Singapore branch assets – including the foreign reserves – to a statutory body of another country; the assets would be entirely subject to Malaysian legislation and control. The issue of the Singapore branch being a separate legal entity had indeed surfaced during the formal negotiations but there appears to have been some ambiguity and, therefore, scope for Singapore to pursue in future discussions the ability of the local branch to own assets.[18] That ambiguity had now disappeared.[19]

The Singapore government wrote to Governor Ismail on 15 July, pointing out that during the negotiations it had been accepted that all the assets of the bank in Singapore should belong exclusively to the branch. The government wanted this fundamental agreement to be given full legal effect. Moreover, after full consideration, it was not clear that it was possible to achieve this beyond any doubt within the framework of a single legal entity.[20]

Ismail met with Lim on 21 July 1966 and told him that as far as he was concerned such assets must remain vested in BNM. Lim Kim San said that his position would be untenable if the reserves were legally vested in an institution created by a foreign government and that he could not recommend the draft agreement to the Singapore cabinet. Although Governor Ismail appreciated Singapore's position, he was of the opinion that 'nothing could be done except

Yang di-Pertuan Negara (later President) Yusof bin Ishak gives an address at the opening of the Singapore branch of Bank Negara at Empress Place in 1964.

for the two governments to break off negotiations and proceed to issue their own currencies'.[21]

With the expectation that Governor Ismail would be more conciliatory, the Singapore officials were willing to continue with the negotiations. Certainly, they had good reason to do so in the hope that Malaysia would eventually accede to its terms; the Singapore leaders felt that breaking off negotiations might well reduce Malaysia's willingness to collaborate on other economic matters in the future. This was probably more important for Singapore's future prosperity than for Malaysia. However, the Malaysian position was confirmed on 23 July when Tan Siew Sin said that as far as he was concerned, the only outstanding issue was the name of the organisation of BNM in Singapore. He was prepared to recommend the draft agreement to the Malaysian cabinet, and the institution's name as Bank Negara Malaysia, Singapore.[22]

In an attempt to resolve the legal impasse over the ownership of reserves, Lim Kim San wrote to Tan on 4 August, handing the letter personally to him in Kuala Lumpur. He proposed that the currency reserves of both countries be deposited with an agreed third-party trustee, such as the Bank of England or the IMF, a plan that had been conceived originally by the IMF itself. Alternatively, the Singaporean deputy governor could be legally incorporated as a 'corporation sole' so that the assets of the Singapore bank could be vested in him personally. In this way, the currency reserves of Singapore would belong to the country at all times. The government would also be prepared to consider other alternatives.[23] When Tan hosted Lim to dinner on the same day, he said that the loss of ownership of its reserves that Singapore feared 'was really a remote possibility'.[24] Tan replied formally on 8 August 1966 that the use of trustees was impracticable: it would make BNM inoperative since every transaction would have to be effected by the foreign trustee, and no self-respecting central bank could accept such a position. Also, designating the deputy governor as a corporation sole amounted, in effect, to having two central-banking organisations.

With no clear way out of this impasse, the door to further negotiations ultimately closed. Malaysia had already postponed the issue of its currency by a whole year, and it was of the view that even if the draft agreement had been accepted and implemented, it would require a considerable amount of understanding and goodwill on both sides to make it work. 'We have had to agree to disagree ultimately.'[25] After the split, a headline in the *Straits Times* suggested that 'The essential fact was distrust.' The IMF, in its report on the negotiations released on 1 March 1966, found that although both countries were keen to preserve a common currency and banking system, it had the impression that there was a certain 'mutual disenchantment' following the political separation that did not help to create the cordial atmosphere important for the negotiation of an agreement.[26]

Beyond a lack of political trust, there were also deep, underlying economic differences. In the IMF mission's opinion, 'a satisfactory currency arrangement could have been worked out' and indeed, given the existing economic links, having a common unit of measure and means of transaction made sense. However, in the long run, a currency union would have proven unworkable if both countries had not been prepared to establish ever-closer cooperation in economic and financial policies on a broad front.[27] In retrospect, although the reserves issue dominated the discussions, it seems clear that there was little chance that a joint monetary authority could have been agreed after the political separation in 1965, given the two countries' very different economic philosophies and competing economic goals. Ultimately, the gulf between the two countries proved to be too wide and, with hindsight, it is surprising that the talks continued for as long as they did.

And so it was that having shared a common currency for decades, Malaysia and Singapore were to undergo a 'currency split'.

On 17 August 1966, the public in both countries were informed that Malaysia and Singapore would issue their own currencies on 12 June 1967, and the Malaya and British Borneo currency board's currency-issuing powers would cease on that day. Brunei, which had earlier announced plans to issue its own currency, would do so on the same day. The Malaysian announcement was made by Deputy Prime Minister Tun Abdul Razak after the weekly cabinet meeting, the Singapore announcement by Radio Singapore at lunchtime and later that day on television. The joint announcement noted that no satisfactory formula for currency and central-banking arrangements acceptable to both and compatible with their status as two independent countries could be found. However, the respective monetary authorities of Malaysia and Singapore would continue to cooperate to the fullest extent possible.[28]

The news was greeted with widespread dismay. Stock prices fell sharply, and the following day the *Straits Times* reported that after the announcement business people and bankers 'immediately huddled together in conference rooms to discuss the news', lamenting that there had been no consultation or discussions in Parliament. There were last-minute attempts to get the two governments back to the negotiating table.[29] This was followed up by a more detailed critique of both governments in the same newspaper on 20 August, which pointed to the uncertainty created 'from Change Alley to postage stamps and the payment of taxes on income', and wondered whether Singapore and Malaysia would actually be able to cooperate on monetary and banking matters. Bankers and businessmen had no idea why the negotiations had broken down; the two governments had agreed to say nothing. Questions arose: if it was understood that a common currency would not work since Singapore and Malaysia had divergent trade and economic policies, why was this not brought up earlier if both countries had already agreed on a draft?[30]

On 26 August 1966, Singapore brought out its White Paper on Currency including selected letters and memoranda (a number of which were marked 'Secret'), to clarify the issues from the government's point of view and to reassure the banking and business communities. The following day, both finance ministers made different statements to their respective parliaments and the day after that, the Malaysian Ministry of Finance released the text of the 'final draft agreement' and two letters that had been exchanged between Singapore and Malaysia over the course of the negotiations to the *Straits Times* under the headline 'Out – that secret draft'.[31]

Unloading rubber at Boat Quay, 1969.

In Singapore, Prime Minister Lee Kuan Yew made a number of speeches where he laid out the issue in street-level terms, justifying the break. He referred to coffee-shop talk which said Singapore was finished and that it would be left with 'banana notes' reminiscent of the worthless Japanese currency still in circulation in 1945 when the British returned to the island (see p. 164). He reminded Singaporeans that Malaysia had natural resources in the form of rubber and tin but Singapore had none. To drum up confidence in Singapore's soon-to-be-issued currency, he stressed the advantages of retaining the currency board system for the country and by implication the weaknesses associated with having a central bank, joint or otherwise.[32]

In Malaysia, the official attitude initially was 'the less said the better', but remarks deriding the credibility of central banks relative to currency boards did not go down well, and the Malaysians also felt it necessary to shore up confidence. In September, Tan Siew Sin made a formal statement about the breakdown of the negotiations. Malaysia, with its balance of payments surplus, had little to worry about in terms of confidence, he said. But for BNM, the failure to reach agreement on a common currency and banking arrangements between the two countries was a great disappointment.[33]

Singapore retains the currency board system

While Singapore had from the outset expressed a preference for continuing with the currency board system, there was in fact significant debate as to whether this or a central bank would be more appropriate for Singapore given its economic circumstances.

Singapore was familiar with the benefits and workings of currency boards, as the currency in circulation on the island had been issued by such boards since the turn of the 20th century, beginning with the Straits Settlements dollar (see p. 93). In fixing to a strong and stable reserve currency, such as the pound sterling, the local currency would be 'as good as sterling'. For newly independent Singapore, a currency board represented continuity, stability, and credibility at a time when the world was uncertain about the longer-term prospects for the country.

The main advantage of a central bank was that, unlike a currency board, it could adjust monetary policy flexibly to insulate the economy from the ups and downs of the business cycle. If there were a downturn, it could increase the supply of money to the banking sector and reduce the cash that the banks were required to keep in their vaults or the reserves with the central bank as a precaution against a bank run. It could also provide funds to the government in exchange for government securities to finance longer-term development programmes. This was an important reason for setting up central banks in developing countries such as Malaysia, Ghana and Nigeria when they became independent in the 1950s, since at least some of their reserves formerly 'locked up' in London could now be used to invest in economic development.[34]

Moreover, unlike a currency board, a central bank could act as 'lender of last resort' to banks and other financial institutions which needed help during a financial crisis. One of the reasons why the Great Depression of the 1930s was so damaging in the United States was that this type of lending was not generally available.

The idea that a central bank would be able to adjust monetary policy flexibly in response to the business cycle, and to serve the development needs of the economy, was attractive to Malaysia; it was one of the factors behind the formation of Bank

Negara Tanah Melayu in 1959. Although Malaysia was also relatively young as an independent nation, it had abundant natural resources, and there would clearly be global demand for its exports. The concern about being irrelevant and bypassed by the world was not as pressing an issue in Malaysia as it was in Singapore, and thus the credibility-boosting properties of the currency board were less crucial to the former than to the latter.

Dr Goh Keng Swee played a key role in the debate. In his judgement Singapore had no experience in central banking, and he was sceptical about the ability of a central bank to carry out monetary policy in an economy that was so open to trade and capital flows.

In particular, Goh Keng Swee saw a currency board as a safeguard against profligate governments that would run irresponsible deficits and generate excessive inflation, as had happened in many other newly independent countries.[35] He had emphasised in 1960 that governments should not resort to monetary authorities to finance their deficits, and he remained adamant: 'We wanted to indicate to academics, both local and foreign, that what was fashionable in the West was not necessarily good for Singapore.'[36] There would be no expectation of a free lunch. Government spending would have to be financed by taxation, through the accumulation of overseas assets, or by the proceeds of foreign loans raised on the collateral of those assets.[37]

This meant that if the government was willing to tie its fiscal hands in order to maintain the currency board, the discipline imparted would feed back to ensuring a stable value for the Singapore dollar; this would promote trade and inward foreign investment and reduce the risk of capital flight and speculative attacks. The same argument had been made during the currency negotiations between Singapore and Malaysia in 1966–7 and was all the more relevant now that Singapore had to signal its credibility as a newly sovereign nation eager to integrate with the global economy.

The Singapore government rejected the central-bank option in favour of a more conservative solution – a currency board to issue the currency, while banking supervision would be undertaken by a banking commissioner. This was primarily to minimise disruption and retain confidence in the local economy. At the time there was uncertainty about how the new currency would be received by the people and whether Singapore was really viable as an independent state. To make matters worse, unemployment

Minister for Finance Dr Goh Keng Swee points out a key feature of the Jurong Industrial Estate to Malaysia's Deputy Prime Minister Tun Abdul Razak (right) and Chairman of the Economic Development Board Hon Sui Sen.

Dr Goh Keng Swee: economic architect of modern Singapore

No one has been more influential in Singapore's modern monetary and currency history than Goh Keng Swee in his role as Singapore's first Minister for Finance. He held that post in the years 1959–63 and again in 1967–70. He was directly involved in the decision to retain the currency board system in August 1967, when Singapore issued its own currency, and in setting up the Monetary Authority of Singapore (MAS) in 1971. He became deputy prime minister and chairman of MAS in 1980, at a critical time in the history of the central bank; and deputy chairman of Singapore's sovereign wealth fund – the Government of Singapore Investment Corporation (GIC) – in 1981.

Dr Goh Keng Swee

Dr Goh was born in 1918 in Malacca (Melaka). When he was two years old the family moved to Singapore. Goh's father was a rubber-planter in Pasir Panjang during the 1930s, and when he was young Goh was made acutely aware of the economic devastation caused by the Great Depression. He graduated from Raffles College in 1939 with a Diploma in Arts with a special distinction in Economics. After World War II, he was awarded a scholarship to study statistics at the prestigious London School of Economics (LSE), graduating in 1951 with First Class Honours. In 1956 he returned to LSE and received his PhD in Economics, choosing for his thesis the problem of national income accounting in developing countries.

Goh Keng Swee became a founding member of Singapore's People's Action Party (PAP) in 1954, and in 1958 at the age of 41 was elected as a Member of Parliament. He was a leading exponent of a development strategy for Singapore that was based on an eclectic mix of socialism and capitalism.[38] As Minister for Finance, he established himself as a firm opponent of government financing through budget deficits and foreign aid. He prioritised spending on education and healthcare and reduced budget deficits by cutting the salaries of ministers and civil servants, and increasing taxes on tobacco.

Dr Albert Winsemius, Singapore's chief economic advisor from 1961 to 1984.

A key feature of Goh was pragmatism: 'You do not have to reinvent the wheel.' He was always open to ideas from abroad which could be adapted to Singapore's circumstances. In 1960, the United Nations Development Programme visited Singapore to advise on industrialisation. The mission was led by a Dutch economist, Dr Albert Winsemius, who became a regular visitor to Singapore for 23 years and, despite having no formal contract with the government, was to play a major role in the nation's economic planning as 'economic engineer', and in particular, in setting up the Economic Development Board in May 1961 to promote manufacturing.[39, 40, 41]

A more controversial strategy was the establishment of the Jurong Industrial Estate in southwest Singapore to attract foreign manufacturing companies. At the time, many people called it 'Goh's folly', unconvinced it would succeed given the associated costs, a lack of local entrepreneurs, and industrial disputes with the trade unions. Events proved the doubters wrong. Jurong was to become the heart of high-quality manufacturing in Singapore.

Those who worked with Dr Goh respected him. Although he was not always easy to get along with, he had high standards. He was a diabetic and a smoker, and he liked his whisky. He had a sense of humour. As defence minister in the 1970s, he was worried that Singapore's armed forces might become complacent and sloppy – that anyone could slip a chunk of statistics into an army document and no one would notice. To test this theory, he inserted into a general circular an extract from the Bible's Book of Genesis and circulated it widely in the Ministry of Defence. Most recipients were perplexed. Some took it seriously, interpreting 'You shall bring two of every sort into the ark' and 'The rain was on the earth forty days and forty nights' as an instruction to send two representatives from each company to assemble 40 days later.[42]

Goh Keng Swee stepped down as a Member of Parliament in 1984, and passed away in 2010.

Members of the
new Board of
Commissioners of
Currency Singapore,
1967. Minister for
Finance Lim Kim San
is seated third from
the right.

was high. The cabinet wanted to make sure there would be no doubt about the government's intentions.[43] Traders and investors would know that every Singapore dollar was backed by an equivalent amount of external reserves and was fully convertible at a fixed rate into sterling. The new currency would be as prudently managed as its predecessor, the Malaya and British Borneo dollar, had been. Singapore's leaders at the time aimed to develop Singapore into a regional financial centre and believed that a stable and strong currency under a currency board system would help in this endeavour.

The strategy coincided with the ruling PAP's emphasis on prudence and hard work. The road to greater wealth was through thrift, enterprise and effort. These sentiments were expressed in a speech by Prime Minister Lee Kuan Yew to the General Printing Workers' Union. 'For every dollar we issue, there will be a currency board which guarantees that there is that amount in gold or foreign exchange in London or New York or some other place to back it. So the money won't go down. But I will tell you what will go down – employment will go down if you don't work hard.'[44]

Singapore's decision to retain a currency board system in 1967 was seen as rather unusual.[45] Indeed, when the Ministry of Finance sought advice on the type of monetary authority Singapore should have, the IMF suggested a central bank.[46] An IMF mission visited Singapore from 20 November to 6 December 1966, and despite the fact that the government had already announced its intention to continue with a currency board system, the IMF again recommended a central bank 'which would be more commensurate with the sophistication of the country's banking and credit structure'.[47] Even Singapore's currency adviser, R.W. Groenman, said he preferred a central bank or at least 'an institution with wider powers in the field of monetary management'.[48] The Minister for Finance at the time, Lim Kim San, may also have been receptive to the idea of a monetary authority with credit-creating powers.[49]

Nevertheless, Singapore went its own way and adopted the currency board system, eschewing the formation of either a central bank or an alternative monetary authority. The Board of Commissioners of Currency, Singapore (BCCS) was established on 7 April 1967 under the Currency Act passed in that same month, and two weeks later, BNM closed its branch on the island. Henceforth, BCCS would serve as the sole currency-issuing authority for the Republic. Before this, the issuance of money for Singapore had always been subsumed under that of a larger political entity, whether the Straits Settlements, or a broader set of colonial territories under Britain. In June that year, BCCS issued Singapore's own currency notes. For the first time in its history, the country had a currency of its own: the Singapore dollar.

The new currency was fully backed by the external assets of the BCCS and was fully convertible into sterling at 2s 4d and into gold at 0.290299 grams per Singapore dollar. The BCCS was chaired initially by finance minister Lim Kim San, but in August 1967 Goh Keng Swee took over. To signal that the board of the BCCS would be subject to scrutiny by independent and experienced people from outside government, three bankers from the Chartered Bank, Overseas Union Bank and Bank of America, together with the president of the Singapore Indian Chamber of Commerce and Industry, were selected as directors for one year.

Pounds, shillings and pence

Before Britain converted to a decimal currency system on 15 February 1971, the pound was divided into 20 shillings (s) to the pound (£); a shilling was divided into twelve pennies (d). There was a halfpenny coin (pronounced ha'penny), and, until 1961, a farthing coin (quarter of a penny). When Singapore issued its own

currency in June 1967, the Singapore dollar was a decimal currency, with 100 cents to the dollar, but fixed to the pound in the foreign exchange market at 2s 4d.

Britain's decision to go decimal was made in 1967 under the Decimalisation Currency Act partly for convenience and partly because most countries in the world had always used such a system or had converted to it. For example, the United States adopted the decimal system in 1792 when it became independent of Britain, and Australia went decimal in 1966. Decimalisation made money calculations simpler, quicker, and less liable to error, benefitting both people and machines, and less time was needed in the schools teaching children how to make fearsomely complicated financial calculations.

Britain goes decimal: Lord Fiske, chairman of the Decimal Currency Board, displays information about the new currency, 1971.

The BCCS's main task was to ensure sound management of the foreign assets backing the Singapore dollar, but instead of keeping all the external reserves in liquid assets – for instance, gold, cash bank deposits, and fixed interest securities denominated in major reserve currencies, such as sterling and the US dollar – a small portion was held in equities. This was unusual at the time and was a forerunner of the idea of wealth preservation that was to become an important cornerstone of Singapore's reserve-management approach in the 1980s (see p. 301).

Singapore therefore found itself in the unique position of being the only newly independent former British colony to issue its currency under the currency board system which, as Dr Goh Keng Swee later acknowledged, was in every sense of the phrase 'a colonial relic'.[50]

The decision to retain the currency board and the fix to the pound sterling in 1967 can thus be explained given Singapore's positive interpretation of how the colonial currency board system had worked throughout its history. The currency board would signal to the world that the Singapore dollar would be strong and convertible and a sound basis for an economy increasingly reliant on manufacturing and financial services, as well as attracting foreign investment.

Producing Singapore's own money

On 12 June 1967, the BCCS issued Singapore's first set of currency notes for general circulation. Known as the Orchid series, these notes are still in use today. This was an important milestone in the nation's journey after independence, represented by the appearance of a new symbol for the Singapore dollar: S$. The motifs and designs of the new notes were not just an embodiment

Minister for Finance and chairman of the newly established Board of Commissioners of Currency Lim Kim San displays Singapore's new currency notes to the press, 20 May 1967.

of sovereignty but also an expression of self-determination and a specifically Singaporean national identity that was multiracial, multicultural, multilingual and secular.[51] The note designs were beautiful and predated the selection of the Vanda Miss Joaquim orchid as Singapore's national flower in April 1981.

Singapore's own circulation coins were introduced to the public on 30 November 1967. The coins were designed by Stuart

The 'money ship', SS *Comorin*.

Devlin, an Australian artist and metalworker who had designed coins for many countries around the world. He had moved to London in 1965 and in 1982 became goldsmith and jeweller to the British monarch Queen Elizabeth II. Unlike earlier coins that had typically borne the profile of the reigning British monarch, these new coins had the denomination, year of issue, two stalks of paddy symbolising the staple food, rice, and the name 'SINGAPORE'.

Every effort was made to ensure that the issuance of the new Singapore dollar notes and coins would proceed smoothly and securely. The notes were printed in the British plants of Bradbury Wilkinson & Co. Ltd and Thomas De La Rue & Co. Ltd. The latter company, in consultation with the BCCS, had improved the method of banding the packs of notes. This involved using a nylon strap known as 'bandamatic strapping', which held the notes tightly together so that individual notes or bundles of 100 notes could not be removed without cutting the strap, which thereafter could not be reused.[52] The coins were initially minted at the Royal Mint in the United Kingdom.

The first batch of new dollar notes arrived by ship on 30 March 1967 and was distributed to the banks in heavily guarded vans for issuance in June. In November 1967 a 'money ship' – the P&O cargo liner SS *Comorin* – was unloaded under strict security at the Port of Singapore Authority wharves. It contained seven million dollars' worth of notes and coins weighing 63 and 4.5 tons, respectively.[53] There were 1,175 boxes of notes and ten cases of coins. The new Singapore coins were first issued on 20 November that year.

Contrary to expectations, there was no rush by people at the banks to exchange old notes for new. After all, the Malaya and British Borneo dollar remained legal-tender and continued to circulate alongside the Singapore dollar – it was only due to be withdrawn by 16 January 1969. Moreover, its value was the same as the Singapore dollar, and there were plenty of new notes to replace the old ones.[54] Likewise, when coins were issued, the queues for exchange at community centres and post offices were orderly.[55]

Independent Singapore's first circulation notes

Singapore's first circulation notes after the separation from Malaysia, the Orchid series, were released to the public on 12 June 1967. There were six denominations: 1, 5, 10, 50, 100 and 1,000 dollars.

The motif on the front (obverse) of each was an orchid hybrid native to the country. The back (reverse) bore symbols of Singapore's national identity, such as four clasped hands on the ten-dollar note signifying racial harmony and housing estates on the one-dollar note to symbolise economic development and prosperity for all citizens. Other notes depicted key landmarks on the island such as the Istana and scenes of the Singapore River, as a reminder of Singapore's beginnings as a seaport. The notes also incorporated the national coat-of-arms, a lion-head watermark and the signature of Lim Kim San, Minister for Finance.

In August 1972 the Orchid series was supplemented with a 25-dollar note and a 500-dollar note. Both had improved security features in the form of fluorescent printing visible only under ultraviolet light. On 29 January 1973, a brown 10,000-dollar note was added with a hand-engraved vignette that could not be copied. The 10,000-dollar note had two security threads.

S$1 (dark blue), issued 12 June 1967

Front: Orchid *Vanda* Janet Kaneali

Back: blocks of flats in a housing estate

S$5 (green), issued 12 June 1967

Front: Orchid *Vanda* T.M.A.

Back: busy scene on the Singapore River

S$10 (red), issued 12 June 1967

Front: *Dendrobium* Marjorie Ho 'Tony Pek'

Back: four clasped hands with map of Singapore in the background

S$25 (brown), issued 7 August 1972

Front: *Renanthopsis* Aurora

Back: Supreme Court Building

S$50 (blue), issued 12 June 1967

Front: *Vanda rothschildiana* 'Teo Choo Hong'

Back: Singapore seafront and Clifford Pier

S$100 (mid-blue and mauve), issued 12 June 1967

Front: *Cattleya*

Back: a peaceful scene along the Singapore waterfront

S$500 (green), issued 7 August 1972

Front: *Dendrobium* Shangri-La

Back: government offices at St. Andrews Road

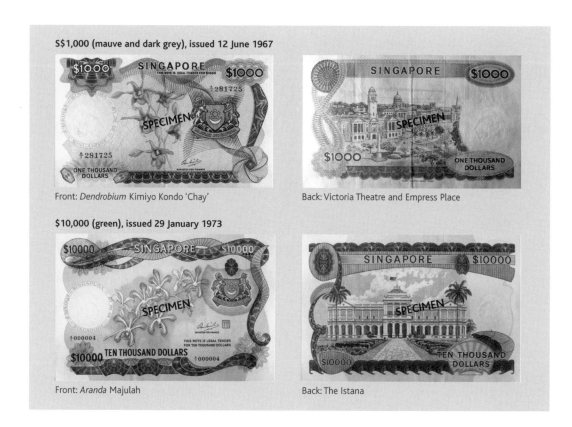

S$1,000 (mauve and dark grey), issued 12 June 1967

Front: *Dendrobium* Kimiyo Kondo 'Chay'

Back: Victoria Theatre and Empress Place

$10,000 (green), issued 29 January 1973

Front: *Aranda* Majulah

Back: The Istana

Yet, some hiccups were encountered in the rollout of the new dollar notes. The different orchid sprays featured on the notes were not always familiar to the man on the street, and many people found it difficult to tell at a glance whether the note was genuine or not. The wide variety in design and motif made forgery easier and detection harder. In contrast, the new Malaysian notes bore the face of the first Sultan of Malaysia, which was easily recognisable and made the notes more difficult to forge.[56] Some Singaporeans were puzzled that the new notes did not have a date of issue on them. The then deputy chairman of the BCCS, Chua Kim Yeow, had to explain that this was of no significance – Singapore was simply following the Australian system, whereas Brunei, for example, followed the American system of serial numbers for the year of issue.[57]

Printing mistakes occurred in some instances, and issued notes with imperfections quickly became collectors' items. A five-dollar note that belonged to a Miss Veronica Ong had an orchid with a yellow top half instead of orange.[58] She reportedly received an offer of S$150 for her 'freak note'. In another instance, a ten-dollar note obtained from a bank by a cook named Alex Pereira had the reverse of the letters 'ore' printed directly below the big word 'Singapore' on both sides of the note. As a keen philatelist, Pereira said he would sell it to anyone who could offer him an attractive price.[59] By August 1967, the number of notes with imperfections had risen to three, and all were apparently up for sale 'at the right price'.[60] In 1971, some 100,000 of the 1,000-dollar notes printed were delivered with the finance minister's signature but lacked the seal.[61] The BCCS took these problems in its stride.

As was the case in the colonial era, the government would at times produce money that the general public did not find convenient to use. In August 1972, 25-dollar- and 500-dollar-denomination notes were added to the Orchid series. The release was accompanied by great publicity to coincide with Singapore's National Day celebrations,[62] and specimens were duly sent to BNM so they could distribute them to bank branches in Malaysia for reference purposes.[63]

A lunchtime crowd at the Chartered Bank in Battery Road waits to exchange old notes for the new Singapore dollar, officially released to the public for the first time, 1967.

An article in the *Straits Times* on 30 June 1973 ran the headline: 'Issue of fifties suspended to boost use of 25-dollar notes.' A senior official of the BCCS was quoted as saying that he did not think this would cause inconvenience to the public as those who wanted bigger-denomination notes could always ask for 100-dollar notes. However, the 25-dollar notes were unpopular, as the public clearly preferred to use 50-dollar notes instead as an intermediate denomination between 10 dollars and 100 dollars. Because people were reluctant to accept 25-dollar notes, banks were left holding large stocks, preferring instead to keep 50-dollar notes on hand to disburse to customers.

As well as legal-tender coins produced for everyday use, Singapore, in common with many other countries, has issued commemorative coins to celebrate major political, commercial or sporting events. The first was struck in 1969 – a 150-dollar gold coin to commemorate the 150th anniversary of the founding of colonial Singapore by Sir Stamford Raffles in 1819. According to a telegram from the British High Commission to the Commonwealth Office, the idea of a gold commemorative coin came to Dr Goh Keng Swee following a trip to Bangkok, where he had been presented with three gold coins commemorating the birthday of the Queen of Thailand.[64]

Independent Singapore's first circulation coins and commemorative coin

Singapore's own circulation coins were introduced to the public on 30 November 1967 in denominations of 1, 5, 10, 20, and 50 cents, and 1 dollar. Except for the one-cent coin, which was struck in bronze, the coins were made of cupronickel – an alloy of copper that contains nickel and strengthening agents such as iron and manganese.

The first commemorative coin was minted in 1969 – a 150-dollar gold coin to commemorate the 150th anniversary of the founding of colonial Singapore by Sir Stamford Raffles in 1819.

1 cent bronze copper-clad steel with plain edge

Reverse: denomination and year date, two stalks of
    paddy, and the word 'Singapore' on the right
Obverse: high-rise public housing block with a
    fountain and clouds

5 cents, cupronickel from aluminium

Reverse: denomination and year date, two stalks of
    paddy and the word 'Singapore' on the right
Obverse: snakebird in its nest preening its feathers
Obverse: a pomfret with inscriptions around it (1971,
    aluminium with plain edge)

10 cents, cupronickel with milled edge

Reverse: denomination and year date, two stalks of
    paddy and the word 'Singapore' on the right
Obverse: seahorse with stylised version of seaweed

20 cents, cupronickel with milled edge

Reverse: denomination and year date, two stalks
    of paddy and the word 'Singapore' on the right
Obverse: swordfish against background
    symbolising water

50 cents, cupronickel with milled edge

Reverse: denomination and year date, two stalks of
    paddy and the word 'Singapore' on the right
Obverse: a lionfish

S$1 cupronickel with milled edge

Reverse: denomination and year date, two stalks of
    paddy and the word 'Singapore' on the right
Obverse: Singapore lion flanked by sheaves of rice

150th anniversary of the founding of Singapore S$150-dollar commemorative gold coin

Reverse: Singapore coat of arms and denomination.
Obverse: Raffles Lighthouse

Even as the new currency was being rolled out, a question remained: what was to become of the old Malaya and British Borneo dollar? It continued to circulate in Singapore, although it was to be withdrawn by 16 January 1969 and would then no longer be legal-tender. Over time, the assets and liabilities of the Malayan and British Borneo currency board would automatically be transferred to the three new currency-issuing authorities: BNM, the Brunei Darussalam Currency Board and the BCCS, in proportion to public demand for the new dollars. There was no need for a prior agreement on the division – the process would take place automatically as each monetary authority recalled the old notes and coins circulating within their territories and redeemed them at the currency board for the equivalent amount in sterling or sterling securities valued at current market prices. While the Board of Commissioners of Currency, Malaya and British Borneo no longer supplied notes and coins, it would continue to redeem the old notes and coins until, by unanimous agreement of the three governments, the redemption process was completed.

The Board began the redemption of the old currency on 12 June 1967 when the new issuing authorities commenced operation. The old dollars were withdrawn from circulation as they came into the hands of the banks which could tender them either to the Board in exchange for sterling or to any of the new currency authorities in exchange for Malaysian, Singapore, or Brunei dollars. In the latter case, the relevant authority would pass on the old notes to the Board and receive sterling in exchange. While the coins were shipped to London for disposal at the Royal Mint, old notes were destroyed in the country where they were being redeemed. The notes had to be burnt, and the only incinerators available for this in Singapore were at the Board office. As one Board employee, Heng Hung Chang, put it, 'For two years I was burning money.'[65]

The redemption process proceeded smoothly. In 1967, the gross circulation of old dollar notes and coins amounted to about 1,545.3 million Malaya and British Borneo dollars. By the end of 1968, old notes and coins redeemed by the three territories totalled 1,476.5 million dollars, of which Singapore had redeemed 520.1 million (35.2 per cent), Malaysia 932.7 million (63.2 per cent), and Brunei 23.7 million (1.6 per cent). All in, about 95.5 per cent of the stock of old currency had been redeemed by then.[66] Destroying the old money was also a straightforward process.

However, distributing the small amount of residual assets held by the old currency board proved more challenging. According to the Currency Agreement of 1960, a reserve had to be put aside for the currency notes and coins that were to be redeemed; the remaining surplus would be distributed among the participating governments according to the profit-sharing ratio in the financial year prior to the first Notice of Replacement being lodged. Since the first notice was lodged by Malaysia in December 1964,[67] this meant the remaining surplus would be distributed in the proportions of 74 per cent to Malaysia, 18.3 per cent to Singapore, and 7.7 per cent to Brunei, in line with distribution of the Currency Surplus Fund at the end of the previous financial year.

Malaysia was happy to go along with this procedure,[68] but Singapore wanted the assets to be distributed according to the percentage of total currency actually redeemed in the three countries. This formula would have substantially increased the shares going to Brunei and Singapore at the expense of Malaysia. Malaysia maintained that one reason Singapore's percentage was higher on this count was that the old dollars circulating in Indonesia, Thailand and Hong Kong had been redeemed in Singapore.

No agreement could be reached until, on 4 May 1972, it was decided at a meeting of the Board of Commissioners of Currency, Malaya and British Borneo that the surplus assets would be distributed, after all, according to the formulation in the 1960 agreement. After a reserve was kept aside to cover unredeemed currency and pension liabilities for former staff, currency profits from 1968–71 and the residual assets of the currency board were distributed on 16 May 1972. The total came to 292.95 million dollars, of which Malaysia received 216.74 million, Singapore 53.62 million and Brunei 22.59 million.

With the question of asset and profit distribution largely settled by the early 1970s, and with Malaysia, Singapore and Brunei having operated their own currency-issuing monetary authorities for a few years, all that remained was to decide what to do with the old currency board. Singapore held that it should not be dissolved, as it could remain as a vehicle for the redemption of any remaining old currency. It could also provide a convenient forum in which the Malaysia and Singapore finance ministers and the State Financial Officer of Brunei could discuss other matters relating to finance and monetary affairs. Malaysia disagreed, describing the old currency board as an 'anachronistic organisation' whose continued existence would be inconsistent with the existence of a central bank or monetary authority as a currency-issuing body.[69] After a legal opinion had been obtained from a Queen's Counsel in the UK, the Board was finally dissolved on 31 May 1975. The sum of 53.1 million dollars was transferred to the Crown Agents (investment agents for the colonies, including Singapore, in London) to cover the unredeemed currency, while the surplus of 3.5 million dollars was distributed according to the percentages adopted in 1972. The rate of redemption had by now diminished to a trickle. With the dissolution, the last vestige of the old joint-currency board system, and indeed the currency union that had once existed between Singapore, Peninsular Malaya, and British territories on Borneo, ceased to be.

New money, old crimes

The switch to the new Singapore dollar triggered criminal incidents of the kind typically associated with currency. Shortly after its launch, boxes of redeemed Malaya and British Borneo coins were sent on the P&O steamship SS *Comorin* to the Royal Mint in London to be destroyed. However, on 31 August 1967 it was reported to the Board of Commissioners of Currency, Malaya and British Borneo that 180 boxes of coins had been stolen. The driver of the lorry loaded with the coins had been kidnapped at gunpoint about 30 miles from its destination. The coins had been insured for their intrinsic value only.

Then, on 17 September the Board was advised that 2000 Malaya and British Borneo dollars'-worth of ten-cent coins and 384 dollars in 50-cent coins had been recovered, which left 357,616 dollars still missing. The police had obtained convictions against those receiving the stolen coins, but the missing coins had still not been recovered. Since the thieves had probably expected to find more valuable coins, such as silver, rather than the cupronickel coins actually stolen, and since it would have been hard for the thieves to dispose of the coins in Britain and risky to ship them back to Malaysia, the BCCS decided that it would not be worthwhile to offer a reward for the coins' recovery.

There was also the case of the 'man who tried to shop with a 10,000-dollar note'. In May 1973, roadsweeper Mohsin bin Shaik Omar was detained when he went to buy some shirts, and offered the note for payment. The shopkeeper was suspicious because he had read in the newspaper that such a note had been stolen from a businessman in North Bridge Road. Mohsin was jailed for two years. In mitigation he said he did not steal the note but was asked to change it for a man on the promise of a commission.[70]

'Dollar for dollar': the Currency Interchangeability Agreement

The authorities were aware that a currency split would have significant impact on business and finance. On 18 August 1966, one day after the joint announcement by Malaysia and Singapore that they would issue their own currencies, Malaysian finance minister Tan Siew Sin said, 'We intend to make arrangements to enable some form of interchangeability so that firms and individuals having trading connectivity with both countries will be able to conduct their business with the minimum inconvenience.' The currency split would not be 'the end of the world'.[71]

On 6 September, in a speech in Parliament on the Central Bank of Malaysia Amendment Bill, Tan recommended the 'Caribbean' customary-tender system adopted by Jamaica, Trinidad and Tobago and Guyana, which had a single banking institution to facilitate access to each other's notes and coins at par. Customary tender differed from legal-tender in that only legal-tender could be used to pay a financial obligation or debt. However, customary tender meant that the banks in each country would accept without charge notes and coins issued by the currency authority of the other countries at the existing par value, and would exchange these notes and coins into their own currency. The following day, an article in the *Straits Times* referred to a campaign by the Singapore Chinese Chamber of Commerce and Industry to persuade the two governments to

Minister for Finance
Lim Kim San opens
the new factory of
Jurong Tile Works Ltd
at 11½ milestone,
Jurong Road.

reconsider their decision not to proceed with a common currency, and to discuss the interchangeability arrangement operating in the West Indies.[72]

There seemed, initially, to have been a communication problem between the Malaysian and Singapore governments over the issue. On 26 October 1966, Tan Siew Sin told the Malaysian Parliament that there had been no reaction from Singapore in response to his suggestion for some form of currency interchangeability between Malaysia and Singapore.[73] He repeated this when interviewed in Singapore on 11 December – the Malaysian government had proposed to the Singapore government that a customary-tender system could be considered which 'has proved to be a success in the Caribbean and other countries', but that Singapore had yet to reply.[74] Similar remarks were made in his budget speech to the Malaysian Parliament on 16 January 1967.[75]

However, on 9 September 1966 Singapore's finance minister Lim Kim San had stated publicly at the opening of a new factory that he was willing to consider any system which would make for easy convertibility and movement of funds between the two currencies. Lim had added: 'The people of Singapore and Malaysia would no doubt be pleased to hear from Minister Tan himself what sort of arrangements he envisages for the interchangeability.'[76]

This uncertainty did not go down well with the business community in either country. On 11 December 1966, the Association of Chinese Chambers of Commerce, which represented Chinese business interests throughout the Federation of Malaysia, passed a resolution at their annual general meeting appealing to the two governments to reopen talks on a common currency. Again, there was support for something similar to the Caribbean arrangement but little information had been provided about how it worked and whether it was suitable.[77]

On 25 December 1966, Malaysia's Prime Minister Tunku Abdul Rahman said he was willing to cooperate with Singapore on matters of exchange to simplify the use of currency,[78] and shortly afterwards the Singapore government said that Prime Minister Lee Kuan Yew and the governor of BNM had agreed on the principle of customary tender.[79] In Malaysia the idea was met with enthusiasm. In Minister Tan Siew Sin's view, once there was agreement in principle, the details would not be formidable and would be a matter for the experts. Malaysia and Singapore had previously failed to agree on a common currency. 'We cannot afford to let this happen again,' he said.[80]

Singapore consulted the IMF on the next steps. They recommended that the system should be as flexible as possible, similar to the Caribbean arrangement, with no written agreement, but merely an exchange of letters which they would draft. Implementation-wise, there would be periodical repatriation of the currency of the other country with the issuing authority bearing the cost of repatriation.[81] The IMF wanted to know if they should go to Kuala Lumpur to discuss the issues with the Malaysians and Singapore said 'yes'. Negotiations would begin once the legislation for the new Singapore currency was ready by around February 1967. The IMF advised that both sides should avoid further public discussion until the negotiations had taken place.[82]

Brunei had made plans to issue its currency separately. Nevertheless, Brunei thought it was 'highly desirable that the currencies of Malaysia, Singapore and Brunei should circulate freely in each of the territories'.

Empress Place, when it was home to the Board of Commissioners of Currency, Singapore. Painting by Liu Kang.

An agreement in principle between all three countries was reached on 7 January 1967 at a meeting of the Board of Commissioners of Currency, Malaya and British Borneo. The details were to be worked out by experts and a report would be made by the three governments.[83] As a testimony to how seriously the West Indies system was being considered, Singapore's currency adviser R.W. Groenman discussed the interchangeability system with the governor of the Central Bank of Trinidad and Tobago twice that month.[84]

In contrast to the failed negotiations between Malaysia and Singapore in 1966 to preserve the common currency, which had been detailed and sometimes intense, there was a strong consensus among the three countries that a simple arrangement based on customary tender was in the best interests of all parties. On 5 June 1967, there was a joint statement by the Singapore and Malaysian governments that a currency interchangeability arrangement would come into force on 12 June 1967, as letters had been exchanged between the governor of BNM and the chairman of the BCCS.[85] A few days later Brunei agreed to join the arrangement and committed to exchanging letters with BNM and BCCS to this effect.[86]

And so it came to pass that when Malaysia, Singapore and Brunei began issuing their own currencies on 12 June 1967, the governments of the three countries concurrently adopted a system of free interchangeability between their new currencies, beginning on the same date. This interchangeability was possible because all three currencies were pegged at the same sterling value of 2s 4d, so that a Singapore dollar would be at par with the Malaysian dollar and a Brunei dollar.

Under the Currency Interchangeability Agreement, each country would issue, manage and own its own currency; and each country's currency, while not legal-tender in the other two countries, would be customary tender.[87] For instance, individuals could make purchases from a shop in Malaysia using Singapore dollars, and the shop-owner could then deposit the currency without charge at his local bank. The bank would credit the Malaysian dollar equivalent to his account. BNM would then arrange for the repatriation of the currency in exchange for the equivalent in sterling or some other agreed currency. While the agreement did not *require* businesses and individuals to accept all three currencies in transactions, the fact that the other currencies could always be readily exchanged into the local currency should make them more acceptable. In this way, the interchangeability arrangement provided a degree of assurance to individuals and businesses used to dealing with a common currency across borders. By reducing the friction of transacting in different currencies, the transition to individual currencies was smoother.

'Dollar for dollar' ran the press headlines. You could use a Singapore dollar to pay for a taxi in Kuala Lumpur; a Malaysian dollar to buy satay in Bandar Seri Begawan; and a Brunei dollar to buy a newspaper in Singapore.[88] Moreover,

'Dollar for dollar',
Straits Times,
6 September 1966.
This catchphrase
would be used in
subsequent headlines
on the currency
interchangeability
arrangements.

since all three currencies were still fixed to the pound sterling, they were interchangeable at the par values declared by their governments. Thus, in practice, the convenience afforded by the old currency board remained to a certain degree – the three currencies circulated as one in the marketplace.[89]

It is perhaps surprising that the customary tender approach had not figured as a last resort in the earlier negotiations over the common currency, given that it would have been a convenient compromise and would have made the transition to separate currencies much smoother, not least by reassuring the public.

The announcement of the interchangeability agreement was greeted with great relief amongst bankers and traders as well as the general public. It was more than just a matter of convenience, but of considerable psychological importance, that there should be acceptance of the three currencies as payment for goods and services in the shops without the need for conversion.

Working out the specifics of the agreement proved to be challenging. Problems arose over the currency-clearance system. The agreement provided for the physical collection of notes and coins by each monetary authority and the periodic repatriation against settlement in sterling or some other agreed currency. Singapore would have preferred the transfers to be primarily between the commercial banks, which would have borne the foreign exchange risk, rather than the BCCS, which was not supposed to bear risk. The Bank of England recommended the East African Currency Board settlement system, which held accounts in the name of several central banks and cleared balances through them, settling at the end of each week.[90] Malaysia favoured this arrangement but Singapore considered it inappropriate for the BCCS to accept a holding account for BNM.[91] So the system was incomplete, and the banks themselves had eventually to set up their own clearing system across the national borders.

The Singapore branch of the Hongkong and Shanghai Bank (today's HSBC) was especially critical of this process,[92] alleging that neither government appeared to have considered the implications of the changeover sufficiently before it took place; and no arrangements existed whereby banks could exchange the respective currencies directly with the monetary authorities, the only medium for settlement being through sterling or other foreign currencies.[93] Finally, in mid-March 1968, interchangeability was extended to bank balances. To facilitate this, BNM opened an account in Singapore currency with the accountant-general in Singapore, while the latter opened a mirror account in Malaysian dollars with BNM.[94]

The sterling devaluation of 1967

By the second half of 1967 a devaluation of sterling was widely expected because of Britain's balance of payments difficulties. Internal documents show that in the run-up to this event, the Singapore government had assessed the likely impact of a sterling devaluation and was concerned about how the rest of the world might respond, especially Malaysia.[95] Prior to the devaluation there were two speeches in Parliament by Minister for Finance Goh Keng Swee, in which he explained that for more than a year, sterling had been 'an ailing currency' despite drastic

Minister for Finance Dr Goh Keng Swee (at the head of the table) speaks to the press, October 1967.

attempts by the British to maintain its value through a very unpopular austerity programme. The blocking of the Suez Canal during the Egypt-Israel Six Day War, which began on 5 June 1967, had increased the cost of Britain's imports. A strike by dock workers in October seriously slowed British export earnings. Goh's conclusion was that 'there is a significant risk of a devaluation this year'.[96]

Although the writing appeared to be on the wall, the British provided repeated assurances that they would not devalue, and applied political pressure on Sterling Area countries such as Malaysia and Singapore not to liquidate their sterling reserves. This made both Malaysia and Singapore vulnerable, especially since they were holding substantial foreign reserves in London which would be worth less in terms of other foreign currencies if the pound sterling were to be devalued.

Britain devalues the pound – the news headlines in London, 18 November 1967.

Nevertheless, on 16 November 1967 the Chancellor of the Exchequer, James Callaghan, recommended to the British Parliament that the pound should be devalued. He had Prime Minister Harold Wilson's backing for the move. Approval was obtained and at 9.30 p.m. GMT on Saturday 18 November 1967 (5.30 a.m. Singapore time, Sunday 19 November), following strong speculative selling of the pound on the expectation that the British balance of payments deficit was unsustainable, the British government announced that the pound sterling was devalued by 14.3 per cent.[97] It was now equal to US$2.4 instead of US$2.8. Prime Minister Wilson's 'the pound in your pocket' broadcast was widely derided for suggesting that the value of the pound in people's pockets, purses or the bank in Britain had not changed, even though the pound was now worth 14.3 per cent less abroad in terms of foreign currencies.[98] Since import prices were likely to rise as a consequence of the devaluation, the buying power of a pound in the pocket would certainly be hit in the longer run. It was no coincidence that three years later Wilson's Labour Party lost the November 1970 general election to the opposition Conservative Party.

Singapore and Malaysia were given advance notice of a few hours. At 5.30 p.m. Singapore time on Saturday 18 November, the British officially informed the government that the pound would be devalued. In a message from James Callaghan to Singapore's finance minister Goh Keng Swee,[99] reasons for the devaluation were given, including the likelihood of a large balance of payments deficit for 1967 and 'little or no prospect of restoring confidence in the present parity'. This was accompanied by political pressure on both Singapore and

Malaysia not to follow suit or diversify the composition of their external reserves held in sterling. The British view, expressed in a memo from the Chancellor of the Exchequer to Singapore's Minister for Finance, was that the devaluation would be quite sufficient to re-establish a strong pound and balance of payments, so there was no need for changes in the parities of other major currencies and 'no one need regret having held reserves in sterling over the years, or be in doubt as to the advantages of continuing to do'.[100]

The choices facing Malaysia and Singapore in response to the sterling devaluation were stark: to do nothing and let their currencies appreciate automatically by 14.3 per cent against the currencies of Britain and those countries which also devalued in tandem with Britain; maintain the existing parity against sterling and so devalue against the rest of the world; or partially devalue against the rest of the world. Goh later said that partial devaluation was not an option for Singapore and in the event, both countries chose the first option.

A few hours after Malaysia had been informed by the British, Malaysia's finance minister Tan Siew Sin informed Goh Keng Swee at 7.45 p.m. Singapore time that Malaysia would not follow suit to devalue its dollar.[101] Then on 19 November, at 4 p.m. local time, the Singapore government announced that the Singapore dollar would not be devalued either.[102] The Brunei government subsequently announced that it also would not devalue.

The economic considerations for Malaysia and Singapore in relation to devaluation were slightly different. Singapore exported manufactured goods and could ramp up production quickly to take advantage of a weaker exchange rate, but Malaysia was less able to do so (see **To devalue or not to devalue**, opposite). Certainly, Singapore Prime Minister Lee Kuan Yew personally leaned in favour of devaluing, while Goh subsequently acknowledged in a speech to a group of industrialists on 20 November that devaluation would have allowed Singapore's exporters 'to compete more keenly in the export markets for manufactured goods'.[103]

However, authorities in both countries ultimately placed more emphasis on the reasons not to devalue. For Malaysia, it was a matter of pride to preserve the value of its new dollar and send a positive signal to foreign investors. After all, it would have been embarrassing to have issued a new currency and then devalue it just six months later! For Singapore, the fear was that devaluation would have significantly increased import prices and costs and destabilised labour relations, ultimately negating any price benefits to the country's exports.[104] The fact that Malaysia would not devalue was also a key consideration in Singapore's decision. Interchangeability would have been disrupted by an exchange rate change between Singapore and Malaysia and could have harmed trade and financial flows between the two countries.

To devalue or not to devalue – that is the question

Devaluation is the official lowering of the value of a currency fixed in terms of another currency, a basket of currencies, or an international reserve asset such as gold. It contrasts with 'depreciation', which is a market-determined fall in the value of a currency.

Devaluation can be undertaken to try to improve a country's competitive position in international markets at least in the short term, and can be effective as long as other countries do not devalue at the same time and to the same extent. It has been a predatory tactic to gain a trade advantage over economic rivals. However, devaluation is more typically undertaken to correct a persistent balance of payments deficit, as was the case with Britain in November 1967. It can also be justified if a monetary authority is unable to support the fixed value of its currency because of heavy volatility in the foreign exchange market, or has insufficient reserve assets or access to international borrowing. This was also the case for Britain in 1967.[105]

The justification for Malaysia not to devalue in November 1967 following the sterling devaluation was that its exports consisted largely of primary products, such as rubber and tin, making it difficult for Malaysia to benefit from devaluation. Agricultural output was subject to predetermined production plans which could not be changed quickly, unlike factory-produced manufactured goods. At the same time, the international tin price was regulated by the International Tin Council, which imposed export quotas on its members, including Malaysia. Moreover, there was anyway no need to devalue since Malaysia's balance of payments was in surplus, international debt was not a problem and it had ample reserve assets with which to defend the parity of its currency against sterling.

In principle, Singapore had more to gain from devaluing and more to lose by not devaluing than Malaysia, because the proportion of manufactured goods in the former's total exports was much higher. Moreover, the amount of local currency that the Board of Commissioners of Currency, Singapore (BCCS) could issue after devaluation for each pound held in its reserves would have been reduced, and this could have had deflationary effects on the economy unless the BCCS had been in a position to increase the amount of reserves it held to back the Singapore dollar.

But there was another, overriding reason not to devalue. A substantial portion of Singapore's exports contained a large amount of imported raw materials, and devaluation would have made these imports more expensive. The increase in import prices brought about by a devaluation would have had a much more powerful upward effect on domestic prices in Singapore than in Malaysia, and would eventually have increased the prices of exports and offset the initial competitive gains from the devaluation. At the same time spending by the government and consumers on imports was very high, so import demand would not have fallen significantly following the devaluation; instead, the rise in import prices would have quickly and strongly 'passed through' to consumer prices. As with Malaysia, there was no compelling reason for Singapore to devalue since its balance of payments was in surplus, the value of its external debt was negligible, and the BCCS had ample external reserves to back the currency fix to sterling.

Singapore and Malaysia agree not to devalue: the *Straits Times*, 20 November 1967.

However, the sterling devaluation created an immediate currency problem for the three countries vis-à-vis the Malaya and British Borneo dollar, which was still in the process of being removed from circulation. The old dollar, which had previously been on a par with the Malaysian, Singapore, and Brunei dollars, was still redeemable at the fixed rate of 2s 4d. It therefore automatically devalued against the new currencies by 14.3 per cent, equivalent to the sterling devaluation.[106] This affected about 600 million dollars of old currency which was still in circulation then; the banks in all three territories had to exchange them at only 85 cents to the new dollar. If the amount of old currency circulating in Singapore was proportional to its 18.3 per cent share in the assets divided when the Malayan and British Borneo currency board was wound up, there would have been 110 million dollars of old currency still on the island, worth approximately S$93 million in new currency. This would have been equivalent to 22 per cent of the currency in active circulation in Singapore as at end-1967, or 9.5 per cent of money supply (M1). Not surprisingly, people became anxious to exchange

Workers at Chartered Industries of Singapore working on a coin machine while others polish bullets.

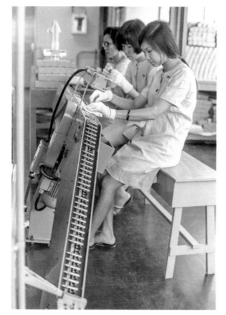

old dollars for new in case they were devalued further. Goh Keng Swee had been aware of this problem when he explained publicly why Singapore did not devalue. He admitted that the devaluation of the old coins had created 'a nasty situation' but he thought that eventually a solution could be found.[107]

The sudden rush to change old currency for new coincided with an inadequate supply of Singapore dollar notes, as Singapore's British printers faced a shortage of the security paper used to print the notes, which was required to prevent forgery.[108] The BCCS, in response to long queues at its office, was forced to announce a limit on the amount of the old currency that could be exchanged[109] to five old dollars per person and their staff worked over the weekend to ensure there was sufficient currency available.[110]

The demand for the new coins increased far beyond what had been supplied to date. On 22 November 1967, Goh Keng Swee wrote to Britain's Chancellor of the Exchequer requesting his personal assistance. He asked him to intervene on Singapore's behalf with the Royal Mint in London 'with whom we intend to place an immediate order worth S$20 million of new coins to be minted immediately' – would it be possible for Britain's Royal Air Force Transport Command to fly them out to Singapore?

Goh pointed out that the new coins had only been issued on 20 November and the present stock was only expected to last about a week![111]

Two days later, the BCCS was informed that the Royal Mint would indeed deliver 25 million coins per week starting from 1 December, up to a total of 100 million. Since the approximate weight to be delivered was 450 tons the Royal Air Force could not help, as they were engaged in the withdrawal of troops from Aden and were on 'stand-by' in Cyprus.[112] On 30 November, Goh thanked the Chancellor for helping Singapore get out of what could have been a difficult situation.[113] Singapore would find other ways to get the coins to the island: in December ten planeloads of airlifted coins – equivalent to 180 tons – arrived via chartered aircraft at a cost of nearly a million Singapore dollars.[114, 115]

The costs and logistical challenges of shipping coins from an overseas mint to Singapore, which had plagued it even during the colonial era, were resolved shortly after. On Goh Keng Swee's initiative, the Singapore Mint was established in March 1968 in Jurong as a division of the government-owned Chartered Industries of Singapore, and coins minted in Singapore gradually replaced those imported from Britain. They were exactly the same but local production eliminated freight and foreign exchange costs. Today Chartered Industries of Singapore is a division of Singapore Precision Industries Pte Ltd.[116]

After the announcement of the sterling devaluation, there was substantial confusion surrounding all transactions involving the old currency in both Singapore and Malaysia.[117] The hardest hit were people holding old dollars who kept their savings in cash at home. They felt cheated and betrayed. They could not understand the legal technicalities but had simply trusted their governments that one old dollar would be equal to one new dollar. 'When they said that one old dollar was equal to 85.7 new cents only, they were shocked!'[118] The manager of the Hongkong and Shanghai Bank branch in Kuala Lipis, Malaysia, the only bank in the town, recounted his own experience: 'We had long queues of unhappy people. One farmer with 40 years' worth of coins saved for his pilgrimage to Mecca was in tears.'[119]

There were quarrels between bus conductors and passengers as to the exact amount of change they were entitled to, and abuse from the public when they were unable to change old notes at their pre-devaluation value. In Singapore, the *Straits Times* reported that the Ministry of Finance had met with operators of bus companies to hammer out a solution: bus companies would continue to accept coins for fares 'at normal value', i.e. old coins would have the same value as new coins in payment for fares.[120] Confusingly, however, the article went on to state that 'there will be no change in the value of old coins used on any business in Singapore', which was clearly not the case. Shopkeepers were accused of rounding-off change, effectively increasing prices by 5 or 10 cents across the board.[121]

A bus is attacked in Penang on 24 November 1967 following the devaluation of the old Malaya and British Borneo dollar.

To make matters worse, riots broke out in Penang, Perak, Kedah and Selangor in Malaysia, resulting in bloodshed and the introduction of curfews. On 24 November 1967, a peaceful protest by the Malaysian Labour Party in Penang turned violent. Five people were killed and 92 injured.[122] The protesters stopped buses and lorries and attacked shops and breakfast cafés which refused to participate in the protest. A 24-hour curfew was imposed the same day. According to the British High Commission in Kuala Lumpur, the riots initially arose from the devaluation of the old dollar but 'were serious because they became racial'.[123]

There did not seem to have been any public demonstrations in Singapore.[124] However, local pressure groups, including the National Trades Union Congress, pointed to the devaluation's disproportionate impact on lower income groups; they lobbied the government to redeem the old currency at par with the new. The Chinese Chamber of Commerce and Industry said that the sterling devaluation and the divergences in the value of old and new notes and coins had caused 'much difficulties and inconvenience to the people'. They sent a memo to finance minister Goh Keng Swee expressing their concerns, and pointed to disputes between exporters and importers and the banks over exchange rates.

Public dissatisfaction in Singapore spilled over into the political domain when on 22 November a Member of Parliament, Lim Soo Peng, wrote to Dr Goh to inform him that he planned to put a question to him in Parliament over the confusion.[125] The left-wing political party in Singapore, the Barisan Sosialis, described the whole episode as 'a big imperialist plot to allow the British to plunder this region'.

Goh Keng Swee had been considering measures to ease the dislocation and hardship experienced by people holding old currency – he feared undesirable political repercussions. He now suggested that the three governments agree to change old coins into new coins at the rates existing before the sterling devaluation, with the losses incurred from redeeming the coins from the Malaya and British Borneo currency board at a lower rate to sterling than the new ones to be borne by the three governments.[126]

Finally, in response to public discontent, on 24 November the Malaysian and Singaporean governments agreed to a partial solution: they announced simultaneously that the value of the old five- and ten-cent coins would be the same as that of the new. However, Brunei decided not to change the parity of the old coins since it 'would have caused confusion'.[127]

Was the decision to allow the old currency to be devalued against the new the right one? A partial devaluation would have been a quick and sure way to drive the old currency out of circulation and wind up the affairs of the former currency board. However, the Malaysian government argued that it was illegal for it not to let the old dollar automatically devalue against the new since any change in the official rate between the Malaya and British Borneo dollar vis-à-vis sterling required a change in the Currency Acts of Malaysia, Singapore and Brunei.[128]

Ironically, it was illegal for Singapore to allow the old dollar to be automatically devalued in terms of the new because the 1967 Currency Act stipulated that the old currency should be exchangeable at par with the new notes issued by the BCCS. This was intended to strengthen confidence in the new Singapore dollar and ensure it would not be worth less than the old.[129] Thus, on 23 November 1967, the Singapore cabinet was obliged to approve an emergency amendment to the 1967 Currency Act that was moved in Parliament on 5 December. Unusually for parliamentary procedures, it would take effect retrospectively – from 19 November, when the sterling devaluation had occurred in Singapore time.[130]

Regardless, the sterling devaluation did impose genuine financial losses on Malaysia, Singapore, and Brunei. It reduced the purchasing power of sterling reserves in countries which did not devalue, and more sterling assets would now be needed to back the new currencies, since the local-currency value of the reserves would have fallen. For Singapore, there was an immediate shortfall in the value of the external assets of the BCCS, and this had to be transferred from the Consolidated Fund to the Currency Fund to maintain the 100 per cent backing of Singapore notes and coins in circulation as required by law.[131] The Singapore government questioned whether in showing a lack of initiative before devaluation, the Crown Agents were putting the interests of the British government above those of their clients.[132]

Unknown to the British government, Singapore had been diversifying its foreign reserves since July 1966, leaving the sterling reserves in London intact but investing other government funds in non-sterling currencies.[133] Dr Goh noted that: 'What is of relevance to us is that before July 1966, the entire external reserves of the Singapore Government were held in London in sterling. It is obvious that devaluation of sterling would inflict an inescapable loss to us unless

Public housing changed the face of Singapore: early HDB flats at the MacPherson Estate. Flat ownership became the main financial asset for a large proportion of Singaporeans.

we took out some of this money and converted into gold or into non-sterling foreign currency.'[134] In a nod of respect to Britain, the diversification was gradual because Singapore did not want to be seen to be weakening sterling by withdrawing reserves from London in a substantial way. Consequently, while the Singapore government had by November 1967 reduced its sterling holdings to about 50 per cent of its reserves, down from 90 per cent, Singapore was still the fifth-largest holder of sterling in the world, after Australia, Hong Kong, Kuwait and Malaysia.[135]

The issue of Singapore's diversification of its reserves out of sterling led to an exchange of letters between the British and Singapore governments. Britain's Chancellor of the Exchequer – by now Roy Jenkins – expressed concern about Singapore's announcement that only 50 per cent of its reserves were kept in sterling. He argued that this would not only weaken the Sterling Area but also encourage others to follow, and he regretted that Singapore had not consulted him on this matter.[136]

In his reply on 12 December, Dr Goh said that three-quarters of the funds Singapore kept overseas were not monetary reserves but various deposits and surpluses on the government's account, mainly the outcome of prudent financing over the years and surpluses in Singapore's overall balance of payments.[137] On 18 December, Prime Minister Lee Kuan Yew himself wrote to Prime Minister Harold Wilson confirming that Singapore had 'never moved any of her sterling reserves over the previous three years but did place some of her budget surpluses in non-sterling securities'.[138] The British view was that this did not make any difference to the damage it did to the Sterling Area.[139]

The diplomatic exchanges were complicated by Britain's announcement in January 1968 that it would withdraw its military personnel from Singapore by end-April 1971, earlier than the 'mid-1970s' date previously announced in July 1967. Just one month earlier, in December 1967, Lee had written to Wilson expressing concern over the effect of the withdrawal on confidence in Singapore's future, especially since a large number of Hong Kong industrialists had recently been attracted to the country to set up subsidiaries.[140]

There was no doubt that the economic impact of the withdrawal would be substantial since the bases employed about 23,000 workers, accounting for a tenth of Singapore's land area and almost 20 per cent of gross domestic product (GDP). The *Financial Times* estimated that 45,000 people would lose their jobs and quoted Goh Keng Swee's budget statement that the Singapore government would have to spend £10 million more for each of the next three years to redress the issue. The rise in unemployment and loss in confidence was particularly worrying at a time when Singapore's population was growing fast, and large numbers of school-leavers were entering the workforce. But there would be some relief from the fact that a third of the retrenched workers would be non-citizens, the naval dockyard could be converted into a commercial service centre for tankers, and Americans serving in the Vietnam War were taking their 'rest and recreation' in Singapore.[141]

Perhaps concerned that the issue of reserves diversification was being conflated with the British motivation for withdrawal, Goh Keng Swee explained in his letter of 12 December 1967 that the proportion of Singapore's reserves held outside London was not substantial. He reminded Jenkins that, furthermore, neither he nor any of his colleagues had uttered a single word of recrimination against the British government's decision to devalue sterling, unlike other countries. Dr Goh also pointed out that because Singapore's foreign reserves held in pounds were now worth less in terms of other currencies, the country had lost a total of S$157 million, 'substantial losses for a small underdeveloped country to sustain'.[142]

Wilson and his defence secretary Denis Healey were clearly sympathetic to Singapore's plight and the compensation in the end was quite generous, but they made it conditional on Singapore's continued support for the Sterling Area and no further diversification of its reserves.[143] Lee would subsequently acknowledge that 'the considerate manner and measured pace of the withdrawal', the fact that the military installations could quickly be converted to civilian use and the £50 million aid package were enough to make for 'a boost in morale'.[144]

The topic of Singapore's sterling reserves and its participation in the Sterling Area would continue to dog relations between Singapore and Britain. On 25 September 1968, the British were forced by their Group of Ten partners[145] to negotiate bilateral agreements with Singapore, Hong Kong and other holders

Singapore Prime
Minister Lee Kuan
Yew with UK Prime
Minister Harold
Wilson after
discussions in London
over the withdrawal
of British troops from
Singapore, 1968.

of sterling that guaranteed the US dollar value of their sterling foreign exchange reserves in the event of a further British devaluation. However, the weakness of sterling was to lead to further currency problems for Singapore in the early 1970s after the pound was allowed to float, and the British government eventually unilaterally dismantled the Sterling Area (see p. 265).

In retrospect

Despite Singapore's political separation from Malaysia in 1965, negotiations to retain some vestige of a common currency lasted for nearly two more years, about as long as Singapore's membership of the Federation of Malaysia. After all, the social, business, and financial ties linking Singapore and the rest of the federation were deep and extensive. From this perspective, having one currency to serve as a common unit of account and means of transaction between the two entities was natural, sensible and desirable.

Although the politicians were unable to avert a currency split, support for maintaining currency interchangeability was strong within each country, culminating in the Currency Interchangeability Agreement of 1967. This was critical in preventing disruptions to trade, banking and finance across the three countries, and was widely celebrated at the time. Nevertheless, scepticism about the durability of this arrangement remained.

While the currency interchangeability arrangement survived the challenges posed by the devaluation of the pound sterling in November 1967, other strains were coming to bear, arising from different policy objectives on either side of the Causeway. Meanwhile, Singapore was actively soliciting foreign direct investment to enhance its manufacturing base and absorb the substantial pool of unemployed labour. Malaysia was keen to promote its own manufacturing sector and, in line with other developing countries at the time, was prepared to protect its 'infant industries' with tariffs and other forms of protection. It was also less welcoming to foreign multinational corporations than Singapore and was eager to build up its own financial and transportation services.

In its commentary on 12 June 1967, the *Straits Times* argued – presciently, as it would turn out – that 'the currency was split because of political distrust and the weakening of economic co-operation. These factors remain, and they will govern the future that matters.' The policy differences between Singapore and Malaysia would become more evident thereafter, and as the next chapter will show, they would significantly shape the two countries' responses to turmoil in the international monetary system in the early 1970s.

CHAPTER 07

FOUNDING MAS;
THE END OF BRETTON WOODS
(1970–1979)

Singapore thrived after separation from Malaysia, defying expectations and despite the economic impact of Britain's military withdrawal. In 1971, the Monetary Authority of Singapore was founded. Its main challenges were external, as some developed economies were hit by balance of payments problems and pressures on their currencies. This led to the breakdown of the Bretton Woods system of fixed exchange rates. The Singapore dollar was then pegged to the US dollar rather than sterling. The Sterling Area ceased to exist when the British pound floated in June 1972. With the gradual relaxation of capital controls that followed, a key hindrance to Singapore's development as an international financial centre was removed. Singapore and Malaysia placed different emphases on their economic development agenda, and the currency interchangeability arrangement with Malaysia came to an end (although that with Brunei continues to this day). External events again hit the headlines: severe inflation in 1972/3 was exacerbated by the OPEC oil embargo. Singapore's response was financial discipline and credit restraints to curb excess growth in the money supply. The year 1977 brought the Bird series of currency notes. As the decade neared its end, the arrival of the first ATM in Raffles Place ushered in a new era of banking technology.

Defying naysayers' expectations, Singapore thrived in the years immediately after separation from Malaysia. According to a World Bank report, 'In 1968 Singapore entered a new phase of accelerated growth with boom conditions in private investment, a decline in unemployment, buoyancy of government revenues, the emergence of an overall surplus of savings over investment, and a significant build-up of external reserves.'[1] Gross domestic product (GDP) growth was strong, averaging nearly 13 per cent annually in 1966–70. Despite concerns about the withdrawal of the British military, which was completed in 1971, the economy avoided a recession, and there were even shortages of labour in some sectors. There were no queues outside employment exchanges, but business was brisk at centres processing work permits for non-citizens.[2] Immigration laws were relaxed to bring in foreign labour on short-term work permits.

There was notable progress in the general welfare of Singapore's population. Slums were cleared and social infrastructure was put in place, such as improved public transport and public flats built in neighbourhoods that became known as 'new towns': the aim was to make Singapore 'clean, green and beautiful'. Real income per head, S$5,319 in 1965, had risen to S$8,878 by 1970. The World Bank and International Monetary Fund (IMF) reported that in the Singapore of 1970 there was 'a general atmosphere of ebullience and optimism'.

With the most pressing issues of national survival addressed, 1971 seemed as good a year as any for Singapore to set up a monetary authority to handle the functions that would more typically be carried out by a central bank. Currency issuance, however, remained within the purview of the Board of Commissioners of Currency, Singapore (BCCS).

However, this optimism would quickly dissipate, and the fledgling Monetary Authority of Singapore (MAS) would have its work cut out, as a number of external shocks buffeted the island state in quick succession. US President Richard Nixon's decision to suspend the convertibility of the US dollar into gold in 1971 was followed by flotation of the pound sterling and the dissolution of the Sterling Area in 1972. The year 1973 saw flotation of the US dollar, the termination of the Currency Interchangeability Agreement between Malaysia and Singapore, and the flotation of the Singapore dollar, just as the first global oil-price shock struck.

These events had the potential to cause significant harm to Singapore, but with judicious management they were turned to the country's advantage. Favourable circumstances allowed MAS to adopt a discretionary monetary policy, while at the same time advancing Singapore's ambition of becoming a regional financial hub.

Chapter opening picture: Boat Quay, 1974. Twakows (lighters serving larger ships in the harbour) are still moored in the river, but the OCBC bank building under construction is evidence of economic change.

Founding MAS

Following the currency split of 12 June 1967, the BCCS was set up to issue the first-ever currency specific to Singapore. Nevertheless, there were other functions typically carried out by central banks that needed to be performed domestically. For instance, there was a need for an institution to act as banker to the government and to supervise the banking system. Dr Goh Keng Swee, who had returned to the Ministry of Finance in August that year, did not think that a central bank was necessary for Singapore at that time. Apart from his concern that central banks could be held hostage to irresponsible fiscal policy, he was doubtful, for instance, that the key instrument for central banks – 'open market operations', or the buying and selling of government securities from the primary banks to increase or decrease the money supply – would make for effective monetary policy in Singapore. Consequently, having or not having a central bank would make no practical difference.

Instead, Dr Goh held the view that the main central-banking functions could be carried out effectively by existing government bodies and departments. Unusually, therefore, in Singapore the Accountant-General's Department held the deposits that banks had to maintain with the government, issued treasury bills, and ensured that there was sufficient bank liquidity; the Commissioner of Banking enforced the Banking Ordinance; the Department of Overseas Investment within the Ministry of Finance managed Singapore's external assets; and the Ministry of Finance directed and coordinated the whole system. As Dr Goh subsequently reflected, 'It is an untidy system, consisting of units that grew up *ad hoc* in the course of time in response to urgent requirements but in the aggregate, they can be said to perform central banking functions.'[3] In sum, the system was doing well.

Nevertheless, Goh Keng Swee was clear that Singapore's reasons for establishing a currency board rather than a central bank would only prevail in the short term as the newly independent country sought to establish the credibility and stability of the Singapore dollar. Accordingly, he did not rule out the possibility that Singapore could establish its own central bank at some future date.[4] However, the move to a fully fledged central bank, he said, should be taken in two steps: first, organise the existing units into a central monetary authority under the direction of the Ministry of Finance. From that body, over time, a 'proper' central bank would emerge as an independent monetary institution when 'the world has moved into a period of tranquillity'.[5]

The demands of an increasingly complex banking and monetary system in the 1970s necessitated a streamlining of the multiple agencies conducting central-banking functions, so as to enable a more dynamic and coherent policy on monetary and financial matters. The need for consolidation became increasingly

Michael Wong
Pakshong, first
managing director
of MAS.

obvious. Accordingly, in January 1971, MAS was set up under the terms of the 1970 Monetary Authority of Singapore Act.[6] The initial draft legislation was produced by Dr Goh with advice from the International Monetary Fund (IMF), although he had moved to the Ministry of Defence by the time the legislation was ratified by the Singapore Parliament in December 1970.

The establishment of MAS consolidated the traditional central-banking functions previously performed by government departments.[7] Crucially, the job of issuing currency was left with the BCCS. This was an unusual arrangement, as the 1971 IMF mission to Singapore had noted;[8] it was not until 2002 that the issue of currency was finally transferred to MAS (see p. 353). Accordingly, the Authority's objectives as specified in the 1970 Act were to act as banker to, and financial agent of, the government; to promote monetary stability and credit and exchange conditions conducive to economic growth; and to supervise Singapore's financial system and manage its reserves. Reflecting the reality that MAS did not initially conduct discretionary monetary policy given the Singapore dollar's peg under the currency-board system, the Authority was, operationally, much more focused on financial supervision and reserve management. In fact, when MAS was first set up it only had three departments, covering Banking and Financial institutions, Investment and Exchange Control, and Banking Operations and Administration. They were split between offices at City Hall and the currency board building at Empress Place.

MAS's first managing director was Michael Wong Pakshong, a South African-born Chinese, who guided the Authority through its first decade. Its first chairman was Hon Sui Sen, who had replaced Goh Keng Swee as Minister for Finance in August 1970. It was unusual for a monetary authority to be chaired by the finance minister. The arrangement ran contrary to World Bank advice that such

Minister for Finance
Hon Sui Sen (centre)
meets with MAS
officials, 1971.

an arrangement would compromise policy independence: the Bank feared that MAS could be put under political pressure to finance government budget deficits. However, Dr Goh argued that appointing nominally independent bank chiefs did not itself guarantee the ability of central banks to make policy independently. For example, US President Richard Nixon had put political pressure on Federal Reserve Chairman Arthur Burns to engage in expansionary monetary policy before the 1972 presidential election.

In Singapore the 100 per cent backing of the currency by the BCCS effectively ruled out the financing of government budget deficits anyway. Government spending in Singapore would be paid for out of government revenue and there would be budget surpluses, if possible, to provide resources 'for a rainy day'. Therefore, the argument went, Singapore did not need a central bank whose independence was guaranteed by statute. Instead, the government would adhere strictly to the principle of fiscal prudence, and this would confer the necessary policy and operational independence on the BCCS and MAS.[9]

Singapore's external reserves were transferred from the Department of Overseas Investment (DOI) in the Ministry of Finance to the Investments and Exchange Control Department at MAS, with a small amount left at the BCCS. By 1970, foreign reserves per capita had almost tripled compared to 1965. Goh Keng Swee had correctly foreseen that Singapore's reserves would continue to grow as a result of substantial balance of payments surpluses. Once provision had been made for MAS to have sufficient liquid reserves to be able to intervene when necessary in the foreign exchange market, there was a desire to invest the 'excess reserves' in a diversified portfolio for longer-term wealth preservation; this should include equities, as well as the low-risk, low-return cash, bonds and gold typically held by central banks. There was a concurrent need to diversify away from the pound sterling and US dollar to currencies such as the Japanese yen and the deutschmark, for which there was both liquidity and scope for appreciation.

It was not clear whether MAS would be able to build up the special risk-management skills needed to actively manage the portfolio of reserves and at the same time develop expertise in other day-to-day central banking responsibilities, which were also starting from a low base. Moreover, central bankers and fund managers were usually compensated and incentivised differently – typically fund managers' remuneration was based primarily on the performance of their investments. There could be a conflict of interest between on the one hand MAS's requirement for a substantial stock of liquid reserve assets with which to intervene in the foreign exchange market and so maintain the Singapore dollar's peg to sterling, and the need to invest these reserves for longer-term returns.

The Bretton Woods system breaks down

Shortly after MAS was established, it had to confront 'a crisis undermining the fabric of the international monetary order',[10] namely the breakdown of the system of fixed exchange rates that had been in place since 1945. Under the

Bretton Woods rules, the Singapore dollar was pegged to sterling, which itself was fixed to the US dollar, which in turn was fixed to gold[11] (see p. 162). Throughout the 1960s and early 1970s, however, the system showed increasing signs of strain. With the benefit of hindsight, there were clearly some flaws built into the system that eventually led to its demise.

To begin with, countries found it increasingly difficult to keep their currencies within the required exchange rate band vis-à-vis the US dollar without sacrificing their domestic economic goals, namely an acceptable level of unemployment consistent with low consumer price inflation. This difficulty of achieving domestic goals and at the same time keeping the exchange rate fixed was compounded by asymmetrical

John Maynard Keynes, the economist, who played a key role at the Bretton Woods Conference.

policy pressures: countries with balance of payments deficits, such as Britain, France and Italy, were unwilling to introduce policies that would restore balance as the system required. Cutting domestic spending, allowing unemployment to rise and/or devaluing their currencies were politically unpopular at home. Meanwhile, countries with persistent balance of payments surpluses, such as West Germany and Japan, were reluctant to stimulate their economies through monetary and fiscal policy because that could lead to higher inflation, while revaluing their currencies would make their exports less competitive in international markets.[12] The asymmetry arose from the fact that countries with deficits would eventually run out of reserves to meet their balance of payments needs and would inevitably have to adjust policies, whereas countries in surplus could postpone adjustment almost indefinitely. The funding available to the IMF to help deficit countries was also inadequate.

A more fundamental flaw in the system became known as the Triffin Dilemma, named after Robert Triffin, a Yale University professor of economics, who testified before the US Congress in 1947.[13] The US dollar had become a 'global reserve currency', meaning that it was the predominant currency in which central banks held their reserves, as well as the currency in which most global trade and financial transactions were denominated. Triffin pointed out that global demand for US dollars would keep increasing, given the growth in international trade. With an insufficient supply of gold, central banks would need increasing amounts of US dollars as liquid reserve assets to back their currencies as their economies grew. The global demand for US dollars could only be met if the US ran a balance of payments deficit, i.e. it was injecting more US dollars into the global economy than it was receiving, for example by purchasing more from the world than it was selling to the world. But if the US balance of payments went increasingly into deficit, central banks might lose confidence in the ability of the US Federal Reserve to provide gold, if requested, at the fixed rate of US$35 an ounce. The situation was compounded by a sharp rise in the US balance of payments deficit from the mid-1960s, when the government increased its spending to pay for the war in Vietnam and for domestic social programmes.[14]

But the straw that broke the back of the Bretton Woods system was a rise in short-term capital mobility in the 1960s that introduced large swings in exchange rates. Capital markets such as the Eurodollar Market had developed rapidly as financial technology improved and multinational corporations transferred funds globally. At the same time, capital controls had become increasingly ineffective and made it more difficult for central banks to defend their exchange rate parities.[15] Speculators thus found avenues through which to attack weak currencies such as the pound sterling and Italian lira in anticipation of devaluation, and take refuge in stronger currencies such as the Japanese yen and the deutschmark.

In May 1971, within months of the formation of MAS, the US dollar came under intense pressure in international currency markets as confidence waned in the Federal Reserve's ability to maintain the dollar's fix to gold at the official price of US$35 an ounce. There were heavy speculative flows out of the US dollar into currencies such as the deutschmark, Japanese yen and Swiss franc. The inability to neutralise these inflows and defend their fixed rates against the US dollar led to the float of the deutschmark, while other currencies such as the Austrian schilling and the Swiss franc were revalued.

Then, in August 1971, US President Nixon 'closed the gold window' so that central banks were no longer able to exchange US dollars for gold with

The Mount Washington Hotel, setting for the Bretton Woods Conference.

the Federal Reserve. Nixon's actions fundamentally undermined the basis of the Bretton Woods gold exchange standard. This rocked the international monetary system. In one stroke, he had made the US dollar a fiat currency, i.e. one no longer backed by gold or any other precious metal.

In an attempt to reform the international monetary system, the authorities of the Group of Ten industrial countries and the IMF organised a series of meetings that took place at the Smithsonian Institution in Washington in September and December 1971. This culminated in the Smithsonian Agreement, whereby the US dollar was devalued by 8 per cent against gold, and stronger currencies such as the Japanese yen were revalued. The deutschmark, which had floated in the face of the Nixon shock, returned to a revalued parity. The limits within which currencies were allowed to fluctuate on either side of the central parity were widened from 1 per cent under Bretton Woods to 2.25 per cent to give central banks more flexibility in dealing with speculative currency flows.

On 19 December, both the Malaysian and the Singapore governments announced that they would maintain the parities of their currencies to the pound sterling, and thus to gold, at one local dollar to 0.290299 grams. Brunei quickly followed suit. Hence all three currencies automatically appreciated against the US dollar by 8 per cent.

The parity between the Singapore, Malaysian and Brunei dollars was unchanged and consequently the currency interchangeability arrangement remained in force. Although the foreign exchange markets of the three countries were closed for two days, there appears to have been no significant disruption when they were reopened. Had Malaysia devalued and Singapore not followed suit, or vice versa, this would have led to immediate practical complications for the 'customary tender' arrangement (see p.239). For example, revenue collection from telephone booths and vending machines could have involved losses if individuals used Malaysian coins in place of Singapore ones: while the size of the coins was the same in both countries, their relative values would have changed. If Singapore were to have replaced all coins in circulation to circumvent this problem, this would have cost approximately S$12 million.[16]

MAS's main consideration at the time was to maintain confidence in the Singapore dollar. As in November 1967, when the pound was devalued, there were no strong grounds for Singapore to devalue along with the US dollar. The balance of payments was in surplus and therefore did not justify devaluation under IMF rules; in any case devaluation would have done little to increase the competitiveness of Singapore's exports and would have quickly resulted in an increase in domestic prices and export prices as well.

The pound floats; the end of the Sterling Area

On 8 March 1972 Minister for Finance Hon Sui Sen in his budget speech said that 1971 had been 'a good year'. Despite the international monetary crisis, including the 'Nixon shock', the economy had grown at 14 per cent, only just below the target of 15 per cent.[17] However, the respite offered by the Smithsonian Agreement was brief. On 24 June 1972, following heavy speculative attacks and capital outflows, the British treasury announced that it would let the pound sterling float in value. Britain had lost a large amount of gold and foreign exchange reserves as the Bank of England tried unsuccessfully to support sterling at a fixed parity with the US dollar. The decision to float the pound was not unexpected given Britain's mounting trade deficit and accelerating inflation. Chancellor of the Exchequer Anthony Barber described the flotation as temporary, and he intended that the pound should return to operating within fixed trading bands around parity as per the Smithsonian Agreement as soon as possible. However, this was not to be.

The authorities in both Singapore and Malaysia decided to switch their currency pegs from sterling to the US dollar to counter the inflationary pressures that a depreciating pound would have generated. At the same time, the parties to the Currency Interchangeability Agreement – Singapore, Malaysia and Brunei – agreed to redeem their currencies from 26 June at a par value of 2.81955 to the US dollar.[18]

The US dollar thus became the main reserve currency for these countries. This was a significant step since the three territories had a long history of fixing their currencies to sterling, and of holding reserve assets in sterling, mostly in London.

The decision to shift the anchor currency of the peg was sensible. In the same way that countries had over time shifted to the gold standard over the late 19th century and the turn of the 20th because others were using gold-backed currencies, so more and more countries were now using the US dollar rather than the pound as their reserve currency, including Singapore's Southeast Asian neighbours such as Indonesia and the Philippines. The importance of the US dollar in the global monetary system had grown by the mid-1950s so the peg to the US dollar brought Singapore closer to what had become the dominant international practice, and, in the longer run, helped to further integrate Singapore into international financial markets.[19] More practically, the shift to a US dollar peg better matched the foreign exchange needs of the local banking and business community that had long been using it in international trade and financial transactions.

The flotation of the pound marked the end of the Sterling Area, to which both Singapore and Malaysia belonged. Countries in the Sterling Area had pegged their currencies to the pound; settled payments among themselves in sterling; and agreed to remove foreign exchange controls against each other but retain them against non-members. The flotation of the pound meant the Sterling Area no longer conferred stability on the exchange rates of member countries.

It had become increasingly evident over the 1950s and '60s that the Sterling Area was losing relevance for its members as Britain's global influence waned.[20] Member countries such as Australia, South Africa and Pakistan had begun to diversify their trade away from Britain, and concomitantly started to diversify their external reserves away from sterling, typically towards the US dollar. Singapore began diversifying its reserves from 1966. Some members, such as India and Pakistan, also began to introduce their own exchange controls within the Sterling Area itself. At the same time, the attraction of London as a source of funds or destination for lending was diminishing as access to other money and capital markets, such as those of West Germany and Switzerland, became easier. Decolonisation was loosening the political ties between Sterling Area countries and Britain. Indeed, the 'hub' was looking more like the periphery, as Britain increasingly relied on borrowing from the Group of Ten advanced countries through the Bank for International Settlements (BIS).

The growing sense of irrelevance was no doubt increasingly clear to Britain as well, given the prospect that trade with continental Europe was expected to be more important to the nation than trade with its former colonies within the Commonwealth. Britain had begun the process of applying to join the European Economic Community (EEC). However, there was an impediment: France was of the view that the pool of sterling reserves in London, which had come about as a result of the Sterling Area, posed a threat to the stability of the pound. Winding down the sterling balances – which would effectively bring the Sterling Area to an end – was to become one of the preconditions of Britain's membership.

In any event, the devaluation of the pound in 1967 generated some resentment on the part of Sterling Area countries such as Malaysia and Singapore because of a lack of consultation and the drop in the value of their sterling reserves. Indeed, Singapore had for some time been considering what disengaging from the Area would mean: it had consulted the IMF in 1969 on the implications of leaving the Sterling Area.[21]

To protect the value of the pound, in 1968 the British government reached formal agreements (through exchanges of letters) with members of the Sterling Area, that they should keep a minimum proportion of their external reserves in sterling. In return, Britain was given a US$2 billion line of credit by the BIS on condition

Workers in London's financial district read about the UK government's decision to join the European Economic Community (forerunner of the EU).

The Sterling Area

When Britain left the gold standard in September 1931, a diverse group of over 70 countries decided to use the pound sterling as their own currency or peg their currencies to the pound. This arrangement became known as the 'Scheduled Territories', the 'Sterling Area' or the 'Sterling Bloc'.

The Sterling Area brought benefits to Britain and its members. During the Great Depression, many countries yearned for some stability in their currencies, but did not want to return to the rigidity of the gold standard. Pegging to sterling together with other countries brought about this stability.

Since the sterling reserves of Sterling Area countries were pooled in London, they were available to meet members' legitimate demands for balance of payments financing without the quota restrictions imposed by the IMF. Members also benefitted from access to financial resources in London and from settlement of their international payments in sterling with other Sterling Area countries without cumbersome foreign exchange controls. At that time, capital controls prevented them from borrowing freely in Europe and the United States.

From Britain's point of view, the Sterling Area ensured a consistent supply of cheap imported raw materials and export markets for its manufactured goods. Britain could also use the pool of sterling reserves in London to protect the value of the pound which was fixed to the US dollar under the Bretton Woods system.

The benefits to Singapore of belonging to the Sterling Area came with some anomalies. For example, transfers of funds to Malaysia and Sterling Area member countries in Africa were free of controls, but transfers to Thailand, a fellow member of the Association of Southeast Asian Nations (ASEAN), were controlled. If a Singapore resident went on holiday to Jamaica he or she could transfer money and spend freely; but she would need approval to transfer funds for a holiday in neighbouring Bangkok. There was also the burden of paperwork for the banks, in implementing the exchange controls.

that the British government guaranteed the US-dollar value of up to 90 per cent of the sterling reserves held by Sterling Area countries in the event of another devaluation. Both Malaysia and Singapore agreed to keep 40 per cent of their reserves in sterling. A collapse in the value of the pound would not have been in their interest, and they needed time to disengage from the Sterling Area.

Despite a desire to further diversify the external reserves away from sterling, Singapore renewed the agreement with the British government for another two years in 1971, and the sterling portion of its reserves was reduced to 36 per cent of the total. However, when the pound floated, Britain now applied exchange controls to most members, including Singapore, even as it still abided by the agreements to guarantee the US dollar value of reserves held in sterling. Britain paid compensation to Singapore three times during the early 1970s when sterling depreciated against the US dollar.[22]

When the Sterling Area formally came to an end in June 1972 this opened up an opportunity for Singapore to revisit the issue of capital controls. A few options were on the table: Singapore could maintain the status quo and retain the controls on non-Sterling Area territories or remove controls on all countries.

The case for retaining the Sterling Area controls was not strong. Singapore had no significant economic or political ties with most members; its external reserves were by now substantially diversified out of sterling; it could access money and capital markets, such as Switzerland and West Germany, other than London; and, crucially, its strong balance of payments and ample external reserves mitigated the risks of a surge in capital outflows if controls were removed.

In contrast, the arguments *against* retaining the controls were strong. Importantly, capital controls were a stumbling block to Singapore's ambition to become a regional, and ultimately global, financial centre, since they hampered the free flow of funds in and out of the country compared to potential competitors such as Hong Kong. Indeed, liberalising controls was something that Singapore had seriously considered for several years now. In April 1972, even before the flotation of the pound, MAS had examined the legal requirements for further developing Singapore into a regional financial centre, building on the Asian Dollar market which had been established in Singapore in October 1968. The 1972 exercise took as its starting reference MAS's 1967 consultation with the IMF, whereby the Fund's representative Franz Ballmann had drafted legislation for the further relaxation of exchange controls.[23] Specifically, the IMF advice was to retain only selective controls and allow freedom of foreign exchange transactions unless explicitly ruled out. This was a reversal of, and simpler than, the existing legislation that ruled out all foreign exchange transactions unless they were explicitly allowed.

On this front, there were differing views in the Singapore government, which were reflected in a series of written exchanges and meetings among officials between 15 October 1975 and 3 January 1976.[24]

Most wanted some liberalisation to promote Singapore as a regional financial centre. There was an acknowledged need for MAS to improve the statistics it collected to monitor the balance of payments and exchange rate movements so that it would be better able to deal with the capital flows and currency fluctuations that had become more volatile in the 1970s.

However, some were inclined towards full liberalisation and no new restrictions on former Sterling Area countries, while others preferred to retain the existing controls for the time being but extend preferential treatment to ASEAN countries as a first step towards full liberalisation. Some parties favoured a number of new controls to make the system more coherent. MAS was concerned that there would be costs to removing all existing controls immediately, because doing so would expose Singapore to increased volatility in currency movements and capital flows, and there could be a destabilising conversion of domestic bank deposits into higher-return Asian Currency Unit deposits (see p. 277). It would also be hard to reimpose controls if they were needed in the future. Given that

MAS was new to central banking and needed time to build up the necessary expertise in dealing with a more volatile global environment, this caution was understandable.

There was also debate about the extent to which macroeconomic policies could mitigate the impact of more volatile capital flows, should controls be relaxed. Given the openness of the Singapore economy, some were sceptical about the effectiveness of monetary and fiscal policy in insulating the economy from large fluctuations in trade, currency and capital flows. There was the view that the Singapore economy could adjust automatically to external shocks, as had happened under the 1920s gold standard, given its strong balance of payments position and a currency backed by substantial reserve assets. In contrast, others within the government, including MAS, were more optimistic about the efficacy of monetary and fiscal policy. They were more wary of the gold-standard type of adjustment to changes in the balance of payments insofar as this would make it more difficult to control inflation and unemployment if the balance of payments were to deteriorate.

Removing all controls immediately was seen as risky, while retaining all existing controls would hinder the development of Singapore as a regional financial centre. A compromise was thus reached: Singapore would retain free payments and capital flows within the countries that had made up the Sterling Area as an interim solution but gradually remove controls on payments and capital flows for other countries. A more extensive relaxation of capital controls would only come a few years later, driven by the imperative to grow the Asian Dollar Market.

Our dollar and their dollar

By the early 1970s, the Currency Interchangeability Agreement between Singapore, Malaysia and Brunei introduced after the currency split in 1967 was working well. It had survived challenges to the international monetary system, including the sterling devaluation in 1967, the breakdown of the Bretton Woods system in 1971, and the flotation of the pound in 1972. When MAS was formed in 1971, Singapore wanted to transfer responsibility for the settlement of funds within the agreement from the Accountant-General to MAS. The Singapore Ministry of Finance prepared new terms of agreement and these were duly agreed by Malaysia and Brunei.[25]

The issue of the currency to be used in settling transfers of funds between the respective monetary authorities had been a long-standing area of concern. The net flow of funds had always been in favour of Singapore, but when the pound sterling was weak, Singapore made a loss when funds received from the other two countries were converted into Singapore dollars. Singapore would have preferred the settlement to be made in local currency and wanted to push for change. However, the sentiment within MAS shifted, with internal reports recommending that since the potential financial losses arising from settlement in sterling were not a big problem, it would be best not to reopen discussions with Bank Negara Malaysia (BNM). After all, Singapore benefitted from interchangeability and the net transfer of funds was broadly in its favour. MAS did not want to jeopardise the arrangement.[26] The participating countries agreed to switch to local currencies for settlement in February 1973 when the US dollar floated and the Bretton Woods pegged exchange rate system collapsed.[27]

Overall, it seems that Singapore was reasonably pleased with the arrangement. However, it was concerned that developments in the international monetary system – specifically the flotation of the US dollar in February 1973 – might lead to different par values for the Singapore and Malaysian currencies (see p. 274). While the need to maintain the interchangeability arrangement kept the currencies of both countries at par, the internal thinking then was that Singapore should prepare to adopt a more independent approach on policy matters, such as interest rates.

This preparation was important, as there was a certain precariousness to the interchangeability arrangement. The agreement included a provision whereby it could be terminated by any party simply upon giving three months' notice in writing. Concerns thus arose in the early days of the arrangement as to what would happen during the notice period: the Malaysians wanted the currencies to be redeemed at par value, and this was agreed by Singapore; it was also agreed that the two monetary authorities would bear the transport costs and that the point of exchange would be Johor Bahru.[28] The Association of Banks in Malaysia and Singapore had also been assured that should the agreement be terminated, the currencies would continue to be redeemed at par during the notice period.[29] But some public doubt remained as to what would actually happen in the event.

All speculation would soon be put to rest. On 8 May 1973, Malaysia made a surprise announcement: finance minister Tan Siew Sin told the Malaysian Parliament that he was unilaterally giving notice of termination of the Currency Interchangeability Agreement with Singapore. Although the agreement covered only notes and coins, and while the Singapore and Malaysian dollars remained at par value by virtue of their common peg to the US dollar, the termination signalled that Malaysia would likely go its own way with respect to its interest rates and the exchange rate of its currency. This was reflected in a broader breakdown of the financial links between the two countries. The exchange rate quotations by the Association of Banks in Malaysia and

Singapore announced the following day were the same in both countries, but these would diverge subsequently, and the organisation would split as well. Tan also announced on 8 May that Malaysia would establish its own stock exchange in Kuala Lumpur independent of the joint stock exchange in Singapore, ostensibly to serve local companies. Accordingly, the stock exchange in Singapore was closed temporarily, and the Kuala Lumpur and Singapore offices

opened as independent units on 13 May.[30] A few weeks later, Brunei and Malaysia's interchangeability arrangement came to an end, although Brunei maintained the status quo with Singapore.

Under the Termination Agreement currency notes were to be exchanged at par without charge until 7 August 1973, as long as the parity of either currency was not changed in terms of gold. But Malaysia decided that the Singapore dollar could be exchanged in Malaysian banks on these terms only until 19 May. As the *Straits Times* reported on 20 May, 'From midnight yesterday the Singapore dollar will be treated like any other foreign currency by the Malaysian authorities and it will be changed at banks and money changers at market rates fixed by the Association of Banks after normal commission.'[31]

Despite this, the Singapore government decided to continue exchanging the Singapore dollar with the Malaysian currency as per the terms of the Termination

Above: Minister for Finance Hon Sui Sen (left) officially opens the Stock Exchange of Singapore, June 1973.

Below: The trading floor of the exchange, ready for the commencement of operations.

Changing Singapore currency for Malaysian dollars and vice versa at the Causeway, 1973.

Agreement until August. The decision was welcomed by the public, and it helped to quash rumours that there would be a sudden change in the rate of exchange before that date. Exchange booths at the Causeway and Paya Lebar Airport – including those set up by the BCCS – to exchange notes (not coins) until the grace period expired were welcomed since they reduced inconvenience for frequent travellers between the two countries. According to press reports, the booths at the Causeway were very busy with average daily transactions of S$70,000. Bernama, the Malaysian national news agency, reported that Malaysia had repatriated S$90 million to Singapore since 8 May, and 19 million Malaysian dollars had been repatriated back to Malaysia. As the *Straits Times* commented, 'The public have taken it in their stride,'[32] although some housewives in the rural areas of Singapore were not so happy: some people had been persuading them to sell their Malaysian dollars for 99 Singapore cents on the grounds that the Malaysian currency was weak.

The Singapore government itself did not seem to be overly concerned about the termination. The *Straits Times* of 12 May 1973 reported that the government was taking steps to avoid inconvenience to the public. It also carried a statement made by Prime Minister Lee Kuan Yew in Tokyo the previous day: 'No one is ruffled. It is not likely to produce any instability in either country on account of it being part of a trend continuing since 1965.' The 'trend' he referred to included the gradual unravelling of Singapore-Malaysia linkages, such as Malaysia's ban on log exports to Singapore; the political separation from Malaysia in 1965; the splitting-up of Malaysia-Singapore Airlines; and the disagreement over settlement of outstanding balances arising from the repatriation of each country's currency under the Currency Interchangeability Agreement.[33]

In the event, parity of the Singapore dollar with the Malaysian dollar could only be maintained until 23 June as events subsequently overtook both Malaysia and Singapore (see p. 274–5).

Why did Malaysia terminate the Agreement in May 1973? Expediency appears to have determined the timing to an extent – the break had to come sooner or later and now was the best time since the Malaysian currency was strong.[34] Both economies were in a healthy state and were expected to remain so for some time.[35]

However, there were a number of reasons why the Malaysian authorities decided to initiate the termination in the first instance,[36] and in that sense there

The rubber hits the road

The Malaysian authorities felt that continuing with the interchangeability arrangement would inhibit the development of the country's financial and commercial institutions and favour Singapore as the financial and trading centre. After all, Singapore had the incumbent advantage, having developed the institutions for rubber trading, foreign banking and foreign-exchange trading from colonial times. Indeed, Singapore had provided auxiliary commodity-processing and financial services to Malaysia's commodity-producing hinterland (see p. 115–7). 'Surgery to separate the interdependent economies' was Malaysia's way of promoting its own sustained economic growth.[37]

Without the dollar-for-dollar exchange rates dictated under the interchangeability arrangement, it would now be inconvenient for Malaysian firms to export and receive foreign exchange via Singapore. Consequently, Malaysian finance minister Tan Siew Sin sought to move more of Malaysia's merchandise through its own ports at Klang and Penang, and to promote a Malaysian rubber market. He was advised that special efforts should be made to attract brokers and dealers to Kuala Lumpur to establish it as the dominant international rubber market. The Malaysian Rubber Exchange held a special board meeting on 12 May 1973, and decided that in future, all exports to or through Singapore would be settled in Malaysia in the latter's currency, and all official prices quoted by either the Malaysian Rubber Exchange or the Rubber Authority of Singapore should be in that currency. Subsequently both countries agreed to joint quotes in Malaysian dollars except for physical rubber *in situ* in Singapore which could have come from a range of sources and would continue to be quoted in Singapore dollars.

There was, however, no reason to think that Malaysia's desire to develop its own economy was designed to be at the expense of Singapore. Tan himself believed that the impact on Singapore would be minimal since Singapore's reliance on regional entrepôt trade had fallen substantially by that time and the economy was diversifying into manufacturing and financial services.[38]

Internal MAS briefing documents suggested that Singapore would lose its competitive advantage in rubber trading to the advantage of Taiwan and Hong Kong.[39] However, the termination of the interchangeability agreement and the policies that Malaysia adopted in fact had little effect on Singapore's economic growth and trade.

was an element of inevitability. In the official announcement, Minister Tan Siew Sin said that the agreement was only ever meant to be temporary and characterised it as an aberration against the reality of the differences between the two economies. Malaysia was mainly a producer of primary commodities, though it was making significant progress in industrialisation; Singapore was a city–state depending largely on trade and the provision of services, although it too had made substantial industrial progress. In his view, the economies of Malaysia and Singapore were so different that 'monetary union between our two countries can, therefore, be likened, in so far as finance is concerned, to a pair of Siamese twins trying to grow together normally'.[40] From this perspective, the Agreement was a monetary straitjacket that confined both Malaysia's and Singapore's future development paths. Without political reunification, it could become a potential source of conflict between the two nations, and terminating it seemed best.

Like Malaysia, the Singapore government felt that the agreement had constrained the country's development. Together with the requirement that Sterling Area members impose capital controls vis-à-vis non–Sterling Area members, Singapore's ability to intermediate funds from international capital markets and thus grow its financial services sector was hampered. Singapore's determination to become a manufacturing base for multinational corporations and to grow its financial services sector also pushed the two economies further apart in terms of their development objectives. Freed from both the shackles of the Currency Interchangeability Agreement and the Sterling Area requirements, Singapore could now go its own way and promote itself as the 'Zurich of the East'.[41]

Despite the termination of the agreement, it was not until the early 1980s that a significant divergence in the market value of the two currencies became evident, when global exchange rates became especially volatile.

Floating the Singapore dollar

Barely eight months after Singapore, Malaysia and Brunei chose to abandon the pound sterling and peg their currencies to the US dollar, the latter came under heavy speculative attack. On 12 February 1973, the US currency was devalued by 10 per cent; the official price of gold between central banks was simultaneously increased from US$38 per ounce to US$42.22. Soon afterwards there was another speculative attack on the US dollar, forcing foreign exchange markets all over the world to be closed on 2 March, and they remained so for 17 days. When the markets were reopened the world woke up to a new international monetary order: the US dollar was now free-floating, while other major currencies, including sterling, the deutschmark and Japanese yen, were no longer fixed to the US dollar and were floating as well.

There were rumours that the Singapore dollar might be devalued against the US dollar and the Malaysian currency revalued based on the strength of the Malaysian economy compared to that of Singapore.[42] In reality, Singapore had not seriously contemplated devaluation.[43] On 17 May 1973, two economists from the National University of Singapore were asked by MAS for their views on the implications for Singapore of a further weakening of the US dollar. The arguments they gave for not devaluing were similar to those advanced when the pound sterling was devalued in August 1967 and floated in June 1972. Both the Singapore dollar and the Malaysian dollar remained pegged to the US dollar.

However, foreign exchange market pressures intensified, and on 20 June 1973, Singapore decided to let its currency float. Malaysian finance minister Tan Siew Sin was informed of the move by his Singapore counterpart Hon Sui Sen over the telephone, after Singapore had made its official announcement.

The next day Malaysia announced that it would do likewise and float the Malaysian dollar.

For both countries, there seemed little choice in the matter.

In Singapore's case, trying to defend the original peg against the US dollar would have been unsustainable. Before the float MAS had supported the US dollar at the floor price of S$2.4805 per US dollar by buying US dollars and selling Singapore dollars in the foreign exchange market. MAS's foreign exchange intervention operations thus injected a significant amount of Singapore dollars into the economy, leading to concerns about domestic prices rising, especially in the equity and property markets. Trying to defend the peg would have led to even more liquidity and thus asset and price inflation in the Singapore economy. Moreover, the turmoil in the international monetary system remained and was likely to get worse before it got better. It would have been impossible for MAS to have intervened on a daily basis in such foreign exchange market conditions to keep the local currency at any sort of fixed rate. Finally, there was the concern that if the Malaysian currency had floated down with the US dollar while the Singapore dollar remained at its pre-devaluation level, the price of Singapore's products would have been misaligned in export markets.

In a treasury press statement released afterwards, the Malaysian government said that their decision to float had been made in view of the Singapore government's decision;[44] it would have been pointless for BNM to continue to lose foreign exchange by buying the US dollar as the Singapore float would have diverted even more US dollars into Malaysia. In any case, the Malaysians expected their currency to appreciate 'to a slightly higher level than the Singapore dollar'.[45] In the end, it made sense for both Singapore and Malaysia to float their respective currencies.

With the float, neither the Singapore dollar nor the Malaysian dollar remained pegged to a common currency at the same rate of exchange. Consequently, the parity between the two currencies ceased. The Currency Interchangeability Agreement lapsed before the terms of the notice period could be fulfilled. At 11.30 a.m. on 23 June 1973, the banks in Singapore stopped accepting the Malaysian dollar at par, and at 5 p.m. the BCCS followed suit. Banks would now only accept the Malaysian dollar on payment of a 'normal' commission and, as banks could now quote their own exchange rates, businessmen were advised to shop around for the best rate. In the event there was no rush to exchange the Malaysian dollar into the Singapore dollar.[46]

The first five days of floating were quite orderly, much less chaotic than had been generally expected;[47] but there was some misunderstanding by the banks as to how active MAS had been in intervening in the foreign exchange market. There were rumours that the unusual stability of the Singapore dollar had been due to MAS intervention, but MAS was clear that they had only intervened to support the US dollar on 21 June, the first day of floating, when volatility was high; and that they had withdrawn from the market the following day since the market clearly wanted the US dollar to be substantially lower.[48]

It was not the intended policy of Singapore and Malaysia to have floating exchange rates but they were compelled by circumstances to do so. Thrust into this new operating environment, MAS would try to ensure a more orderly foreign exchange market by making available from time to time the Singapore dollar against the US dollar and vice versa at rates more in keeping with the relative strengths of the two currencies in world markets, rather than direct its operations to maintaining a new parity. Flotation made the transition from the Currency Interchangeability Arrangement more difficult, as banks, firms, and individuals would now have to contend with a significantly higher degree of volatility in the rate of exchange between Singapore and Malaysian dollars than they had previously known.

Initially at least, both countries expected to return to a fixed exchange rate in the near future.[49] Public sentiment in favour was strong, especially among businessmen, since they had benefitted for a long time from the increase in trade and inward capital flows that fixed rates had facilitated, while businesses had no experience of floating rates. MAS itself expected that the local currency would appreciate against the US dollar, and that when the international currency situation had stabilised, the Singapore dollar would return to a fixed parity.[50]

But this was not to be. The Nixon shock in 1971 had precipitated what would turn out to be an irrevocable breakdown in the global system of fixed exchange rates in 1973. From MAS's point of view, the best outcome would have been for the Singapore dollar to appreciate enough to keep the cost of living from rising too fast without making Singapore's exports too expensive when priced in world markets.[51] In this sense, for the first time, MAS was trying to find an intermediate path between a freely floating currency and a fixed exchange rate peg.

The floating of the Singapore dollar pointed to MAS's need to build up its exchange rate management infrastructure. It no longer had an 'anchor currency' to fix to automatically, and so benefit from its stability, as it had done for a long time with its fix to sterling and then briefly to the US dollar. By 1975, MAS had abandoned any idea that the Singapore dollar would return to a fixed parity. This prompted MAS to develop a framework for 'managing' the Singapore dollar more actively. In 1975, an exchange rate policy band was applied to the trade-weighted Singapore dollar[52] and movements within that band were monitored by MAS. This represented a first, exploratory step towards the more formalised, managed floating exchange rate system that would eventually be introduced by MAS in 1981 (see p. 303).[53]

Building bridges: the Asian Currency Market

The end of the Sterling Area, the termination of the Currency Interchangeability Agreement, and the shift towards greater exchange rate flexibility precipitated by the failure of the Bretton Woods system paved the way for MAS to liberalise capital controls. These would prove key to Singapore's ambition to become first a regional financial centre, and eventually a global one.

From as early as 1 October 1968, the Singapore government had allowed both domestic and foreign-owned banks in Singapore to apply to open special departments called Asian Currency Units (ACUs). ACUs could accept non-resident currency deposits of up to US$50 million and lend these, or other foreign currencies, to finance activities outside Singapore. The thinking was that Singapore's financial sector could channel funds from all over the world into regional development projects.[54] This facility became known as the Asian Dollar Market (ADM), because it provided a market in the Asian time zone for offshore US dollars. In that sense, it was modelled on the Eurodollar Market based in London, where the US dollar was also the most traded currency. However, as it was also an offshore market for other major currencies such as the deutschmark and the pound sterling, it has also been called the Asian Currency Market.

A bridge in time

Most accounts of the origins of the Asian Dollar Market emphasise the role of the Dutch economist Albert Winsemius, chief economic advisor to the Singapore government from 1961 to 1983.[55] In later interviews, Winsemius himself recalled how J. D. van Oenen, who was to become vice-president of the Bank of America branch in Singapore, took a globe and pointed to a gap in the financial markets of the world to show how the island could provide round-the-clock trading.[56] Unlike Hong Kong and Tokyo, Singapore was in a time zone that meant it could bridge the gap between East and West and achieve a crucial 'first-mover' advantage. As US markets closed at about 5 a.m. Singapore time, Singapore could trade with other Asia-Pacific centres, such as Hong Kong, Tokyo and Sydney; with London it began trading at 4.30 p.m. Singapore time; and with the rest of Europe as their markets gradually opened.[57] Dealers in the foreign-exchange market in Singapore could complete transactions without having to wait for overnight execution, useful when overnight interest rates and exchange rates could be volatile, as they were at that time.

Albert Winsemius wrote to Hon Sui Sen, the then chairman of the Economic Development Board, who approached Lee Kuan Yew with the suggestion that foreign exchange restrictions be lifted on all currency transactions between Singapore and territories outside the Sterling Area (see p. 267).

Beginning with just a few million US dollars, mainly from existing depositors at Bank of America branches in Southeast Asia, many of whom were overseas Chinese, van Oenen himself started operationalising what could perhaps be considered a small-scale version of the ADM as early as 1963.[58] Bank of America eventually became the first bank to be licensed to operate an Asian Currency Unit, followed by First National City Bank (today's Citi), Chartered Bank (now Standard Chartered), the Hongkong and Shanghai Bank (now HSBC), and Bank of Tokyo. The US dollar was by far the most important currency used and interest rates were closely linked to those in the Eurodollar Market.[59]

At the time, this innovation was seen as a surprising move, since Singapore had relatively little financial infrastructure for such an ambitious undertaking compared to other regional financial centres, such as Hong Kong. Nevertheless, it made sense for Singapore to be a regional financial centre given its history and geography. It had long been a regional trading hub providing entrepôt and banking services, including the remittance of funds by Chinese merchants back to China; and since the 19th century it had hosted many local and international banks engaged in trade and finance for Southeast Asia, particularly in the rubber and tin trades of the Malay Peninsula. By 1965, there were 34 commercial banks in Singapore, including 24 foreign bank branches.[60] Rapid regional growth had created attractive lending and borrowing opportunities, so for investment purposes Singapore could take advantage of the pool of foreign currency deposits of residents in Asia, and the increase in funds coming into Asia.

In an interview in 1970, Singapore's finance minister Hon Sui Sen explained the government's thinking on welcoming foreign funds and deploying them for use in the region. 'I believe that money which suffers from ill-treatment should be allowed a safe refuge just as persecuted religious minorities deserve a sanctuary. Hitherto, refuge has been provided in countries such as Switzerland and to this extent the capital is lost for economic development in the region. When it remains in Singapore, it will be available when suitable investment opportunities arise.'[61]

Other financial centres such as London and New York had developed spontaneously and evolved organically. In contrast, despite Singapore's natural advantages, the ADM was essentially a creation of the government; it would not have been viable without the deliberate measures to promote it.[62] Crucial in this respect was the 1969 abolition of the 40 per cent withholding tax on interest paid on deposits, since there was no such tax on competing currency markets outside Singapore. There was also a reduction of tax on loan interest and offshore income to 10 per cent, and a large reduction in the duty on ACUs to ½ per cent. In fact, taxation in the Singapore offshore banking system, even in this early period, was lower than that in the domestic banking system.

The ADM started from a low base of activity in 1968 but progressed side-by-side with the domestic banking system as the number of ACUs and the volume of transactions rose quickly from 1970 onwards in line with rapid growth in international finance and banking. At the end of 1969 there was only one ACU but by 1976 there were 69. The volume of transactions had grown from US$123 million to US$17 billion over the same period. When the Korean Exchange Bank opened a branch in Singapore and transferred its eurodollar holdings to the ADM in May 1973, among the reasons it gave were Singapore's time-zone advantage and its political stability.[63]

Announcing plans for a multinational regional merchant bank to link the money markets of the US, the UK, Switzerland and France with that of Singapore. Present is J.D. van Oenen of Bank of America (far right).

Most transactions in the ADM initially involved deposits collected in the Asian region by the ACUs and remitted to London or New York for investment. However, over time, the ADM increasingly assumed a regional character as funds began to be channelled from Europe and the United States for investment in the Asian region. Funds were sourced from within and outside Singapore via commercial and central banks, non-bank corporates such as multinational corporations, and wealthy overseas Chinese, and they were utilised both by businesses for investment and by governments. ACUs also began to participate in the recycling of oil revenues generated by the sharp rise in the price of crude oil in 1973–4. As the originator and hub of the ADM, Singapore was becoming Southeast Asia's financial centre.

In Singapore, the reception to the ADM was generally upbeat. According to an article in the *Straits Times* on 7 February 1971, Singapore held the prospect of becoming the financial centre of the whole of Asia and not just of the immediate region. However, new competencies would be required before it could rival the Eurodollar Market as a money-market centre.[64] There was even some optimism that Singapore would join an ambitious Economic Commission for Asia and the Far East initiative to set up an Asian currency union that would clear intraregional dollar settlements and allow parties to provide credit to each other via a clearing house.[65]

Promoting the further development of the ADM became one of the main priorities of the newly set-up MAS. It was unorthodox at that time for a central bank to undertake a promotional role, as opposed to financial regulation and supervision. Moreover, Singapore was still a developing country new to central banking and financial supervision. As Lee Kuan Yew put it in his memoirs, 'The history of our financial centre is the story of how we built up credibility as a place of integrity and developed the officers with the knowledge and skills to regulate and supervise the banks, security houses and other financial institutions so that the risk of systemic and financial failure is minimised.' [66]

In 1972, MAS gradually lifted the barriers for resident individuals and companies wishing to participate in the ADM.[67] Minister for Finance Hon Sui Sen rationalised this as putting Singapore on the money-market map of the world.[68] Subsequently, Singapore's departure from the Sterling Area, as well as the termination of the Currency Interchangeability Agreement with Malaysia, provided it with the space to liberalise progressively capital controls vis-à-vis its neighbours and the rest of the world. By June 1978, nearly all exchange controls in Singapore had been removed, and there was a free flow of funds in and out of Singapore for investment and payment purposes.

This was quite a bold move; after all, it was highly unusual for developing countries to remove all controls and even advanced countries generally retained some as a precaution. Concerns that Singapore would lose control over currency movements and experience greater exchange rate volatility proved unfounded; instead, liberalisation served to help grow the Asian Dollar Market.

Stormy seas – inflation and oil shocks

When MAS was formed in 1971, one of its objectives was to promote monetary stability and credit and exchange conditions conducive to economic growth. However, MAS did not conduct discretionary monetary policy in any conventional sense.

MAS had no specific monetary targets but instead monitored a range of indicators, including interest rates, exchange rates, the money supply and loan growth.[69] To ensure that domestic monetary and credit conditions were broadly conducive to economic growth, MAS began developing an 'eclectic' toolbox of monetary and other instruments. In January 1973, for instance, the Straits Times reported that MAS was planning to introduce a bank rate (or discount rate) within a year, and this would be followed by the use of open-market operations, perhaps within a year or two.[70] Over time, the toolbox came to include financial market instruments and institutions for the implementation of monetary policy, including treasury bills and discount houses. However, there were blunter direct measures for restraining credit, including raising the cash reserves that banks were required to hold with the MAS, supplemented by the use of 'moral suasion', and on occasion raising interest rates.

The need and capacity for effective discretionary monetary policy emerged amidst the upheavals in the international and domestic monetary systems in the early 1970s. From late 1972 Singapore was experiencing net inflows of foreign

Singapore's first post-Independence bank run

Following the oil-price shock in late 1973, there was significant financial and economic uncertainty in 1974. Banks all over the world were affected. For instance, there were reports that the Franklin National Bank of New York as well as the Lugano branch of Lloyds Bank of London had suffered huge foreign currency losses. Towards the end of the year, rumours about the soundness of some of the local banks started to emerge. In September, rumours spread that the Oversea-Chinese Banking Corporation (OCBC) had suffered 'big losses' in its foreign exchange dealings. MAS stated that the rumours were unfounded, and emphasised that the bank had substantial financial backing and was 'a well-managed and properly run bank'.[71] OCBC's operations continued as normal.

On 3 October, rumours began to spread that Chung Khiaw Bank, a member of the United Overseas Banking Group (UOB), was in a tight liquidity position. A few days earlier, long queues had been seen at some branches of the UOB Group, including those of the Chung Khiaw Bank. It turned out later that they were just the normal 'end of the month' queues as workers went to cash out wages and pay bills.[72] Nevertheless, amidst the general jitters over banks, rumours soon spread and large numbers of depositors lined up at the Group's branches to withdraw their money. MAS issued a statement emphasising that the Group's financial and liquidity position was 'very strong and sound'. UOB announced that the Geylang branch of the Chung Khiaw Bank would remain open until all customers had been served. While other branches stuck to the official closing time of 3 p.m., people already inside the branches by then would be served. The Jalan Kayu branch of UOB stayed open until the last customer was served at 7 p.m. Over at Geylang, a 300-strong crowd was still waiting to withdraw their money at 7.50 p.m. The last customer was served at 10.30 p.m.[73]

Next day, the queues returned. The rumours that had prompted the run on the bank had no basis, but they would have been self-fulfilling if the withdrawals had continued unabated: Chung Khiaw Bank would have had no choice but to close, and the whole UOB Group might have been badly affected. Support for the UOB Group and Chung Khiaw came out in full force. Both the Association of Banks and the Chinese Chamber of Commerce chimed in, urging the public not to make panic withdrawals. MAS reiterated its statement that the bank was fundamentally sound.[74]

By 8 October, the panic had died down. Heads were cooled thanks to these various reassurances and the closure of bank branches over the weekend. Business returned to normal at Chung Khiaw and other members of the UOB Group. Singapore's first post-Independence bank run had been successfully quelled.

Anxious customers at the Alexandra branch of Chung Khiaw Bank, October 1974.

funds, and the surfeit in liquidity was creating the conditions for rising inflation in the economy into 1973. This prompted a comment in the *Straits Times*: 'The need for a more vigorous monetary policy has become apparent as Singapore pushes towards her goal of becoming the "Zurich of Asia".'[75]

In the face of the surge in liquidity, in February 1973 MAS hiked the statutory reserve ratio (the ratio of reserves to deposits that banks and finance companies needed to keep with the MAS) from 5 per cent to 9 per cent.[76] It also raised the ratio on net borrowed funds from abroad to the same extent. It imposed credit ceilings on banks and finance companies, together with selective credit guidelines. 'Moral suasion' came in the form of circulars that urged financial institutions to exercise 'care and caution' and to pursue a 'prudent and conservative policy' when extending credit in particular cases.[77]

Compounding the shocks caused by the surge in liquidity was a sharp rise in global inflation accompanied by rising unemployment (a combination known as 'stagflation') in advanced countries, which put upward pressure on Singapore's import prices and reduced the volume of its exports. For example, annual inflation in the United States, which in 1964 had been around 1 per cent, rose to 12 per cent in 1974; while unemployment at 5 per cent in 1964 rose to over 7 per cent in 1974. Average consumer price inflation in the 1970s in Singapore was almost 6 per cent, relatively high compared to later decades.

The 'Great Inflation' in advanced countries can be traced back to a number of factors. A major cause was excessive monetary growth permitted by their central banks. Policymakers thought at the time that they could promote economic growth without bringing about inflation through interest rate policy, which turned out to be an illusion. As inflation rose, workers revised upwards their expectations of future inflation and hence wage demands, thus generating a self-fulfilling wage-price spiral.

The inflation caused by 'too much money chasing too few goods' was exacerbated by the oil shocks of the 1970s. In October 1973, members of the Organization of Petroleum Exporting Countries (OPEC) introduced an oil embargo targeted at countries such as the United States, Japan, and the United Kingdom, which were perceived to be supporting Israel during the Yom Kippur War. The fighting had begun on 7 October 1973 when Egypt and Syria mounted an offensive to regain the Sinai Peninsula and the Golan Heights occupied by Israel during the 1967 Six Day War, and it lasted until a ceasefire took effect on 25 October.

By the end of the embargo, the price of crude oil had quadrupled, which benefitted the major oil exporters such as those in the Middle East, but caused the trade deficits of oil-importing countries to balloon, thus creating balance of

Singapore's currency and the Great Inflation

Financial discipline was a crucial component in Singapore's attempts to curb accelerating inflation over 1973/4. For instance, finance minister Hon Sui Sen argued that it would be 'no less than madness' to subsidise utility bills. Instead, he emphasised that people and businesses should find ways to cut down on their consumption of oil and electricity; in fact, the government increased taxes on petrol precisely to reduce non-essential car usage.[78] Hon felt that it was to Singapore's credit that it had accepted the discipline inherent in the currency board system. Accordingly, the government would not resort to excessive and unhelpful spending, such as on subsidies, that would not resolve the underlying inflation problem.

This discipline was expressed at the individual level by a concerned citizen who wrote pseudonymously to the *Straits Times* urging fellow Singaporeans to 'cut off all spending in all respects on luxury items and concentrate mainly on the necessities of life, and instead save the money available in banks to earn interest'. This would keep 'unnecessary cash' from entering the market and would help to dampen inflation, thereby preventing the Singapore dollar from becoming 'worthless and equivalent to the banana dollar of the Japanese Occupation of Singapore'.[79]

The public understood broadly that Singapore's reliance on imports meant that rising prices were unavoidable, but there was palpable anger directed at 'hoarding, the creation of artificial shortages, price fixing and collusion among traders',[80] which pushed prices up excessively. Prime Minister Lee Kuan Yew and the Secretary-General of the National Trades Union Congress, Devan Nair, urged the people to 'strike back' by changing shopping and consumption patterns and boycotting offenders. The NTUC also opened its first co-operative supermarket in July 1973 to increase competition and lower prices for consumers.

There was some profiteering. Some shopkeepers were found to have rounded prices up to the nearest five or ten cents when smaller increments would arguably have sufficed, and were justifying the move by saying that the government had sanctioned the price increases. Hon declared in Parliament in March 1974 that there was 'no excuse' for such a large rounding-up, since one-cent coins were in abundance and more could be put into circulation if necessary.[81]

A housewife haggles with a hawker in Pagoda Street in 1975.

payments difficulties for the latter. Essentially, this amounted to a huge transfer of wealth from oil importers to oil exporters.

Although there had been significant discoveries of oil in Malaysia and Indonesia, it was costly to refine. Instead, Singapore was very reliant on Middle East oil for its refineries and rapidly growing domestic demand. For instance, 45 per cent was imported from Kuwait alone.[82]

Prime Minister Lee Kuan Yew called the end of 1973 'a turning point in the history of the world' when the price of oil rose from under US$3 per barrel in 1972 to over US$12 by the end of the embargo. However, Lee took some comfort in the fact that substantial supplies of oil in Southeast Asia, apart from Singapore, meant that most of its neighbours in the region were less affected than many other developing countries.[83]

The combination of surging domestic liquidity and high imported inflation, especially from skyrocketing oil prices, drove consumer price inflation in Singapore to 20 per cent in 1973 and nearly 30 per cent in the first half of the following year. The pain of sharp price increases was keenly felt among the public.

In the face of inflation shocks, MAS kept the various monetary and credit levers under its purview on a tight setting. The statutory reserve ratio remained high at 9 per cent.[84] To absorb the excess liquidity in the domestic economy, bond issues were accelerated, and local companies were encouraged to go public quickly, while already-listed companies were urged to have rights issues.[85] MAS also hiked interest rates in October 1974 by two percentage points.

All things considered, Singapore weathered the inflation shock of the 1970s relatively well. Although the manufacturing sector slipped into negative growth in 1975 as the higher oil costs hit production processes with a lag, the overall

Sheikh Yamani (second from left), oil minister of Saudi Arabia, at the negotiations between OPEC and western oil companies, Vienna 1973.

Pumping oil.

economy avoided recession in both 1973 and 1974, and it managed to grow by 4 per cent in 1975. Consumer price inflation subsequently moderated to an average of 2.6 per cent in 1975.

Currency in the 1970s

With the tumult of the first half of the 1970s in the past, 1976 was perhaps an opportune year for BCCS to introduce its second series of currency notes since Independence – the Bird series. Ten years had elapsed since the Orchid series was issued in 1967. Particular thought was put into issuing the Bird series: within the currency board, a 1969 US Treasury-authored paper was circulated detailing the history of American money, including the first coins issued in April 1792, with information on how more recent American currency was coined and printed, brought into circulation, and destroyed.[86]

The notes were well received by the public, and initially even treated as collectors' items. When they were first launched, in August 1976, more than 2,500 people queued up at the BCCS's premises in Empress Place to exchange old Orchid series notes for new ones. A week later, there was still a marked absence of the new notes in circulation, which according to the *Straits Times* 'clearly indicates that a fair amount of hoarding is taking place'.[87] There were reports that the notes were being sold at inflated rates on the black market, to which BCCS replied that there was no need for this as they could be readily obtained from the Board and the commercial banks.

As with the Orchid series, mistakes in printing did occur but they were rare. In 1982, a Mr M.S. Vasudevan wrote to the *Straits Times* asking why his one-dollar note did not bear the red seal and the signature of the Minister for Finance.[88]

The Bird series notes

The Bird series currency notes included nine denominations. The 1-, 5-, 10- and 50-dollar notes were issued first on 6 August 1976, followed by the 100- and 500-dollar notes on 1 February 1977. Subsequently, a 1,000-dollar note was put into circulation on 7 August 1978; a 20-dollar note on 6 August 1979; and a 10,000-dollar note on 1 February 1980. BCCS had learnt from the 25-dollar note fiasco of the Orchid series, and decided to issue a 20-dollar note instead.

As the name suggests, the dominant design theme of this series was 'birds', which symbolised strength, adaptability and independence – traits said to characterise the young Republic of Singapore 'soaring to greater heights'. Pictured on the notes were birds native to Singapore. On the back of the notes were representations of Singapore's achievements over the previous decade, such as public housing on the 10-dollar note and Changi International Airport on the 20-dollar note. There were also the country's scenic attractions such as the Singapore River on the 10,000-dollar note and cable cars above the harbourfront on the five-dollar note. Cultural activities were represented by dancers on the 100-dollar note and a school band on parade on the 50-dollar note. Major industries were also celebrated through images such as the container terminal on the 1,000-dollar note.

New security features were added to the Bird series, including the perfect alignment of the lion symbols on the front and back of the notes.

S$1 (blue), issued 6 August 1976

Front: black-naped tern

Back: National Day Parade

S$5 (green), issued 6 August 1976

Front: red-whiskered bulbul

Back: cable cars and aerial view of the harbour

S$10 (red), issued 6 August 1976

Front: white-collared kingfisher

Back: garden city with high-rise public housing

S$20 (brown), issued 6 August 1979

Front: yellow-breasted sunbird

Back: Changi International Airport with Concorde in the background

S$50 (blue), issued 6 August 1976

Front: white-rumped shama

Back: school band on parade

S$100 (blue), issued 1 February 1977

Front: blue-throated bee-eater

Back: dancers

S$500 (green), issued 1 February 1977

Front: black-naped oriole

Back: oil refinery

S$1,000 (purple), issued 7 August 1978

Front: brahminy kite

Back: container terminal

S$10,000 (green), issued 1 February 1980

Front: white-bellied sea eagle

Back: scenes of the Singapore River

The BCCS responded that this appeared to have been a misprint, and the Deputy Manager for Currency Operations invited Mr Vasudevan to call on him at the BCCS office (which by then had moved to Robinson Road).[89]

A few forgeries also occurred, with reports indicating that the 5-, 50-, and 100-dollar notes had been counterfeited. The fakes were typically very poor reproductions. Although they caused inconvenience and some degree of hardship to those that ended up with the notes, forgery did not become so systemic a problem that it threatened the integrity of the Bird series or the public's trust.

Notes from the Bird series were dispensed through automated teller machines (ATMs). The technology underpinning ATMs had evolved in Europe and the United States over the 1960s before eventually landing on Singapore's shores in the late 1970s.

On 17 August 1979, media reports mentioned a race between commercial banks, such as the Chartered Bank (today's Standard Chartered Bank) and the Hongkong and Shanghai Bank (today's HSBC), and the Post Office Savings Bank (POSB), to set up the first ATM in Singapore.[90] The three had applied to MAS for permission to introduce the machines: as the ATMs were capable of performing most bank-branch functions, they were considered to be sub-

New banking technology: Minister Hon Sui Sen (holding the printout) at the inauguration of a computer facility at the DBS building, Shenton Way, 1973.

branches, and thus needed MAS's approval. Although POSB announced plans the next day to install the machines by December,[91] Chartered Bank beat them to it by two months, opening Singapore's first ATM at its main office in Raffles Place on 15 October 1979. The machine dispensed cash in multiples of S$10 and had a withdrawal limit of S$1000. Current account holders could use it from 9 a.m. to 4 p.m. on weekdays, and up to 12 noon on Saturday; ATM services were not available on Sunday.[92]

The use of ATMs took off exponentially, and more banks joined in offering the service, innovating along the way. Within two years, POSB had extended its network to 40 machines while the six publicly listed local banks had installed more than 50. Orders were placed for several more. The 24-hour ATM was pioneered by the United Overseas Bank (UOB).[93] By 1982, POSB alone had up to 150 ATMs handling 41,808 transactions per terminal per year, up from 738 transactions handled by its debut machine in 1979.[94]

It is no exaggeration to say that the ATM transformed the way the public interacted with money. In the same way that financial innovations of the past such as paper notes (first issued by chartered banks in the colonial era, and subsequently by governments) and money orders made it much easier to obtain and transport currency and carry out transactions, so the ATM significantly reduced the time and inconvenience involved in withdrawing cash and conducting basic banking services. Previously, customers had to queue up at a bank branch, and

Moneychanger Noor Mohamed bin Muthu Marican, winner of the Singapore Sweep, lost most of his winnings after someone used a forged cheque to draw S$48,000 from his bank account, 1973.

they could only obtain cash during business hours. Comparing the ATM to other financial innovations that followed it, Paul Volcker, former chairman of the US Federal Reserve, would quip in 2009 that 'the ATM has been the only useful innovation in banking' in the past few decades.[95]

No new coin series were issued with the Bird series of notes in the 1970s, but a number of limited-edition and commemorative coins were minted. The policy seems to have been that commemorative coins should be minted only for very significant events of national importance. In July 1977, the BCCS decided against issuing a coin to mark the official opening of the Singapore Science Council on these grounds.[96] There was also a sharp rise in the price of silver in the late 1970s which would have increased minting costs, although the Board did consider reducing the fineness and size of the coins to deal with this – they could still have been classed as silver coins so long as the percentage of silver exceeded that of any other metal.

The BCCS was keen to distribute numismatic coins both locally and globally.[97] It wanted to create a larger pool of local coin collectors, market the coins overseas, and issue them in more convenient ways through standing-order deposit accounts, mailing lists and distribution centres rather than just over the counters of the BCCS.[98] In 1976, the Board set up the Standing Order Deposit Account (SODA) scheme to facilitate coin collecting by local numismatists. Under the SODA scheme, collectors would, for an annual deposit of S$150, enjoy an allocation of all coins issued by the Board, and have access to a direct mailing service informing them of new coin issues. They could subscribe to a mailing list for a lower fee of S$10. To gain further insight on the types of coins that collectors were interested in, and to understand better how the Board could improve on future commemorative coin issues, the BCCS surveyed SODA and mailing list members in 1979.[99]

The BCCS also explored the possibility of selling selected numismatic currency notes with a certificate of authenticity. They had observed that Singapore's notes were among those offered to worldwide collectors by Paramount, one of the largest numismatic corporations in the world, and they concluded that the notes must have been obtained from local dealers since no approach had been made to the BCCS. However, internal BCCS memos in November 1978 and August 1981 suggest that no concrete progress had been made in the creation of such an issue.[100]

Numismatic interest in the limited-edition coins issued in this decade was very strong. Singapore's first uncirculated ten-dollar silver coin was minted by Chartered Industries in 1972, and about 80,000 were put into circulation. They were very popular and forgeries soon emerged.[101] A ten-dollar silver proof coin was issued in November, and Chartered Industries had to mint 3,000 coins to

Seven thousand people queue at the BCCS premises, Empress Place, to buy the new ten-dollar silver coins, 1972.

Admiring a ten-dollar uncirculated silver coin purchased at BCCS, 1975.

The second Annual Assay Commission carries out verification of coins at the Singapore Mint, 1979.

meet numismatic demand.[102] Even then, queues still formed when the coins were reissued in 1973. The BCCS would eventually issue ten-dollar uncirculated and proof silver coins every year within the decade. Sales of the coins were often restricted to one or two per person.

A joint commemorative philatelic-numismatic set to commemorate the opening of the National Stadium and the seventh Southeast Asian Peninsular Games was issued in 1973. Orders exceeded the maximum issue of 10,000 sets even before they went on sale. To cater to the growing interest in commemorative coins, the Singapore Mint established a mailing list to inform collectors of future coin issues.[103]

In February 1975, the BCCS announced four coins – three gold and one silver – to commemorate Singapore's tenth anniversary as an independent nation. The face values of the gold coins were S$100, S$250, and S$500, while that of the silver coin was S$10. The coins came in uncirculated and proof versions. The uncirculated silver coins, which were issued first in February, were snapped up quickly – 50,000 were purchased within a week of their issue. There were reports that black-market syndicates had recruited 'housewives, schoolchildren, hawkers and grandmothers' to buy the coins on their behalf. The strong response prompted the BCCS to think of ways to reduce the risk that coin-buyers would be pickpocketed if they turned up to purchase coins with a large amount of cash.[104] When the uncirculated gold coins went on sale in August, the BCCS issued application forms for purchase, in the hope of limiting queues to people who had ordered them. In any event, long queues still formed, and the coins were in such high demand that the BCCS reissued them in November the same year.[105]

Coins minted abroad to commemorate global events also sold well in Singapore. For instance, a 1972 'Nixon-Mao' coin commemorating President Richard Nixon's visit to China 'sold like hot cakes' when the local branch of a German bank put them up for sale. All 500 coins were sold out, and hundreds of unsuccessful buyers stormed the branch in the belief that the bank had stocks of the coins but were refusing to

Counterfeit birds

In 1980 the police and BCCS investigated fake five-dollar notes from the Bird series that had ended up in the possession of a few taxi-drivers and commuters. The counterfeits were black-and-white photocopies painted with watercolour, with no security thread.[106]

The first fake 100-dollar note was discovered in September 1981, and ten months later it was reckoned that a one-man forgery operation passed off 151 notes to an unsuspecting public. They were black-and-white photocopies, embellished with watercolours and crayon, and outlined with blue ballpoint ink. However, this time the forger took pains to include the security thread and lion-head watermark. The notes ended up in the possession of banks, merchants, wholesalers and shops which had received them from their customers. In one case, a woman claimed that she had received a fake 100-dollar note from a bookie at the Turf Club, and it was only found to be counterfeit when the Public Utilities Board rejected it as payment for a bill! The S$5,000 reward offered for information on the forger was left unclaimed.[107]

Forged 50-dollar notes became a problem towards the mid-1980s. In April 1983, six members of a gang were arrested on suspicion of faking currency notes. They had used some counterfeits at shops on 5 February when an eight-hour power failure had made it difficult for retailers to verify visually their authenticity.[108] Then, between January and September 1985, 167 fake 50-dollar Bird series notes were handed over to the BCCS, having been discovered by banks, the Changi Airport Duty-free Emporium, and members of the public. Although the notes bore serial numbers, they were printed on inferior paper and had a line printed where the security threads should have been.[109]

It was believed that fake notes were being recirculated by people who had received them, as they did not want to be saddled with a counterfeit. A taxi-driver interviewed by the *Straits Times* said, 'If I'm paid with a fake 50-dollar note and don't find out about it until later, what do I do? If I go to the police, I lose 50 dollars. I can't afford to lose this money. Times are bad.' Others were worried that the process of reporting the notes might take up too much time. The BCCS treated these attitudes seriously and said, 'Holding on to fake currency might be taken as intention to pass it on to other people.'[110]

sell them. Police had to be called in, and MAS eventually advised the bank to stop selling coins, as this was not one of the core functions of a banking institution.[111] The strong interest in commemorative and numismatic coins would bump up against the problem of rising minting costs. In August 1977, the BCCS queried a 37 per cent rise in the quotation for the one-, two- and five-cent coins from the Singapore Mint.[112] In the event, they decided to accept a quote for minting the 1980 Chinese New Year numismatic nickel coins from the Royal Canadian Mint, on the grounds that the their quote was 60 per cent lower than that of the Singapore Mint; its security was better; and the coins were of higher quality. The Canadian High Commission in Singapore was approached to help transfer the coin dies from the Singapore Mint to the Canadian Mint by diplomatic bag.[113]

There were further difficulties with the 1980 proof set. According to the Singapore Mint there had been a delay in the arrival of a polishing machine

Treasure at Sago Street

On 19 January 1976, while construction works were going on at a vacant plot of land between Sago Lane and Sago Street, a cache of silver coins was discovered. These were mainly ten-cent coins dating from 1916 to 1941. While the records do not state what coins these were, the dates suggest that they would likely have been Straits Settlements coins and possibly Malayan coins. Work was halted, and hundreds of passers-by rushed to grab the coins and to dig for more with their bare hands. A black market sprung up on the spot; within a short time, enterprising finders of the coins were selling them on to those unable to find any, and the price soon exceeded S$1 per coin. Fifteen-year-old Chin Oi Lin and her brother reaped a grand profit of S$27 by selling 90 coins. After about an hour, the police came to disperse the crowd.

A Mr Leong Yat Sun claimed that the coins belonged to his parents. They had lived in a shophouse that had previously occupied the now-vacant plot; the building had been torn down for urban renewal works. He recalled as a child seeing his parents bury items in the floor of their room, which he said was located where the coins were found. However, he made no attempt to claim any of them. The police were given instructions to confiscate all the coins as they had been found on state land.[114]

After a bulldozer unearthed a cache of coins between Sago Lane and Sago Street in January 1976, crowds flocked to scoop them up. They were mainly ten-cent coins dating from 1916–41.

purchased from Italy, and the manual polishing of the blanks by less experienced staff had resulted in a slower rate of production. There was also a high rejection rate (more than 40 per cent) for the ten–dollar coin 'due to the complexity of its design'.

In retrospect

In 1979, a second oil shock hit the world. Oil production fell sharply following the Iranian revolution in early 1979, when the Shah of Iran was deposed and fled abroad. The world price of crude oil more than doubled over the next 12 months and in advanced countries inflation rose on average to 11 per cent. As with the 1973 oil shock, inflation in Singapore also rose, reaching 8.5 per cent in 1980, and exports fell as Singapore's major trading partners went into recession.

It was a gloomy end to a challenging decade that saw the fundamental reshaping of Singapore's monetary arrangements. The flotation of the pound sterling marked the formal end of British dominance over Singapore's exchange rate and reserve management policies. With Malaysia's termination of the Currency Interchangeability Agreement with Singapore, the last vestiges of the colonial system of a currency shared by all three territories – Singapore, the

Malay Peninsula, and the former British territories in Borneo – came to an end. The Bretton Woods system of fixed exchange rates revolving around the US dollar and supervised by the IMF had given way to a much less disciplined system of floating exchange rates between the major countries. Singapore was cast adrift into what British economist John Williamson would later famously describe as 'the international monetary non-system'.[115]

These same events, however, had a silver lining. Singapore could now liberalise capital controls as it deemed fit, which, together with the greater degree of exchange rate flexibility won through the flotation of the Singapore dollar, bought MAS significant room for manoeuvre in setting monetary policy. It allowed MAS to mount as good a response as it could to the inflationary shocks over the decade using its 'eclectic' toolbox. This policy shift was important – whereas previously the story of Singapore's 'money' had been dominated by the evolution of physical currency, from the 1970s it would have more to do with exchange rate and monetary management by MAS, and the actions of foreign and local commercial banks, than it would with notes and coins, important as they were.

Nevertheless, the eclectic toolbox eventually proved inadequate for MAS's purposes, and a need for effective monetary policy remained. The difficulty MAS had in taming inflation planted the idea in the mind of Goh Keng Swee – who had been serving as Deputy Prime Minister since March 1973 – that a more effective and coherent monetary policy framework was necessary. The events of the 1970s would come to influence MAS's approach to its monetary policy in the next decade.

CHAPTER 08

MANAGING THE CURRENCY IN TURBULENT TIMES

(1980–1999)

MAS adopted a monetary policy framework centred on managing a trade-weighted basket of currencies to secure low and stable inflation. The establishment of the Government of Singapore Investment Corporation brought a more professional approach to managing the foreign reserves. As the world economy experienced volatility on the foreign exchange markets, and the US dollar became overvalued, five developed nations signed the Plaza Accord, facilitating a depreciation of the dollar and pledging closer cooperation in their macroeconomic policies. Nevertheless, tensions arose between the United States and newly industrialised economies in Asia, and the US 'graduated' Singapore from its Generalized System of Preferences. Debate over exchange rates extended into the 1990s, until the region was hit by the Asian Financial Crisis. Singapore was comparatively unscathed, due to strong underlying economic fundamentals. Within Singapore, more and more financial transactions – even for the general public – became cashless, with the introduction of the EFTPOS system and other technological developments. For Singapore's workers, paying wages in cash was no longer the norm. This period saw two currency note issues: the Ship series and the Portrait series, as well as Singapore's second coin series.

O n 1 January 1980, the *Business Times* reported on the previous day's activity in the foreign exchange markets: the Singapore dollar had ended 1979 at the level of S$2.16 to the US dollar. Despite the fact that the Smithsonian Agreement (see p. 264) had already lapsed, the exchange rate that would have prevailed under the agreement was still being published. The US dollar was some 23 per cent weaker than would have been the case had Singapore abided by the parity agreement and continued its peg with the US dollar.[1]

Over the course of the next two decades, the Singapore dollar would continue to appreciate significantly against global and regional currencies, including the US dollar. A trade-weighted basket comprising the currencies of Singapore's major trade partners would become the focus of the Monetary Authority of Singapore's (MAS) new monetary policy framework, introduced in 1981. By end-1987 the Singapore dollar had touched just below S$2 per US dollar, an eight per cent appreciation from end-1979. The gyrations in the bilateral exchange rate would cause much consternation to the US – the American view was that the Singapore dollar had not appreciated enough against the US dollar – while at home it led to complaints about Singapore's loss of competitiveness, especially in the manufacture of final products such as garments. However, MAS would focus on the trade-weighted exchange rate to secure low and stable consumer price inflation in Singapore. MAS would abide closely by this mandate even in the face of economic stresses caused by Singapore's first two recessions since Independence.

The 1980s and 1990s also saw important innovations concerning money. Technological advances that had facilitated the electronic transfer of funds in the 1970s would be extended for use in day-to-day payments by the general public. This would broaden people's conception of 'money' to include their bank deposits, and not just cash in the wallet. The beginnings of a move away from physical currency would become a feature of these two decades, paving the way for further changes after the end of the millennium.

Reforming monetary policy

On 1 August 1980, Dr Goh Keng Swee was appointed chairman of MAS, replacing Hon Sui Sen. This was a departure from precedent, since the chairman of MAS had hitherto been the Minister for Finance and Hon remained in that role. Dr Goh was concurrently First Deputy Prime Minister and chairman of the Board of Commissioners of Currency, Singapore (BCCS).

Goh's return to MAS heralded reform on the issues of exchange rate and reserve management. One of the first things he did was to commission a team from the Management Services Department of the Ministry of Finance to review the objectives, functions, organisation and operations of MAS and

Chapter opening picture: The skyscrapers of the Central Business District in striking contrast to the low-rise shophouses of Chinatown, 1998

The iconic control tower at Changi Airport. Terminal One commenced operations in July 1981, and was officially opened on 29 December that year. Widely regarded as one of the world's best, Changi Airport has come to symbolise Singapore's interconnectedness with the region and the world at large.

BCCS.[2] In December 1980, a confidential report, circulated only to the Cabinet, recommended that MAS concentrate on two areas: developing Singapore as a financial centre and investing its reserve assets.[3] The BCCS would continue to issue the nation's currency – there were no plans at this juncture to transfer this function to MAS.

As a consequence of that report, Singapore's reserve management practices underwent a major shift. MAS would still be responsible for the foreign reserves needed for exchange rate management, but the rest – including foreign reserves held by the BCCS – would be professionally managed to achieve higher longer-run returns. To this end, in 1981 Goh established the Government of Singapore Investment Corporation (since renamed GIC Private Ltd). To be sure, Singapore was not the first country to establish an investment corporation to manage its reserves; but at that time such enterprises were generally rather opaque and set up largely to invest the surpluses from commodity exports, such as oil, rather than to invest surplus reserves.

Despite the Management Services Department's recommendation that MAS just focus on developing Singapore as a financial centre and investing reserve assets, Goh had other plans: specifically, he wanted to overhaul MAS's approach to monetary policy.

From its founding up to this point, MAS had managed monetary and credit growth in the economy largely through an 'eclectic' toolbox comprising multiple instruments such as interest rates, reserve ratios, credit ceilings and 'moral suasion'. But there was increasing focus on the exchange rate, particularly as the Singapore dollar began floating in June 1973. MAS initially aimed to let market forces determine the exchange rate, but it would intervene to smooth large fluctuations in the currency and to ensure there was sufficient liquidity in the banking system. In 1975, policy switched to monitoring the level of the Singapore dollar trade-weighted exchange rate within a band during a quarterly review of monetary policy. The idea was that MAS should dampen currency fluctuations and at the same time inject sufficient liquidity into the money market to stabilise domestic interest rates.

However, it was increasingly apparent that the instruments in the monetary and credit toolbox were no longer as effective. Simultaneously stabilising the exchange rate and domestic interest rates was becoming more difficult, and was further complicated by the abolition in 1975 of the bank cartel that fixed interest rates, as well as the liberalisation of foreign exchange controls by 1978. Freeing capital flows into and out of Singapore meant that domestic interest rates became more volatile; and because they were set by market forces, MAS had to rely on its individual relationships with the banks to guide their behaviour on interest rates and to monitor inflows and outflows of capital.

A key turning point came in 1979, when the second oil shock led to a sharp rise in Singapore's inflation. It remained relatively high at 8.5 per cent in 1980 and 8.2 per cent in 1981. Much of this was 'imported' through higher import prices, especially for food and raw materials. At the same time, capital inflows were putting upward pressure on the prices of property and securities. MAS had allowed the Singapore dollar to appreciate after the 1979 oil shock and this convinced Goh that strengthening the exchange rate would ultimately be more effective in dampening inflationary pressures than tightening interest rates or controlling credit availability. A more coherent monetary policy framework was needed if Singapore was to prevent a repeat of the high-inflation experiences of the previous decade, and Goh Keng Swee was clear that the exchange rate should be the main instrument in such a framework.

Making the exchange rate the main instrument of monetary policy was sensible given Singapore's openness to trade: by 1980, imports accounted for about 60 per cent of total expenditure and exports 70 per cent. Other countries in the world were also very open to trade; what made Singapore different was its negligible tariffs and quotas on exports and imports and the very high import content of its domestic expenditure and exports. So compared to other countries, changes in Singapore's exchange rate had a more direct pass-through to, and powerful influence on, domestic costs and prices.

Centring the monetary policy framework on the exchange rate was not a foregone conclusion. During the sterling and US dollar devaluation episodes in the 1960s and early 1970s, the Singapore government had been aware that any short-term boost to competitiveness arising from a weaker exchange rate would have been quickly whittled away if higher import, and thus consumer, prices had

Managing Singapore's reserves

When Singapore became an independent nation in 1965, it had around 1 billion Malaya and British Borneo dollars of external reserves (also known as official foreign reserves). These grew rapidly from the 1970s onwards due to persistent balance of payments surpluses arising from a high domestic saving rate and regular government budget surpluses as well as an inflow of foreign capital.[4]

Singapore's official foreign reserves

After Singapore separated from Malaysia, the Singapore government argued that because the nation did not have any natural resources, it needed to build up a 'war chest' of reserves in anticipation of military and financial threats that could disrupt trade and capital flows. This was in addition to the foreign assets needed for 'monetary' purposes, i.e. to meet the legal obligations of the BCCS in backing or managing the Singapore dollar.

Goh Keng Swee's thinking was that Singapore would in all likelihood continue to accumulate foreign assets, and it would have reserves in excess of what was required for 'monetary' purposes. These 'excess reserves', he felt, should not be managed in the traditional low-risk, low-return asset portfolios typically held by central banks. This line of thought was reminiscent of that revealed in Goh's exchanges with Britain's Chancellor of the Exchequer Roy Jenkins in 1967 following the sterling devaluation. Goh's argument then was that 'non-monetary reserves' could be invested differently for long-term gain (see p. 252).

In September 1980, Goh travelled to Europe to meet central and commercial bankers, including his former London School of Economics tutor Sir Claus Moser, who was by this time with the Rothschild bank in London. Moser invited him to visit Rothschild, where he met the head of fixed income and currency, Richard Katz. Katz recommended that the Singapore government hold equities in its reserve portfolio, as equities over the long term typically achieved a greater return above inflation than cash and bonds. He suggested that an investment organisation separate from MAS be made responsible for such investment – after all, central banking and asset management required different types of expertise.

Dr Goh invited Moser and Katz to submit a consultancy proposal, with a view to recommending a reserve-management portfolio suitable for the long term, and a structure for an investment-management company designed to achieve this end. The bankers accepted the invitation, and co-opted a third person, Kate Mortimer, also from Rothschild. The three were appointed for a six-month period and on 27 February 1981, Dr Goh released a press statement announcing the establishment of GIC.

GIC was duly incorporated on 22 May 1981 with an authorised capital of S$2 million. Three American fund managers were appointed, each a specialist in a particular investment field. The new company would be the only one in Singapore with ministers as its directors and the prime minister as its chairman. That alone would signal the importance the government attached to the endeavour.[5]

Singapore's reserves comprise the assets of GIC, MAS and Temasek Holdings. These assets include not only official foreign reserves, but foreign assets that are managed for longer-term returns, as well as domestically focused investments in areas deemed strategic to the nation.

The Economic Development Board hosts a meeting of the National Wages Council, 1984.

encouraged workers to press for wage increases. Indeed, this chain of events was a major cause of the 1970s 'Great Inflation' in the major industrial countries, and the effects had spilled over into Singapore through rising import prices. Goh was keen to avoid a repeat of this situation. However, as Singapore developed its export sectors during the 1970s, there was a growing view within the broader government that a weaker currency could perhaps be beneficial for export growth. Indeed, during the period in the mid-1970s when inflation was relatively quiescent, MAS's thinking was that since inflation was not a problem, the Singapore dollar could be allowed to depreciate within the band to keep exports competitive.

Goh Keng Swee's return to MAS put an end to this mindset. He reinforced the view that long-term growth could not be achieved by a weakened exchange rate but depended on improvements in productivity. At around the same time, there was a growing sense at the Ministry of Finance that the negative effect of an appreciating Singapore dollar on exports was probably less important than was once thought. After all, a rising currency would not affect exports much if they had a high import content; indeed, imported inputs would be cheaper if the currency strengthened. In contrast, a weaker Singapore dollar would hurt the export sector in the long run as it would subsidise inefficient firms and industries and keep them from innovating and increasing productivity. This led to the conviction that even if MAS were to intervene to depreciate the Singapore dollar, this would not yield enduring improvements in export competitiveness. Separately, MAS's own research also suggested that Singapore's export sales depended more on changes in real income in destination countries than on changes in export prices brought about by a change in the value of the currency. Other government agencies eventually came around to support this alternative view of the role of the exchange rate.

A further change in thinking, supported by the International Monetary Fund (IMF), was that a stronger Singapore dollar could replace the 'high wage policy' pursued by the government between 1979 and 1981. This policy had been designed to persuade producers to invest in capital- and skill-intensive activities rather than relying on the low-wage, labour-intensive manufacturing that had driven the economy in the 1970s. Switching to a stronger-dollar policy would make 'traditional' lower-value-added exports less price-competitive and encourage producers to switch to higher-quality goods; labour productivity would then increase to match wage increases.

In August 1980, an internal meeting at MAS concluded that imported inflation was the main problem facing Singapore; the economy was not at risk of a significant slowdown, since there was an ample supply of infrastructure projects in the pipeline that would help shore up GDP growth. The time was ripe for a shift in MAS's approach to monetary policy.

And so, as 1981 began, MAS introduced an exchange rate-centred monetary policy framework. Under this new framework, the Singapore dollar was neither fixed to any one currency nor allowed to float freely. Rather, it was managed against an index comprising a weighted basket of the currencies of Singapore's major trading partners and competitors. This index was known as the Singapore dollar nominal effective exchange rate (S$NEER) or trade-weighted index (TWI).

The impact of the exchange rate-centred monetary policy [6]

MAS's formal exchange rate-centred monetary policy would primarily target imported inflation. For example, if consumer price inflation was expected to rise due to higher import prices, such as from crude oil, MAS would tighten monetary policy. However, instead of raising interest rates, as other central banks might have done, MAS would let the trade-weighted Singapore dollar appreciate more quickly, which would lower import prices and consequently domestic wholesale and consumer prices. This 'direct imported inflation channel' was especially important to a country that had no natural resources and had to import almost all of its food and energy needs.

The anti-inflationary effects of the exchange rate would also filter through a second 'derived demand' channel. Insofar as the currency appreciation reduced the revenues of Singapore-based exporters, it lowered their demand for factor inputs, such as manpower and capital goods, and put downward pressure on domestic costs and consumer price inflation.

MAS has some advantages not always available to other central banks when implementing its monetary policy. Because the government usually runs a budget surplus and does not accumulate foreign debt, there is no need for the MAS to finance government debt. It can therefore concentrate on its main task of preserving the value, and thus the purchasing power, of the Singapore dollar. In particular, the fiscal surpluses of the government, combined with the balance of payments surpluses in the economy, will underpin a trend appreciation of the Singapore dollar, which the MAS manages in such a way as to keep inflation low over the medium term.

The MAS building, opened in 1985.

The TWI would be managed within a prescribed policy band. Market forces would be allowed to drive fluctuations in the index within the band, but the degree of volatility would be lower than if the currency were to float freely. It was a sensible compromise between the restrictive fixed exchange rates under the Bretton Woods system and the volatility that could potentially occur under the free-floating system.

What made this monetary policy framework unique at the time was that the TWI was not something that MAS monitored as by-product of a more conventional monetary policy targeting the money supply or interest rates. Nor was it a framework for intervening in the foreign exchange market for other purposes – whether to keep the currency weak and so boost export competitiveness; or strong and so reduce capital inflow into the domestic economy. Rather, exchange rate policy was *in itself* Singapore's monetary policy.

MAS's first monetary policy decision under the new exchange rate framework was made in January 1981: the TWI would be managed along a gradually appreciating trend for six months. The significance of the change in policy was then made public in the MAS Annual Report of 1982. Monetary policy, it said, differed somewhat in 1981 in that the policy direction was aimed largely at maintaining a strong exchange rate for the Singapore dollar while ensuring that there was sufficient liquidity in the money market to facilitate economic growth.

The strong Singapore dollar was quickly opposed by manufacturers, who found that an appreciating currency eroded their profits. Within a month, the media reported on the plight of local garment manufacturers who were already facing stiff competition from Taiwan, Hong Kong and Korea; critically, competitors in those economies were helped by the fact that their currencies moved in line with, rather than strengthened against, the US dollar.[7] In one commentary, the *Business Times* made the case for a weaker Singapore dollar. It questioned whether having cheaper imports and lower consumer price inflation in the near term was worth the long-term implications of the loss in export competitiveness, especially at a time when the global economy was weakening. 'All factors argue for the Singapore dollar to tread a middle, moderate path – and for the MAS to resume its restraining role in the foreign exchange market.'[8] In the subsequent years, the nominal and inflation-adjusted TWI appreciated significantly, and manufacturers' complaints grew. The Singapore Australian Business Council in 1984 put it bluntly: manufacturing in Singapore had declined over the past three years, they

MAS finds its footing

Given the new and – all things considered – unorthodox monetary policy framework, MAS also had to find its footing in communicating and implementing monetary policy.

First, communications around MAS's new exchange rate-centred monetary policy framework were sparse. Certainly, reluctance on the part of MAS to share information was not unexpected at that time, especially since it was a relatively new central bank still in the early stages of implementing a new monetary policy. The lack of information – particularly around the currencies in the trade-weighted basket – prompted speculation and overreactions to rumours about the extent of MAS intervention. In December 1987, The *Asian Wall Street Journal* reported that 'because of the tight control maintained by the authority over the republic's currency and its past record in controlling speculation against the Singapore dollar ... the market is obliged to take even the rumour of intervention very seriously. In the past, currency traders have found the Authority is ready to intervene in the market to curb speculation in the local currency and keep it within what the government deems its correct trading range'. The *Journal* also reported that the Singapore dollar had suddenly weakened against the US dollar, and foreign exchange traders were blaming the drop on intervention by MAS. Officials at MAS apparently could not be reached for comment and treasury officers at local banks, through whom intervention would have taken place, were unwilling to comment. Nor would local traders confirm reports of intervention. A senior dealer at a local bank acknowledged that he was under specific instructions not to confirm or deny that MAS had acted through his bank.

The way interest rates were determined within the new framework was puzzling to some market participants. Because MAS targeted the exchange rate as its primary monetary policy, it could not at the same time target the domestic money supply or fix local interest rates: these were therefore determined largely by international interbank rates. However, MAS *did* manage liquidity in the domestic banking system to ensure that banks had sufficient money to carry out their daily lending and borrowing operations.[9] MAS would also at times ask the banks to reconsider proposed changes to their lending and borrowing rates. For instance, in November 1986 the Development Bank of Singapore (DBS) had wanted to cut its prime lending and deposit rates and widen the spread between the two. MAS advised DBS to cut deposit rates by only 0.5 per cent since it did not want the bank to create the impression that interest rates were plunging headlong downwards: this might lead to a capital outflow. All these moves added to confusion as to whether MAS was trying to control domestic interest rates as well.[10]

said, largely due to the 'sustained rise' in the Singapore dollar, and 'no amount of normal productivity gain will redress this'.[11]

MAS's new monetary policy would soon be tested. In 1985, the domestic economy experienced its first recession since Independence as well as a speculative attack on the Singapore dollar.

The economy contracted by 0.6 per cent in 1985 and expanded by only 1.3 per cent in 1986; these were sharp drops from the average 9 per cent growth rate over the previous five years. The main cause of the slump was a significant fall in exports in 1985 and 1986 due to an economic downturn affecting the US and several of Singapore's major trade partners including Malaysia, Indonesia, and Hong Kong. Exports of electronics were badly hit, as were ship-repairing and tourism services. The appreciation of the trade-weighted exchange rate would

MAS board meeting in the early 1980s. From left to right, J.Y. Pillai, Chairman Goh Keng Swee, Richard Hu.

have exacerbated the drag on exports: Singapore's inflation-adjusted effective exchange rate had risen rapidly and by early 1985, it was around 15 per cent higher than its level in 1980. This was due in part to MAS tightening monetary policy to contain inflation – the nominal trade-weighted exchange rate rose by 25 per cent over the same period.[12] However, other factors weighing on GDP growth included rising business unit costs due to the government's earlier high-wage policy and a steady increase in the employers' compulsory contribution rate to the Central Provident Fund (CPF), which peaked at 25 per cent in July 1985.[13] Reflecting all the above factors, unemployment rose from 2.7 per cent in 1984 to more than 4 per cent in 1985, and then to over 6 per cent by 1986.

In the midst of the recession, on 16 September 1985 there was a severe speculative attack on the Singapore dollar. This was driven in part by the perception that the dollar was overvalued, and that MAS would eventually ease monetary policy and intervene to weaken the currency.

Despite the downward pressures on the exchange rate, Dr Goh Keng Swee – who by this time had retired from politics (he stepped down from Parliament on 3 December 1984) and transited to the role of deputy chairman of MAS – was determined not to let speculators have their way. He instructed MAS to buy Singapore dollars using its US dollar reserves and to raise short-term interest rates, and so punish speculators expecting a currency depreciation. Around US$100 million, less than 1 per cent of the external reserves, were spent, but the tight liquidity pushed the overnight interbank rate up to 105 per cent on 17 September and 120 per cent the following day, well above their usual level of about 5 per cent.[14] Goh issued a statement that same day to dispel the 'widespread belief in financial markets that the Singapore Government wants a cheaper Singapore dollar'[15] and later warned speculators to 'leave the Singapore dollar alone'.[16] The

Singapore's nominal and real effective exchange rates

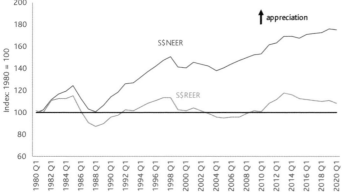

Source: International Monetary Fund, International Financial Statistics.

sum of these actions was that the Singapore dollar strengthened by about 5 per cent against the US currency in just four days. This was dramatic but effective in reversing the speculative attack, while at the same time causing heavy and widespread losses to foreign exchange dealers.[17]

In early 1986, global crude oil prices collapsed, and imported inflationary pressures moderated. Both the nominal and real trade-weighted Singapore dollar indices depreciated over the course of 1986. At the same time, the government introduced a number of cost-reduction measures, including cutting civil servants' bonuses, lowering the employers' CPF contribution rate from 25 per cent to 10 per cent, and imposing a two-year wage-restraint policy targeted largely at the public sector. The resultant recovery in real GDP in 1987 was quick and robust, with growth reaching 10.8 per cent, driven largely by a turn-round in exports.

Towards a cashless society

The average Singaporean was doubtless concerned that the Singapore dollar notes and coins in his or her pocket should retain their purchasing power. On this count there was not much to fear, as MAS's new exchange rate-centred monetary policy delivered. Between 1980 and 1989, consumer price inflation rose by an average of 2.8 per cent per year, and only exceeded 5 per cent in the first two years of the decade. This was lower than the 5.8 per cent per annum average inflation of the 1970s, when capital inflows and the first oil shock drove inflation up to around 20 per cent in 1973–4.

Over the 1980s, however, other developments would fundamentally reshape the public's interaction with money. Financial innovation opened up the possibility of conducting transactions without cash. To make payments, Singaporeans were increasingly able to draw directly on their 'money' in the bank – that is, bank deposits – instead of physical currency. As money, bank deposits differ crucially from physical currency. They are created by banks and not by the government, and as such are the liabilities of the former, not the latter. In this sense, money in the bank is more closely aligned with the paper banknotes issued by chartered banks in the 19th century (see p. 76) than with the physical notes issued by Singapore's various currency boards over the course of its history.

As the 1980s began, the use of physical currency was still a dominant way of life for most Singaporeans. Payment of wages in cash had been codified into law since 1955 but this had become increasingly dated; as at late 1983, two-thirds of all workers were still paid in cash. The government handled 40 million transactions in which taxes, fees and charges were collected each year, and nearly three-quarters of this was done in cash either through 'multi-revenue centres' – centres set up so that individuals could pay various government dues using notes and coins – or through payment counters at government offices. In all, there were 1,930 counters manned by 3,000 staff.[18] At that time, cashless payments were restricted to cheques and credit cards. However, not many Singaporeans had current accounts that offered chequing facilities; and while credit cards were more popular, they were typically only available to those earning more than a specified monthly income.

The Singapore government sought to encourage the transition to a 'cashless' society. The shift began quietly. In January 1984, a task force was set up comprising representatives from the government, employer associations, banks and the National Trades Union Congress (NTUC). Its mission: to minimise cash transactions for manpower savings and make cashless transactions 'a way of life

Banking goes to the people: the Chartered Bank's branch in a bus.

The campaign to minimise the use of cash in transactions was launched in March 1985 by Minister for Labour Lee Yock Suan (centre).

for Singaporeans by 1987'. This was only feasible because Singaporeans already had fairly decent access to banking services: by end-1980, the Post Office Savings Bank (POSB) alone had nearly 1.9 million savings accounts in a population of 2.4 million people. The local banks and POSB[19] had installed automated teller machines (ATMs) in various parts of the island, and although initially their main function was to dispense physical notes, the ATMs were later to play an important part in the transition *away* from cash.

In February 1984, the Singapore Parliament amended the Employment Act to encourage – but not compel – employers to pay workers' wages through banks or by cheques. The benefits of cashless paydays were touted: workers would run a lower risk of mislaying their pay or having it stolen. There was also the convenience of not having to carry large amounts of cash or go to the bank to deposit it. If workers were paid through bank accounts, and only withdrew what they needed, then their bank balances would be higher on average, and they would earn more interest. In pragmatic Singaporean fashion, it was trumpeted that 'An efficient pay system means a general rise in productivity.'[20]

The hardware was ready, but the people were not. The fact that, with cashless paydays, individuals would have to go to banks or ATMs to withdraw cash was itself a concern. While the banks had extended the ATM network significantly since the machines first appeared in 1979, they could often only be accessed during business hours, and distribution of the machines across the island was uneven. Even before the law was passed, NTUC secretary-general Ong Teng Cheong said that while workers did not object to the move, the transition 'should be handled with care', citing the very real fears of some workers that their ATM

POSB 'Cash-on-Line' automated teller machine, 1989.

cards would be 'swallowed' by the machine if they accidentally keyed in the wrong security code.[21] NTUC conducted a survey and found that only 15 per cent of workers paid in cash would be comfortable receiving their pay through their bank accounts or by cheque. Nearly 30 per cent said that cashless payments would be inconvenient, citing concerns such as the need to queue up at the ATM or bank to withdraw cash, machine errors, or the early closure of banks, which meant workers would not be able to withdraw cash unless they were given time off. Some respondents also commented that if they were not paid in cash, they would incur additional travelling costs if they had to go to the bank to cash a pay cheque or to an ATM for cash.[22, 23] Lower-wage workers, including daily-rated employees, were found disproportionately to favour being paid in cash. Of the daily-rated workers surveyed, nearly two-thirds did not know how to use ATMs, while up to 13 per cent stated they would have difficulty completing forms in the bank (to apply for an ATM card and banking services, for instance) because they were illiterate.

The legislation was debated in Parliament, and members suggested ways to ease the transition: extend banking hours, have all banks share a common ATM network, integrate a proposed Electronics Fund Transfer at Point of Sale (EFTPOS) card with the ATM card.[24] Some of these suggestions would eventually be taken up. Banks tried to encourage employers and employees to make the switch, and these efforts bore fruit. A group of banks came together to develop an inexpensive computerised salary payment system. Employers using this system could submit payroll diskettes and magnetic tapes containing salary payment instructions to their banks, and payment would be processed by the banks on payday.[25] Banks took steps to assuage workers' concerns. For instance, POSB expanded the ATM network to cover more workplaces such as factory spaces and shipyards. The number of ATM card-holders increased; and in the first half of 1984, more than 30,000 people opened current accounts with POSB and so acquired cheque books.[26]

The amendments to the Employment Act were duly passed. To support the cashless payday initiative, MAS did away with the regulations requiring banks to seek its permission before installing an ATM, so that the network of teller machines could be rapidly expanded.[27] To minimise the risk of a crush at ATMs and banks, the government announced that paydays should be staggered. The public sector would lead by example – from January 1985, all civil servants would be paid on or about the 12th of each month rather than at the end.[28]

If workers' bank accounts could be automatically credited with their wages, then it made sense that they should also be able to pay bills and buy things through an electronic direct-debit service. Since 1974, customers of the Post Office Savings Bank could have their utilities, telephone bills, and later, property taxes, debited from their bank accounts. However, the number of organisations on this bill payment system was limited. From 7 April 1984, a true General Interbank Recurring Order (GIRO) bill payment system was established when the network was widened to include the local banks and a larger range of organisations as payees. Both POSB and local bank customers could now handle the bills listed above, as well as pay for subscriptions, insurance premiums, rents or loan repayments through a computerised standing-order service. The commercial banks went one step further. In October 1984, Overseas Union Bank (OUB) pioneered a bill-payment facility at its ATMs. To complement the development of GIRO and encourage the 'cashless' payment of bills, the Singapore government announced in 1985 that over the course of a year it would gradually do away with the 20 multi-revenue centres. Payment counters at government offices would remain, but they would be reduced in number and manned by fewer staff.

Some bills you need never bother with ever again.

When you use Giro.

POSB encourages bank customers to use GIRO for regular payments.

What of cashless purchases? At about the same time that Parliament started to discuss amendments to the Employment Act, POSB and the four major local banks – United Overseas Bank, DBS, Oversea-Chinese Banking Corporation, and OUB – formed a steering committee to examine the feasibility of an EFTPOS system. This meant that consumers could immediately access the full purchasing power of their bank balances and make transactions without having to carry around cash, while sales receipts would go directly into retailers' bank accounts. EFTPOS offered reduced administrative costs related to cash sales, lower security risks, and greater convenience.[29]

Payment using an EFTPOS card: how the system works. *Business Times*, 21 March 1984.

Even before the committee had finished its deliberations, the NTUC Fairprice chain of supermarkets computerised its checkout system, in anticipation of the day when it would be linked up to an EFTPOS system. NTUC then put its existing cash registers up for sale.[30]

In June 1985, the five banks launched a two-month pilot shopping scheme whereby their staff would be able to make purchases using EFTPOS. The recommendation in Parliament to have the ATM card double up as an EFTPOS card was implemented: two staff from DBS were highlighted in the media for using their ATM cards to purchase one-dollar pens from a Times bookshop at Centrepoint. The pilot was successful, and the service was opened up to the public in January 1986. The EFTPOS system that Singaporeans have come to know as NETS (Network for Electronic Transfers) came into being, and it became an integral part of the payments landscape.

It is clear that some of the aims of the task force set up in 1984 were met: cash transactions were reduced, if not absolutely minimised. In the decade that followed, Singaporeans had plenty of time to adapt to electronic banking and fund transfers and the conveniences that came with these and other financial innovations. The stock of physical currency in active circulation when normalised by GDP fell steadily from 12 per cent in 1980 to around 7 per cent by the end of the millennium.

Currency for the 1980s and 1990s

The release of Singapore's third currency note issue, the Ship series, was prompted by demand for a note that was not routinely used for day-to-day transactions. The 1000-dollar note was the first in the series to be issued, on 22 October 1984, because stocks of notes from the earlier series had become depleted. Singapore's second circulation coin series was released on 2 December 1985.

All monetary authorities face the problem of currency counterfeiting, but in the 1980s it worsened and became more globalised. According to an internal BCCS memo in 1982, the problem had become so acute that the US Secret Service had set up an office in Paris. The US dollar had by then earned the ignominious distinction of being the most widely forged currency in the world, accounting for about 85 per cent of the total known counterfeits. In 1980, US$65 million in greenbacks had been seized in the United States, and US$17 million globally. The most counterfeited US dollar denominations were the 100-dollar, 50-dollar and 20-dollar notes. These were printed with only two colours, all the denominations were the same size, and there was no watermark or security thread. A number of different portraits of former US presidents appeared on the notes, not all of whom were easily recognisable. All these factors made it harder to distinguish the counterfeits from the authentic notes.[31]

Within Singapore, counterfeiting notes had come a long way from the time when fake Bird-series notes took the form of black-and-white photocopies marked with watercolour paint (see p. 293). However, action by the BCCS and the police – including the somewhat extreme measure of controlling the import of colour photocopiers – sharply reduced the incidence of forgery. In December 1988, there were a total of 23 cases of forged Ship series notes but by August 1989 this had been reduced to zero.[32]

The Ship series notes

The Ship series was released to the public by the BCCS on 22 October 1984 in the form of a 1000-dollar note. The remaining denominations were released between August 1985 and January 1991. The series had nine denominations: the 20-dollar note of the Bird series was not replaced, and a new two-dollar note was introduced. The two-dollar note was red when it first appeared in January 1991, similar to the colour of the ten-dollar notes in this and previous note series. The colour caused some confusion with the public and there were anecdotes of hawkers giving the wrong change. The red note was eventually replaced with a purple one in December that year.

The Ship series paid tribute to the role of merchant shipping in Singapore's development from an entrepôt trading centre into one of the busiest ports in the world. The fronts of the notes depict vessels that have plied the waters of Singapore over the centuries. All the notes bore the Singapore coat of arms, a lion's head watermark, and the signature and seal of the Minister for Finance and Chairman of the BCCS. On the front centre panel of all except the two-dollar note were colour lithographic offset-printed images of creatures from Chinese mythology.

The back celebrated Singapore's achievements in the fields of communications, housing, defence, and port management. Also on the back of the notes was the orchid Vanda Miss Joaquim, the national flower of Singapore.

The design originated at the Basingstoke office of the British security printer De La Rue, but the notes were actually printed by the company's branch in Jurong – this was the first time that currency notes had been printed in Singapore. They were printed on a new paper that crackled when rustled, had a 'raised' feel, and was capable of incorporating very fine detail. Security features included intaglio printing, a clear watermark, and the perfect registration of the fish printed on the bottom right-hand corner of some of the notes. There was also a security thread embedded vertically across each note. Special colours and fluorescent inks were used, and the lower right-hand corners of all the denominations except the one-dollar and 10,000-dollar notes had raised concentric rings to facilitate reading by the blind.

S$1 (blue), issued 12 January 1987

Front: 'Sha Chuan'

Back: Sentosa satellite earth station

S$2 (red, purple)
Red issued 28 January 1991

Purple issued 16 December 1991

Front: tongkang

Back: ethnic groups at the Chingay procession

S$5 (green), issued 21 August 1989

Front: twakow

Back: PSA container terminal

S$10 (red), issued 1 March 1988

Front: barter trading vessel 'Palari'

Back: public housing

S$50 (blue), issued 9 March 1987

Front: coaster vessel 'Perak'

Back: Benjamin Sheares bridge

S$100 (brown), issued 1 August 1985

Front: passenger liner 'Chusan'

Back: Changi Airport

S$500 (green), issued 1 March 1988

Front: cargo vessel 'Neptune Sardonyx'

Back: Singapore's armed forces and civil defence

S$1,000 (purple), issued 22 October 1984

Front: container ship 'Neptune Garnet' and quay cranes

Back: ship repair yard

S$10,000 (red), issued 21 August 1989

Front: bulk carrier 'Neptune Canopus'

Back: National Day parade, 1987

How currency notes are printed[33]

All Singapore's currency notes except for the Ship series have been printed overseas. In 1984, De La Rue Currency and Security Print Pte Ltd (formerly known as Thomas De La Rue (Singapore) Pte Ltd) opened its printing plant in Singapore and started printing the majority of the Ship series currency notes locally.

Currency notes are printed using a combination of intaglio (right) and lithographic (left) printing processes, as seen here in two proofs, together with the finished note.

An approved proof note by the then Board of Commissioners of Currency, Singapore (BCCS).

Design and origination

The first stage in the creation of a currency note is the design. Currency notes should be aesthetically pleasing but the various denominations must also be distinctive in some way so they can be quickly differentiated by the public. It is also important to include security features at this early stage for authentication and protection against counterfeiting. Such features can vary across the denominations and are planned into the aesthetic elements of the design. A different colour may be used for each denomination and the physical size of the paper can vary, depending on the value of the notes.

Based on the artworks provided by MAS, the currency-note printer will convert the approved designs together with different graphic elements (carefully assembled using a special computer system) into original digital files containing all the security elements incorporated in a currency note. These design origination files are printed out on high-resolution inkjet printers as 'Digital Proof Prints', which are then submitted to MAS for preliminary approval. Changes may then be made speedily using computers before the actual engraving and plate-making processes begin. In order to ensure that currency notes printed from the approved designs are in line with MAS' expectations, fully printed proof currency notes are produced using the same printing methods as full production, but on a smaller scale.

Plate-making

Once the fully-printed proofs are approved by MAS, the mass-production process begins with the making of the printing plates. The digital files that were used to produce the proof prints are sent to high-precision laser machines which produce the plates used for lithographic/offset printing and the master plates for the intaglio printing process. Intaglio printing plates are then made from the master plates by an elaborate multi-stage process. For lithographic printing, multiple plates are made using the digital files created within the computer design studio. Each plate contains different elements of the design which are then combined at the point of printing. The lithographic content generally forms the background design.

The three stages in the lithographic printing of the 500-dollar Bird series note. These proofs are known as 'progressives'.

Printing

The paper or polymer substrate supplied for the currency notes is in sheet form for 28–60 single notes, depending on the denomination. At each successive stage of the printing process, the printing substrate stock is subject to rigorous counting to ensure that every single sheet is accounted for.

Sheets of currency notes are produced by up to five separate and different printing processes. The substrate sheets are first run through a high-speed rotary process, which prints the lithographic content on the front and back of the notes during a single pass of the substrate through the machine. This process is known as 'lithographic printing' or 'offset printing'. Perfect registration of the design elements on each side is achieved by this process.

The second stage incorporates the intaglio print on the back of the notes. This process produces subtle tonal variations with remarkable fineness of detail. The substrate is brought into contact with the engraved plate under heat and pressure and ink is transferred to produce a very distinctive three-dimensional relief-type representation and print lines

The engraved part of the design is printed by intaglio in several colours. The printer has marked out the areas and indicated the inks used.

which feel rough to the touch. The incredible precision of the intaglio can also be used to produce extra-small printing. To the naked eye, this appears as a line; but when viewed through a magnifying glass, the lines are actually texts in micro-print.

In the case of paper notes, after the back intaglio printing, the kinegram (the octagonal security foil) is applied on the currency sheet using a die. The size of the die depends on the denomination of the note. The application of the kinegram is a hot-stamping process where temperature and pressure are applied to the paper substrate.

After the hot-stamping process, the currency sheet is ready for the front intaglio printing. The process is similar to the back intaglio printing.

Finally, two sets of serial numbers are printed on each note by the letterpress method.

Varnishing

In the case of polymer substrate, the currency notes are varnished as an additional protection to the finished product.

Finishing

The last step in the production of currency notes is the finishing. In this phase, the fully printed sheets are first counted in sheets of 100 before being cut into single notes. Each note is then fed into a quality inspection machine and checked for flaws. Notes that do not meet the required quality standard are sorted out for destruction. Notes that pass the quality inspection process are banded into packs of 100. Ten packs are combined and counted before being strapped and shrink-wrapped in bundles of 1,000 notes. These bundles are packed into cartons for delivery.

Polymer notes

In 1990, Singapore produced its first polymer note – a 50-dollar commemorative note to celebrate 25 years of independence.[34] Polymer notes are secure and difficult to counterfeit. They are cleaner and more durable than paper notes, as they wear out less easily.[35]

Intaglio (left) and the lithographic (right) printing proofs for the two-dollar Ship series note.

The image on the intaglio engraving plate (in this case for the S$50 Ship series note) is reversed.

The second series of coins

The second series of coins (1985–90) consisted of six denominations. The 5-cent, 10-cent, 20-cent and 50-cent coins were introduced on 2 December 1985. Two more denominations, one cent and one dollar, were introduced on 28 September 1987. The metallic composition of the one cent coin was changed to copper-plated zinc, and the five cent and one dollar coins were now made of aluminium-bronze. A floral theme representing local plants and flowers was adopted to show Singapore as a 'garden city'. The rationale behind the new design was to make Singaporean coins easily distinguishable from foreign coins, and smaller, lighter and easier to carry and handle, especially as people needed to carry more coins for coin-operated machines, as on public transport for example. From 1 April 2002, the one cent coin was no longer issued as it was not widely used by the public. However, at the time of writing those still in circulation remain legal-tender.

The obverse (front) of the coins bore the Singapore arms in the centre, surrounded by the word 'SINGAPORE' in the four official languages (English, Malay, Mandarin and Tamil) around the circumference. The year date was below the Singapore arms. A ring of dashes surrounded the Singapore arms on both the 10 cent and 50 cent coins. There was an octagonal frame around the circumference of the one-dollar coin; its milled edge bore the inscription 'REPUBLIC OF SINGAPORE' and a lion symbol. Since 28 May 1990, the 50-cent coin has been minted with a plain edge with the inscription 'REPUBLIC OF SINGAPORE' and a lion symbol.

1 cent, copper-plated zinc with plain edge, issued 28 September 1987

Reverse: orchid (*Vanda* Miss Joaquim)

5 cents, aluminium bronze with milled edge, issued 2 December 1985

Reverse: fruit salad plant (*Monstera deliciosa*)

10 cents, cupronickel with milled edge, issued 2 December 1985

Reverse: star jasmine (*Jasminum multiflorum*)

20 cents, cupronickel with milled edge, issued 2 December 1985

Reverse: powder-puff plant (*Calliandra surinamensis*)

50 cents, cupronickel with milled edge, issued 2 December 1985; with plain edge issued 28 May 1990

Reverse: yellow allamanda (*Allamanda cathartica*)

1 dollar, aluminium bronze with milled edge, issued 28 September 1987

Reverse: periwinkle (*Lochnera rosea*)

How coins are minted

Most of Singapore's first and second series circulation coins were minted by The Singapore Mint, which was founded in 1968. It also designs, manufactures and sells local and foreign numismatic/commemorative coins and souvenirs. The first batch of the third series circulation coins was minted by the Royal Canadian Mint.

The processes involved in coin production can be broken down into three main parts: producing coin blanks, creating coinage tools and striking coins.

Producing coin blanks

Blanking is the process of producing coin blanks. Metal coils are fed through a press, which punches out round discs of metal without any designs. In the case of numismatic coins, precious metals such as silver or gold are used to create the coin blanks. For circulation coins, blanks are usually made of alloys, such as cupronickel, or a base metal like steel that is electroplated with nickel, brass or bronze. Before each blank is struck, it goes through a polishing process called burnishing, to create a shiny exterior.

Creating coinage tools

Once the coin designs are finalised, the details are transferred onto a master die. The master die is a critical coinage tool, as it is used to reproduce many working dies that are to be used during coin production. Working dies are created in an extremely high pressure process called hobbing. These working dies are then treated with heat and polished prior to the coin striking process.

Striking coins

The minting process follows. The designs of the working dies are struck onto the blanks, turning them into coins. The working dies are mounted in high speed presses that can strike hundreds of coins per minute. The coins are then inspected, and packed as coin rolls into boxes before being for distribution.

The threat of the colour printer

One security measure against the counterfeiting of notes affected the public directly: a bar on the free use of colour copying technology. This technology had been available commercially since 1974, and the colour resolution and quality had improved substantially since. It was also becoming more easily available to the public. Controls on the import of colour copiers into Singapore were introduced in 1979 under the Control of Import and Export Act.

It seems rather extreme to ban a general-purpose technology such as colour photocopying in order to curb counterfeiting. One possible alternative was to strengthen the security features embedded in currency notes. However, while the anti-counterfeiting measures incorporated in Singapore's notes were clearly useful for trained retail and bank staff and for organisations using machine recognition such as commercial banks, the public could not be expected to recognise all the security features that ought to be present in a genuine note. Moreover, counterfeiters had become increasingly skilled, for example simulating intaglio printing by giving a rough texture to the notes. The BCCS accepted that they could not expect members of the public to carry magnifying glasses just to check on notes they received as change.[36] Consequently, controls on the colour photocopiers remained until the late 1990s.

In Singapore itself, the two most popular denominations for forgery purposes in the late 1980s were the 50-dollar and 100-dollar notes of the Ship series. During 1988, eight pieces of forged 1,000-dollar notes were discovered as well.

The BCCS adopted numerous measures to curb counterfeiting, including liaising with other currency-issuing authorities, currency-paper manufacturers, mints, and security printers, to keep abreast of newly developed or introduced security features and other measures. The board also provided expert advice on Singapore's currency and counterfeits, and supplied specimen currency to other monetary authorities on request. For instance, BCCS and Bank Negara Malaysia exchanged information on forgeries to help both countries better detect counterfeits of each other's notes.[37, 38]

To meet growing demand from numismatists,[39] in December 1983 the BCCS issued its first gold-bullion commemorative coins in weights of 1, $^1/_2$, $^1/_4$ and $^1/_{10}$ troy ounces, and so offered the public a convenient way to invest in gold.[40] The Singapore Mint was appointed as the sole marketing agent.

Five-dollar commemorative coin celebrating 25 years of independence, 1965–1990.

To celebrate Singapore's 25 years since Independence, in 1990 an aluminium-bronze five-dollar coin was issued for circulation, as well as four numismatic coins: a silver 10-dollar coin, a gold 250-dollar coin and a platinum 500-dollar coin. The design chosen for all the coins, which incorporated an airliner, the Central Business District skyline and a container ship, celebrated the nation's achievements – its airline, its financial centre and its port.

While BCCS would issue commemorative coins throughout the 1980s and 1990s, the 25th anniversary of Independence prompted the wish to produce commemorative notes and coins that would have a greater chance of reaching everyone in the country. Australia, for example, had issued a special currency note to mark the 1986 bicentennial of the first convict ships' arrival from Britain in 1786. They were made with a plastic base, or substrate, something that no other country had used for money before. Why not create a similar note for Singapore's 25th anniversary?

50-dollar note, with a hologram of President Yusof bin Ishak as a security feature.

After much discussion of possible themes and designs, the BCCS issued Singapore's first commemorative note in 1990, a 50-dollar note using a polymer synthetic plastic substrate. It featured scenes of Singapore in the early days, juxtaposed with 1990. A unique element was a holographic image of Singapore's first president, Yusof bin Ishak. The notes were printed in Australia and the artist was Singaporean Chua Mia Tee. Chua is one of Singapore's best realist painters, having spent his childhood in Chinatown and taken inspiration from the Singapore River. He painted portraits of former Prime Ministers Lee Kuan Yew and Goh Chok Tong.[41] To ensure that everyone could have at least one note, 5.1 million pieces were printed, including 4.8 million for circulation.[42] Commemorative coins for the occasion were likewise struck, and a million five-dollar circulation coins were made available to the public.

There was much to commemorate on the monetary front in the 1990s. By then BCCS and MAS had notched up more than 20 years of experience in currency-issuance and central-banking operations. In 1992, BCCS issued special two-dollar notes to commemorate its 25 years of issuing currency. The notes had as their base design the two-dollar note of the Ship series, but they were overprinted with text marking the board's 25 years. Single commemorative two-dollar notes were distributed with the book *Prudence at the Helm*, a history of the BCCS since its establishment in 1967. Separately, uncut sheets of 25 two-dollar notes could also be purchased by collectors. Four years later, MAS issued 300,000 commemorative 25-dollar notes to celebrate its 25th anniversary. In 1997, BCCS issued another note to commemorate two occasions jointly: its 30th anniversary, as well as 100 years of currency-board operations in Singapore. The latter dated back to 1897 when the Board of Commissioners of Currency, Straits Settlements was formed to issue the Straits Settlements dollar (see p. 93). The commemorative issue comprised an uncut sheet of 28 100-dollar notes. Again, the equivalent note from the Ship series was adopted as the base, and each note was overprinted with additional logos.

Commemorative note, celebrating 25 years since the founding of MAS.

Fighting forgery

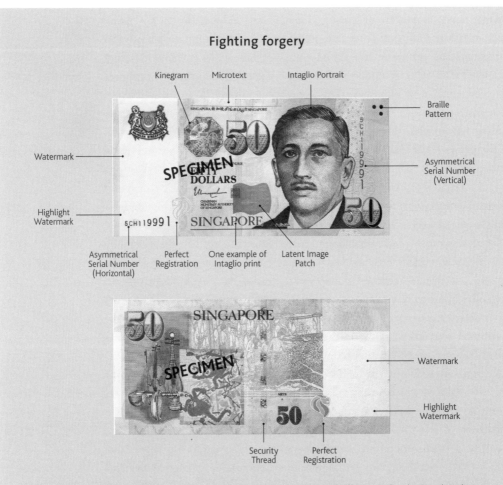

Producing, circulating or paying with fake Singapore currency is a criminal offence under the Penal Code.

Reproducing images of the currency is permitted but only under strict conditions. For example, no permission is required if you want to use an image for advertisement, publication or educational purposes provided a number of conditions are met. These include ensuring that the images do not 'detract from the dignity, integrity and image of the note or coin'; that there is no risk of any confusion with the real currency; that there is no distortion of the images of the President or any national symbol; that the word 'SPECIMEN' in bold black lettering is placed diagonally across the image.

Approval is required for using currency images for any other purpose, such as importing or manufacturing products with currency designs.

Although, according to MAS, the amount of counterfeiting is very low, it does occur. On 23 June 2019, the Singapore police issued a press release on the arrest of a 30-year-old woman for her suspected involvement in using counterfeit S$50 notes at convenience stores and retail outlets.[43] In February 2021 a man was jailed for conspiring to deposit a fake S$10,000 note at a local bank in return for a commission.[44]

Intricate micro-lettering is incorporated into the design of currency notes – it is hard to replicate, even with modern-day colour photocopiers, but it can still be recognised by the public. Reflective patterns or 'kinegrams' may be added which have transformational effects when the note is tilted. A combination of flat 'offset' printing and embossed rough-edged 'intaglio' printing, which can be detected by rubbing the note, is also used, as in the Ship series of notes.

A machine-readable watermark can be printed into the paper showing the full range of shades from light to dark and three-dimensional images when held up to the light, such as in the lion's head featured on the Orchid series notes.

Crucially, a machine-readable security thread can be embedded as a continuous line in a note. This can also be detected by running a fingernail across the note to expose counterfeit two-sided notes glued together or paper shred inserted between two pieces of paper.

Until the 19th century, currency notes were mostly printed using only one coloured ink on a white background. In more recent times, mixed colours and tones have been used. To counter forgeries produced by means of colour photography and colour photocopiers, special inks are used together with special effects. These may be invisible words in fluorescent inks which show up only under ultraviolet light, as in the Ship series of notes; or magnetic and fluorescent serial numbers or signatures.

Fake coins are probably harder to produce and easier to detect than fake notes.

Each denomination will have a precise thickness and weight, as well as a unique electromagnetic signature. A simple magnifying glass should be sufficient to spot imperfections, such as irregular millings around the edge or artificial edging produced by using chemicals. Patterns on the coin may be worn or uneven or the designs on the obverse and reverse sides not matched. Bi-metallic coin forgeries are often made with paint rather than using two types of metal. More sophisticated security features include laser micro-engraving, so that a dense micropattern can be seen under magnification.

Exchange rate and trade woes

Singapore's monetary policy framework was very unusual at the time and often misunderstood both inside and outside Singapore. Being centred on the exchange rate, it was bound to come up against developments in the international monetary and global trade systems.

A few days after the speculative attack on the Singapore dollar in September 1985, while the country was still in the throes of recession, finance ministers and central bank governors of the Group of Five (France, West Germany, Japan, the United Kingdom and the United States, also known as the G5) nations met some 15,000 kilometres away at the Plaza Hotel in New York. On 22 September, they signed what came to be known as the Plaza Accord, whereby they agreed on closer economic cooperation, especially with respect to exchange rate intervention by central banks. The aim

Signatories to the 1985 Plaza Accord (from left): Gerhard Stoltenberg (West Germany); Pierre Bérégovoy (France); James Baker (USA); Nigel Lawson (UK); Noboru Takeshita (Japan).

of the Accord was to reduce the US balance of payments deficit and halt the relentless rise in the US dollar against major currencies such as the Japanese yen and the deutschmark.

Major currencies against the US dollar in the 1980s

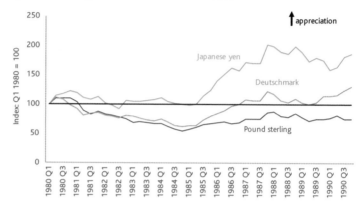

Source: International Monetary Fund, International Financial Statistics

Asian currencies against the US dollar in the 1980s

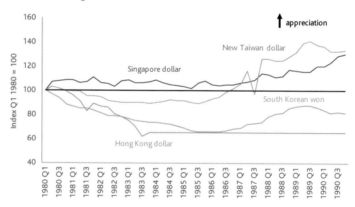

Source: International Monetary Fund, International Financial Statistics

The Plaza Accord was successful insofar as the US dollar did fall substantially against the yen and the deutschmark. However, the US administration, Congress, and American businesses became concerned that the dollar had not depreciated sufficiently against the currencies of the Newly Industrialising Economies (NIEs) in Asia – Taiwan, South Korea, Hong Kong and Singapore – and that US trade deficits with these economies continued to widen.[45] Up to that point, Japan had been the key target of criticism in Asia, but now the Asian NIEs were being regarded by the US administration as 'mini-Japans'.

The Plaza Accord and the floating-rate dollar standard[46]

Following the breakdown of the Bretton Woods System in the early 1970s and the move by the major industrial countries to float their currencies, the US dollar remained the dominant international currency despite the strength of the Japanese yen and the deutschmark. A system known as the 'floating-rate dollar standard' developed.[47] As advanced countries pursued independent monetary policies while being open to international capital flows, their central banks would intervene periodically to smooth fluctuations in their currencies against the dollar. However, there was no fixed par value, unlike in the Bretton Woods system.

The Plaza Hotel, New York City, after which the Plaza Accord was named.

However, by the 1980s there were two fundamental problems. First, exchange rates had become excessively volatile. The Europeans and Japanese attached relatively greater importance to exchange rate stability; in contrast, the US Federal Reserve had more faith in the virtues of market-determined exchange rates.[48] This led to differences in views between the major countries over the role of exchange rate policy in achieving domestic economic goals, such as low and stable inflation and a high level of employment while, at the same time, maintaining a sustainable balance of payments surplus or deficit.

Second, the lack of any effective mechanism to coordinate policies between nations meant that there were significant spill-over effects from one country's policies on those of other countries. Governments did not always work together to reconcile their macroeconomic policy differences and the IMF only played a limited role in coordinating and urging policy adjustment.

All this came to a head between December 1980 and February 1985, when the US dollar appreciated substantially against the yen, the deutschmark and the pound sterling. The United States had made reducing inflation a high priority, and tight monetary policy by the Federal Reserve led to a sharp rise in interest rates. At the same time the Reagan administration introduced cuts in personal income taxes and increased military spending. As the budget deficit widened, US interest rates rose further and foreign capital was attracted, which drove up the US dollar.

The US government began considering international negotiations with a view to coordinating exchange rate policies. At the Plaza Hotel on 22 September 1985, the finance ministers and central bank governors of the G5 agreed to 'talk the dollar down' from its overvalued rate. They issued a joint statement on the desirability of an 'orderly appreciation of non-dollar currencies'; they said they would act in concert to keep their currencies within agreed, flexible, but unpublished, boundaries and adjust them as economic fundamentals changed. The day the communiqué announcing the Plaza Accord was released, the dollar fell against the yen and the deutschmark and it continued to decline thereafter. Yet there was no significant change in monetary and fiscal policies on the part of the countries concerned.

The Federal Reserve Building, Washington DC.

Left: Richard Hu Tsu Tau, chairman of MAS 1985–1997, Minister for Finance 1985–2001.

Right: US Treasury Secretary James Baker.

Three charges were levelled at these four economies. First, that they had deliberately undervalued their currencies to boost their exports. Second, that their macroeconomic policies had artificially increased savings rates and depressed the growth of domestic demand. Third, that they had introduced restrictive trade policies by means of tariffs, quotas and subsidies to support their exports while curbing imports. However, this last accusation was rarely applied to Singapore and Hong Kong given their reputation as free-traders.

Rumours that the United States was considering action against the NIEs started around August 1986, when a *Colby's* report said it was common knowledge that the US administration sensed that a weaker US dollar was the key to dealing with the country's trade deficit in the longer run.[49] According to the article, the US was moving beyond the Plaza agreement and would seek a weaker dollar against currencies other than those of the G5: it was now pressing Taiwan and South Korea to revalue their currencies, and it might move against Singapore and Hong Kong.

Then, on 11 September, the Singapore embassy in Washington sent a telex to MAS reporting that Singapore and the other Asian NIEs faced the prospect of the US naming them as currency manipulators who were intervening in their exchange rates to gain a competitive advantage in trade. The US Commerce Secretary had presented these views at a House of Representatives sub-committee on unfair trade practices.

A week later MAS chairman and finance minister Richard Hu met with US Treasury Secretary James Baker in Washington. The private meetings left Singapore with the impression that the Treasury understood its position. However, the Treasury's outward position was that the Asian NIEs were manipulating their currencies to gain a competitive advantage for their exports. According to the Treasury's public stance, Singapore was guilty of this as its currency had appreciated by only 7.5 per cent against the US dollar since the Plaza Accord in September 1985. In fact, since the Japanese yen and the German mark had gained 78 and 71 per cent respectively against the US dollar, the Singapore dollar had depreciated against these currencies and Singapore had gained competitiveness in the US at the expense of these countries as well. The Americans saw the exchange rate as a major factor in the growth of Singapore's trade surplus with the US – a jump of 65 per cent in the first eight months of 1987 compared to the same period in 1986. They also referred to research which suggested that the currencies of the Asian NIEs as a group needed to appreciate by 10–15 per cent if they were to be correctly valued. Publicly, Baker named Singapore specifically when raising the issue of the Asian NIEs in a speech in November, and emphasised that they needed to 'allow their currencies to better reflect economic fundamentals'.[50] Not only were Singapore's official foreign reserves large and growing, populist sentiment within the US meant that the Asian NIEs would be viewed as a bloc and be treated in a similar fashion across the board.

Subsequently, the Singapore government received intelligence that while the US Treasury understood Singapore's situation, the Americans were closely watching the Singapore dollar as the US dollar declined in value. US officials did not want the former to follow the latter down, as such a drop would negate the competitive benefits to the US from the Plaza Accord.[51] Yet, in a speech on 17 November 1987, Mulford said that Singapore and Hong Kong were models of free trade, so the Treasury's main focus was on Taiwan and South Korea as far as trade policy was concerned.[52]

The political economy of Singapore's trade with the US shifted again in early 1987 when the Omnibus Fair Trade and Competitiveness Bill, which would give fast-track powers to the President to sign trade deals and take retaliatory action against countries suspected of unfair trade practices, began making its way through the chambers of Congress. Although Japan was the main target of the bill, other countries that had large bilateral trade surpluses with the US were also singled out, and eight countries would be the subject of negotiations to prevent them obtaining an unfair advantage. When Singapore asked US officials why the country had been cited as a major competitor of the US in the trade bill, no direct explanation was forthcoming. Nevertheless, Singapore again came away with the view that the US administration understood Singapore's use of the exchange rate in its monetary policy and its commitment to free trade.[53]

Meanwhile, further changes were afoot in the international monetary system. There was a growing sense that the adjustment in the US dollar following the Plaza Accord had been excessive. To bring its decline to a halt and to stabilise currency markets, the Group of Six (the G5 and Canada) met at the Louvre in Paris on 22 February 1987. In the resultant Louvre Accord, the six countries agreed to establish loose 'reference' or 'target' zones between the US dollar, the deutschmark and the Japanese yen with rules for managing these currencies. The central banks agreed to undertake foreign exchange interventions to keep their currencies within the target zones. The US for its part would cut government spending and reduce its budget deficit for the fiscal year 1988, and keep interest rates low. There was some optimism at this point that the Louvre Accord would prove to be a major step towards international policy coordination.

In August 1987, a congressional task force visited Singapore and praised the country for its vigorous free-trade policies, adding that they appreciated Singapore's unique circumstances. A member of the task force said that it would try to explain Singapore's economic structure and policies to Congress.[54]

In the later part of the year, Singapore officials met with their Treasury counterparts again to express their concern on the exchange rate issue. The key impression from these meetings was that the trade bill had taken on a life of its own as the issue had become highly politicised. The protectionists in Congress believed that the Asian NIEs as a whole were taking advantage of the situation to increase their shares of the US market. If Singapore were to notionally allow its currency to appreciate more, this would serve to encourage Taiwan and South Korea to do likewise.[55]

Then, on 6 October, the key congressmen responsible for the trade bill admitted to having been mistaken about Singapore's status as a competitor to the United States. They assured Singapore that they would seek to remove it from the final bill currently going through the Senate. However, pressure would continue to be put on the country concerning its trade surplus with the US.[56]

It appeared that the US and Singapore had reached a kind of equilibrium. Singapore would in public discourse be inevitably lumped with the Asian NIEs, though the American policy establishment seemed to appreciate Singapore's position and had no quarrel with it. The US Congress would, for political reasons, be more hard-line than the Treasury. While the American administration was reluctant, also for political reasons, to distinguish Singapore publicly in their rhetoric, they did not formally request the Singapore government to appreciate the Singapore dollar.[57]

It helped that the IMF was broadly supportive of Singapore. Following consultations, the Fund had said that it was satisfied that the Singapore dollar was not undervalued against the US dollar, and they did not recommend an appreciation.[58]

On 22 October 1987, any semblance of a détente was shattered. On what became known as Black Monday, a stock-market crash occurred in New York and spread across the world. The US administration and other governments scrambled to take action to limit the impact on their economies. The policy coordination agreed under the Louvre Accord was shelved, as governments reverted to doing what they needed to do from a domestic political standpoint. Barely a week later, Singapore received the news that US officials were recommending that the Asian NIEs be 'graduated' from the General System of Preferences (GSP). This would send a signal to Congress that the administration was serious about reducing the US trade deficit.[59]

The GSP was a non-reciprocal tariff arrangement which offered duty-free or preferential access to a particular developed-country market, such as the United States, for specific countries and products.[60] It was originally designed to allow developing countries access to developed-country markets on a country-by-country basis, to promote the former's export-driven industry growth and enable them to diversify away from dependence on the export of primary products. The arrangement was not supposed to be permanent; countries would be 'graduated' when they had reached a threshold level of per capita income. But since the graduation criteria were not precisely specified, there was some discretion for the advanced country to decide when to apply it.

Singapore and the other three Asian NIEs had enjoyed preferential access to US markets under the GSP. The US proposal came as a surprise to the Singapore government. In the previous year, South Korea and Taiwan had been threatened with graduation if they did not appreciate their currencies against the US dollar, but the administration had persuaded Congress to drop graduation proposals in that year's trade bills on the grounds that they would not make much difference to the US deficit.[61]

The Singapore government made several points in response to the proposed graduation. The key one was that the United States was in fact reneging on the commitments it had made to Singapore during the last GSP General Review, in which Singapore was given an excellent score and awarded the best country package. The American move would 'cast doubt on the ability of the administration to abide by its commitments in future trade negotiations'. A second point was that the US had insisted on changes to Singapore's copyright law and had given assurances that the package of waivers obtained in return would remain in effect for the duration of the GSP programme. In any case, Singapore's graduation would make almost no difference to the US trade deficit and would harm US companies operating in Singapore.[62]

There was also the issue of reciprocal arrangements. In 1985, 96 per cent of US exports entered the Singapore market free of tariffs and quotas, but only 25 per

Investors in Tokyo, Japan, watch the electronic board as stock prices plunge after Black Monday, 20 October 1987.

cent of Singapore's exports to the United States received the same treatment even after GSP concessions had been taken into account.

In early November 1987, the US administration wrote to Singapore and confirmed that it was reviewing the status of the major GSP beneficiaries in terms of their level of development and export competitiveness. While American officials conceded that Singapore had a strong point on the issue of US commitments, they argued that the arrangement was always intended to be temporary and not applicable to countries which had become internationally competitive.

The Singapore government responded that the US Trade Act of 1984 already provided a mechanism for graduation when a threshold per capita income level had been reached, although this was not a very useful criterion in Singapore's case. Compared to the other NIEs, Singapore had little indigenous industrial know-how, and the economy was very much linked to international business through multinational corporations. That made it more like a city such as New York or London than a country. Anyway, on the basis of the income-per-capita criterion, the US would have to skip over both Brazil and Mexico if they were to graduate Singapore – as a percentage of GDP, Brazil had a larger trade surplus with the US than did Singapore.[63]

US Assistant Treasury Secretary David Mulford subsequently lambasted the Asian NIEs publicly, warning that they could no longer disregard the problem of global imbalances. The NIEs would have to 'adapt; and adaptation will require cooperation, not predatory behaviour'.[64] Clayton Yeutter, the US Trade Representative, presented a more conciliatory front to local media. In an interview published on 2 November 1987, Yeutter conveyed that Congress had become more cautious following the stock-market crash, and, referencing two protectionist politicians of the 1930s, said that the congressmen 'do not wish to become the Smoot-Hawleys of the 1987s [sic]'. On whether Singapore would be graduated from the GSP programme, Yeutter was comforting: 'No decision has been made. I assure you there are few failures of institutional memory in the US. Singapore will not be maltreated. It is a credible nation.'[65] To the American and international media, however, Yeutter would be more hawkish: he confirmed to the *Washington Post* in December that the Reagan administration was considering a broad attack on the duty-free privileges of the Asian NIEs, including graduating all four of them from the GSP 'when a broad range of a country's products are competitive in the United States and when nations reach a certain stage of development'.[66] This was followed a few weeks later by a *Business Week* article arguing that the decision to take the duty-free privileges away from the NIEs shows 'a new resolve to stop coddling the four like poor, vulnerable allies and force them to start behaving as mature trading nations'.[67]

Minister for Trade and Industry Lee Hsien Loong addressed Parliament on 2 December 1987, reiterating that Singapore had not adopted restrictive and devious barriers to trade in pursuit of unfair advantage, nor had it artificially depressed the value of the Singapore dollar to build up a trade surplus. He added that Singapore had no need to apologise for being more competitive than some of her trading partners.

Meanwhile the US authorities continued to deliberate on how to deal with the Asian NIEs. In April 1988, a written testimony to the House Banking Subcommittee hearing highlighted that these economies had orientated their exchange rate policies heavily towards the US dollar rather than the stronger yen; and that the rise in the yen had benefitted them by making exports to Japan cheaper as well as in markets, such as the US, where they were competing with Japan. But the testimony was otherwise generally complimentary about the economic success of the four. It also recognised that there were differences between on the one hand Singapore and Hong Kong, which were free-market economies, and on the other hand South Korea and Taiwan. Importantly, it acknowledged that the frictions with the United States had led to some misunderstanding, such as when the House Banking Committee had previously described Singapore as a major trade competitor.[68]

The US Treasury continued, however, to put administrative pressure on Singapore. When Prime Minister Lee Kuan Yew and Dr Hu met Baker and Mulford on 15 April 1988, they came away with the message that global imbalances were a major problem and Singapore had to share responsibility.[69] In a *Straits Times* article in December 1987, the US assistant treasury secretary conceded that, taken separately, Singapore's part in the NIEs' overall trade surplus was not great, but that they had to look at the whole picture: Singapore represented part of the growing US trade deficit with the NIEs overall. The economic power of the NIEs might be small in a global context, he wrote, but 'they are important trading nations with a substantial impact on world trade'.[70] Consequently, Singapore would still be expected to appreciate its currency, though by not as much as Taiwan and South Korea.

The Omnibus Foreign Trade and Competitiveness Act was eventually passed in 1988, and the US chose to name Taiwan and Korea as currency manipulators under the act. Singapore and Hong Kong were spared, although the issue of currency manipulation was to rear its head again in the new millennium when Singapore became caught up in a trade dispute between the US and China and the broader issue of 'global imbalances' (see p. 364–6).

However, Singapore was not spared as far as the GSP was concerned. The loss of benefits under the GSP was announced to the press on 29 January 1988. In a last-ditch attempt to halt the process, on 4 February Singapore, South Korea and Hong Kong complained to the council of the General Agreement on Tariffs and Trade (GATT) that the graduation violated GATT rules. The council took note but no action,[71] and eight days later Yeo Cheow Tong, Singapore's Minister of State for Foreign Affairs, was quoted by the *Business Times* as saying that the US decision to graduate Singapore from the GSP cast doubt on the Americans' credibility and reliability and was 'detrimental to the long-term relations between ASEAN and the US'.[72] Mr Yeo's audience included US Secretary of State George Shultz. The same paper ran a second article on the same day entitled 'George Shultz lashes out in response'. Shultz said, 'If that's what you believe, there's very little basis for a genuine dialogue.' He added: 'The special treatment for Singapore's goods aren't your rights …, they're your privileges in our market; it's not your market, it's our market.'[73]

Singapore, together with Hong Kong, Korea and Taiwan, 'graduated' on 2 January 1989. This was a low point for US-Singapore relations and Singapore experienced its first ever anti-American demonstration. Graduation imposed some costs on Singapore – a loss of exports to the US, further pressure on Singapore to graduate to developed-country status at the GATT, and the risk of a relocation of multinational companies to neighbouring countries. However, in the event, the exchange rate and trade dispute with the US turned out to have a minimal overall impact on the Singapore economy.

The 1990s: sailing through choppy waters

Trade and the exchange rate would become issues of concern again in the 1990s, but this time the voices speaking up were from within. To be sure, the Singapore economy had recovered quickly from the 1985–6 recession. Meanwhile, the period from 1990 up to the Asian financial crisis of 1997–8, was in retrospect a golden age of strong growth averaging just under 8 per cent per annum and low unemployment. However, the side-effect of this success was a rise in costs and prices. This contributed again to the perception that Singapore was losing cost-competitiveness to other countries in East and Southeast Asia, especially in labour-intensive manufacturing sectors such as textiles, electronics and chemicals.[74]

There was perhaps good reason to be concerned about cost-competitiveness. Singapore had arguably not yet reached the stage where it could compete with the developed countries in skill-intensive manufacturing. The loss of relatively more labour-intensive manufacturing if foreign multinationals relocated their plants to lower-cost economies within the region meant that Singapore faced the spectre of 'de-industrialisation', or the 'hollowing out' of the manufacturing sector. Manufacturing would consequently shrink as a percentage of GDP.

Given its price stability mandate, MAS would not bow to pressure to soften or reverse a currency appreciation to placate exporters. Instead, to offset the build-up of inflationary pressures both from domestic sources and from abroad, MAS allowed the trade-weighted Singapore dollar index to appreciate significantly from 1990 to the eve of the Asian Financial Crisis. Estimates suggest the nominal effective exchange rate increased by around 30 per cent, while the inflation-adjusted rate rose nearly 20 per cent.

Despite Dr Goh Keng Swee's efforts to delink the exchange rate from competitiveness, the concept still loomed large in the minds of businesses and there was public concern about the strength of the Singapore dollar. MAS had consistently argued that there was no evidence that overall exports had been negatively affected and advised producers to take into account compensating benefits from the fall in the costs of their imported intermediate inputs due to the trend appreciation of the Singapore dollar. As the figure below clearly shows, Singapore's real non-oil domestic exports grew steadily following its recovery from the 1985–6 recession, with few periods of persistent quarterly falls until the Asian financial crisis of 1997–8.

Singapore's real non-oil domestic exports, 1980–2015

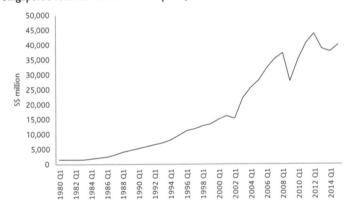

Source: SINGSTAT

However, the fact that overall exports grew does not mean that Singapore had not become less competitive in labour-intensive manufacturing by the 1990s. The evidence was clear: Singapore did lose ground in this area compared to its regional competitors. This was primarily due to the appreciation of the Singapore dollar relative to the currencies of its competitors rather than because of a rise in relative costs.[75]

Dr Goh had emphasised in the 1980s that artificially keeping the exchange rate weak would subsidise inefficient firms and disincentivise them from innovating and becoming more efficient. The fact that firms involved in more labour-intensive production eventually left Singapore proved him correct: in the absence of a weak exchange rate, they could not survive.

As debates about the strength of the Singapore dollar intensified in 1995, finance minister Dr Richard Hu asserted in Parliament that MAS had acted appropriately in letting the exchange rate appreciate. 'By curtailing labour demand and achieving lower CPI inflation, wage growth has been lower than what it would otherwise have been without an appreciation of the currency,' he said. 'Productivity growth has also been stronger, as the strong Singapore dollar has propelled businesses to upgrade and automate.'[76] Instead, Singapore's overall exports continued to grow because the manufacturers that remained on the island had invested and shifted to higher-value-added production. They were therefore exporting higher-quality, sophisticated intermediate inputs and components such as integrated circuits and pharmaceuticals, rather than low-value-added final goods.

Thus, the fear at the time that Singapore would 'de-industrialise' did not materialise. To be sure, Singapore's manufacturing sector was shifting to higher value-added activities. Clothing and textile production left the island, disk-drive producer Seagate laid off workers in Singapore in 1998, and in 1999 Western Digital moved its production to Malaysia. Nevertheless, in 2000 manufacturing still represented a significant 26 per cent of GDP, which suggests that the Singapore economy did restructure and manufacturing managed to avoid hollowing out. These structural changes were not unique to Singapore. During the same period, in Hong Kong, one of Singapore's closest competitors, entrepreneurs engaged in low-cost manufacturing literally closed down their factories on a Saturday, dispatched their machinery and equipment across the border to mainland China, and began work again the following week employing cheaper Chinese workers.

With the aid of hindsight, it is clear that the change in the structure of Singapore's exports in the 1990s may have been part of a broader and longer process whereby a regional production network centred on China would eventually emerge, with Singapore providing more specialised and sophisticated inputs and components. If Singapore ceased to export final goods to a particular market, such as the United States, it did not matter as long as this was offset by growth in exports of intermediate inputs to other markets. Singapore benefitted in particular from the growth of its neighbours in the longer run, and from increased regional trade in intermediate parts and components. These began to account for a substantial proportion of Singapore's non-oil domestic exports as the 1990s unfolded.

The Barings debacle

The 1990s saw substantial efforts to speed up the globalisation of Singapore's financial sector.[77] The Singapore International Monetary Exchange (SIMEX) had been set up in 1984 to broaden the equities market. It offered currency futures contracts alongside other financial futures, and currency options. MAS adopted a tighter approach to regulation and supervision than in the 1970s. Its priorities were to allow only reputable financial institutions into Singapore, to reduce

Financial trader Nick Leeson arrives at Changi Airport, after being sent back from Germany to stand trial, 23 November 1995.

exposure to global risks and financial contagion, and to show zero-tolerance as regards institutions that did not operate in a sound or prudent way.

Despite these reforms, incidents occurred that potentially threatened the stability of financial institutions. In April 1992, Barings, a London-based merchant bank with more than 200 years' history, decided to open a Futures and Options office in Singapore to conduct and clear transactions on SIMEX. Within three years the bank announced that it was going into administration. It emerged that Nick Leeson, the 28-year-old general manager of the Singapore office, had lost US$1.3 billion on futures contracts based on Japan's Nikkei-225 stock market. The losses had been concealed and had just come to light. Despite an attempted bailout by the Bank of England, Barings was declared insolvent and administrators brought in to manage its finances. Following the Barings announcement, in Britain's House of Commons the Chancellor of the Exchequer, Alan Johnson, would describe Leeson as a 'Rogue Trader'.[78] Leeson was arrested in Frankfurt on 2 March 1995, and returned voluntarily to Singapore on in late November. He pleaded guilty to two offences of 'deceiving the bank's auditors' and of 'cheating the Singapore exchange' and was sentenced to six-and-a-half years in prison.

That Leeson's trading had led to such huge losses for Barings was surprising since he was supposed to be 'arbitraging', or seeking to profit from, differences in the prices of Nikkei-225 futures contracts listed on the Osaka Securities Exchange and SIMEX. This was not usually very risky and should not on its own have broken Barings.

However, Leeson had deviated from his mandate. To recoup losses which had been logged into an errors account numbered 88888, he started making speculative trades that were unauthorised. His trading strategy moved well beyond arbitrage: he began to gamble on the future direction of the market by selling options where there was some risk involved. Initially he was successful. Then the losses mounted. On 17 January 1995 disaster struck. The Tokyo stock market plunged 1175 points in the aftermath of the Kobe earthquake. Leeson bet on a rapid recovery for the Nikkei and bought futures on a huge scale in an attempt to push the price up. This failed and his losses escalated. To prevent the London office from receiving accurate daily reports on his true trading position, Leeson doctored the accounts of the branch.

Fundamentally, Barings had failed to put in place adequate checks and balances on the Singapore branch's trading activities. Contrary to normal accounting and audit safeguards, Leeson was both head of the 'frontline' derivatives trading desk and the 'backroom' clearing, settling, and accounting operations. As he later admitted, this was a bizarre situation since he had 'one foot on the dealing floor' and was also 'in charge of the girls in the back office'. As he put it, 'Nobody knew who I reported to, and they tended to let me get on with my job.'[79] With the authority to settle his own trades, Leeson was able to falsify trading records, invent fictitious clients and a bogus bank account at Citibank, and cover his shortfalls by reporting losses as gains to Barings in London.

Both internal and external auditors had had some concerns about Leeson's dual role and his frequent and sizeable funding requests from London. However, they failed to carry out basic checks, especially of the fact that the positions he reported to SIMEX in Singapore, including those in the error account, did not match the funding he requested from London. In February 1995, even when the auditors found a discrepancy in Leeson's accounts to the tune of £50 million and wanted to see supporting documents, he fooled them with a concocted audit put together with scissors and glue.[80] The auditors gave him an unqualified Audit Report which meant that he had been 'vetted and cleared'.

After the collapse, the Board of Banking Supervision at the Bank of England acknowledged that there had been losses due to unauthorised and concealed trading in Singapore, and a serious failure of controls and managerial confusion not detected by external auditors, supervisors and regulators. But they did not find the Bank of England itself guilty of failing in its duty as a regulator and were reluctant to prosecute senior Barings staff.[81]

The Singapore Ministry of Finance was critical of Barings, and of Barings' head of investment banking Peter Norris in particular. 'In our view the Baring Group's management either knew or should have known about the existence of account 88888 (the error account) and of the losses incurred from transactions booked in this account.... Mr Norris' explanation after the collapse, namely that the senior management of the Baring Group believed that Mr Leeson's trading activities posed little (or no) risk to the Baring Group, but yielded very good returns, is implausible and in our view demonstrates a degree of ignorance of market reality that totally lacks credibility.'[82]

While the Barings collapse was shocking, Singapore was not harmed. Because Barings had been required by MAS to trade futures in Singapore through an entity separate from its merchant-banking arm and reporting directly to London, the bulk of Leeson's trades had been for the accounts of Barings Securities (London) and Barings Securities (Tokyo). Consequently, there was no systemic financial threat to Singapore. SIMEX dealt with the open positions quickly and reforms were introduced subsequently to strengthen regulation and the lines of communication between SIMEX and MAS. Singapore would not get off as lightly in the next crisis to hit the island.

The Asian Financial Crisis [83]

By 1989, Singapore, together with fellow 'graduates' from the United States' preferential tariff systems – Hong Kong, Korea and Taiwan – as well as Japan, had been labeled 'East Asian Miracle Economies',[84] in recognition of their rapid GDP growth and improvement in living standards within a span of 30 years. Over time, other economies were added to the group: Indonesia, Malaysia and Thailand. The performance of these eight economies attracted the attention of social scientists of all stripes seeking to explain whether it was policies, the type of government, or culture that could explain the miracle. The World Bank paid the eight a significant compliment in 1993 when it reviewed the policies underpinning their growth.[85] While the bank's report concluded that there was no single 'East Asian model' of development, it highlighted the factors that worked to secure strong and sustained growth. In doing so, it unwittingly gave credence to the vast range of policies adopted in these economies at that time without paying much heed to the vulnerabilities inherent in the growth models in place. A veritable cottage industry of research soon sprang up, debating whether to characterise the economies as 'miracle' or 'myth'.

Within a few years, the 'miracle' did prove to have certain mythical elements to it. The Asian Financial Crisis began on 2 July 1997, when the Bank of Thailand was forced to relinquish the baht's peg to the US dollar: it had run low on the foreign reserves needed to defend the currency. The Thai economy had been weakening for some time, and the float of the baht marked the culmination of waves of speculative attacks that had begun in May, betting that the currency would be devalued. The baht depreciated rapidly on floating, triggering capital outflows and a domestic banking crisis. On 11 August, the IMF announced a US$16 billion rescue package for Thailand, followed by a further US$3.9 billion bailout nine days later.

The crisis quickly spread to other countries in Asia, including Indonesia, South Korea, Malaysia and the Philippines. Clearly, even the 'miracle' economies would not be spared. The crisis in each country typically started with speculative attacks that led to falls in the exchange rate, stock market indices, and property prices. These, in turn, prompted capital flight and banking crises. Comparing the values of exchange rates from prior to the baht devaluation to one year after (June 1997 and July 1998), the Indonesian rupiah weakened by a massive 81 per cent, followed by the Malaysian ringgit (39 per cent), and the Thai baht (37 per cent). By the end of 1997 the Kuala Lumpur and Bangkok stock exchange indices had lost more than 50 per cent of their values compared to the beginning of the year; Jakarta saw a similarly devastating 42 per cent decline.

Many of the affected economies had loosely pegged their currencies to the US dollar. In the run-up to the crisis, lulled by misplaced confidence in the fixed exchange rates, the private sector had built up significant debt denominated in foreign currencies. The subsequent speculative attacks on their own currencies and the eventual depreciations (or devaluations) increased the burden of servicing this debt, wiping out debtors and leaving creditors empty-handed. Businesses and banks collapsed, unemployment rose rapidly, and many people fell below the poverty line as economies entered severe recessions. The hardest-hit was Indonesia, with GDP shrinking by 13.1 per cent, followed by Thailand and Malaysia (more than 7 per cent each) and South Korea (5.1 per cent). In Indonesia, the marked drop in the value of the rupiah and the subsequent rise in food prices led to riots throughout the country and eventually forced the resignation of long-serving President Suharto. The 1998 recession was Malaysia's first in many years. In response, the IMF stepped in with a US$40 billion rescue package for

Protesting the effects of the Asian Financial Crisis, Silom Road, Bangkok, Thailand.

South Korea, Thailand and Indonesia. Malaysia rejected the IMF's assistance package. It opted instead to impose capital controls to stem the outflows, and to devalue its currency to 3.8 ringgit to the US dollar, from approximately 2.5 ringgit previously.

Even economies such as those of Hong Kong and Singapore, which were among the stronger ones in the region and had robust financial systems, were afflicted. The Hong Kong dollar came under intense speculative attack; its fixed peg to the US dollar was saved only by heavy intervention by the Hong Kong Monetary Authority, which had substantial foreign exchange reserves thanks to its currency-board system. The Singapore dollar fell from S$1.43 per US dollar in June 1997 to as low as S$1.78 in August 1998, a depreciation of 20 per cent. This marked a reversal of the long-term appreciation of the Singapore dollar against the US dollar that had taken place since the second half of the 1980s. The worst of the economic impact hit Singapore in 1998: real GDP contracted by as much as 5 per cent in the third quarter of that year compared to the same period the year before, and shrank by 2.2 per cent for 1998 as a whole. Much of this was due to falling investment as business confidence deteriorated. There was also a sharp fall in exports, especially of electronics – this was not so much through direct trade links with crisis-hit countries such as Thailand, Indonesia and Malaysia as through indirect links with economies with large trade volumes, such as Japan, Hong Kong and South Korea.[86]

The Sathorn Unique Tower (nicknamed the 'Ghost Tower'), Bangkok, unfinished and derelict.

Asian currencies against the US dollar, Q1 1990 to Q4 2000

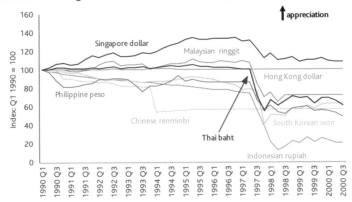

However, compared to the other affected economies, the impact on Singapore was relatively mild, partly due to its strong fundamentals. Foreign reserves were high and there was no official foreign debt, while domestic banks had not built up significant liabilities in foreign currency not matched by foreign-currency assets. Policy frameworks that MAS had put in place served Singapore well. One of the key precursors of the crisis was an influx of foreign capital over the earlier part of the decade. Singapore coped with this inflow relatively successfully; the exchange rate-centred monetary policy framework gave MAS a greater degree of flexibility than the pegged currencies of other regional economies, and Singapore had not fallen into the trap of trying to manage the currency too tightly against the US dollar to maintain export competitiveness in the American market. Instead, it was prepared to allow the Singapore dollar to appreciate in the face of capital inflows, especially since this also served MAS's inflation objective by keeping import prices down.

While MAS had liberalised nearly all controls on foreign exchange in 1978 (see p. 280), there were a few remaining restrictions on Singapore-dollar lending by domestic banks to foreigners. The aim was to prevent the build-up of a large pool of dollars outside Singapore that could be used for speculative purposes. It was thought that this policy – also known as the 'non-internationalisation of the Singapore dollar' – reduced the scope for a speculative attack on the currency. MAS also recognised the emergence of a bubble in the domestic property market and imposed pre-emptive regulations to temper it. This helped to cushion the impact of falling prices when the economy subsequently fell into recession. It helped too that the bulk of capital inflows into Singapore were dominated by foreign direct investment, which was longer-term by nature and translated ultimately into economic production, rather than 'footloose' short-term capital seeking returns in the property and securities markets.

Once the Asian Financial Crisis was in full swing, the Singapore government responded with expansionary monetary and fiscal policies. Inflation had begun slowing with the onset of the recession, and in June 1998 the economy slipped into deflation. MAS maintained an accommodative monetary policy stance during the crisis, specifically, keeping the slope of the trade-weighted exchange rate policy band at zero per cent. This was supplemented by a wider band to allow the trade-weighted exchange rate to fluctuate by a greater degree in this climate of heightened financial volatility and economic uncertainty. However, the much sharper depreciation in the exchange rates of some of the regional economies – which were also Singapore's major trade partners – compared to the Singapore dollar led initially to a perverse pattern in the trade-weighted index (TWI): despite MAS's policy stance, the TWI appreciated through to 1998. However, as in the past, there was no active attempt to force the TWI to depreciate in line with regional currencies. That could have triggered a speculative attack on the Singapore dollar and reduced confidence in the exchange rate as the

The (non-)internationalisation of the Singapore dollar [87]

An internationalised currency is one that is held and used beyond the borders of the issuing country for transactions with that country's residents, as well as between non-residents.[88] For example, both a Singapore exporter and a foreign exporter to Singapore could invoice their goods in Singapore dollars. Foreigners could buy Singapore-dollar-denominated financial assets, such as bonds and securities, both in Singapore and in the rest of the world.

If the Singapore dollar were to be used in transactions by non-residents, a pool of the currency would build up outside Singapore's borders. In the 1980s, concerns grew at MAS about such a build-up as it could potentially be used to destabilise the Singapore dollar and undermine the effectiveness of MAS's newly introduced exchange rate-centred monetary policy (see p. 303). In November 1983, MAS formally announced Regulation 621 to discourage the use of the Singapore dollar abroad for activities that had no apparent benefits for the domestic economy.

The Singapore government did not feel that its desire to develop Singapore into an international financial centre required the dollar to be internationalised in the long run.[89] This reluctance to internationalise was not unique. Japan discouraged internationalising the yen before June 1973 because it was concerned that it would compromise its monetary and exchange rate policy. West Germany's restrictions on offshore issues of deutschmark bonds were only liberalised when domestic financial markets matured and the economy was better insulated from external shocks.

Over time however, MAS came to regard its policy of discouraging the internationalisation of the Singapore dollar as a 'rearguard' action at best. It became increasingly clear that in the context of globalised financial markets, the restrictions would not make much difference as the rules could be easily circumvented by financial institutions that did not rely on bank borrowing, while new financial instruments could be created to get around the restrictions. Moreover, the restrictions could not address the problem of speculation by locals, such as had occurred in Thailand in the run-up to the Asian Financial Crisis. Thus, even in the thick of the crisis, MAS concluded in an internal policy review in January 1998 that the restrictions would not have been effective in the absence of Singapore's strong economic fundamentals, namely, its sizeable balance of payments surplus, large stock of external reserve assets,[90] prudential supervision of the financial sector, and credible monetary and fiscal policies. The IMF would subsequently conclude that the non-internationalisation policy could not 'be disentangled from the impact of the [Singapore government's] solid policy track record and credibility.'[91]

Critically, even if the Singapore dollar were to be internationalised, there was a relatively low risk of its becoming widely used for transactions abroad. Singapore's share of global trade and real income was too small compared to those of other major economies with internationalised currencies, such as the United States and the Eurozone. This meant that Singapore-dollar loans extended abroad tended to be converted into foreign exchange,[92] which reduced the risk of a large pool of Singapore dollars building up abroad.

By this time, the prevalent view in MAS was that the restrictions made Singapore marginally less attractive as an international financial centre. There were concerns that some investment might have gravitated to Hong Kong as a result of the non-internationalisation stance.[93]

In the 1998 review, MAS concluded that the risks of liberalisation were manageable. It therefore moved to gradually liberalise existing restrictions. This shift was marked by the issuance of MAS Notice 757, replacing Notice 621. All restrictions on non-residents relating to Singapore dollar equity listings and company bond issues were relaxed. There was further liberalisation in the subsequent years, and by 2004 nearly all restrictions had been lifted. However, Singapore dollar futures were still not allowed because they might facilitate speculation and undermine the integrity of MAS's exchange rate-centred monetary policy framework.[94]

long-run nominal anchor for inflation. Instead, MAS maintained the flat and wider policy band throughout 1999. As financial instability and volatility in the TWI receded, the policy band was restored to its narrower, pre-crisis level.

The decision to stick closely with the existing exchange rate framework did not pass without some controversy. A *Straits Times* editorial published on 13 January 1998 made the case that Singapore should peg the Singapore dollar to the US dollar – something not done since the Singapore dollar floated in 1973. This would be a temporary crisis measure, similar to what Hong Kong had done in fixing the exchange rate of its own currency to the US dollar in 1983 as anxieties rose when China and Britain began negotiations over the return of Hong Kong to the People's Republic. After the financial turmoil had stabilised, the exchange rate could transit away from the peg, to prevent it from becoming fundamentally misaligned.[95] Economist Professor Augustine Tan concurred, and wrote to the *Business Times* stating his belief there was a lot of merit to the suggestion. He thought that as the foreign exchange market was expecting a continued slide in the Singapore dollar, it would be a good idea to peg it to the US dollar for the time being to maintain confidence.

However, MAS made it clear that it would stick to managing the Singapore dollar against a basket of currencies as this policy had served Singapore well thus far. In a reply to the media, MAS argued that it was not obvious at what rate and for how long a US dollar peg would be required; if the wrong rate were chosen, the local currency could become vulnerable to a speculative attack. Moreover, thus far there had been no speculative attack against the Singapore dollar, because it was perceived by the market to have adjusted to the new circumstances and remained in line with the economy's long-term fundamentals.[96]

The BCCS was of the view that fixing to the US dollar would give the impression that Singapore was going back to a full currency board system. Notwithstanding the fact that all notes and coins were fully backed by foreign assets, the BCCS had technically not operated a fully fledged currency board system since the floating of the Singapore dollar in 1973.

In normal times, Singapore's fiscal policy had hitherto been aimed primarily at longer-term goals, such as attracting foreign multinationals, enhancing Singapore's value proposition as a trade and transportation hub, and improving the public transportation infrastructure. However, the seriousness of the economic downturn meant that government spending would have to be directed at stimulating the economy to offset the weakness in aggregate demand.

When the budget was first announced in February 1998, the Singapore economy was still not doing too badly. However, as the situation deteriorated, additional fiscal support was forthcoming. In June 1998, the government announced S$2 billion in off-budget measures, followed in November by a further S$10.5 billion package. Overall government spending for 1998 was increased to 19 per cent of GDP compared to 15 per cent the year before, and this certainly helped to prevent a greater slowdown than would otherwise have occurred.

The crisis took a toll on the labour market: redundancy rates nearly tripled in 1998 compared to the year before, and the number of unemployed in 1999 was double that for 1997. The resident unemployment rate rose from 1.9 per cent in 1997 through 1998, reaching 3.6 per cent in 1999. Consequently, an important feature of the government's policy response was to supplement the monetary policy stance and the modest fiscal stimulus with direct measures to reduce labour costs. This would encourage hiring and boost competitiveness. The first cuts were announced in late 1998, and included a halving of the employers' Central Provident Fund contribution rate to 10 per cent. This complemented the market-driven fall in wages which, together with other cost reductions, led to a fall in business costs by about 12 per cent in 1999.[97] In the manufacturing sector, real labour costs per unit of output fell by almost 20 per cent between 1998 and 2000.[98]

The CPF Building, Shenton Way.

Within the broader region, however, it was not apparent that the worst was over. Stock-market indices in Malaysia, Indonesia and Thailand fell by another 30–40 per cent from end-1997 to September 1998. Risk aversion towards emerging markets rose further following Russia's default on its domestic government debt. The effects of the Asian Financial Crisis and the Russian crisis on emerging-market asset prices forced hedge funds such as Long-Term Capital Management L.P. (LTCM) to unwind their positions. Many of these funds, including LTCM, had borrowed heavily in Japanese yen at very low interest rates to invest in emerging-market securities and derivatives. When the funds were forced to liquidate their positions and purchase Japanese yen to repay their loans, this led to the unwinding of the 'yen carry trade'. Over the few weeks between end-September and 19 October, the Japanese yen strengthened by around 15 per cent against the US dollar.

The fall in the US dollar stemmed depreciation pressures on the regional currencies. At the same time, it helped that the affected Asian economies had taken measures to rid banks' balance sheets of the bad assets that had arisen during the banking crisis. As the rest of the developed world, principally the US economy, had been largely unaffected, the tide for Asia turned once the worst of the financial turmoil eased. Singapore and its neighbours were on a much stronger footing to ride an upturn in global demand in 1999.

Overall, Singapore emerged from the Asian Financial Crisis relatively unscathed. The economy recovered quickly as external demand picked up, with GDP growth of 5.7 per cent in 1999 and 9 per cent in 2000. In less than a year, it was back on its growth trajectory. Although the financial and property markets remained moribund for a while and higher unemployment persisted for a number of years, these eventually recovered as the worst of the crisis passed and the millennium came to an end.

Currency for the new millennium

In the 1990s, controls on the import and export of colour photocopying machines were still in place. Both the security issues and the lack of access to colour photocopiers were acknowledged in a speech made by Minister for Finance and Chairman of BCCS Dr Richard Hu at the 30th Anniversary Dinner of the BCCS in November 1997. He said that the upcoming fourth note series due to be released in 1999 would have 'refreshing new designs' and 'new innovative security features'. In particular, they would utilise the latest anti-colour-copier and anti-scanner security features.[99] In light of this, the BCCS planned to lift all existing controls on the use and import of colour copiers in advance of the note issue.[100] Singaporeans would now have access to cheaper full-colour copying.

In September 1999, the Portrait series of currency notes was launched. The portrait in question was that of Singapore's first president, Yusof bin Ishak, in honour of his contribution to nation-building. This was the first time a portrait was the main design element on a Singapore note. A single portrait can be an

Puan Noor Aishah, wife of Singapore's first president, Yusof bin Ishak, receives a memento at the launch of the Portrait series of currency notes, 9 September 1999.

effective anti-counterfeiting feature. Unlike flora, fauna, or inanimate objects, facial portraits, made up of distinctive fine lines, are instantly recognisable and difficult to reproduce. Any slight change – a tiny variation in a line, a dot, or even a colour – can alter the expression on a face.

The durability of the Portrait series of notes has been remarkable. The Orchid series was replaced after ten years, the Bird series after eight, and the Ship series after 15. At the time of writing, the Portrait series has been in place for more than two decades. The notes have endured not only because they are difficult to counterfeit, but also because of MAS's decision to issue polymer versions of the high-use, lower-denomination notes – the two-, five-, and ten-dollar notes. The ten-dollar polymer note was first issued in 2004, and the others were released subsequently. Over time, these came to replace the paper versions. Singapore would now have currency notes fit for the new millennium. In the 2000s, the high-denomination notes would come under the spotlight as a potential vehicle for money-laundering and for financing terrorist activities – an unwanted testimonial to their value. As a pre-emptive measure, from 1 October 2014 MAS stopped issuing the Portrait-series S$10,000 note, and on 1 January 2021 the S$1000 note.

In retrospect

The Singapore dollar had come a long way since 1967: it had become a coveted store of value. The credibility derived from the backing of currency issued under the BCCS, as well as MAS's management of the exchange rate-centred monetary policy framework in pursuit of low and stable inflation, meant that the currency's purchasing power had been preserved domestically and abroad. Singapore's unique monetary-policy framework had survived conflicting political pressures – on the one hand to appreciate the currency to smooth ruffled foreign feathers; and on the other hand to keep it conducive for activities in parts of the business sector. In all this, MAS remained true to Dr Goh Keng Swee's vision.

On 1 January 1980 the *Straits Times* published an article heralding an electronic mail service that would allow letters to be sent in and out of Singapore 20 times faster than the prevailing telex system.[101] This was a sign of things to come: over the 1980s and '90s, Singaporeans would become familiar with the distinctive, high-pitched buzz of a modem making a network connection as dial-up Internet spread across the country. By the late 1990s, Singapore would take preliminary steps to make broadband Internet access a reality. Telegraphic cables, first laid in the 1850s, had transformed the way information and capital flowed across borders in the 19th and 20th centuries; fibre-optic cables were first laid in the 1980s and for the story of money they would prove just as revolutionary.

The Portrait series notes

The Portrait series (1999–present) was launched on 9 September 1999.

All the notes in the series featured the same portrait of President Yusof bin Ishak. Other design elements on the front included the Singapore coat of arms, a watermark of the portrait, the Singapore lion symbol, and the word 'Singapore' in the four official languages, as well as the signature and seal of the chairman, Board of Commissioners of Currency, Singapore. After the BCCS's merger with MAS in 2002 (see p. 353), the signature was that of the MAS chairman. The designs on the back represented education, Singapore as a garden city, sports, the arts, youth, government, and the economy.

There were seven denominations: 2 dollars, 5 dollars, 10 dollars, 50 dollars, 100 dollars, 1,000 dollars, and 10,000 dollars. There were no one-dollar or 500-dollar notes in this series. The one-dollar note had been fully displaced by the one-dollar coin from the second series of circulation coins, and the public had by now got used to two-dollar notes for smaller-value transactions.

The 2-, 5- and 10-dollar notes were issued in both paper and polymer form. The polymer notes have a transparent white coat-of-arms in the top left corner; on the paper version, the coat of arms is printed in the colour of the note (as in the other denominations shown here). The paper versions also have the kinegram (see p. 322). All the denominations of S$50 and above were issued only in the paper version.

S$2 (purple), issued 9 September 1999 (paper), 12 January 2006 (polymer)

Front: Singapore's first President, Yusof bin Ishak   Back: pupils with teacher in a 'borderless classroom'

S$5 (green), issued 9 September 1999 (paper), 18 May 2007 (polymer)

Front: Singapore's first President, Yusof bin Ishak   Back: Garden City landscape

S$10 (red), issued 9 September 1999 (paper), 4 May 2004 (polymer)

Front: Singapore's first President, Yusof bin Ishak   Back: sporting activities

S$50 (blue), issued 9 September 1999 (paper)

Front: Singapore's first President, Yusof bin Ishak

Back: Singapore arts scene

$100 (orange), issued 9 September 1999 (paper)

Front: Singapore's first President, Yusof bin Ishak

Back: youth activities

$1,000 (purple), issued 9 September 1999 (paper)

Front: Singapore's first President, Yusof bin Ishak

Back: buildings of the Singapore executive, legislature and judiciary

$10,000 (gold), issued 9 September 1999 (paper)

Front: Singapore's first President, Yusof bin Ishak

Back: future direction of the Singapore economy driven by knowledge and technology

CHAPTER
❧ 09 ❧

MONEY IN THE
NEW MILLENNIUM
(2000–)

In the new millennium, Singapore would be confronted with multiple shocks in fairly rapid succession over the first two decades. Although the Y2K 'bug' proved less disruptive to financial institutions than feared, the dot-com bubble burst shortly after, and expectations of quick riches for many would-be digital entrepreneurs were dashed. As the SARS epidemic spread across Asia, the Singapore economy faltered but quickly recovered. More impactful was the Global Financial Crisis, starting in the United States. Fortunately, Singapore came through it without major systemic damage, as MAS (now merged with BCCS) applied lessons learned from history, easing monetary policy settings, ensuring that the banking system had adequate liquidity, and using fiscal policy as its main weapon in countering the downturn. Controversy over the role of exchange rates in global imbalances emerged again, and in a move reminiscent of the 1980s, MAS explained that it did not, and could not, use the exchange rate to gain an export advantage or achieve a current account surplus. On the currency issuance front, Singapore saw a new series of coins. Electronic payments came to play an increasing role in daily economic life. As almost every Singaporean had a computer or a mobile phone, and had become familiar with the Internet, electronic payments between individuals and institutions became routine; cash cards and 'e-wallets' presented alternatives to physical currency. Quick Response (QR) codes were becoming ubiquitous. Privately issued digital currencies that could potentially compete with 'traditional' forms of money – coins and notes and bank deposits – emerged. How digital currencies will shape the evolution of money in Singapore remains to be seen.

Technological advances linked to the spread of electronic banking and Internet access brought challenges with them at the turn of the millennium. For a start, countries faced a potentially crippling programming issue: the Y2K bug. This came about because many computer programmes used only two digits to represent a year, making it impossible to distinguish between 2000 and 1900. Dating errors could cause severe problems, such as for time-based billing. In many cases, programmed machines could malfunction severely enough to pose a threat to critical economic infrastructure such as telecommunications networks, power grids and the banking system. Banks might fail to pay the correct interest on savings accounts; pre-scheduled GIRO bill payments might not go through; or ATM cash withdrawals might fail.

Singapore was alerted to the problem well in advance and began tackling it as early as 1995. The Monetary Authority of Singapore (MAS) made sure that the financial sector was prepared for the transition, and on 30 December 1999 it announced that 99 per cent of banks were Y2K-ready. Despite the assurance, businesses and households stockpiled cash. Currency in active circulation picked up in the last two months of the year and rose above S$11 billion for the first time by the end of December 1999 to $11.32 billion. By the end of March, when it was clear that the Y2K bug had not raised any systemic banking issues, the cash was redeposited, and currency in active circulation fell back to S$10.97 billion.

However, another technology-related problem was already looming. As the old millennium was drawing to a close, Internet fever hit, and new companies offering Internet-based services mushroomed. Many of these proved to be 'pie in the sky' – the firms themselves were never going to be financially viable. Things came to a head for financial markets in 2001. As the dot-com bubble burst, the share values of such companies collapsed. Some of the investment made in broadband networks and other electronics-enabled capabilities was deemed excessive. Global semiconductor chip sales plummeted, recording their largest fall in 20 years. As a key exporter of semiconductors and other electronics products, Singapore went into a full-blown recession in 2001.

With its two decades of experience using an exchange rate-centred monetary policy framework, MAS was ready to tackle the recession. In light of the shock to the domestic economy, it eased monetary policy settings, and subsequently accommodated the increased exchange rate volatility that followed the 9/11 terrorist attacks in New York in 2001. Recovery from the recession turned out to be quick, helped by a slew of fiscal and cost-cutting policies as well as MAS's loosened monetary policy stance.

These two incidents set the tone for the next two decades. Negative shocks to the global and domestic economies would feature regularly. Singapore would be threatened by a global financial crisis as well as coronaviruses leading to an epidemic in 2003, and a pandemic from 2020. The 'noughties', specifically, would see three downturns in the space of a decade, whereas only two had occurred in the three-and-a-half decades leading up to the millennium. In slightly over two decades, Singapore would be beset by two crises so severe they would draw comparison with the Great Depression of the 1930s.

Yet not all was gloom. The dot–com bust turned out to only be a brief detour in Singapore's journey towards the Internet age. The Internet itself would fundamentally reshape the nature of money, as well as the way people use it to make payments, in Singapore and globally.

A tale of two monetary authorities

When the 'currency split' from Malaysia occurred in 1967 and Singapore began to issue the Singapore dollar, the government had insisted on retaining the currency-board system, which had been in place since 1897 when Singapore was part of the Straits Settlements (see p. 93). Thus the BCCS was born and for a number of years it was Singapore's sole monetary authority. Even after MAS was established in 1971, currency issuance remained firmly under the BCCS's control.

Yet, as far as MAS was concerned, there had always been a plan for Singapore to have a full-purpose central bank with the power eventually to issue currency. Internal documents indicate that as early as 1974 there had been government approval in principle for a merger of the two. Draft legislation had been prepared and administrative arrangements finalised; but in 1980 Dr Goh Keng Swee, by then deputy prime minister and chairman of MAS, decided against it.[1]

The issue of a merger was revived in the latter half of the 1990s. In the end, the debate was settled as the two institutions discussed five fundamental questions relating to the currency-board system. What was the reserve currency against which the Singapore dollar was pegged? At what rate could the local currency be converted into that reserve currency or to gold? Who was allowed to obtain the reserve currency or gold from the issuer of the local currency? Could the

Staff at work at the BCCS office.

currency-board system prevent the monetisation of budget deficits? And, finally, what ultimately underpinned confidence in the Singapore dollar?

In 1996, MAS and BCCS were prompted to discuss the issue more directly when the first three questions were raised in a book published in the same year on the Singapore economy.[2] The authors argued that Hong Kong, which had a currency-board system underpinning the Hong Kong dollar's peg to the US dollar, could answer the first three questions readily. As far as Singapore was concerned, however, on a day-to-day basis the Singapore dollar was not fixed against any reserve currency. Indeed, there had been no such fixing in the period either after the Singapore dollar floated in June 1973, or under the exchange rate-centred monetary policy framework adopted in 1981 (see p. 303). Meanwhile, the obligation of the BCCS to convert the Singapore dollar into foreign currency or gold had been abolished in 1982.[3] Seen from the authors' perspective, Singapore had a currency board but in practice it no longer operated a currency-board system.

The BCCS took the view that the three questions did not impinge on the currency board. Even though there was no bilateral reserve currency against which the Singapore dollar was pegged, it was managed against a basket of currencies, and to an extent this would serve the same purpose of anchoring the exchange rate. There was no need for the BCCS to commit to providing a specific reserve currency at a fixed rate against the Singapore dollar; what mattered more was that individuals and firms could exchange the domestic currency for foreign currency at any time at prevailing market rates, and the fact that one could do so was well-known to the public. While the system operating in Singapore might not be 'the so-called true currency-board system', Singapore nonetheless did, in practice, still have a currency-board system.[4]

MAS raised the fourth and fifth questions in an exchange of letters with the BCCS in 1997. It wondered whether the discipline mechanism associated with a currency board had diminished in relevance. Referring to the fourth question, MAS observed that the BCCS only constrained the printing of physical currency. This technically would not rein in the government's ability to 'print money' to finance spending, since it could just issue bonds, run down its foreign-exchange reserves, or borrow from abroad. On the fifth question, there was a growing recognition that confidence in the Singapore dollar was underpinned by the country's policies and institutions rather than by the currency board itself. For instance, it was the government's adherence to the principle of fiscal prudence that boosted confidence in the Singapore dollar. Although a currency board could be useful during a banking crisis, MAS had by then strengthened prudential regulation and supervision, and these, rather than the currency board, would ensure a resilient domestic banking sector and prevent crises. The credibility imparted to the currency by a full backing of external assets could be done under a different organisational set-up and did

Singapore's financial district, overlooking Marina Bay.

not require a currency board *per se*. In accordance with central-bank thinking, an inflation target plus an independent central bank would be sufficient to ensure the credibility of monetary policy and safeguard the value of the currency.[5] Although MAS did not have an inflation target or institutional independence, it had established a track record of keeping inflation low, and had proven itself to be fiercely independent on that front (see p. 332–4).

Critically, full reserve backing of currency issued did not preserve the value of the Singapore dollar in any meaningful sense, since the stock of notes and coins in circulation by 1997 accounted for less than 10 per cent of the money supply. This compared to 19 per cent in 1967, when the BCCS was first established. The BCCS had no oversight of the remaining 90 per cent of bank-issued money. MAS, which could exercise its power in money markets, determined the way banks lent as well as the composition of their balance sheets. It could affect the non-currency part of the money supply and thus the value of the Singapore dollar in a much more comprehensive way than could the BCCS.

The shift in thinking continued into the new millennium. In January 2002, the Ministry of Finance, which was then the parent ministry of both BCCS and MAS as statutory boards, announced that the government had decided that by 31 March 2003 the two should be merged. The statement acknowledged that 'Singapore has progressively evolved' away from the system of fixed exchange rates prevailing when the BCCS was first established in 1967. The merger, it was envisioned, would rationalise 'common functions and realise efficiency gains, without compromising the overriding objective of managing confidence in the Singapore dollar'.[6]

The Singapore-Brunei Currency Interchangeability Agreement [7]

Following the BCCS and MAS merger, two institutional remnants of the currency board system were retained. One was the requirement that all currency issued be backed by foreign assets; the other was the continuation of the Currency Interchangeability Agreement between Singapore and Brunei (see p. 242).

Currency cooperation between the two countries had roots stretching back to the Straits Settlements dollar created at the turn of the 20th century, which circulated widely in Brunei also. After Brunei had become a British Protectorate in 1888, its political and economic links with the Straits Settlements meant that the Straits dollar became its *de facto* currency of choice. The Currency Ordinance of 1938 (see p. 131) formally linked Singapore and Brunei through the Malayan dollar. This arrangement continued in spirit, if not in form, after Brunei and Singapore issued their own currencies in 1967: the Currency Interchangeability Agreement kept the value of the currencies at par with one another.

The monetary arrangements in both countries have evolved over the decades. MAS was established in 1971. The Singapore dollar eventually floated in 1973, and MAS shifted to managing the Singapore dollar trade-weighted index within its monetary policy framework in the 1980s. Brunei maintained its peg to the Singapore dollar throughout this period. In 2004 the Brunei Darussalam Currency Board was dissolved and re-chartered as the Brunei Currency and Monetary Board. In 2011, it was reconstituted as Brunei's central bank, the Autoriti Monetari Brunei Darussalam (AMDB).

In 2017, MAS and AMBD commemorated the 50th anniversary of the Currency Interchangeability Agreement. Over this half-century, the agreement has contributed to preserving and deepening the economic and financial linkages between the two countries. Indeed, following the signing of the agreement in 1967, trade between the two countries grew steadily from under US$20 million in 1968 to close to US$1,000 million in 2017.

The agreement has also reduced the costs of doing business between them and enhanced their bilateral investment flows. The currency peg has effectively eliminated the transaction costs of converting the Singapore dollar into the Brunei dollar and vice versa and the need to hedge against exchange rate risk. Brunei can access Singapore's onshore and offshore money markets without currency risk; and since Singapore is a

Celebrating the Currency Interchangeability Agreement
after 40 years (opposite) and after 50 years (above).

major foreign exchange trading centre, the arrangement has also facilitated the convertibility of the Brunei dollar into other currencies.

The agreement has stood the test of time and has been resilient in the face of economic challenges, such as the Asian Financial Crisis of 1997–8 and the Global Financial Crisis of 2008–9.

On the 40th anniversary of the agreement in 2007, a S$20 note was introduced into circulation together with a collectors' set of one Singapore-dollar note and one Brunei-dollar note with matching serial numbers. Then in 2017, on the occasion of the 50th anniversary, both countries made available to collectors a set of 50-dollar notes.[8]

On 1 October 2002, the merger was formalised. There was little controversy, since it was seen as just an administrative reorganisation. The legal-tender status of currency issued by the BCCS was unaffected. The Currency Fund was incorporated into MAS's balance sheet and was formally dissolved in 2017 as the transfer of all its assets and liabilities to MAS's accounts had been completed. However, the backing of notes and coins remained unchanged in substance – the only difference now was that all notes and coins issued could not exceed the value of MAS's full assets. Any shortfall would have to be made good from the government's Consolidated Fund.

With the absorption of the currency-issuance function, it might be thought that MAS was now finally a full central bank. It is telling that when the two academics raised the merger question in their book in 1996, they were of the opinion that 'there would be no great loss of confidence in the Singapore dollar if it were to be issued by the central bank, which is consistently voted one of the most successful central banks in the world'. This characterisation shows how far MAS had come in establishing its credibility since Dr Goh Keng Swee's insistence that Singapore should in the first instance have a monetary authority but not a central bank. MAS had, through its conduct of functions within its purview over the decades, long been recognised as a credible central bank in its own right. There was certainly no pressing need to change its name either to reflect what had already *de facto* been its role.

Financial Crisis redux

In early 2003, Severe Acute Respiratory Syndrome (SARS) hit Singapore. The coronavirus quickly infected close contacts of those who were ill, although its spread was curbed once restrictions were imposed. In total, Singapore had recorded close to 250 cases; with over 30 deaths, the fatality rate was very high at nearly 15 per cent. In the second quarter of 2003, SARS caused GDP to fall by 1.4 per cent from the previous quarter as people shunned public transport and avoided going out. However, as the disease came under control the economy quickly rebounded, supported by easier monetary and fiscal policies. In the three years that followed, the Singapore economy rode on a wave of strong global growth to expand by 8.7 per cent annually between 2004 and 2006.

In 2007, the Singapore economy grew by an impressive 9 per cent, marking the fourth consecutive year of strong GDP growth. The seasonally adjusted unemployment rate in December was at a decade low of 1.7 per cent. If there

Faced with SARS, travellers take protective measures.

was a problem, it was consumer price inflation, which had rapidly risen from −0.6 per cent at the beginning of the year to nearly 5 per cent by November. This acceleration was due to rapidly rising global food and oil prices and, at the same time, increases in local wages and rentals.

Not all was well on the external front either. There were rumblings that the US economy, which had been experiencing a housing boom for several years, would see a slowdown in growth. The house-price index in the US had peaked in the first quarter of 2007 and was gradually declining. A gentle correction seemed to be on the cards, notwithstanding concerns raised by some analysts and economists about wider ramifications if the property bubble were to burst and prices were to 'correct' more rapidly.

By September 2008, the situation facing policymakers in Singapore had changed dramatically. Home prices in the US began to fall sharply, triggering losses on a wide range of mortgage-related derivatives. Investors in these, including hedge funds, banks, insurance companies, pension funds, government agencies and others, made severe losses. On 15 September, the US Federal Reserve declined to bail out investment bank Lehman Brothers, and the company filed for bankruptcy. Shocked by the immediate fallout, on 16 September the Federal Reserve announced that it was providing US$85 billion in funds to shore up insurance company AIG, and so prevent it from inflicting further stresses on the financial system and the global economy. What had hitherto been a crash in the housing market in the United States had escalated into a full-blown worldwide financial crisis.

Fortunately for Asia, the Global Financial Crisis did not match either the Great Depression or the Asian Financial Crisis in 1997–8 in its impact on the region. To be sure, asset markets did weaken throughout Asia over 2008–9. Overall however, financial sectors in the countries neighbouring Singapore were relatively less affected this time round. According to the Asian Development Bank, this was partly because their financial systems were dominated by domestically owned banks with relatively little exposure to US mortgage-related assets. Arguably, the Asian Financial Crisis had also made banks more wary about taking much risk onto their balance sheets, and this had helped reduce fallout. The widespread failures of financial institutions and the resultant pullback in credit that decimated the business sectors in 1997–8 did not reoccur. Interbank borrowing accounted for a smaller share of Asian banks' overall funding, while regional interest rates generally did not spike in the latter part of 2008. All in all, the economies and financial systems of Singapore's neighbours were not as affected by the seizing-up of global lending markets, which, if anything, seems to have been more a credit 'hiccup' than a 'crunch'.[9]

The Global Financial Crisis

US Treasury Secretary Timothy Geithner and Federal Reserve Bank Chairman Ben Bernanke give evidence on 20 April 2010 before the House Financial Services Committee enquiry about the collapse of Lehman Brothers.

The 2008–9 recession was genuinely global, unlike the Asian Financial Crisis of 1997–8, which largely impacted Asian countries, or the bursting of the dot-com bubble in 2001, centred on advanced economies.

The primary trigger of the Global Financial Crisis was the 2007 fall in US property prices following a bubble that began in 2000 and peaked in early 2007. This led to widespread defaults on mortgages and a sharp deterioration in the balance sheets of financial institutions holding mortgage-related assets. There were financial failures within the United States and the effects spread to the rest of the world, generating a 'credit crunch'. As lending between banks all but dried up, financial institutions began to fail. The Global Financial Crisis led to what commentators have subsequently called the Great Recession; not a few dubbed it 'the Great Depression redux'.

One of the reasons why the Great Depression of the 1930s had such a severe impact on the financial system and the real economy was that the US Federal Reserve at that time did not step in decisively enough to avert a collapse in the money supply. As bank runs occurred, an inadequate supply of liquidity and physical currency led to the failure of financial institutions. Credit seized up, causing firms to go insolvent and default on their financial obligations, creating a vicious feedback loop. Deflation went unchecked, and as prices and wages fell, it became more difficult for borrowers to repay debts of which the nominal values remained unchanged. This exacerbated corporate and bank insolvencies and financial distress.

This time around, central bankers in the US and other major economies had learnt their lessons well. The situation demanded unprecedented emergency policy responses by governments in both the developed and the developing worlds.[10] The Federal Reserve led the way in cutting policy rates to nearly zero per cent, resolving banking-sector stresses, and undertaking unconventional monetary policy in the form of large-scale purchases of US Treasury bonds and distressed assets such as mortgage-backed securities. Quantitative easing – whereby the central bank purchased long-term securities to keep borrowing rates low and encourage credit and thus money-supply growth – went from being an unorthodox instrument of monetary policy to become a regular part of the central bank's toolkit.

The world economy thus weathered a severe financial crisis and recession. Prompt global central-bank action prevented the money supply from collapsing. Together with other expansionary policy actions, this helped to stave off a second Great Depression. Nevertheless, the economic contraction suffered by the US and global economies was serious enough to merit the 'Great Recession' label.[11]

Despite reforms to liberalise the banking sector in the 1990s, Singapore too escaped the financial fallout. Its banks were not heavily exposed to toxic assets linked to the US property market, such as mortgage-backed securities. Their financial fundamentals were sound, and the regulatory regime prevented the banks from taking on excessive risk.

MAS's priority was to ensure that financial institutions in Singapore had access to Singapore-dollar and US-dollar liquidity if needed, and that viable banks remained solvent. MAS carried out routine money-market operations to stabilise interest rates and provide sufficient liquidity to the banking system.[12]

A more critical need was to prevent a mass withdrawal of bank deposits. In October 2008, the government announced that it would guarantee all Singapore-dollar and foreign-currency deposits of individual and non-bank customers of banks, finance companies, and merchant banks until December 2010. This deposit guarantee was backed by S$150 billion of Singapore's national reserves. Without it, if customers had fled from one bank to another domestically or abroad, bank runs could have spiralled out of control and become self-fulfilling panics. Solvent banks caught in a temporary but severe liquidity shortage could have been forced inadvertently into insolvency. The scheme therefore provided a fundamentally different playing field compared to the situation in the 19th century when runs had taken place on Singapore-based banks, and the stronger banks had had to help the distressed ones (see p. 83). In the absence of a private-sector solution at that earlier time there had been no public recourse. This time, the government stepped in to back bank-issued money in a big way.

In October 2008, a temporary US$30-billion swap line with the Federal Reserve was established to provide US dollars for financial institutions in Singapore.[13] The knowledge that the swap line existed quelled fears and prevented a severe US-dollar liquidity crunch; in fact, the signalling effect of the swap line was so strong that in the end there was no need for MAS to draw on the funds.

Despite being a relative newcomer compared to major central banks that were several centuries old, MAS took lessons learnt from the Great Depression to heart. In ensuring that the financial system was flushed with liquidity, MAS prevented a collapse in the money supply comprising both government-issued currency in active circulation and bank-issued money in the form of deposits. This was in contrast to the Great Depression years, when the money supply of Malaya, as proxied by the value of Straits Settlements dollars issued, nearly halved. The economic downturn, and the deflation that ensued, were severe (see p. 120).

Growth of currency in active circulation, deposits and money supply

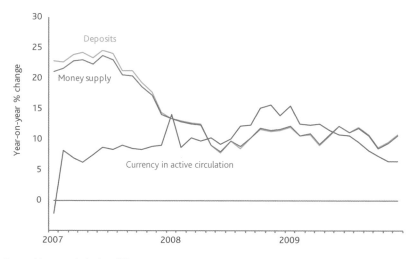

Source: Monetary Authority of Singapore

Thus, while the failure of Lehman and the stresses on AIG precipitated a global credit crunch, the region was largely spared, and in Singapore's financial sector these incidents led to isolated rather than systemic problems. For instance, retail investors in Singapore, including the elderly and those with lower investment risk tolerance, had been mis-sold Lehman's 'structured notes'[14] as 'safe and conservative' savings vehicles that promised in the event of a failure to pay back investors all their initial investment plus any profits accruing at the time. Lehman's collapse meant that the notes would default on their scheduled interest payments. A forced early redemption of the notes occurred, and given the turmoil in financial markets the underlying assets were liquidated at a great loss. Consequently, most investors lost nearly all their money. As at October 2008, 9,750 retail investors had bought the notes. MAS investigated the complaints of mis-selling and found some non-compliance. It subsequently banned ten financial institutions from selling the notes for periods ranging from six months to two years, and the selling rules were tightened up.[15]

Following news of the AIG bailout, policyholders in Singapore flocked to the customer service centre of its local subsidiary AIA in Finlayson Green. To calm them, MAS issued a statement on 17 September 2008 making it clear that AIA's assets were ring-fenced and could only be directed to meet AIA's obligations to its clients – i.e. AIA's money could not be used to shore up AIG abroad. MAS emphasised that AIA had sufficient funds to meet all its liabilities to policyholders, and it made clear that it would not tolerate rumours about the soundness of particular financial institutions.[16] As it turned out, AIA was largely unaffected by the collapse of its parent AIG, and the impact on Singapore policyholders was minimal, much to everyone's relief.

However, the impact on the Singapore economy was much more severe this time round compared to the Asian Financial Crisis. Rather than the failure of regional financial institutions and systems weighing on economic growth, the slowdown in Asia occurred as the recession in the advanced economies led to the collapse of exports from the region. Singapore's exports fell by 18 per cent for 2009 as a whole. The economy shrank for four consecutive quarters from the second quarter of 2008 to the first quarter of 2009. GDP growth did not turn negative in either 2008 or 2009, but the depth of the crisis showed in annual GDP growth rates averaging 1.0 per cent per year over the two years. This compared to an average growth of 3.1 per cent in the two years of the Asian Financial Crisis. Inflation, which had hit a high of 7.6 per cent year-on-year in the second quarter of 2008, began decelerating rapidly. The resident unemployment rate rose steadily from the third quarter of 2008 to reach nearly 5 per cent a year later.

As the growth outlook deteriorated, the prospect of deflation loomed. Consequently, MAS eased its monetary policy settings in October 2008 and April 2009, and maintained an accommodative policy stance until it was clear that the worst was over. As in past downturns, there was no desire to depreciate the currency artificially to boost export competitiveness; indeed to do so would have made no sense. In the midst of a financial crisis, it was all the more important to stabilise confidence in the Singapore dollar. MAS did not believe in competitive devaluation. In a global recession when demand was shrinking across the world, there was even less reason to believe that currency depreciation could help any country export its way out of a crisis.

Singapore's Great Recession and Great Recovery

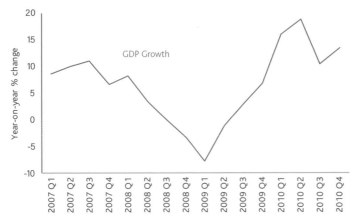

Source: SINGSTAT

Consequently, Singapore's main way of addressing the downturn was through fiscal policy. Ahead of schedule in January 2009, a S$20.5 billion 'Resilience Package' was introduced in the budget. The budget included targeted transfers to households and businesses; a 'Special Risk-sharing Initiative' to stimulate bank lending; and, of crucial importance, a 'Jobs Credit Scheme' to provide subsidies to employers for the retention of local workers and to prevent a spike in retrenchments. This involved drawing for the first time since Independence – with the required consent of the President of Singapore – on the nation's past reserves. The money was returned in full when the economy recovered even though there was no legal obligation to do so.

As governments around the world successfully stemmed the crisis in their economies and global demand began to recover, international trade resumed. Consequently, the trade-related activities that had collapsed earlier bounced back. The Singapore economy rebounded in the second half of 2009 and annual growth in 2010 was an astounding 14.5 per cent, substantially higher than after the previous two recessions.[17] Indeed, by the fourth quarter of 2009 all the output lost during the downturn had been recovered. The labour market proved resilient, thanks in no small part to the Jobs Credit Scheme that encouraged employers to hold on to their local workers, even as the foreign workforce bore the brunt of any softening in labour demand. Damaging deflationary pressures moderated and prices stabilised by the first quarter of 2010. By the fourth quarter of 2009, the resident unemployment rate had fallen to 3.3 per cent.

Singapore and the US Treasury's Monitoring List

Following the Global Financial Crisis, it became clear that the world was in a two-speed recovery mode: the worst-hit advanced economies were growing very slowly due to the ravages of the crisis, whereas GDP growth in the less-affected emerging market economies had rebounded rapidly. The unconventional monetary policies unleashed by the major central banks to prevent a meltdown in global financial markets and shore up their economies brought interest rates to near-zero for an unprecedented length of time. Amid the abundant liquidity, investors began to 'search for yield', or higher returns. This led to a surge of capital abroad, principally into emerging markets, which caused the latter's currencies to appreciate rapidly.

In Singapore, by April 2010, the worst of the crisis was over. The Singapore economy was staging a very strong recovery. Faced with the prospect of rising inflation and runaway asset prices, fuelled in part by the near-zero domestic interest rates 'imported' from abroad and the surge of foreign capital inflows into the economy, MAS tightened monetary policy in three successive

Pro-Government demonstrators during the Greek debt crisis, June 2015.

policy meetings by allowing the trade-weighted index (TWI) to appreciate at a faster pace.

In July 2011 however, capital was coming into Singapore for a different reason: a flight to safety, rather than the search for yield. During this period, financial markets were spooked by the potential failure of the US Congress to raise the national debt ceiling. The debt ceiling was a legislative limit on the stock of US Treasury debt that determined the total sum the American government could borrow at any time. The limit had been reached several years previously, but it was typically increased every year by Congress without much fanfare. In 2011, however, the Republican-dominated Congress threatened not to raise it unless Democrat President Barack Obama's administration negotiated to reduce the budget deficit. A failure to raise the ceiling would, in the absence of alternatives, cause the US government to default on its debt. This would send shockwaves around the world as the US Treasury bond was the *de facto* risk-free asset of the world that determined the pricing and yields of many other assets.

The sudden uncertainty around the US government's ability to fulfil its obligations sent investors into a flight to safety. Other economies with solid credit ratings, such as Switzerland and Singapore, suddenly found themselves deluged with capital inflows as risk aversion rose. The Swiss franc had already been strengthening for some time against the euro, given growing jitters about Greece's fiscal problems, and the Swiss National Bank had emphasised that it would come in against any 'excessive' appreciation of its currency against the euro. The US debt ceiling problem compounded the pressures on the Swiss franc to strengthen further. The Singapore dollar appreciated to an unprecedented S$1.20 to one US dollar on 27 July, two days before the US debt ceiling was due to expire. It had risen by 14 per cent since end-2009 and 7 per cent since end-2010. The Singapore dollar TWI appreciated by 8.3 per cent and 3.4 per cent over the same period. At the last hour, Congress lifted the debt ceiling and the Singapore dollar depreciated as safe-haven capital inflows receded.

These events demonstrate how Singapore's openness to global capital flows has led to challenges. While liberalising capital flows was a critical precondition in the development of the city-state as a regional financial centre, the large and volatile capital flows that characterised the years preceding the Global Financial Crisis as well as the years following it posed problems for Singapore. Left unchecked, excessive capital inflows could have led to a sharp appreciation of the TWI and a recession. MAS thus found itself in a very different situation from the 1980s, when speculators were selling Singapore dollars amid an economic downturn (see p. 305–6). In the face of speculative inflows, MAS would have found it necessary to purchase US dollars and sell Singapore dollars in return to ensure that the TWI remained in line with the domestic economy's fundamentals.

In 2019, the international political context of MAS's monetary policy shifted. Major economies, principally the US, China, and the European Union, entered a trade war. In the US, there was now heightened scrutiny of governments' interference in trade, especially through the exchange rate. On 29 May, the US Treasury released its biannual report on the foreign exchange and macroeconomic policies of the US's trade partners. This time round, it had broadened the number of economies to be assessed to include all countries whose bilateral goods trade with the US exceeded US$40 billion annually. Singapore therefore came under assessment. Due to the size of Singapore's overall current account surplus, as well as the Treasury's estimates of its net purchases of foreign exchange, Singapore was put on the report's Monitoring List, a move signalling that the country concerned had met a number of criteria that took it a step closer to being declared a currency manipulator.[18]

While trade was the impetus behind many of the US administration's actions in 2019, it was not an issue of contention as far as Singapore was concerned. Since the early 2000s, Singapore had recorded goods trade deficits, not surpluses, vis-à-vis the US. Accusations of 'currency manipulation' this time round were more reminiscent of the 1980s 'global imbalances' debate where countries such as Singapore were deemed to have 'excessive' current account surpluses, while others, such as the US, had the counterpart deficits. In this respect, the roots of the dispute could even be traced back to the collapse of the Bretton Woods agreement in the early 1970s.

The US Treasury recognised that the Singapore economy had some special structural characteristics. For instance, it was expected that Singapore would need to build up saving in anticipation of spending by, and on, its ageing population. Unlike in the 1980s, there was a much better appreciation this time round that the country's unique exchange rate-centred monetary policy was credibly directed at ensuring low and stable inflation. In this context, the Treasury understood that foreign exchange interventions were part and parcel of implementing monetary policy, and that a tighter monetary policy stance – through an appreciation of the Singapore dollar nominal effective exchange rate – could lead to deflation in the economy.

While the US accepted that the above characteristics might lead to Singapore having a current account surplus, and might warrant net purchases of foreign exchange under certain exchange rate market conditions, they felt that these considerations were not sufficient to justify the *size* of the surplus or the *extent* of intervention. If MAS's net purchases of foreign exchange were deemed by the Treasury to be excessive, the implication was that MAS was deliberately keeping the Singapore dollar weak in order to boost Singapore's current account surplus. The government's other macroeconomic policies that contributed to the high rate of saving in the economy and thus the surplus, namely, the mandatory contributions to the national pension scheme (the Central Provident Fund), as well as the government's adherence to fiscal prudence, also came under the spotlight. To reduce the current account surplus, the report contended that Singapore's currency should appreciate more and the government should increase spending to strengthen social safety nets and boost consumption spending.

Singapore's official reply to the report, as conveyed in a press release by MAS on 29 May 2019, was strongly worded.[19] It emphasised that MAS did not, and could not, use the exchange rate to gain an export advantage or achieve a current account surplus. Recalling the principles established by Dr Goh Keng Swee when MAS first adopted the exchange rate-centred monetary policy framework, the Authority emphasised that a deliberate weakening of the Singapore dollar would cause inflation in Singapore to spike and compromise MAS's price-stability objective.[20] Second, the current account balance was ultimately determined by saving and investment behaviour rather than by the exchange rate. In the early years of nation-building (1965–84), Singapore had recorded large and persistent current account deficits averaging 10 per cent of GDP. However, as the economy matured, investment needs tapered off and national saving increased. Consequently, the current account moved into surplus around the mid-1980s as saving began to exceed investment. With rising affluence, domestic consumption should increase over time and the current account surplus would be expected to fall naturally, as public and private savings were drawn down to meet

Deputy Prime Minister
Heng Swee Keat,
June 2019.

the needs of an ageing population. Indeed, according to MAS, this had already begun to happen.

The headline in the *Business Times* the following day was 'Singapore refutes US accusation of currency manipulation'.[21] Many local commentators viewed the inclusion of Singapore as unwarranted, and the general public, commenting on social media, by and large felt that the move simply reflected the protectionist sentiment prevalent in the White House at the time. In the event, there were no immediate consequences for Singapore's being placed on the 'List' and no obvious panic in Singapore's financial markets.

The currency manipulation issue had been intimately linked with exports in the 1980s when it first arose, and the then Minister for Trade and Industry, Lee Hsien Loong, had defended Singapore's position in the media. This time round, the concerns were still very much with exports and imports, what with the US, China, Europe and other major economies in the midst of a trade war. However, the issues had broadened, touching on the very foundational principles of a broad swathe of Singapore's government policies. As a consequence, Deputy Prime Minister Heng Swee Keat, who was concurrently Minister for Finance as well as a former managing director of MAS, came out publicly to reiterate that 'Singapore is not a currency manipulator', and '[it] is not in our short-term nor long-term interests to manipulate the currency.. if we manipulate our exchange rate for some short-term gains, we will set ourselves further behind.'[22]

MAS's explanations lay at the heart of the dispute with the US over Singapore's large current account surplus and persistent accumulation of foreign assets. The issue from the global imbalances perspective was that Singapore's high saving rate imposed costs on deficit countries such as the United States.

Arguably, a case could be made that there *should* be a shared responsibility for reducing global imbalances between *both* surplus *and* deficit countries. If this was so, then surplus countries should also adjust their policies to facilitate rebalancing, no matter how desirable their policy objectives might be for their citizens. Indeed, a number of attempts have been made to create a system whereby surplus countries would bear some of the burden of adjustment as well. For instance, when designing the Bretton Woods system in 1944, the economist John Maynard Keynes incorporated a means for surplus and deficit countries to address imbalances or face sanctions.[23] A second attempt to 'discipline' surplus countries was made by the IMF Committee of Twenty, which met from late 1972 to mid-1974 after the collapse in the Bretton Woods system (see p. 262). The United States, a deficit country, proposed symmetrical penalties on any surplus or deficit countries that failed to take the necessary policy actions to solve their balance of payments problems.

Yet, these proposals quickly came to nothing. The bottom line was that a collective solution to share the burden of dealing with global imbalances was unlikely to succeed if the major surplus countries did not agree to it. The United States, which had a balance of payments surplus in 1944, rebuffed Keynes's suggestion, while Japan and West Germany did not agree to the IMF's arrangement in the 1970s. As the Eurozone crisis showed, surplus countries were unlikely to agree to such a proposal, especially since it was not self-evident that the deficits were primarily due to policies adopted by surplus countries themselves rather than the excesses of deficit countries. Likewise for the United States: faced with insufficient private saving and budget deficits every year since 1980 except for 1999–2001 (towards the end of the Clinton presidency), the United States has relied on a continuous inflow of foreign capital to finance its current account deficits. Until the 1980s, the United States was the largest creditor country in the world, but by 2012 its net foreign debt had reached US$3.9 trillion, or 23 per cent of GDP.

One could say that the US's persistent external deficits are a by-product of the dollar's role as the pre-eminent global reserve currency. From this perspective, the US is providing an international 'public good' by allowing its dollar to be used in global trade and financial transactions. This is a role that no other country's currency could ever match, least of all the currencies of small, surplus economies such as the Swiss franc or the Singapore dollar. Singapore and Switzerland have had a foretaste of what would happen to their own currencies if global investors fled to them for safety when existing reserve currencies were shaken during the US debt ceiling crisis. The appreciation pressures on the two currencies would have been overwhelming for such small, open economies in the absence of offsetting policy action.

Physical currency

Although the BCCS did not know it at the time, the Portrait series of notes introduced in 1999 was its swansong as far as note series issuance was concerned. The enduring quality of these notes has meant that, as at the time of writing, no new note series have been issued since. Following the merger of the BCCS and MAS in 2002, it was MAS that issued Singapore's third series of circulation coins in 2013. MAS would also issue commemorative notes to mark moments of national significance, just as the BCCS had done in the years before the merger. The Singapore Mint would continue to mint coins both for circulation and for sale as commemorative coins.

The 'stylised' and 'official' versions of the Singapore coat of arms on the one-dollar coins from the second series.

The latest series of coins featured a version of Singapore's coat of arms different from that on the second series when it was first issued in 1985. The 1985 series used a 'stylised version' on the obverse, with the shield bearing the crescent and five stars rising above the heads of the lion and tiger supporting it. But in 1992, the Coin Advisory Committee recommended to the board of BCCS that the 'stylised' version be replaced with the 'official' version in which the shield was positioned lower. This official version was used on all coins from that date and was consistent with the coat of arms on all currency notes issued since 1967. [24]

Coins were legal-tender, meaning that they could be used to fulfil any financial obligation. However, the Currency Act placed limits on the number of coins that could be used in one transaction. Vendors were only obliged to accept coins up to certain limits. 5-cent, 10-cent and 20-cent coins could be used to make payment for amounts not exceeding S$2, while the limit set on 50-cent coins was S$10. There was no limit on the number of dollar coins that could be used.

In 2014, however, cases of the excessive use of coins were widely reported in the local media. In several instances, a mobile phone shop was reported as making refunds to customers in coins running up to over a thousand dollars. One lady was due a refund of S$1,010. The shop paid S$460 in notes; the remaining S$550 was paid in coins reportedly weighing some 18kg. In another instance, a man was ordered by a court to pay a car dealer S$19,000. The payment was made in coins – many of them 20-cent denomination – and weighed more than 350kg in total. On being interviewed, the man said he was displeased with both the court verdict and the car dealer, and he had decided to pay in coins to make his unhappiness clear.[25]

While these incidents were rare, they led MAS to consider whether the rules governing the use of coins should be tightened further and simplified. In particular, there was a loophole in the existing legislation – the lack of a limit on the amount that could be paid using dollar coins. MAS proposed a revised limit of ten coins per denomination per transaction, and sought the public's feedback. An online poll by the *Straits Times* found that nearly 65 per cent of respondents were

The third series of coins

On 25 June 2013, the first series of circulation coins since 1985 was issued, the third since Independence. For the first time they were the work of a local designer, Fabian Lim. There were five denominations: 5 cents, 10 cents, 20 cents, 50 cents and 1 dollar. The coins depicted local icons and landmarks familiar to Singaporeans – the Esplanade performing arts centre, Changi Airport, the port, and a public housing block.

The new designs brought the coins in line with the Portrait series of notes issued in 1999, which featured the image of Singapore's first President, Yusof bin Ishak, on the obverse and scenes depicting the nation's development on the reverse. The new coins had larger denomination numerals and progressive sizing by denomination to allow users to recognise the coins more intuitively; there were also tactile features such as different edge patterns on each denomination. These features were developed in consultation with special interest groups such as the Singapore Association for the Visually Handicapped.

Security was enhanced in the form of a customised electromagnetic signature for each denomination; and for the dollar coin a laser micro-engraving of the Vanda Miss Joaquim, Singapore's national flower.

5 cents, multi-ply brass-plated steel with plain edge

Reverse: the Esplanade

10 cents, multi-ply nickel-plated steel with interrupted milled edge

Reverse: public housing

20 cents, multi-ply nickel-plated steel with milled edge

Reverse: Changi Airport

50 cents, multi-ply nickel-plated steel with micro-scalloped edge

Reverse: the Port of Singapore

1 dollar, the inner circle is made of multi-ply nickel-plated steel and the outer ring of multi-ply brass-plated steel, with milled edge

Reverse: the Merlion

against the proposal.[26] In the end, it was decided that the limit should be 20 coins per denomination. Coins would only be legal-tender for paying an amount not exceeding 20 times their face value: S$1 coins could be used only for paying an amount of up to S$20; 10-cent coins, up to S$2. These changes were enshrined in law when the Currency Act was amended in 2017.

Although MAS did not issue new circulation note series, it issued polymer version of the 2-dollar, 5-dollar, and 10-dollar notes in the 2000s. MAS also issued commemorative notes. On 13 August 2015, six commemorative polymer notes were issued – a 50-dollar note and five 10-dollar notes – to celebrate the 50 years of nation-building since Singapore separated from Malaysia. The notes were all designed by local artists: Chua Mia Tee, Eng Siak Loy, Weng Ziyan and Fabian Lim.[27] The front of both denominations featured a portrait of Singapore's first president, Yusof bin Ishak, different from the one on the Portrait series already in circulation. A novel security feature was a 'see-through' security stripe with image movement. In particular, the stripe on the 50-dollar note displayed '1965' or '2015' when held at different angles. Visible on both the front and back of the note was the iconic image of Singapore's first prime minister, Lee Kuan Yew, on the steps of City Hall in 1959 with his fist raised and leading the crowd with the Malay rallying call 'Merdeka!' ('Independence!'). The reverse depicted the first National Day parade on 9 August 1966 and the new town of Punggol. The public were advised not to rush to obtain them, quotas were imposed on the number of transactions per person, and priority was given to Singaporeans.

The 50th anniversary of Independence in 2015 was also marked by commemorative coins on the themes of education and nation-building. They consisted of a two-dollar cupronickel coin, a five-dollar silver coin and a 50-dollar gold coin.

The release of the commemorative notes was not without incident. MAS had presented the notes in a folder with an explanatory booklet. However, after banks had begun issuing the notes, it was discovered that there was a spelling mistake in Yusof bin Ishak's name in both the folder and the booklet. MAS apologised, initially printing stickers to be pasted over the misspellings, and subsequently reprinting the folders.[28] In addition, demand for the notes turned out to be much lower than expected. The notes had been launched with much fanfare and initially long queues had formed outside participating bank branches, partly in response to MAS's decision to ration the supply. However, demand turned out to be underwhelming – less than half of the stock produced was actually distributed to buyers. It seemed that banks, merchants and consumers did not want them, even as gifts or *hongbao* at Chinese New Year; they could only be deposited over the counter and not in cash-deposit machines, which were not configured to recognise them. As the *Business Times* headline went: 'SG50 notes. Too much of a good thing.'[29]

Commemorative notes

Commemorative 50-dollar note celebrating
50 years of nation-building, 2015

In 2015, five different versions of the 10-dollar note were
issued to mark 50 years of nation-building.

Digital payments and digital currencies

The technological advances of the 21st century were no doubt significant, but a much greater sea change in monetary systems had happened during the previous century. The days when customer deposits and withdrawals were recorded physically in a bank's ledger book, or when nations cleared outstanding gold balances under the gold standard by means of physical movements of bullion, were long gone. By the turn of the millennium, monetary systems – comprising customer deposits held with commercial banks, and reserves held by financial institutions directly with central banks – were already mostly digital.[30]

Many technological advances in the way people pay for goods and services took place over the 19th and 20th centuries. For instance, the 1800s saw the beginning of payment by telegraphic wire; cheques became popular in the latter half of the 20th century as automated cheque-processing technologies were developed; and modern credit cards emerged in the 1950s. Since the 1980s, Singaporeans have been able to use bank deposits rather than physical notes or coins to make purchases, pay bills, and transfer money electronically to one another. Automated teller machines also provided a convenient way to deposit and withdraw cash.

Easier access to the Internet, in particular with the introduction of smartphones and broadband data plans, has transformed the ability to use digital money as a means of payment. The demand for digital money grew alongside a burgeoning user base built up by regional and global technology firms such as Alibaba, Amazon, Apple, Google, Grab and Shopee. Their technologies brought economic processes, transactions, interactions and other activities based on digital technologies[31] to the forefront of Singaporeans' minds. Not all these firms accepted physical currency in exchange for goods and services, and they contributed to a significant shift towards the use of digital money. Besides bank-based digital money, 'e-money' issued by non-bank financial institutions has also become ubiquitous in Singapore.[32] The instruments on which e-money is stored have evolved over the years, from the Nets CashCards first introduced in the mid-1990s to the phone-based electronic wallets ('e-wallets') of today, such as Singtel Dash and GrabPay.

At the same time, the ability to draw on bank-based digital money as a means of transaction improved by leaps and bounds in the 2010s and 2020s, as banks and payment platforms upgraded back-end payment infrastructure.

In 2014, Singapore launched the Fast And Secure Transfers (FAST) system, one of the first 24-hour, real-time interbank fund-transfer systems in the world. When a transaction involving sending funds was executed, payment could be received by the bank accounts of individuals or businesses almost immediately, at any hour of the day. This was much faster than processing cheques or interbank GIRO transfers, which could take two or three business days. FAST was certainly efficient. However, the payer still needed to know the payee's bank-account details. This limitation was soon overcome. In 2017, MAS brought banks together to create PayNow.[33] By linking an individual's or company's account with a unique identifying number, users could now make instant payments using just the recipient's mobile phone or identity card number, or a company's unique entity number. As the use of e-wallets gained traction, MAS decided to open up access to the FAST and PayNow systems to major non-bank payment providers. From 2021, this enabled users of e-wallets to make real-time funds transfers between bank accounts and e-wallets as well as across different e-wallets. Electronic payments were becoming ever more seamless.

A symbolic SGQR label with various QR payment options.

Ironically, the proliferation of electronic payment modes brought its own challenges. For instance, the payment modes accepted by a particular business might not match what the customer was using. Many businesses were run by sole proprietors on a relatively small scale. For them, physical currency was the most convenient means of transaction – they did not want the hassle or costs of managing multiple electronics payments systems. Consequently, in 2016 MAS and the financial industry introduced the Unified Point of Sale (POS) terminal, a single device that could accept payments from all electronic modes, including NETS, regular debit or credit card, contactless cards, ApplePay or Google Pay. The year 2018 saw the launch of the Singapore Quick Response Code (SGQR). This was the world's first QR code designed to unify QR codes for multiple electronic payment schemes into a single label. With these initiatives, merchants no longer needed to provide multiple payment infrastructures or put up different QR codes corresponding to individual systems. Digital payment was becoming much more convenient.

The 2017/18 Household Expenditure Survey found that 92 per cent of all Singapore resident households performed at least one e-payment transaction during the year.[34] Users were increasingly using cashless payment methods at the point of sale, be they debit and credit cards or e-wallet solutions. New digital services (e.g. ride-hailing) were seamlessly integrating electronic payments to create better user experiences. With the rise of e-commerce, households were buying more goods and services online, for which payment with physical cash was a less convenient option. The shift to digital money occurred at the expense of physical cash: the total value and volume of cashless transactions in Singapore rose over the period 2015–19, whereas ATM withdrawals over the same period declined.

A parallel development has been the emergence of privately issued digital currencies, also known as cryptocurrencies. In terms of the technology underpinning them, cryptocurrencies differ significantly from the digital bank-issued money and e-money discussed above.

One such private-sector initiative came from the pseudonymous 'Satoshi Nakamoto'. Evidence suggests that Nakamoto began working on computer code

Left: ATMs are ubiquitous in Singapore, in public venues and shopping malls, and throughout many HDB housing estates.

Right: The DBS PayLah personal mobile wallet as advertised on an ATM screen.

for a digital currency as early as 2007. On 31 October 2008, Nakamoto published a white paper describing a system offering two distinct innovations. The first was a new digital currency – 'bitcoins' – that would be 'mined' by computers, not created by governments or banks; highly competitive miners would be rewarded with bitcoins as they helped maintain the integrity of the transaction history on the network. The second innovation was the underlying blockchain infrastructure. It brought together a unique set of technologies to enable anyone with an Internet connection to participate in this fledgling financial network.

Most significantly, the blockchain relied on a novel system of incentives and encryption allowing the recording of peer-to-peer transfers without the need for trusted intermediaries or a centralised ledger-keeper. The system conferred a degree of 'immutability'; that is, since there was no single, centralised ledger, it was very difficult to amend records or falsify a transaction. By being less reliant than conventional monetary systems on such gatekeepers, it aimed to lay the foundation for more inclusive and privacy-preserving financial services.

Led by bitcoin, the first generation of these private digital currencies demonstrated the innovative potential of the underlying blockchain. However, they failed to gain credibility as a form of money because their values were extremely volatile. Moreover, the capacity of these cryptocurrency systems to handle large numbers of transactions was limited, which further reduced their usefulness as a means of payment. Instead, thus far these first-generation cryptocurrencies have mostly served as speculative assets. MAS was concerned enough that in 2017 it cautioned the public to 'act with extreme caution' and 'understand the significant risks' involved in investing in cryptocurrencies. The anonymity they offer have also attracted illicit activities. However, governments have started to recognise the advantages in fighting financial crime afforded by a global transaction history that is immutable.

The failure of the first generation of digital currencies to become widely accepted as 'money' spurred the emergence of subsequent generations of private digital currencies. These sought to address the limitations of earlier iterations while keeping the best of their innovations. Stablecoins emerged, built on crypto-based networks: these sought to overcome price volatility by linking the digital currency's value to a pool of financial assets where the exchange rate was well established by financial markets. For example, the value of a cryptocurrency called the USD Coin was linked to the US dollar. This harkened back to the earlier idea that the credibility of new, government-issued national currencies emerging on the global scene could be anchored by pegging their value to an external and well-established currency. As we saw in an earlier chapter, when Singapore, Malaysia and Brunei first issued their own dollars in 1967, they were pegged to the pound sterling. As stablecoins were anchored to something whose value was well understood, their own value was more stable than that of the first generation of cryptocurrencies, and they offered greater potential as a means of payment.

One of the highest-profile developments in the stablecoin space was Facebook's announcement in June 2019 that it had organised a consortium of technology and payment companies with a view to launching a stablecoin denominated in a new unit of account, Libra.[35] The value of a Libra would be pegged to a basket of major currencies. Many more firms would be able to access the underlying blockchain-based financial infrastructure to offer Libra-denominated financial services. Libra was by no means the first stablecoin proposal, but stood out because it could make use of the existing platforms of its issuers, which promised to drive adoption at an unprecedented speed and scale. Facebook alone had a network of over 1.5 billion active users and had managed to bring into the project partners such as Spotify and Uber. Libra sparked discussions of how the financial landscape might be reshaped by the emergence of a 'global stablecoin' – a stablecoin with the serious potential to emerge as an alternative to national currencies. Governments and central banks all over the world sat up and took notice, including in Singapore.

The fact that alternative digital currencies – whether new units of account such as bitcoin and the original Libra proposal, or new mediums of exchange for existing currencies such as USD Coin – began to emerge in the face of well-established incumbent currencies may be due partly to some shortcomings of government- and bank-issued money and associated payment systems.

Privately issued digital currencies would be denominated in their own unique units (e.g. bitcoin) rather than national legal-tender (e.g. the US dollar). However, proponents of the newer digital currencies argued that this did not matter. In nearly all countries, there was nothing concrete to anchor the value of existing money. To be sure, central banks have aimed to preserve the purchasing power of both central-bank- and commercial-bank-issued money by keeping inflation

Representation of the bitcoin currency

close to a defined target. However, given the assumption that most governments and banks created money 'out of nothing' in the first instance, and that the value of those currencies were dictated by fiat, one can argue nothing makes a currency such as the US dollar inherently more valuable than a cryptocurrency, except that everyone believes that everyone else is willing to accept the dollar in exchange for goods and services.

The second factor was trust, or the lack thereof. This was a privacy issue. It was closely tied to the processes underlying the banking systems and payment platforms connected with them. Money passing through them left digital trails. It was not only criminals who wanted to conceal their transactions; there were private individuals who simply disliked the idea that the government or a bank could have access to, and potentially profit from, knowledge of a person's financial transactions and the preferences they revealed. If no one could be trusted to hold all this data confidentially, then perhaps a decentralised ledger similar to that underpinning many cryptocurrencies would be the way forward.

Thirdly, there was the cost of financial transactions. As most transactions today have relied almost exclusively on intermediaries (e.g. to prevent double-spending), charges and fees could be levied along the way to the profit of banks and existing payment platforms. Banks were also subject to significant anti-money-laundering checks and regulations, and these could add to costs and delays in cross-border transactions. Even where seamless, low-cost, and easy-to-use digital banking and payments systems were already available to the average citizen, they mostly offered transactions within countries. Alternative digital currencies built with a global, interconnected system in mind from the outset, which would allow for transactions both within and across borders to be conducted almost instantaneously at minimal cost, were an attractive proposition.

Singapore did not suffer from doubts about the central bank or the Singapore dollar as a credible store of value. There was little direct concern about bank-created digital money. MAS's prudent regulation and supervision of the local banks, the financial institutions' strong capital base, together with the deposit-guarantee framework put in place after the Global Financial Crisis, meant that the public had a high degree of confidence in the soundness of the domestic banks. Both MAS and the private sector had worked to create increasingly seamless means of electronic payments to spur the use of digital bank-issued money. And on the issue of cross-border transfers, in 2021 MAS and the Bank of Thailand announced that in a world first, they had linked up Singapore and Thailand's real-time retail payment systems, PayNow and PromptPay. Up to S$1,000 or 25,000 Thai baht per day could be transferred seamlessly to a counterparty identified by a mobile phone number – the transaction could be completed in a few minutes. While these transactions would incur fees, they would be 'affordably priced'.[36]

MAS envisioned that one day a similar system for 'simple, swift and secure cross-border payments' across the other ASEAN economies would be available.

Even so, privately issued digital currencies, such as bitcoin, Ethereum and stablecoins like Tether and USD Coin, were making their presence felt in Singapore. In 2014, the first bitcoin ATM in the country was installed in a pub on Boat Quay.[37] A growing, albeit small, number of retailers tentatively accepted bitcoin and other cryptocurrencies in payment. If trends abroad were anything to go by, more widespread retail acceptance of crypto-based digital currencies seemed likely. In 2021, VISA became the first major payments network to accept payments made directly with USD Coin.[38]

It may be that physical cash as a medium of transaction is becoming increasingly irrelevant in a digital economy. This begs the questions: should MAS simply allow it to be phased out over time? Or should it ensure the continued use of coins and notes? Should it digitise physical currency by creating a central-bank digital currency (CBDC) for retail use?

The view of many central banks is that even if the world were to become increasingly digitised, it would still be important for the general public to have direct access to some form of government-issued money, be it in the form of physical cash or retail CBDC.

In the first instance, central-bank money is the safest and most liquid asset in the economy, even though bank deposits come close, with the protection conferred by sound regulation, deposit insurance and the central bank's backing. Households and firms should therefore be given the option of holding central-bank money if they wish to, rather than traditional commercial-bank money, e-money, or any other privately issued digital currencies.

Government-issued money would also serve as a competitor to privately issued money. This would help keep issuers of private money disciplined and ensure that the money they issued was safe. For instance, a bank would take care to ensure that risks on its balance sheet were well-managed if it knew that at the slightest sign of trouble, depositors would rush to exchange their deposits for cash, as has happened in bank runs in Singapore historically (see p. 82). A CBDC would be as safe as its physical counterpart, cash, and would have similar disciplining effects on commercial banks and other private issuers of digital currencies.[39]

Further, central-bank-issued money would be a critical 'back-up' mode of payment in the event of a failure in private networks. Imagine a cyber attack on banking networks: the economy would collapse if the ability to buy and sell, and to send and receive money, were compromised with no alternatives available!

Physical cash is the most accessible and inclusive mode of payment in existence. Anyone is able to use it, regardless of age, education or familiarity with information technology. This is unlike digital money and electronic payments, where adoption in certain segments of the population, such as the elderly, faces significant impediments.

For all these reasons there would still be a place for government-issued money; not only in the form of physical currency but perhaps in a digital form as well. At the time of writing, it is clear that central banks' interest in a digital form of cash has grown enormously – over 80 per cent of central banks around the world are studying or experimenting with CBDCs.[40] However, few central banks have come to a decision on the issuance of a digital equivalent to cash. Retail CBDCs could have profound implications for the structure of the banking system which must be addressed before they are launched. The case for a retail CBDC remains open and will depend on country-specific circumstances.

In retrospect

Is there ever a good time to set up a central bank? Dr Goh Keng Swee envisioned it would happen in times less turbulent than the 1970s. However, over subsequent decades the severity of economic crises would intensify. Within the first decade of the new millennium, MAS had to deal with the most serious financial crisis since the Great Depression in the 1930s.

But a far more severe shock was just around the corner. Going into the third decade of the millennium, Singapore and the world were confronted by a 'bug' with far greater consequence than Y2K or SARS. A novel coronavirus had begun to spread within Asia in late 2019, and in January 2020, Singapore recorded its first case of COVID-19.[41] The virus spread rapidly within and across borders and the world was soon in the grip of a pandemic. By the end of 2020, more than 80 million people had been stricken globally, and nearly 2 million had died as a result.

To curb transmission of the virus, Singapore, together with many other countries, closed borders to most international travel and shut down large swathes of the economy except for services deemed 'essential' to daily living. The world experienced its worst recession since the Great Depression of the 1930s and Singapore's economy shrank by 5.4 per cent in 2020, the biggest drop since Independence. The worst-hit sectors of the economy were travel-related and consumer-facing businesses, such as aviation, retail, and food services, because of restrictions on people's movements; and construction, due to the stoppage of work as the virus spread among migrant-worker dormitories. The government allocated nearly S$100 billion in measures to combat the impact of the pandemic, and obtained the President's permission to draw on up to S$52 billion from the nation's reserves to fund these policies. As with past recessions, MAS eased monetary policy to soften the downturn but again, as in past downturns, fiscal policy bore the brunt of the responsibility for shoring up the economy's productive capacity and offsetting the social impact of the pandemic.

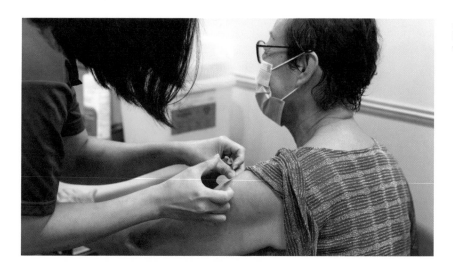

A senior citizen gets her jab at a COVID-19 vaccination centre.

The pandemic had the effect of accelerating the shift away from the use of physical currency in transactions towards electronic payments. When shopping in-store, many buyers and sellers opted for 'contactless' e-payment methods instead, as notes and coins are 'high contact' items that can potentially transmit the virus. During the circuit breaker,[42] many businesses were forced to adopt an online presence, while Singaporeans turned to purchasing goods and services more frequently online. On such platforms, the means to pay in currency is limited or non-existent. The bank DBS noted that 100,000 of their customers started online spending for the first time in the first quarter of 2020 as the virus began to spread.[43] However, the amount of currency in circulation has not declined; during uncertain times like these, the demand for physical notes as a store of value has risen instead, as we have previously seen in history.

MAS has played a pivotal role in managing and shaping the monetary and payments landscape, as it moved on from the physical into the digital era. As the preceding chapters have made clear, in the history of Singapore's money, the importance of physical currency and its issuance has waned over time while the importance of bank-created money and the role of central banks and monetary policy has become more prominent. Central banks and their monetary policies adopted in light of the Global Financial Crisis have had a long-term impact on the monetary and currency developments of the 2000s. At the same time, privately issued digital currencies have emerged, and they could potentially compete with 'traditional' forms of money – coins, notes and bank deposits. How digital currencies will shape the evolution of money in Singapore in the post-pandemic world remains to be seen.

The story continues – of money in all its myriad forms, the policies put in place by governments, the institutions that issue it, and the sociopolitical milieu of which it is a vital part.

NOTES

CHAPTER 1: CURRENCY AND TRADING NETWORKS IN EARLY SOUTHEAST ASIA

1   Liu (1988), p. 19; Boardman (2000), pp. 717–29.
2   Nishijima (1986), pp. 579-80.
3   Hall (1985), p. 36.
4   Hansman (1985), p. 25.
5   Hall (1985), pp. 36-38.
6   Suresh (2001), pp. 976-85; Higham (1991), p. 244; *International Business Times* 4 October 2016; Li (2015), pp. 284-5; Hall (1985), p. 36.
7   Hall (2010), p. 111; Hall (2016), p. 388.
8   Stavorinus (1798), p. 225; Osbeck (1771), Vol 2, pp. 105–106, 110, 142.
9   Osbeck (1771), pp. 41, 142; Stavorinus (1798), p. 224.
10   Kearney (2004), pp. 2, 12; Tuckey (1815), p. 144.
11   Baldaeus (1672), p. 573.
12   Ng (2017), pp. 6-15.
13   Ng (2017), pp. 7, 11.
14   Qin and Xiang (2011), pp. 308-336; Nik Hassan Shuhaimi Nik Abd Rahman (1991), p. 7. It was noted that under Srivijaya, ships sailing through the Straits of Malacca and the east coast of the Malay Peninsula had relatively safe passage.
15   Nik Hassan Shuhaimi Nik Abd Rahman (1991), pp. 7, 23, 26. The centralising of the Indies trade at a single node at Palembang, and the order brought about by Srivijaya's extension of control, had made the region more conducive to foreign trade. Song China had noticed this and to show its approval, Srivijaya was granted 'preferential status'.
16   Lehman (2013).
17   van Aelst (1995), p. 363.
18   van Aelst (1995), pp. 361–2.
19   Miksic and Goh (2017), p. 447.
20   van Aelst (1995), p. 362.
21   Christie (1996), pp. 268–9.
22   Christie (1996), pp. 268–9; van Aelst (1995), pp. 361–8. After 1127, less than 200 million copper coins were produced annually.
23   van Aelst (1995), pp. 367–8.
24   van Aelst (1995), p. 362.
25   van Aelst (1995), p. 368.
26   Christie (1996), p. 270; van Aelst (1995), pp. 361–9.
27   van Aelst (1995), p. 361.
28   According to Arjan van Aelst: 'There is mention of coins with a Chinese appearance, which are certainly not Chinese, however, as their inscriptions read "pang-ki-lan pao" and "su-tan ju-hao". The Chinese characters for this are a phonetic rendering of the Javanese words for "coin of the prince" and "treasure of the sultan"'. See van Aelst (1995), pp. 377, 387.
29   van Aelst (1995), p. 369.
30   Hall (2011), p. 273. In Kenneth Hall's view, the copper coins mixed with tin and lead were the local Chinese traders' response to China's ban on exporting copper.
31   Hanitsch (1903), p. 184.
32   van Aelst (1995), p. 372.
33   Ng (2017), pp. 16-18. Malacca declined as an entrepôt following its 1511 subjugation by the Portuguese, who practised monopolistic policies at the port city.
34   Dakers (1939), pp. 1-12.
35   Dakers (1939), p. 10.
36   Hanitsch (1903), p. 185; Shaw and Mohd Kassim Haji Ali (1970), p. 15. William Shaw and Mohd Kassim noted that cowrie shells were also current in ancient Malacca as subsidiary currency used for 'minor purchases'. Vasco da Gama observed in 1498 that 'native money' was composed of the staple commodity of the Straits, namely tin. See Chalmers (1893), p. 381.
37   Miksic and Goh (2017), p. 500. All the coinages of the Malaccan Sultanate are described and discussed in Dakers (1939).
38   Rasanubari Asmaramah (1999/2001), p. 298.
39   Rasanubari Asmaramah (1999/2001), p. 299. For a more detailed description of all coinage minted at Trengganu, see Bucknill (1923).
40   Asmaramah (1999/2001), p. 300.
41   Borschberg (2018), para 6.
42   While the Malay Annals were written in the 17th century, many of its interpretations are based on readings of translations.
43   Crawfurd (1820), p. 481; Anderson (1824), pp. 22–3; Phipps (1836), p. 261; Montgomery (1837), pp. 138–9, 157; Newbold, p.273; Cameron, (1865), pp. 6–7.
44   Linehan (1947).
45   Wolters (1970).
46   de Barros, J. and de Couto, D. (1788) , pp. 3-4.
47   *Daoyi zhilüe*, p. 27 (including the cover); quoted in Winstedt (1969), p. 8. This state of affairs had not changed by the 17th century. Jacques de Coutre, a Dutch trader who travelled the Malayan Archipelago in the early 1600s, noted the presence of numerous Orang Laut along the old Straits of Singapore. They were also fishermen who traded provisions (barter) for goods on board passing vessels. Coutre's cautionary remarks about these boat people is telling: 'They are treacherous people by nature; for this reason we deal with them very carefully and with weapons in our hands, because it has happened that they were allowed to come aboard our ships in such numbers, ostensibly to sell fresh fish, and in the blink of an eye they rose and killed everyone aboard.' Quoted in Borschberg (2014), pp. 78–9.
48   Cortesão (1944), p. 229.
49   Cortesão (1944), p. 264.
50   Rouffaer and Winstedt (1922), p. 258; Linehan (1947), p. 123.
51   Cortesão (1944), p. 264.
52   A line from *Suma Oriental*. See Cortesão (1944), p. 232.
53   Miksic (2013), pp. 266, 287.
54   Miksic (2013), p. 20.
55   Low Mei Gek, Cheryl-Ann, 'Singapore from the 14th to 19th Century', in Miksic and Low (2004), pp. 20, 31; Miksic (2013), pp. 351–2.
56   Heng Thiam Soon, Derek, 'Economic networks between the Malay region and the hinterlands of Quanzhou and Guangzhou: Temasek and the Chinese ceramics and foodstuffs trade', in Miksic and Low (2004), pp. 73–85.
57   Raffles's letter to Marsden, 31 January 1819. Raffles noted that the Old Lines of Singapore could still be traced. See Raffles (1830), p. 376.
58   Crawfurd (1828), p. 44.
59   (1820), *Asiatic Journal and Monthly Register for British India and its Dependencies, July-December*, p. 477. Besides the Chinese coins, China-ware and shells were also found. The Chinese inscription on the coin was translated by Rev. Samuel Milton, the resident English missionary in Singapore who was operating the printing press of the London Missionary Society. See O'Sullivan (1984), pp. 73-79. The coins were from the last years of the Northern Song (960–1127) period.
60   Iron rusts, while bronze does not.
61   Crawfurd (1828), p. 47; Crawfurd (1856), p. 402. Crawfurd repeats his error on the year 967 coin in his *Descriptive Dictionary of the Indian Islands* (1856). Also, Chinese coins would still be found (dug up) in great numbers throughout Java (1820s). Bali was still using Chinese money in the early 1820s.
62   (1836), *Asiatic Journal and Monthly Register for British and*

Foreign India, China and Australasia, January-April, p. 203.

63 (1820), *Asiatic Journal and Monthly Register for British India and its Dependencies*, July-December, p. 477.

64 (1820), *Asiatic Journal and Monthly Register for British India and its Dependencies*, July-December, p. 477.

65 For example, Bantam, Malacca, Acheh, Palembang, etc. Western colonial polities such as Batavia, Penang, Rhio and Bencoolen had the same settlement pattern. The chief of the Chinese in the latter would normally be called Captain (Kapitan) China.

66 One may cite Wang Dayuan's *Daoyi zhilüe*, compiled in 1349, as a counterexample. He observed that the 'Tan ma-hsi [Temasek] barbarians', the Orang Laut (aborigines), had mixed with the Chinese – 'the natives and the Chinese dwell side by side'. Quoted in Colless (1969), p. 2. Wang's statement and observation here is ambiguous and problematic. First, could Wang have meant that the two different communities were next to each other or the peoples lived side by side? In either case, it was most unlikely since the aborigines were 'boat people' (living on in small boats), and the Chinese were not. Secondly, these aborigines were known to have engaged in piracy when needed. How would they have co-existed with economically active neighbours?

67 Heng (2006), pp. 195, 198–9. Derek Heng contends that this explains why large quantities of such coins were excavated in Kota Cina on the northeast coast of Sumatra. It also had a substantial domiciled Chinese population. Heng also argues that Temasek's status as a regional emporium necessitated the use of copper coins for trade with its two other major partners, Vietnam and Java.

68 Heng (2006), p. 201.

69 Although the founding of Singapura by Sang Nila Utama is dated as coming before the island was known as Temasek, the island is named 'Temasek' in some of the earliest contemporary accounts of the island, such as Wang Dayuan's *Zhilüe* in the 14th century. The Malay Annals, which introduced the term 'Singapura', were composed later, between the 15th and 16th centuries. *Singapore Free Press*, 29 June 1837.

70 *Singapore Free Press*, 29 June 1837.

71 A number of Chinese porcelain items were dredged up in the Kallang basin in the 1960s. These date from the late 16th century (Wan Li period), when the capital was at Johor Lama. See Miksic (2013), pp. 409-10; Kwa Chong Guan, '16th-century underglaze blue porcelain sherds from the Kallang Estuary', in Miksic and Low (2004), pp. 86–94.

72 Kearney (2004), pp. 94–5. During Admiral's Cheng Ho great Ming voyages to visit the major cities of the Indo-Pacific region, he stopped over at Malacca in 1405. Malacca was already well-known to the Chinese prior to this visit. China made Malacca its preferred port of call in the East Indies as the region's rice and pepper produce had been exported from this port city.

73 The Portuguese conquered Malacca in order to outflank Venice; as the Portuguese Tomé Pires wrote in 1515, 'Whoever is lord of Malacca has his hand on the throat of Venice.' See Cortesão (1944), p. 287.

74 Ziegenbalg (1718), Part 2, pp. 3, 9.

75 Shaw and Mohd Kassim Haji Ali (1970), p. 16.

76 Codrington (1924), p. 92.

77 Kerr (1824), Vol. VIII, pp. 141, 178.

78 Kerr (1824), Vol. VIII, pp. 258-9.

79 António Galvão, 'The Discoveries of the World from their First Original, unto the Year of Our Lord 1555', in Clarke (1803), p. 306.

80 Biswas (2007), pp. 147–9. See also Deyell (2010). In fact, cowries were valued from ancient times. They have been found in Shang period tombs in Henan. See Yang (2011), pp. 3–4.

81 Stavorinus (1798), pp. 460-62.

82 Cowrie shells were one of the items listed (in the press) in the Price Currents of 1830s Singapore.

83 Codrington (1924), p.102.

84 Moisés (2005), pp. 82–3.

85 Moisés (2005), p. 76.

86 Moisés (2005), p. 75.

87 Codrington (1924), p. 92. Gold specie was only struck at the Goa mint.

88 Boxer (1970), pp. 459-60.

89 By the mid-16th century, Portugal's empire was in decline. While its export of gold from West Africa had diminished, the import of Asian spices to Lisbon had fallen from two million cruzados (silver) to 3,000 in the 1630s. The Portuguese Crown was in debt, owing three million cruzados in the 1550s, and was bankrupt by 1560. Meanwhile, the maintenance of its North African outposts and requirements of its navy added to the financial strain on the empire. Even the produce of its colonies could hardly cover half of their expenses, let alone the cost of transporting goods from the East. See Scammell (1981), pp. 290–94.

90 Barnes (1911), p. 30.

91 Kerr (1824), Vol. VIII, pp. 183–4.

92 Baldaeus (1672), Vol. 3, p. 731.

93 Stavorinus (1798), pp.71–2; Kerr (1824), Vol. VIII, p. 223. British shippers were advised that they ought to use their shipment of rice or opium as ballast, or if these had been sold, '24,000 dollars in species' would suffice. And when specie was not available, they could use 'sand or red stones' which could be got at Penang. See Elmore (1802), pp.164–5, 305. In the mid-17th century, the Dutch had also used copper imports from Japan as ballast, instead of stones, in the homeward-bound vessels. See Blussé (1996), p. 70.

94 Borschberg (2018), para. 25.

95 Borschberg (2018), para. 32, quoting Kwa (2017), p. 53.

96 It was during the Eighty Years War of Dutch Independence (1568–1648) that the nations of Northern Europe broke free of Spanish rule. Holland's emergence as a strong trading nation during the conflict and the period of truce (1609-1621) saw the balance of trade between the two nations favour the Dutch. This resulted a trade deficit for Spain and a northward drain of Spanish silver. It was during the truce that Holland was able to secure Spanish silver (bullion) which it used strategically in its trades. See Israel (1990), pp. 3-7, 140–41. Geoffrey Scammell added that Holland also acquired silver from Spain through 'piracy and illicit trade and then directly from Cadiz after the peace of 1648'. See Scammell (1981), pp. 294, 393, 406.

97 Rahusen-de Bruyn Kops (2002), pp. 536–57.

98 Scammell (1981), p. 393.

99 Rahusen-de Bruyn Kops (2002), pp. 537-8.

100 Bucknill (1931), pp. 18–35, 50.

101 Rahusen-de Bruyn Kops (2002), pp. 538, 540, 576; de Vries and van der Woude (1997), pp. 430–33. By the 1650s, the VOC's share of Japanese bullion was significantly smaller than Zheng's. From 1656, Zheng's fleet of junks were trading directly with the East Indies, and in 1662, the VOC lost to Zheng its strategic base at Formosa (Taiwan). Zheng's revolt in China also led to such turmoil that it ended the VOC's direct silk trade with China after 1666. By 1670–80, the share of the Japanese and Holland bullion at Batavia had fallen to 37.2–33.9 per cent.

102 Scammell (1981), p. 408.

103 Rahusen-de Bruyn Kops (2002), pp. 538, 540, 576; de Vries and van der Woude (1997), pp. 430–33.

104 van Zanden and Marks (2012), p. 39.

105 Wolters (2015), pp. 113–14.

106 Raffles (1830), pp. 244, xxvii.

107 See Bligh (1792), pp. 257–9.

108 Elmore (1802), pp. 49–50. European traders were told that

they would receive payment in specie, tin or pepper if they smuggled (privately) in the Indies. Contraband trade was conducted by Chinese junks coming from the Philippines and the Celebes.

109　A rixdollar was a denomination of the Dutch currency in Holland that was of greater value than a stiver. In the East Indies, however, it served as an accounting unit.

110　Stavorinus (1798), Vol. 1, pp. 266–7.

111　Wolters (2015), p.114.

112　Wolters (2015), p.114.

113　Wolters (2015), p.114.

114　Wolters (2015), p.114.

115　Wolters (2015), pp.114-15.

116　Wolters (2015), p.115.

117　Marsden (1811, reprinted 2012).

118　Osbeck (1771), Vol. 1, pp. 177–8, 234, 241, 243.

119　Osbeck (1771), Vol 1, pp. 261–2.

120　Wolters (2015), p.116.

121　van Zanden (2007), p. 171.

122　'Java currency and finance', in Moor (1837), pp. 163–71; *Singapore Chronicle*, 7 June 1827.

123　Pridmore (1975), p.10.

124　A country trader was one who had received a licence from the East India Company to trade.

125　Hamilton (1727, 1739), Vol. 2, p. 98.

126　Hayes (1754), p. 413; Kelly (1835), p. 101; Mortimer (1766), section on *Mon* (Money), *East Indies* (to mean Eastern India).

127　Wilkinson (1941), p.109.

128　Tuckey (1815), Vol. 3, p. 491.

129　Hill (1922), p. 60; see also Bucknill (1931), pp. 163, 179-80, 184, 186.

130　Pridmore (1975), pp. 10, 13, 17. For fractional parts of a Spanish dollar, the silver coinage had ½ dollar, ¼ dollar and $^{1}/_{10}$ dollar, while the copper pice were in denominations of $^{1}/_{10}$, ½ and 1 cent.

131　Pridmore (1975), pp. 11, 17. The imported copper coins were worth 50 per cent less than current coins. As a result, the higher-value copper coins were carried off the island, and the less-valued imported coins filled the Penang treasury.

132　Ellis (1895), p. 135.

133　Ellis (1895), p.136.

134　Bucknill (1925), p. 3.

135　Bucknill (1931), p. 243.

136　Ellis (1895), pp. 135-53.

137　The Malayan islands provided a vast range of goods. Among them were gold dust, ivory, tin, birds' nests, wax, dammer, rice, rattan, sharks' fins, maws, pepper, dragon's blood, camphor, sago, mace, cloves, nutmegs, copper, cinnamon, wood oil, benzoin, sandalwood, etc. See Tuckey (1815), p. 490. At the heart of the region's spice cultivation were the Moluccas (Motir, and Makian). See Kearney (2004), pp. 4, 44, 59.

138　Pridmore (1975).

CHAPTER 2: COMPANY, EMPORIUM AND EMPIRE

1　C.O. Blagden, 'The foundation of the settlement', in Makepeace et al (1991), p. 8.

2　In the Malay world, the Temenggong would have held a cabinet-level position in the Sultan's kingdom, being in charge of local security, akin to a police chief.

3　Yule and Burnell, (1996), pp. 345–46.

4　Chew and Lee (1996), pp. 36–7.

5　A Presidency was an administrative district of British India. Each Presidency had its own governor. The main Indian Presidencies in the 19th century were Madras, Bengal and Bombay. Penang was raised to a Presidency

in 1805. British Bencoolen was an Indian Presidency from 1763 to 1785.

6　This honorific title was first seen throughout the Indian papers and English magazines in the early 1820s. See *Calcutta Monthly Journal* (1822), p. 703.

7　Buckley (1984), p. 71.

8　As seen in Chapter 1, although Malacca was a vibrant port city while under Portuguese rule, the Dutch chose to develop Batavia instead of Malacca after they had gained control of the Portuguese possessions in the Malay Archipelago.

9　Mercantilism was an economic model of trade, favoured in the 16–18th centuries, that encouraged nations to accumulate wealth by maximising exports. The aim was to achieve a net positive inflow of precious commodities such as silver and gold. Mercantilism also promoted the use of trade controls such as the imposition of monopolies on items of trade. It favoured strong state control and regulation.

10　Towards the latter part of the 18th century, a new thinking arose amongst western philosophers and economists with regard to the very nature of imperialism, politics and the economy in Europe. They argued against the old mercantilist system and championed free trade. The proponents of free trade believed that unrestricted commerce and deregulation would encourage individual effort and prosperity, and this would promote the prosperity of the nation as a whole.

11　Thomas Stamford Raffles (1781–1826), in his two-volume *The History of Java*, referred several times to economist and philosopher Adam Smith (1723–1790) and his landmark work, the *Wealth of Nations* (1776). See Raffles (1817). Some scholars have questioned the extent of Raffles's liberalism as he was also an imperialist – they cite the invasion of Java and the occupation of Singapore. See Ng (2018).

12　Hall (2010), p. 388.

13　In early 1820, there were usually 30–40 proas and junks in the harbour waiting to offload pepper and tin to EIC ships sailing to China. At this point, the Dutch became restrictive, not even allowing boats filled with fruits to sail to Singapore. See (1820) *Asiatic Journal and Monthly Register for British India and its Dependencies*, July-December, p. 293.

14　Phrase taken from Frost (2005).

15　Also reported in the *London Paper*, according to correspondence from Singapore dated 21 October 1821, the monthly imports several months before the letter was 'calculated to exceed $580,000 [Spanish dollars] on the average'. See (1822) *Asiatic Journal and Monthly Register for British India and its Dependencies*, January–June, p. 620.

16　Master Attendant Statements of Import and Export in Singapore, April 1820–April 1821, produced in Cowan (1950), pp. 112–17. According to Buckley, quoting the Marquis of Lansdowne, the trade at Singapore in 1822 (imports and exports) was $8,468,000. See Buckley (1902), p. 71. The Asiatic Journal estimate for Singapore's 1822 trade value was $8,496,172, with imports at $3,610,206 and exports at $3,172,332, and the amount not on official returns having been at $1,713,634. See (1823) *Asiatic Journal and Monthly Register for British India and its Dependencies*, July–December, p. 246. The Chinese junks arriving at Singapore in the early 1820s were from Canton, Amoy, Cochin-China and eastern islands. See Finlayson (1826), p. 69.

17　Crawfurd (1828), p. 536.

18　(1825), *Asiatic Journal and Monthly Register for British India and its Dependencies*, July–December, p. 467.

19　(1825), *Asiatic Journal and Monthly Register for British India and its Dependencies*, July-December, p. 709; Cowan (1950), pp. 112–18. European ships had yet to carry large volumes of opium through and from Singapore in 1821, as is reflected in the returns of 'square-rigged vessels' for August 1821. Officially, the three items most shipped by European vessels between China and the Straits in that year were tobacco, cotton and sundries. In reality, as the EIC still had a monopoly over the tea and opium trade with China, many private traders dealing in these commodities had to resort to smuggling, and would not have declared such cargo to the Master Attendant at Singapore. The English exported tobacco to China from the 18th century to earn much-needed revenue. Yet, it was still necessary to trade opium for tea at Canton to help finance their China Trade. However, due to the harm caused by opium addiction, the Chinese emperors proclaimed this import an illegal commodity in a series of edicts (1723, 1799, 1814 and 1831). In 1796, the Chinese government threatened to ban the trade in tea if the EIC did not cease exporting opium to China. The Company circumvented this obstacle by selling the opium in India to private English merchants who then smuggled the illegal commodity into China. See Miron and Feige (2005).

20 (1827), *Asiatic Journal and Monthly Register for British India and its Dependencies*, July-December, p. 380; *Singapore Chronicle*, 1 March 1827.

21 The EIC had to use bullion from the home country to purchase Chinese tea. This was essentially an outflow of silver for Britain. However, the tea monopoly held by the EIC allowed it to set the price for the tea it sold without fear of competition, thereby earning it significant profits.

22 Thornton (1825), pp. 319, 324, 344, 346.

23 Under the East India Company, a Resident was an official in charge of a Residency, an administrative unit subordinate to a Presidency. When Singapore came under the control of the Colonial Office in London, the post of Resident was replaced by that of Governor.

24 Crawfurd (1828), pp. 40–41.

25 Thornton (1825), pp. 319, 324, 344, 346.

26 *The London Paper*, 18 December 1820.

27 Correspondence in *The Asiatic Journal*, 10 August 1820.

28 Buckley (1902, 1984), p. 69.

29 Even to ship cargo or items from Singapore, the shipping charges needed to be in the currency of the destination. Rupees and annas had to be paid for shipping to India, Spanish dollars for shipping to China and guilders for Batavia (East Indies). See shipping rates in *Singapore Chronicle*, 9 January, 3, 17 April 1834.

30 *Straits Times*, 26 June 1855. A case in point: when Spanish authorities at Manila acquired an EIC ship there, the Spanish Governor-General transferred payment for the ship, $2,159, to the Singapore treasury. See *Singapore Chronicle*, 23 February 1829.

31 Straits Settlements Record L15, No. 43, 22 April 1823, Farquhar to Messrs. Harrington & Guthrie. The business of Alexander Guthrie and Thomas Talbot Harrington started in 1821 when Guthrie arrived to work for Harrington. The firm was named Harrington & Co. They became partners on 1 February 1823, selling British piece goods to the merchants of Singapore. However, the partnership did not survive its first year, and Guthrie then ran the company on his own. The company was renamed Guthrie & Co. in 1833.

32 Such transactions were essentially a source of income for the administration.

33 In 1822, Singapore's export of gold and silver bullion to Bengal amounted to $424,025. This increased to $539,864 a year later. See (1825), *Asiatic Journal and Monthly Register for British India and its Dependencies*, January-June 1825, p. 709.

34 Raffles's instructions to Farquhar, 6 February 1819, para. 8, 10, 14, 22, 23. Quoted in Buckley (1984), pp. 40, 42–44, 49.

35 *Straits Times*, 26 June 1855. The pay of the Assistant Resident, Assistant Engineer, Assistance Master Attendant, among others, were all in Spanish dollars.

36 Straits Settlements Records L4, 251–52, 247; L5, 330-32, 447-48, 348; L7, 98-99; L8, 140-41, 200-201; L9, 58. The funds collected were in Spanish Dollars.

37 *Singapore Free Press*, 16 January 1845; *Straits Times*, 28 October 1845.

38 *Straits Times*, 26 June 1855. This is likely to have been at Raffles's request or on his instruction, since payment of local wages and the accounts of Singapore submitted to him were to be in Spanish dollars. Besides, since the Indian Presidencies preferred rupees, there would have been no issue sending Spanish dollars to the eastern colonies where the currency had been the main trade dollar.

39 This is distinct from the funds of the Municipal Committee, which had its own treasurer. During the EIC period, the municipality deposited most of its surplus funds in the Oriental Bank. The Singapore treasury would have kept most of its holding liquid because it supported the movement of specie and bullion used in the China Trade. Traders on the island could purchase specie they required directly from the treasury. The Singapore treasury also sold bills of exchange or other government securities issued by the Indian treasury, to be paid in India. The distribution or circulation of specie or subsidiary coinages issued by the British authorities would also have been through the Singapore treasury, whether directly or through appointed banks. In all these transactions, the treasury would earn on the fees or discounts.

40 Buckley (1984), p. 60.

41 The pepper and gambier plantations operated by the Chinese were established mostly on grounds that were not allotted, or on previously occupied grounds that had not been surveyed by government revenue surveyors. By the mid-1830s, many of these gambier and pepper enterprises had become 'exhausted' and new plantations were started further north on the island. See Jackson (1968), p. 11.

42 Provisional Treaty 6 February 1819, Article 9. See Buckley (1984), pp. 39-40.

43 Raffles's instructions to Farquhar, 6 February 1819, paragraph 12. See Buckley (1984), p. 43.

44 Buckley (1984), pp. 59-60.

45 Straits Settlements Records L10, 314–15, 20 March 1820, 367–72, 5 May 1820; Buckley (1984), p. 63. Raffles did not respond immediately, but not because he rejected Farquhar's plan. He wanted more details of the regulations governing the licences to ensure that free trade was not affected.

46 Data collated from the following sources: *Singapore Chronicle*, 22 April 1830, 26 April 1832, 25 April 1833, 24 April 1834, 16 April, 9 July 1836; *Singapore Free Press*, 21 April 1836, 25 April 1839, 22 April 1841. The data for 1837 have yet to be found.

47 When currencies had to be purchased or imported for use locally, a premium on the actual value had to be added to cover the cost of transport, supply and demand considerations, etc. For example, if silver rupees were needed, a local merchant had to have Spanish dollars to purchase the equivalent in rupees, and he might receive as rupees 10 per cent less in value. This difference is the discount (rate).

48 This was made possible following the 1824 Anglo-Dutch Treaty which saw the British giving up Bencoolen in exchange for Dutch Malacca and Singapore confirmed as part of the British sphere of influence.

49 It was at this point that the Residents of each settlement became known as Resident Councillors (the three settlements' Residents had formed a council that advised the Governor at Penang).

50   Indian Currency. Hansard, HL Deb. 21 April 1856 vol. 141 cc. 1248–51; *Singapore Free Press*, 12 June 1856.

51   Cowan (1950), p. 21. The three main rupees in India were: Bengal (sicca rupee), Bombay (surat rupee), Madras (arcot rupee). See Laughlin (1893), p. 593.

52   Francis Light founded Penang on the principle of free trade in 1786. However, after a few years, import duties had to be introduced to cover the expenses of the settlement. See Das Gupta (1946), pp. 341, 349. In 1801, the free port experiment was abandoned by Governor George Leith as customs duties on imports and exports were required for government revenue. See Drake (2017), pp. 2–3; Chiang (1978), p. 4.

53   Buckley (1984), p. 71.

54   *Singapore Free Press*, 24 August 1837, 19, 26 October 1837; *Singapore Chronicle*, 24 January 1833. Till the mid-1830s, British India itself provided all kinds of rupees; each Presidency of India had its own rupee – Bengal Presidency (capital at Calcutta), Bombay Presidency (capital at Bombay), and Madras Presidency (capital at Madras). Even Penang, an Indian Presidency from 1805 to 1830, had its own coinage, albeit not a rupee nor widely circulated. The Indian rupees also had their subsidiary coinage (one rupee was equal to 16 annas, and each anna was worth 4 paisas).

55   *Singapore Chronicle*, 7 June 1827. The circulation of paper notes reached a peak in the late 18th and early 19th centuries when the wars in Europe led to a shortage of silver specie across the continent. Most European nations, including Britain, had issued paper money to cover the shortage of specie. Most of it was still in circulation after the end of the conflict.

56   Crawfurd had noted as early as 1825 that there had already been a great demand for bills by the 'public' as well as government (Crawfurd's letter dated 21 October 1825 – see *Straits Times*, 26 June 1855). Sub-treasuries also used private bills, especially when there were no government bills (from India) to be had, as 'paper currency' with which they too could remit monies without having to ship actual species, which carried risk as well as incurring cost.

57   In June 1828, private bills on London, 4 shillings and 2 pence (4s 2d) per Spanish dollar. In March 1827, private bill on Bengal at 198 sicca rupees for $100 at 80 days sight, on England at 4s 2d per $1 at 6 months sight, on Bombay at 210–212 rupees for $100. See *Singapore Chronicle*, 15 March 1827; (1828), *Asiatic Journal and Monthly Register for British India and its Dependencies*, July-December, p. 759.

58   *Singapore Chronicle*, 7 June 1827. Changing 'paper for silver', it was estimated, normally incurred a loss of 10–12 per cent.

59   *Singapore Chronicle*, 24 January 1833; India Office Record F/4/1730 Collection 69913, 1839. In 1839, the Governor of the Straits Settlements authorised the use of 'Mitchell's tables of exchange rates of Spanish dollars'.

60   The scarcity of money was said to have affected the opium trade. See *Singapore Chronicle*, 13 March 1828.

61   Unfortunately, Singapore was also exporting more doits than were imported for local use. See *Singapore Chronicle*, 7 October 1830. The figures exclude transactions with Penang and Malacca. In the 1830s, the natives of the East Indies also brought copper doits to Singapore to trade, and these were quickly taken up by Chinese and local merchants. See *Singapore Chronicle*, 21, 28 November 1835. It was in the context of this shortage that Merchant Tokens were minted for the conduct of the East Indies trade.

62   Wolters (2015), p. 118.

63   *Singapore Chronicle*, 7 June 1827, 13 March 1828.

64   *Singapore Chronicle*, 10 April 1828; (1828), *Asiatic Journal and Monthly Register for British India and its Dependencies*, July–December, p. 508.

65   *Singapore Chronicle*, 14 August 1834. It was remarked in the *Singapore Chronicle* three years earlier: 'In Consequence of the deficiency of the *Circulating Medium*, and the peculiar mode in which business is conducted in this settlement, scarcely any sales are made for cash; and, it being therefore impossible to give the cash price for almost any article, it must be observed that the quotations in Price Current are invariably made on supposition, that all sales are affected on a credit of three to six months, for payment in produce upon the principle the majority of the sales take place in this Market.' See *Singapore Chronicle*, 20 January 1831.

66   Headline statements attached to the *Commercial Remarks in the Singapore Chronicle* across 1835. In the Price Current in *Singapore Chronicle*, 1 January 1835: 'The majority of the sales which takes place in this Market, are effected on the principle of Barter for Produce, on Credit; and the quotations in this Price Current are made on that supposition. The Cash Price of Produce may be said to be 10 per cent, under the rates following; and if Piece Goods & etc are sold for cash (which is seldom practicable), it must 10 to 20 per cent under them. The Currency in which commercial transactions are calculated, is the Spanish Dollar divided into Cents.' In the Price Current in the *Singapore Chronicle*, 7 November 1835: 'It having been agreed at a Public Meeting of the Merchants of this Settlement, held on the 23rd April last, that all sales shall be effected on the principle of Cash, we shall in future – instead of barter quotations – give them at Cash rates. Almost all goods (more especially European manufactures) are sold at a credit of 2, 3 or 4 months, and all produce brought from natives, is for ready cash. The Currency in which commercial transactions are calculated, is the Spanish Dollar divided into Cents.' In the Report on the Market, *Singapore Chronicle*, 31 December 1835: 'All sales of European imports, can now be effected for payment in cash, and returns made in Bullion or Bills when produce is not preferred.'

67   *Singapore Chronicle*, 21 February 1835. The merchants realised that the market and godowns had been overstocked because the goods of the failed businesses had flooded the market, causing a fall in prices. Also, the credit system allowed local merchants to borrow to trade instead of using their own capital, and they took their time to repay these loans. So businesses in Singapore became heavily indebted, and when they folded, they threatened the financial viability of other firms. Consequently, in addition to the merchants' resolution that future trades should be in cash, they also specified that no credit should be given more than three months for settlement. If promissory notes were used in a transaction, the loan had to be paid within three days. These measures were to be strictly enforced. See also (1836), *Asiatic Journal and Monthly Register for British and Foreign India, China, and Australasia*, January-April, p. 28–29.

68   (1822), *Asiatic Journal and Monthly Register for British India and its Dependencies*, January-June, p. 620.

69   See *Singapore Free Press*, 23 January 1845; *Straits Times*, 22 April, 13 June 1846.

70   See *Singapore Free Press*, 3 March 1836.

71   See *Singapore Chronicle* 1 April 1837.

72   *Singapore Free Press*, 26 November, 3 December 1840; 11 November 1841; 3 February, 12 May 1842.

73   *Singapore Free Press*, 14 September 1843. There was no run on the bank.

74   *Straits Times*, 5 August 1845; 25 April, 13 May, 21 November 1846; March 1847; *Singapore Free Press*, 12 February, 15 October 1846. While the first banknote with the 'Singapore' imprint was issued by the Union Bank

of Calcutta when it established a branch on the island in 1840, the first locally incorporated bank to issue Singapore banknotes was the Oriental Bank (India) in 1849.

75 *Straits Times* 24 July 1849; *Singapore Free Press*, 10 May 1849.

76 *Straits Times*, 11 November 1851, 10 October 1854; *Singapore Free Press*, 7 November 1851.

77 Bank Charter Act, 1844, chapter 32: IV. 'All Persons may demand of the Issue Department Notes for Gold Bullion.' https://www.legislation.gov.uk/ukpga/Vict/7-8/32/enacted. The government had the authority to suspend the Act temporarily. It did so during the economic crises of 1847, 1857 and 1866.

78 Bank Charter Act 1844, chapter 32: III. 'Proportion of Silver Bullion to be retained in the Issue Department.' https://www.legislation.gov.uk/ukpga/Vict/7-8/32/enacted. Strictly speaking, the bullion requirement under the Bank Charter Act was applied to the Bank of England as part of the legislation giving it note-issuing powers. However, this had a ripple effect on other note-issuing institutions.

79 Bank Charter Act 1844, chapter 32: XVIII. 'Issuing Banks to render Accounts.' https://www.legislation.gov.uk/ukpga/Vict/7-8/32/enacted.

80 *Straits Times*, 23 October, 27 November 1855.

81 *Straits Times*, 8 January 1848.

82 *Singapore Free Press*, 24 August, 26 October 1849; 11 October, 6 December 1850. The Act IX of 1848 paved the way for the creation of a local Municipal Fund.

83 Wolters (2015), p. 121.

84 See *Singapore Free Press*, 28 November 1844.

85 *Singapore Free Press*, 27 July 1837; 3, 15 November 1838.

86 The Act XXII of 1844.

87 *Singapore Free Press*, 20 November 1862.

88 *Singapore Free Press*, 3 October, 12 December 1844; 16 January 1845.

89 *Singapore Free Press*, 16 June, 17, 24 July 1845; *Straits Times*, 22 April 1848.

90 Indian Office Records G34.

91 See *Singapore Free Press*, 23 October, 8 November 1845; *Straits Times*, 28 October 1845.

92 Section II of Act No. VI of 1847.

93 *Singapore Free Press*, 10 June 1847, 27 April 1848; *Straits Times*, 18 November 1846.

94 *Singapore Free Press*, 17 February, 27 April 1848.

95 *Singapore Free Press*, 17 February 1848.

96 Wolters (2015), p. 118.

97 Wolters (2015), p. 135.

98 *Singapore Free Press*, 10 June 1847.

99 *Singapore Free Press*, 10, 17 February 1848; 23, 30 March 1848; 27 April 1848.

100 Seah (1847), pp. 34–37.

101 *Singapore Free Press*, 26 November 1835; 10, 17 December 1835.

102 *Singapore Free Press*, 14 January 1836.

103 *Singapore Free Press*, 21 January 1836.

104 *Singapore Free Press*, 28 January, 21 April 1836.

105 *Singapore Chronicle*, 6 February 1836; *Singapore Free Press*, 4 February 1836. Meanwhile, fellow merchants in China lent their support to Singapore by publicly expressing the view that Bengal and the British government should 'pay their share' in the fight against piracy and should 'not just tax the colonies'! *Canton Register*, 12 March 1836; *Singapore Free Press*, 31 March 1836.

106 (1836), *Asiatic Journal and Monthly Register for British and Foreign India, China, and Australasia*, September-December, p. 268.

107 *Singapore Chronicle*, 25 March 1830. By mid-1836, the Glasgow East India Association had also petitioned the India Board in London against customs duties for Singapore.

108 In 1833, Calcutta announced plans to equalise the silver currency of India by creating a uniform Indian Rupee currency. See *Singapore Chronicle*, 1 August 1833.

109 Fort William, Proclamation of New Rupee, Act XVII of 1835 – The creation of the Company Rupee. See *Singapore Chronicle*, 24 October 1835; *Singapore Free Press*, 19, 26 November 1835. All Indian silver coinage rupees were standardised to the Madras rupee (180 grains and 11/12 fine), and the new Company rupee became the basis for the Indian currency system till 1893. Following this, merchants in Singapore held another public meeting in 1836 to discuss the implications of Calcutta's efforts to create a single rupee currency, which could be applied to Singapore. See *Singapore Free Press*, 23 June 1836.

110 *Singapore Chronicle*, 26 November 1836.

111 *Singapore Free Press*, 19 October 1837, 3 May 1838.

112 Act XI of 1854. *Singapore Free Press*, 17 November 1854, 3 July 1886.

113 *Straits Times*, 31 January 1854.

114 *Singapore Free Press*, 17 February 1854.

115 *Straits Times*, 10 October 1854.

116 *Singapore Free Press*, 1 December 1854.

117 *Singapore Free Press*, 25 June 1857. Straits Settlements Administrative Report for 1855-56.

118 *Singapore Free Press*, 16 October 1856.

119 *Straits Times*, 26 June 1855. This was the second time the Indian Government had attempted to ram through the imposition of a Stamp Act to raise revenue. The first was in March 1827. *Singapore Chronicle*, 29 March 1827.

120 *Singapore Free Press*, 29 January 1856; 19 February, 1, 21 May, 25 June 1857; 20 November 1862.

CHAPTER 3: FROM COMMODITY MONEY TO TOKENISATION

1 The First Opium War (1839–1842) was fought between China and Britain. In the Second Opium War (1856–1860), also known as the Arrow War, China fought Britain and France. The first war ended with the Treaty of Nanjing (1842) which ceded Hong Kong to Britain and the opening of 'treaty ports' to foreign trade: Canton, Amoy (Xiamen), Foochowfoo (Fuzhou), Ningpo (Ningbo) and Shanghai. This ended the Canton System, which had been operating since 1760. The Second Opium War ended in 1860. The Treaty of Tianjin (1858) led to more Chinese ports opening for foreign trade: Niuzhuang, Tamsui, Hankou, Nanjing, Haicheng and Penglai, Yantai and Yingkou. The 1860 Convention of Peking added Tianjin as a treaty port.

2 Cameron (1865), p. 179. Straits Settlements total imports-exports before and after the Opium Wars: 1833 £4,777,000; 1843 £6,727,000; 1863 £16,908,000. Singapore's share of the Straits Settlements China trade during these periods was consistently more than 80 per cent of the total.

3 Pioneering Singapore historian Mary Turnbull identified the period when the empire peaked as between 1867–1914. See Turnbull (1992), p. 76.

4 Klein (1968), pp. 53-68; Hall (1981), pp. 592–612.

5 Sadka (1968); Chew (1996), pp. 182–84.

6 The four Residential States were Selangor, Perak, Negeri Sembilan and Pahang.

7 Dollarisation refers to the situation where the currency of one territory – such as a dollar – is adopted as the currency of another territory. The latter would have no part in the decision processes behind the issuance and management of the currency, and its economy is said to be 'dollarised'.

8 The Government of India Act 1858 (21 and 22 Vict. c. 106) passed on 2 August 1858. It provided the powers for the liquidation of the EIC and the transfer of its functions in India to the British Crown.

9   Turnbull (1992), pp. 69–70.
10   The EIC copper coin issued in 1847 was dated 1845, the year the coin was sanctioned.
11   *Singapore Free Press*, 28 May 1857. Point made by the Singapore Chamber of Commerce in their petition to government dated 20 May 1857.
12   Essentially, India had refused to provide the Straits a decimal copper coinage. The Governor of Singapore added his voice to the chorus and stated that 100,000 dollars' worth of copper coins was needed. See *Singapore Free Press*, 28 May 1857; 13 May 1958; 22 January, 6 March 1859; *Straits Times*, 26 May 1857.
13   As one of its last acts, the EIC administration in India declared in March 1858 that it was aware of the dire situation faced by the Straits community. In fact, the Governor of Hong Kong, Sir John Bowring, had also made a similar request for local mints. Bowring requested the establishment of a mint in Hong Kong because Mexican dollars shipped to China from Britain incurred great costs – commission, insurance and freight charges. It was cheaper to have a mint at Hong Kong where sycee silver was in abundance. This request was also rejected. See *Singapore Free Press*, 4 October 1858. Due to the possibility that the Straits Settlements might be transferred to the Colonial Office, the Indian government was unwilling to expend resources on the Straits to create a mint and new dollar. See Pridmore (1975), p. 39.
14   *Singapore Free Press*, 13 May 1858.
15   *Singapore Free Press*, 22 January 1859.
16   *Singapore Free Press*, 3 March 1859.
17   *Singapore Free Press*, 3 January 1861.
18   This refers to the standardised Indian rupees issued from 1835. *Singapore Free Press*, 9 August 1860.
19   *Straits Times*, 18 May 1861.
20   The Indian Income Tax Act, Act XXXII of 1860, taxed income earned from landed property (rent and sales), from earnings of professionals and traders, income from capital gains from securities and income from salaries and pensions. See https://taxguru.in/income-tax/history-evolution-income-tax-act-india.html.
21   *Singapore Free Press*, 13 September, 30 August 1860.
22   *Straits Times*, 23 January, 1864.
23   *Singapore Free Press* 17 July, 23 October 1862.
24   *Singapore Free Press*, 23 Oct, 8 November 1862.
25   *Singapore Free Press*, 3 January 1865.
26   *Singapore Free Press*, 2 February 1865.
27   See *Singapore Free Press*, 9 August, 13 September 1860, 7 November 1864. Observations of Lord Canning, 9 November 1859. Minutes, Revenue of the Straits Settlements and the Straits Settlements Administrative Reports for 1858–9 and 1859–60. For revenue farm collections 1864–5, see *Singapore Free Press*, 9 April 1864.
28   *Straits Times*, 4 February 1908.
29   *Straits Times*, 7 May 1903, 4 February 1908.
30   Colonial troops were not necessarily stationed in the Straits for local defence. As a naval station, a role which Penang also played, Singapore was a stopover and logistic hub for the British military in the East. The convict establishment at Singapore housed prisoners convicted in India. It was not a local jail but functioned as a penal station outside India. This was the context of the local merchants' petition against the implementation of the Indian Income Tax Act in Singapore: see *Singapore Free Press*, 30 August 1860. For Straits Settlements Revenue and Civil, Convict, Military Liabilities 1858–64, see *Straits Times*, 1 June 1861, 1 July 1865; *Revenue and Expenditure of the Straits Settlements*, 1862–1863, 1863–1864.
31   See *Straits Times*, 1 June 1861, 1 July 1865.
32   *Singapore Free Press*, 28 April 1864.
33   Turnbull (1992), p.72.
34   Turnbull (1992), p. 73.
35   *Singapore Free Press*, 2 August 1866.
36   Turnbull (1992), p. 73.
37   Provision 2. '… no Dollar shall be legal-tender unless it be of the same fineness and intrinsic value as the Hong Kong Dollar, and be of not less than 415 grains Troy weight, and not injured or defaced.'
38   See de Soto (2009), p. 485.
39   Piatt (1904), p. 356.
40   *Singapore Free Press*, 19 January 1863. The actual coin was minted at the Heaton Mint in Birmingham under a contract from the Royal Mint. See http://ykleungn.tripod.com/anetviga/hk10c.htm.
41   *Straits Times*, 27 October 1865.
42   *Straits Times*, 27 October 1865.
43   These new subsidiary silver coins were popular and had been widely circulated. See *Singapore Free Press*, 20 December 1866.
44   *Singapore Free Press*, 10 March, 29 September 1864; *Straits Times*, 7 May 1903; Pridmore (1975), p. 40.
45   *Singapore Free Press* 10 March, 29 September 1864; *Straits Times* 7 May 1903.
46   *Straits Times*, 4 February 1908.
47   *Straits Times Overland Journal*, 20 May 1871. Straits Settlements Legislative Council Proceedings.
48   The Colonial Treasury came under the Colonial Office.
49   *Straits Times Overland Journal*, 25 October 1871.
50   *Straits Times*, 3 August 1872.
51   *Straits Times Overland Journal*, 1 February 1872; *Straits Times*, 27 January 1872.
52   The exception was the Post Office Savings Bank, which was a truly Singapore (Straits Settlements government) bank.
53   *Straits Times Overland Journal*, 9 August 1873.
54   *Singapore Free Press*, 20, 27 September 1855.
55   *Straits Times*, 23, 25 April 1846.
56   The three exchange banks in Singapore often mentioned by scholars were the Chartered Bank, Oriental Bank and Mercantile Bank. According to Drake, '…these were "exchange banks" rather than deposit and loan institutions'. See Drake (1969), p. 14. In fact, most bank branches in Singapore offered a full range of services and not just exchange.
57   For example, the Mercantile Bank bought and sold bills of exchange, granted letters of credit, had current deposit accounts (no commission and interest), fixed deposits with 3, 6, 12 months offering 4, 5, and 6 per cent interest respectively, discount local bills if two sureties were provided or if secured by deposit of collateral security, and issued Circular Notes to travellers – payable in Europe, Egypt and Australian colonies. See *Straits Times*, 23 October 1855.
58   *Singapore Free Press*, 24 February 1859.
59   *Singapore Daily Times*, 12 May 1882.
60   '… "exchange banks" were restricted to providing the means of making transactions between traders using different currencies': see Citizendium in https://en.citizendium.org/wiki/Banking; Malavika Nair give emphasis to the 'chartered' nature of these banks - the 'Exchange Banks' were 'chartered to handle foreign exchange'– see Nair (2011). 'Workings of a nineteenth century indigenous banking system: a case in support of free banking', workshop paper, Economics Department, Suffolk University, published 2011 in https://econfaculty.gmu.edu/pboettke/workshop/Spring2011/Nair.pdf.
61   Bank Charter Act 1844, chapter 32: IV: 'All Persons may demand of the Issue Department Notes for Gold Bullion.' https://www.legislation.gov.uk/ukpga/Vict/7-8/32/enacted. The government had the authority to suspend the Act temporarily. It did so during the economic crises of 1847, 1857 and 1866.
62   Bank Charter Act 1844, chapter 32: III: 'Proportion of Silver

Bullion to be retained in the Issue Department.' https://www.legislation.gov.uk/ukpga/Vict/7-8/32/enacted.

63 Bank Charter Act 1844, chapter 32: XVIII. 'Issuing Banks to render Accounts.' https://www.legislation.gov.uk/ukpga/Vict/7-8/32/enacted.

64 See *Straits Times*, 25 November 1876; *Straits Times Overland Journal*, 30 November 1876. In reality, the 'world' was undergoing another economic downturn – the Panic of 1873. The Long Depression (1873–96) saw a global recession that precipitated the demise of the silver dollar, the transition onto the gold standard for many nations, and the emergence of government notes as a more viable paper currency than banknotes. See Klitgaard and Narron (2016).

65 The Mercantile Bank had a profit of £102,613 in 1875, offered 8% to each shareholder. The Chartered Bank, with a profit of £71,988 for the year passed, gave 5%, while the Oriental Bank Oriental Bank, with a profit of £174,070, offered 11%. See *Straits Times*, 27 May 1876.

66 *Straits Times Overland Journal*, 2 June 1878; *Straits Times*, 1 June 1878.

67 Muirhead (1996), chapter 10.

68 A year prior to 1878, the Mercantile Bank was already laden with bad debts. It had advanced a great sum to a Batavia firm which provided its sugar as security. Then sugar prices fell. The bank then sold a large portion of the sugar to another firm which also failed. See *Straits Times Overland Journal*, 2 June 1878; *Straits Times*, 1 June 1878.

69 *Straits Times Overland Journal*, 27 May 1879.

70 *Straits Times Overland Journal*, 13 May 1876.

71 For example, Eichengreen and Flandreau (1998), and Meissner (2005).

72 N. Shivam, 'History of Indian currency: five periods', in https://www.economicsdiscussion.net/india/indian-currency/history-of-indian-currency-5-periods/21246

73 *Straits Times Overland Journal*, 2 June 1878; *Straits Times*, 1 June 1878.

74 *Straits Times Overland Journal*, 27 May 1879; *Daily Times*, 23 May 1879.

75 *Singapore Daily Times*, 15 March 1880.

76 *Singapore Daily Times*, 15 March 1880.

77 *Singapore Daily Times*, 12 May 1882.

78 *Singapore Daily Times*, 9 November, 6, 29 December 1877.

79 *Singapore Free Press*, 13 December 1884.

80 *Straits Times Overland Journal*, 31 October, 19 November 1881. *Straits Times Weekly Issue*, 6 August 1884. It was specified that the notes were to be fully payable in specie coins on demand.

81 *Straits Times Overland Journal*, 3, 10, 17 March 1880; *Straits Times Weekly Issue*, 14 May 1884.

82 *Straits Times Weekly Issue*, 14 May 1884. The withdrawal of the one-dollar HSBC banknotes in circulation being made a condition for opening a branch in Singapore perhaps implies that these notes were also to be found circulating in Singapore. Merchants who had business tractions with Hong Kong were unlikely to reject these notes when they received them, especially when subsidiary currencies were generally in short supply.

83 *Straits Times Weekly Issue*, 14 May 1884.

84 *Singapore Daily Times*, 4 May 1880; *Singapore Daily Times*, 25 March 1881; *Straits Times Weekly Issue*, 20 June 1883; *Straits Times*, 19 May 1884; *Straits Times Weekly Issue*, 20 August 1884; *Daily Advertiser*, 7 October 1890; *Singapore Free Press* (weekly), 1 September 1891; *Singapore Free Press*, 7 July 1893; *Singapore Free Press*, 16 December 1893; *Singapore Free Press*, 20 May 1893; *Straits Times*, 6 Sep 1894; envelopes 1,000 pc 75 cents 1896 *Singapore Free* (Weekly) 24 Mar 1896; *Mid-Day Herald and Daily Advertiser*, 15 November 1897.

85 *Daily Advertiser*, 12 June 1891.

86 See *Straits Times*, 9 November 1872; *Singapore Free Press*, 13, 17 June 1892.

87 *Straits Times*, 29 June 1897.

88 See *Singapore Daily Times*, 13 May, 10 June 1882; *Straits Times Weekly Issue*, 29 January, 31 May, 9 August, 4 October, 3 November, 8 December, 29 December 1883, 23 February, 1 March 1884.

89 *Straits Times Overland Journal*, 3, 10, 17 March 1880. Banknote circulation reached a milestone in mid-1886. By May 1886, Straits banks had 4,346,417 dollars' worth of banknotes in circulation. By September 1892, the total value of banknotes circulated had fallen to 3,438,088 dollars. See *Straits Times Weekly Issue*, 1 July 1886, 7 June 1889; *Straits Times* 30 August 1886, 28 October 1889; *Singapore Free Press* 26 June, 21 August, 4 September 1886; *Daily Advertiser*, 31 October 1892. The general decade-long economic slowdown and run on banks in 1892 were probably responsible for the decline in the use of banknotes. When the British trade dollar was introduced in the latter half of the 1890s, banknotes in circulation would decline even further.

90 *Straits Times Overland Journal*, 3 March 1880.

91 Muirhead (1996), chapter 10. Following a falling off in business in 1878, the Oriental Bank was inundated by bad debts the year after. Its investments in coffee crops in Ceylon also failed at this time. Losses mounted and continued into 1882. *Straits Times Weekly Issue*, 17 November 1883.

92 *Straits Times Weekly Issue*, 28 May 1884.

93 *Singapore Free Press* (weekly), 8 December 1896.

94 *Straits Times*, 5 May 1884.

95 This accolade was universally acknowledged in the Straits. See *Straits Times Overland Journal*, 2 June 1878; *Straits Times*, 1 June 1878.

96 *Straits Times Weekly Issue*, 21 May 1884.

97 *Straits Times Weekly Issue*, 28 May 1884.

98 *Straits Times Weekly Issue*, 7 May 1884.

99 *Straits Times Weekly Issue*, 7, 14 May, 16 July 1884; *Straits Times*, 5, 7 May, 11 October 1884.

100 Muirhead (1996).

101 *Singapore Daily Times*, 13 May, 10 June 1882; *Straits Times Weekly Issue* 29 January, 31 May, 9 August, 4 October, 3 November, 8 December, 29 December 1883, 23 February, 1 March 1884.

102 *Singapore Free Press*, 13 June 1892; *Singapore Free Press* (weekly), 14 June 1892; *Daily Advertiser* 14 June 1892.

103 http://bankingmergers.blogspot.com/2018/09/great-britain-india-hong-kong-bank_7.html; *Straits Times Weekly Issue*, 11 June 1893.

104 *Singapore Free Press*, 13 December 1884.

105 *Straits Times*, 30 September, 31 December 1895; *Singapore Free Press* (weekly), 3 November 1896.

106 *Straits Times*, 10 July, 21 May 1898.

107 The first Savings Bank in Malaya was started in Penang in 1833, following the establishment of a similar institution at Calcutta. See Buckley (1984), pp. 231–32; *Singapore Chronicle* 14, 21 November, 12, 19 December 1833; 9, 16 January 1834; *Singapore Free Press*, 26 November 1846.

108 *Straits Times*, 8 August 1874.

109 Straits Settlements Government Gazette, 1, 8 September 1876; Bill to incorporate Savings Banks, the Savings Bank Ordinance, 1876. See *Straits Observer* (Singapore), 24 May 1875, 20 September 1876; *Straits Times*, 9, 16 September 1876.

110 The oft-cited 1 January 1877 opening date was a projection. The bank actually opened in 16 January 1877. See *Straits Observer* (Singapore), 4 November 1876; *Straits Times Overland Journal*, 20 February 1878.

111 *Singapore Daily Times*, 18 May, 13 November 1877; *Straits Times*, 8 June 1878. The loans took the form of mortgages. See *Straits Times*, 7 September 1878; *Straits Times*

Overland Journal, 7 September 1878.

112 *Straits Times*, 30 November 1878.

113 *Singapore Daily Times*, 7 May 1877.

114 The Colonial Office's budget was also very tight. For instance, when Joseph Chamberlain took over as Colonial Secretary in 1895, the department's budget was a mere £130,000. See Pakenham (1979), p. 27.

115 *Straits Times*, 7 September, 16 November 1878; *Straits Times Overland Journal*, 7 September 1878.

116 *Straits Times*, 7 September, 16 November 1878; *Straits Times Overland Journal*, 7 September 1878.

117 *Straits Times*, 15 May 1880; *Singapore Daily Times*, 8 May 1880.

118 *Straits Times Overland Journal*, 4 April, 9 June 1881.

119 Correspondence to the press in 1881 actually referred to the drawdown of deposits as a run on the bank, while not naming the institution. See *Straits Times Overland Journal*, 19 November 1881. Even before the savings bank was reconstituted, a number of depositors had already closed their accounts. It was believed that remitting funds (savings) to England to be invested in government securities would result in the termination of all local loans issued at low rates by the bank. Investments in England would only draw an interest of 3% at this time (early years of the Long Depression in Europe), and the returns might be even lower after including exchange rates and Crown Agent's commission. For savings bank depositors, remaining with the bank might mean they would receive less than half the returns which could be gotten from other investments in Singapore. Fearing this 'calamity', a number of depositors withdrew their savings in late 1878, and this nearly created a run on the bank. See *Singapore Daily Times*, 1 April 1879; *Straits Times Overland Journal*, 28 December 1878. Legislative Council Proceedings, 16 December 1878.

120 *Straits Times*, 13 April 1901.

121 Straits Settlements Government Gazette, Vol XLII, No.29, 'An Ordinance to amend the law relating to the Government Savings Bank', 18 June 1907.

122 *Singapore Free Press* (weekly), 22 April 1909; *Singapore Free Press*, 4 January 1907.

123 *Straits Times*, 25 October 1907.

124 While financial instruments of the exchange banks were all subject to revenue stamp payments (stamp duty), the Postal and Government bank documents were exempt from this tax, making the use of money orders and postal orders and money transfers or remittances through the Savings Bank cheaper for the man on the street. The Straits Settlements Government Gazette Ordinance No. I of 1879 had already exempted the Savings Bank's documents from stamp duty.

125 *Malaya Tribune*, 5 February 1920; *Singapore Free Press*, 5 February 1920.

126 *Malaya Tribune* 5 January, 5 February 1920; *Singapore Free Press*, 5 February 1920, 19 March 1920.

127 *Straits Times* 16, 22 February, 17, 18, 22 March 1921; *Malaya Tribune*, 22 March, 1 November 1921.

128 *Singapore Free Press*, 14 May 1863. As early as 1864, there were already calls for the establishment of a mint in Hong Kong which could also supply coins to Straits Settlements. See *Singapore Free Press*, 10 March, 29 September 1864. While championing the transfer of the Straits Settlements in London in 1861, former Resident John Crawfurd produced a pamphlet on the Straits Settlements. It indicated that the merchants of the Straits supported coining a local British silver dollar of the same value of the Spanish *peso duro* (Spanish dollar 370.9 grains of pure silver – decimal coinage, divisible to 100 copper coins). See *Straits Times*, 18 May 1861.

129 See *Straits Times Overland Journal*, 17 December 1874; *Straits Times*, 12 December 1874.

130 *Straits Times Overland Journal*, 14 July 1872.

131 *Straits Times*, 7 May 1903, 4 February 1908, 19 April 1954; *Daily Advertiser*, 21 July 1893.

132 It is not clear from the source what territory the Auditor General served.

133 *Straits Times Weekly Issue*, 29 November 1886.

134 *Straits Times Weekly Issue*, 25 July 1893.

135 Order of Queen's Council dated 21 October 1890, Straits Settlements Government Gazette, Government Notification No. 647, 5 December. *Straits Times*, 7 May 1903. The Governor had already granted the American Dollar and Japanese Yen legal-tender status in January 1874; but this new Order repealed all previous Orders, and reinstated the American dollar and the yen with qualification relating to weight and fineness. See *Straits Times*, 7 May 1903.

136 *Daily Advertiser*, 21 July 1893.

137 *Straits Times Weekly Issue*, 10, 17 October 1893.

138 *Singapore Free Press* (Weekly), 11 December 1894.

139 *Singapore Free Press*, 11 December 1894.

140 *Straits Times*, 21 May 1898; *Singapore Free Press* (Weekly), 20 October 1898. *Singapore Free Press* (weekly), 17 April 1894.

141 *Straits Times*, 5 April, 21 May 1899; *Singapore Free Press* (weekly), 28 September, 5 October 1899.

142 Straits Times, 24 July 1897. The average value of banknotes circulation in 1897 was 7,326,693 dollars; in 1898 it was 7,737,057 dollars. See *Singapore Free Press* (weekly), 28 September 1899.

143 *Straits Times*, 23 March 1895; *Singapore Free Press* (weekly), 8 December 1896.

144 *Singapore Free Press* (weekly), 8 December 1896.

145 *Singapore Free Press* (weekly), 8 December 1896.

146 Straits Settlements Government Gazette, Ordinance VIII of 1897.

147 Amongst the first commissioners appointed were: L.M. Wood, see *Singapore Free Press* (weekly), 27 April 1899; J.O. Anthonisz, see *Straits Times*, 8 July 1899; W.L. Carter, see *Straits Times*, 27 October 1899; A.H. Capper, see Straits Settlements Government Gazette, 25 August 1898, No. 596.

148 *Straits Times*, 7 December 1896. This body was the genesis of the currency board system under which Singapore's currency matters were managed till 2002.

149 *Straits Times*, 27 August 1897.

150 *Singapore Free Press* (weekly), 14 December 1898.

151 *Straits Times*, 26 March 1900; *Singapore Free Press*, 3 October 1899.

152 *Singapore Free Press* (weekly), 8 December 1896.

153 *Straits Times*, 21 May 1898.

154 *Singapore Free Press* (weekly), 20 April 1899; 1 March 1900; *Straits Times*, 25 July 1900.

155 *Straits Times*, 18 July 1905.

156 *Straits Times*, 7 May 1903.

157 Negeri Sembilan had already declared the Straits Settlements coin legal-tender in 1890. Straits Settlements Government Gazette, Legislation 1890, XXVII 24 June 1891. See *Straits Times*, 7 May 1903.

158 *Singapore Free Press*, 4, 11 May 1899; *Straits Times*, 4 May 1899.

159 Straits Settlements Government Gazette, No.21 – Bill to be introduced into the Legislative Council: An Ordinance to provide for the Issue of Government Paper Currency, 'Objects and Reasons'. The issues were significant enough for the old ordinance to be rewritten and introduced as a new ordinance, instead of simply amending the ordinance of 1897. See also *Singapore Free Press*, 10 January, 1 March 1899; 26 January 1901; *Singapore Free Press* (weekly), 12 January, 2 February 1899; *Straits Times* 3 January, 7 May 1903.

160 *Singapore Free Press*, 26 January 1901, *Straits Times*, 29 November 1901, 7 May 1903.

161 *Singapore Free Press*, 16 August, 3 October 1900, 23 May 1901; *Straits Times*, 17 May 1901.

162 George Robinson, 1st Marquess of Ripon.

163 Kemmerer (1904), p. 643.

164 *Straits Times*, 21 February 1903.

165 *Singapore Free Press* 13, 19 November 1902; *Straits Times*, 7 May 1903. On 16 July 1902, the Governor asked the Secretary of State for the Colonies to refer the gold standard matter to an expert. The Secretary, accordingly, appointed a Commission to look into it. The British Secretary of State for the Colonies at this time was Joseph Chamberlain, in office 1895–1903. *Straits Times*, 12 February 1903.

166 *Straits Times*, 12 February 1903.

167 *Straits Times*, 18 November 1902, 10 February 1903.

168 The Commission's report was published in full in the press, see *Straits Times*, 7 May 1903. For more details, see Kemmerer (1906), pp. 663–98.

169 *Straits Times*, 7 May 1903.

170 Lee (1990).

171 *Straits Times*, 30 May, 2, 4 July 1903. The Council approved going onto the gold standard on 29 May 1903.

172 *Straits Times*, 18, 24 July, 26 September 1903.

173 *Straits Times*, 18 July 1903; *Singapore Free Press*, 18 July 1903.

174 Straits Settlements Government Gazette Supplement No. 18, 30 March 1906. Report on the Working of the Currency Note Issue, 1905, the Treasury, 15 February 1906.

175 Kemmerer (1904), p. 665. *Singapore Free Press*, 18 July 1903; 24 November 1904; *Straits Times*, 18 July 1903, 4 February 1908.

176 *Straits Times*, 18 July 1903. In July 1903, 1.9 million dollars' worth of old coins was taken from the Currency Note Reserve and sent to Bombay. The dies used for re-coining came directly from London. See *Straits Times*, 10 July 1903.

177 *Straits Times*, 3 October 1903.

178 *Straits Times*, 26 January 1904.

179 By October 1904, a year after the first Straits dollars were returned from re-minting in Bombay, the Commissioners of Currency at Singapore had already received 33.1 million dollars' worth of re-minted coins from the mint, close to their circulation target of 35.9 million dollars. *Singapore Free Press*, 24 November 1904.

180 Straits Settlements Government Gazette, 31 March 1905, no. 421, Ordinance No. III of 1905, 'The Currency Note Ordinance 1899 Amendment Ordinance 1905'.

181 Ordinance No. 1 of 1906. 'The Currency Ordinance 1899, Amendment Ordinance 1906' (29 January 1906), in Straits Settlements Government Gazette No. 5, Vol. XLI, 29 January 1906, no. 98 Ordinance No. I of 1906. Lee Sheng-Yi states the date as 29 February 1906 on p. 13, but as 29 January 1906 on p. 14. See Lee Sheng-Yi (1990), pp. 13–14. A month later, the Ordinance was amended once more to fine-tune the management of the profits made from the investment of the Note Guarantee Fund.

182 *Straits Times*, 24 December 1909.

183 Banks issuing notes had not proven stable during trade depressions, hence the lack of guarantee for their notes as well.

184 See *Singapore Free Press*, 26 February 1904.

185 The official narrative for the period is that up till 1903, the Straits Settlements had been on the silver standard. The gold standard phase starts in 1906. However, there is no description of the period between 1903 and 1906. See Monetary Authority of Singapore (2000), pp. 15–18. Lee Sheng-Yi labels these years as the 'period of currency reform'. See Lee (1990), p. 12.

186 *Straits Times*, 11 June 1903.

187 *Straits Times*, 9 December 1904.

188 *Straits Times*, 17 May 1904.

189 The extension of the time frame for certain territories to continue exporting the old coinage to Singapore was given so as to not disrupt trade in the region. See *Singapore Free Press*, 22 September 1904.

190 *Straits Times*, 21 October 1903.

191 *Straits Times*, 12 November 1906.

192 *Straits Times*, 21 March 1906.

193 Since the mid-1880s, many residents of Singapore had refused to accept Sarawak, British North Borneo and Hong Kong copper coins, which had up to that time had supplemented the small local change. See *Straits Times Weekly Issue*, 18 October 1886.

194 *Singapore Free Press* (weekly), 1 October 1890; *Daily Advertiser*, 30 December 1890.

195 *Daily Advertiser*, 4 August 1891; *Straits Times Weekly Issue*, 4 August 1891.

196 *Singapore Free Press*, 17 June 1892; *Straits Times Weekly Issue*, 6 December 1892.

197 The Foreign Coin Prohibition Ordinance 1891, in Straits Settlements Government Gazette, 15 January 1892.

198 *Straits Times Weekly Issue*, 6 December 1892; *Daily Advertiser*, 18 April 1892.

199 *Straits Times Weekly Issue*, 6 December 1892.

200 *Daily Advertiser*, 18 April 1892.

201 *Straits Times*, 20 July 1892.

202 *Singapore Free Press* (weekly), 23 February 1897.

203 *Straits Times*, 19 October 1903. British North Borneo copper coins would remain in circulation till 1908 when they were entirely withdrawn.

204 Lee (1990), p. 14.

205 *Straits Times*, 2 October 1900. Riots had broken out in many parts of India at this time.

206 In 1902, while the investment in gold saw an appreciation of 78,063.24 dollars in value, they were reduced as the value of the currency board's Indian securities depreciated by 35,572.06 dollars. See *Straits Times*, 30 March 1903.

207 Straits Settlements Government Gazette, Supplement No. 11, 10 March 1905: Report on the Working of the Currency Note Issue, 1904. In January 1904, the value of gold securities fell by 454,347.53 dollars, while the value of Indian securities lost 106,974.32 dollars. See Report on the Working of the Currency Note Issue, 1905.

208 Straits Settlements Government Gazette 1906, 23 February 1906, no. 199, Ordinance No. V of 1906, passed 16 February 1906.

209 Straits Settlements Government Gazette, 31 March 1905, no. 421, Ordinance No. III of 1905, 'The Currency Note Ordinance 1899 Amendment Ordinance 1905'.

210 Lee (1990), p. 14.

211 *Singapore Free Press* (weekly), 17 October 1907. The process of reminting the 1903 coinage and releasing a smaller one gave the government a surplus of 1,647,026 dollars. See *Straits Times*, 4 February, 7 November 1908; *Singapore Free Press*, 8 October 1908; *Straits Times*, 2 October 1908.

212 *Eastern Daily Mail and Straits Morning Advertiser*, 27 March 1907.

213 Lee (1990), p. 14.

214 *Straits Times*, 21 January 1905; 30 January 1906; *Eastern Daily Mail and Straits Morning Advertiser*, 16 September 1905.

215 *Singapore Free Press* (weekly), 18 October 1906.

216 *Straits Times*, 11 December 1906.

217 *Straits Times*, 2 October 1908.

218 Lee (1990), p. 14.

219 *Singapore Free Press*, 3 October 1908; Lee (1990), p. 14.

220 *Straits Times* 2 October 1908.

221 Straits Settlements Government Gazette, 15 May 1908 no. 575 and 12 June 1908 no. 677 – Statement of Account by Currency Commissioners, 30 April and 31 May 1908.

222 *Straits Times*, 2 October 1908.

223 *Singapore Free Press*, 3 January 1910.

224 Schenk (2009).
225 *Straits Times*, 15 September 1914.
226 *Straits Times*, 1 October 1917. The currency board's coin reserve had 50,957,272 dollars and 29,121,272 dollars in its Guarantee Fund. The Currency Ordinance was also amended to allow the Governor to defer cashing notes.
227 *Malayan Tribune*, 6 October 1917; *Straits Times*, 22, 25 September 1917; *Singapore Free Press*, 27 September 1917.
228 *Straits Times*, 15 October 1917.
229 *Singapore Free Press*, 10 October 1917.
230 *Straits Times*, November 1918; *Singapore Free Press*, 19 June 1947.
231 *Malayan Tribune*, 5 February 1918.
232 *Singapore Free Press*, 29 January 1917; *Straits Times*, 24 January 1918.
233 *Straits Times*, 25 February 1918.
234 *Malayan Tribune*, 29 January 1920.
235 *Straits Times*, 31 October 1921.

CHAPTER 4: CURRENCY AND FINANCES IN CRISES AND WAR

1 Britain's national debt in 1914, when World War I commenced, stood at £650 million. By the end of the war the debt had mushroomed to £7 billion, owing mainly to war bonds issued from 1917. This 'war loan' was not fully paid off until 9 March 2015. See Cosgrave (2015) and British Broadcasting Corporation (2014). 'UK finally finishes paying for World War I', published 9 March 2015 in https://www.cnbc.com/2015/03/09/uk-finally-finishes-paying-for-world-war-i.html; BBC News online, 'Government to pay off WW1 debt', 3 December 2014, in https://www.bbc.com/news/business-30306579.
2 Reibel (2018).
3 In 1919, for instance, the British faced revolutionary unrest sparked in Egypt, rioting in Punjab, a bloody insurgency in Ireland. The Third Anglo-Afghan war (the War of Independence) also began in the same year. More episodes of unrest occurred in the following years. See Kitchen (2014).
4 Boyce (2010).
5 Boyce (2010).
6 The heavy reparations for which Germany was liable under the Treaty of Versailles severely damaged the country's postwar economy and paved the way for the emergence of right-wing parties such as the Nazi Party, which promised to reject the Treaty of Versailles and restore German glory. See Pruitt (2018). By 1933, the Nazi Party was in power, and the prospect of another war in Europe was becoming very real.
7 For instance, the French built the Maginot Line, a defensive wall stretching from Switzerland to Luxembourg to the Strait of Dover; and the British stationed troops at Singapore and completed construction of the colossal Naval Base. The building of the former started in 1930 and was completed in 1939 at a cost of three billion French francs, while the latter, completed in 1938, cost the British £60 million. This cost did not include all other defensive works across the island of Singapore, which included shoreline pillboxes, multiple airfields (bases) and massive gun positions protecting Singapore's waterways.
8 See Mokyr (1999).
9 Besides steam shipping, advances in telegraphic communications also made the world more connected than before. Chiang Hai Ding has also identified other factors contributing to the expansion of world trade: the opening of the Suez Canal, and the dismantling of trade barriers in Europe in the second half of the 19th century. See Chiang (1978), pp. 69–71. Pascali (2017). The period 1870–1913 has been labelled as 'the birth of the first era of trade globalisation'.
10 Chiang (1978), pp. 68–69.
11 For more details, see Bogaars (1956), pp. 128–31.
12 See Survey Map of New Harbour, 1891, Singapore Maritime Museum AC HC000087.
13 Chiang (1978), p. 73.
14 The British Residential system was established in these four states. A British administrator, the Resident, was appointed for each state, akin to William Farquhar and John Crawfurd, the first two Residents of Singapore. Politically and legally, the Residents were only advisors to the sovereign of each Malay State. In reality, they became *de facto* heads of the State administrations within the British colonial system.
15 Chiang (1978), p. 92.
16 Chiang (1978), p. 92. See McKillop and Ellis (1932).
17 Chiang (1978), pp. 92–93.
18 Khoo (1999), p. 17.
19 Chiang (1978), p. 90. Trade would have been denominated in the silver dollars of the day in 1870, and in Straits Settlements dollars in 1915. When the Straits Settlements dollar was created, it was equivalent in value to the silver dollars, which gradually ceased to be used.
20 Malaya produced more than half the world's tin in 1904, spurred by surging demand in Europe for tin cans to preserve food. See overview of Sultan Nazrin Shah (2017) in https://www.ehm.my/publications/books/charting-the-economy-early-20th-century-malaya-and-contemporary-malaysian-contrasts.
21 In 1897, only 345 acres of Malayan lands were planted with rubber plants. By 1922, this had increased to 2.3 million acres. Much of this growth was driven by the rising prices of rubber which western industries, in particular the American automobile industry, required to manufacture rubber tyres. John Drabble, 'Change in the Malaysian economy circa 1800–1990' in https://www.ehm.my/publications/articles/change-in-the-malaysian-economy-circa-1800–1990. In Chiang Hai Ding's estimation, there were 500 acres planted in 1897. He may have included plots in the Straits Settlements. He added that the extent of rubber lands increased to 50,000 acres in 1905, and by 1914 there was more than 1 million acres of grounds planted with rubber. See Chiang (1978), p. 75.
22 Drake described the creation of the Straits dollar as having achieved a 'uniform and unified domestic currency'. See Drake (1981), p. 8.
23 *Singapore Free Press* (weekly), 8 September 1896; *Straits Times*, 3 October 1931.
24 Colonial Secretary Report, 1908, *Straits Times*, 3 October 1931.
25 Chiang (1969).
26 'Report of D. Milton Figart, Vice Consul General, Singapore, Straits Settlements, 10 July 1912', in Huebner (1913), pp. 212-15.
27 Straits Settlements Legislative Council Proceedings No. 26, 1911. Minutes of Meeting 25 May 1911.
28 *Singapore Free Press* (weekly), 24 June 1925.
29 Bower (2019), pp. 100-102; Horton (2010).
30 See *Straits Times*, 28 November 1913; *Malaya Tribune*, 18 November 1914. *Straits Times*, 25 September 1913.
31 See *Malaya Tribune*, 2 November 1922; *Straits Times*, 31 December 1925. The failure of the Dutch to join the Stevenson Scheme had contributed to its failure. See 'Rubber export restriction scheme', House of Commons Debates, 26 April 1928, Vol. 216, cc 1161–222, section 1209. However, Shimomoto points out that the scheme had only restricted the small holders' production (Chinese and Malays) and not the large (British) estates. See Shimomoto (1980), pp. 99–100.
32 The price of rubber per lb: $0.50 (June 1924), $1.09½

(June 1925), $0.32¾–$0.33 (October 1929), $0.27¾ (November 1929), $0.07 ¹⁄₁₆ (January 1933). See *Straits Times*, 29 September 1925, 4, 7 October 1929, 18 November 1929, 11 January 1933. The price of tin per picul: $141 (September 1925), $90 (November 1929), $75.12½ (January 1933). See *Straits Times*, 29 September 1925, 7 October, 18 November 1929, 11 January 1933.

33 From 1926 to 1928, the years leading up to the abandonment of the Stevenson Scheme, duties collected from the export of rubber fell from 11.2 million Straits dollars to 8.6 million dollars in 1927, reaching 3.7 million dollars in 1928. However, the duties collected from tin increased in 1927–8. See *Straits Times* 5 November 1928, 4 November 1929; *Malaya Tribune* 14 September 1929.

34 In the 1920s, more than 90 per cent of the FMS's imports and exports were shipped through the Straits ports. *Straits Times*, 31 December 1925.

35 *Malaya Tribune*, 26 June 1929.

36 *Malaya Tribune*, 28 August 1930.

37 *Malaya Tribune*, 2 October 1932.

38 *Malaya Tribune*, 11 May 1931, 26 May 1934.

39 Section 16 (3) of the Currency Ordinance allowed the Currency Guarantee Fund to provide its reserves to cover depreciations due to the lower price of silver. See *Malaya Tribune*, 29 September 1930.

40 *Malaya Tribune*, 11 May 1931.

41 *Straits Times Weekly Issue*, 24 February 1892, 10 April 1894, 11 August 1896, 12 January 1899; *Singapore Free Press* 7 January 1899; *Mid-Day Herald and Daily*, 8 August 1896; *Straits Times*, 23 September 1897; Tarling (1971), p. 1.

42 *Malaya Tribune* 31 October 1932.

43 The economic interests of the Malay States and Straits Settlements were very different. See *Malaya Tribune*, 31 March 1933.

44 Sources: http://www.rhodesianstudycircle.org.uk/1932-imperial-economic-conference/; https://www.nationalarchives.gov.uk/cabinetpapers/themes/great-depression.htm; https://www.britannica.com/topic/imperial-preference#ref115604; Stewart (1932).

45 For a more detailed discussion, see Ngono Fouda (2012), p. 351.

46 The original budget planned for 1932 was $71,000,000. This was trimmed to $56,789,994 in late 1931. See *Straits Times*, 12 November 1931. The FMS railway led one of the first mass retrenchment exercises, laying off 200 staff in early 1931. See *Straits Times*, 2 March 1931. The plan for the year was to retrench 25 per cent from all government departments: see *Straits Times*, 5 May 1931. Despite these efforts, it was estimated in 1932 that the deficit would reach 10 million Straits dollars in 1933, and 24 million the year after. The stagnation of trade, and thus revenues, persisted in 1932, necessitating further retrenchments. See *Malaya Tribune*, 27 April, 25 July 1932; *Straits Times*, 1 November 1932.

47 *Malaya Tribune*, 26 May 1934.

48 In 1929, the FMS's main source of import duties was taxes on liquors, tobacco, petrol. For exports, the main taxed items were rubber and tin (smelted, manufactured and ore). The possibility of raising duty rates came with the Ottawa Conference. See Boyce (2010).

49 Boyce (2010).

50 Boyce (2010).

51 Boyce (2010).

52 *Straits Times*, 1 November 1932.

53 *Singapore Free Press*, 8 December 1932.

54 *Singapore Free Press*, 14 June 1933.

55 *Singapore Free Press*, 28 May 1932.

56 *Straits Times* 25 March 1933; *Straits Times* 6 January 1934; Koh and Tanaka (1984), citing the *Report of the Commission appointed by His Excellency the Governor of the Straits Settlements to enquire into and report on the Trade of the Colony*, 1933-1934. See also *Straits Times*, 25 March 1933.

57 *Straits Times*, 6 January 1934.

58 *Malaya Tribune*, 30 March 1933.

59 Anti-Japanese sentiments amongst the diaspora Chinese eventually weighed on the import of Japanese produce in Malaya following a successful boycott of Japanese goods.

60 For a more detailed discussion, see Ngono Fouda (2012), p. 351.

61 *Straits Times*, 11 July 1930.

62 *Singapore Free Press* (weekly), 19 June 1929.

63 *Malaya Tribune*, 7 October 1930.

64 The Perak River Hydro-Electric Power Company, which opened in 1930 during the Great Depression, was one such asset. Due to the difficulties associated with the depression, the company went into liquidation in 1935 and had to be restructured. The Colonial Office intervened in this instance, since the British government was its largest shareholder. In the process of reorganising the company, the FMS suffered huge losses; its £425,000 preference shares were cancelled, £212,000 in interest arrears were waived, and the £850,000 capital loaned to the company were all turned into shares. See *Straits Times*, 10 July, 14 November 1935. In Diana Kim's account of the affair, there is no mention of the FMS's opium revenue fund. Kim contends that the Straits Settlements Opium Revenue Replacement Fund was used to 'support the Perak Electric Power Company, which had long supplied electricity to the Kinta Valley', and that the opium funds were used 'to transform the loan into an investment to avoid losses from the company's possible liquidation or restructuring'. See Kim (2020); *Malaya Tribune*, 7 October 1930; *Straits Times*, 1 November 1932; *Singapore Free Press*, 3 November 1932.

65 Warren (1986), p. 242.

66 Warren (1986), p. 244.

67 *Singapore Free Press* (weekly), 31 January 1907.

68 *Singapore Free Press* (weekly), 12 August 1909.

69 *Straits Times*, 3 July 1916.

70 See *Malaya Tribune*, 24 August 1925; *Singapore Free Press*, 26 August 1927; *Malaya Tribune*, 18 October 1934; *Malaya Tribune*, 14 December 1925; *Straits Times*, 15 December 1925.

71 *Malaya Tribune*, 24 January 1933. Even then, the FMS government's financial situation remained weak as the reserves were largely invested and there was very little liquidity to draw on at short notice. See *Singapore Free Press*, 24 April 1933.

72 The Straits government transferred 20 million dollars from the colony's Currency Guarantee Fund to top up the Government's revenue surplus before drawing 30 million dollars from this surplus to start the Straits' Opium Revenue Replacement Reserve Fund. See *Malaya Tribune*, 24 August 1925; 24 March, 2 July 1927; 12 April 1928; *Straits Times*, 16 July 1926, 28 June, 2 July 1928.

73 Growth of the Straits Settlements Opium Revenue Replacement Reserve Fund: July 1928 – $43,000,000, October 1929 – $44,000,000, May 1930 – $44,500,000, September 1932 – $46,000,000, October 1933 – $57,600,000, October 1935 – $62,000,000. See *Malaya Tribune*, 22 July 1930, 3 October 1933; *Straits Times* 29 October 1929, 27 September 1932; *Singapore Free Press*, 17 May, 3 October 1933, 29 October 1935.

74 *Straits Times*, 29 October 1929; *Malaya Tribune* 22 July 1930.

75 The deficit was ultimately funded through the following: 10 million dollars from the surpluses of the Currency Guarantee Fund; 2.25 million dollars in interest earned by the opium replacement fund; 2 million dollars in extra revenues collected from the consumption of tobacco, petrol, liquors, and a 2% tax on all totalisator bets and

sweepstakes; saving 1 million dollars by ending temporary allowances to government officers. The remainder was covered by general government revenue surpluses. *Straits Times*, 29 September 1931.

76   See *Straits Times*, 27 September 1932; *Malaya Tribune*, 3 October 1933; *Malaya Tribune*, 25 September 1934; *Singapore Free Press*, 3 October 1933. See *Straits Times*, 3 October 1933.

77   *Malaya Tribune*, 18 September 1937.

78   *Malaya Tribune*, 25 September 1934.

79   *Malaya Tribune*, 10 October 1927.

80   *Straits Times*, 6 December 1933. Detractors of this idea stressed that Malaya was not a country, hence there was no scope for discussion of 'citizenship' in this instance.

81   *Malaya Tribune*, 5 December 1933.

82   *Straits Times*, 18 December 1933; See *Singapore Free Press*, 13 February 1934. Some scholars have argued that the Malayanisation policy manifested itself in educational policies (for example, making Malay the official language for all), in order to eventually forge a common Malayan citizenship. See Blackburn and Wu (2019), pp. 30–45.

83   *Malaya Tribune*, 23 January 1934.

84   *Malaya Tribune*, 14 February 1934.

85   *Singapore Free Press*, 13 February 1934.

86   *Straits Times*, 1 December 1933.

87   *Straits Times*, 18 July 1935. In Johor's view, 'Malayanisation is a nebulous thing. It seems to march with the stride of the particular Governor and High Commissioner in office; it has never been defined in writing and has never been put forward to Johore as a general policy.' Also, 'Some Malayanisation is merely co-operation, some merely co-ordination, while the rest is either unification or tending to unification. Johore ... should resist unification.' See *Straits Times*, 18 July 1939.

88   *Malaya Tribune*, 30 July 1934; *Straits Times*, 30 July 1934; *Singapore Free Press*, 31 July 1934.

89   *Malaya Tribune*, 11 May, 2 December 1933.

90   *Malaya Tribune*, 7 December 1933.

91   *Malaya Tribune*, 22 December 1933, 30 July 1934; *Straits Times*, 30 July 1934; *Singapore Free Press*, 31 July 1934.

92   *Malaya Tribune*, 30 July 1934. See also *Malaya Tribune*, 11 May, 2 October 1933.

93   Currency Ordinance 1937 (Chapter 219), Straits Settlements Government Gazette 1937, 19 February 1937, pp. 519–31. See *Straits Times*, 23 January 1939. The new Board of Commissioners of Currency, Malaya included representatives from the Straits Settlements. All the assets of the old currency board were transferred to the new board. See *Malaya Tribune*, 16 September 1937.

94   Currency Ordinance, 1938 (No. 23 of 1938), 21 October 1938, in *Supplement to the laws of the Straits Settlements, 1939*, pp. 238, 414–27. One main amendment in the new Ordinance was to change all references to the 'Treasurer' (to Government), to 'Financial Secretary'.

95   *Straits Times*, 19 September 1935.

96   *Malaya Tribune*, 16 October 1939.

97   *Singapore Free Press*, 16 February 1937; *Straits Times*, 19 March 1940.

98   *Straits Times*, 2 July 1939.

99   When the Straits Settlements dollar notes were first issued, they bore the image of King Edward VII. However, new Straits dollar notes issued after King George V ascended to the throne in 1910 bore his image instead.

100   *Singapore Free Press*, 19 March 1940.

101   *Straits Times*, 23 December 1940; *Singapore Free Press*, 23 December 1940. In March 1940, the design for $50, $100, $1,000 and $10,000 notes were not yet ready. War in Europe had also delayed their printing. See *Straits Times*, 24 March 1940.

102   *Straits Times* 25, 29 March 1941. By mid-1941, the government had halted issuing any more new notes. A lack

103   of new notes in January 1941 led to no new notes being issued for Chinese New Year, the first time since the Straits dollar was launched. See *Malaya Tribune*, 18 January 1941. *Straits Times*, 22 August 1939. In August 1939, the new Board issued $10,000-worth of Straits notes to replace soiled ones.

104   *Straits Times*, 1 May 1939.

105   *Straits Times*, 27 January 1841.

106   These accounts cannot be verified against historical documents, but they have circulated in the numismatic community. See https://www.realbanknotes.com/news/30-malaya-paper-money-issues-1940-1941; https://enacademic.com/dic.nsf/enwiki/1834048; https://notescollector.eu/pages/en/notes.php?noteId=1101.

107   *Sunday Tribune*, 30 March 1941.

108   *Malaya Tribune*, 26 May 1934, 5 December 1938.

109   *Straits Times*, 7 April 1941. Although the Board of Commissioners of Currency, Malaya was already in operation by this time, the Straits Settlements dollar was still widely used and kept in circulation, as the issuance of the Malaya dollar had been delayed.

110   *Morning Tribune*, 23 January 1940.

111   *Singapore Free Press*, 8 February 1941.

112   Sources: (1851) *The Journal of the Indian Archipelago and Eastern Asia*, Vol 1, p. 35; Warren (1986); *Chinese Heritage, history of the Chinese clan associations in Singapore*.

113   *Morning Tribune*, 20 February 1940.

114   *Straits Times*, 14 January 1941.

115   *Singapore Free Press*, 11 July 1940; *Straits Times* 12 July 1940.

116   *Straits Times* 12 July 1940.

117   *Straits Times*, 20 July 1940.

118   *Straits Times*, 23 July 1940.

119   *Straits Times*, 23 July 1940.

120   *Singapore Free Press*, 19 July 1940; *Straits Times*, 20 July 1940, 'Only notes can relieve shortage'.

121   *Malaya Tribune*, 9 September 1940.

122   *Malaya Tribune*, 8 August 1941.

123   *Sunday Tribune* (Singapore), 24 August 1941.

124   *Malaya Tribune*, 28 August 1941.

125   Winston Churchill had believed that Singapore was the 'Gibraltar of the East'. Gibraltar, a British colony, was a heavily defended fortress and seaport located at the southern point of Spain. It is strategically positioned to guard the narrow entrance into the Mediterranean Sea from the North Atlantic Ocean. See Glueckstein (2015).

126   *Straits Times*, 16, 19 January 1942.

127   *Singapore Free Press*, 16 January 1942; *Straits Times*, 16, 19 January 1942.

128   *Straits Times*, 9, 15 January 1942; *Singapore Free Press*, 9, 17 January 1942.

129   *Singapore Free Press*, 17 January 1942.

130   *Singapore Free Press*, 19 January 1942

131   *Singapore Free Press*, 20 December 1941.

132   *Straits Times*, 3 January 1942.

133   *Morning Tribune*, 11 December 1941.

134   One reason why the Japanese targeted the Hongkong and Shanghai Bank as well as the Chartered Bank might have been because they had facilitated the implementation of the 1939 Anglo-Sino Chinese Currency Stabilisation Fund. The Fund was created to lend support to the Chinese dollar so as to facilitate Britain's trade with China while the latter was at war with Japan.

135   *Singapore Free Press*, 18, 20 December 1941; *Malaya Tribune*, 17 December 1941.

136   *Singapore Free Press*, 16 January 1942.

137   *Malaya Tribune*, 22 December 1941. The main British banks affected were the Chartered Bank, Hongkong and Shanghai Bank, Mercantile Bank and Eastern Bank.

138   *Singapore Free Press*, 19 December 1941.

139   *Straits Times*, 30 January 1942.

140   *Singapore Free Press*, 27 February 1942

141 *Straits Times*, 17 January 1942.

142 *Singapore Free Press*, 15 January 1942.

143 *Malaya Tribune*, 26 February 1941; *Morning Tribune*, 26 February 1941.

144 *Malaya Tribune*, 19 December 1941.

145 *Straits Times*, 15 January 1942.

146 *Straits Times*, 23 January 1942.

147 *Singapore Free Press*, 27 January 1942; *Straits Times*, 22 February, 24 July 1941; *Singapore Free Press*, 27 January 1942.

148 *Singapore Free Press*, 29 January 1942. See *Straits Times*, 24 January 1942.

149 *Straits Times*, 30 January 1942; *Singapore Free Press*, 26 January 1942.

150 *Straits Times*, 31 January 1942.

151 *Straits Times*, 27 February 1948 (Percival's account).

152 *Straits Times*, 13 February 1942.

153 *Straits Times*, 14 February 1942.

154 Territories Japan ruled or administered prior to World War II: Taiwan and the Penghu Islands (1895–1945); Korea (1910–1945); Karafuto Prefecture (South Sakhalin) (1907–1949); Manchuria (1932–1945); Micronesia (1914–1945) (1920–1936, under the Mandate of the League of Nations); and Concessions in China: Kwantung leased territory/South Manchuria Railway Zone (1905–1945); Kiautschou Bay leased territory – Qingdao (1914–1922); Tianjin (1898–1943); Hankou (1898–1943); Chongqing (1897–1943); Suzhou (1897–1943); Hangzhou (1897–1943); Shashi (1898–1943).

155 *Singapore Free Press*, 7 January 1942.

156 *Syonan Shimbun*, 23, 24 February, 28, 21, 29 May, 30 October, 7 November, 28 December 1942; 1 January, 6 March, 29 April, 16 August, 20 September, 8 December 1943; 11 November 1944.

157 *Syonan Shimbun*, 21 May 1942. In reality, not many of these old notes would have been in active circulation during the Occupation. The banks transferring assets and deposits out of Singapore before its surrender to the Japanese would have taken a significant amount of these notes with them. Much of the rest of these notes remaining in Malaya were either retained by the Japanese or hoarded by individuals.

158 *Straits Times*, 20 May 1948; *Singapore Free Press* 20 August 1948.

159 *Straits Times*, 24 October 1946, 14 February 1948. The goal of the trial prosecutors was to demonstrate that 'the Japanese obviously intended to use this Occupation money [since 1940] ... it could not be used unless the Japanese planned to attack areas where the money could be spent.' They concluded that this was proof enough that the attack on Pearl Harbor had been premeditated.

160 *Straits Times*, 10 October 1945.

161 Singapore Memory Project, memory of Yeo Hong Eng (10 July 2014) in https://www.singaporememory. sg/contents/SMB-c2edec4b-0658-403e-bc53-8861632a346c; and 'Heads of Executed Malay and Chinese Civilians displayed in a Syonan [Singapore] Street, 1942', Imperial War Museum, https://www.iwm.org.uk/collections/item/object/24259.

162 *Syonan Shimbun*, 11 November 1944. The first banana notes distributed from 1942 were in denominations of 1, 5, 10 and 50 cents, $1, $5 and $10.

163 The Malayan Currency Commissioners reported that they had $219,800,000 notes in circulation in 1941. See *Straits Times*, 10 October 1945.

164 *Indian Daily Mail*, 9 April 1946.

165 See Chia (2006) for more information on the Overseas Chinese Association.

166 While the Japanese would have had intended to make use of the OCAs to serve their own agenda, the OCAs became the *de facto* community leaders of the Chinese in Malaya.

Beyond the propaganda, the OCA had in effect also become the wartime institution with the 'mandate' to organise aid for the Chinese at large. In October 1942, for instance, the Singapore OCA found charitable persons who donated $3,000 and 800 coffins to aid the community's funeral needs. Each bereaved family was given $10 burial expenses. See *Syonan Shimbun*, 4 October 1942.

167 *Syonan Shimbun*, 9 September 1942.

168 *Syonan Shimbun*, 29 May, 13 September 1942.

169 *Syonan Shimbun*, 5, 9 September 1942. According to the Japanese military administration, the 1942 lottery had removed $700,000 from circulation.

170 *Syonan Shimbun*, 19 February, 9 April 1943; 3 January 1944; 1 January, 1 June, 16 July 1945. The Japanese military administration declared that the Konan Saiken was also raising funds for the relief of the poor and for sanitary and health improvements.

171 The lottery in Sumatra, the Sumatra Tomikuzi Syoken, was started in 1942. See *Syonan Shimbun*, 12 September 1942. Another lottery also started in Kuching in 1942. See *Syonan Shimbun*, 25 August 1942.

172 *Syonan Shimbun*, 24 November 1942. The two Japanese banks reopened on 20 March 1942.

173 *Syonan Shimbun*, 30 April, 15 May 1942.

174 The Japanese declared that they had discovered that the Hongkong and Shanghai Bank had abnormally 'expanded' their paper currency issuance just before the fall of Singapore. The Japanese-operated banks, as well as the restarted Chinese banks were tasked to tackle this monetary surplus in circulation so as to prevent inflation. Yet, at the same time, the Japanese authorities also decried the 20 million dollars missing from the vaults of the Post Office Savings Bank in Singapore. Of course, they knew that the British had transferred the money out of Singapore before the surrender. See *Syonan Shimbun*, 23 March, 20 April, 19 May, 24 November 1942. OCBC was the first Chinese bank to reopen, on 28 April 1942.

175 *Syonan Shimbun*, 24 November, 15 December 1942.

176 *Syonan Shimbun*, 24 November, 15 December 1942.

177 *Syonan Shimbun*, 16 October 1942.

178 *Syonan Shimbun*, 27 November 1942, 2 June 1943. See *Syonan Shimbun*, 23 February 1944. See *Syonan Shimbun*, 3 August 1943.

179 *Straits Times*, 7 September 1935, 'Japanese currency near danger point'.

180 *Morning Tribune*, 25 October 1939.

181 *Syonan Shimbun*, 24 November, 15 December 1942.

182 *Straits Times*, 23 January 1942.

183 *Syonan Shimbun*, 9 July 1942.

184 *Syonan Shimbun*, 25 September 1942.

185 *Syonan Shimbun*, 25 September 1942. The 1942 New Regulation allowing exchange of currency between Malaya and Sumatra: Tomi Kanrei No. 2 – Regulation for the Exchange of Malaya and Sumatra Currencies. See *Syonan Shimbun*, 20, 30 October 1942.

186 *Syonan Shimbun*, 27 September 1943.

187 *Syonan Shimbun*, 14 July 1942.

188 *Syonan Shimbun*, 13 October 1942.

189 *Syonan Shimbun*, 11, 12, 14 December 1942.

190 *Syonan Shimbun*, 27 September 1943.

191 *Syonan Shimbun*, 24 July 1944.

192 *Syonan Shimbun*, 25 February 1942.

193 *Syonan Shimbun*, 17 Mar 1942. Retailers must keep a book recording the name and address of new customers.

194 *Syonan Shimbun*, 10 July 1942.

195 *Syonan Shimbun*, 21 March 1942.

196 *Syonan Shimbun* 22, 30 December 1942.

197 *Syonan Shimbun*, 23 February 1944, 3 May 1944.

198 *Syonan Shimbun*, 7 August 1943.

199 In April 1942, the JMA declared that it was the Nippon goal to attain self-sufficiency in food for Malaya by

increasing rice production. In August that year, the JMA revealed its new food policy: to speed up self-sufficiency in foodstuffs by cultivating all available land, including idle farms. They were also prepared to produce farming implements. See *Syonan Shimbun*, 28 April, 7 August 1942.

200 *Malaya Tribune*, 28 January 1941.
201 *Morning Tribune*, 27 October 1941.
202 *Syonan Shimbun*, 10 July 1942.
203 *Syonan Shimbun,*, 24 September 1942.
204 *Syonan Shimbun*, 18 November 1943.
205 *Straits Times*, 1 August 1980.
206 *Syonan Shimbun*, 3 February 1944.
207 *Syonan Shimbun*, 15 August 1944.
208 *Syonan Shimbun*, 15 August, 21 November 1944.
209 *Syonan Shimbun*, 14 April 1944.
210 *Syonan Shimbun*, 17 May 1944, 10 July 1942.
211 *Syonan Shimbun*, 11 August, 1 September, 2 November 1943.
212 *Syonan Shimbun*, 16 August 1943.
213 *Syonan Shimbun*, 16 August 1943, 11 November 1944.
214 *Syonan Shimbun*, 4 January 1945.
215 *Straits Times*, 7 October 1945.
216 *Syonan Shimbun*, 10 February 1944.
217 *Syonan Shimbun*, 31 January, 9 February, 6, 17 March, 26 April 1944.
218 *Syonan Shimbun*, 19 February 1945.
219 *Syonan Shimbun*, 23 February 1945.
220 *Syonan Shimbun*, 23 July 1945.
221 *Syonan Shimbun*, 10 April, 20 June 1945.
222 *Syonan Shimbun*, 13, 18 August 1945.
223 *Syonan Shimbun*, 7 February and 9 June 1945.

CHAPTER 5: FROM LIBERATION AND RECOVERY TO SELF-RULE

1 Following the capitulation of Corregidor in the Philippines on 6 May 1942, the Japanese Imperial Navy was unopposed in the Pacific. However, the tide subsequently turned. The American and Allied naval forces were able to hold back further Japanese advances following the Battle of the Coral Sea (4–8 May 1942), and the Battle of Midway (4–7 June 1942), which saw the sinking of Japan's four main aircraft carriers. The Allied losses, in terms of vessels and men, were much lower. It would take another three years to defeat Japan completely in the Pacific. During the Battle of Guadalcanal (7 August 1942–9 February 1943), the Japanese sustained critical losses that allowed the Americans to regain naval supremacy. See Morgan (2019).
2 While the war in the Pacific was reaching a turning point in 1943, events in Europe also created the conditions for change. By mid-1943, the sentiment was growing amongst the Allies that the Axis Powers would eventually be defeated. In July-August 1943, the Axis alliance appeared to flounder when Italy indicated that it wanted to sue for peace unilaterally. The Germans arrested the Italian leader Benito Mussolini. In early September 1943, the Allies invaded Italy. Soon after that, Stalin, Churchill and Roosevelt met at Tehran to co-ordinate their war efforts. On 6 June 1944, D-Day, the Allies launched the re-invasion of Europe. By 25 August 1944, Paris had been liberated.
3 For the history of the Malayan Planning Unit, see Lau (1986), pp. 80–5. By early 1944, the Malayan Planning Unit had already put together plans for the formation of a Malayan Union when British rule returned. See War Office, WO 32/15036, Public Records Office, National Archives of the United Kingdom.
4 See Adams (1946).
5 See United States Department of State (2001-9).

6 Malay nationalists objected to the liberal citizenship terms given to non-Malays in the Union. The creation of the Federation also restored the status of the sultans of the Malay States.
7 Also known as partial internal self-government.
8 *Syonan Shimbun*, 20, 22, 25, 26, 28 August; 2, 3 September 1945.
9 *Straits Times*, 10 September 1945.
10 *Straits Times*, 8 September 1945.
11 One-dollar coins would be legal-tender for a maximum amount of ten dollars, while smaller denomination coins would be legal-tender for up to two dollars.
12 *Straits Times*, 10 September 1945.
13 *Straits Times*, 8 September 1945.
14 *Straits Times*, 10 September 1945.
15 *Straits Times*, 10, 14 September 1945.
16 *Straits Times*, 10 September 1945.
17 *Straits Times*, 10 September 1945.
18 *Straits Times*, 11 September 1945.
19 *Straits Times*, 7, 8, 10, 14, 15, 25 September, 6, 8, 10, 24 October, 15, 17, 19 November 1945; 9, 21, 24, 30 December 1945; *Malaya Tribune*, 24 October 1945.
20 *Straits Times*, 7, 11 September 1945.
21 The *Straits Times* quoting the *Malaya Times* reporting a British Official's opinion. See *Straits Times*, 8 September 1945.
22 *Straits Times*, 14 September 1945.
23 See *Straits Times*, 11, 14 September 1945.
24 Western banks had remained closed throughout the Occupation years. The BMA planned to disburse the new currency to the public through these banks when they opened. See *Straits Times*, 11 September 1945.
25 *Straits Times*, 6 February 1946.
26 *Singapore Free Press*, 12 November 1947.
27 *Singapore Free Press*, 5 October 1948; *Straits Times*, 27 August 1947.
28 *Straits Times*, 26 January 1946.
29 *Straits Times*, 25 April, 30 November 1946; 5 January, 10 February 1947.
30 Britain left the gold standard during the Great Depression.
31 *Sunday Tribune*, 8 December 1946; *Malaya Tribune*, 16 December 1946; *Singapore Standard*, 28 July, 23 August 1951.
32 *Singapore Free Press*, 12 November 1947.
33 *Straits Times*, 31 March 1950. The payment in kind comprised 500,000 dollars' worth of foodstuff, 500,000 dollars' worth of textiles, and 140,000 dollars' worth of sundries.
34 See *Straits Times*, 25 January 1948; *Singapore Free Press*, 2 August 1947.
35 *Straits Times*, 10 February 1947.
36 *Straits Times*, 17 September 1945. See also *Singapore Free Press*, 26 November 1948; *Straits Times*, 5 January 1949; 12 January, 11 November 1951.
37 *Singapore Free Press*, 19 June 1947.
38 *Straits Times*, 5 April 1947, 18 July 1948; *Singapore Free Press*, 2 August 1947.
39 *Singapore Free Press*, 26 November 1948.
40 *Straits Times*, 25 January, 20 May, 22 October 1948; *Singapore Free Press*, 20 August 1948. The problem with paper currency, especially subsidiary notes, was that it got damaged quickly and needed constant replacement.
41 *Singapore Free Press*, 26 November 1948; *Straits Times*, 5 January 1949.
42 *Straits Times*, 12 January, 11 November 1951. *Straits Times*, 17 September 1945. Even though the 1917 ten-cent notes printed locally and 1919 notes printed in London were still legal-tender, they had ceased to be accepted on the street. The 1919 issue was officially withdrawn in 1921 following the government release of more copper and silver coins. In 1940, when coins were in short supply

again, the government issued 25-cent notes. See *Singapore Free Press*, 19 June 1947. In August 1948, coins replaced all subsidiary paper notes issued from 1917 to 1919. However, due to a shortage of 10-cent coins in January 1950, the Singapore treasury had to re-issue 10-cent notes.

43 Pridmore (1975), p. 90.

44 *Straits Times*, 14 September, 10 October 1945.

45 *Straits Times*, 5, 9 October 1945.

46 *Morning Tribune*, 9 October 1946; *Malaya Tribune*, 9 October 1946.

47 *Straits Times*, 22 May 1948.

48 *Straits Times*, 3 August 1946.

49 *Straits Times*, 25 September 1945

50 *Malaya Tribune*, 3 November 1945; *Straits Times*, 25 September 1945.

51 *Malaya Tribune*, 3 November 1945, *Straits Times*, 2 November 1945.

52 HMS *Rotherham* was part of a fleet led by HMS *Sussex* that proceeded to Singapore to accept the surrender of 77,000 Japanese troops there. Her commander, Captain Hilary Worthington Biggs, personally accepted the surrender of 34,000 men of the Imperial Japanese Navy at the Singapore Naval Dockyard at Sembawang. In commemoration of the event, the main entrance of the dockyard was renamed 'Rotherham Gate'.

53 CO 953/4/4 no.51349 – Singapore, currency surrendered by the Japanese.

54 *Straits Times*, 25 September 1945.

55 *Straits Times*, 11, 20 September 1945.

56 *Straits Times*, 15 September 1945.

57 *Straits Times*, 27 September 1945.

58 *Straits Times*, 30 September, 2 October 1945.

59 *Straits Times*, 23, 25 October 1945.

60 *Straits Times*, 25, 26 October 1945.

61 Siam's wartime status was complicated. While, officially, after an initial phase of hostilities, Siam became 'allied' with the Japanese, not all Siamese had agreed with the alliance. As a result, a resistance movement grew within the nation. At its peak, the movement had 90,000 men under arms, and they were supplied by the Allies. Japan, on the other hand, had stationed 150,000 troops in the kingdom. The United States considered Siam an 'occupied state' during World War II. See Tarling (1978), p. 22.

62 *Straits Times*, 2 October 1945. Of course, one could guarantee supplies from these territories if higher prices were offered.

63 *Sunday Tribune*, 21 October 1945.

64 *Straits Times*, 13 September, 10 November, 3 December 1945, 13 February 1946.

65 *Straits Times*, 26 November 1945; *Malayan Tribune*, 26 November 1945.

66 *Straits Times*, 6 November 1945.

67 *Morning Tribune*, 1 May 1946.

68 *Singapore Free Press*, 27 June 1946; *Malaya Tribune*, 27 June 1946; *Straits Times*, 28 June 1946.

69 *Malaya Tribune*, 27 June 1946; *Indian Daily Mail*, 27 June 1946.

70 *Singapore Free Press*, 17 June 1948.

71 *Singapore Free Press*, 25 January 1949.

72 *Straits Times*, 28 June 1946.

73 *Malaya Tribune*, 23 December 1946.

74 *Singapore Free Press*, 14 December 1946; *Malaya Tribune* 14 December 1946; *Straits Times* 14, 19 December 1946.

75 *Singapore Free Press*, 8 January 1947.

76 *Singapore Free Press*, 20 January 1947. See *Straits Times* 25 September 1948.

77 *Singapore Free Press*, 20 January 1947.

78 *Indian Daily Mail*, 8 October 1946.

79 *Indian Daily Mail*, 28 January 1947. See also White (1997) and Kratoska (1988). 'The post-1945 food shortage in British Malaya', *Journal of Southeast Asian Studies*, Vol. 19,

No. 1 (March 1988), pp. 27–47.

80 See *Indian Daily Mail*, 9 December 1946.

81 See *Singapore Free Press*, 1 July 1949.

82 *Straits Times*, 17 July, 28 August, 17 December 1948.

83 *Straits Times*, 4 September 1948.

84 *Malaya Tribune*, 25 January 1949; *Singapore Free Press*, 26 January 1949.

85 *Malaya Tribune*, 5 February 1949.

86 *Singapore Free Press*, 28 April 1949; *Straits Times*, 16 November 1949.

87 *Singapore Free Press*, 30 March 1949.

88 *Straits Times*, 27 September 1945.

89 *Straits Times*, 17, 20 November 1945.

90 *Straits Times*, 11 January 1946.

91 *Indian Daily Mail*, 7 March 1946.

92 Transactions recorded in the current account include the export and import of goods and services, and incomes payable to factors of production abroad and receivable by factors of production locally, such as debt payments and disbursements and remittances.

93 *Straits Times*, 16 August 1950, 23 January 1951; *Telegraph*, 8 October 2001.

94 *Straits Times*, 14 September 1945.

95 *Morning Tribune* 1 May 1946; *Straits Times*, 14 July 1946.

96 *Straits Times*, 7 September 1945.

97 *Straits Times*, 26 April 1950.

98 *Singapore Free Press*, 25 April 1950; *Straits Times*, 26 April, 16 August 1950.

99 *Straits Times*, 23 January, 22 June 1951.

100 *Straits Times*, 26 February 1946.

101 *Malaya Tribune*, 12 August 1947.

102 *Straits Times*, 31 August 1947.

103 *Straits Times*, 10 February 1947.

104 *Straits Times*, 13 February 1947.

105 *Singapore Free Press*, 12 August 1947.

106 *Morning Tribune*, 28 July 1947.

107 *Singapore Free Press*, 16 April 1948.

108 *Morning Tribune*, 31 July, 16 October 1948, 13 July 1949.

109 *Malaya Tribune*, 18 September 1947; *Singapore Free Press*, 30 August 1948.

110 *Malaya Tribune*, 13 July 1949.

111 *Singapore Free Press*, 14 July 1949.

112 *Sunday Times*, 11 November 1945.

113 Up to the beginning of 1942, more than 90 per cent of the world's natural rubber supply had come from Singapore-Malaya. See *New York Times*, 15 May 1991. For some time, with the synthetic rubber industry in the US still in its infancy in 1942, the Americans turned to the wild rubber trees in Brazil for supplies of this strategic stock: https://historyofrubber.weebly.com/wwii.html.

114 *Straits Times*, 6 February 1946.

115 Lepoer (1989).

116 *Straits Times*, 21 August 1957, 18 February, 7 March, 24 April 1958; *Singapore Free Press* 21 February 1958.

117 *Straits Times*, 9, 11 August 1957, 1 April 1960.

118 *Morning Tribune*, 20 July 1946; *Straits Times*, 20 July 1946.

119 House of Commons debate 27 September 1949, Hansard, vol. 468, columns 7–144.

120 *Straits Times*, 1 September 1949.

121 *Straits Times*, 1 September 1949. Opinion of Lee Kong Chian, OCBC chairman.

122 *Sunday Tribune*, 26 October 1947.

123 Lepoer (1989).

124 *Singapore Free Press*, 26 December 1947; *Straits Times*, 25 December 1947.

125 The 1938 formula for the Malayan dollar currency board was: Straits Settlements (37%), Federated Malay States (37%) and the Unfederated Malay States (26%).

126 *Straits Times*, 12 July 1951.

127 *Straits Times*, 23 December 1951. The currency agreement for the creation of this common currency was

promulgated in these laws: The Currency Ordinance No. 44 of 1952 of the Crown colony of Singapore; No. 33 of 1951 of the Federation of Malaya; No. 10 of 1951 of the British North Borneo; and No. 1 of 1951 of the Crown colony of Sarawak. See (1952), *Colonial Reports. North Borneo 1951*, pp. 25, 61.

128   *Straits Times*, 14 June, 12 July 1951, 22 July 1953.
129   *Straits Times*, 25 November 1952.
130   *Straits Times*, 24 January 1952, 3 January 1953; *Singapore Standard*, 9 January 1952; *Singapore Free Press*, 3 January 1953.
131   *Singapore Free Press*, 27 May 1952.
132   *Straits Times*, 8 December 1954.
133   *Straits Times*, 8 December 1954. See *Singapore Standard*, 5 September 1950; *Straits Times*, 22 July 1952.
134   *Straits Times*, 14 June, 12 July 1951, 24 January 1952, 22 July 1953; *Singapore Standard*, 9 January 1952.
135   *Singapore Standard*, 9 January 1952; *Straits Times*, 24 January 1952.
136   *Singapore Free Press*, 3 January 1953; *Straits Times*, 3, 25 January 1953. See *Singapore Free Press*, 19 June 1947, 26 November 1948; *Straits Times*, 17 September 1945, 5 January 1949, 12 , 11 January November 1951.
137   George (2016).
138   *Morning Tribune*, 3 May 1946.
139   *Malaya Tribune*, 16 December 1946.
140   *Singapore Free Press*, 26 August 1947.
141   *Straits Times*, 10 October 1946.
142   *Singapore Free Press*, 26 August 1947.
143   The city centre of Singapore was conferred 'City Status' on 22 September 1951, under the authority of the City Council. The rest of Singapore was under the authority of the Singapore Rural Board.
144   *Singapore Standard*, 28 October 1950.
145   *Singapore Standard*, 28 October 1950.
146   *Singapore Standard*, 31 October, 10 November 1956; *Straits Times*, 9 November 1956.
147   *Singapore Free Press*, 26 August 1947.
148   *Singapore Free Press*, 26 August 1947.
149   The budget would typically be presented for debate and approval. Depending on the outcome of the legislative debate, a different set of numbers would have been approved. Towards the end of the calendar year, during the tabling of the following year's budget, revised estimates of revenue, expenditure, and the budget position for the current year would also be tabled. Actual budget outturns were not always reported in the media.
150   *Straits Times*, 22 October 1949.
151   *Singapore Free Press*, 12 November 1960.
152   *Singapore Free Press*, 16 August 1954.
153   *Singapore Free Press*, 16 August 1954.
154   *Straits Times*, 28 September 1953.
155   *Singapore Free Press*, 16 October 1951.
156   *Straits Times*, 12 May 1955.
157   *Straits Times*, 8 August 1960.
158   *Straits Times*, 10 June 1962, 11, 12 April 1963.
159   See *Straits Times*, 3 February, 21 September 1971.
160   *Singapore Free Press*, 4, 14, 17 July 1951; *Straits Times*, 14 June 1951.
161   *Straits Times*, 4 March 1940.
162   *Malaya Tribune*, 17 December 1947.
163   *Straits Times*, 31 December 1947.
164   *Singapore Standard*, 5 September 1950.
165   *Straits Times*, 27 November 1953, 1 January 1954.
166   *Straits Times*, 18, 25, 26 November 1953; *Singapore Free Press*, 24 November 1953. It has been suggested that apart from wanting to support the Malayan government as part of its Cold War conflicts in the Southeast Asia theatre, the contribution was also to show appreciation to Malaya for its part in contributing to the Empire's 'pot' of US dollars over the years. By 1954, Britain's export to

dollar areas had also seen significant improvements. See *Straits Times*, 30 December 1953.
167   *Straits Times*, 18 November 1954, 13 February, 11 November 1956.
168   *Straits Times*, 22 February 1956.
169   *Straits Times*, 19 March 1959.
170   *Straits Times*, 16 September 1956; See HistorySG, 'World Bank announces mission to Singapore and Malaya', 13 August 1954. https://eresources.nlb.gov.sg/history/events/f1ac6a2f-7300-4896-9d10-db04f06780b0. 'Company tax' refers to corporate income tax.
171   *Straits Times*, 4 December 1954.
172   *Straits Times*, 4 December 1954.
173   *Singapore Standard*, 10 January 1955. Not all the people of Malaya supported this 'inaction' on their government's part. In February 1956, as a result of the colossal budget deficit faced in that year, a rumour that the Malayan dollar might be devalued gained traction. The government denied this, and suggested instead that the new central bank, when it was established, might reduce the reserves backing the currency by 250–300 million dollars, and that the sum might be diverted instead to financing development spending. See *Straits Times*, 22 February 1956.
174   See *Straits Times*, 16 October 1957.
175   *Straits Times*, 9 May 1957.
176   *Straits Times*, 8, 10 May 1957; *Singapore Free Press*, 7 May 1957.
177   *Straits Times*, 15 June 1957; *Singapore Free Press*, 26 June 1957.
178   *Singapore Standard*, 4 December 1958.
179   *Straits Times*, 21 October 1953.
180   *Singapore Standard*, 4 December 1958.
181   *Singapore Standard*, 7 September 1953.
182   FCO 141/14930 & FCO 141/14931, 1957–1959: Singapore: Malayanisation Commission; Malayanisation of the Public Service. National Archives of the United Kingdom.
183   See *Straits Times*, 17 October 1957; *Straits Times*, 19 March 1959.
184   *Straits Times*, 25 July 1959.
185   *Singapore Free Press*, 17, 23 June 1959; *Singapore Standard*, 24 June 1959; *Straits Times*, 24 June 1959.
186   *Straits Times*, 11 April 1957.
187   *Straits Times*, 14 August 1957, 30 April 1958.
188   *Straits Times*, 20 May, 13 June 1958; *Singapore Standard*, 13 June 1958.
189   *Straits Times*, 19 October 1958.
190   *Straits Times*, 19 October 1958.
191   *Straits Times*, 15 June 1957, 5 December 1958; *Singapore Free Press*, 26 January 1957.
192   *Straits Times*, 13, 22 January 1959.
193   *Straits Times*, 23 July 1959.
194   *Singapore Free Press*, 5 September 1960.
195   *Straits Times*, 28 October 1960.
196   *Straits Times*, 5 June 1953.
197   *Singapore Free Press*, 10 November 1951.
198   *Straits Times*, 12 April 1955.
199   *Singapore Free Press*, 20 September 1955.
200   *Straits Times*, 21 March 1954.
201   *Straits Times*, 17 November 1954, 3 July 1955.
202   *Straits Times*, 13 February, 24 March 1956.
203   *Straits Times*, 5 May 1957.
204   *Straits Times*, 18 September 1924; 8 February 1994; Cornelius-Takahama, V. and Lim, F. (2004).
205   *Straits Times*, 15 July 1959.
206   *Straits Times*, 1 March 1959.
207   *Singapore Free Press*, 24 September 1955.
208   *Straits Times*, 27 September 1955.
209   *Singapore Standard*, 9 February, 30 June 1956.
210   *Straits Times*, 30 June 1956; *Indian Daily Mail*, 30 June 1956.
211   *Singapore Standard*, 3 July 1956.
212   *Straits Times*, 29 May 1958.

213 *Singapore Standard*, 24 October 1958.
214 *Straits Times*, 22 November 1960, 27 August 1961, 13 December 1962, 20 February 1964.
215 *Singapore Free Press*, 14 July 1836; *Straits Times*, 21 December 1939; *Malaya Tribune*, 27 March 1931.
216 *Straits Times*, 9, 14 February, 25 June, 22 September 1960.
217 *Singapore Free Press*, 5 October 1960; *Straits Times* 14 February 1960.
218 George (2016), pp. 12–13.
219 *Straits Times*, 16 September 1963.
220 George (2016), p. 13.

CHAPTER 6: NEW NATION, NEW CURRENCY

1   Lau (1998), p. 258.
2   MAS internal records.
3   MAS internal records.
4   MAS internal records.
5   Schenk (2013), p. 500.
6   Tun Tan Siew Sin, speech to National Press Club, Kuala Lumpur, 15 September 1965. Quoted in Tan Siew Choo's letter to the *Straits Times*, 17 October 2000.
7   Singapore Government White Paper on Currency (1966), Annex A.1, contains some of the key correspondence between the Malaysian government and itself on currency issues.
8   Singapore Government White Paper on Currency (1966).
9   MAS internal records.
10   Singapore Government White Paper on Currency (1966), Annex A.4.
11   *Straits Times*, 28 January 1966.
12   Singapore Government White Paper on Currency (1966), Annex B.5.
13   Singapore's team also included Ngiam Tong Dow and Elizabeth Sam from the Ministry of Finance, the Attorney-General, Tan Boon Teik, and the Accountant-General Chua Kim Yeow. Other representatives from Malaysia included Tan Sri Chong Hon Nyan and Dato Malek Ali Merican from the Treasury, the Solicitor-General Tan Sri Salleh Abas, the Deputy Governor of BNM Choi Siew Hong, and the Manager of its Singapore branch Hooi Kam Sooi.
14   Singapore Government White Paper on Currency (1966), Annex B.9.
15   'Legal-tender' means that the coins and banknotes must legally be accepted if offered in payment of a debt.
16   Singapore Government White Paper on Currency (1966), Annex B.9.
17   MAS internal records.
18   The relevant extracts of these minutes are reproduced in the White Paper on Currency, Annex B.7.
19   The archived files contain two sets of minutes of the 11th meeting at which this issue was raised. Both show that Malaysia had maintained that there should not be two legal entities (BNM and BNM, Singapore), but in one set there was no record of the Singapore team challenging this assertion. In the other set, Singapore maintained that it was essential to show beyond doubt that the assets belonged to BNM, Singapore.
20   Singapore Government White Paper on Currency (1966), Annex C.2.
21   Singapore Government White Paper on Currency (1966), Annex C.3.
22   Singapore Government White Paper on Currency (1966), Annex C.3.
23   Singapore Government White Paper on Currency (1966), Annex C.4.
24   MAS internal records.
25   Singapore Government White Paper on Currency (1966), Annex C.7.
26   Singapore Government White Paper on Currency (1966), Annex B.1.
27   Singapore Government White Paper on Currency (1966), Annex B.1.
28   Singapore Government White Paper on Currency (1966), Annex C.9.
29   *Straits Times*, 18 August 1966.
30   *Straits Times*, 20 August 1966.
31   *Straits Times*, 28 August 1966.
32   Singh (1984), p. 137.
33   Singh (1984), p. 138.
34   Although they chose at the start of their independence to retain 100 per cent sterling backing for their currencies. Schenk (1997).
35   This was the theme of a public speech by Minister for Finance Lim Kim San at the opening of Jurong Tile Works on 9 September 1966.
36   Board of Commissioners of Currency, Singapore (1992), p.34.
37   Speech by Dr Goh at the 13th anniversary dinner of the Economic Society of Singapore, 20 September 1969, p. 5.
38   For some background on this, see Peebles and Wilson (2002), p. 34.
39   Lee (1998), p. 347.
40   *Straits Times*, 23 September 1996.
41   For an in-depth assessment of his life and contributions to Singapore see Quah (forthcoming).
42   Tan (2007), p. 145.
43   Orchard (2016), p. 39.
44   Lee Kuan Yew, speech at 54th Anniversary of the Singapore General Printing Workers' Union, NTUC Conference Hall, 25 August 1966. Quoted in Orchard (2016), p. 42.
45   Hong Kong also had a currency board at this time but, unlike Singapore, it was still a British colony.
46   Letter from Mr Tun Thin (Acting Director, Asian Department, IMF) to Mr Ngiam Tong Dow (Ministry of Finance, Singapore), 25 August 1966. Source: International Monetary Fund.
47   Schenk (2013), p. 510.
48   'A currency board, even adulterated to the effect that it may grant credit up to a fixed sum to the Government, is not sufficient for an economy in an advanced stage of development...one can definitely not count on the foreign banks in Singapore to bring in considerable amounts of liquid foreign funds should they be in need of cash here.' MAS internal records.
49   Schenk (2013), p. 15.
50   Board of Commissioners of Currency, Singapore (1992), p. 31.
51   For useful background on Singapore's first currency notes and coins, see Soh (1990), Ho (2016), and Lim (2019).
52   MAS internal records.
53   *Straits Times*, 10 November 1967.
54   *Straits Times*, 6 June 1967.
55   *Straits Times*, 13 December 1967.
56   Lim (1969), p.35.
57   *Straits Times*, 13 June 1967.
58   *Straits Times*, 4 July 1967.
59   *Straits Times*, 28 July 1967.
60   *Straits Times*, 2 August 1967.
61   MAS internal records.
62   MAS internal records.
63   MAS internal records.
64   Telegram from the British High Commission to the Commonwealth Office, 24 August 1967 – HYE 4/2.
65   Singh (1984), p. 161.
66   Lee (1990), p. 58.
67   Board of Commissioners of Currency, Malaya and British Borneo (1968).

68   According to Singapore's finance minister Tan Siew Sin:
      Straits Times, 17 September 1966.
69   *Straits Times*, 7 December 1966.
70   *Straits Times*, 12 May 1973.
71   *Straits Times*, 18 August 1966.
72   MAS internal records; *Straits Times*, 6 September 1966 and
      7 September 1966.
73   *Straits Times*, 26 October 1966.
74   *Straits Times*, 11 December 1966.
75   *Straits Times*, 16 January 1967.
76   MAS internal records.
77   *Straits Times*, 9 December 1966, 11 December 1966,
      7 January 1967, and 16 January 1967.
78   MAS internal records.
79   *Straits Times*, 7 January 1967.
80   *Straits Times*, 7 January 1967.
81   MAS internal records.
82   Schenk (2013).
83   MAS internal records; *Straits Times*, 7 January 1967.
84   MAS internal records.
85   MAS internal records.
86   *Straits Times*, 9 June 1967.
87   If it were legal-tender, coins and banknotes would have to
      be accepted if offered in payment of a debt.
88   *Straits Times*, 16 January 1967.
89   Lim (1969), p. 34 offers a succinct contemporary view of
      what the Currency Interchangeability Agreement meant
      for Malaysia and Singapore: 'So if both are equivalent
      to 0.29029 grams of fine gold and 2s and 4d, one
      Malaysian dollar equals one Singapore dollar. According
      to Euclid, two things that are equal to the same thing
      are equal to each other. So when the two countries
      agreed to use each other's currency as customary
      tender and there was to be no commission then they
      were freely interchangeable as well as freely convertible.
      In a strictly economic sense, therefore the currency
      union continued.'
90   FCO1 1/64, TNA.
91   FCO1 1/ 65, TNA.
92   HSBC Group Archive, GH0238: Singapore Half Yearly
      Reports 1956–67.
93   Schenk (2013), p. 512.
94   The problem was that the banks had to transfer funds
      in sterling or by mutual settlement of balances in the
      three currencies across the border and there could be
      shortages of a particular currency. Now the two monetary
      authorities would at least ensure the banks could obtain
      the necessary currencies to carry out the transfer on
      behalf of their clients.
95   MAS internal records.
96   MAS internal records.
97   National Archives of the United Kingdom, 'The 1967
      devaluation of the pound'.
98   His exact words can be found at https://www.youtube.
      com/watch?v=mIQnpoGBS1I.
99   The Executive Board of the IMF was being asked to meet
      at 5 pm GMT on Saturday 18 November, to approve the
      British decision. The following Monday was declared to be
      a bank holiday in Britain and all financial markets were to
      be closed.
100   MAS internal records.
101   MAS internal records.
102   National Archives of Singapore, 1ky/1967/ky1119.doc.
103   *Straits Times*, 21 November 1967.
104   As Dr Goh said in a speech to Parliament: 'If we had
      devalued, then the cost of imports will scale up to such an
      extent as to lead to higher cost of living, higher wages and
      consequently lower profits and lesser employment. These
      rising costs would also lead to higher export prices and
      eventually will eliminate the benefits of devaluation.' MAS
      internal records.

105   In the 1960s, under the Bretton Woods system of fixed
      exchange rates countries could not legitimately devalue
      unless the balance of payments was in 'fundamental
      disequilibrium' and it was approved by the IMF. This was to
      prevent predatory devaluation.
106   The Secretary of BNM was clear that the old currency
      could not be exchanged one-for-one with the new
      because the Currency Act of 1960 had no provision for
      this. The old dollar would have to be exchanged at 2s 4d or
      0.29029 grams of gold. So when the pound was devalued
      against gold the old dollar was worth less. *Straits Times*,
      12 December 1967.
107   *Straits Times*, 21 November 1967.
108   MAS internal records.
109   MAS internal records.
110   MAS internal records.
111   MAS internal records.
112   MAS internal records.
113   MAS internal records.
114   *Straits Times*, 7 December 1967.
115   Board of Commissioners of Currency, Singapore (1992), p. 2.
116   *Straits Times*, 27 April 1968.
117   Singh (1984).
118   Drake (1969), p. 226.
119   Wong (2004), p. 127.
120   *Straits Times*, 20 November 1967.
121   MAS internal records.
122   *Straits Times*, 25 November 1967.
123   National Archives of the United Kingdom, HS/4/551/1.
124   Based on a meeting between Lee and the Commonwealth
      Secretary on 3 March. FCO 15/149.
125   MAS internal records.
126   MAS internal records. There is also a record of a speech to
      Parliament by Goh on this matter on 5 December 1967 in
      the National Archives of the United Kingdom; and a BCCS
      document – MAS internal records.
127   MAS internal records.
128   *Straits Times*, 21 November 1967.
129   MAS internal records.
130   Under the Government Gazette, Acts Supplement,
      15 December 1967, a new section was added to absolve
      the BCCS from any claim as a result of the devaluation
      and subsection (4) of section 14 was amended by deleting
      the words 'up to their face value'.
131   Soh (1990) p. 28.
132   MAS internal records.
133   On 18 November 1967, Singapore's reserves amounted to
      US$326.9 million. The BCCS immediately instructed that
      15 per cent of sterling deposits be invested in the United
      States, Canadian and Japanese securities of up to two
      years' maturity.
134   MAS internal records.
135   ThinkSpace, 21 February 2020.
136   National Archives of the United Kingdom. Letter from
      Roy Jenkins, Chancellor of the Exchequer, United Kingdom
      to Goh Keng Swee, Minister for Finance, Singapore,
      6 December 1967.
137   National Archives of the United Kingdom. Letter from Goh
      Keng Swee, Minister for Finance, Singapore, to Roy Jenkins,
      Chancellor of the Exchequer, United Kingdom,
      12 December 1967.
138   National Archives of the United Kingdom. Letter to Harold
      Wilson from Lee Kuan Yew, 18 December 1967.
139   National Archives of the United Kingdom. Letter to Goh
      Keng Swee, Minister for Finance, Singapore, from Roy
      Jenkins Chancellor of the Exchequer, United Kingdom,
      6 March 1968.
140   National Archives of the United Kingdom. Letter to Harold
      Wilson from Lee Kuan Yew, 18 December 1967.
141   *Financial Times*, 1 January 1968. The income generated
      by the visits of the American troops and the spending

activities of the British expatriate community in Singapore are described in the novel *Saint Jack* by Paul Theroux. Theroux, himself an American, taught English at the National University of Singapore in the late 1960s.

142 National Archives of the United Kingdom. Letter from Dr Goh Keng Swee, Minister for Finance, Singapore, to Roy Jenkins, Chancellor of the Exchequer, United Kingdom, 12 December 1967. The newspaper articles he cites are in the *Straits Times*, 21 November 1967 and 22 November 1967. He also explains that the diversification exercise was conducted gradually and over a long period of time.

143 National Archives of the United Kingdom. Letter to PM Lee Kuan Yew from PM Harold Wilson, 25 February 1968.

144 Speech by Prime Minister Lee Kuan Yew at the dinner in honour of the Rt. Hon. Sir Harold Wilson and Lady Wilson, at the Istana, 10 January 1978. National Archives of Singapore.

145 These were advanced developed countries which had agreed to provide the International Monetary Fund with additional funds to lend under the 1962 General Agreement to Borrow.

CHAPTER 7: FOUNDING MAS; THE END OF BRETTON WOODS

1 Turnbull (2009), p. 311.
2 *Straits Times*, 9 August 1971.
3 Speech at the 13th Anniversary Dinner of the Economic Society of Singapore on 20 September 1969. National Archives of Singapore.
4 When the Cabinet decided to establish a currency board instead of a central bank the reasons were short-term: 'As such, the subject of establishing a central bank will no doubt have to be seriously considered at some time in the future.' Speech at the 13th Anniversary Dinner of the Economic Society of Singapore on 20 September 1969. National Archives of Singapore, p.5.
5 Speech at the 13th Anniversary dinner at the Economic Society of Singapore, 20 September 1969. National Archives of Singapore.
6 Dr Goh insisted it be called the Monetary Authority of Singapore to distinguish it from a central bank. In his view central banks in developing countries at the time often financed government deficits through the printing of money and thereby generated excessive price inflation.
7 The Act was also amended in November 1972 to empower MAS to act more effectively as 'lender of last resort' by making available loans to banks or other eligible institutions that were experiencing financial difficulty or were considered highly risky or near collapse.
8 International Monetary Fund Concluding Statement, International Monetary Fund Article VIII Consultation (1971). Quoted in Orchard (2016), p. 81.
9 There is also the argument that this arrangement gave the MAS a stronger voice in overall policymaking than it might otherwise have had, and its strong economic record in keeping inflation low and stable as well as achieving rapid economic growth over successive decades justified this decision. Orchard (2016), p. 84.
10 Monetary Authority of Singapore (1971), Annual Report.
11 Because only the US dollar was fixed to gold the exchange rate mechanism became known as the Gold Exchange Standard rather than the Gold Standard where all member countries fixed to gold directly.
12 Britain devalued in 1949 and 1967, as did France in 1957 and 1959, while Italy did not devalue at all. West Germany revalued in 1961 and 1969, but Japan did not revalue at all.
13 Triffin (1960).
14 This caused problems for other countries since the increase in the US demand for imports led to a rise in their exports

and put upward pressure on their domestic price levels.
15 Capital mobility was also high in the 19th century and interwar years, but governments had more domestic political freedom to take the necessary action to defend their currencies and could use capital controls. After World War II, the rise of trade unions, universal suffrage and parliamentary labour parties committed to the welfare state, together with the fact that it became harder to enforce capital controls, made this increasingly difficult. Eichengreen (1996).
16 MAS internal records.
17 *Straits Times*, 8 March 1972.
18 MAS internal records.
19 This would build on the offshore Asian Dollar Market which Singapore had established in Singapore in 1968.
20 A detailed account of this, including the implications for Singapore, can be found in Schenk (2010).
21 Paper by Franz Ballmann on 'The implications and consequences of Singapore leaving the Sterling Area', 25 August 1969. Source: International Monetary Fund.
22 Schenk (2010).
23 Draft legislation prepared for Singapore by Franz Ballmann, titled 'An Act for the regulation and control of transactions in foreign commerce, gold and foreign exchange, 1 March 1967. Source: International Monetary Fund.
24 MAS internal records.
25 MAS internal records.
26 MAS internal records.
27 MAS internal records.
28 MAS internal records.
29 MAS internal records.
30 Schenk (2013), p. 20.
31 *Straits Times*, 20 May 1973.
32 *Straits Times*, 12 May 1973.
33 *Straits Times*, 12 May 1973.
34 *New Nation*, 9 May 1973.
35 *Straits Times*, 22 May 1973.
36 For Tan it was the biggest decision of his 15 years as Minister for Finance. Singh (1984).
37 Schenk (2013), p. 516.
38 Tan Siok Choo, letter to the *Straits Times*, 7 October 2000.
39 MAS internal records.
40 *Straits Times*, 9 May 1973.
41 *Straits Times*, 14 May 1973.
42 MAS internal records.
43 MAS internal records.
44 MAS internal records.
45 MAS internal records.
46 *New Nation*, 23 June 1973.
47 The President of the Singapore Foreign Exchange Club said: 'We have the foreign exchange expertise and are well-equipped to handle the new situation.' (*Straits Times*, 22 June 1973). Merchants were, however, concerned about the effect of the increased uncertainty caused by swings in the exchange rate on imports and exports and Singapore's attractiveness to foreign investors (*Straits Times*, 9 July 1973).
48 MAS internal records.
49 The Ministry of Finance said that the Singapore dollar 'will return to fixed parity when the international currency situation is stabilised'. *Straits Times*, 21 June 1973.
50 MAS internal records.
51 MAS internal records.
52 Instead of monitoring the Singapore dollar against individual currencies, the idea was to monitor a basket of currencies with their importance or 'weights' determined by how much trade Singapore did with those countries.
53 MAS internal records.
54 This was in line with a general increase in capital mobility in the 1960s and 1970s as opportunities were created to diversify the geographic location of financial activity. The

best example of this was the London-based Eurodollar Market. The devaluation of the pound sterling in 1967 also encouraged Asian bankers and traders to switch to offshore US dollars instead of sterling as their preferred foreign currency. Schenk (2020).

55 For an up-to-date account of the origins and development of the Asian Dollar Market, see Schenk (2020).

56 In his memoirs, Lee Kuan Yew also recalled the idea as coming from Winsemius, who sought out van Oenen for advice. Lee (2000).

57 In the 1960s, Singapore's 'clock' was seven hours and thirty minutes ahead of Greenwich Mean Time. Today Singapore Standard Time is eight hours ahead, so the London markets now open at 5 pm Singapore time.

58 Schenk (2020), p. 7.

59 Emery (1975).

60 Lee (1990), Table 1.

61 Interview with *The Banker* in 1970.

62 Emery (1975), p. 6.

63 *Straits Times*, 28 May 1973.

64 *Straits Times*, 7 February 1971.

65 *Straits Times*, 23 November 1970.

66 Bank licences were issued only to branches of foreign banks and not their subsidiaries, so their head offices were obliged to make up any shortfall in liquidity, thus reducing the risk of insolvency.

67 This was done by eliminating a 20 per cent liquidity-ratio requirement on ACU deposits and reducing the income tax on offshore loans and ACU business incomes from 40 to 10 per cent.

68 *Straits Times*, 13 October 1972.

69 Monetary Authority of Singapore (2012).

70 *Straits Times*, 19 January 1973.

71 *Straits Times*, 6 September 1974.

72 *Straits Times*, 28 December 1974.

73 *Straits Times*, 4 October 1974.

74 *Straits Times*, 5 October 1974.

75 *Straits Times*, 19 January 1973.

76 *Straits Times*, 14 February 1973.

77 *Straits Times*, 7 February 1973.

78 *Straits Times*, 5 March 1974.

79 *Straits Times*, 21 August 1974.

80 *Straits Times*, 23 February 1974.

81 *Straits Times*, 27 March 1974.

82 *Straits Times*, 10 August 1973.

83 Address to the Pacific Basin Energy Conference on 9th December 1974. National Archives of Singapore, lky/1974/lky1209.doc.

84 *Straits Times*, 19 December 1973.

85 *Straits Times*, 5 December 1973.

86 MAS internal records.

87 *Straits Times*, 13 August 1976, p. 8.

88 *Straits Times*, 2 February 1982.

89 *Straits Times*, 11 February 1982.

90 *Straits Times*, 17 August 1979.

91 *Straits Times*, 18 August 1979.

92 *New Nation*, 13 October 1979.

93 *Business Times*, 10 October 1981.

94 *Business Times*, 3 April 1984.

95 As quoted in *Financial Times*, 23 June 2017.

96 MAS internal records.

97 MAS internal records.

98 MAS internal records.

99 *Straits Times*, 6 April 1979.

100 MAS internal records.

101 *Straits Times*, 19 September 1972.

102 *Straits Times*, 29 December 1972.

103 *Straits Times*, 7 July 1973.

104 *Straits Times*, 6 February 1975.

105 *Straits Times*, 14 November 1975.

106 *Straits Times*, 17 May 1980.

107 *Straits Times*, 21 July 1982.

108 *Straits Times*, 2 April 1983.

109 *Straits Times*, 28 September 1985.

110 *Straits Times*, 18 May 1985.

111 *Straits Times*, 27 February 1972.

112 MAS internal records.

113 MAS internal records.

114 *Straits Times*, 19 January 1976.

115 Williamson (1977).

CHAPTER 8: MANAGING THE CURRENCY IN TURBULENT TIMES

1 *Business Times*, 1 January 1980.

2 On the reorganisation of MAS and history of the GIC, see Orchard (2016).

3 Orchard (2016), p. 104.

4 The official foreign reserves include foreign exchange, monetary gold and Special Drawing Rights and reserves held at the International Monetary Fund.

5 This invoked the headline: 'Kim San MAS Managing Director, PM to Head Top Government Company.' *Straits Times*, 28 February 1981.

6 For an overview of Singapore's monetary policy, see Monetary Authority of Singapore (2000), and Wilson (2015).

7 *Business Times*, 4 February 1981.

8 *Business Times*, 4 February 1981.

9 Singapore's high savings rate, including the compulsory contributions by employers and employees to the CPF, and persistent government budget surpluses, tended to drain liquidity from the domestic banking system so MAS periodically injected liquidity back into the money market so long as this did not conflict with its monetary policy centred on the exchange rate.

10 MAS internal records.

11 *Singapore Monitor*, 13 September 1984.

12 Some academics in Singapore suggested that the fall in the money supply in 1984 may have generated a liquidity squeeze and was a factor in the recession. This was disputed by MAS, who argued that the fall in the money supply was a result of a drop in demand for credit and a more cautious lending policy by banks in Singapore, together with a deterioration in consumer and business creditworthiness once the downturn had begun. MAS internal records.

13 The employee contribution rate was also 25 per cent so the total withdrawal from spending was 50 per cent. CPF is not strictly a tax, as employees get it back when they reach retirement age; but it acts like a tax in the short run, since it takes away purchasing power.

14 *Business Times*, 18 September 1985.

15 *Straits Times*, 17 September 1985.

16 *Straits Times*, 19 September 1985.

17 Monetary Authority of Singapore (2012), p. 74; MAS internal records.

18 *Straits Times*, 13 March 1985.

19 POSB, which had previously been a branch of the Postal Services Department, became a statutory board under the Minister of Communications in 1972. In 1974, it was transferred to come under the Ministry of Finance. As a statutory board, it was not typically referred to in the media as a 'local bank'.

20 *Singapore Monitor*, 22 February 1984.

21 *Straits Times*, 7 March 1984.

22 *Business Times*, 21 March 1984.

23 *Straits Times*, 4 May 1984.

24 *Straits Times*, 21 March 1984.

25 *Straits Times*, 27 March 1984.

26   *Straits Times*, 17 May 1984.
27   *Straits Times*, 4 November 1984.
28   *Singapore Monitor*, 13 November 1984.
29   *Business Times*, 15 February 1984.
30   *Singapore Monitor*, 22 April 1984.
31   MAS internal records.
32   MAS internal records.
33   For some background on the making of Singapore's notes and coins see Soh (1990) and the Board of Commissioners of Currency Singapore (1992).
34   See Ida Bachtiar, 'Plastic Fantastic', in the Board of Commissioners of Currency, Singapore (1992).
35   See Ida Bachtiar, 'Plastic Fantastic', in the Board of Commissioners of Currency, Singapore (1992).
36   MAS internal records.
37   MAS internal records.
38   MAS internal records.
39   Numismatics is the study and collection of coins, tokens and other objects used as currency, although originally it referred only to coins or metals. Commemorative currency can be for circulation or for collectors and is intended to draw attention to specific historical events or people. All commemorative and numismatic currency in Singapore can be redeemed at face value at the commercial banks in Singapore.
40   A variety of numismatic coins had been issued since 1967 to celebrate lesser events. For a full list see Monetary Authority of Singapore: mas.gov.sg; https://www.mas.gov.sg/currency.
41   https://eresources.nlb.gov.sg/infopedia/articles/SIP_1010_2008-07-30.html.
42   Soh (1990), Chapter 7.
43   *Straits Times* 23 June 2019.
44   *Straits Times* 20 February 2021.
45   A newly industrialising economy is one where its level of economic development ranks it somewhere between 'developing' and 'developed'.
46   For an overview of the problems of floating exchange rates at this time see Reinert *et al* (2009), and Feldstein (1994), pp. 306–309.
47   McKinnon (1993), p. 26.
48   Eichengreen (1996), p. 146.
49   *Colby's Monthly Report* No. 8, 7 August 1986.
50   James A. Baker, speech to the Asia Society Washington Centre, 18 November 1986.
51   MAS internal records.
52   David Mulford, speech to the Asia-Pacific Capital Markets Conference in San Francisco, 17 November 1987.
53   MAS internal records.
54   MAS internal records.
55   MAS internal records.
56   MAS internal records.
57   MAS internal records.
58   *Singapore – Staff Report for the 1985 Article IV Consultation* and *Singapore – Staff Report for the 1986 Article IV Consultation*. Source: International Monetary Fund.
59   MAS internal records.
60   Background on the GSP can be found at https://unctad.org/en/Pages/DITC/GSP/Generalized-System-of-Preferences.aspx.
61   MAS internal records.
62   MAS internal records.
63   MAS internal records.
64   *Business Times*, 30 November 1987.
65   *Business Times*, 2 November 1987.
66   *Washington Post*, 18 December 1987.
67   *Business Week*, 15 February 1988.
68   MAS internal records.
69   MAS internal records.
70   MAS internal records.
71   http://www.sunsonline.org/trade/areas/agricult/02040088.htm.
72   Opening statement of H.S. Mr Yeo Cheow Tong, Acting Minister for Health and Minister of State for Foreign Affairs, and Spokesman of the ASEAN Delegation at the 8th ASEAN-US Dialogue, 10-11 February, 1988. Reported in *Business Times*, 12 February 1988.
73   *Business Times*, 12 February 1988.
74   For an overview of the debate about Singapore's international competitiveness in the 1990s, see Abeysinghe and Wilson (2002), and Toh and Tan (1998).
75   Abeysinghe and Lee (1998).
76   *Straits Times*, 15 March 1995.
77   Monetary Authority of Singapore (2012).
78   *Hansard*, Volume 263, 18 July 1995.
79   Leeson (1996), p. 61.
80   Greener (2006), p. 433.
81   *The Economist* (1995) and *Financial Times*, 7 January 1997.
82   *Financial Times*, 7 January 1997.
83   For assessments of the impact of the Asian financial crisis on Singapore, see Ngiam (2000) and Peebles and Wilson (2002).
84   McCord (1989), p. 74.
85   World Bank (1993).
86   Abeysinghe and Tan (1998).
87   For an overview of the issues surrounding the internationalisation of the Singapore dollar, see Ong (2000) and Chow (2008).
88   For some background on international money and currency internationalisation see Kenen (2011), He and McCauley (2010), and Frankel (2011).
89   In an interview with Reuters in May 1988, finance minister Richard Hu noted, 'It would be a mistake to allow the use of the Singapore-dollar-denominated assets to enhance the growth of Singapore's financial centre, even though the financial institutions themselves would no doubt welcome it.'
90   Singapore's external reserves amounted to about 80 per cent of GDP in the 1990s. International Monetary Fund (2001).
91   International Monetary Fund, *Selected Issues, Singapore*, 9 October 2001.
92   By 1998, the Singapore dollar was used to invoice only 26 per cent of Singapore's total trade. MAS internal records.
93   MAS internal records.
94   MAS had opposed the setting up of a Singapore dollar futures contract on the New York Cotton Exchange in 1997. MAS internal records.
95   *Straits Times*, 13 January 1998.
96   *Straits Times*, 22 January 1998.
97   Ministry of Trade and Industry (1999).
98   It is interesting to note that when the employer's contribution rate was raised again in the first quarter of 2001, labour costs rose significantly.
99   Dr Richard Hu, speech at the 30th Anniversary of the Board of Commissioners of Currency, Singapore, 18 November 1997.
100 MAS internal records.
101 *Straits Times*, 1 January 1980.

CHAPTER 9: MONEY IN THE NEW MILLENNIUM

1   MAS internal records.
2   Peebles and Wilson (1996).
3   MAS internal records.
4   MAS internal records.
5   MAS internal records.
6   Ministry of Finance press release, 'Merger of the Board of Commissioners of Currency, Singapore (BCCS) with the Monetary Authority of Singapore (MAS)', 23 January 2002.
7   For an overall assessment of the agreement, see Monetary Authority of Singapore (2017).

8   MAS.gov.sg/currency.
9   Asian Development Bank (2009).
10 For an overview of the impact of the global financial crisis on Singapore, see Bhaskaran and Wilson (2011).
11 This is clearly the case for the US. See Monetary Authority of Singapore (2016).
12 Chow and Wilson (2011).
13 See MAS media release 'Monetary Authority of Singapore Announces Swap Facility with US Federal Reserve as part of Coordinated Central Bank Actions', 30 October 2008. According to former MAS managing director and present Deputy Prime Minister Heng Swee Keat, 'We spent several nights building on work that was done earlier, to go through all the fine details to craft a scheme that was credible and which did not put the whole of the government's balance sheet on the line.' Monetary Authority of Singapore (2012), p. 193.
14 A structured note is a debt obligation rather like a bond from the issuing bank with an embedded financial derivative component which tracks equities, currencies or interest rates. This means there is some risk involved and if the issuer fails there is no guarantee investors will get all or even some of their money back.
15 Monetary Authority of Singapore press release, 3 February 2010.
16 Monetary Authority of Singapore press release, 7 July 2009.
17 Monetary Authority of Singapore (2011).
18 The US Department of the Treasury (2019).
19 Monetary Authority of Singapore media release, 29 May 2019.
20 This argument has been made consistently by MAS. According to its online Frequently Asked Questions, a deliberate depreciation would not work for Singapore because its exports and imports are not sensitive enough to changes in their prices following a devaluation, and Singapore's exports are driven more by global income. It is better, therefore, to focus on increasing productivity and the quality of exports.
21 *Business Times*, 30 May 2019.
22 *Straits Times*, 31 May 2019.
23 Moggridge (1980).
24 Mas.gov.sg/currency.
25 *Asiaone*, 6 November 2004.
26 *Straits Times*, 17 March 2017.
27 Other numismatic sets were also made available for sale. Details on these can be found at mas.gov.sg/currency.
28 *Straits Times*, 21 August 2015.
29 *Business Times*, 19 February 2016.
30 Monetary Authority of Singapore (2019), Macroeconomic Review, April.
31 Monetary Authority of Singapore (2018), Macroeconomic Review, April.
32 'e-money' refers to any electronically stored monetary value apart from bank deposits.
33 PayNow is an overlay central addressing service that runs on top of the FAST payment system.
34 Including bus and MRT/LRT fares, the share of households with electronic payment expenditure would be even higher at 97.4 per cent given the widespread usage of EZ-link cards for public transportation.
35 Libra was rebranded as Diem in December 2020.
36 MAS media release, 'Singapore and Thailand launch world's first linkage of real-time payment systems', 29 April 2021.
37 It accepted currency in exchange for bitcoin but did not dispense cash in return for the cryptocurrency. *Straits Times*, 15 September 2014.
38 VISA, 29 March 2021.
39 There are concerns that it would be so much easier to switch to holding digital cash than physical cash since the costs involved in storing, transporting and securing large amounts of the former would be much lower than the latter. In turn, the banking system could become more vulnerable to runs during periods of financial stress.
40 Bank of International Settlements (2021).
41 COVID-19 refers to the Coronavirus Disease 2019, as the virus causing it was first identified in 2019.
42 The 'circuit breaker' was a period of elevated safe distancing measures in Singapore aimed at significantly reducing the movements and interactions of people in public and private places. This set of measures was in place from 7 April 2020 until 1 June. Schools moved towards full home-based learning and most physical workplace premises were closed, save for those providing essential services or those in selected economic sectors deemed critical for Singapore's local and global supply chains.
43 *Straits Times*, 15 April 2020.

BIBLIOGRAPHY

Abeysinghe, T. and Forbes, K. (2001), 'Trade linkages and output multiplier effects: a structural VAR approach with a focus on Asia.' *NBER Working Paper*, No. 8600.

Abeysinghe, T. and Lee H.C. (1998), 'Singapore's cost competitiveness in the region: a technical note on RULC', *Singapore Economic Review*, 43(2), pp. 12–23.

Abeysinghe, T. and Tan L.Y. (1998), 'Exchange rate appreciation and export competitiveness', *Applied Economics*, vol. 30 issue 1, pp. 51–55.

Abeysinghe, T. and Wilson, P. (2002), 'International competitiveness', in Chng M.K., Hui W.T., Koh A.T., Lim K.L. and Rao B. (eds.), *The Singapore Economy in the 21st Century: Issues and Strategies*. Published by McGraw-Hill, Singapore.

Adams, T.S. (1946), papers on Malaya; Constitutional Working Committee, School of Oriental and African Studies (SOAS) Archives, University of London. Accessed at https://archiveshub.jisc.ac.uk/search/archives/b470af35-4de8-3702-b793-db96bd370edb

Anderson, J. (1824), *Political and Commercial Considerations Relative to the Malayan Peninsula and the British Settlements in the Straits of Malacca*. Published by William Cox, Prince of Wales Island.

Asian Development Bank (2009), *Enduring the Uncertain Global Environment, Asian Development Outlook*.

Baldaeus, P. (1672), *A True and Exact Description of the most Celebrated East-India Coasts of Malabar and Coromandel, as also of the Isle of Ceylon*, vol. 3. Translated from high Dutch.

Bank of International Settlements (2021), 'Ready, steady, go? Results of the third BIS survey on central bank digital currency', *BIS Papers*, no. 114.

Barnes, W.D. (1911), 'Singapore Old Straits and New Harbour', *Journal of the Straits Branch of the Royal Asiatic Society*, No. 60, December, pp. 25–34.

Bhaskaran, M. and Wilson, P. (2011), 'The post-crisis era: challenges for the Singapore economy', in Wilson, P. (ed.), *Challenges for the Singapore Economy After the Global Financial Crisis*. Published by World Scientific, Singapore.

Biswas, A (2007), *Money and Markets from Pre-colonial to Colonial India*. Published by Aakar Books, Delhi.

Blackburn, K. and Wu Z.L. (2019). *Decolonizing the History Curriculum in Malaysia and Singapore*. Published by Routledge, London.

Bligh, W. (1792). *A Voyage to the South Sea, undertaken by command of his majesty, for the purpose of conveying the bread-fruit tree to the West Indies, in His Majesty's ship the Bounty*. Published by George Nicol, London.

Blussé, L. (1996). 'No boats to China. The Dutch East India Company and the changing pattern of the China Sea Trade, 1635-1690', *Modern Asian Studies*, vol. 30 no. 1, February, pp. 51–76.

Board of Commissioners of Currency, Malaya and British Borneo (1968), *Report of the Board of Commissioners of Currency Malaya and British Borneo 1966*.

Board of Commissioners of Currency, Singapore (1968), *Currency Report*.

Board of Commissioners of Currency, Singapore (1992), *Prudence at the Helm: Board of Commissioners of Currency, Singapore 1967–1992*.

Boardman, J. (ed.) (2000), *The Cambridge Ancient History: The High Empire, AD 70–192*. Published by Cambridge University Press, Cambridge.

Bogaars, G. (1956), 'The Tanjong Pagar Dock Company, 1864–1905.' *Memoirs of the Raffles Museum*, No. 3. Published by Government Printing Office, Singapore.

Borschberg, P. (2014), *The Memoirs and Memorials of Jacques de Coutre: Security, Trade and Society in 16th- and 17th-century Southeast Asia*. Published by NUS Press, Singapore.

Borschberg, P. (2018), 'Three questions about maritime Singapore, 16th–17th centuries', *Ler História*, vol. 72, pp. 31–54.

Boxer, C.R. (1970), 'Plata es sangre: Sidelights on the drain of Spanish-American silver in the Far East, 1550–1700', *Philippine Studies*, vol. 18, no. 3, July, pp. 457–78.

Bower, A.K. (2019), 'Rebranding Empire: Consumers, Commodities, and the Empire Marketing Board, 1926-1933', History MA Dissertations (Theses, Paper 5397), Portland State University.

Boyce, R. (2010), 'The significance of 1931 for British imperial and international history', *Histoire@Politique*, vol. 11, no. 2, page 8 in https://www.cairn.info/revue-histoire-politique-2010-2-page-8.htm.

Buckley, C.B. (1984), *An Anecdotal History of Old Times in Singapore*. First published 1902 by Fraser & Neave Ltd. Reprinted 1984 by Oxford University Press, Oxford and New York.

Bucknill, J.A.S. (1923), 'Observations upon some coins obtained in Malaya and particularly from Trengganu, Kelantan, and Southern Siam', *Journal of the Malayan Branch of the Royal Asiatic Society*, Vol. 1 No. 1 (87), April, pp. 195–210.

Bucknill, J.A.S. (1925), 'A note on some coins struck for use in Tarim, Southern Arabia', *Journal of the Malayan Branch of the Royal Asiatic Society*, Vol. 3 No. 1 (93), pp. 1–4.

Bucknill, J.A.S. (1931), *The Coins of the Dutch East Indies*. Published by Spink & Son, London.

Cameron, J. (1865), *Our Tropical Possessions in Malayan India: being a descriptive account of Singapore, Penang, Province Wellesley, and Malacca; their peoples, products, commerce, and government*. Published by Smith, Elder and Co., London.

Cary, J. (1808), *Cary's New Universal Atlas, containing distinct maps of all the principal states and kingdoms throughout the World. From the latest and best authorities extant*. London: Printed for J. Cary, Engraver and Map-seller, No. 181, near Norfolk Street, Strand.

Chalmers, R. (1893), *A History of Currency in the British Colonies*. Published by Her Majesty's Stationery Office, London.

Chew, E. (1996), 'The first state council in the Protected Malay States', *Journal of the Malaysian Branch of the Royal Asiatic Society*, vol. 39 no. 1 (209), pp. 182–184.

Chew, E. and Lee, E. (eds.) (1996), *A History of Singapore*. Published by Oxford University Press, Singapore.

Chia, J.Y.J. (2006) 'Oversea Chinese Association', article on Singapore Infopedia in https://eresources.nlb.gov.sg/infopedia/articles/SIP_1222_2006-12-09.html

Chiang H.D. (1969), 'The early shipping conference system of Singapore, 1897–1911', *Journal of Southeast Asian History*, vol. 10 issue 1, January, pp. 50–68.

Chiang H. D. (1978), *A History of Straits Settlements Foreign Trade, 1870–1915*, Memoirs of the National Museum , no. 6. Published by National Museum of Singapore.

Chow, H.K. (2008), 'Managing capital flows: the case of Singapore', *Asian Development Bank Institute Discussion Paper* no. 86.

Chow H.K. and Wilson, P. (2011), 'Monetary policy in Singapore and the Global Financial Crisis', in Wilson, P. (ed.), *Challenges for the Singapore Economy After the Global Financial Crisis*. Published by World Scientific, Singapore.

Christie, J.W. (1996), 'Money and its uses in the Javanese states of the ninth to fifteenth centuries A.D.', *Journal of the Economic and Social History of the Orient*, vol. 39, no. 3, *Money in the Orient*.

Clarke, J.S. (1803), *The Progress of Maritime Discovery, From the Earliest Period to the Close of the Eighteenth Century, Forming an Extensive System of Hydrography,* vol. 1. Published by T. Cadell & W. Davies, London.

Codrington, H.W. (1824). 'Ceylon coins and currency', *Memoirs of the Colombo Museum*, Series A, no. 3.

Colless, B. E. (1969), 'The ancient history of Singapore', *Journal of Southeast Asian History*, vol. 10, no. 1, Singapore Commemorative Issue 1819–1969, March, pp. 1–11.

Cornelius-Takahama, V. and Lim, F. (2004), 'Change Alley', article on Infopedia, National Library Board. Accessed at https://eresources.nlb.gov.sg/infopedia/articles/SIP_223_2004-12-17.html

Cortesão, A. (ed.) (1944), *The Suma oriental of Tomé Pires: an account of the East, from the Red Sea to Japan, written in Malacca and India in 1512-1515; and, the book of Francisco Rodrigues, rutter of a voyage in the Red Sea, nautical rules, almanack and maps, written and drawn in the East before 1515*, vol. II. Published by The Hakluyt Society, London.

Cosgrave, J. (2015), 'UK finally finishes paying for World War I debt', 9 March, in https://www.cnbc.com/2015/03/09/uk-finally-finishes-paying-for-world-war-i.html

Cowan, C.D. (1950), 'Early Penang and the rise of Singapore, 1805–1832', *Journal of the Malaysian Branch of the Royal Asiatic Society*, vol. XIII, Part 2, March, pp. 2-210.

Crawfurd, J. (1820), *History of the Indian Archipelago. Containing an account of the manners, arts, languages, religions, institutions and commerce of its inhabitants*, vol. 2. Published by Archibald Constable & Co., Edinburgh.

Crawfurd, J. (1828), *Journal of an embassy from the Governor-General of India to the courts of Siam and Cochin China, exhibiting a view of the actual state of those kingdoms.* Published by Henry Colburn, London.

Crawfurd, J. (1856), *A Descriptive Dictionary of the Indian Islands and Adjacent Countries.* Published by Bradbury & Evans, London.

Dakers, C.H. (1939), 'The Malay coins of Malacca,' *Journal of the Malayan Branch of the Royal Asiatic Society*, vol. 17, no. 1 (133), October, pp. 1–12.

Das Gupta, S.N. (1946), 'Some aspects of the history of Penang from 1786 to 1805', *Proceedings of the Indian History Congress*, vol. 9, pp. 339–349.

de Barros, J. and de Couto, D. (1788) *Da Asia, Década Segunda, Parte Segunda*. Liv. VI. Cap. I.

de Soto, J.H. (2009), *Money, Bank Credit, and Economic Cycles*, 2nd ed. (English, translated by Melinda A. Stroup). Published by the Ludwig von Mises Institute, Auburn.

de Vries, J. and van der Woude, A. (1997), *The First Modern Economy: Success, Failure, and Perseverance of the Dutch*. Published by Cambridge University Press, Cambridge.

Deyell, J. (2010), 'Cowries and coin: The dual monetary system of the Bengal Sultanate', *Indian Economic & Social History review*, 47, 1, April, pp. 63-106.

di Varthema, L. (1610), *Hodeporicon Indiae Orientalis*, translated by Hieronymus Megiser.

Drabble, J. (n.d.), 'Change in the Malaysian economy circa 1800–1990' in https://www.ehm.my/publications/articles/change-in-the-malaysian-economy-circa-1800–1990

Drake P.J. (1969), *Financial Development in Malaya and Singapore*. Published by Australian National University Press, Canberra.

Drake, P.J. (1981), 'The *evolution of money in Singapore since 1819'*, in Monetary Authority of Singapore, *Papers on Monetary Economics*. Published by Singapore University Press, Singapore.

Drake, P.J. (2017), *Merchants, Bankers, Governors. British Enterprise in Singapore and Malaya, 1786–1920*. Published by World Scientific, Singapore.

Eichengreen, B. (1996), *Globalizing Capital: A History of the International Monetary System*. Published by Princeton University Press, Princeton.

Eichengreen, B., and Flandreau, M. (1998), 'The geography of the Gold Standard', *Currency Convertibility: The Gold Standard and Beyond*, ed. de Macedo, J.B., Eichengreen, B. and Reis, J. Published by Routledge, London.

Ellis, H.L. (1895),'British copper tokens of the Straits Settlements and Malayan Archipelago', *The Numismatic Chronicle and Journal of the Numismatic Society*, third series, vol. 15, pp. 135–53.

Elmore, H.M. (1802), *The British Mariner's Directory and Guide to the Trade and Navigation of the Indian and China Seas. Containing Instructions for Navigating from Europe to India and China, and from Port to Port in those Regions, and Parts Adjacent: With an Account of the Trade, Mercantile Habits, Manners, and Customs of the Natives*. Published by Blacks & Parry, London.

Emery R.F. (1975), 'The Asian Dollar Market.' *International Finance Discussion Papers*. Washington D. C. Published by the Federal Reserve Board.

Feldstein, M. (1994), 'American economic policy in the 1980s: a personal view', in Feldstein, M. (ed.), *American Economic Policy in the 1980s*. Published by University of Chicago Press, Chicago.

Finlayson, G. (1826), *The mission to Siam and Hue, the capital of Cochin China, in the years 1821–2, from the journal of the late George Finlayson; with a memoir of the author by Sir Thomas Stamford Raffles*. Published by John Murray, London.

Frankel. J. (1995), 'Still the lingua franca', *Foreign Affairs*, vol. 74, no. 4.

Frost, M. R. (2005), 'Emporium in Imperio: Nanyang networks and the Straits Chinese in Singapore, 1819–1914', *Journal of Southeast Asian Studies*, vol. 36 no. 1, February, pp. 29–66.

George, J. (2016). 'The Malayan Currency Board, 1938–1967', *Studies in Applied Economics*, No. 53, March.

Glueckstein, F. (2015), 'Churchill and the fall of Singapore', *Finest Hour*, issue 169, Summer. Accessed at https://winstonchurchill.org/publications/finest-hour/finest-hour-169/churchill-and-the-fall-of-singapore/

Greener I. (2006), *Nick Leeson and the Collapse of Barings Bank: Socio-technical Networks and the Rogue Trader*. http://org.sage.pub.com.

Gualtieri, N. (1742), *Index testarum conchyliorum quae adservantur in museo Nic. Gualtieri … et methodice distributae exhibentur tabulis CX*. Published by Caetano Albizzini, Florence.

Hall, D.G.E. (1981), 'The British Forward Movement in Malaya and Borneo', in *A History of South-East Asia*. Published by Palgrave, London.

Hall, K.R. (1985), *Maritime Trade and State Development in Early Southeast Asia*. Published by University of Hawaii Press, Honolulu.

Hall, K.R. (2010), 'Ports-of-trade, maritime diasporas, and networks of trade and cultural integration in the Bay of Bengal region of the Indian Ocean: c. 1300-1500', *Journal of the Economic and Social History of the Orient*, vol. 53, no. 1/2. Empires and Emporia: The Orient in World Historical Space and Time, pp. 109-145.

Hall, K. R. (2011), *A History of Early Southeast Asia: Maritime Trade and Societal Development, 100–1500*. Published by Rowman & Littlefield Publishers, Lanham.

Hall, K.R. (2016), 'Commodity flows, diaspora networking, and contested agency in the Eastern Indian Ocean c. 1000-1500', *Trans-Regional and -National Studies of Southeast Asia*, Vol. 4 No. 2, July.

Hamilton, A. (1727, 1739). *A New Account of the East-Indies: Being the Observations and Remarks of Capt. Alexander Hamilton, who resided in those parts, From the Year 1688, to 1723*. First edition 1727, published by J. Mosman, Edinburgh; second edition 1739, published by A. Bettesworth & C. Hitch, London.

Hanitsch, R. (1903). 'On a Collection of Coins from Malacca', *Journal of the Straits Branch of the Royal Asiatic Society*, no. 39, June, pp. 183–202.

Hansman, J. (1985). *Julfār, an Arabian Port*. London: Royal Asiatic Society.

Hayes, R. (2010). *The Negociator's Magazine*. London. First published 1754. Reprinted 2010 by Gale ECCO, Print Editions.

He D. and McCauley, R. (2010), 'Offshore markets for the domestic currency: monetary and financial stability issues', *BIS Working Papers* No. 320.

Heng, D. T. S., (2006), 'Export commodity and regional currency: the role of Chinese copper coins in the Melaka Straits, tenth to fourteenth centuries', *Journal of Southeast Asian Studies*, Vol. 37 No. 2, pp. 179-203.

Higham, C. (1991), *The Archaeology of Mainland Southeast Asia: From 10,000 BC to the Fall of Angkor*. Published by Cambridge University Press, New York.

Hill, G.F. (1922), *A Guide to the Department of Coins and Medals in the British Museum*, 3rd ed. Published by Trustees of the Museum, London.

Ho, S. (2016), *History of Singapore Currency.* Singapore National Library Board e-resources. nlb.gov.sg/infopedia!articles!SIP_20l 6-03-09_11 4438.html.

Horton, M. (2010), 'Propaganda, Pride & Prejudice: Revisiting the Empire Marketing Board Posters at Manchester City Galleries', PhD Dissertation, The Manchester Metropolitan University, 2010.

Huebner, S.S. (ed.) (1913), *Special Diplomatic and Consular Reports: Prepared for the Use of Committee on the Merchant Marine and Fisheries, in Answer to Instructions from the Department of State, and Practices of Steamship Lines Engaged in the Foreign Carrying Trade of the United States*. Published by U.S. Government Printing Office.

International Monetary Fund (1971), Concluding Statement Article VIII Consultation.

Jackson, J. (1968), *Planters and Speculators: Chinese and European Agricultural Enterprise in Malaya, 1786–1921*. Published by University of Malaya Press, Kuala Lumpur.

Jonathan, I. (1990), *Empires and Entrepots: The Dutch, the Spanish Monarchy, and the Jews, 1585–1713.* Published by The Hambledon Press, London.

Kearney, M. (2004), *The Indian Ocean in World History*. Published by Routledge, London.

Kelly, P. (1835), *The Universal Cambist and Commercial Instructor*. London: printed for the author.

Kemmerer, E.W. (1904), 'A gold standard for the Straits Settlements', *Political Science Quarterly*, vol.19 no. 4, pp. 636–649.

Kemmerer, E.W. (1906), 'A gold standard for the Straits Settlements II', *Political Science Quarterly*, vol. 21 no. 4, pp.663–698.

Kenen, P. (2011), 'Currency internationalisation: an overview', in Bank for International Settlements (ed.), *Currency Internationalisation, Lessons from the Global Financial Crisis and Prospects for the Future in Asia and the Pacific*, vol. 61, pp. 9–18.

Kerr, R. (1824), *A General History and Collection of Voyages and Travels, Arranged in Systematic Order: Forming a Complete History of the Origin and Progress of Navigation, Discovery and Commerce, By Sea and Land, From the Earliest Ages to the Present Time*. Published by W. Blackwood & T. Cadell, Edinburgh and London.

Khoo K. K. (1999), 'Developments relevant to Malayan agriculture in the post-rubber crisis era (1920-1921)', *Journal of the Malaysian Branch of the Royal Asiatic Society*, vol. 72 no. 2 (277), pp. 17–47.

Kim, D.S. (2020), 'The sticky problem of opium revenue', *BiblioAsia*, vol. 16 issue 3, October–December. Published by National Library Board.

Kitchen, J. E. (2014), 'Colonial empires after the war/decolonization', *International Encyclopaedia of the First World War* in https://encyclopedia.1914-1918-online.net/article/colonial_empires_after_the_wardecolonization

Klein, I. (1968), 'British expansion in Malaya, 1897–1902', *Journal of Southeast Asian History*, vol. 9, Issue 1, March, pp. 53–68.

Klitgaard, T. and Narron, J. (2016), 'Crisis chronicles: the Long Depression and the Panic of 1873', report by Liberty Street Economics, 5 February, in https://libertystreeteconomics.

newyorkfed.org/2016/02/crisis-chronicles-the-long-depression-andthe-panic-of-1873.html.

Koh, D.S.J. and Tanaka K. (1984), 'Japanese competition in the trade of Malaya in the 1930s,' Japanese Journal of Southeast Asian Studies, vol. 21 no. 4, March, pp. 374–99.

Kratoska, P.H. (1988), 'The Post-1945 Food Shortage in British Malaya', vol. 19 issue 1, March, pp. 27–47.

Kwa C.G. (2017), Singapore Chronicles: Pre-colonial Singapore. Published by Institute of Policy Studies (IPS) and Straits Times Press, Singapore.

Kwa C.G., Heng, D., Borschberg, P., and Tan T.Y. (2019), Seven Hundred Years: A History of Singapore. Published by National Library Board and Marshall Cavendish, Singapore.

Lau, A. (1998), A Moment of Anguish: Singapore in Malaysia and the Politics of Disengagement. Published by Times Academic Press, Singapore.

Laughlin, J. L. (1893), 'Indian monetary history', Journal of Political Economy, vol. 1, no. 4, September, pp. 593–596.

Lee K.Y. (1998), The Singapore Story: Memoirs of Lee Kuan Yew 1923–2015. Published by Times Editions, Singapore.

Lee K. Y. (2000), From Third World to First: The Singapore Story 1965–2000. Published by Marshall Cavendish and Straits Times Press, Singapore.

Lee S.-Y. (1990), The Monetary and Banking Development of Singapore and Malaysia, 3rd edition. Published by Singapore University Press, Singapore.

Leeson, N. (1996), Rogue Trader: How I Brought down Barings Bank and Shook the Financial World. Published by Little, Brown, Boston.

Lehman, D. Jr., (2013), The Rise and Fall of Southeast Asia's Empires. Published by Lulu.com.

Lepoer, B.L. (ed.) (1989), Singapore: A Country Study. Published by U.S. Government Printing Office for the Library of Congress. http://countrystudies.us/singapore/9.htm.

Printing Office for the Library of Congress. http://countrystudies.us/singapore/9.htm.

Li Q. (2015), 'Roman coins discovered in China and their research', Eirene. Studia Graeca et Latina, Vol. 51 Issue 1-2, pp. 279-299.

Lim C.Y. (1969), Money and Monetary Policy. Published by Eastern Universities Press, Singapore.

Lim K.S. (2019), 'Singapore issues its first currency.' Singapore National Library eresources.nlb.gov.sg/history/events/b6bb3Ofe-3f57-4328-955d-fcl 530ede37f.

Lim, M.C.S., Tan N.K. and Price Waterhouse (1995), Baring Futures (Singapore) Pte Ltd: investigation pursuant to Section 231 of the Companies Act (Chapter 50): the report of the inspectors appointed by the Minister for Finance. Published by the Ministry of Finance, Singapore.

Linehan, W. (1947), 'The kings of 14th-century Singapore', Journal of the Malayan Branch of the Royal Asiatic Society, vol. 20, no. 2 (142), December, pp. 117–127.

Liu X. (1988), Ancient India and Ancient China: Trade and Religious Exchanges: AD 1–600. New York: Oxford University Press.

Makepeace, W.E., Braddell, J. and Brooke, G.S. (eds.) (1991), One Hundred Years of Singapore, vol. 1. First published 1921 by

John Murray, London. Reprinted 1991 by Oxford University Press, Singapore.

Marsden, W. (2012), The History of Sumatra: Containing an Account of the Government, Laws, Customs and Manners of the Native Inhabitants. First published 1811, reprinted 2012. Published by Cambridge University Press, New York.

McCord, W. (1989), 'Explaining the East Asian Miracle', The National Interest, No. 16, Summer, pp. 74–82. Published by Center for the National Interest.

McKillop, J. and Ellis, T.F. (1896), 'Tin-smelting at Pulo Brani, Singapore', Minutes of the Proceedings of the Institution of Civil Engineers, vol. 125 issue 1896 pt. III, pp. 145–62.

McKinnon, R. (1993), 'The rules of the game: international money in historical perspective', Journal of Economic Literature, vol. XXXI, March, pp. 1–44.

Meissner, C.M. (2005), 'A new world order: explaining the international diffusion of the gold standard, 1870–1913', Journal of International Economics, 66(2): 385–406.

Miksic, J. N. (2013), Singapore and the Silk Road of the Sea: 1300s–1819. Published by NUS Press and National Museum of Singapore.

Miksic, J.N. and Goh G.Y. (2017), Ancient Southeast Asia. Published by Routledge, London.

Miksic, J. N. and Low M. G. C-A. (eds.) (2004), Early Singapore: 1300s–1819. Published by Singapore History Museum, Singapore.

Miron, J.A. and Feige, C. (2005), 'The Opium Wars, opium legalization, and opium consumption in China', NBER Working Paper no. 11355, May, pp. 2–3.

Moggridge, D.E. (1980), Keynes. Published by Macmillan, London.

Moisés, R.P. (2005), 'The rise of the Spanish Silver Real', Sigma: Journal of Political and International Studies, vol. 23, article 5.

Mokyr, J. (1999), 'The Second Industrial Revolution, 1870–1914', in Valerio Castronovo (ed.), Storia dell'economia mondiale. Published by Laterza Publishing, Rome. Accessed from http://faculty.wcas.northwestern.edu/~jmokyr/castronovo.pdf.

Monetary Authority of Singapore (1971), Annual Report.

Monetary Authority of Singapore (2000), 'A survey of Singapore's monetary history', Occasional Paper No. 18, Economics Department, Monetary Authority of Singapore.

Monetary Authority of Singapore (2011), Macroeconomic Review, April.

Monetary Authority of Singapore (2012), Sustaining Stability, Serving Singapore. Published by Straits Times Press, Singapore.

Monetary Authority of Singapore (2016), Macroeconomic Review, April.

Monetary Authority of Singapore (2017), Macroeconomic Review, April.

Monetary Authority of Singapore (2018), Macroeconomic Review, April.

Monetary Authority of Singapore (2019), Macroeconomic Review, April.

Montgomery, M.R. (1837), History of the British possessions in the Indian & Atlantic Oceans: comprising Ceylon, Penang, Malacca, Sincapore, the Falkland Islands, St. Helena, Ascension, Sierra

Leone, the Gambia, Cape Coast Castle, &c. &c. Published by Whittaker, London.

Moor, J.H. (1837), *Notices of the Indian Archipelago and Adjacent Countries*. Published by F. Cass & Co., Singapore

Morgan, H.B. (2019), 'Guadalcanal 1942–1943: a critical turning point in the pacific and window to multi-domain operations', *The Bridge*, 10 December. Accessed at https://thestrategybridge.org/the-bridge/2019/12/10/guadalcanal-1942-1943-a-critical-turning-point-in-the-pacific-and-window-to-multi-domain-operations

Mortimer, T. (1766), *A New and Complete Dictionary of Trade and Commerce: containing a distinct explanation of the general principles of commerce; an accurate definition of its terms*. Published by Thomas Mortimer, London.

Muirhead, S. (1996), *Crisis Banking in the East: The History of the Chartered Mercantile Bank of India, London, and China, 1853–93*. Published by Scolar Press, Aldershot.

Nair, M. (2011), 'Workings of a nineteenth century indigenous banking system: a case in support of free banking', workshop paper, Economics Department, Suffolk University, in https://econfaculty.gmu.edu/pboettke/workshop/Spring2011/Nair.pdf

Newbold, T.J. (1839), *Political and Statistical Account of the British Settlements in the Straits of Malacca, viz. Pinang, Malacca, and Singapore: with a history of the Malayan states on the peninsula of Malacca*, vol. 1. Published by John Murray, London.

Ng C.K. (2017), *Boundaries and Beyond: China's Maritime Southeast in Late Imperial Times*. Published by NUS Press, Singapore.

Ng T.S. (2018), 'British conceptions of wealth and property in the East Indies and their influence on governance and society: 1807–1924', PhD dissertation, Australian National University.

Ngiam K.J. (2000), *Coping with the Asian Financial Crisis: The Singapore Experience*. Published by Institute of Southeast Asian Studies, Singapore.

Ngono Fouda, R.A. (2012), 'Protectionism and free trade: a country's glory or doom?' *International Journal of Trade, Economics and Finance*, Vol. 3 no. 5, October, pp. 351–55.

Nik Hassan Shuhaimi Nik Abd Rahman (1991), 'Port and polity of the Malay Peninsula and Sumatra (5th–14th centuries AD).' International Seminar for UNESCO Integral Study of the Silk Roads: Roads of Dialogue 'Harbour cities along the Silk Roads', Surabaya, Indonesia: 9–14 January.

O'Sullivan, L. (1984), 'The London Missionary Society: A written record of missionaries and printing presses in the Straits Settlements, 1815–1847', *Journal of the Malaysian Branch of the Royal Asiatic Society*, vol. 57, 247, no. 2, pp. 73–79.

Ong C.T. (2000), 'Singapore's policy of non-internationalisation of the Singapore dollar and the Asian Dollar Market', *BIS Papers* no. 15.

Orchard, F. (2016), *Safeguarding the Future: The Story of How Singapore Has Managed Its Reserves and the Founding of GIC*. eBook from gichistory.gie.com.sg/download.html.

Osbeck, P. (1771), *A Voyage to China and the East Indies*, vol. 2. Translated from German by John Reinhold Foster. Published by Benjamin White, London.

Pakenham, T. (1979), *The Boer War*. Published by Weidenfeld & Nicolson, London.

Pascali, L. (2017), 'The Wind of Change: maritime technology, trade, and economic development', *American Economic Review*, 107 (9), September, pp. 2821–54.

Peebles, G. and Wilson, P. (1996), *The Singapore Economy*. Published by Edward Elgar, Cheltenham.

Peebles, G. and Wilson, P. (2002), *Economic Growth and Development in Singapore: Past and Future*. Published by Edward Elgar, Cheltenham.

Phipps, J. (1836), *A Practical Treatise on the China and Eastern Trade: Comprising the Commerce of Great Britain and India: Particularly Bengal and Singapore, with China and the Eastern Islands*. Published by W.H. Allen, London.

Piatt, A.A. (1904), 'The end of the Mexican dollar', *The Quarterly Journal of Economics*, vol. 18 no. 3, May, pp. 321-56.

Pridmore, F. (1975), *Coins and Coinages of the Straits Settlements and British Malaya, 1786 to 1951*. Published by National Museum of Singapore.

Pruitt, S. (2018), 'How the Treaty of Versailles and German guilt led to World War II', *History*, in https://www.history.com/news/treaty-of-versailles-world-war-ii-german-guilt-effects, 29 June. Updated 3 June 2019.

Qin D. and Xiang K. (2011), 'Sri Vijaya as the entrepôt for circum-Indian Ocean trade: evidence from documentary records and materials from shipwrecks of the 9th-10th centuries', *Études Océan Indien*, 46-47, pp. 308–336.

Quah, E. (forthcoming), *Albert Winsemius and Singapore: Here, It Is Going to Happen*. Published by World Scientific, Singapore.

Raffles, S. (1830), *Memoir of the Life and Public Services of Sir Thomas Stamford Raffles*, vol. I. Published by John Murray, London.

Raffles, T.S. (1817), *The History of Java*, vols I and II. Published by John Murray, London.

Raffles, T.S. (1830), *The History of Java*, vol. I, 2nd ed. Published by John Murray, London.

Rahusen-de Bruyn Kops, H. (2002), 'Not such an "unpromising beginning": The first Dutch trade embassy to China, 1655–1657'. *Modern Asian Studies*, vol. 36, no. 3, July, pp. 535–578.

Rasanubari Asmaramah (2001), 'Gold and tin coins of the Malay States', proceedings of the ICOMON meetings held in Madrid, Spain, 1999. Published by Museo Casa de la Moneda, Madrid.

Reibel, Lucius (2018), 'Economics Cost of WWI in Britain', *The Saint*, 23 November, in http://www.thesaint.scot/2018/11/economics-cost-of-wwi-in-britain/

Reinert, K.A., Rajan, R.S., Glass, J.A. and Davis, L.S. (2009), *The Princeton Encyclopaedia of the World Economy*. Published by Princeton University Press.

Rouffaer, G.P. and Winstedt, R.O. (1922), 'The early history of Singapore, Johore and Malacca', *Journal of the Straits Branch of the Royal Asiatic Society*, Vol. 86, pp. 257–260.

Sadka, E. (1968), *The Protected Malay States, 1874–1895*. Published by University of Malaya Press, Singapore.

Scammell, G.V. (1981), *The World Encompassed: The First European Maritime Empires*. Published by University of California Press, Berkeley.

Schenk, C.R. (2009), 'The retirement of sterling as a reserve currency after 1945: Lessons for the US dollar?', May.

Schenk, C.R. (2010), *The Decline of Sterling: Managing the Retreat of an International Currency, 1945–92*. Published by Cambridge University Press, Cambridge.

Schenk, C.R. (2013), 'The dissolution of a monetary union: the case of Malaysia and Singapore, 1963–1974' *Journal of Imperial and Commonwealth History*, 41:3, pp. 496–522.

Schenk, C.R. (2020), 'The origins of the Asia Dollar Market 1968–86: regulatory competition and complementarity in Singapore and Hong Kong', *Financial History Review*, 27 (1), pp. 17–44.

Seah E.C. (1847), 'Annual remittances by Chinese immigrants in Singapore to their families in China', *Journal of the Indian Archipelago and Eastern Asia*, vol., pp. 34–37.

Shaw, W. and Mohd Kassim Haji Ali (1970), *Malacca Coins*. Published by Muzium Negara, Kuala Lumpur (online version https://myrepositori.pnm.gov.my/bitstream/123456789/3550/1/MIH_1970_Dis_03.pdf)

Shimomoto Y. (1980), 'Agricultural development policy in West Malaysia', *Japanese Journal of Southeast Asian Studies*, vol. 18 no. 1, pp. 92–109.

Singh, S. (1984), *Bank Negara Malaysia: The First 25 years 1959–84*. Published by Bank Negara Malaysia, Kuala Lumpur.

Soh, D. (1990), *From Cowries to Credit Cards: Stories of Singapore's Money*. Published by Federal Publications, Singapore.

Stavorinus, J.S. (1798), *Voyage par le Cap de Bonne-Espérance à Batavia, à Bantam et au Bengale, en 1768, 69, 70 et 71*. Published by Chezh J. Jansen, Paris.

Stavorinus, J.S. (1798), *Voyages to the East Indies*, vol. 1. Translated from Dutch by Samuel Hull Wilcocke. Published by G.G. & J. Robinson, London.

Stewart, K. (1932), 'The Ottawa Conference', *Foreign Policy Reports*, vo. VIII no. 21, 21 December. Published by the Foreign Policy Association, New York.

Sultan Nazrin Shah (2017), *Charting the Economy: Early 20th Century Malaya and Contemporary Malaysian Contrasts*, published by Oxford University Press, Shah Alam. Overview accessed from https://www.ehm.my/publications/books/charting-the-economy-early-20th-century-malaya-and-contemporary-malaysian-contrasts

Suresh, S. (2001), 'Countermarks on Roman coins found in India: chronology and significance.' *Proceedings of the Indian History Congress*, vol. 62, pp. 976–85.

Survey Department, Singapore (1885), Map of Singapore and its Dependencies. Prepared and published by J. Von Cuylenburg, Surveyor-General's Office, Singapore, Major H.E. McCallum, Colonial Engineer and Surveyor-General, Straits Settlements.

Tan S.S. (2007), *Goh Keng Swee: A Portrait*. Published by Editions Didier Millet, Singapore.

Tarling, N. (1971), 'Sir Cecil Clementi and the Federation of British Borneo', *Journal of the Malaysian Branch of the Royal Asiatic Society*, vol. 44 no. 2 (220), pp. 1–34.

Tarling, N. (1978), 'Atonement Before Absolution: British Policy Towards Thailand During World War II', *The Journal of the Siam Society*, vol. 66 no. 1, January, pp. 22–65

Thornton, T. (1825), *Oriental commerce, or, The East India trader's complete guide: containing a geographical and nautical description of the maritime parts of India, China, Japan, and neighbouring countries, including the eastern islands, and the trading stations on the passage from Europe, with an account of their respective commerce, productions, coins, weights and measures, their port regulations, duties, rates, charges, &c., and a description of the commodities imported from thence into Great Britain, and the duties payable thereon*. Originally compiled by William Milburn, 1813, Reprinted 1825 by Kingsbury, Parbury and Allen, London.

Toh M.H. and Tan K.Y. (1998), *Competitiveness of the Singapore Economy: A Strategic Perspective*. Singapore: Singapore University Press and World Scientific.

Triffin, R. (1960), *Gold and the Dollar Crisis: The Future of Convertibility*. Published by Yale University Press, New Haven.

Tuckey, J.H. (1815), *Maritime Geography and Statistics*, vol. 3. Published by Black, Parry & Co., London.

Turnbull, C.M. (1992), *A History of Singapore, 1819–1988*, 2nd ed. Published by Oxford University Press, Singapore.

Turnbull C.M. (2009), *A History of Modern Singapore 1819–2005*. Published by NUS Press, Singapore.

Twitchett, D. and Loewe, M. (eds.) (1986), *Cambridge History of China: the Ch'in and Han Empires, 221 BC–AD 220*, vol. 1. Published by Cambridge University Press, Cambridge.

United States Department of State (2001-9), 'The Bretton Woods Conference 1944'. Article archived at https://2001-2009.state.gov/r/pa/ho/time/wwii/98681.htm

United States Department of the Treasury (2019). *Report to Congress Macroeconomic and Foreign Exchange Policies of Major Trading Partners of the United States*, May.

van Aelst, A. (1995), 'Majapahit picis; the currency of a "moneyless" society 1300–1700', in *Bijdragen tot de Taal, Land- en Volkenkunde* (Journal of the Humanities and Social Sciences of Southeast Asia and Oceania), 151(3), July, pp. 357–393.

van Zanden, J.L. (2007), 'Linking two debates: money supply, wage labour, and economic development in Java in the nineteenth century', in Lucassen, J. (ed.), *Wages and Currency: Global Comparisons from Antiquity to the Twentieth Century*. Published by Peter Lang, Bern.

van Zanden, J.L. and Marks, D. (2012), *An Economic History of Indonesia: 1800–2010*. Published by Routledge, New York.

Warren, J.F. (1986), *Rickshaw Coolie: A People's History of Singapore, 1880–1940*. Published by Oxford University Press, Singapore.

White, N.J. (1997), 'The frustrations of development: British business and the late colonial state in Malaya, 1945–57', *Journal of Southeast Asian Studies*, vol. 28 issue 1, March, pp. 103–119.

Wilkinson, R.J. (1941), 'More on Bencoolen', *Journal of the Malayan Branch of the Royal Asiatic Society*, vol. 19, no. 1 (138), February, pp. 101–119.

Williamson, J. (1977), *The Failure of World Monetary Reform, 1971–1974*. Published by New York University Press, New York.

Wilson, P. (2015), 'Monetary policy and financial sector development', *Singapore Economic Review*, 60(3):1550031.

Winstedt, R.O. (1969), 'Tumasik or Old Singapore', *Journal of the Malaysian Branch of the Royal Asiatic Society*, vol. 42, no. 1 (215), July, pp. 5–9.

Wolters, O.W. (1970), *The Fall of Srivijaya in Malay History*. Published by Cornell University, Ithaca and London.

Wolters, W. (2015), 'The "doit infestation in java": exchange rates between silver and copper coins in Netherlands India in the period 1816–1854', in Leonard, J. K. and Theobald, U. (eds.), *Money in Asia (1200–1900): Small Currencies in Social and Political Contexts*. Published by Brill, Boston.

Wong, D. (2004), *HSBC: Its Malaysian Story*. Published by Editions Didier Millet, Kuala Lumpur.

World Bank (1993), *The East Asian Miracle: Economic Growth and Public Policy: Main Report*, MacDonald, L. (ed). Published by World Bank Group, Washington D.C.

Yang B. (2011), 'The rise and fall of cowrie shells: the Asian story', *Journal of World History*, Vol. 22, No. 1 (March), pp. 1–25.

Yule, H. and Burnell, A.C. (1996), *Hobson-Jobson: The Anglo-Indian Dictionary*. First published 1886 by John Murray, London. Reprinted 1996 by Wordsworth Editions, Ware.

Ziegenbalg, B. (1718), *Propagation of the Gospel in the East. Being an Account of the success of Two Danish Missionaries, lately sent to the East Indies for the conversion of the Heathens in Malabar*. Part 1, 1713; Part 2, 1718. Published by Joseph Downing, London.

See also:

Asiatic Journal and Monthly Register for British India and its Dependencies, vol. X, July–December 1820.

Asiatic Journal and Monthly Register for British India and its Dependencies, vol. XIII, January–June 1822.

Asiatic Journal and Monthly Register for British India and its Dependencies, vol. XVI, July–December 1823.

Asiatic Journal and Monthly Register for British India and its Dependencies, vol. XIX, January–June 1825.

Asiatic Journal and Monthly Register for British India and its Dependencies, vol. XX, July–December 1825.

Asiatic Journal and Monthly Register for British India and its Dependencies, vol. XXIV, July–December 1827.

Asiatic Journal and Monthly Register for British India and its Dependencies, vol. XXVI, July–December 1828.

Asiatic Journal and Monthly Register for the British and Foreign India, China and Australasia, vol. XIX, New Series, January–April 1836.

Asiatic Journal and Monthly Register for the British and Foreign India, China and Australasia, vol. XXI, New Series, September–December, 1836.

Calcutta Monthly Journal, Vol. 42, August–December 1822.

Colonial Secretary Report, 1908.

Colonial Reports, North Borneo 1951, (1952). Published by Her Majesty's Stationery office, London.

Hansard, HL Deb, vol. 141 cc.1248-51, 21 April 1856.

Hansard, vol. 468, columns 7–144, House of Commons debate, 27 September 1949.

Hansard, vol. 263, 18 July 1995.

History of the Chinese clan associations in Singapore (1986), Published by Singapore News & Publications Ltd, Singapore.

Imperial Gazetteer of India, vol. 26, 1908. Published by Oxford University Press.

Journal of the Indian Archipelago and Eastern Asia, vol. 1, Jan. (1851).

Report of the Commission appointed by His Excellency the Governor of the Straits Settlements to enquire into and report on the Trade of the Colony, 1933-1934, (1934).

Report on the Working of the Currency Note Issue, 1904, 8 February. Published as No. 11 Supplement to the Straits Settlement Government Gazette, 10 March 1905, in the Straits Settlements Government Gazette v. 40, no. 1-25 (Jan. 6-Apr. 28, 1905).

Report on the Working of the Currency Note Issue, 1905, 15 February. Published as No. 18 Supplement to the Straits Settlement Government Gazette, 30 March 1906, in the Straits Settlements Government Gazette, v. 41, no. 1-21 (Jan. 5-Mar. 30, 1906).

Singapore Government White Paper on Currency, (1966).

Straits Settlements Government Gazette, Government Notification No. 257, 24 November 1876.

Straits Settlements Government Gazette, Government Notification No. 155, 9 May 1879.

Straits Settlements Government Gazette, Government Notification No. 674, 5 December 1890.

Straits Settlements Government Gazette, 1937

Straits Settlements Legislative Council Proceedings No. 26, 1911. Minutes of Meeting 25 May 1911.

Supplement to the Laws of the Straits Settlements, 1939.

PICTURE CREDITS

Every effort has been made to trace copyright holders for images used. In the event of error or omissions, appropriate credit will be made in future printings of the work. The images in this book appear by courtesy of the following:

AFP/Getty Images: 284

Apichart Weerawong/Reuters: 338

Archive PL/Alamy Stock Photo: 45 (top)

Art Collection 2/Alamy Stock Photo: 22

Arthur B. Reich Collection, courtesy of National Archives of Singapore: 200 (top)

Asahi Shimbun/Getty Images: 329

Bettmann/Getty Images: 263

Bloomberg/Getty Images: 374 (right), 379

British Library Board (Foster 887): 37

BTEU/RKMLGE/Alamy Stock Photo: 7 (top)

Bukit Panjang Government School Collection, courtesy of National Archives of Singapore: 192 (bottom)

Business Times, © Singapore Press Holdings Ltd, reproduced with permission: 311 (bottom)

Cabinet Office collection, courtesy of National Archives of Singapore: 215

Chew Chang Lang Collection, courtesy of National Archives of Singapore: 148, 149 (top)

Chip Somodevilla/Getty Images: 358

Clement Liew collection: 14, 60, 202

Collection of the Monetary Authority of Singapore: 241

De La Rue plc: 316-7 (all)

DEA/Biblioteca Ambrosiana/Getty Images: 63

Ded Pixto/Shutterstock: 285

Dragan Ilic/Alamy Stock Photo: 93 (top left)

FineArt/Alamy Stock Photo: 8

Frank Goon Collection (reproduced with permission): 75 (top, both), 93 (bottom), 94 (all), 108 (top), 121 (10-dollar note), 134 (5-dollar note), 184 (1-dollar note)

George W. Porter Collection, courtesy of National Archives of Singapore: 224

Heritage Image Partnership Ltd/Alamy Stock Photo: 36 (bottom)

Hirarchivum Press/Alamy Stock Photo: 120

HSBC Holdings plc (HSBC Archives): 79 (all except 50-dollar note), 80, 83

Hulton-Deutsch Collection/Getty Images: 266

Imperial War Museum, London: 143, 160 (SE 4659)

incamerastock/Alamy: facing contents list

Jan Fritz/Alamy Stock Photo: 93 (top right)

Jimlop Collection/Alamy Stock Photo: 39

John Macdougall/AFP/Getty Images: 335

Keystone Press/Alamy Stock Photo: 254

Keystone/Getty Images: 245

Kumar Sriskandan/Alamy Stock Photo: 374 (left)

Lee Brothers Studio Collection, courtesy of National Archives of Singapore: 135 (top)

Library of Congress: 139 (top, Control No. 2013650311), 139 (bottom, Control No. 2013650277), 140 (Control No. 2013648902).

Lim Kheng Chye Collection, courtesy of National Archives of Singapore: 85 (bottom)

Loh Teck Cheong Collection, courtesy of National Archives of Singapore: 154 (bottom)

Mario Cabrera/AP/Shutterstock: 323

MAS Heritage Collection (photographer: Calvin Yeo): 18 (bottom, both), 20 (both), 24 (top), 54 (top), 57 (bottom), 66, 68 (left and right), 72, 73 (lower coin), 76 (top, both), 79 (50-dollar note), 90 (top right), 96, 103, 105 (both), 108 (two lower notes), 121 (all notes except 10 dollars), 132 (all), 134 (1-dollar and 10-dollar notes), 138 (all), 145 (serialised 1-dollar, 5-dollar and 10-dollar notes), 166 (all), 170 (all), 184–5 (all except 1-dollar note), 206 (all)

MAS Heritage Collection: 19, 45 (bottom), 121 (all coins), 144 (10-cent, 50-cent, 1-dollar notes), 232–3 (all), 234 (all), 236 (all except obverse of 1971 5-cent coin and commemorative coins), 286–7 (all), 288 (all), 313 (all), 314–5 (all), 318 (all), 320–1 (all), 346–7 (all), 354–5 (all), 369 (all), 371 (all)

Ministry of Information and the Arts Collection, courtesy of National Archives of Singapore: 176, 180, 189, 193, 198 (top), 201, 203, 208, 209 (all), 212, 214, 218, 226, 228, 230, 240, 244, 260 (bottom), 271 (bottom), 289 (top), 292 (bottom), 302, 309, 310, 344

Monetary Authority of Singapore: 260 (top), 306, 322 (both), 326 (left), 351 (both), 373

Museum of Applied Arts and Sciences: 57 (second row, item N9561), 73 (upper coin, item N10535) (both gifts of Australian Museum, 1961, photographer Laura Moore)

Museums Victoria: 28 (left, photographer Heath Warwick, https://collections.museumsvictoria.com.au/items/69947), 28 (right, photographer Heath Warwick, https://collections.museumsvictoria.com.au/items/70554), 46 (left, photographer Heath Warwick, https://collections.museumsvictoria.com.au/items/51831), 46 (right, photographer Heath Warwick, https://collections.museumsvictoria.com.au/items/1368253), 54 (lower, photographer Jennifer McNair, https://collections.museumsvictoria.com.au/items/83416), 57 (top, photographer Heath Warwick https://collections.museumsvictoria.com.au/items/1368263), 68 (centre, photographer Heath Warwick, https://collections.museumsvictoria.com.au/items/55274), 71 (left, photographer Jennifer McNair, https://collections.museumsvictoria.com.au/items/44757), 71 (right, photographer Jennifer McNair, https://collections.museumsvictoria.com.au/items/56341), 91 (photographer Jennifer McNair, https://collections.museumsvictoria.com.au/items/75874)

National Archives of the Netherlands, Kaartcollectie Buitenland Leupe, 4.VELH, 619.67: 18 (top)

National Archives of Singapore: 41, 62, 107, 116 (top), 128, 135 (bottom), 173, 191 (left), 227 (bottom)

National Archives of Singapore, reproduced with the permission of POSB/DBS: 311 (top)

National Archives of the UK: 76 (bottom), 131, 167, 188, 190, 191 (right), 192 (top), 194 (both)

National Library Board: 39, 47 (top), 50, 84, 85 (top), 90 (bottom), 95 (both), 102 (all), 133, 143 (bottom), 149 (bottom), 150, 152, 153, 155, 157, 175, 179

National Library of Australia, Rex Nan Kivell Collection, object nla.obj-230712560: 4–5

National Maritime Museum, Greenwich, London, Caird Collection: facing p. 1.

National Maritime Museum, Greenwich, London, Daniel Bolt Collection: 36

National Museum of Singapore, National Heritage Board: 32, 35, 42, 59, 69, 125, 136, 154 (top), 154 (middle)

National Museum of Singapore, National Heritage Board – gift of Mr Woon Wai Yoong: 172

National Numismatic Collection, National Museum of American History: 90 (top left)

NurPhoto/Getty Images: 375

OrhanCam/Shutterstock: 325 (bottom)

P&O Heritage Collection, www.poheritage.com: 231

Paula Bronstein/Getty Images: 356

Photo12/Universal Images Group/Getty Images: 207

Picture Art Collection/Alamy Stock Photos: 26

Pigphoto/iStock: 348

Popperfoto/Getty Images: 229

Prasit Rodphan/Alamy Stock Photo: 353

Registry of Co-operative Societies Collection, courtesy of National Archives of Singapore: 177

Rob Crandall/Shutterstock: 326 (right)

Robert Kawka/Alamy Stock Photo: 53

'Singapore Facts and Figures, 1966', published by the Ministry of Culture: 252

Singapore Free Press and Mercantile Advertiser, © Singapore Press Holdings Ltd, reproduced with permission: 47 (bottom)

Singapore Free Press and Mercantile Advertiser (Weekly), © Singapore Press Holdings Ltd, reproduced with permission: 101

Singapore Mint: 236 (obverse of 1971 5-cent coin and commemorative coin): 368

Standard Chartered Singapore: 130, 308

Talisman Archive: 16

The Straits Times, © Singapore Press Holdings Ltd, reproduced with permission: 124, 165 (all), 171, 198 (bottom), 204, 220,

227 (top), 235, 243, 247, 248 (both), 250, 271 (top), 272, 279, 281, 283, 289 (bottom), 291, 292 (top), 294, 343, 366

Timothy Auger: 15, 110, 114, 115 (both), 116 (bottom), 118, 126, 133 (top), 142 (both), 144 (5-cent, 5- and 10-dollar notes), 145 (100- and 1000-dollar notes), 178, 196, 197, 199, 205, 299, 339

TkKurikawa/iStock: 304

Universal History Archive/Getty Images: 262

Universal Images Group North America LLC/Alamy Stock Photo: 64–5

Urban Redevelopment Authority, all rights reserved: 256, 296

Wikimedia Commons/Hong Kong Museum of Art: 73 (top)

Wikimedia Commons, image courtesy of Heritage Auctions: 24 (bottom)

Wikimedia Commons, image courtesy of National Numismatic Collection at the Smithsonian Institution: 23

Wikimedia Commons/Jean-Michel Moullec: 7 (bottom), 12 (all)

Wikimedia Commons/Osama Shukir Muhammed Amin FRCP (Glasg): 51

Wikimedia Commons/ Paweł Marynowski: 325 (top)

Wikimedia Commons/Universiteitsbibliotheek/Vrije Universiteit: 21

Wikimedia Commons /University of Birmingham Collection: 97

Wikimedia Commons/Windrain: 98

Yiorgos G.R./Shutterstock: 363

Yusof Ishak Collection, courtesy of National Archives of Singapore: 222

INDEX